Canadian Income Taxation

Planning and Decision Making

SEVENTH EDITION

W.J. BUCKWOLD

University of Victoria

McGraw-Hill
Ryerson

Toronto   Montréal   Boston   Burr Ridge, IL   Dubuque, IA   Madison, WI   New York
San Francisco   St. Louis   Bangkok   Bogotá   Caracas   Kuala Lumpur   Lisbon   London
Madrid   Mexico City   Milan   New Delhi   Santiago   Seoul   Singapore   Sydney   Taipei

CANADIAN INCOME TAXATION
Planning and Decision Making
Seventh Edition

ISBN: 0-07-092719-7

1 2 3 4 5 6 7 8 9 10 TCP 0 9 8 7 6 5 4

Printed and bound in Canada

Care has been taken to trace ownership of copyright material contained in this text; however, the publisher will welcome any information that enables them to rectify any reference or credit for subsequent editions.

Vice President, Editorial and Media Technology: Patrick Ferrier
Sponsoring Editor: Rhondda McNabb
Marketing Manager: Kim Verhaeghe
Developmental Editor: Brook Nymark
Production Coordinator: Kelly Selleck
Supervising Editor: Anne Nellis
Copy Editor: Kelli Howey
Cover Design: Sharon Lucas
Cover Image Credit: © Digital Vision; © Brand X Pictures;
                    © Photographer's Choice/Bryan Mullennix
Composition: Greg Devitt
Printer: Transcontinental Printing Group

National Library of Canada Cataloguing in Publication

Buckwold, W. J.
        Canadian income taxation: planning and decision making / W.J. Buckwold. -- 7th ed.

Includes index and footnotes.
ISBN 0-07-092719-7

        1. Business enterprises--Taxation--Canada. 2. Income tax--Canada.
3. Tax planning--Canada. I. Title.

HD2753.C3B64 2004   343.7105'268   C2003-903334-1

To Ricki, Jordana, and Benjamin

If Patrick Henry thought taxation without representation was bad, he should see it with representation.
≈ HANDY NEWS

Author Biography

W.J. Buckwold has extensive experience in academic and professional tax education. A chartered accountant and graduate of the University of Western Ontario's School of Business Administration, with cross studies at the Faculty of Law, he currently is a member of the Faculty of Business at the University of Victoria. He has lectured extensively across Canada for various provincial Institutes of Chartered Accountants, the Canadian Society of Management Accountants, the Banff School of Advanced Management, and the Bar Admission program of the Law Society of Manitoba. Before joining the academic community on a full-time basis, he was self-employed, providing tax consulting services to accounting and legal firms. From 1983 to 1986, Professor Buckwold served as a governor of the Canadian Tax Foundation. He has received numerous awards, including the University of Manitoba's prestigious Olive Beatrice Stanton Award for Excellence in Teaching and the Board of Advisors Distinguished Educator Award at the University of Victoria's Faculty of Business. Professor Buckwold has served as a member of the Council of the Institute of Chartered Accountants of Manitoba and as a member of the Professional Development Committee of the Canadian Institute of Chartered Accountants.

Summary of Contents

Contents

Preface   Taxation is exciting, interesting, and less complex than it is reputed to be. This seventh edition of *Canadian Income Taxation: Planning and Decision Making* is written in a manner consistent with this view. The textbook is for the student of taxation as well as for the interested layperson and business executive. It develops the fundamental principles of the Canadian income tax laws and examines their effect on business decision making and financial planning.

What's New in the Seventh Edition   This new edition incorporates the changes initiated in the 2003 federal budget. These include the reduction in corporate tax rates, the increase in the small-business deduction limit, changes to the RRSP limits, and the revision of certain non-refundable personal tax credits. This edition also exposes the changing relationship between individuals and corporations resulting from the decline in personal and corporate marginal tax rates. All relevant examples, demonstration problems, and the Instructor's Manual have been revised to reflect these changes and ensure the text is current. Some of the changes announced in the 2003 federal budget are to be phased in over several years. Where appropriate, examples in this edition have jumped forward to reflect the ultimate change in the legislation.

Audience

This text is applicable to a wide range of academic programs; it's also a general-interest text and reference for the interested layperson and business executive. Business schools, professional accounting programs, law schools, community colleges, and executive training programs all offer tax courses with different objectives. Whether used as a primary text for courses that emphasize taxation and business decision making, an easy-to-read background for other interpretive materials, or an adjunct to other texts written in a technical style, this book will educate in the fundamental principles of Canadian income tax laws as well as their effect on business decision making and financial planning.

While the book follows a traditional sequence of topics, it departs from other texts in both its comprehensive approach to the learning process and in its accessible style. Each chapter emphasizes the fundamental principles of the topic and their relationship to the overall framework of the Canadian tax system. Any revisions to the tax laws will not render the reader's knowledge obsolete; rather, it will require only minor adjustments.

A major component in learning taxation involves the development of a **decision-making approach** that emphasizes **problem recognition**. To this end, each chapter in the text relates the basic principles to business and investment decision situations. Through numerous situational examples, together with a number of case study analyses, the reader can develop and enhance decision-making skills. These skills will permit the student to approach business decision making in terms of alternative actions and alternative tax consequences, while at the same time integrating the results with relevant non-tax considerations.

Written in an expository style, and refraining, as much as possible, from the use of technical jargon and descriptions of the Income Tax Act, *the book allows the student to begin each chapter with a clear understanding of the objectives. The student will find the chapter easy and enjoyable to read, and will finish reading with a sound understanding of the fundamental issues. By adhering to the fundamental framework, complex issues are presented in a clear and concise manner and tied to their practical applications.*

What makes this text stand out from the competition:

- Reader- and learner-friendly format and style
- Strong links between tax law and its application to business and investment transactions and decision making
- Immediate adaptation of recent budget changes to tax planning and decision-making issues
- Extensive individual examples and integrated end-of-chapter demonstration problems with detailed solutions and explanations
- Tax-planning references throughout each chapter, plus an end-of-chapter summary of tax-planning issues
- Powerful review questions at the end of each chapter, focussing on the primary issues of that chapter and providing an efficient guide for student study and review
- Wide variety of problems and cases that focus on both the technical calculations and the broader tax planning and decision-making issues
- Fully referenced by footnote to the *Income Tax Act* and Interpretation Bulletins, providing a direct link to specific tax laws without disturbing the text's flow
- Numerous problems adapted from professional accounting exams

Content Overview

Part One: Introduction: A Management Approach to Taxation (Chapters 1, 2) develops the concept of a business-decision approach to taxation from a management perspective. It also outlines the fundamentals of tax planning by stating the techniques and skills required to apply tax knowledge.

Part Two: An Overview of Income Determination and Tax for the Two Primary Entities (Chapters 3–11) provides an overview of the fundamentals of income determination for the two primary taxable entities: individuals and corporations. These chapters develop the basic principles of the tax system and discuss their impact on cash flow and on management decisions.

Part Three: The Corporate Structure (Chapters 12–14) considers the corporate entity, which is the primary business structure.

Part Four: Other Forms of Business Organization (Chapters 15, 16) develops the fundamental principles and implications of other business structures such as joint ventures, partnerships and limited partnerships.

Part Five: Selected Topics (Chapters 17–22) deals with a number of specific business-decision problems; it also integrates and further applies the fundamentals developed in the first four parts of the text.

Throughout the seventh edition I've employed **review questions, problems, and cases** to develop the student's fundamental knowledge of the Canadian income tax system, and to nurture the skills they require to effectively consider tax implications in business decision making and financial planning. These learning tools range from easy to difficult, and, depending on course objectives, may be used as assignment material or for class discussion.

Review questions follow the text's flow and test the reader's understanding of the main tax principles developed in each chapter.

Problems demonstrate specific applications and also show, in a directed manner, the impact of taxation on business decision making.

Cases require the student to identify particular problems, to determine how tax factors may affect those problems, to consider alternative courses of action, and to make a decision.

The text's questions, problems, and cases are designed so the student will be able to:
- Develop a basic understanding of tax
- Identify situations in which taxation has application to business decision making
- Structure alternative courses of action, and recognize that each course of action may result in additional problems which must be solved
- Determine the tax impact of decisions on investment returns, earnings per share, risk, and share values
- Anticipate the effect of current decisions on possible future events

Other learning tools featured in this text:
- **Tax Planning Checklists**
- **Chapter Summaries and Conclusions**
- **Reading Lists**
- **Demonstration Questions**

Exposure to actual business and investment scenarios is of great importance in the development of tax knowledge. The material in this textbook includes a significant number of actual business and investment situations. The student not only is guided to solve real problems, but also develops the crucial ability to define what those problems are.

Acknowledgments I'm grateful to the Certified General Accountants Association of Canada and the Canadian Institute of Chartered Accountants for granting permission to adapt a number of their national exam questions for the text. Specific permissions from the Canadian Institute of Chartered Accountants are included within the text. Permissions from the Certified General Accountants Association of Canada are listed in the following reference chart.

Text Reference			CGA Reference*	
Chapter	Demonstration Question	Problem	Examination	Question #
4		7	September 1994	1
4		8	March 1994	3
4		9	September 1997	3
4		10	September 1998	3
4		12	Practice Exam 1992	
4	1		March 1995	2
4	2		September 1996	3
5	1		September 1997	2
5		5	Practice Exam 1992	
5		7	June 1995	1
5		8	June 1995	2
5		9	June 1994	3
6	1		March 1996	2
6	2		March 1993	2
6		5	Practice Exam 1992	
6		9	June 1992	3
6		11	March 1999	3
7	1		June 1995	4
7		7	June 1993	2
7		8	June 1998	3
7		9	March 1998	2
8	1		September 1994	4
8		7	March 1994	1
8		8	March 1996	1
9		7	June 1992	4
10		2	March 1992	2
10		3	June 1992	1
10		6	June 1996	4
10		7	September 1999	4
11		2	Practice Exam 1992	
11		6	Practice Exam 1992	
13	1		June 1996	3
13		8	June 1997	2
17		1	June 1999	3

*Extracts from Taxation 1 examinations (dates specified above), published by the Certified General Accountants Association of Canada (©CGA – Canada, 1992–1999), reprinted by permission.

Whatever merit this book may have must be attributed to those people who have most influenced me in the taxation field. Four stand out and deserve special mention: Professor Brian Arnold of Goodman, Phillips and Vineberg, Toronto, whose challenging instructional approach sparked my interest in the dynamics of taxation; Joe Hershfield of the Tax Court of Canada, Ottawa, whose inquisitive and analytical mind forced us into long hours of debate on tax policy, interpretation, and planning; Hans Pintea of Deloitte and Touche, Winnipeg, who continually pushed me back to basics when I was faced with complex business situations; and Cy Fien of Fillmore and Riley, Winnipeg, whose interpretive skills set a standard of excellence that I admire and seek to attain.

The task of completing this manuscript was made easier by those who worked closely with me on the project. Nicole Lukach, Executive Sponsoring Editor, and Brook Nymark, Developmental Editor at McGraw-Hill Ryerson, provided advice and encouragement. Their efforts and professionalism are the reasons for the changes in the seventh edition. Anne Nellis, Supervising Editor, has made the transition from manuscript to finished product the smoothest part of this project. Special thanks to Kelli Howey for her careful proofreading of the text. I also acknowledge Mathew Kudelka, copy editor of past editions, who transforms complex sentences and paragraphs into flowing, understandable text. His wizardry with words amazes me. More than anyone else, he has assisted in making this a highly readable text.

I also acknowledge the excellent staff and partners of PricewaterhouseCoopers who developed the online Tax News Network (www.ca.taxnews.com). Their research, tax planning ideas, and timely exposure of tax law changes have been invaluable to me.

A special thanks must also go out to the reviewers whose thoughts and comments have guided this work through numerous editions. Reviewers for the seventh edition include: Brian Winter (Southern Alberta Institute of Technology), Alex Gelardi (Simon Fraser University), Ralph Gioia (British Columbia Institute of Technology), Ann Powell (Sir Sanford Fleming College), and George Cummins (Memorial University).

Of course, a large part of the burden associated with the preparation of this text has been shared by my wife and children, to whom this book is dedicated. Their lives have been uprooted by my constant focus on this project. In spite of this, they have been ever supportive and have made many sacrifices. I am extremely grateful.

And finally, I am most proud to acknowledge the thousands of students who, over the years, have been both critical and appreciative. From them I have received my greatest reward.

BILL BUCKWOLD

LearningCentre

www.mcgrawhill.ca/college/buckwold

FOR THE STUDENT

- Want to get higher grades?

- Want instant feedback on your comprehension *and* retention of the course material?

- Want to know how ready you *really* are to take your next exam?

- Want the extra help at *your* convenience?

Of course you do!

Then check out your
Online Learning Centre!

- Online Quizzes
- Literary Links
- Chapter Summaries and Reviews

Canadian Income Taxation

SEVENTH EDITION

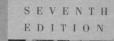

FOR THE INSTRUCTOR

- Want an easy way to test your students prior to an exam that *doesn't* create more work for you?

- Want to integrate current events into your lectures *without* all the searching and extra work?

- Want an *easy* way to get your course on-line?

- Want to *free up more time* in your day to get more done?

Of course you do!

Then check out your
Online Learning Centre!

- Downloadable Supplements
- PageOut
- Online Resources
- Microsoft® PowerPoint® Presentations

Mc Graw Hill **McGraw-Hill Ryerson**

Higher Learning. Forward Thinking.™

Introduction: A Management Approach to Taxation

Management's job is to see the company
not as it is . . . but as it can become.

John W. Teets

part one

Chapter 1   Taxation—Management's Forgotten Responsibility

Taxation has an important effect on business decision making. Decisions on the form of business organization, expansion, the raising of capital, wage and salary settlements, and business acquisitions and divestitures are significantly influenced by alternative tax treatments. While the structure of the tax system is highly technical, its application to business decision making is not. But in spite of all this, few enterprises have developed a formal process to integrate taxation into the decision-making process.

This chapter discusses the role of taxation in the business decision process, examines the issue of tax complexity and its significance to management issues, defines management's role in the process, and outlines the requirements for the development of an efficient management approach to taxation.

I. The Role of Taxation in the Business Decision Process

Business enterprises are subjected to many forms of taxation by municipal, provincial, and federal authorities. The most significant form of taxation affecting return on investment is the federal and provincial income tax. This form of taxation, by its nature, taxes more heavily those enterprises that are more successful at maximizing profits. Ultimately, an investor's return on investment is measured by the cash flow returned after the payment of all related taxes. Obviously, decisions that reduce or postpone the payment of tax will make it easier to maximize the total earnings of an enterprise—and ultimately increase the overall wealth of its owners.

Managing an enterprise involves making many important decisions at different levels of management in all functional areas of that enterprise. Decisions about marketing, production, finance, labour relations, policy strategy, and expansion are all made with the common goal of maximizing long-term wealth by cash-flow enhancement. Cash flow exists only on an after-tax basis; therefore, every decision necessarily has a tax impact, whether or not the ultimate result of that decision is successful.

Normally the decision-making process involves identifying alternative courses of action and analyzing the short-range and long-range costs and benefits for each alternative. The quantitative portion of a cost/benefit analysis consists of determining the amount and timing of cash outflows and inflows. The amount of tax payable and the timing of the payment may vary significantly between alternatives. However, functional managers tend to ignore and take no responsibility for the ultimate tax effects of their particular decisions.

Consider the following marketing-expansion situation, which is typical:

Situation: A wholesale enterprise that has, to date, marketed its product line exclusively within its home province is considering an expansion into a neighbouring province. Three strategy options are being considered as a means to gain initial market penetration.

1. The new territory could be serviced with a *direct sales* approach by home-based sales personnel, who would travel regularly to the neighbouring province.

2. A small *branch sales office* could be established in the neighbouring province and staffed by local personnel familiar with the territory.

3. A *separate corporation* could be established in the new market province to house a small sales office staffed by local personnel.

Analysis: Provincial income tax rates vary considerably among provinces. The neighbouring province may have a higher or a lower rate of tax on profits subject to its jurisdiction. Each of the above-mentioned options affects, in a different way, the amount of income to be allocated and taxed in each province. If the provincial rates of tax vary, then the resulting after-tax cash flow will vary, and this variance must be included in the related cost/benefit cash-flow analysis.

Under the direct-sales option, all income earned in the new province is taxed in the home province. However, if a branch sales office is established, a portion of the organization's total profits is allocated to the new province by an arbitrary formula based on the ratio of sales and wages paid in the new province to the sales and wages paid by the total entity. As a result, the profits (or losses) allocated under the branch-sales option may have no relationship whatsoever to the actual operating results in the new territory. If a separate corporation is utilized, the actual profits (or losses) in the new province will be attributed to that jurisdiction.

Each of the above options is subject to different tax costs, as well as to different selling, administrative, and overhead costs. The added cost of maintaining a small branch office, for example, may be partly or fully offset by a reduction of provincial income taxes, because the formula for allocation (based on sales and wages—not on profits) has captured profits that were realized in one jurisdiction and allocated them to another jurisdiction.

In addition to the provincial tax cost, each option has other, broader federal and provincial tax implications. For example, if the new territory suffers losses for several years before the full potential of the territory is realized, then the direct-sales or the branch-sales office approaches permit an enterprise to use the losses incurred in the new province to reduce immediately the profits of home-based operations. This offset reduces annual tax and enhances annual cash flow, which assists in funding the loss requirements. If a separate corporation were utilized instead, such losses would be locked in to the new corporation and could not be utilized until the new territory became profitable or the separate corporation was formally amalgamated with its parent corporation.

Clearly, each alternative has a different impact on the amount of tax and the timing of the payment of tax. Even though the decision is primarily a marketing one, it has a direct effect on the long-term tax cost of the firm and thus on its profits and value. Thus, tax costs are relevant when alternative marketing strategies are being considered.

The above situation demonstrates that tax is an important consideration in the business decision process. It is important to recognize that this is true at all levels of management, in all functional areas of business, and in a broad range of problems, from union negotiations to business acquisitions and divestitures.

Individual managers, who must take responsibility for making decisions and living with the results, cannot ignore the impact that their decisions have on their organization's tax status. Including taxation as a part of the formal decision-making process leads to improved cash flows and the long-term maximization of the value of the enterprise.

II. The Complexity Issue—Mountain or Molehill?

A major roadblock to entrenching taxation in the formal decision process at all levels of management is the perception that our tax laws are extremely complex. Because of this perception, tax issues are often delegated to professional advisors outside the organization. While outside advisors have strong technical knowledge, they are often not in tune with the strategic decision-making process of the particular organization. In addition, functional managers often do not have a direct line of communication with the outside advisor. The result is that fundamental aspects of taxation are often ignored at the time decisions are being made.

While a certain amount of complexity exists in Canada's tax system, the issue is highly overemphasized. It is true that the *Income Tax Act* is written and presented in a complex manner; however, its fundamental structure and concepts are *not* complex and certainly are not beyond the comprehension of responsible managers. Approximately two-thirds of the *Income Tax Act* deals with special areas and exceptions, and with items that do not regularly affect business decisions. The remaining one-third has a logical flow, and a close-knit structure that includes a limited number of variables that have an impact on the business decision process. The major variables include the following:

- **Taxpayers** There are only three entities subject to tax in Canada, of which two are fundamental to the business process.

- **Types of income** Each of the taxpayer entities can earn five types of income, of which four have general application to business activity.

- **Business structure** There are five basic forms of organization in which a business activity can take place. Of the five, only two are directly subject to tax.

- **Tax jurisdictions** A Canadian business is normally subject to two taxation authorities, unless it extends its operations to international markets.

The key variables that are relevant to the business decision process are summarized in Exhibit 1-1.

Exhibit 1-1: Fundamental Tax Variables in the Business Decision Process	Primary types of income	Entities subject to taxation on income	Alternative forms of business structures used by taxable entities	Tax jurisdictions
	Business Property Employment Capital gains	Individuals Corporations Trusts	Proprietorship Corporation Partnership Limited partnership Joint venture	Provincial Federal Foreign

The basic tax rules relating to each of the four areas in Exhibit 1-1 are neither complex nor lengthy. Each variable encompasses a handful of general concepts that, once understood, are sufficient to enable managers to recognize which items affect normal business decisions. More important, however, is the *interaction* among these major variables: tax, type of income, and form of organization. When the variables are changed in each of the major categories, alternative tax structures are created that can then be applied to the decision process. For example, consider the variables in the following three situations:

1. Two investor *corporations* (the taxpayers) jointly entering into a new venture that will earn *business income* (type of income) could utilize a *partnership*, a *joint venture*, or a *separate corporation* (business structure). Each alternative structure may affect the amount and timing of tax on operating results.

2. A *corporation* that earns *business income* and requires new capital could expand either its equity base or its debt structure. Equity capital is serviced by dividend distributions, which are not deductible by the payer and constitute *property income* taxed in a certain way to the investor. Debt capital is serviced by interest payments, which are deductible by the payer and constitute *property income* to the recipient.

Regardless of whether debt or equity is used, the investor providing the capital may be an *individual* or a *corporation,* and, therefore, taxed differently on the receipt of dividends or interest. Identifying the variables permits a global analysis to be made that identifies costs and benefits to both the corporation and its supplier of capital, thereby permitting an informed decision.

3. A *corporation* earning *business income* can compensate employees in different ways. Simply understanding that the payment of compensation by the corporation reduces its *business income* for tax purposes, but at the same time increases the employee's *employment income*, can assist in ascertaining the true costs and benefits of compensation packages for all levels of staff. Employment income is subject to a completely different set of general rules from business income. In addition, corporate tax rates differ from individual tax rates. Identifying these variables and their different applications lets managers examine alternatives for compensating executives as well as union and non-union staff, with a view to reducing the after-tax costs of employee benefits while increasing the after-tax income to the employees.

While the details of our tax system are presented in a maze of complex legal jargon, this cannot be used by the business community as an excuse for ignoring the importance of tax on decision making. In the tax process there is a role for the manager as well as for the professional tax advisor. Managers need only acquire a basic knowledge of the tax structure and its key variables in order to fulfill their role, and can obtain this knowledge and understanding without having to learn how to interpret specific tax laws. Managers continually work under the umbrella of many legal statutes, and the tax statute is no different: its fundamentals can be readily understood and applied. In addition, it is important to note that the areas of tax law that apply to the internal day-to-day decisions of the business enterprise are among the least affected by the annual changes in federal budgets. Therefore, one can be comforted by the fact that a study of the fundamentals will have long-lasting benefits and will not be subject to regular major adjustments.

III. Management's Role and Approach to Taxation

Management's role in the tax process is to *apply* known tax law to the special types of decisions faced by the particular enterprise. It is not the role of management to *interpret* tax law; that is the function of external tax advisors and other interpretive bodies, who can provide, at the request of management, information relating to specific issues. While managers do not have to be tax experts, it *is* their role and responsibility to be aware of tax issues that affect decisions for which they are responsible.

It is essential to recognize that applying tax law to business decisions is no different from applying any other variable. If it affects profit and cash flow, then it is relevant and must be analyzed, understood, and applied. Applying tax law does not mean using tax avoidance techniques, nor does it result in the enterprise paying less than its "fair share" of the country's tax bill. Instead, the enterprise benefits by understanding the real costs of all business alternatives requiring management decisions. In some circumstances it may even be desirable to pay *greater* tax in order to achieve other definable benefits, but such decisions cannot be made without adequate consideration of the tax implications.

In short, the management process is enhanced when the decision maker is aware of the amount and timing of the related tax consequences. Application of the fundamentals of the tax structure is the issue here—not the pursuit of elaborate reorganization schemes or so-called tax "loopholes." When this specific role and direction is kept in mind, the complexity issue is overcome, and management can have a positive and productive attitude toward taxation.

IV. Development of a Management Approach to Taxation

The management team of a business entity can develop an efficient management approach to taxation by establishing attitudes and relationships in the following areas.

A. Controllable Expense

The tax cost to a business enterprise must be regarded as an *expense of doing business* similar to other relevant costs. Managers continually attempt to understand and control costs that are affected by decisions within their spheres of responsibility. An intimate knowledge of product costs, occupancy costs, selling costs, and other costs is fundamental to the success of any business organization. Tax costs must also be looked on as controllable. As such, the components of the tax cost must be analyzed in order to determine which actions or activities have a greater or lesser impact on the resulting cost.

Consider an enterprise whose business includes manufacturing activities. Manufacturing profits are subject to a federal income tax reduction. Several provinces also offer tax rate reductions for manufacturing profits. However, manufacturing profits for tax purposes are not determined by calculating the actual manufacturing profits, but rather are determined arbitrarily, by a formula that is based on the ratio of manufacturing capital (tangible assets) and manufacturing labour employed to the entity's total capital and labour employed. Clearly, a number of management decisions will affect the end product of the formula, thereby increasing or decreasing the formulated manufacturing profit and the related tax reduction. Below are two brief examples.

1. The formula favours the labour input, and, as a result, all decisions that change the ratio between capital employed and labour employed will have an impact on the manufacturing tax reduction. Therefore, the incremental impact of such decisions on the manufacturing tax reduction becomes a relevant cost for analysis.

2. Combining manufacturing and retail, wholesale, or service activities into a single entity, or dividing a single entity into those multiple entities, will affect the ratio of manufacturing capital and labour to total capital and labour; it will also affect the profits to which the ratio applies. Therefore, decisions relating to corporate structure, vertical integration, and business acquisitions may significantly alter the entitlement to manufacturing incentives (see Chapter 11).

The above examples demonstrate the importance of regarding tax as an integral part of profit maximization, as well as the need to analyze and understand tax as a controllable expense.

Even when reporting financial information, the tax cost must be included—at least for internal purposes—as an expense "above the bottom line." The reference "profit before income taxes" should not exist when operating results are being given. In many respects it is a matter of attitude; the method by which tax is reported in financial statements is indicative of the manner in which it is treated by management.

B. Cash Flow after Tax

All cash flow, whether it relates to revenue, expense, asset acquisition or divestiture, or debt or equity restructuring, should be considered *after tax*. Cash flow before tax has no relevance whatsoever to the value of an enterprise, or when it comes to analyzing the alternative courses of action that affect value. Most business decisions are quantitatively analyzed by examining the timing of cash inflows and outflows; to the extent that the net present value of future cash flows is positive, the action is considered to be favourable. If the decision involves choosing among several alternative courses of action, the net present value of each option is compared and ranked. Such analysis cannot be of value unless the real tax impact is included. It is necessary for each manager to think "after tax" for every decision at the time the decision is being made. In addition, it is necessary to seek out alternative courses of action that will minimize the tax impact, in the same way that one would seek out alternative production or procurement methods to minimize the cost of products manufactured or acquired for resale. Consider the following:

- The cost of a 10% wage increase to an employer in a 40% tax bracket is really 6% after tax, and the value of the raise to an employee in a 45% tax bracket is 5.5% after tax. The real cost to one party is different from the real benefit to the other (see Chapter 22).

- The cost of a 12% interest-bearing debt instrument is 7.2% to a business subject to 40% tax rates; the value to an investor in a 45% tax bracket who receives the interest is 6.6%. On the other hand, a dividend on equity capital of 7% that is *not* deductible to the business has a real cost of 7% after tax, and its net value to an individual investor subject to a 45% tax rate is 4.9%, after applying the dividend tax credit (see Chapter 10). The cost of debt (as opposed to equity) to the business, and its value to the investor, has meaning to the parties involved only when it is viewed on an after-tax basis (see Chapter 21).

- The after-tax cash returns as a result of expansion through the acquisition of new ventures will vary considerably depending on the method of acquisition. Acquiring the assets (land, equipment, inventory, goodwill, and so on) and assuming the liabilities of the target entity, instead of acquiring the shares of the corporation that houses those assets and liabilities, will dramatically alter the amount and timing of taxable income and therefore the after-tax cash flows on profits realized after acquisition (see Chapter 17).

- The value of a business is usually based on its potential for after-tax profits. Therefore, the value of a "for sale" subsidiary may vary considerably, since it depends on a given potential buyer's particular tax structure compared with that of the present owner. It is just as important to target potential buyers when selling a business as it is to target potential vendors when acquiring a business (see Chapter 19).

- The after-tax returns and funds available for reinvestment may vary considerably for a company attempting to expand sales volume by penetrating markets in out-of-province or foreign jurisdictions. Much depends on the strategy involved, as described earlier in this chapter (see also Chapter 20).

Failure to take an after-tax approach at the time a decision is being considered may impose a permanently inefficient tax structure, or result in decisions that appear favourable on a pre-tax basis but are, on an after-tax basis, unfavourable or marginally favourable.

C. Management Responsibility

Effective after-tax decision making will result only when responsibility for the tax effects of decisions is allocated directly to the functional manager involved. This does not mean, for example, that the manager responsible for retailing operations should bear the burden of the higher tax rate on retail income compared with the lower tax rate on manufacturing income. However, it *does* mean that the managers responsible for particular areas within the organization should be negatively judged on performance if they fail to

(a) consider the tax impact of alternative strategies under investigation;
(b) seek out alternative structures within their sphere of influence that will minimize tax without creating an overpowering negative impact on non–tax-related areas; or,
(c) justify in terms of non-tax or non-quantitative reasons the choice of a higher-tax alternative.

Generally, the tax burden of an enterprise is broadly based, so it is difficult to carve up and allocate the total cost among managers according to internal responsibility. However, on a selective basis, the real cost of the failure to consider any of the responsibilities listed above can be allocated to specific management departments. Similarly, compliance with those responsibilities can quantitatively improve departmental performance results when the tax reduction involved in choosing one alternative outweighs the additional other costs of choosing that course of action. In many cases, the selective allocation, for performance purposes, of the results of one decision will affect many future years; as a result, the impact can be significant.

Normally the overall responsibility for tax matters lies with a financial executive or the chief executive officer. It is imperative that such responsibility be spread out to all functional areas of management in order to stimulate the timely consideration of taxation and enhance cash flow.

It is recognized that each manager will not have a full and intimate knowledge of tax law. That, of course, would be inefficient and impractical. However, managers should be aware of those tax laws that affect decisions within their areas of responsibility, and either apply that knowledge directly or know when to seek out advice on certain decisions.

D. Interpretation to Application

The management approach to taxation requires that the gap be bridged between interpreting data and applying that data to business problems. It is management's responsibility to

(a) gather together, from a variety of sources, information that interprets provincial, federal, and foreign tax statutes;
(b) analyze those interpretations and apply them specifically to the enterprise's particular business structure; and,
(c) inform the relevant decision makers within the organization.

Interpretive data can be obtained from publications; conferences and seminars sponsored by various bodies, including the Canadian Tax Foundation (an independent tax research organization sponsored by the Canadian Bar Association and the Canadian Institute of Chartered Accountants); various publishing houses that specialize in tax and other legal publications; international, national, and local accounting firms; Canadian law firms; professional accounting bodies; Canada Customs and Revenue Agency (formerly Revenue Canada); and various independent newsletters. In addition, tax law interpretation can be obtained by retaining competent tax advisors from the legal and accounting professions.

The quantity of information is substantial and is seldom presented in a form that is directly applicable to analyzing business problems. It is, therefore, essential that management develop a formal process of identifying the types of decisions that occur within the organization and matching those decisions to the collected interpreted tax data. Management must also categorize these types of decisions by functional responsibility, and inform each manager of the related tax issues that concern his or her area of responsibility. In addition, anticipated major strategy decisions of a long-term and infrequent nature, when possible, should be identified so that an information-gathering process can be established.

E. Utilizing the Tax Advisor

Typically, an external tax advisor's relationship with an enterprise is restricted to areas of tax compliance, filing requirements, and complex reorganization of corporate structures. The input of such advisors into the management decision process is limited, primarily because they are retained for interpretive purposes. Furthermore, an external advisor cannot be expected to be fully aware of the decision-making process faced by each client, or the types of decisions arising from that process. While management can develop a process of applying taxation to the decision structure, it can enhance the positive results of this by engaging independent advisors with that specific process in mind. The advisor can play a role in developing a management approach to taxation, as well as contribute to its ongoing success. The tax advisor can

(a) while helping to initiate a management tax program, work closely with the financial executive to develop a tailored program by identifying the types of decisions typically made within the organization and coordinating them with the relevant areas of taxation;
(b) provide initial seminars that increase the functional managers' overall understanding of the basic tax structure;
(c) assist in communicating to all sectors of management the tax areas that require consideration within their spheres of responsibility;
(d) provide updated information on changes in tax laws that may alter the tailored program;
(e) review major policy and strategy alternatives before they are implemented; and,
(f) from time to time, complete a tax decision audit by reviewing internal documentation of past decisions within departments, and follow with a report on how to improve the process, providing expanded information where relevant.

Involving the independent tax advisor in the development of a management approach to taxation will permanently open direct lines of communication with decision makers and create an atmosphere in which the tax factor is given timely consideration.

V. Conclusion

The thrust of a management approach to taxation is *not* to place tax planning in a vacuum as a separate function of management, but rather to include, in a formal way, taxation as a major variable to be considered in decisions made regarding all functional areas of business. Obviously, decisions are not made solely for tax purposes, but if the tax consequences are excluded as a contributing variable, the full impact of decisions will not be understood and wealth will not be maximized. This concept applies to both small and large organizations. Certainly, the larger the organization, the greater the requirement to formalize and control the function; however, the concept is always the same.

The next chapter reviews the basic concepts of tax planning. The remaining chapters of this text are devoted, first, to developing a broad understanding of the fundamental principles of each of the variables outlined in Exhibit 1-1, and second, to applying those principles to decisions that confront business managers in various functional areas.

Review Questions

1. If income tax is imposed after profits have been determined, why is taxation relevant to business decision making?

2. Most business decisions involve the evaluation of alternative courses of action. For example, a marketing manager may be responsible for choosing a strategy for establishing sales in new geographical territories. Briefly explain how the tax factor can be an integral part of this decision.

3. Many businesses simply delegate all taxation issues to outside professional advisors. Why? And is it a satisfactory method of dealing with tax matters? Explain.

4. Must business decision makers be able to interpret the *Income Tax Act* in order to include the tax factor in their decisions? Explain.

5. What are the fundamental variables of the income tax system that decision makers should be familiar with so that they can apply tax issues to their areas of responsibility?

6. Why is the perceived complexity of the income tax system an overrated excuse for ignoring tax issues in the business decision process?

7. What is an "after-tax" approach to decision making?

8. Briefly explain what is required for a business entity to develop a management approach to taxation.

9. Is it realistic to assume that the tax costs of an entity can be allocated, for performance evaluation purposes, to those responsible for incurring them? Explain.

10. How can management bridge the gap between the interpretation and the application of tax law?

11. How can an outside professional tax advisor be used to enhance an entity's decision-making process?

Chapter 2   Fundamentals of Tax Planning

The previous chapter discussed how to integrate taxation into the business decision process. Improving cash flow by means of tax planning involves taking actions that result in a reduction, elimination, or change in the timing of tax. A knowledge of the fundamentals of the income tax system is essential if one is to understand the tax planning process, and the bulk of this text will be devoted to those fundamentals. However, it is important first to introduce some of the basic tax planning techniques that are used throughout the text. This will provide a foundation upon which tax planning skills can be developed.

This chapter explains what tax planning is and how to go about it. Specifically, this chapter covers the following areas:

1. The meaning of tax planning and how it is distinguished from tax avoidance and tax evasion.

2. The basic types of tax planning and the skills required to implement them.

3. The formal limitations to tax planning.

I. What Is Tax Planning?

A. Tax Planning Defined

Tax planning is the legitimate arranging of one's financial activities in a manner that reduces or defers the related tax cost. The difficulty with this definition lies in the term "legitimate." Certainly, if the tax authorities do not attempt to prevent certain transactions, then those transactions can be considered legitimate. A number of years ago, Canada Customs and Revenue Agency (CCRA) described legitimate tax avoidance as

> cases in which a taxpayer, in seeking a beneficial result, has merely selected a certain course of action that is either clearly provided for or not specifically prohibited in law and has implemented that decision in a real way.[1]

The *Income Tax Act* has now been changed to include what is called the general anti-avoidance rule, which attempts to indicate what is not legitimate tax planning. (This rule is discussed later in the chapter.) Concurrent with this change, CCRA has removed the preceding quote from its official publication. Even so, its principle forms part of the new anti-avoidance rule.

An example of a legitimate tax planning activity is presented in the following situation:

Situation:

A Canadian-controlled private corporation will earn a profit of $150,000 in 20X1. Included in the calculation of that profit is a deduction of $20,000 as a reserve for the anticipated non-collection of certain accounts receivable (bad debts). The corporation has recently signed a new contract and anticipates that profits for the following year (20X2) will be $400,000. The following tax rules are assumed to be applicable:

1. A taxpayer is given the choice of deducting or not deducting a reserve for bad debts in any particular year (see Chapter 5).

2. The corporation pays tax at the rate of 20% on the first $300,000 of annual business income and 40% on income above that amount (bracket and rates assumed).

---

1 IC 73-10R2. Revised IC 73-10R3 excludes this quote.

Analysis: Because the reserve deduction is optional, the corporation can choose not to deduct it in 20X1. Not claiming the deduction in 20X1 does not mean that it is lost, because the taxpayer has the option of deducting the reserve in 20X2 or a subsequent year (see Chapter 5).

Based on the income levels for each year, all of the 20X1 income will be taxed at 20%, whereas part of the 20X2 income will be taxed at 40%. If the $20,000 deduction is not claimed in 20X1, the profits for 20X1 will increase to $170,000 from $150,000, causing a tax increase of $4,000 (20% of $20,000). However, when the amount is deducted in 20X2, the expected profit in that year will decline to $380,000 from $400,000, creating a tax saving of $8,000 (40% of $20,000). Therefore, the decision to pay more tax in 20X1 results in an overall tax reduction of $4,000 ($8,000 − $4,000 = $4,000).[2]

The above tax planning action is clearly provided for in the *Income Tax Act* and constitutes a legitimate tax planning activity.

To better appreciate what tax planning involves, it is useful to understand the terms "tax evasion" and "tax avoidance."

B. Tax Evasion

CCRA's definition of tax evasion is very clear: it is the commission or omission of an act with the intent to deceive. This includes knowingly failing to report revenue, or claiming the deduction of a false expense, or both. It also includes knowingly omitting material facts from tax records.[3]

Tax evasion is so removed from the concept of tax planning that distinguishing between the two is not difficult.

C. Tax Avoidance

Between tax planning and tax evasion lies a grey area referred to as tax avoidance. Generally, tax avoidance involves transactions which, while legal in themselves, are planned and carried out mainly to avoid, reduce, or defer tax payable under the law. In some cases the transactions do not reflect the real facts of the situation and may be regarded as an abuse of the system. What constitutes such an abuse is debatable. Consider the following example:

Losses accumulated within a corporation become restricted as to their use when control of the corporation is transferred to a new party. The purpose of this restriction is to prevent the new owners from using these losses to reduce their otherwise taxable income. However, such restrictions do not occur within a related group of corporations—for example, between two corporations owned by the same shareholders.

Now, assume that two corporations are owned by the same shareholders and that one has unused losses while the other has taxable profits. If these two entities carried out a series of legal steps to shift income to the loss corporation, would that constitute an abusive avoidance transaction? Likely not, because the spirit of the *Income Tax Act* and its various provisions pertaining to losses are designed to permit flexibility for loss utilization within a group of commonly owned corporations. Therefore, this series of transactions to avoid tax would not be challenged.

However, if the two corporations described above were not initially related, a different result might occur. For example, if steps were taken to cause the two unrelated corporations to become related for the sole purpose of circumventing the loss restriction rules, then the transaction might well be considered abusive.

---

2   The analysis has ignored the time value of money, which is discussed later in the chapter.
3   IC 73-10R3.

The distinction between the two situations is important. In the first, the steps were carried out between two *already related* corporations to take advantage of the rules and did not run counter to the spirit of the system; in the second, the steps taken were designed to alter the facts by causing two unrelated corporations to be related to circumvent the intended rules, and went *against* the spirit of the system.

When CCRA perceives tax avoidance transactions to be abusive, it will attempt to deny the resulting benefits. The general means at their disposal are reviewed in Part III of this chapter.

Often, it is difficult to distinguish between legitimate tax planning and abusive tax avoidance. When the line is unclear, the tax planner must choose between passing up the opportunity and embracing it. The latter course means risking an adverse ruling by CCRA.

Unless otherwise indicated, the suggestions offered in this text are legitimate tax planning techniques.

II. Types of Tax Planning

The objective of tax planning is to reduce or defer (or both) the tax cost of financial transactions. There are many specific tax planning opportunities; all of them fall into one of three categories.[4]

1. Shifting income from one time period to another.

2. Transferring income to another entity or alternative taxpayer.

3. Converting the nature of income from one type to another.

A. Shifting Income from One Time Period to Another

In most cases, there is a very definite time frame for recognizing income for tax purposes, so there is little opportunity to choose between discretionary alternatives. However, a taxpayer can sometimes choose to recognize income or claim a deduction from income in a different time period. Even when this opportunity exists, however, it does not inevitably follow that wealth will be enhanced if those discretionary choices are exercised.

Future tax rates may be greater than, less than, or the same as current tax rates. If current tax rates are lower than the expected future rates, the absolute tax cost can be reduced by recognizing income now rather than later. However, this reduction in tax cost incurs another cost—the cost of financing the payment of tax in advance of when it would otherwise occur. As long as the tax saving is greater than the related financing cost, a wealth enhancement will result for the taxpayer. This can be demonstrated by reconsidering the situation described on pages 14–15.

Situation:

Summary of previous facts:

- The assumed corporate tax rate is 20% on the first $300,000 of annual business income and 40% on the remainder.

- The 20X1 income of the corporation is $150,000 after a deduction of $20,000 is claimed as a reserve for doubtful accounts receivable.

4 *Taxes and Business Strategy—A Planning Approach*, Scholes and Wolfson, Prentice-Hall, 1992, pp. 15–18.

- The 20X2 income is projected to be $400,000, so some of that income will be subject to a 40% tax rate.

- The $20,000 reserve can be delayed until 20X2 at the taxpayer's discretion.

Also, the company is using its available cash resources to take advantage of early payment discounts on purchases of merchandise. Specifically, these invoice costs can be reduced by 2% by paying the supplier within 10 days instead of the normal 30 days.

Analysis: If the corporation chooses to delay the deduction of $20,000 until 20X2, the 20X1 profits increase and the 20X2 profits decrease. Shifting income from 20X2 back to 20X1 in this way takes advantage of the lower tax rate. As stated previously, the overall tax cost is reduced by $4,000, as follows.

Increase in 20X1 tax (20% × $20,000)	$4,000
Decrease in 20X2 tax (40% × $20,000)	(8,000)
Tax reduction	$4,000

However, to achieve this, $4,000 of tax must be paid one year in advance. This reduces the cash available for securing purchase discounts over the next year. The value of the purchase discount is 2% for prepaying invoices by 20 days. As there are eighteen 20-day periods in a year, the opportunity savings cost is 36% (2% × 18 periods). This means that the cost of prepaying tax one year in advance is $1,440 (36% × $4,000). This, of course, is before tax. The additional purchasing costs would be deductible in 20X2 and would save tax at the rate of 40%. The net cost is therefore $864 ($1,440 − 40% of $1,440).

After costs associated with reduced cash flows are taken into account, the net advantage of shifting income in this situation is seen to be $3,136 ($4,000 − $864).

Clearly, in the above situation the corporation would be wise to shift income from 20X2 to 20X1. When making this judgment, it was necessary to determine

(a) future tax rates, or income levels that will cause those tax rates, or both;
(b) the discretionary opportunities within the tax system; and,
(c) the time value of money.

Of the above variables, only (b) can be determined with a reasonable degree of certainty. Tax information on discretionary items can be obtained, though this may require some effort. The other two variables are more difficult to determine, in that both involve predicting future activities.

The above situation and analysis required that profits and cash flows be predicted over several years. Specifically, the planner had to realize that paying out $4,000 in 20X1 would reduce cash flows for a one-year period, thereby increasing the cost of inventory owing to a weakened ability to claim prepayment discounts. However, the actual cash cost of failing to obtain a discount is the after-tax cost, which can be reduced if the corporation still has borrowing capacity. In this case, the $4,000 could be financed with increased debt without disturbing the purchase discount opportunities.

In this situation, the magnitude of the tax saving is obvious. Even so, the tax planner must consider the impact, if any, of not having $4,000 of cash available for business use. In some cases, especially when a business is subject to the risk of sudden market fluctuations or is in clear financial difficulty, the benefits of keeping cash available as added insurance must be considered, whatever the numbers say. In other words, the realities of the specific business must prevail, and common sense may sometimes override the quantitative results.

As a general rule, if future tax rates will likely be the same as or lower than the current tax rate, one should seek to delay income recognition. When tax rates are expected to rise, the decision to delay the recognition of income must be made in the context of the potential use of those funds in the shorter term.

In some cases, the shifting of income from one period to another may simply involve choosing a *type* of investment. Consider the following situation:

Situation: A taxpayer has $100,000 to invest for three years. Two investments are available:

1. A secure corporate bond paying annual interest of 12%.

2. Secure corporate shares that have no annual dividend but have an anticipated growth rate of 12% per year.

   Annual after-tax cash flow can be reinvested in bank deposits earning 10%. The taxpayer has a tax rate of 45%.

Analysis: The interest income on the bond investment is subject to tax annually (see Chapter 7) at the rate of 45%. The after-tax annual return is therefore 6.6% (12% − [45% of 12%] = 6.6%). Similarly, the interest income on the bank deposits has an annual after-tax return of 5.5% (10% − [45% of 10%] = 5.5%). Based on this, the bond investment provides the following value at the end of three years:

Initial investment	$100,000
End of year 1:	
Bond interest received (6.6% of $100,000)	6,600
End of year 2:	
Bank deposit interest (5.5% of $6,600)	363
Bond interest received (as above)	6,600
	13,563
End of year 3:	
Bank deposit interest (5.5% of $13,563)	746
Bond interest (as above)	6,600
	20,909
Total value of bond investment	$120,909

The share investment is taxed differently. Its annual growth of 12% will not be recognized for tax purposes until the shares are sold at the end of year 3. In addition, the growth will likely be considered a capital gain (see Chapter 8), and, as a result, only one-half of the gain will be taxable. The share investment provides the following value after three years:

Initial investment	$100,000
End of year 1:	
Growth—12% of $100,000	12,000
	112,000
End of year 2:	
Growth—12% of $112,000	13,440
	125,440
End of year 3:	
Growth—12% of $125,440	15,053
	140,493
Tax at end of year 3:	
45% (½) ($140,493 − $100,000)	(9,111)
Total value of share investment	$131,382

The return on the share investment is greater by $10,473 ($131,382 − $120,909). Much of this is because only one-half of the return on the shares is taxable. The advantage to be gained by shifting the income for tax purposes from years 1, 2, and 3 (bond) to year 3 (shares) can be isolated as $1,362, as follows:

Total advantage (above)	$10,473
Tax preference (non-taxable portion):	
45% (½) ($140,493 − $100,000)	(9,111)
	$1,362

This analysis shows that delaying the recognition of income for tax purposes permits the annual returns to accrue and compound without annual tax cost. The longer the delay, the greater the advantage.

This section has demonstrated two simple examples of the benefits that can be gained by shifting income from one time period to another. (Many other examples will be offered throughout this text.) Also demonstrated here has been the importance of considering the time value of money and of anticipating financial scenarios related to a particular issue.

B. Transferring Income to Another Entity

Only individuals can enjoy the benefits of accumulating wealth. However, they can do so by using several different entities, all of which ultimately lead back to themselves or to members of their families. For example, an individual may own all or part of one or more corporations (see Chapters 11, 12, and 13), which in turn may hold several types of investments or operate businesses. Also, the individual or his or her corporation may participate in partnerships or joint ventures with other individuals or their corporations (see Chapters 15 and 16). As well, individuals may direct their income into various types of trusts. A trust can be created during one's lifetime or upon death. Some trusts—registered pension plans, registered retirement savings plans, and so on—may not be taxable. Finally, in certain circumstances it may be possible to arrange for income to be earned by other members of a family.

The tax treatment often varies with the entity chosen. There may be many non-tax reasons for choosing a particular structure to carry out certain financial activities, but the tax factor is always an important one—sometimes the only one. Shifting income to another entity may reduce or significantly delay the amount of tax otherwise payable.

Consider the following simple example of shifting income from one entity to another:

Situation: An individual operates an unincorporated service business that generates annual pre-tax profits of $100,000. She requires approximately $39,000 to meet her personal financial obligations. The *assumed* personal tax rates (federal plus provincial) are as follows:

On the first $30,000	25%
On the next $30,000	35%
On the next $40,000	40%
On income over $100,000	45%

Any cash generated in excess of personal needs and income taxes is generally used to expand the business operations.

Corporate tax rates for a Canadian-controlled private corporation are *assumed* to be 20% on the first $300,000 of annual business profits and 40% on the excess.

Analysis: Under the existing structure, the individual has annual excess cash of $27,000 available for business expansion, as follows:

Business profits		$100,000
Tax: 25% of $30,000	$ 7,500	
35% of $30,000	10,500	
40% of $40,000	16,000	(34,000)
$100,000		66,000
Personal expenditures		(39,000)
		$ 27,000

As an alternative, she could create a separate corporation to operate the service business. She would be a shareholder and also would be employed by the corporation and earning a salary. In order to provide for her personal financial needs, the corporation would have to pay her an annual salary of $55,400 (after-tax amount—$39,000).

Salary		$55,400
Less tax:		
25% of $30,000	$ 7,500	
35% of $25,400 (tax rounded)	8,900	16,400
Personal requirements		$39,000

Consequently, the corporation would be able to retain after-tax profits of $35,700 for business expansion, as follows:

Business profits	$100,000
Salary to shareholder	(55,400)
Corporate business profit	44,600
Tax (20% of $44,600)	(8,900)
Available for expansion	$ 35,700
Cash-flow enhancement ($35,700 – $27,000)	$ 8,700

In the above situation, shifting income to the corporation results in a new tax base that permits a lower tax rate on a certain amount of annual income. Notice, however, that a tax reduction is not achieved on the full $100,000 of business income. This is because the corporation had to shift income back to the individual in order to provide her with cash for personal needs. In other words, a tax reduction was achieved only to the extent that the profits could be retained in the corporation and only as long as the corporate profits were below $300,000 (the level at which the tax rate increases to about 40%).[5]

In order to fully appreciate the implications of the above tax planning activity, certain other factors must be considered—for example, the tax implications if the following should occur:

- The shareholder requires further cash distributions from the corporation.

- The corporation earns profits in excess of $300,000 that will incur a higher rate of tax.

- Losses are incurred by the corporation.

- The business fails to survive.

- The business is sold by the corporation.

- The shares of the corporation are sold.

- The shareholder dies or leaves the country.

This is another reminder that tax planning must involve anticipating possible future events. When income is shifted from one entity to another, the cash-flow map is altered. However, the map always eventually leads one back to the original source. Usually, any change in plans will affect the treatment of a number of future events that were not originally targeted for change. In some cases, transferring income from one entity to another may have beneficial results in one area but negative results if certain future events should occur. Potential events must therefore be considered.

C. Converting Income from One Type to Another

The third general type of tax planning activity involves the conversion of one type of income into another. As was stated in Chapter 1, the income tax system recognizes five general types of income, of which four have substantial application—employment income, business income, property (investment) income, and capital gains. The amount of taxable income to be claimed and the timing of that claim for tax purposes can depend greatly on the type of income being claimed. This means that the amount of tax and the timing of its payment can be altered by adjusting a financial transaction so that it generates one type of income instead of another.

It is not always simple to convert one type of income to another. For example, one cannot simply choose to call business income a capital gain. In most cases converting income also involves shifting that income from one entity to another, as was discussed previously. Consider the following situation:

Situation:

Individual A is the sole shareholder of Opco, a Canadian-controlled private corporation. Opco operates a successful wholesale business. The shares of Opco were recently valued at $410,000. These shares were acquired by A several years ago for $10,000. A intends to sell all of the shares of Opco. In 20X1, after the share valuation but just before the share sale, A arranged for Opco to pay a dividend of $40,000 to himself in order to remove excess cash from the corporation.

---

5   As will be shown in Chapter 13, this tax saving is not permanent because additional tax may be payable when the amount is eventually distributed to the shareholder or the shares are sold.

Two years earlier, A had incurred a loss of $500,000 on the sale of shares of another corporation. That loss could not be used at the time for tax purposes, so A has been carrying it forward.

The assumed marginal tax rate (federal plus provincial) in 20X1 is 45% on all income other than Canadian dividends. Dividends from Canadian corporations are subject to an assumed special tax rate of 30%.

Analysis: First of all, notice that A has already taken the tax planning step of shifting income from himself to another entity by operating the business from within a corporation. It should also be explained that the loss on the previous share sale was a capital loss, which means it can be offset only against a capital gain and not against other sources of income (see Chapter 3). Unused capital losses can be carried forward indefinitely until a capital gain is realized (see Chapter 10). Also, only one-half of a capital gain is included in taxable income (see Chapter 9).

In the above situation, the corporation paid a dividend of $40,000 *after* its shares were valued at $410,000. Consequently, the value of the company and therefore of its shares declined by $40,000, so the sale price of the shares must be reduced to $370,000 ($410,000 − $40,000). A has realized his full value of $410,000 as follows:

Dividend	$ 40,000
Share price	370,000
	$410,000

His tax cost on the above is $12,000, as follows:

Dividend (30% × $40,000)		$12,000
Capital gain:		
Price of shares	$370,000	
Cost	(10,000)	
Capital gain	$360,000	
Taxable portion (½)	$180,000	
Loss carry-over	(180,000)	
Taxable income	–0–	
Tax on capital gain		–0–
Total tax cost		$12,000

Notice that the tax treatment of the capital gain is more to A's advantage than the tax treatment of the dividend. This is because he has a loss carry-over of $250,000 (½ × $500,000) from a previous year that can only be used against new capital gains.

If A had not declared himself a dividend, the share value would have remained at $410,000 and the total tax would have been zero, as shown at the top of the next page.

The decision to pay or not to pay a dividend belonged to A. By choosing not to pay the dividend he would have converted dividend income (property income) into a capital gain that in this case had a preferred tax treatment.

Dividend	–0–
Capital gain:	
Price of shares	$410,000
Cost	(10,000)
Capital gain	$400,000
Taxable portion (½)	$200,000
Loss carry-over	(200,000)
Taxable income	–0–
Tax on capital gain	–0–
Total tax cost	–0–

It is important to appreciate that tax planning does not consist of a definitive list of rules. In the above situation, an advantage would have been achieved by converting property income (dividends) into a capital gain, but this does not mean that it is always better to convert dividends into a capital gain.

Because tax planning does not consist of a definitive list of rules, one must test alternative courses of action, with a view to achieving specific financial goals. In the situation being discussed, A sought to receive the value from his corporation and had two fundamental choices—distribute dividends or sell shares.

It is also worthwhile to approach tax planning decisions in the context of expenditures. Advantages may be gained when the cost for acquiring a good or service is converted from one type of expenditure to another, just as it is when income is converted from one type to another. Consider the following situation:

Situation: Corporation X requires more land to provide parking facilities for its staff at one of its branch locations. Two options are available: it can purchase land for $100,000 or lease it for $10,000 per year. The corporation's long-range restructuring plans call for the closing of the branch after five years. Real estate studies indicate that land values will likely continue to increase at 4% annually.

Corporation X has limited borrowing capacity, so if it uses current funds, it will have to forgo certain business opportunities. Typically, the corporation's investments provide a minimum pre-tax return of 20%. The corporation's tax rate is 40%.

Analysis: Whether the land is purchased or leased, Corporation X will obtain the right to use the property to fulfill its objective of providing more parking facilities. If the land is purchased, the expenditure will be classified as a capital item and will not be deductible for tax purposes from the company's business income. Instead, when the land is sold, the cost will be deducted from the selling price to determine the amount of the capital gain or loss at that time. One-half of that gain or loss will be applicable for tax purposes.

The real cost of purchasing the land is thus the initial cash outflow of $100,000 less the cash proceeds (net of tax) from the sale of the land at the end of five years. Because the cash received from the sale occurs at year 5, its value must be discounted at an appropriate discount rate, which in this case may be 20% pre-tax or 12% after-tax (20% − [40% of 20%] = 12%). The cash flows from this alternative are as follows:

Beginning of year 1:	
Cash outflow (purchase)	$100,000
End of year 5:	
Value of land sold ($100,000 + (4% × 5 years))	$121,665
Tax on gain (40%)(½)($121,665 − $100,000)	(4,333)
Net cash inflow	$117,332

The net cost of the land acquisition is **$33,423**, as follows:

Purchase price	$100,000
Recovered from future sale:	
Present value—$117,332 discounted at 12% for 5 years	66,577
	$ 33,423

In comparison, if the land is leased, the annual rent cost of $10,000 is deductible from business income for tax purposes as a current expenditure rather than a capital expenditure.

Effectively, the expenditure for land has been converted from one type to another. Because the rent is deductible, tax savings of 40% will occur annually, resulting in a cash cost of only $6,000 for the lease ($10,000 − 40% of $10,000 = $6,000). The actual cost of this alternative is the present value of five payments of $6,000.

| Present value—$6,000 annually for 5 years, discounted at 12% | $21,629 |

In the above situation, converting the land costs from a capital item to an expense item results in an overall cost reduction of $11,794 ($33,423 − $21,629).

This example can also be used to demonstrate that the tax planning process can involve considerable uncertainty. In the above example, the following factors require significant speculation:

- The rate of growth of the value of the land.
- The appropriate discount rate.
- The anticipated tax rate at the end of year 5.
- Whether the planned branch closure will occur after five years, and if not, how the lease option will be affected.

Each of these items is important but uncertain. For example, if the corporation still has borrowing capacity and can borrow funds at 11% interest, the appropriate discount rate can be reduced to 6.6% after tax (11% − 40% of 11% = 6.6%), in which case the outcome of the analysis can be completely reversed and, all else being equal, purchase would be the least costly alternative.

III. Skills Required for Tax Planning

This chapter has emphasized three basic types of tax planning. In order to implement tax planning activities, it is necessary to develop certain skills. Certainly one of these is an ability to understand the fundamentals of the Canadian income tax system and how they relate to domestic and international transactions. But there are others, which are summarized below.

• **Anticipation**   All financial investments have a beginning, an activity period, and an end. From the outset one must try to envision the complete cycle, even if the time frame is long. For example, when investing in a corporation, one must envision the returns that it will yield as well as the disposal of that investment at some future time.

• **Flexibility**   Any objective can be achieved in a number of different ways. It is therefore highly worthwhile to seek out alternative methods of achieving particular goals. For example, an asset used in the operation of a business can be leased or purchased. As another example, consider a situation in which three separate entities plan to pool their resources to operate a new business venture. The new venture can be organized as a partnership of three partners or as a corporation having three shareholders. Once the alternatives have been identified, the future activities can be predicted and the tax and financial implications can be examined and compared.

• **Speculation**   One must be able to anticipate the tax effects, if any, should events turn out in a different way than expected—for example, if losses should occur for a period of time, or if the activity should fail completely.

• **Applying the eighth wonder of the world**   It has been said that the eighth wonder of the world is compound interest.[6] Achieving a good return on investment is important, but the ability to reinvest that return is essential for wealth accumulation. Obviously, the amount that is available for reinvestment is affected by the tax cost. For example, if a taxpayer invests $6,000 every year for 30 years ($6,000 × 30 = $180,000) and obtains an annual return of 16% on the invested amount, the accumulated value is $3,691,000. However, if that same taxpayer is subject to a 50% tax rate, the annual return will be only 8%, and the invested amounts will accumulate to only $734,000 after 30 years. Notice the enormous difference: even though the return has dropped by one-half, wealth accumulation over the 30-year period has declined fivefold.

Respect for the time value of money is central to tax planning. Most people are familiar with the saying that "a dollar received today is worth more than a dollar received in the future." Even so, few people appreciate the magnitude of this value until the simple calculation of compound interest is made.

• **Perspective**   Another skill needed for tax planning is the ability to put the tax factor in perspective. Taxation is only one of many considerations in financial decision-making. Whenever a tax-driven course of action is being considered, common sense and general business judgment must prevail. The participants in the activity must understand the transactions and accept them for business as well as tax reasons.

• **Global approach**   Yet another skill that has not been previously referred to is the ability to view transactions in a global context. Financial transactions always involve more than one party. For example, the sale of a business involves a buyer and a seller. Each attempts to carry out tax planning activities to improve its own position. A buyer that can take steps

---

6   Professor E. Vogt, professor of Actuarial Mathematics, University of Manitoba.

to assist the seller in achieving its tax planning goals may gain an advantage in price or other specific terms. For this to happen, the buyer must take a global approach and attempt to understand the tax implications for the seller. This concept is applicable in many types of transactions. An employer should consider the tax position of its employees, a corporation should consider the tax position of its bondholders and shareholders, and so on.

How difficult is it to develop all these skills? On the surface, very. But in fact, there is a common factor that binds them together, and remembering what it is will make the task achievable. This common factor, which is the essence of financial decisions, is *cash flow*. Cash flow has three factors:

- the amount of money coming in;
- the amount of money going out; and,
- timing.

By considering these factors, tax planners can develop or greatly improve their decision-making skills.

IV. Restrictions to Tax Planning

Earlier in this chapter, it was indicated that the benefits from certain tax avoidance activities may be denied. Consequently, tax planning is divided between acceptable and unacceptable activities.

The *Income Tax Act* specifically prohibits a number of activities. These prohibitions are referred to as anti-avoidance rules. In addition, the act has a general rule that attempts to state in general terms what is considered to be unacceptable activity. This section cannot examine all of these rules in depth. Instead, it provides a brief overview to suggest the general flavour of the types of restrictions that exist. Many of these restrictions will become even clearer as you proceed through the text.

A. Specific Anti-Avoidance Rules

It should be noted at the outset that there are two general types of financial transactions. There are those in which the parties have a close relationship, such as a parent and child or two corporations owned by members of the same family. These taxpayers, who are specifically defined in the *Income Tax Act*, are said to be not at arm's length. And there are those in which the parties are completely independent of each other. These taxpayers are at arm's length.[7]

The tax authorities are more concerned with transactions between taxpayers who are closely associated (not at arm's length), because these often are not motivated by normal market forces. In contrast, transactions between arm's length or opposing parties usually reflect economic realities, so the structure of such transactions is usually consistent with their substance. Outlined below are several examples of provisions that have been designed to limit certain tax avoidance activities.

- When a person transfers property to a party who is not at arm's length, the transaction price normally cannot be less than the fair market value of the property transferred.[8] This prevents taxpayers from avoiding taxable gains by simply altering the transaction price.

- When a Canadian taxpayer sells property or services to a non–arm's length foreign entity for an amount that is less than what would have been reasonable if it were sold

7 ITA 251, 252; IT-419R.
8 ITA 69(1)(b); IT-405.

on the open market, the reasonable price is imposed for tax purposes. A similar treatment applies to expenses between such parties.[9] This rule prevents a Canadian entity from avoiding tax by shifting Canadian taxable income to its foreign parent corporation.

- A taxpayer who directs an anticipated taxable receipt to be paid directly to another person must still include that amount in his or her income.[10] This rule prevents a person from shifting taxable amounts to other parties. For example, one cannot avoid tax by directing that one's salary be paid to a creditor.

- A taxpayer cannot transfer a right to income to a related party.[11] For example, an individual who has earned consulting income cannot simply transfer the right to that income to his or her own corporation. For a corporation to earn that income, it must be under contract to do so.

- When property is transferred to a spouse, the future income from that property is included in the income of the original owner for tax purposes.[12] Similar rules apply for the transfer of property to children who are less than 18 years old (see Chapter 9). This rule prevents taxpayers from shifting income to family members who may be subject to lower tax rates.

The above list is far from complete. It does, however, suggest which types of transactions are unacceptable.

B. The General Anti-Avoidance Rule —GAAR

The Canadian tax authorities have enacted a broadly based general anti-avoidance rule (GAAR) to supplement the more specific rules.[13] GAAR stipulates that when a person is involved in an "avoidance transaction," tax will be adjusted to deny the benefit that would have resulted from the transaction or from the series of transactions. This rule raises two questions: what is an avoidance transaction? and what is the nature of the benefit referred to in the rule?

A *tax benefit* is a reduction, avoidance, or deferral of tax, or an increase in the refund of tax. Obviously, all tax planning activities attempt to achieve one or more of these, so the key to understanding the anti-avoidance rule lies in establishing whether a transaction is an *avoidance transaction*.

A transaction is not an avoidance transaction simply because it results in the achieving of a tax benefit. In order for a transaction not to be considered an avoidance transaction, its primary objective must be other than to obtain a tax benefit; in the words of Canada Customs and Revenue Agency (CCRA), "a transaction will not be an avoidance transaction if the taxpayer establishes that it is undertaken primarily for bona fide business, investment or family purposes."[14] In effect, this establishes a business purpose or economic reality test to distinguish between acceptable and unacceptable planning activities.

It would appear that the business purpose test described above eliminates the principle that an individual can organize his or her affairs in such a manner as to pay the least amount of tax required by law.[15] However, the anti-avoidance rule maintains this basic

9 ITA 69(2), (3); 247.
10 ITA 56(2); IT-335R.
11 ITA 56(4); IT-440R2.
12 ITA 74.1; (2), (3); IT-510, -511R.
13 ITA 245.
14 IC 88-2.
15 *Stubart Investments Ltd. v. The Queen*, 84 DTC 6305 (SCC).

principle by tempering the business purpose test with what it refers to as the "misuse or abuse" criteria. Effectively, these state that even when an avoidance transaction occurs, the anti-avoidance rule will not be applied if it may reasonably be considered that the transaction would not result in a misuse or abuse of the provisions of the *Income Tax Act* as a whole. *Therefore, for a tax plan to be rejected, it must fail the business purpose test and, in addition, must be extreme to the extent that it is not within the "spirit" of the tax system as a whole.*

All of this is very subjective and places a responsibility on taxpayers to develop their own degree of certainty by adequately investigating the circumstances in which a misuse or abuse may occur.

V. Summary and Conclusion

Tax planning is the conscious effort of directing one's financial activities in such a manner as to eliminate, reduce, or defer the incidence of tax on those activities. It is important to recognize that the tax system provides a certain degree of flexibility in determining income and organizational structures. This means that taxpayers can, within certain limits, take planned steps to convert one type of income to another, shift income from one time period to another, and transfer income to a different entity for tax purposes.

In many cases these actions are consistent with prudent business activities, as may be the case when, for example, a proprietorship is transferred into a corporation. In other situations the activities are undertaken mainly for tax reasons, in which case potential tax advantages may be denied if the activities are considered to be a misuse or abuse of the income tax system.

Businesspeople must recognize that the ability to tax plan is not based solely on the acquiring of a certain amount of tax knowledge; any such knowledge must be combined with certain general skills if decisions are to be effective and creative. Those skills, and the factor common to all of them—cash flow—were discussed in this chapter. Generally, good tax planning involves applying the business basics.

As the reader proceeds through this text and acquires knowledge of the fundamentals of the tax system, he or she should try to relate the principles of this chapter to the particular item being reviewed. At the end of most chapters, a checklist of tax planning items is provided.

Reading List

Income Tax Act References

	Section
General anti-avoidance rule	245(2)
Benefit conferred on a person	246(1)
Offences—tax evasion	239(1), (1.1), (2)
Attribution rules—spouse and children	74.1(1), (2)
Inadequate consideration	69(1)
Unreasonable consideration	69(2)
Arm's length	251
Allocation of amounts in consideration for the disposition of property	68
Agreement to share income so as to reduce or postpone tax otherwise payable	103(1), (1.1)
Indirect payments	56(2)
Transfer of rights to income	56(4)
Capital gain deduction not permitted	110.6(11)
Benefit conferred on shareholder	15(1)
Transfer pricing	247

Canada Customs and Revenue Agency Publications

IC88-2	General anti-avoidance rule, plus supplement.
IC73-10R3	Tax evasion.
IT-432R2	Benefits conferred on shareholders.
IT-335R	Indirect payments.
IT-440R2	Transfer of rights to income.
IT-405	Inadequate consideration.
IT-510, -511R	Attribution rules—income splitting.
IT-453	Conferral of benefits.
IT-419R	Meaning of "arm's length."

Major Court Decisions

Stubart Investments Ltd. v. The Queen, 84 DTC 6305 (SCC)—Tax avoidance and the business purpose test.
McNichol et al. v. The Queen, 97 DTC 111—General Anti-Avoidance Rule.
RMM Canadian Enterprises Inc. et al. v. The Queen, 97 DTC 302—General Anti-Avoidance Rule.
Granite Bay Charters Ltd. v. The Queen—General Anti-Avoidance Rule (TCC).
Donahue Forest Products Inc. v. The Queen—General Anti-Avoidance Rule (TCC).

Other Publications

Davison, Kent, "Avoidance, Evasion, and the Problem Client," Report of Proceedings of the 50th Tax Conference (1998), Canadian Tax Foundation, p. 7.1.
Lawlor, W., "GAAR Challenges by Revenue Canada: An Update," Report of Proceedings of the 49th Tax Conference (1997), Canadian Tax Foundation, p. 6.1.
Thomas and Bowman, "GAAR: It's Alive, It's Alive!" *Canadian Tax Journal*, Vol. 45, No. 5 (1997), p. 1117.
MacNaughton and Mawani, "Tax Minimization Versus Good Tax Planning," *CA Magazine*, Jan./Feb. 1997, p. 40.
Explanatory notes on "General Anti-Avoidance Rule," Bill C-139, Clause 186, June 30, 1988, Department of Finance.
Arnold and Wilson, "The General Anti-Avoidance Rule," *Canadian Tax Journal*, Part 1: July/August 1988, pp. 829–871; Part 2, September/October 1988, pp. 1123–1185; Part 3, November/December 1988, pp. 1269–1410.

Review Questions

1. "Tax planning and tax avoidance mean the same thing." Is this statement true? Explain.

2. What distinguishes tax evasion from tax avoidance and tax planning?

3. Does Canada Customs and Revenue Agency deal with all tax avoidance activities in the same way? Explain.

4. The purpose of tax planning is to reduce or defer the tax costs associated with financial transactions. What are the general types of tax planning activities? Briefly explain how each of them may reduce or defer the tax cost.

5. "It is always better to pay tax later rather than sooner." Is this statement true? Explain.

6. When corporate tax rates are 30% and tax rates for individuals are 40%, is it always better for the individual to transfer his or her business to a corporation?

7. "As long as all of the income tax rules are known, a tax plan can be developed with certainty." Is this statement true? Explain.

8. What basic skills are required to develop a good tax plan?

9. An entrepreneur is developing a new business venture and is planning to raise equity capital from individual investors. Her advisor indicates that the venture could be structured as a corporation (i.e., shares are issued to the investors) or as a limited partnership (i.e., partnership units are sold). Both structures provide limited liability for the investors. Should the entrepreneur consider the tax positions of the individual investors? Explain. Without dealing with specific tax rules, what general tax factors should an investor consider before making an investment?

10. What is a tax avoidance transaction?

11. "If a transaction (or a series of transactions) that results in a tax benefit was not undertaken primarily for bona fide business, investment, or family purposes, the general anti-avoidance rule will apply and eliminate the tax benefit." Is this statement true? Explain.

An Overview of Income Determination and Tax for the Two Primary Entities

You're acting like a thing from
a different tax bracket.

From *Buffy the Vampire Slayer* ≫

part two

Chapter 3   Liability for Tax and Income Determination

The Canadian income tax system has a two-part structure: one part states which parties are subject to tax; the other, how to determine the income to which the tax is applied. It is essential to understand this, because every financial activity involves a particular type of transaction by certain parties, and activities or parties that are not within the scope and parameters of the fundamental structure are not subject to Canadian income taxation. This chapter briefly outlines the sources of Canadian tax law, and explains which entities fall within its scope and how those entities determine their income for tax purposes. The chapter also explains how the income tax relates to the goods and services tax.

I. Sources of Canadian Tax Law

There are three separate sources that govern income tax law in Canada:

- statute law
- common law
- international tax conventions

A. Statute Law

The Canadian federal income tax system is developed in the legal statute known as the *Income Tax Act*. The statute is lengthy, and its form is complex as the result of its authors' efforts to be precise and equitable. Notwithstanding the complex presentation, all taxpayers are responsible for assessing their liability for tax on various types of income earned.

In addition, all provincial jurisdictions impose a tax on income, and each province has enacted its own separate provincial income tax act. However, every province with the exception of Quebec has adopted the federal *Income Tax Act*, with minor variations, as the basis for its own particular provincial statute.

B. Common Law

Disputes regarding the application and interpretation of various sections of the *Income Tax Act* and related provincial statutes are often settled within the Canadian court system. While many cases settled before the courts deal with a narrow set of facts, over the years sufficient jurisprudence has been developed in many areas that it is now the primary source of definitions and interpretations. For example, the *Income Tax Act* does not provide a definition of business income and capital gains, but substantial jurisprudence has developed general guidelines for distinguishing between the two. Common law is, therefore, an integral source of tax law.

C. International Tax Conventions

Canadian taxpayers often invest, carry on business, or are employed in foreign jurisdictions that also impose income tax. In addition, foreign entities engage in similar activities in Canada. As a result, Canada has entered into reciprocal tax treaties with many foreign countries in order to

(a) rationalize and define the jurisdictional authority on transactions of an international nature; and,
(b) avoid the incidence of double taxation resulting from applicable provisions of tax legislation in two or more jurisdictions.

In many cases, provisions of international treaties are in conflict with the *Income Tax Act*. When this occurs, the international treaty takes precedence.

Federal tax law is the responsibility of the Department of Finance. However, assessing and collecting tax is the job of Canada Customs and Revenue Agency (CCRA). In order to assess tax, CCRA must interpret the law, and its interpretations may sometimes conflict with the intentions of the designers. CCRA's interpretations of complex or controversial sections of the *Income Tax Act* are made public through two primary publications—Interpretation Bulletins and Information Circulars.

It is important to recognize that the interpretations published by CCRA are not law and can be disputed through the court system. However, they do reflect current assessment policy and should always be an important factor when tax planning activities are being considered.

Except on rare occasions, the body of this text will not make reference to specific provisions found in the above sources of tax law; rather, it will explain the structure of the tax system in layperson's terms to provide a broad understanding of its general principles for the purposes outlined in Chapter 1. However, to provide a trail for further study and review, appropriate references to the *Income Tax Act* and other sources of tax law are provided by footnote. In addition, a reading list of ITA sections, case law, Interpretation Bulletins, and other publications is provided at the end of each chapter.

II. Liability for Tax

Federal and provincial income taxes are imposed on only three basic types of entities:[1]

A. The Entities

- individuals
- corporations
- trusts

Trusts have limited application to business and investment structures; therefore, this text will direct most of its discussion to the two primary entities—individuals and corporations.

There are other forms of business organizations such as proprietorships, partnerships, joint ventures, and limited partnerships (reviewed in Chapters 15 and 16). None of these entities is directly taxable; rather, they are organizational structures whose profits (or losses) are allocated to the participating owners for tax purposes. The participating owners of the nontaxable structures mentioned above are either individuals or corporations, and therefore all income, regardless of the organizational structure that is used to earn it, is eventually subject to tax.

A corporation is considered to be an artificial person having the same legal rights and responsibilities as an individual. Its affairs are formally separate from the affairs of its owner or owners—the shareholder(s). A building owned by a corporation is not the property of the corporation's shareholder even though the shareholder may control its use and disposition. Similarly, for tax purposes, corporate profits earned or losses incurred belong to the corporation. At some point individual shareholders will realize the profits of the corporation by receiving dividends and/or by disposing of their shares, if and when they rise in value.

While the individual and the corporation are separate taxable entities, there is only one ultimate recipient of profit and cash flow—the *individual*. This means that the separate taxation of the two primary entities is only temporary, and that ultimately the two will be integrated.

Exhibit 3-1 shows two simple organizational structures. Structure A consists of an *individual* operating a business as a proprietorship. The proprietorship itself is not a taxable entity, and all income earned by it is taxed directly in the hands of the individual. Structure B, on the other hand, consists of an *individual* as a shareholder of a *corporation* that

1 ITA 2(1), 104(1), 248(1).

operates a business; this structure involves both primary taxpayers. The corporation, as a taxpayer, is subject to tax on its business income. If and when the individual shareholders receive the remaining after-tax profits as dividends, or sell their shares in the corporation, they are subject to further tax treatment. Both structures are created for the same purpose—to permit an owner to carry on a business—but the amount of tax, as well as the point in time at which that tax is paid, may vary considerably.

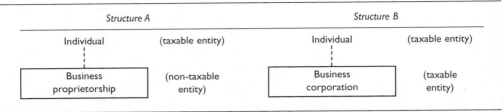

Exhibit 3-1:
Simple Structures of the
Two Primary Taxpayers

In summary, the Canadian income tax system taxes two primary entities—the individual and the corporation. While at times decisions with respect to each can be made in isolation, they generally must be considered as integrated in order for taxpayers to appreciate the impact on cash flow decision making.

B. Resident Individuals and Corporations

Both individuals and corporations are subject to the full thrust of Canadian tax laws if they are considered to be *resident* in Canada.[2] As will be outlined in Part III of this chapter, Canadian residents, whether individuals or corporations, are subject to tax on their *world income*, the scope of which is very broad.[3] Non-resident entities may also be subject to tax in Canada, but in such cases the scope of that income is limited to particular types of income earned only in Canada. This means that residency is an important factor in determining how an entity is taxed in Canada, especially with regard to investments and business expansion abroad. Each of the two primary taxpayers is subject to its own particular definition of residency; the term is often a point of confusion.

1. Individuals

The concept of "residency," although it is key to the process of determining an individual's obligation to pay tax, is left virtually undefined in the *Income Tax Act*. Past court decisions provide a common-law definition, though even that in itself is not specific.

A perspective can be gained by first considering what the definition of residency does *not* include. Residency does not refer to one's domicile; that is, one is not considered a resident of Canada simply by virtue of being present at a particular address. Also, residency does not mean citizenship; individuals who are not citizens can be resident, while individuals who are citizens can be non-resident. The United States uses citizenship as the primary basis for taxing individuals, but Canada does not.

To be a resident of Canada, an individual must maintain a "continuing state of relationship" with the country.[4] While the fact that one is present in the country indicates a state of relationship, it is only one of the factors that must be considered. Even when an individual is present in the country for only a short period annually, other factors may provide a set of circumstances that show a continuing relationship. It is, therefore, a question of fact whether one is resident or not, and each case is judged on its own special circumstances.

---

2 ITA 2(1).

3 ITA 3.

4 ITA 250(3); IT-221R2.

The courts have concluded that a number of factors must be collectively considered when determining residency.[5] The factors include

(a) the amount of time spent in Canada on a regular basis;
(b) the motives for being present or absent;
(c) the maintenance of a dwelling place in Canada while away, and its accessibility;
(d) the origin and background of the individual;
(e) the general mode and routine of the individual's life; and,
(f) the existence of social and financial connections with Canada.

For example, consider an individual who resides and works in another country, but who maintains a dwelling place in Canada which, although rented out, is accessible on short notice, and who maintains formal social ties with clubs and other associations, and who holds Canadian investments and visits Canada for short periods regularly. That person may be considered a resident of Canada because a continuing state of relationship exists. As a result, all world income of that individual would be taxable in Canada.

Individuals who do not exhibit a continuing state of relationship but do spend time sojourning in Canada are automatically deemed to be Canadian residents if their presence exceeds 182 days in the year.[6]

Residency is determined on a year-to-year basis. Once the criteria are met, one is considered a resident throughout the entire year. The only exceptions to this occur when an individual, at some time during the year, severs all previous ties with the country; or when a non-resident establishes new ties with the country. In such cases the individual is considered a resident for the relevant portion of the year and accordingly is taxed on world income for that portion.[7]

2. Corporations

Determining a corporation's resident status is significantly less complicated than determining an individual's. Basically, all corporations *incorporated* in Canada are considered residents of Canada and consequently are subject to tax on world income.[8] Therefore, any corporation incorporated under the federal or a provincial jurisdiction is a Canadian resident regardless of where the controlling shareholders reside—they may be in Canada or in any foreign jurisdiction.

It is also possible for a foreign corporation to be considered a Canadian resident. Under Canadian common law, a company incorporated in a foreign jurisdiction may be resident in Canada if it can be established that the "central management and control" over the major policy affairs of the entity's business is exercised from within Canada.[9] This common-law test is seldom applied, however, due to the obvious difficulties of enforcement and the negative effects it would have on international trade with respect to Canadians carrying on business abroad. Rather, it seems to be used to combat tax avoidance schemes and usually does not affect normal international business or investment structures.

3. Dual Jurisdictions

That an individual or corporation has achieved Canadian-resident status—making that entity's world income taxable in Canada—does not preclude other foreign jurisdictions from claiming the right to tax the same activity and income generated within their boundaries. In such cases the process is rationalized by the application of both the International

---

5   *Thomson v. MNR*, 2 DTC 812 (1946).

6   ITA 250(1).

7   ITA 114; IT-193R; *Schujahn v. MNR*, 62 DTC 1225.

8   ITA 250(4). This rule applies to companies incorporated after April 26, 1965. Companies incorporated prior to that date should consult paragraph 250(4)(c) of the *Income Tax Act*.

9   *De Beers Consolidated Mines Ltd. v. Howe* (1906) AC 455.

Tax Treaty and Canada's *Income Tax Act*. The International Tax Treaty determines the rights of the foreign jurisdiction to tax the particular income; the *Income Tax Act* offers, in most cases, a reduction of Canadian tax by the amount paid to the foreign jurisdiction on the same income.

For example, consider the situation of a Canadian corporation that carries on business in Canada but also operates a major branch operation in the United States. As the corporation is a resident of Canada, the foreign-branch income is part of its world income and is therefore taxable in Canada. The branch is also subject to taxation in the United States. The Canada/U.S. tax treaty permits the United States to tax the branch profits at its applicable rates and according to its rules of income determination. While Canada also includes the branch income in its tax calculation, the resulting Canadian tax can be reduced by the amount of tax paid in the United States. Although double taxation is avoided when income is taxed simultaneously by Canada and a foreign country, the result is that the rate of tax paid on foreign income by the Canadian entity will always equal the tax rate imposed by the country with the higher tax rate (see Chapter 20).

C. Non-Resident Individuals and Corporations

As mentioned previously, non-residents of Canada (both individuals and corporations) are not subject to tax in Canada on their world income but are, at times, taxable on specific activities that occur within this country. A review of this topic may at first appear to be of little value to a Canadian reader; however, Canada treats the activities of foreign entities in much the same way that other countries treat the activities of Canadian entities. This review will help the reader to understand how taxation affects a Canadian entity's international business activities.

International business transactions can be placed in two broad categories:

1. Transactions that are started and are completed in the foreign host country.

2. Transactions that originate in one country but are concluded in a second country.

For example, the payment of interest on a debt by a Canadian resident to a foreign creditor would fall within the second category, since the payment originates in Canada but the transaction is not completed until the interest is received by the non-resident. Similarly, the purchase of a product by a Canadian resident directly from a foreign supplier is also of the second category. On the other hand, the selling of merchandise in Canada by a foreign enterprise via the establishment of a branch warehouse and sales office would come under the first category, as each sale would originate and conclude within the Canadian branch. Income in the first category can generally be determined on a net basis, being the revenues minus the expenses incurred to earn the revenues, whereas transactions that originate in one country and conclude in the other, such as the payment of interest, relate only to the revenue component of net income. Both types of activity are taxed in Canada on a selective basis.

1. Tax on Net Income

Non-residents are taxed in Canada on the net income (revenues minus expenses permitted for tax purposes) arising when the non-resident

(a) carries on business in Canada;

(b) disposes of certain Canadian property; or,

(c) is employed in Canada.[10]

---

10 ITA 2(3); IT-176R2, IT-420R3.

Notice that in order for a foreign entity (individual or corporation) to be taxed in Canada on business activities, that entity must carry on business in Canada. While the term "carrying on business in Canada" has broad scope within the *Income Tax Act*, most international tax treaties between Canada and other countries indicate that it applies only when the business is being carried on through a "permanent establishment" in Canada.[11] A permanent establishment is regarded as either a fixed place of business or an agency relationship where a resident party has authority to regularly contract on behalf of the non-resident entity. Therefore, the method by which a foreign entity does business in Canada (it might involve direct sales to customers, or sales to independent contractors who resell to customers, or the establishing of a warehouse and/or a branch sales office, or the creation of a separate corporate entity) has a significant impact on how that entity is taxed in Canada and in turn on the amount and timing of income taxes.

2. Tax on Canadian Source Income

The tax on an amount that originates in Canada but is paid directly to a non-resident is referred to as a "withholding tax," because the payer must withhold a portion of the obligated payment and remit it directly to the Canadian tax authorities. Normally this type of tax is calculated at a flat rate and is based on the gross amount paid, without consideration of any related expenses that may have been incurred by the recipient.

The rate of withholding tax has been set at 25% by the *Income Tax Act*.[12] Most negotiated international tax treaties, however, have reduced the rate to 5%, 10%, or 15% on most types of revenues. Listed below are the *major* types of payments that may be subject to Canadian source tax when paid to non-residents:[13]

- interest
- dividends
- rents
- royalties
- pension benefits
- certain management and administration fees

The above list is not complete, and there are major exceptions within each category. Notice that the direct sale of goods and services across international boundaries between independent parties is not subject to this form of taxation.

D. Decision Making and the Residence Issue

The issue of who is liable for tax in Canada has a significant impact on decisions Canadians make about investing abroad or expanding a business enterprise into international markets. The knowledge that the two primary entities are subject to tax on world income only if they are resident in Canada provides an insight into which international transactions are taxable in Canada. In addition, knowledge of the Canadian framework for taxing non-residents carrying on business in Canada can be reversed and applied to Canadian activities in foreign jurisdictions, thereby permitting a general appreciation of the foreign taxes that affect such activities.

Always, the intention is to create an organizational structure that will meet the desired business objectives with a minimum of cash requirements and permit the maximum repatriation of generated funds for reinvestment. While international tax issues are complex and extensive (see Chapter 20), the areas reviewed to this point provide a sufficient base to appreciate the relationship between cash flow and organization structure. Consider

---

11 ITA 253.

12 ITA 212.

13 IC 76-12R5 provides agreed withholding tax rates with treaty countries.

Exhibit 3-2, which outlines three simple alternative structures for accomplishing the same basic objective—to expand Canadian business operations into a foreign market. By applying Canada's residence rules and using the framework of Canadian taxation of non-residents as a guide to Canadian expansion, the following analysis on cash flow can be made.

Structure A

Under this structure, penetration into the foreign market is achieved by direct sales from the Canadian business entity to the foreign customer. Payments for all sales are made directly to Canada.

Operations in the foreign country are not carried on from a permanent establishment; therefore, they are not subject to tax by the foreign jurisdiction. Both the individual and the Canadian corporation are resident in Canada and subject to tax on world income. As they are separate entities, the profits of the corporation, if and when they are distributed to the individual shareholder, are included in the individual's taxable income as dividends.

Therefore, under structure A, foreign profits are taxed in Canada at Canadian corporate tax rates and are then available for reinvestment in Canada and the foreign country, or for distribution to shareholders.

Structure B

In structure B, foreign operations are conducted out of a branch location that houses inventory and personnel for selling and administration. Payments for all foreign sales are made to the branch location.

The branch operation constitutes a permanent establishment, and the profits (if any) attributable to it are subject to tax in the foreign country. (In addition, some foreign jurisdictions annually impose a low, flat rate tax on after-tax branch profits accumulated.) Within Canada, the Canadian corporation is considered a Canadian resident and is taxed on its world income. The branch operation is considered a separate entity by the foreign jurisdiction, but is not a separate taxable entity for Canadian purposes since it is not one of the two primary entities. As a result, any profits it makes constitute part of the corporation's *world income*. Branch profits are, therefore, simultaneously taxable in Canada, at Canadian corporate tax rates, and in the foreign country. However, Canadian corporate taxes can be reduced by the amount of tax that was paid in the foreign jurisdiction. Also in this structure, any *losses* incurred by the foreign branch can be offset against Canadian income to reduce tax, which would enhance corporate cash flow and assist in funding the branch operations.

In summary, the branch alternative directs cash flow from the customer to the branch and then to the Canadian corporation, with branch profits being taxed annually at either the Canadian or the foreign corporate tax rate, whichever is greater.

Structure C

Under this alternative, the foreign operations are based formally in a foreign corporation as a subsidiary of the Canadian corporation.

As a foreign corporation is one of the two primary entities, a determination must be made as to its residence status. It was pointed out earlier that to be a resident of Canada by statute law, a corporation must be incorporated in Canada. The foreign corporation, even though its shareholders are based in Canada, is not resident and accordingly is not taxed on world income in Canada. This means that profits earned by the foreign entity are taxable only in the foreign country at the foreign rates of corporate tax, which are likely to differ from Canadian rates. As well, any losses incurred by the foreign operation belong exclusively to the foreign corporation and cannot be offset against profits in Canada.

Exhibit 3-2:
Basic Structures for
Foreign Expansion

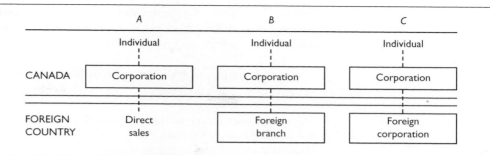

If and when after-tax profits of the foreign entity are distributed to the Canadian shareholder (also a corporation), they flow as dividends and are subject to a source-withholding tax by the foreign jurisdiction.

With this structure, funds flow from the foreign customer to the foreign corporation and are subject to tax at foreign corporate rates. The after-tax profits in the foreign corporation can be used for investment in the foreign country or distributed to the Canadian corporate shareholder. If funds are distributed to Canada as dividends, the amount—net of foreign withholding tax—is then available for reinvestment by the Canadian corporation, or for distribution, with further tax, to the individual Canadian shareholders.

The above alternatives illustrate the substantial tax differences that can occur as business structures are changed. More importantly, they demonstrate a framework for utilizing basic tax principles in the decision process. Cash flows along many different paths and at various speeds before it finally comes to rest with the ultimate investor. When applying the tax factor to business and investment decisions, the key is to *identify the point* along that path at which the cash flow and the power to reinvest are going to be reduced. Cash flow must therefore be charted and anticipated, and always in terms of the basic entities. While business structures can be extensive and complicated, cash flow is taxed only as it enters one of the two primary entities—the individual and the corporation—each of which is separately taxed.

In order to complete the process of charting cash flow, it is also necessary to appreciate the fundamentals of two additional variables as they apply to each of the two primary entities:

(a) the types of income that are taxable; and,
(b) the rates of tax.

III. Determination of Income

Each of the primary entities is required to pay a rate of tax on its *taxable income* in each taxation year.

"Income," by itself, is a broad term, and its definition varies with the point of view of the person defining it. The economist's concept of income is different from a professional accountant's concept of income, and both are different from the dictionary definition. Some parties would restrict the definition so that it includes only wealth enhancement in terms of money or money's worth, and only as the result of labour or enterprise; others would include such items as inheritance and windfalls (lottery winnings, gifts, and the like). "Income for tax purposes," while embracing parts of both definitions, does not subscribe wholly to either; rather, it stands by itself as a separate concept. In order to understand the consequences of financial decisions, it is necessary for one to cast off other views of income determination and develop an appreciation of the concept of *income for tax purposes*.

This concept has no concise definition. (In fact, the *Income Tax Act* does not specifically provide a single definition of income.) Instead, it more closely resembles a framework, which includes the following:

1. Each entity subject to tax determines its taxable income on the basis of a taxation year.

2. Income for each entity includes and is restricted to the world income generated from five general categories. Each category of income is determined in accordance with its own brief set of fundamental principles.

3. The net incomes (revenues minus expenses) for each of the five categories are aggregated in accordance with a strict formula, the sum of which is referred to as *net income for tax purposes.*

4. The sum of the five categories of income is then reduced by a limited number of specific items. Such items differ for the two primary entities. This total is referred to as *taxable income* and is the base to which the rate of tax is applied.

The taxable income for a taxation year of an entity subject to tax in Canada can be expressed in the following simple formula.

$$TI = Net\ income - Special\ reductions$$

A. The Taxation Year

Taxable income is determined and assessed on the basis of an entity's taxation year. The term "taxation year" is defined differently for the two primary entities.[14]

• **Corporations**   The taxation year of a corporate entity is regarded as its fiscal period, being any time period not exceeding 53 weeks (one year) for which the entity accounts for its financial affairs.[15] This means that corporate taxpayers can choose the annual period for which tax will be assessed. It is accepted practice for corporations to account to their shareholders on an annual basis, and this same fiscal period is normally used for tax purposes. Once a corporation chooses a fiscal period, it must continue with the same period in the future unless concurrence is given by CCRA. Such concurrence is normally not withheld if the primary purpose of the change is business related as opposed to tax related.[16]

A fiscal period, and therefore a taxation year, may be less than 12 months in the year in which a corporation comes into existence or ceases to exist, or in which a change in year end is granted. For example, a corporation that is created on June 1 may choose an October 31 fiscal year end, in which case the first taxation year would include only the five months from June 1 to October 31.

• **Individuals**   The taxation year for an individual taxpayer is simply the calendar year, and therefore includes the 12-month period ending on December 31 of every year.

---

14 ITA 249.
15 ITA 249.1.
16 IT-179R.

The choice of a 12-month period for both individuals and corporations to determine taxable income is arbitrary and does not necessarily coincide with the timing of revenues earned and expenses incurred. Transactions often straddle more than one taxation year. For example, a taxpayer with a taxation year ending on December 31 may

(a) earn salary in one year but receive payment in the next;
(b) invest in a bond bearing 10% interest on September 1 but not receive the interest payment until August 31 of the next year; and/or,
(c) buy shares of a public company in year 1 for $10,000 and sell them for $15,000 in year 6.

Certainly, the income over the life of the above transactions is recognizable; even so, the arbitrary imposition of a 12-month taxation year is a common source of confusion and may require a departure from economic reality when the tax input and its effect on return on investment are being considered. The effect is most dramatic when the income process involves long-term depreciable assets. Consider the simple situation of a business entity purchasing a truck to earn revenue over several years. If the truck cost $10,000 in year 1 and earned revenues of $5,000 annually for six years before being scrapped, the profit over the six years (ignoring operating and maintenance costs) can be determined exactly, as shown below.

Revenues (6 y × $5,000)	$30,000
Expense (cost of truck)	10,000
Profit	$20,000

However, the arbitrary use of a taxation year requires profits to be determined annually. In the above example, this presents no problem for the revenues ($5,000 annually), but it does present a problem when it comes to determining annual expenses. A logical solution would be to estimate the useful life of the asset at the time of its purchase and allocate the total cost over that period. Since it is difficult to estimate accurately the useful life of long-term assets, this procedure would certainly result in some degree of error. Whether an error is made or not, the final profit will be $20,000 over the six years. The tax system removes the need for estimating the useful life of assets by providing a uniform allocation rate for certain types of assets (see Chapter 6). This uniform procedure may allocate the cost of depreciable property over a period of time in a way that does not correspond to either the owner's estimate of useful life or the asset's active life span. As a result, profits for tax purposes, which over the life of the asset will total the proper amount, will in many cases differ every year from economic reality.

The impact of different taxation years on cash flow must also be examined in terms of the business structure. For example, consider the structure outlined in Exhibit 3-3, which concerns an individual who owns 100% of a corporation that carries on an active business. That corporation has entered into another venture in the form of a partnership, of which the corporation owns 50% and some other entity owns the balance.

There are three entities within the structure, and all three earn income independently. However, only *two* of the entities—the individual and the corporation—are subject to tax. The partnership is a non-taxable entity whose annual income is allocated to the partners (in this case, 50% of the profits are annually allocated to the corporation) and taxed in their hands. Even though the partnership is a non-taxable entity, it is entitled to account for its income on a fiscal-period basis, and is considered to have allocated its computed income to the partners on the last day of its fiscal year (see Chapter 15). Notice that each entity

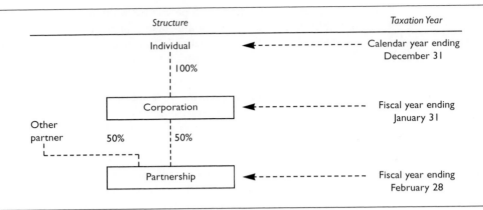

Exhibit 3-3:
Taxation Years and
Business Structure

has a different taxation year, even though each is part of the same business structure. This means that the timing of the taxation of income is different for each entity in the group, and that the impact of that timing on cash-flow decision making is important.

Cash flow can be enhanced by a prudent choice of fiscal periods when creating a structure. In Exhibit 3-3 the choice of February 28 as the partnership fiscal period delays the payment of tax until the corporate year end, which is January 31 of the next year. For example, partnership income for the year from March 1, 2000 to February 28, 2001 is allocated to the corporation on February 28, 2001, and therefore falls within the corporation's taxation year lasting from February 1, 2001 to January 31, 2002. This is demonstrated in the following diagram.

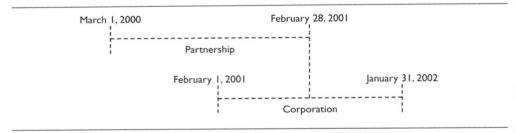

Notice also that the movement of cash within the structure from one entity to another for reinvestment is affected by the timing of the distributions. For example, consider the decision to move realized profits from the partnership venture all the way to the individual shareholder in Exhibit 3-3. One choice might be to distribute the cash at each entity's year end. Accordingly, the partnership would distribute its profits on February 28, 2001 to the corporation, which would hold the cash until its year end of January 31, 2002, at which time a dividend would be paid to the individual shareholders. The cash flow in terms of each entity's taxation year is shown in the diagram on the following page.

The partnership profits, most of which were realized in 2000, are first taxed in the corporation in its year ending January 31, 2002. The related dividend distribution in January 2002 is taxable a second time in the individual's taxation year ending December 31, 2002. Of course, the decision could have been made to distribute the dividend before January 2002, in which case tax on the dividend would have been incurred in the individual's 2001 taxation year. The timing of the dividend distribution has tax consequences and must be weighed in terms of the shareholder's need for funds. A delay in dividend distributions that postpones tax must therefore be compared with the incremental cost of obtaining funds on a temporary basis from other sources. That incremental cost is the after-tax borrowing

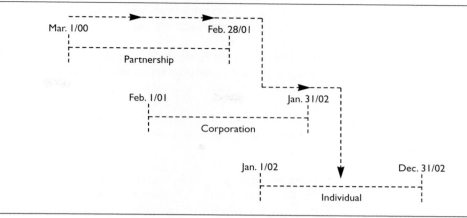

cost (interest) incurred by the shareholder *minus* the after-tax returns to the corporation generated by its use of the funds until the dividend distribution.

The concept of taxation years, although a simple one in terms of tax interpretation, can have a significant impact on the cash-flow process. The choice of year end for each of the various entities within a business structure must be considered whenever expansion activity involves broadening the structural base by including additional entities. As well, the timing of cash-flow activities between entities must be examined in relation to the taxation years in existence at the time.

B. Types of Income

Within the framework of income determination, an entity's world income is derived from five basic sources:[17]

- employment income
- business income
- property income
- capital gains and losses
- other specific sources

Income for each category is determined by applying those basic principles that are special to the particular category. The basic principles determine the extent to which items are included in income, the extent to which deductions from that income are permitted, and the point in time at which the transaction is recognizable for tax purposes. For example, if a transaction giving rise to income falls within the category of "employment income," the application of the basic principles for that category will determine to what extent (if any), and when, the item is to be included.

The basic principles are different for each category, and in some cases these differences are substantial. It is important to note that income determination varies as a function of how the income is earned—whether the entity is an individual or a corporation is normally *not* a factor. The commonly held view is that the corporate taxpayer is entitled to greater deductions than the individual taxpayer. This is untrue: an individual who earns business income determines that income according to exactly the same principles used by a corporation earning business income. It is also important to recognize that both of the primary entities can earn more than one type of income and, therefore, can be subject to several

17 ITA 3.

formats of income determination; for example, an individual could derive income from all five categories in one taxation year and would have to apply different principles to each one.

The first step toward understanding how a specific transaction or an ongoing activity will be taxed is to relate that transaction or activity to one of the five income categories mentioned earlier. The importance of this process is twofold.

1. If the item falls within a particular category, then the process of determining the amount and timing of its income is directed by the basic principles that apply only to that category.

2. If the item does not fall within one of the five categories, it is not subject to tax within the Canadian system. For example, such items as lottery winnings, inheritances, and the receipt of gifts do not fall within the definition of any of the categories and as such are not taxable.

The five types of income will be defined and developed in detail in later chapters. A brief, general definition for each income category is given below. These definitions are not complete and are provided at this point solely to help the reader gain an appreciation of the formula for total income determination, which is developed in a later section of this chapter.

• **Income from employment**   Income from employment[18] is derived when an entity engages the general services of an individual in return for a salary, wage, and/or other fringe benefits. An individual who independently contracts specific services on a fee-for-service basis, and who is not under the general direction and control of an employer, is not receiving employment income.

• **Income from business**   Income from business[19] includes many things. Generally, it includes all enterprise carried out with the intention to profit. It is not necessary that the activity be ongoing or that it provide the physical appearance of a formal business. The once-in-a-lifetime purchase of land for the purpose of trading it at a profit is a business activity and is treated in the same manner as the affairs of a large land-trading company. Similarly, a person who is not in the painting business but who paints a neighbour's fence in return for a quoted fee has derived income from business.

• **Income from property**   Income from property[20] can generally be regarded as the return that is earned on invested capital. It includes items that are normally thought of as investment income, such as interest, dividends, rents, and royalties. It does **not** include the gain that may be realized on the sale of the investment itself, but rather is restricted to the regular return generated from its ownership. Income from property is often referred to as "passive" income because the earning process requires little effort or labour by the recipient.

• **Capital gains**   Capital gains[21] refer to the profit realized on the sale of assets that were acquired for the purpose of generating monetary returns or personal enjoyment over a long period of time. It is not the nature of the asset itself that causes the profit on sale to be

---

18 ITA 5–8.

19 ITA 9–37.

20 ITA 9–37.

21 ITA 38–55.

considered a capital gain; rather, the use of the asset is the important factor. For example, the tractor used by a farmer to generate farm revenue is a capital asset, and a gain on its sale in excess of the original cost would be considered a capital gain. The same treatment may be applied to profits from the sale of land that was originally acquired and used as part of an apartment complex generating annual returns in the form of rent. On the other hand, the profit on the sale of a tractor by an implement dealer would be regarded as business income and not as a capital gain, because the dealer acquired the property in order to profit from its resale. Similarly, the profit realized on the sale of land that was acquired with the intention of trading it at a profit would not be a capital gain.

• **Other income and deductions**   While the title of this category appears to capture all activities that fall outside the previous categories, its scope, in fact, is extremely limited. The term "other income and deductions" cannot be generally defined, except to state that it *includes* and is *limited to* the few specific items referred to in sections 56 to 66 of the *Income Tax Act*. *Other income* includes such items as superannuation and pension receipts (including Old Age Security and Canada Pension Plan benefits), Employment Insurance benefits, alimony payments, receipts from RRSPs, and deferred profit sharing plans. *Other deductions* includes RRSP contributions, alimony payments, child-care expenses, and moving expenses.

C. Net Income for Tax Purposes— The Aggregating Formula

The second step in determining a taxpayer's income subject to tax is to arrive at net income for tax purposes by aggregating the five types of income eligible for inclusion. While this process is not complex, it requires a strict adherence to a basic accumulating formula.[22] The formula is often referred to as the "statutory scheme," as it is the foundation upon which the entire income tax system is based. In effect, the formula is the *definition of net income for tax purposes*, because it establishes the scope of taxable activities and presents the overall method of computation. Its importance cannot be overemphasized, as it is the broom that sweeps away much of the tax system's complexity.

The formula, which is outlined in Exhibit 3-4 on the next page, consists of four segments, each of which is reviewed below. It is important to recognize that *the same formula is used by both individuals and corporations*, which is the same as saying that the determination of net income for tax purposes is identical for all taxable entities.

Segment A
This segment adds together four sources: employment income, business income, property income, and other income. The remaining category, capital gains, is dealt with separately in segment B.

The reference to each of the income items does not allude to the gross income but rather to the *net income* from each source. Therefore, the business income added into segment A is the gross revenue less the expenses incurred to earn that revenue. Similarly, "employment income" refers to employment income after permitted expenses have been deducted for tax purposes.

Keep in mind that each category of income may have more than one source within it.[23] For example, an entity may operate more than one business, in which case the revenues less expenses must be computed separately for each business. Similarly, an individual may be employed at two jobs, in which case the income less the deductions must be computed separately for each. Segment A includes only those specific sources of

22 ITA 3.

23 ITA 4.

A *Determine* the aggregate of:

Employment income	+
Business income	+
Property income	+
Other items of income	+
Subtotal 1 (must be positive or zero)	+ or 0

B *Increase* subtotal 1 by the amount by which:

Taxable capital gains*	+	
exceed		
Allowable capital losses	–	+ or 0
Subtotal 2 (must be positive or zero)		+ or 0

C *Reduce* (but do not exceed) subtotal 2 by:

Other items of deduction	–
Subtotal 3 (must be positive or zero)	+ or 0

D *Reduce* (but do not exceed) subtotal 3 by:

Employment losses	–	
Business losses	–	
Property losses	–	
Allowable business investment losses	–	– or 0
Total—net income for tax purposes (must be positive or zero)		+ or 0

* A small portion of the formula relating to capital gains (losses) on listed personal property has been omitted. The area has limited application and is discussed briefly in Chapter 8. The entire formula is reviewed in more detail in Chapter 9.

income that, net of deductions, result in *positive net income.* Any source that results in a net loss is included later in the formula, at segment D. Consider the situation where an entity operates two businesses. Business #1 has a net profit of $60,000, while business #2 incurs a net loss of $40,000. Even though the entity's combined income from both businesses is $20,000, segment A includes only the net income from business #1—that is, $60,000.

Because only those sources of income that show a positive net income are included in segment A, the subtotal of all items in that segment must be positive or at least zero.

Segment B
This segment deals exclusively with capital property and includes both taxable capital gains and allowable capital losses. Because the term "exceeds" must be adhered to, this segment applies only when total capital gains for a particular year are greater than the total capital losses for that year. As a result, the calculation in segment B cannot be negative and must show a positive or zero amount. Consider the following two examples.

	Situation 1	Situation 2
Taxable capital gains:		
Property A	$10,000	$10,000
Property B	15,000	15,000
Allowable capital losses:		
Property C	(11,000)	(35,000)
Net gains (losses)	$14,000	($10,000)

In situation 1 the capital gains exceed the capital losses by $14,000 and, therefore, the formula under segment B increases net income for tax purposes by $14,000. However, in situation 2 the capital losses are greater than the gains by $10,000. Because *the gains do not exceed the losses*, segment B results in a zero amount, and net income for tax purposes remains unchanged.

Implicit in this segment of the formula is that capital losses incurred by a taxpayer can be offset in the year only to the amount that capital gains were realized in the year, and **cannot** be used to offset any of the other sources of income included in segment A. Unused capital losses as exemplified in situation 2 are available for use in certain other years if other capital gains are realized; however, it is possible that a taxpayer's capital losses may remain unused indefinitely (see Chapters 10 and 11).

The reader may already be aware that only one-half of the actual capital gains and losses are applicable for tax purposes (see Chapter 8). The reference to "taxable" capital gains and "allowable" capital losses in the formula reflects this.

Segment C

This segment simply deducts from all other sources of income a limited number of items referred to as "Other items of deduction." These include RRSP contributions, moving expenses, and the like. The fact that these specific items are located at this point of the formula (that is, after the five sources of income have been included) indicates that they can be offset against any form of income.

Notice that the formula in Exhibit 3-4 does not permit these deductions to exceed the total of income included to that point. If the deductions in segment C are in excess of all other sources of income, such excess is lost and, except in limited circumstances, cannot be used in any other taxation year.

Segment D

This segment further reduces net income for tax purposes. Losses incurred from employment, business, and property, and allowable business investment losses, are stated here. It was indicated previously that these items are specifically excluded from other segments. The fact that they are located as the last item within the formula is significant, because it means that such losses can be offset against all other forms of income previously included. They therefore are of greater value in the tax process than capital losses, which are restricted by segment B.

The term "allowable business investment loss" is introduced for the first time in segment D and requires a word of explanation.[24] An allowable business investment loss refers to a loss on *either* the sale of shares *or* a loan to a small business corporation (see Chapter 8). Such a loss, though a capital loss, is given a special category outside segment B. Its inclusion in segment D means that such a loss can be offset against all other sources of income. (This is not the case with segment B capital losses.) The result is that the risk of investing in this type of capital property is relatively lower, as potential tax savings on a loss are more readily usable.

The losses in segment D can only reduce income for the year to zero. However, the unused amount (if any) is available for use in a limited number of other taxation years (see Chapters 10 and 11).

The process of aggregating income by strict application of the four-step formula provides many answers to questions concerning how an entity's various income activities interact with each other. In turn, these answers can provide assistance in assessing risk factors in

---

24 ITA 38(c).

financial decision making. Almost every investment carries with it some risk of failure. The real loss on any activity is the actual cash loss incurred less the tax savings (if any) that are generated when the loss is deducted against other sources of income. A business loss of $100,000 that can be offset against other taxable income may reduce tax by $45,000 (assuming a 45% tax rate). In such a case, the investor's real risk exposure when considering such a venture is really $55,000, not $100,000.

Consider the following questions, which are often asked:

1. Can a business loss incurred by an individual be offset against that individual's employment income? *Answer:* Yes. Net income for tax purposes is determined by including employment income in segment A and then deducting a business loss in segment D.

2. Can a corporation deduct its business loss against a capital gain realized on the sale of its subsidiary's shares? *Answer:* Yes. Taxable capital gains are included in income first in segment B. The business loss is deducted in segment D.

3. Can an entity's capital loss on the sale of shares be offset against its business income? *Answer:* No. Capital losses are included in the formula only as a deduction against capital gains in segment B.

4. Can interest expense incurred by an individual on loans acquired for investment purposes be offset against pension income? *Answer:* Yes. Pension income, being "other income," is included in segment A. The interest expense in excess of investment returns, being a loss from property, is deducted later, in segment D.

It is apparent that because of the requirement that the formula be used when determining income for tax purposes, the amount of tax and the timing of its payment are both affected by the *type* of income earned as well as by the amount earned. Consider the following two situations, each of which indicates the same total actual income but a considerably different income for tax purposes.

	Situation 1	Situation 2
Business income (loss)	$(200,000)	$200,000
Capital gains (loss)	200,000	(200,000)
Actual net income	NIL	NIL
Income for tax purposes	NIL	$200,000

In each situation the actual cash profit of the entity was zero. In situation 1 the zero profit was generated by a business loss of $200,000 and a capital gain of $200,000. The formula permits business losses to be offset against all sources of income, and therefore income for tax purposes was zero. However, in situation 2 the zero profit was generated by business profits of $200,000 and a capital loss of $200,000. Since the formula restricts the use of the capital loss because there is no capital gain, income for tax purposes was $200,000, and the entity in situation 2 may have incurred taxes of $90,000 (assuming a tax rate of 45%) even though no cash profits were realized in the year. The activities and total results were the same for both entities—that is, both carried on a business and also invested in capital properties; however, their after-tax cash flows and therefore their ability to compete in the marketplace turned out to be greatly different. Such results can be anticipated by constant reference to the formula for net income determination. This kind of advance knowledge may permit steps to be taken to avoid unfavourable outcomes; it may also provide additional insight when it comes to analyzing the downside cash-flow risk associated with alternative investment opportunities.

The formula can also be applied to business structures in order to determine the tax consequences of income flows between the entities within the structure. Each taxable entity (the individual and the corporation) determines its income separately, and each does so according to the formula. Exhibit 3-5 outlines two simple business structures. In both cases the owner contributed $100,000 of capital to fund an enterprise and, after incurring operating losses of $100,000, terminated the venture. Under structure A the owner operated the business as a proprietorship. Since a proprietorship is not one of the two taxable entities, its income—or loss, in this case—was simply allocated directly to the individual owner. The formula, therefore, applied only to the individual, and the business loss of $100,000 could be immediately offset against any other income earned by the individual, with a resulting reduction in taxes.

Under structure B the business was operated in a corporation that had been capitalized by the individual, who contributed $100,000 for share capital. In this case both entities were taxable and determined their income separately. The business loss of $100,000 belonged only to the corporation and could not be offset against any other income earned by the individual shareholder. The individual also suffered a loss due to the decline in value of the corporation's shares. This loss of $100,000 was realized only when the shares were disposed of and included in the formula as a capital loss. Also, only one-half of the loss ($50,000) is allowable to be offset against taxable capital gains or against other income sources if it qualifies as an allowable business investment loss.

Exhibit 3-5: *The Net Income Formula and Business Structures*		

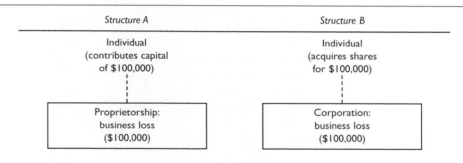

In this example the formula and the concept of taxable entities interacted to significantly alter the tax impact on both structures, even though the unsuccessful ventures were identical.

It can be seen that the formula for determining income for tax purposes has a formidable impact on the tax process. Its simple format, when applied, provides direct answers to many specific questions, as well as a general overview of a broad range of tax issues. Despite its importance, a person who examines the individual or the corporate tax return will find absolutely no hint that such a formula exists. It is hard to understand why the formula is not the primary focus of tax returns; the fact that it is not is likely a major contributing factor to the lack of understanding of the tax process on the part of many taxpayers.

D. Taxable Income

The final step in arriving at the base amount of income to which a rate of tax is applied is to reduce net income for tax purposes (as established by the formula) by a limited number of specified reductions.[25] This final reduced amount is referred to as "taxable income."

---

25 ITA, Part I, Division C, 110–116.

The items that reduce net income for tax purposes to taxable income are different for the two primary taxpayers, which means that the framework of income determination that has so far applied to both individuals and corporations begins to branch at this point. The number of income reduction items in this area is not significant; only a few have a major impact on business and investment decisions. An abbreviated list of the taxable income reductions for individuals and corporations is given below.

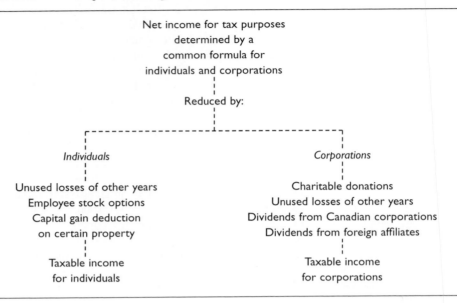

Detailed explanations of the items shown, and their relationship to the decision-making process, are deferred until later chapters (see Chapters 10 and 11). They are identified at this point only to show the limited scope of this part of the income determination process. In later chapters special attention will be given to the utilization of losses and the flow of intercorporate dividend distributions, both of which are significant variables in the management of cash flows.

IV. Income Tax and the GST

In 1991, a national goods and services tax was introduced in Canada. Except for a few exempt items, the GST is imposed at the rate of 7% on the value of all goods or services sold by registered businesses. The tax is charged to businesses as well as to individual consumers. However, most business entities are entitled to a full rebate of the tax on all goods and services purchased, provided that those goods and services were acquired for business purposes. As a result, the tax applies primarily to individuals as the ultimate consumers. In effect, the GST is a sales tax on consumer goods and services. This is demonstrated in the following situation and analysis.

Situation:

A wholesale business purchased inventory from a manufacturer for an invoice cost of $1,000. It then sold that inventory to a retail business for $1,500. The retail business increased the price to $2,500 and sold it to a consumer customer.

Analysis: Both the wholesaler and the retailer will pay GST on their purchases and charge GST on their sales. However, for each business the net cost will be zero, as follows.

	Product sale price (cost)	GST rate	GST collected (paid/remitted)
The wholesaler:			
Sale price to retailer	$1,500	7%	$105
Cost from manufacturer	(1,000)	7%	(70)
Gain	$ 500		35
Remitted to CCRA			35
GST cost			–0–
The retailer:			
Sale price to consumer	$2,500	7%	$175
Cost from wholesaler	(1,500)	7%	(105)
Gain	$1,000		70
Remitted to CCRA			70
GST cost			–0–

The above demonstrates that although wholesalers and retailers are involved in the GST process (collecting, paying, and remitting tax), they merely act as a conduit, passing the tax on to the ultimate consumer. Notice that the wholesaler in this case collected $105 of GST (7% of $1,500) but remitted only $35 to the government. That is because the wholesaler was entitled to claim a GST refund of $70 (7% of $1,000). If costs happen to exceed sales, no tax is remitted and a business is entitled to a GST refund.

Also notice that in this case, the net amount of tax collected and remitted by the wholesaler ($35) was equal to 7% of the value added to the goods that were sold (7% of $500). The same was true for the retailer.

As was pointed out previously, the 7% GST applies to most goods and services. The tax does not apply to items that are classified as either *zero-rated* or *exempt*.

When a vendor business sells goods or services that are zero-rated, the GST is not collected; however, that business can claim credits for any GST paid on costs associated with those items. Zero-rated goods and services include but are not limited to the following:

- prescription drugs
- basic groceries
- agricultural products
- medical devices
- fishery products
- exported items

Vendors that sell goods and services that are classified as exempt also do not collect GST on those items. However, these vendors cannot claim a credit for any GST paid in relation to those exempt items.

Exempt goods and services (as opposed to zero-rated ones) include the following:

- used housing
- education services
- financial services (domestic)
- health-care services
- legal aid services

The above brief outline indicates that, as a general rule, the GST does not create any revenues or expenses for a business entity and has no effect on its income. Consequently, the GST does not have a major impact on income tax. There are, of course, some exceptions to this. For example, businesses that have annual revenues under $30,000 are not required to register as GST participants (though they can elect to do so). Businesses that do not register need not collect GST on their revenues, but neither are they entitled to claim a credit (or refund) for the GST paid on goods and services acquired. In such circumstances, the GST becomes a real cost, and the GST paid on inventory purchases forms part of the inventory cost for income tax purposes and so on. Similarly, many individuals who are not registered GST participants earn investment income and incur related costs. When GST is paid on those costs it becomes part of those items for income tax purposes.

There are several other areas where the GST and the income tax system are closely linked. These are referred to throughout the text in the appropriate chapters.

V. Tax Planning Checklist

This chapter has introduced a number of topics in a very general way. They can be condensed to this short list of tax planning items.

1. When starting a new business or investment venture, consider alternative forms of organization. The structures considered should include the taxable entities (individuals, corporations, and trusts) as well as the non-taxable entities (partnerships, limited partnerships, and joint ventures).

2. From time to time, review existing organization structures and consider making alterations in the context of the changing business environment.

3. When creating an organization, choose the fiscal period carefully in order to optimize timing for the recognition of income or losses.

4. An individual who intends to leave Canada permanently or for an extended period is strongly advised to anticipate the impact of the residence rules—in particular, to identify the relevant dates when his or her status will change. That person should also consider completing certain transactions before or after that date.

5. If capital property has declined in value and a potential capital loss exists, consider when the property should be sold in order to ensure that the capital loss can be offset against any capital gains.

Notice that the first two items deal with a transfer of income from one entity to another. The last three deal with shifting income or losses from one time period to another.

VI. Summary and Conclusion

This chapter has covered an extensive number of topics and has discussed all major areas of the Canadian tax system except the one involving the actual rate of applicable tax. The following summary will be useful in drawing together the topics covered.

Residents of Canada

1. Taxpayers who are resident in Canada are subject to tax on their world income within each taxation year.

2. There are only three categories of taxpayers—individuals, corporations, and trusts—even though other forms of business organization exist.

3. An individual is considered to be a resident of Canada if he or she maintains a "continuing relationship" with the country. A corporation is resident if it is incorporated in Canada.

4. The taxation year normally includes 12 months. For the individual, it is the calendar year; for the corporation, it is the fiscal year chosen by the corporation.

5. World taxable income is limited to five basic sources: employment income, business income, property income, other income, and capital gains. The aggregate of these five sources of income is the taxpayer's net income for tax purposes.

6. Net income for tax purposes is determined in accordance with a four-step formula that applies identically to both primary taxpayers—the individual and the corporation. The formula establishes that losses incurred from business, employment, and property, and allowable business investment losses, can be offset against any of the five types of income earned by the entity. However, capital losses can be offset only against other capital gains.

7. Taxable income is established by reducing net income for tax purposes by a limited number of items. Certain of these items apply only to individuals, others only to corporations.

Non-Residents of Canada

Non-resident individuals and corporations are subject to tax in Canada under two circumstances.

1. If the non-resident carries on business in Canada, is temporarily employed in Canada, or disposes of certain Canadian property, the income from only those particular sources is taxed, in a manner similar to the one faced by Canadian individuals and corporations.

2. Certain income that is paid from a Canadian source is subject to a flat-rate tax, which is withheld by the Canadian payer. Income subject to this tax includes dividends, interest, rents, royalties, and certain management fees paid to non-residents.

The above summary and the preceding comments constitute the full framework of the Canadian tax system, which is predicated on four basic concepts:

*   residency
*   individuals and corporations—two separate taxable entities
*   taxation year
*   net income for tax purposes

An appreciation of these basic concepts by itself provides a significant insight into the tax structure. More importantly, as demonstrated in the brief examples within the chapter, the concepts are tools that can be applied to enhance financial decision making by including the tax impact. In particular, the concepts permit the decision maker to locate the points along the cash-flow path at which the tax factor is relevant. The result is informed decision making leading to the enhancement of cash flow and therefore improved return on investment.

The remaining portion of Part Two is devoted to expanding the general understanding of the framework developed in Chapter 3. A major portion of this (Chapters 4 through 9) defines and discusses the five types of income included in the formula for determining net income.

Reading List

Income Tax Act References

	Section
Tax payable by persons resident in Canada	2(1)
Taxable income	2(2)
Person	248(1)
Individual	248(1)
Corporation	248(1)
Taxation year	249
Fiscal period	249.1
Extended meaning of resident	250(1)
Corporation deemed resident	250(4)
Tax payable by non-residents	2(3)
Residence for part of the year	114
Income for a taxation year	3
Income or loss from a source	4

Canada Customs and Revenue Agency Publications

IT-221R3	Determination of an individual's residence status.
IT-193R	Taxable income of individuals resident during part of the year.
IT-420R3	Non-residents—income earned in Canada.
IT-298	Canada–U.S. Tax Convention—number of days "present" in Canada.
IT-176R2	Taxable Canadian property.
IT-490	Barter transactions.
IT-447	Residence of a trust.
IT-179R	Change of fiscal period.
IC-76-12R5	Withholding tax rates for treaty countries.

Major Court Decisions

Thomson v. MNR, 2 DTC 812 (1946)—Residence. Ordinarily resident in Canada.

Schujahn v. MNR, 62 DTC 1225 (1962)—Full-time and part-time residence.

De Beers Consolidated Mines Ltd v. Howe (1906) AC 455—Corporate residence, central management and control.

Other Publications

Hansen, B., "Individual Residence," Report on Proceedings of the 29th Tax Conference (1977), Canadian Tax Foundation, pp. 682–712.

Pyrcz, O., "The Basis of Canadian Corporate Taxation: Residence," *Canadian Tax Journal*, July/August 1973, pp. 374–390.

Fortin, G., "Economic Reality v. Legal Reality" (meaning of income), Report of Proceedings of the 48th Tax Conference (1996), Canadian Tax Foundation, p. 5.1.

Demonstration Questions

Question One

John Murphy and his family have lived in Winnipeg for 20 years. John owns 100% of the shares of Teulon Ltd., which operates a successful small manufacturing business. 20X0 is shaping up to be a big year for Murphy and his family, as both the business and the family will undergo the following major changes.

1. Teulon plans to expand its operations internationally. To accomplish this, the company will purchase the shares of a Belgian corporation that is manufacturing products similar to those produced by Teulon. The Belgian corporation will generate good profits; it is anticipated that an annual dividend will be paid to Teulon Ltd.

   In addition, Teulon will begin expanding into the United States, by entering into a 50/50 partnership with an American corporation. The partnership will develop a sales and distribution depot in California to market Teulon's products throughout the United States and Central America.

2. Murphy plans to sell 50% of his shares in Teulon to three senior managers. They will purchase the shares with a small cash payment and will pay the balance to Murphy over the next 10 years, with 12% interest.

3. Murphy has indicated that after he sells 50% of the shares of Teulon, he and his family will move to California on a permanent basis. The move will take place on September 30, 20X0. In the United States, Murphy will work part-time for the new American partnership but will also pursue some other business ventures on his own. He will receive regular payments from Canada on the amount owing from the sale of shares. He also hopes to receive dividends on his remaining shares of Teulon.

Required:

Describe briefly how each of the above activities will be affected by Canadian tax laws.

Solution:

Teulon Ltd. is a *resident* of Canada for tax purposes because it is incorporated in Canada. It is subject to tax on its world income. The Belgian corporation is *not* resident in Canada (not incorporated in Canada) and therefore its profits are not taxed in Canada. Dividends received by Teulon from the Belgian corporation are part of Teulon's *world income* and will be included in net income for tax purposes as *income from property*.

The California partnership constitutes a permanent establishment in the United States, and its profits are subject to tax in that country. The partnership is not a separate taxable entity. Therefore, Teulon's share of its profits must be included in Teulon's world income for Canadian tax purposes. Canadian tax will be reduced by taxes paid in the United States.

Murphy is resident in Canada until he leaves to live in the United States. Therefore, he is taxed in Canada on his world income up to the date of departure. Any gain or loss on the sale of Teulon shares is included as part of this world income as a *capital gain or loss*. After his departure, Murphy will be a non-resident for tax purposes. Interest and dividends paid to Murphy after departure are subject to a withholding tax in Canada.

Question Two

Barbara Tomchuk operates a full-time law practice in southern Manitoba. In addition, she owns a 25% interest in a retail store operating as a partnership and has several other sources of income. Her financial information for the taxation year 20X1 is summarized below.

Net income from law practice	$75,000
Taxable capital gains on shares of public corporations	5,000
Withdrawal from a Registered Retirement Savings Plan	2,000
Interest income	1,000
Allowable capital loss from the sale of shares of a small business corporation	18,000
Allowable child-care expenses	3,000
Allowable capital loss on the sale of bonds	7,000
Share of loss from partnership business	22,000
Net rental income from a property in the United States	13,000
Salary from teaching a college course	4,000
Contribution to a Registered Retirement Savings Plan	8,000

Required:

Calculate Tomchuk's net income for tax purposes for the 20X1 taxation year.

Solution:

(a) Employment income—salary		$ 4,000
Business income—law practice		75,000
Property income:		
Interest	$ 1,000	
Net rental income—United States	13,000	14,000
Other income—withdrawal from RRSP		2,000
		95,000
(b) Taxable capital gains—public corporation shares	5,000	
Allowable capital loss—bonds	(7,000)	–0–
		95,000
(c) Other deductions:		
Child-care expenses	3,000	
Contribution to an RRSP	8,000	(11,000)
		84,000
(d) Losses:		
Business loss—partnership	22,000	
Allowable business investment loss—shares of a small business corporation	18,000	(40,000)
Net income for tax purposes		$44,000

Review Questions

1. Which of the following entities are subject to income tax?
    (a) proprietorship
    (b) individual
    (c) joint venture
    (d) trust
    (e) limited partnership
    (f) corporation
    (g) partnership

2. Describe how the income earned by any of the non-taxable entities listed above is included in the Canadian tax system.

3. How and when does income earned by a corporation affect the tax position of the individual corporate shareholder?

4. In describing who is liable for tax in Canada, the *Income Tax Act* simply states, "An income tax shall be paid as hereinafter required upon the taxable income for each taxation year of every person resident in Canada at any time in the year." Accepting that "person" includes both an individual and a corporation, briefly discuss the meaning and ramifications of this statement.

5. In what circumstances are non-residents subject to Canadian income tax?

6. Can a Canadian resident be subject to tax in Canada as well as in a foreign country on the same earned income? If yes, explain how. Also, what mechanism is available to minimize double taxation?

7. Explain the difference between *net income for tax purposes* and *taxable income* for the taxable entities.

8. Explain what is meant by the statutory scheme, and describe the scheme's relevance to the Canadian income tax system.

9. For tax purposes, would you prefer that a financial loss be a capital loss or a business loss? Explain.

10. Explain the difference between *income from property* and a *gain on the sale of capital property*.

11. One often hears that "corporations are entitled to more deductions for tax purposes than individuals." Based on your reading of Chapter 3, is this statement true? Explain.

12. If an individual earns a living as a lawyer, what possible categories of income, for tax purposes, may he or she generate? Describe the circumstances for each possible classification.

13. What types of income for tax purposes may result when a profit is achieved on the sale of property (e.g., land)?

14. Individual A, a Canadian resident, owns and operates a profitable small farm in North Dakota, U.S.A. He also has a large amount of money earning interest in an American bank. Individual B, also a Canadian resident, owns 100% of the shares of an American corporation that operates a profitable small farm in North Dakota. The corporation also has a large amount of money earning interest in an American bank.

Describe and compare the tax positions of these two individuals, who conduct the same activities but use different organizational structures.

15. Jane Q owned an apple orchard for 20 years. During that time she had cultivated a unique brand of apple that was popular with health food fans. Toward the end of the 20X0 growing season, Q became seriously ill and put the orchard up for sale. Q's neighbour agreed to purchase the entire orchard for $250,000. It upset Q to have to sell at that time of year, because that year's crop was of high quality and in three weeks would have been ripe for picking.

What types of property might have been included in the total purchase price of $250,000? For tax purposes, what types of income might have been generated from the sale of the orchard? Explain your answer.

Problems

Problem One

John Day and Carol Knight conduct similar financial activities. Each is employed and has a portfolio of investments, and during the current year each started a separate small business. Their financial results for the year ended December 31, 20X1, are identical, as follows:

Employment income	$40,000
Interest income from investment portfolio	15,000
Loss from new small business operation	(20,000)

The only difference between Day and Knight is that Day operated his business as a proprietorship, whereas Knight operated her business from a wholly owned corporation.

Required:

1. Assuming that individual tax rates are 40%, compare the tax liability of Day with that of Knight for 20X1.

2. How and when may Knight utilize her business loss to reduce her tax liability?

3. What impact may the difference in tax treatment have on Day's and Knight's wealth accumulation and on their long-term returns on investment?

Problem Two

Pierre X owns 100% of the shares of Corporation X. Corporation X owns 50% of the shares of Corporation XY, which holds several investments. The investments in Corporation XY consist of bonds, rental real estate, and a 40% interest in a partnership that operates a chain of retail stores. The remaining 50% of the shares of Corporation XY are owned by Corporation Y. Corporation Y is wholly owned by John Y.

The partnership and all three corporations account for their income on an annual basis at the following fiscal year ends.

Partnership	March 31
Corporation XY	February 28
Corporation X	January 31
Corporation Y	December 31

The partnership and all three corporations distribute their profits to the owners on the last day of the fiscal year.

In April 20X0, the partnership earned an unusually high monthly profit.

Required:

1. Prepare a diagram of the financial structure of these entities from the information provided above.

2. Which entities within the structure are subject to income tax?

3. Based on the activities described, which types of income for tax purposes will be earned by each entity?

4. Individuals must report their income by filing a tax return within four months of the taxation year end. Based on each entity's distribution policy, what is the last date upon which Pierre X can report the unusually high profits earned by the partnership in April 20X0? Provide a brief analysis tracing the April profits through the organization structure.

Problem Three

To what extent, if any, are the following individuals or corporations liable for tax in Canada?

1. An individual who lives and works in Canada received an inheritance from an uncle in France. The inheritance consists of shares, bonds, and French real estate. During the year, the investments generated interest, dividends, and rents, which were retained in France and reinvested.

2. A large corporation based in Alabama operates a branch in Winnipeg that employs Canadian staff, holds a supply of inventory, and sells to the Canadian market.

3. An American citizen who normally resides in New York and has extensive American income, for health reasons takes an extended vacation of six-and-a-half months in Banff, Alberta.

4. A Manitoba corporation is controlled and managed by its British parent corporation.

5. A Canadian individual, who is a student at the University of Saskatchewan, earns income during the summer by operating a street-vending unit in Boulder, Colorado.

6. An individual has been employed in Canada by a large Canadian corporation. He accepts a transfer to manage, on a permanent basis, the corporation's operations in Denver, Colorado. He leaves Canada with his spouse and family on March 31, 20X0.

7. An individual who resides in England receives annual interest income from an investment in a Canadian corporation's bonds.

Problem Four

The Canadian income tax system includes five specific categories of income. Identify the income category to which each of the following pertains.

1. Interest earned on a bond investment.

2. Pension income.

3. Consulting fees.

4. Profit on the sale of shares of a public corporation. The shares were acquired as a long-term investment.

5. Wages from employment services.

6. Share of profits from a partnership that operates a restaurant.

7. Dividends from the shares of a corporation that carries on a retail business.

8. Tips from customers of an employer's business.

9. Rents from tenants of a commercial building.

10. Fees for providing piano lessons to several students.

11. Profit on the sale of land that was used by the owner for farming.

12. Profit on the sale of a summer cottage that was used by the owner for personal enjoyment.

13. Profit on the sale of land that was purchased for resale.

Problem Five

Indicate the category of income under the *Income Tax Act* into which each of the following items falls:

1. Annual stipend received by an individual for serving as a director of a public corporation.

2. Receipt of alimony (spousal support) payments.

3. Receipts from an employer's registered pension plan.

4. Dividends received from a foreign corporation.

5. Proceeds from the sale of land acquired for resale.

6. Loss from a loan to a qualified small business corporation.

7. Moving expenses.

8. Gain from the sale of shares of a public corporation.

9. Fees received for providing legal services.

10. Alimony (spousal support) paid.

11. Gain on the sale of an automobile purchased for resale.

12. Bonus from an employer.

Problem Six

A taxpayer has the following financial results for a particular year:

Business profit—A Enterprise	$10,000
Business loss—B Enterprise	3,000
Other sources of income—pension	12,000
Property income—interest	5,000
Allowable capital losses on sale of land	20,000
Allowable business investment loss	2,000
Taxable capital gains on sale of securities	15,000
Other deductions—alimony payments (spousal support)	3,000
Employment income	30,000

Required:

Determine the taxpayer's net income for tax purposes in accordance with the statutory scheme formula.

Problem Seven

Meadows Enterprises Ltd. is a Canadian corporation located in Regina. The company operates a retail business that has shown consistent profits for several years. Cash generated from those profits has been used to acquire investments. The company prefers two types of investments: real estate and shares in other corporations. Unfortunately, in 20X1 the investments resulted in some losses.

A summary of the corporation's 20X1 financial results is given below.

Retail sales		$1,240,000
Cost of sales		868,000
Gross profit		372,000
Retail administrative expenses		191,000
Income from operations		181,000
Other income (losses)		
Net loss from real estate rentals	$ (22,000)	
Net loss on the sale of shares of other corporations	(170,000)	(192,000)
Net loss for the year		$ (11,000)

The real estate investments include several small commercial buildings that are rented to retail tenants. In 20X1 one of those tenants ceased operations, and a replacement tenant could not be found until the current year. That is the main reason for the $22,000 loss in real estate rentals.

The net loss of $170,000 on shares of other corporations arose from two sale transactions in 20X1, which are summarized below.

	Sale 1	Sale 2
Selling price	$72,000	$ 10,000
Original cost of shares	65,000	187,000
Gain (loss)	$ 7,000	$(177,000)

Both investments, which were in public corporations, had been owned for several years.

An accountant has just completed Meadows's 20X1 tax return and has informed the president that Meadows owes $39,750 in income taxes for 20X1. The president is upset with this and exclaims, "That's impossible! Our company lost 11,000 dollars last year, so it can't owe $39,750 in income taxes! I know that the corporate tax rate for my company is 25%, and 25% of nothing is nothing."

Required:

Briefly explain why the company owes $39,750 in income tax for 20X1. Show your calculations.

Problem Eight

Bendana Corporation is a Canadian company that specializes in the construction of sports facilities. Although its head office is in Edmonton, final approval of all major construction projects is given by the executive officers of Bendana's parent company, Holdings Limited.

Holdings Limited is incorporated in the United Kingdom, and all of its shares are owned by British residents. Holdings owns 100% of Bendana's shares.

The president of Bendana has called a meeting for next week to discuss the company's expansion to the United States. The executives are considering two basic options for the American organization. One is to open an administrative office in Chicago. The office would bid on all American contracts, and service those contracts by hiring American staff and leasing all equipment from American companies. Alternatively, Bendana has an opportunity to acquire the shares of a small construction company that already has an experienced staff and good basic equipment. The president is hopeful that the meeting will settle the issue so that a plan of action can be set in motion.

Whichever option is chosen, Carl Peters, a senior vice-president, will move to Chicago to head up the American operation. Peters intends to leave Edmonton in October 20X0 and rent an apartment in Chicago. His wife and two children will follow in late December when the school break begins. A third child, Carla, will remain in Edmonton to complete her remaining two years at university. Carla will reside at their house near the university until she graduates, at which time the house will be put up for sale. The house is owned by Mrs. Peters. Carla intends to have two boarders staying at the house, who will pay rent monthly to Mrs. Peters.

Peters holds 10% of the shares of a Canadian private corporation. The majority share-holder of that corporation is his brother, Jason. The company pays regular quarterly dividends. Peters has agreed to sell the shares to Jason early in 20X1. The sale will result in a small profit for Peter. Jason will pay 40% of the purchase price in cash and the balance over two years, with interest at 12%.

Bendana has recently been awarded a contract to build a soccer stadium in Regina. The company has asked the British parent company to send its soccer field expert to Regina to consult on the project. Feiffer Thompson will arrive in Regina on November 1, 20X0, and remain there until August 20X1, by which time the project will be substantially fin-ished. She will be paid a salary by Bendana while she is in Canada. Feiffer's husband will remain in the United Kingdom to manage her large investment portfolio, which was left to her by her late father, the Earl of Feiffdom.

Sally Watkins, Bendana's financial expert, works out of the company's Toronto office. Watkins left last month for the Sudan, where she will arrange the financing for a large pro-ject of the Sudanese government. Basically, Watkins is on loan to that government. She is excited about taking a break from her normal duties and pleased to hear that the Sudan does not levy any income tax. She has kept her apartment in Toronto, as she plans to be away only until November 20X1. While she is away, her sister will occupy her apartment.

Required:
Describe briefly how each of the above activities will be affected by Canadian tax laws.

Chapter 4   Income from Employment

Income from employment is the largest single source of Canadian income tax revenue and applies to the largest number of taxpayers. From a business perspective, employee compensation constitutes a significant portion—in many cases, the largest portion—of any enterprise's overall annual expenses. The taxation of income earned from employment is, therefore, a concern to the employer as well as to the employee.

A review of the management and taxation issues surrounding employee compensation is made later, in Chapter 22. This chapter develops a general framework for determining income from employment activities—in other words, it expands on the general formula for calculating net income for tax purposes as outlined in Chapter 3. Specifically, this chapter covers the following areas relating to employment income:

1. The scope of employment activities and the general rules for income determination.

2. The tax treatment of salaries, wages, employee benefits, and allowances.

3. The scope and limitations of deductions permitted in arriving at net income from employment.

4. A sample calculation of employment income.

I. Scope and Structure of Employment Income

A. Definition of "Employed"

An individual's income from providing service can be regarded as income from employment only if that individual is considered to be *employed* by another party. The definition of *employed* is not specifically established within the *Income Tax Act*, and therefore rests on common-law decisions. Normally, people are considered employed when they agree to provide their services, at the full direction and control of the employer, in return for a specific salary or wage. Implicit in this relationship is the employer's right to decide when, where, how, and what work is to be done. In the vast majority of cases, this relationship can be readily identified.

In some cases an individual may provide services to another party as an independent contractor. When service is provided in this manner, the individual is not subject to the same direction and control described above and is paid in the form of a fee for the specifically contracted activities. In such cases the individual is considered to be self-employed rather than employed, and earning business income rather than employment income. This distinction is important, as the rules for determining income for tax purposes differ considerably when an individual is giving service as an employee rather than as an independent businessperson.

When it is not clear whether a person is employed, or self-employed as an independent contractor, the courts consider four primary tests.[1]

• **Control test**   Who determines what is done, where, when, and how? A principal tells a self-employed agent what to do; an employer not only tells an employee what to do, but also how to do it.

• **Ownership of tools test**   A self-employed contractor normally supplies the tools required to do a job; an employer normally provides the tools to an employee.

• **Chance of profit or loss test**   A self-employed contractor normally has a chance to earn a profit on a job, and also bears the risk of realizing a loss on the job. Usually an employer assumes all the risk of profit or loss on a particular job, and the employee normally earns a wage or salary no matter what happens on the job.

---

1   Hoey, G.D., "Shareholder Manager Compensation," Report of Proceedings of the 42nd Tax Conference (1990), Canadian Tax Foundation, pp. 6–14, summarizing *Wiebe Door Services Ltd. v. MNR*, 87 DTC 5025 (FCA).

• **Integration test**   How integral to the business is the worker? A worker who is part of the business, or whose work is an integral part of the business, is probably an employee. If, however, the worker is an accessory to the business, he or she is probably a self-employed contractor.

In many cases these tests will provide conflicting indicators. When that occurs, all four tests are considered and weighed against each other.

It is important to recognize that it is not the *nature* of the service that determines whether or not one is employed; instead, it is the *relationship* that exists between the individual providing the service and the entity receiving the service.

When attempting to establish whether a service is supplied by an employee or an independent contractor, consider which party (the payer or the person providing the service) is responsible for or decides on the following[2]:

- Planning the work to be done.
- Time frame for completion of the work.
- How the work is to be done.
- Hours of work.
- Location of the work.
- Assignment of specific tasks.
- Standards of quality.
- Training.
- Providing and maintaining tools and equipment and their related costs.
- Liability insurance.
- Performance of work.
- Guarantee of quality.
- Costs of worker's benefits such as vacation pay, health insurance, life insurance premiums, and so on.

If the payer is responsible for or decided on most of the above items, an employer/employee relationship may exist.

B. Employment Income— Fundamental Rules and Basic Formula

Compensation for employment services can take several different forms. In addition, some employees are required to incur non-reimbursable expenses as part of the earning process. Four fundamental rules exist that set the general framework of employment income. These rules determine what items are included in employment income, when such items are included for tax purposes, and what items may be deducted against that income. These four fundamental rules are stated below.

1. All remuneration from an office or employment, including salary, wages, commissions, and gratuities, is included as employment income at the point in time that it is *received* by the employee—not necessarily when it is earned.[3]

2. Subject to specific exceptions, *all benefits* received or enjoyed by employees by virtue of their employment are taxable as employment income.[4]

---

2   Revenue Canada RC4110(E) 1219.
3   ITA 5(1).
4   ITA 6(1)(a).

3. Subject to specific exceptions, all amounts received as an *allowance* for personal living expenses or for any other purpose are included in employment income for tax purposes.[5]

4. Except for a specific, limited list of items, *no deductions* are permitted in arriving at net income from employment.[6]

Essentially, the four rules indicate that an employee must include all forms of remuneration in income, and must do so on a cash basis (that is, when received), and is not permitted to deduct expenses incurred. However, as the last three rules indicate, there are a limited number of exceptions, which are the focus of tax planning for compensation programs.

The formula for arriving at net income from employment for tax purposes can be expressed simply as

$$\text{Employment income} = (A + B + C) - D$$

Where:

A = the salary, wages, commissions, gratuities, and other forms of remuneration received
B = the sum of the benefits received or enjoyed
C = the sum of the allowance received
D = deductions that are specifically permitted as exceptions to the general rule

The aggregate of this formula is the net income from employment (income minus deductions), which is included in the overall formula for determining a taxpayer's total net income (see Chapter 3).

Each of the fundamental rules of employment income is reviewed below, together with its major exceptions.

II. Cash Basis
A. Scope

The first fundamental rule for determining employment income concerns the inclusion of the formal compensation arrangements such as salary, wages, commissions, gratuities, bonuses[7] (including bonuses for past performance and signing bonuses[8]), honoraria, and director's fees.[9] This rule is very broad and requires that all items of remuneration earned as a result of a position as an employee or an officer be included. It further requires that an employee include amounts in income for tax purposes in the year they are *received*, which is not necessarily the year they are *earned*. For example, a salary received in January for work carried out in December of the previous calendar year is included in income for tax purposes in the calendar year of receipt.

B. Salary Deferrals

Any gap between the time that employment income is earned and the time that it is received can influence both the rate of tax payable and the pre-tax value of the remuneration. Consider the situation where an employer awards an employee a $10,000 bonus for work carried out in 20X1 but does not make the payment until six months later, on June 30, 20X2. Because the employer must withhold and remit tax for the employee when the bonus

---

5   ITA 6(1)(b).
6   ITA 8(2).
7   ITA 5(1).
8   ITA 6(3); IT-196R2.
9   ITA 6(1)(c); IT-377R.

is paid, that tax payment is also deferred to June 30, 20X2. Whether this deferral is to the advantage of the employee depends on:

(a) the rate of tax applicable to the employee in 20X2 compared with 20X1; and,
(b) whether or not interest is to be paid on the deferred payment.

Both the time value of money and the rate of tax must be considered if one is to properly assess the benefit (if any) of deferring employee remuneration. For example, if the above bonus were paid at the end of 20X1, and taxed at a rate of 45%, and if the balance were then invested at 10% for six months to June 30, 20X2, it would accumulate to $5,653, calculated as follows:

Bonus—end of 20X1	$10,000
Less tax @ 45%	(4,500)
Amount invested	5,500
Add interest @ 10% on $5,500 for six months	
minus tax on the interest	153
Value at June 30, 20X2	$ 5,653

On the other hand, if payment of the bonus were delayed to June 30, 20X2, and taxed at a rate of 45%, and if the employer then paid 10% interest on the deferred amount, the individual would have $5,775 at June 30, 20X2, calculated as follows:

Interest @ 10% on $10,000 for six months	$500
Bonus received on June 30, 20X2	10,000
	10,500
Tax @ 45% on the bonus and interest	(4,725)
Value at June 30, 20X2	$ 5,775

In the above example, delaying the payment enhanced the value of the bonus because interest was earned on the pre-tax value of the bonus rather than on its after-tax value. The outcome of the deferred bonus would be different if the individual's 20X2 tax rate were higher or lower than the 20X1 tax rate. It should be noted that it is not common for an employer to pay interest on a deferred bonus. If no interest is paid, a remuneration delay may be beneficial to the employee only if the future tax rate will decline.

The deferral of remuneration has advantages to the employer as well. The employer's income, which is reviewed in Chapter 5, is calculated on an accrual basis rather than on a cash basis. This means that the employer can deduct employment expenses when they are incurred rather than when they are paid. In the previous example, a bonus payment applicable to 20X1, though deferred to June 30, 20X2, would still be deductible as an expense against the employer's 20X1 income. This would enhance the employer's cash flow by reducing its 20X1 income taxes.

Significant abuses of salary deferral programs have led to the development of two antiavoidance rules that limit the extent to which employers and employees can defer employment benefits. If an employer wishes to deduct deferred compensation on an accrual basis, that compensation must be paid (and therefore included in the employee's income) within 180 days of the fiscal year end in which the expense was incurred. If the payment is delayed beyond 180 days from year end, the employer must delay the deduction of the remuneration until the year in which it is paid.[10] This, of course, makes the employer less interested in using

---

10 ITA 78(4); IT-109R2.

deferred payments. In addition, when an employer and an employee enter into an arrangement the main purpose of which is to defer the receipt of remuneration that would otherwise have been paid, the employee is deemed to have received it in the year that it was earned.[11]

III. Employee Benefits

Employers often provide indirect forms of compensation to their employees, as well as direct ones. Such indirect forms of compensation are commonly referred to as "fringe benefits"; they include such items as employee pension plans, insurance programs, stock options, and automobile benefits. For employees, the tax treatment of such programs varies considerably: some fringe benefits are taxable in the year in which they are received or enjoyed; others are taxable at some future time or are not taxable at all. Most forms of compensation are, however, deductible for the employer. Because the tax treatment varies for these indirect compensation programs, it is essential that compensation decisions be made that maximize the after-tax cash flow to the employee and minimize the after-tax cost to the employer (see Chapter 22).

A. Taxable Benefits

The second general rule for determining income from employment states that the value of all benefits of any kind whatever (subject to specific exceptions), if received or enjoyed in respect of, in the course of, or by virtue of an office or employment, must be included in the taxpayer's income.[12] This means that such benefits as the personal use of an employer's car, the receipt of a substantial gift for a birthday or anniversary, the winning of a prize such as a paid vacation for special efforts, and the free use of an employer's vacation home are all benefits received by virtue of one's employment, and therefore taxable. Even when certain benefits are provided by parties other than the employer—for example, when supplier A of employer B provides prizes for B's employees if A's product is used or sold in certain quantities—a taxable benefit from employment exists. The scope of the general rule is extremely broad. A reasonable starting point is to assume that all benefits are taxable unless a search of the limited list of specific exceptions discloses that the benefit is not taxable.

CCRA's Interpretation Bulletin IT-470R reviews the topic of employee fringe benefits. The following typical benefits are taxable and are discussed in the bulletin:

- Board and lodging provided to employees free or at a reduced price, except at a remote location (IT-91R4).

- Rent-free and low-rent housing.

- Personal use of the employer's motor vehicle (discussed below).

- Gifts from the employer to the employee that are in cash or near cash, including wedding and Christmas gifts. However, up to *two non-cash* gifts annually are *not* taxable to the employee if they do not exceed $500 in total. If the gifts exceed $500 in value the full value becomes taxable.

- Holiday trips and other prizes and incentive awards, including benefits for trips not associated with business and the use of vacation properties.

- Tuition fees paid by the employer, unless the particular course was undertaken at the initiative of the employer for the employer's benefit.

---

11 ITA 6(11), 248(1).
12 ITA 6(1)(a).

- Frequent-flyer programs for personal travel from credits accumulated during business-related travel.

- Travelling expenses of an employee's spouse.

- Premiums under provincial hospitalization and medical care insurance plans.

- Reimbursement from the employer for the cost of tools required to perform duties of employment.

- Interest-free and low-interest loans (discussed below) (IT-421R2).

- Financial counselling and income tax return preparation, except as it relates to the re-employment or retirement of the employee.

- Reimbursement for day-care costs for children, except when the employer provides on-site facilities.

- Club dues when membership in the club provides little or no advantage to the employer's business (IT-148R3).

- Reimbursement by the employer for two specific types of expenses incurred to move to a new work location (discussed below).

The above list is not complete but does provide a sense of how the general rule on employee benefits applies.

The amount of the benefit that must be included in the income of the employee is usually determined as either the cost to the employer of supplying the benefit or the fair market value of the benefit, whichever is lower. If, for example, an employer in the jewellery business gives a retiring employee a gold bracelet that retails for $700 but has cost the employer $400 on a wholesale basis, the value of the taxable benefit is $400. On the other hand, when an employer owns a vacation home that is available to employees, it is the fair rental value of the property that is relevant, not the cost associated with owning the property. In some circumstances the benefit is determined in accordance with a rigid pre-set formula. Special benefit calculations apply to the use of employer automobiles, loans from employers, the reimbursement of specific relocation expenses, and stock-option benefits. These four unusual items are reviewed below.

Automobiles

It is not uncommon, especially at the management level, for an employer to provide an employee with an automobile for business and personal use. To the extent that an automobile is for personal use, a taxable benefit results.[13]

There are two components to the benefit. First, the employer—either by purchase or by lease agreement—has paid for the vehicle and in doing so has relieved the employee of the need to acquire a personal car. This benefit can be referred to as the *capital* portion (the technical term is *standby charge*).[14] Second, the employer may pay for costs associated with operating the vehicle—insurance, repairs, fuel, maintenance, and so on. The benefit to the employee from this activity is referred to as the *operating* portion.

---

13 IT-63R5.
14 ITA 6(1)(e), 6(2).

The taxable benefits from the operating portion and the capital portion are calculated separately. The operating benefit is based on the actual personal use as opposed to business use; the standby charge is based primarily on the *availability* for use.

The operating benefit is determined by multiplying a prescribed rate by the number of personal kilometres driven by the employee for personal use in the year.[15] The prescribed rate changes from time to time. In 2003, the prescribed rate was 17¢.[16] This rate applies whatever the actual expenses incurred by the employer to operate the vehicle. The total value of the operating benefit for personal use is as follows:

Operating benefit = Prescribed rate [17¢ in 2003] × # of personal km driven

For purposes of the above calculation, driving between home and the employer's place of business is considered personal use. In certain circumstances, the operating benefit can be calculated using an alternative method by which the benefit is *deemed* to be one-half of the amount of the standby charge for the capital benefit (see below).[17] The taxpayer can choose, on a yearly basis, the method that results in the lowest taxable benefit. This alternative is available only if the automobile is used primarily in the performance of employment duties (i.e., more than 50% of the total use).

The capital benefit, referred to as the *standby charge*, is normally based on the time period that the automobile was available to the employee for personal use rather than on the number of kilometres driven. It makes a difference here whether the employer owns or leases the automobile. The basic calculations are as follows:

If the employer owns the automobile:

Standby charge = Original cost of the automobile × 2% × # of months available

If the employer leases the automobile:

Standby charge = Monthly lease cost × 2/3 × # of months available

The original cost of the car *includes* any GST and provincial sales tax that is applicable. Note that the original cost of the car, and not the unamortized cost of the car, is used each year for calculating the standby charge.

The value of the standby charge is substantial and in some cases unfair. For example, over a four-year period, 96% (2% × 48 months) of the cost of the car to the employer may be included in the employee's personal income even if the car is used only half the time for personal activity.

The following is provided for demonstration.

Situation: An employer provides a car costing $25,000 to an employee. The car is to be used for business travel and for personal use throughout the year. During the year, the employer expends $5,000 for operating costs relating to insurance, gas, maintenance, and repairs. During the year, the employee drives the car 30 000 km, of which 16 000 km is for personal use and 14 000 km is for business use.

---

15 ITA 6(1)(k).
16 Regulation 7305.1.
17 ITA 6(2.2); IT-63R.

Analysis: The taxable benefit for the year is $8,720, as calculated below.

Operating benefit:*	
16 000 km × 17¢ =	$2,720
Standby charge:	
$25,000 × 2% × 12 months	$6,000
Total taxable benefit for the year	$8,720

* The option of treating the operating benefit as 50% of the standby charge is not available because business use was not greater than 50%.

It is obvious that the benefit relating to the capital portion is considerable. The employer will, over a period of years, deduct the full cost of the car as an expense; however, the employee will take the same amount into income over four years even though 47% of the car's use was for business purposes.

With respect to the standby charge, the after-tax cost to both the employer and the employee is determined in the following calculations (which assume the employer's tax rate is 40%, the employee's tax rate is 45%, and the car has no value after four years).

Employer:	
Purchase price of car	$25,000
Less tax saving on write-off of car over a number of years (40%)	(10,000)
Net cost to employer	$15,000
Employee:	
Cost of car	NIL
Tax cost of employee benefit over four years (6,000 × 4) × 45%	10,800
Net cost to employee	$10,800

In some cases the standby charge can be reduced to reflect a low amount of personal use. The reduction occurs only when the distance travelled is *primarily* for employment duties. CCRA considers "primarily" to mean 50% or more.[18] Even when this is the case, the benefit is fractionalized, as the number of personal kilometres divided by an arbitrary amount of approximately 20 000 km (1 667 km per month).

For example, consider the situation of an employee who drives 30 000 km in a year. Of this amount, 18 000 km (60%) is for business and 12 000 km (40%) is for personal use. If the employer's car has a cost of $25,000, the normal standby charge will be $6,000 ($25,000 × 2% × 12 m). However, because the 50% test has been met, the standby charge is reduced to $3,600 ($6,000 × [12 000 km / 20 000 km]). It is important to recognize that if the number of business kilometres had been 14 000 instead of 18 000, the standby charge would have remained the usual $6,000 because the 50% test had not been met.

---

18 ITA 6(2); IT-63R5.

As a final comment, it is important to recognize that there is a fundamental difference in the way that the benefit is calculated for an *owned* vehicle as opposed to a *leased* vehicle. When the employer owns the car, its full cost is used to calculate the benefit (cost of car—$25,000; benefit—24% of $25,000). However, when the employer leases the car, the benefit is arbitrarily equal to two-thirds of the lease cost. Presumably, this reduction reflects the fact that the lease cost includes some financing costs. Employers should attempt to determine which method (own or lease) reduces their costs, and balance that with the best alternative for the employee.

Employee Loans

Low-cost or non–interest-bearing loans provided by employers are attractive to employees, as most individuals have a need for borrowed funds to finance investments and personal asset acquisitions. The benefit the employee receives from the reduced rate of interest is, of course, taxable.[19] In order to simplify the process in a market of changing and variable interest rates, a prescribed formula is used to determine the value of the benefit to the employee.[20]

Every three months, on a regular basis, CCRA determines a prescribed interest rate that reflects existing financial conditions.[21] The taxable benefit to an employee on a loan made from an employer is the difference between the prescribed rate at the time and the actual interest paid.

This form of compensation can be of significant value to the employee. Consider the following circumstances:

Situation: An employee has a large, outstanding house mortgage bearing 8% interest. Her employer offers her a $20,000 loan bearing interest at 2%. The prescribed interest rate designated at the time by CCRA is 7%. The employee is in the 40% tax bracket.

Analysis: The taxable benefit and tax cost of the loan are $1,000 and $400 respectively, calculated as follows:

Prescribed interest ($20,000 @ 7%)	$1,400
Actual interest paid ($20,000 @ 2%)	400
Benefit for tax purposes	$1,000
Tax cost to employee ($1,000 @ 40%)	$ 400

The actual cost of the $20,000 loan to the employee is 4%, determined as follows:

Actual interest on loan ($20,000 @ 2%)	$ 400
Tax on taxable benefit	400
Total cost of financing	$ 800
Effective rate on financing = $800/$20,000 = 4%	

---

19 ITA 6(9).

20 ITA 80.4.

21 Regulation 4301. For the second quarter of 2003, the prescribed rate was 3% for employee loans.

Usually, the prescribed interest rate will change every quarter of the year for purposes of calculating the benefit. However, in situations like the one just shown, an exception applies: when a loan is used to acquire a house, or to repay an existing house loan, the benefit can be determined using the prescribed interest rate that was in force at the time the loan was made. If the prescribed rate declines, the lower rate can be used. However, if it *increases*, the rate in force at the time the loan was made will remain, for a maximum of five years.[22]

It is important to recognize that in the above situation, the benefit derived from the low-interest loan was equivalent to a salary increase or cash bonus of $1,333. This assumes that the $20,000 loan was used by the employee to reduce an existing house mortgage that bore interest at 8%. See the following calculations:

Value of loan:	
Current interest on mortgage ($20,000 @ 8%)	$1,600
Cost of alternative financing from employer	
(as previously determined)	800
Net savings to employee	$ 800
Value of salary:	
Income from salary	$1,333
Less tax @ 40%	(533)
Net after-tax value of salary	$ 800

The saving of $800 in loan costs is therefore equivalent to a pre-tax cash salary of $1,333 for this particular employee.

An employee sometimes uses the funds borrowed from the employer to invest in shares, or bonds, or the like, that will generate financial returns. In such cases, any taxable benefit (prescribed interest less actual interest) is treated as interest paid by the employee.[23] This means that the employee can deduct the deemed interest when determining investment income for tax purposes. For example, assume that the $20,000 loan in the previous example was used to purchase shares. The employee would include $1,000 as a taxable benefit, as previously calculated. However, when calculating investment income, the $1,000 benefit would be deemed an interest expense and would be deducted from investment income earned in that year. This would apply only when the interest on the loan was otherwise deductible (see Chapter 7).[24]

Sometimes an employer will forgive a loan to an employee. When this occurs, the debt forgiven is a taxable benefit.[25]

It is important that the employee as well as the employer appreciate the real value of certain types of employee benefits in order that realistic compensation decisions can be made (see Chapter 22).

Relocation Expenses

Employers sometimes reimburse employees for all or part of their costs to permanently relocate to a new work location. Generally, the reimbursement of moving costs is *not* a taxable benefit (as discussed in this chapter under the heading "Tax-exempt benefits"). How-

---

22 ITA 80.4(4), (6); IT-421R2.

23 ITA 80.5.

24 ITA 20(1)(c).

25 ITA 6(1)(a), 6(15).

ever, the reimbursement of two specific types of relocation expenses is taxable to the employee. The first type deals with the reimbursement of costs to finance the use of a residence. Here, the full amount of the reimbursement is taxable.[26] The second type deals with the reimbursement of a loss suffered by the employee from the decrease in value or impairment of proceeds of disposition of the employee's residence. The first $15,000 of this type of benefit is *not* taxable to the employee, but *one-half* of any amount above $15,000 is taxable.[27] For example, a $40,000 reimbursement by an employer to an employee for a loss suffered on the sale of a residence caused by a relocation creates a taxable benefit of $12,500 ($\frac{1}{2} \times$ [$40,000 – $15,000]).

Stock Options

Benefits arise under stock option programs when an employee is given the opportunity to acquire shares in the employer corporation at a price lower than the fair market value of the shares at the time of the purchase. Stock options are a unique form of compensation, as they do not require the payment of cash by the employer. In fact, the employee contributes cash to the company treasury, thereby strengthening the employer's resources (although also diluting the existing shareholders' percentage of ownership, because new corporate shares must be issued).

Theoretically, under a stock option plan, employees receive a benefit at the time they purchase the shares, because they have acquired an asset (the shares) that has a market value in excess of the price paid. They can make further gains by continuing to hold the shares for value enhancement. The initial benefit received by acquiring the shares at lower than current value and the gain or loss from subsequent value changes are treated differently for tax purposes. The taxable value of a gain made on a stock option is determined in accordance with specific rules.[28] These rules cover three categories of stock option plans.[29]

1. Stock options of public companies with a designated option price below fair market value at the date the option is granted by the employer.

2. Stock options of public companies with a designated option price equal to or greater than the fair market value at the date the option is granted by the employer.

3. Stock options of Canadian-controlled private companies.

• **First category** When a public corporation offers an employee an option to acquire shares at a specific price that is below those shares' present fair market value, the employee will have tax consequences both at the time the shares are acquired and later on when the shares are sold. Consider the following situation.

An employee of a public company is given an option to acquire 1,000 shares from the company's treasury at a price of $20 per share. At the date that the option contract was offered to the employee, the share value was $22 per share. The contract requires that the employee exercise the option within five years. Stock prices over the next five years increase continuously, as shown in the table at the top of the next page.

---

26 ITA 6(1)(a), 6(23).

27 ITA 6(1)(a), 6(19), (20), (21).

28 ITA 7; IT-113R4.

29 A fourth category applies to employees of mutual fund trusts who receive options to purchase mutual fund trust units.

Date option is offered	$22
Year 1	23
Year 2	26
Year 3	28
Year 4	31
Year 5	33

The employee exercises the option in year 3 and purchases 1,000 shares at $20 per share ($20,000). Although not required to do so, the employee decides to sell all the shares at the end of year 5 for $33 per share ($33,000).

The tax treatment of option benefits from shares of public corporations requires that a taxable benefit be included as *employment* income at the time the option is exercised and the employee purchases the shares. The taxable employment benefit is the difference between the fair market value of shares at the purchase date and the agreed option price. To the extent that the shares change in value after the purchase date, the value change is considered to be a capital gain or loss, of which only one-half is included in income.

In the above situation the tax treatment is as follows:

Year 3 (date of purchase of shares):	
Value of shares (1,000 @ $28)	$28,000
Option purchase price (1,000 @ $20)	20,000
Employment income	$ 8,000
Year 5 (date of sale of shares):	
Selling price (1,000 @ $33)	$33,000
Value at option purchase date (1,000 @ $28)	28,000
Capital gain	$ 5,000
Taxable capital gain (½)	$ 2,500

All of this burdens the employee with a decision concerning when to exercise the stock option. In the previous example, if the option had been exercised immediately at the offer date, the employment income would have amounted to only $2,000 ($22,000 – $20,000) and the subsequent increase in value to year 5 would have been a capital gain that was one-half taxable. This would have reduced significantly the tax cost of the investment but speeded up the requirement for a cash outlay to purchase the shares; as a result, the cost of money would have had to have been considered a negative factor. As an alternative, the decision to exercise the option could have been delayed until year 5, when the share value reached $33, in which case the employment benefit would have amounted to $13,000 ($33,000 – $20,000). This amount would have been fully taxable, with none of the gain considered a capital gain. Such a delay increases the tax cost but reduces the cost of money, as there is no need for an outlay of cash to acquire the shares until just before they are sold.

• **Second category** When a public company offers an employee a stock option without the opportunity of an immediate benefit (that is, when the option price is the same as or greater than the fair market value of the shares at the date the option is offered), the tax treatment is improved over the first category in two ways. First, if the shares do not have special dividend or redemption rights, the normal employment gain calculated when the shares are purchased is reduced by one-half in determining *taxable income*.[30] This

---

30 ITA 110(1)(d).

leaves one-half of the benefit taxable, similar to the way capital gains are treated. Second, on the first $100,000 of stock option value offered to the employee in any year (referred to as the specified value), the stock option benefit from employment can be deferred and included in the employee's employment income in the year the stock is *sold* rather than in the year it was purchased. To receive this deferral, a special election must be filed by the taxpayer. To illustrate: if, in the previous example, the option price granted had been $22 per share (that being the shares' value on the offering date), the tax consequences would have been as follows:

Year 3 (date of purchase of shares):	
Value of shares (1,000 @ $28)	$28,000
Option purchase price (1,000 @ $22)	22,000
Employment income	6,000
Deferred until year of sale	(6,000)
Taxable income in year 3	NIL
Year 5 (date of sale of shares):	
Employment income:	
Deferred from year 3 (above) included in *employment income*	$ 6,000
Reduced by ½ when calculating *taxable income*	(3,000)
Net taxable employment benefit in year 5	$ 3,000
Capital gain:	
Selling price (1,000 @ $33)	$33,000
Value at option purchase date (1,000 @ $28)	28,000
Capital gain	$ 5,000
Taxable capital gain (½)	$ 2,500

Note that the one-half reduction in employment income in the above example is deducted in arriving at *taxable income* rather than net income for tax purposes (see Chapter 3, page 52, and Chapter 10). Thus, the full employment income is included in the aggregating formula for net income for tax purposes and is subsequently reduced by one-half.

The deferral of the employment benefit to the year the shares are sold is available in this situation because the value of the exercisable stock option shares offered to the employee is below the $100,000 specified value limit. This limit is based on the market value of the total stock option shares offered (and vested) to the employee at the date the option was granted, which was $22,000 (1,000 @ $22). If the employer had granted the employee an option to purchase 5,000 shares, the specified value of the offer would have been $110,000. As a result, only 91% ($100,000/$110,000) of the employment benefit would be eligible for a deferral to the year of sale. The remaining 9% would be taxable in year 3 when the option was exercised. The $100,000 specified value limit is an annual limit. This means that an employer can annually grant to an employee up to $100,000 of options that qualify for the deferral. It should be noted that the deferral right is lost if the recipient of the stock option already owns 10% or more of the corporation's shares.

• **Third category** This category relates only to options granted to employees of Canadian-controlled private corporations. Provided that the employee holds such shares for two years after acquisition, the employment benefit is reduced by one-half, and the benefit, rather than being taxable at time of purchase, is not taxable until the shares are sold.[31] Using the same facts as given in the first category, except that a private corporation is the employer, the tax consequences to the employee are as follows:

---

31 ITA 7(1.1), 110(1)(d.1).

Year 5 (date of sale of shares):

Employment income:		
Value of shares at date shares acquired in year 3 (1,000 @ $28)		$28,000
Option purchase price (1,000 @ $20)		20,000
Employment income		8,000
Reduced by ½ (in arriving at taxable income)		(4,000)
Taxable employment benefit in year 5		$ 4,000
Capital gain:		
Selling price (1,000 @ $33)		$33,000
Value at option purchase date		28,000
Capital gain		$ 5,000
Taxable capital gain		$ 2,500*

*May be eligible for the capital gain deduction if the shares are qualified small business corporation shares (see Chapter 11).

The special treatment given to shares of this category is designed to stimulate employee participation in private corporations. However, in spite of the beneficial tax treatment, Canadian-controlled private corporations rarely grant stock options, for the following reasons:

1. The market value of shares is not readily available and is often difficult to determine.

2. Minority shares of private corporations have a low marketability, and buyers, other than the major shareholders, are difficult to find. For this reason the share values are often significantly discounted unless buy/sell agreements are contracted with all shareholders.

3. Controlling shareholders of private corporations normally want to retain full control and flexibility of corporate activity and do not wish to be accountable to minority shareholders for their actions.

It should again be pointed out that in the above examples, when employment income is reduced by one-half, the reduction occurs as part of the taxable income calculation after net income for tax purposes has been arrived at (see Chapter 3).

B. Non-Taxable and Tax-Deferred Benefits

As pointed out previously, the general rule that all benefits received or enjoyed by an employee are taxable has a limited number of exceptions. The *Income Tax Act* specifically allows certain tangible benefits from employment to be excluded from taxable income. Some of the benefits are taxable at a later time, which means their exclusion is actually a deferral. Other benefits are permanently excluded from taxable income. It is important to note that in addition to the excluded benefits described in the *Income Tax Act*,[32] CCRA, by administrative policy, arbitrarily excludes certain other benefits. These items are discussed at the end of this section.

The following specific benefits (described in the *Income Tax Act*) are excluded from income on a deferred or permanent basis:[33]

1. Employer contributions for an employee to a registered pension plan (RPP).

2. Employer contributions on behalf of an employee to a deferred profit sharing plan (DPSP).

---

32 ITA 6(1)(a).
33 ITA 6(1)(a)(i) to (iv).

3. The payment of insurance premiums for group sickness or accident plans that protect the income of employees who are unable to work due to illness or injury.

4. The payment of premiums for private health service plans that provide extended medical coverage beyond public plans. (This applies only to private health plans and not to premiums for public health insurance plans.)

5. The payment by an employer, on an employee's behalf, of premiums for supplementary unemployment insurance plans, including both private and public plans that protect employees in the event of a loss of job.

6. Counselling services relating to the mental or physical health or to the re-employment or retirement of the employee.

Regarding the insurance benefits mentioned above, note that the tax-free benefit relates to the payment of the premium and not to the payments that may be made from the insurance plans when a claim is made. Claims paid out of a private health service plan on an employee's behalf are not taxable. However, when the employer has paid premiums for a sickness or accident insurance plan or an income maintenance insurance plan, claims paid to the employee are considered taxable.[34] The amount taxable is equal to the total payments from the plan in the year *less* the sum of all premiums paid in the current year *and* past years by the *employee*.

The first two benefits listed—RPP and DPSP contributions—are tax deferrals; the remaining four are permanently excluded from taxable income. All six are extremely valuable to employees.

• **Tax-deferred benefits** The registered pension plan is a common form of employee compensation. While several types of plans are used, all involve a contribution by an employer to a trustee on behalf of specific employees. The trustee holds the contributions and invests the funds; at some time in the future both the contributions and the accumulated investment returns are used to acquire a pension for the employee. The funds are taxable to the employee only when they are withdrawn as a pension; they are not taxable while they remain in the plan earning investment income. The two benefits of this arrangement are as follows:

1. An employee is permitted to save and invest a portion of his or her income that has not been subject to tax. Obviously, this creates a larger investment base than if the employee were to receive the benefit as a cash bonus, pay tax, and then invest the after-tax remainder. Investment income earned on money saved is therefore enhanced, since the return is based on pre-tax income as opposed to after-tax income.

2. The annual return on investments accumulated within the plan is also not taxable while the funds remain within the plan. This means that all annual returns that are reinvested also compound on a pre-tax basis rather than on a substantially reduced after-tax basis. A 10% return is compounded at 10% within the plan; if the income had been subject to tax before being reinvested, it would have been compounded at only 5.5% (assumed tax rate of 45%).

The calculations at the top of the next page demonstrate the value of such a tax deferral. The example compares an annual benefit of $3,500 paid to an employee as a cash bonus for 30 years and invested at a 10% return with the same $3,500 paid annually to an RPP and invested within the plan for the same number of years at the same rate of return. The example assumes that the employee is in a marginal tax bracket of 45%.[35]

---

34 ITA 6(1)(f).

35 The compounding calculation assumes that the annual deposit is made at the beginning of each year. This is so throughout the text, unless otherwise indicated.

RPP—$3,500 annual benefit:

$$\$3,500 \times 30 \text{ y @ } 10\% = \underline{\underline{\$633,000}}$$

Cash bonus—$3,500 annual benefit:

	Bonus	Investment return
Pre-tax bonus	$3,500	10.0%
Tax @ 45%	(1,575)	4.5%
Available for investment	$1,925	5.5%

$$\$1,925 \times 30 \text{ y @ } 5.5\% = \underline{\underline{\$147,000}}$$

The compounding of $3,500 @ 10% on a pre-tax basis in the RPP provides an investment value that is four times greater than that achieved on an after-tax basis. While the $633,000 in this example is fully taxable when withdrawn as a pension, its after-tax value still far exceeds the value of the cash bonus arrangement.

In a deferred profit sharing plan, an employer arranges to share, annually, a certain percentage of the business profits with specified employees by contributing to a trustee who holds and invests the funds on the employee's behalf. As with an RPP, a DPSP must be registered with CCRA, and contributions are subject to an annual limit. The tax treatment of a DPSP, from the employee's perspective, is identical to that given RPPs; the benefits, when compared with those of other forms of taxable compensation, are substantial.

• **Tax-exempt benefits** The three insurance and counselling benefits that are fully tax exempt have a lesser dollar value individually than the tax-deferred benefits; nevertheless, in total they are a valuable means of compensation for the employee.

Most individuals are in need of income protection insurance and supplemental health insurance. When such programs are not provided by an employer, individuals have to pay premiums from their after-tax disposable income. For example, an individual in a 40% tax bracket who purchased $1,500 of the above insurance premiums would have to earn salary of $2,500 ($2,500 less tax @ 40% = $1,500) in order to fund the purchase. It is important that the employee and the employer recognize the value of tax-free benefits provided as compensation. When an employer provides the above insurance programs as part of the employee's compensation package, the tax-free benefits can be assigned a pre-tax value. Using the above example, when the employer provides an employee with $1,500 of tax-free insurance benefits, it is equivalent to giving that employee a salary increase of $2,500.

From the employer's perspective, the cost of providing $1,500 in insurance benefits is dramatically lower than it would be to provide $2,500 in salary, even though the employee receives the same value under both alternatives. This substantial saving to the employer can be kept by the employer for business expansion or be given back to the employees, in whole or in part, by expanding other forms of compensation (see Chapter 22).

While the *Income Tax Act* appears to define clearly which benefits are tax exempt, CCRA has, for administrative purposes, chosen to arbitrarily consider certain benefits to be non-taxable. For example, in certain circumstances benefits derived from subsidized meals, merchandise discounts, and moving expenses are considered to be non-taxable. A complete list of tax-free benefits, and the circumstances in which they apply, is given in CCRA's IT-470R, which should be consulted when compensation programs are being designed. Some of these benefits are listed below.

• Discounts on merchandise, except to the extent that the price is reduced below the employer's cost.

• Subsidized meals, provided that the employee pays a reasonable charge.

- Uniforms and special clothing.

- Recreational facilities.

- Club dues, when it is clearly to the employer's advantage to be a member of the club (see IT-148R3).

- Reimbursement of moving expenses for relocating employees to a new work location, except for the two specific items discussed on page 76.

- Employer's contributions under a provincial hospitalization and medicare plan, when these are required by law to be made (i.e., the employer's contribution—if the employer also pays the employee's share of the premium, that amount is a taxable benefit).

- Transportation passes for employees of transportation companies.

IV. Allowances

A. Definition

The third general rule for determining income from employment states that all allowances of any kind whatever, including personal and living allowances, are taxable, subject to specific exceptions.[36] The term *allowance* refers to a fixed, specified amount that is paid to an employee on a regular basis, over and above a normal salary, to cover certain expenses incurred by the employee.[37] The unique aspect of an allowance is that the employee does not have to account for the allowance or provide details of how the money has been spent. The receipt of $300 a month for clothing or for travel, regardless of whether the employee has expended such an amount, is an allowance.

An allowance is not a reimbursement. A reimbursement is the repayment of a specific expenditure incurred by an employee on the employer's behalf. For example, if an employee travels on behalf of an employer and submits an account of travel expenses incurred, the repayment of the specific amount is a reimbursement, which is *not* taxable to the employee.

B. Exceptions

Nine specific allowances are excepted from the general rule and considered not taxable. Only two of the exceptions have broad application; the remaining seven, which include allowances for ministers and volunteer firefighters, apply only in limited situations. The two broader exceptions relate to travel expenses and are reviewed briefly below.

• **Employees selling property or negotiating contracts** Employees engaged in the selling of property (salespeople) or in negotiating contracts for an employer are entitled to a non-taxable allowance for travel expenses provided that the allowance is reasonable.[38] Travel expenses include transportation (by car, plane, and so on), meals, lodging, and other incidental costs. The allowance *must* be reasonable; if it is unreasonably high or low in relation to the actual costs incurred, the allowance is taxable. The most common use of this exception is to provide a car allowance to salespeople who regularly use their car in the performance of their duties. This tax-free allowance is not always beneficial, as its receipt usually eliminates the right to claim expenses that would otherwise be permitted (see the section on salespeople's expenses at the start of this chapter). An allowance, if less than the expenses incurred, may be considered unreasonably low and thus be included in taxable income, in which case expenses can be deducted.

---

36 ITA 6(1)(b).
37 *Ransom v. MNR*, 67 DTC 5235.
38 ITA 6(1)(b)(v).

• **Employees other than salespeople** Employees who are not salespeople are also entitled to receive a tax-free allowance for travel expenses. However, for these expenses to be tax-free, they must meet certain criteria that are more extensive than those for salespeople. In addition, the criteria that apply to travel allowances relating to the use of an automobile are different from those for other travel allowances. A non-salesperson's travel allowance that does *not* relate to the use of an automobile is considered tax-free only if[39]

(a) the allowance is a reasonable amount; and,
(b) the employee travels outside the municipality or metropolitan area in which the employer is located.

Automobile allowances paid to employees who are not salespeople are considered tax-free if [40]

(a) the allowance is for the purpose of travelling in the performance of their duties as employees; and,
(b) the allowance is reasonable and is based solely on the number of kilometres used to conduct employment duties.[41]

The criteria for the automobile allowance are different from the criteria for other travel expenses in that the former are not restricted to travel outside the municipality or metropolitan area of the employer. In addition, the question of reasonableness is more tightly defined, in that it relates to the number of kilometres driven. CCRA does not issue statements on what is "reasonable." However, a reasonable allowance would include those costs that would normally be deductible, such as for fuel, maintenance, insurance, capital cost allowance (depreciation), and so on.

As with salespeople's allowances, if the allowance is considered tax-free, the employee cannot claim certain expenses that are specifically permitted; and the benefit of a tax-free allowance is eliminated if the actual expenses are greater than the allowance. Keep in mind that an allowance can also be considered unreasonable if it is *too low*. In other words, an allowance that is less than the actual reasonable expenses may be considered unreasonably low and included in taxable income. If this happens, the higher actual costs can be used as a deduction.

V. Deductions from Employment Income

The fourth and last general rule for determining net income from employment states that no deductions are permitted except those specifically provided for in the *Income Tax Act*.[42] Since the list of permitted deductions is not extensive, determining employment deductions is a simple procedure that involves merely scrutinizing that list. If an item in question is not on the list, it is not deductible when calculating employment income.

The major items that can be deducted as employment deductions are as follows:

1. Expenses incurred by employees who earn remuneration in the form of commissions from selling or negotiating contracts for an employer.[43]

---

39 ITA 6(1)(b)(vii).
40 ITA 6(1)(b)(vii.1).
41 ITA 6(1)(b)(x).
42 ITA 8(2).
43 ITA 8(1)(f).

2. Travelling expenses, in certain circumstances.[44]

3. Professional membership dues required to maintain professional status in a profession recognized by statute.[45]

4. The cost of supplies consumed directly in the performance of employment duties, provided that the employee is required by the employment contract to be responsible for payment of such items.[46]

5. Annual dues paid to a trade union.[47]

6. Contributions to an employer's registered pension plan.[48]

The above list of deductible items is not complete; however, all of the items omitted have an extremely narrow application. Some of the major deductions require further explanation, as certain criteria must be met before they can be applied. They are discussed below.

A. Travel Expenses

An employee can deduct travel expenses incurred in the course of work-related duties provided that the following circumstances exist:[49]

- The employee is ordinarily required to carry on the duties of employment away from the employer's place of business.

- Under the employment contract, the employee is required to pay the travel costs incurred in the performance of duties.

- The employee has not received a non-taxable allowance designed to cover such costs.

Travel expenses include the costs of all forms of transportation (including automobile costs), meals, lodging, and all other expenses created by the travel activity.

It is sometimes difficult to determine the exact cost of the travel activity when the employee uses his or her own car. The costs include gas, oil, general repairs, insurance, financing costs (interest), and amortization (depreciation) of the automobile from its use.[50] All of these items are accepted for tax purposes and must be determined as they apply to the travel activity. An accepted method for determining travel costs is to total the full costs for the year and prorate the total on the basis of the number of kilometres driven for employment purposes as opposed to personal use. The rate of amortization (depreciation— referred to as *capital cost allowance* for tax purposes) is arbitrarily determined as 30% annually on the undepreciated cost (see Chapter 6). The calculation of capital cost allowance on an automobile is more complicated in a taxation year when a new automobile is purchased and/or a previous one is sold. Special rules apply to these transactions (reviewed in Chapter 6—automobiles costing less than $30,000 are subject to capital cost allowance under class 10; those costing more fall under class 10.1 and are reviewed under the heading "Special Treatment of Passenger Vehicles").

---

44 ITA 8(1)(h), (h.1).
45 ITA 8(1)(i).
46 ITA 8(1)(i).
47 ITA 8(1)(i).
48 ITA 8(1)(m).
49 ITA 8(1)(h), (h.1); IT-522R.
50 ITA 8(1)(j).

Certain of the above travel expenses are subject to an arbitrary reasonableness test which limits the amount that can be deducted against employment income.[51] The imposed limits are subject to regular changes. Currently, the maximum cost of an automobile available for capital cost allowance is $30,000. If an automobile is leased, the maximum lease deduction is $800 per month. The deduction for interest paid on a loan to finance the acquisition of an automobile is limited to an average of $300 per month. And the deduction for meals incurred during travel is limited to 50% of the actual costs incurred. (Specifically, the *Income Tax Act* restricts the amount of the deduction for any "food and beverages consumed or entertainment enjoyed" to 50% of amounts *actually paid*. If the actual costs are unreasonably high, the deduction is limited to 50% of what is reasonable. This applies to all taxpayers and to all types of income. See Chapter 9.)[52]

There is no requirement that the travel costs be incurred away from the metropolitan area of the employer; consequently, costs incurred within the employer's city or town are acceptable for deduction. An exception is meals—an employee must be travelling away from the metropolitan area of the employer for at least 12 hours for this cost to be deductible.

Employees must fulfill all of the three criteria mentioned earlier to be eligible to deduct travel costs. In addition, to the extent the employee is reimbursed, the expenses deducted must be reduced accordingly.

Situation:

An employee is required to use her own automobile for employment duties. She acquired a new car at the beginning of the year for $32,000 and during the year incurred the following expenses:

Gasoline	$2,200
Repairs and maintenance	400
Insurance and registration	800
Meals while away from the office ($200 relates to out-of-town travel)	420
Parking during employment duties	300
Interest on loan to acquire car	3,900

During the year, the employee drove 26 000 km, of which 14 000 were for employment duties and the remaining 12 000 were personal.

Analysis:

First of all, notice that some of these expenses related to both personal and employment activities (e.g., gasoline). Others related only to employment activities (e.g., parking). Also, meal costs were entirely personal, as the employee had to eat whether she was working or not. Remember, however, that meal costs while travelling out of town can be deducted, provided that the time away is greater than 12 hours.

The cost of an automobile can be deducted in the form of capital cost allowance (see Chapter 6). The designated capital cost allowance rate for automobiles is 30%, except in the first year, when it is only 15%. In this case, the rate of 15% applied only to the maximum permitted cost of $30,000 (in 2003), even though the actual cost was $32,000.

Combined personal and employment expenses were as follows:

---

51 ITA 67.2, .3.
52 ITA 67.1.

Gasoline	$ 2,200
Repairs and maintenance	400
Insurance and registration	800
Interest on loan (actual $3,900—limited to $300 × 12 months)	3,600
Capital cost allowance (15% of $30,000)	4,500
	$11,500
Employment portion:	
$\frac{\text{Employment km—14 000}}{\text{Total km—26 000}} \times \$11{,}500 =$	$ 6,192
Total employment expenses:	
Allocated above	$ 6,192
Parking	300
Out-of-town meals (50% × $200)	100
Total expenses	$ 6,592

B. Cost of Supplies Consumed

When the contract of employment requires that the employee pay for supplies used in carrying out the duties of employment, the costs of supplies are deductible only to the extent that they are fully consumed when used.[53] The consumption requirement virtually eliminates the employees' ability to deduct a broad range of items. For example, items such as small tools, books purchased by teachers, and hair dryers purchased by hairdressers are not deductible, even when employees must purchase such items under the employment contract, because they are not consumed by use in a short period of time. Supplies consumed would include such items as postage, stationery, and writing materials. The deductions under this category are extremely limited and in many respects represent an unfair interpretation of the specific tax law.

C. Salespeople's Expenses

Employees who act in a selling capacity or who negotiate contracts for employers fall into a special category, one which permits a broad range of deductions provided that any remuneration includes either some amount of commissions or some other similar amount that is a function of sales volume.[54] In addition, such salespeople must be required to pay their own expenses under the contract of employment; ordinarily, they must also be carrying on their duties of employment away from the employer's place of business; as well, they must not be receiving a tax-free travel allowance.

Effectively, salespeople can deduct *all* amounts expended in the year for the purpose of earning employment income, up to the total amount of commissions or other similar payments. The following, however, constitute exceptions to this:

1. Payments for the use of a yacht, camp, lodge, or golf course.

2. Membership fees or dues in a club, when the main purpose of that club is to provide dining, recreational, or sporting facilities to its members.

3. Expenditures of a capital nature that have a long-term benefit, such as a computer, desk, or filing cabinet. (However, capital cost allowance on an automobile can be deducted.)[55]

---

53 ITA 8(1)(i); IT-352R2.
54 ITA 8(1)(f); IT-522R.
55 ITA 8(1)(j).

Notice that the expenses incurred cannot exceed the amount of the commissions—in other words, a loss from commission activity cannot occur for tax purposes. To the extent that permitted expenses exceed commissions in any year, the excess is lost and cannot be used in other years. It should be pointed out that the capital cost allowance on an automobile, along with any related financing costs, is not subject to the commission limitation and can be deducted over and above commissions earned in a year.

The expenses that can be deducted by salespeople are wide-ranging and include, but are not restricted to, such items as advertising, promotion, telephone, parking, automobile, supplies, accounting costs, fees paid to assistants, the costs of maintaining an exclusive office in a home, and travel expenses. However, such expenses are deductible only if they are incurred solely in an attempt to earn the employment income. They are not deductible if they are for personal use. In addition, the arbitrary reasonableness test limits the amounts that can be deducted for automobiles (cost—$30,000; lease cost—$800 per month; interest—$300 per month) and meals and entertainment (50%), as described in part A above. Consider the following:

Situation: An employee receives a salary of $40,000 and commissions of $4,000 in a taxation year. He is required to use his automobile to earn commissions and receives a travel allowance of $3,000 for this purpose. At the end of the previous year the automobile had an undepreciated capital cost for tax purposes of $18,000. The automobile was driven 24 000 km during the year, of which 16 000 km were for employment purposes. The following additional costs were incurred to earn commissions during the year:

Advertising	$ 1,200
Parking	400
Entertainment—meals for customers	900
Golf club membership for entertaining customers	1,000
Purchase of new home computer	2,000
Automobile operating costs	4,000
Interest on automobile loan (12 months)	3,800
	$13,300

Analysis: First, it is necessary to establish whether the automobile allowance of $3,000 is taxable. It is tax-free if it is considered to be a reasonable allowance.[56] If the allowance is tax-free, no deductions can be claimed for any of the above commission expenses.[57] Here it is apparent that the automobile expenses (operating costs, capital cost allowance, and interest on the loan) far exceed the allowance of $3,000. It can be concluded that the allowance is unreasonably low and therefore is taxable.

The computer is a capital expenditure and cannot be deducted from employment income.[58] Capital cost allowance on the computer cannot be deducted (it could be if the individual was self-employed carrying on a business). However, if the computer is leased, the annual lease costs are deductible. The golf club membership is specifically disallowed as a deduction even if it was used to earn commission income.

The remaining expenses (except the automobile capital cost allowance and related interest on the loan) are deductible, but *only* to the extent of the commission income

---

56 ITA 6(1)(b)(v).
57 ITA 8(1)(f).
58 ITA 8(1)(f).

earned in the year. Capital cost allowance on the automobile and interest on the related loan are deductible (within limits), but are not restricted to the amount of commission income.[59]

Employment income:		
Salary		$40,000
Travel allowance		3,000
Commissions		4,000
		47,000
Salesperson expenses:		
Advertising	$1,200	
Parking	400	
Entertainment—meals—50% × 900	450	
Automobile operating costs		
16 000 km/24 000 km × $4,000	2,667	
	$4,717	
Limited to commission income		(4,000)
Other automobile costs:		
Capital cost allowance—30% × $18,000	$5,400	
Interest on loan—limited to $300 per month		
$300 × 12m	3,600	
	$9,000	
Employment portion—16 000 km/24 000 km × $9,000		(6,000)
Employment income		$37,000

D. Work Space in Home

In some circumstances, certain salespeople and other employees must carry out their duties from a home office. The home in question may be owned or rented. The associated costs are permitted as a deduction from their commission income, provided that certain criteria are met.[60]

A home office deduction is permitted if that office is the "place where the individual principally performs the duties of employment." CCRA has interpreted this to mean more than 50% of the time.

If the above criterion is not met, a deduction may still be permitted if the space is used *exclusively* to earn employment income *and is used on a regular or continuous basis* for meeting customers or clients of the employer.

Both of the above tests may be difficult to meet. When they *are* met, the costs for salespeople are normally the prorated portion of the home's property taxes, insurance, maintenance, and utilities (or the rent cost when the home is not owned). Employees who are not salespeople can deduct only the maintenance and utility costs (not the insurance and property taxes). Such costs cannot be greater than the employment income earned in the year. When they are greater, the excess can be carried forward to the next year. An employee cannot deduct interest on a house mortgage as part of office costs at any time.[61] A self-employed person *can* do so.[62]

59 ITA 8(1)(j).
60 ITA 8(13); IT-352R.
61 ITA 8(1)(f).
62 ITA 20(1)(c).

E. Registered Pension Plan Contributions

It was indicated previously that employers often contribute amounts to a registered pension plan on behalf of an employee and that such contributions, although a benefit, are not taxable until funds are withdrawn from the pension plan. Most RPPs permit the employee to contribute an annual amount to the plan, or require this; as a result, the pension's value is determined by combining the employer and employee contributions. Within specified limits, the contribution made by an employee is deductible in arriving at net income from employment.[63]

The specified limits for employee contributions to an RPP are complex, and integrated with other retirement plans such as deferred profit sharing plans and personal registered retirement savings plans (see Chapter 9). The maximum amount that can be contributed by the employer and employee combined to all of the above-mentioned plans is 18% of the employee's previous year's earned income. For *money purchase RPPs*, the contribution limit is further limited by a dollar amount: $15,500 in 2003, increasing in 2004 to $16,500 and in 2005 to $18,000.[64] Beginning in 2006, the contribution limit will be indexed to increases in the average industrial wage. In most cases the required contribution specified by the employer's pension plan will fall within the designated limits and will be fully deductible by the employee.

The value of investing in tax-deferred pension plans was discussed in Part III of this chapter and will be reviewed more extensively in Chapter 9.

VI. Employment Income and the GST/PST/HST

The *Income Tax Act* rarely refers specifically to the goods and services tax. One of the few times it does so is in the section relating to employment income. There are two important areas where a relationship between the GST and employment income is obvious.

The first relates to taxable employee benefits. When an employer provides an employee with tangible taxable benefits, the employee has, in effect, received a salary and then used it to acquire a particular service or good. Had the employee acquired that item directly, he or she would have paid GST of 7% (unless it was an exempt item such as insurance). This means that the employer must include the value of the GST when calculating the amount of a benefit for an employee.[65] Similarly, the value of any provincial sales tax (PST) or harmonized sales tax (HST) is included in the value of the benefit.

A second GST implication arises when an employee incurs expenses as part of a contract of employment. For example, salespeople who incur promotion, travel, and other expenses must pay GST on those items. However, most employees are not GST registrants and so are not usually eligible for a rebate or credit. Because of this, as a special rule, any employee who has expenses that are deductible for tax purposes can claim a GST rebate on those expenses. For example, an employee who has expenses of $1,070 ($1,000 + $70 GST) can apply for a refund of $70. Because the full $1,070 would have been deducted for income tax purposes, the refund of $70 is taxable to the employee when it is received.[66] An employee has up to four years to claim the refund.

VII. Sample Calculation of Employment Income

Summary of Facts

Ms. X is employed by a Canadian public corporation as a middle-level manager. Information relating to her financial affairs for a particular year is outlined below.

1. Ms. X received a salary of $40,000 during the year. In addition, she was awarded a bonus of $5,000 for her special efforts during the current year. The payment is to be made in two installments during the following year.

---

63 ITA 8(1)(m), 147.2(4).
64 ITA 147.1(1)
65 ITA 6(7).
66 ITA 6(8).

2. Two years earlier, the employer had granted Ms. X an option to acquire 500 shares of the public corporation at $30 per share. At the time the option was granted, the shares were trading at $32. During the early part of the current year Ms. X exercised the option and acquired 500 shares, which at that time had a value of $35 per share. In December of the current year, after their value rose unexpectedly, she sold them for $41 a share.

3. The company had a generous benefit program and during the year provided Ms. X with the following:[67]
   - a contribution to the company pension plan of $3,300
   - a group term life insurance premium of $500 for $50,000 of life insurance for the beneficiaries of her estate
   - a membership valued at $1,000 in a private squash club, to which many of the employer's customers belonged
   - a company car for personal use throughout the year (The car cost the company $20,000 including GST/PST; during the year the company paid $5,000 of operating expenses. The car was driven a total of 20,000 km, of which 11,000 were for personal use.)
   - a gift costing $600 (including GST/PST) in honour of Ms. X's 20th wedding anniversary.

4. During the year, Ms. X made the following payments, some of which were deducted directly from her monthly salary by the employer and paid on her behalf.

Employment Insurance	$ 450
Canada Pension Plan	400
Donations to registered charities	200
Income taxes	8,000
Contribution to the company RPP	3,000
Interest to the employer of 6% on a $10,000 loan	
(CCRA's prescribed interest rate was 10%)	600

5. The contract of employment required that Ms. X acquire, at her own expense, a small portable computer to be used while travelling and at home. During the year she purchased a small computer for $2,000; she also purchased and used $75 worth of special computer paper.

6. From time to time, Ms. X travelled out of town on behalf of the employer. For this reason the company provided her with a monthly travel allowance of $500, which she was not required to account for. During the year she spent $2,000 on airline tickets, $500 on meals, and $1,000 on lodging. This year's travel expenses are similar to amounts spent in previous years.

7. Over several weekends during the year, Ms. X completed a consulting project for her brother-in-law's business, for which she received $3,000.

Employment Income

The net income from employment for Ms. X amounts to $49,915 during the year, determined as shown in the following table.

---

67 It is assumed that the values of the benefits include the appropriate amount of GST/PST if applicable.

A. Remuneration received:		
Salary		$40,000
B. Benefits received or enjoyed:		
Stock option:		
Value at date of acquisition ($35 × 500)	$17,500	
Cost of acquisition ($30 × 500)	15,000	2,500†
Group term life insurance		500
Automobile for personal use:		
Operating costs:		
11 000 km × 17¢		1,870
Capital value, referred to as a "standby charge":		
20 000 × 24% (2% × 12m)§		4,800
Anniversary gift (value exceeds $500)		600
Company loan:		
Prescribed interest ($10,000 @ 10%)	$ 1,000	
Interest paid ($10,000 @ 6%)	(600)	400
C. Allowances received:		
Travel allowance ($500 × 12 m)		
(see explanation below)		6,000
Total remuneration, benefits, and allowances		56,670
D. Deductions permitted:*		
Contribution to company pension plan	$ 3,000	
Computer supplies consumed	75	
Travel costs (including 50% of meal costs)		
—$2,000 + 50% ($500) + $1,000	3,250	6,325
Net income from employment		$50,345

* The cost of GST included in the computer supplies and travel costs will be refunded upon application. The refund is taxable in the year received.

† The stock option benefit is taxable in the year the shares are acquired because the value of the shares at the date the option was granted was higher than the option price.

§ The automobile was not used "primarily" for business use and the standby charge reduction cannot apply.

Explanation of Items Omitted

Several items in the summary of facts are omitted from the determination of income. Their exclusion is explained below.

• **Bonus**   The bonus of $5,000, although earned in the current year, is not received until the following year. As employment income is on a cash basis, it will be included in income in the following year when received.

• **Gain on sale of employer shares**   This is a capital transaction resulting in a capital gain of $3,000, calculated as follows.

Selling price ($41 × 500)	$20,500
Value at date of acquisition ($35 × 500)	17,500
Capital gain	$ 3,000

The taxable capital gain of $1,500 (½ of $3,000) would be included in income within the capital gains area. While this may affect the individual's net income for tax purposes, it is not part of employment income.

- **RPP benefit**   The employer's contribution of $3,300 to the registered pension plan, although a benefit, is excluded because it is one of the specific primary exceptions to the benefit rule.

- **Membership fee**   The payment of a club membership fee is clearly a benefit; however, it is currently a matter of administrative practice that the payment of club dues for employees is not a taxable benefit provided that membership at the club is useful to the employer's income-earning process. In any event, the employer is not permitted to deduct club membership fees for dining, recreational, or sporting activities; this may be CCRA's primary reason for ignoring the benefit to the employee.

- **Donations**   These are not specifically permitted as an employment deduction, and therefore the general rule that no deductions are allowed is in force. Donations, however, qualify for a tax credit, thereby reducing federal and provincial taxes payable (see Chapter 10).

- **Travel allowance**   The travel allowance is included as a taxable benefit because it does not meet the criteria to qualify as an exception to the general rule that all allowances are taxable. As the travel allowance appears to be in excess of a reasonable amount ($6,000 compared with normal travel expenses of $3,500), it remains taxable. Because the allowance is taxable, the actual expenses incurred by the employee can be deducted from employment income. If the allowance had qualified as tax-free, the actual travel costs could not have been deducted.

- **Computer**   While it is a requirement of the contract of employment that the employee acquire a small computer to be used in the performance of duties, the cost of $2,000 does not qualify as a specific deduction permitted, because it does not constitute supplies *consumed* and is thus a capital expenditure. This means that only the $75 spent on paper during the year qualifies as a deduction.

- **Consulting fee**   The consulting fee of $3,000 earned for independent activities does not imply an employer/employee relationship and as such does not constitute employment income. It does, however, qualify as business income and is included in the individual's income within the business income category, which is subject to a separate set of general rules.

- **Canada Pension Plan and Employment Insurance premiums**   These amounts are not deductible, in accordance with the general rule that no deductions are permitted except those specified. However, both items qualify for a tax credit that reduces federal and provincial taxes payable (see Chapter 10).

- **Alternative calculation for operating benefit on automobile**   It is not worthwhile to use the alternative calculation (i.e., 50% of the standby charge), because the result (50% of $4,800 = $2,400) would be greater than the actual benefit of $1,350.

VIII. Tax Planning Checklist

1. Employees should try to maximize their use of employer-provided benefit programs, even when the benefit is taxable, because often the employer can acquire the particular service or good at a lower cost.

2. In lieu of salaries, employers should consider offering a shopping list of benefits from which employees can choose. This way, employees receive only those benefits that are relevant to their personal situation.

3. Salary deferrals may be beneficial when the employer pays interest on the deferred amount. However, employees should consider whether the deferral to a future taxation year will alter the rate of tax that would otherwise be applicable.

4. When provided with an automobile for extensive personal use over several years, an employee should eventually consider purchasing the vehicle from the employer at its depreciated value. The taxable benefit (standby charge) is based each year on the original cost of the car, even when its value is declining. At some point the employee may find it worthwhile to purchase the car rather than incur the tax cost based on the original cost.

5. An employee who wants to take advantage of the reduced standby charge for low personal use of an employer's automobile (i.e., less than 50%) must maintain a careful record of kilometres travelled.

6. An employer who is prepared to fund an employee's personal automobile costs should investigate whether the automobile should be owned or leased, and by which party.

7. When an employee uses his or her own car for employer business, a decision should be made as to the method of employer funding (i.e., allowance or regular reimbursement). In the case of an allowance, the employer should consider including that allowance in the employee's income as unreasonable, so that he or she can deduct the higher actual travel costs.

8. When an employee uses an employer's automobile less than 50% of the time for personal use, and when the employer pays the operating costs (alternative calculation—50% of standby charge), the employee must tell the employer before year end whether he or she wants to use the alternative calculation for the benefit derived.

9. The taxable benefit calculation on low-interest employer home purchase loans is fixed on loans up to a five-year term. When interest rates decline, it may be worth renegotiating the loan to guarantee the lower rate for a new five-year period.

10. Employees who have been granted stock options should consider when such options should be exercised. If the share price is rising, an early purchase reduces the amount of employment income and enhances the amount of the capital gain, of which only one-half is taxable. This benefit must be weighed against the cost of funding the purchase sooner.

11. A commissioned salesperson cannot deduct expenses in excess of commissions earned, and the excess is not available for carry-over to another year. When it would improve the salesperson's tax position, consideration should be given to delaying expenses to the next taxation year.

12. Salespeople cannot deduct capital expenditures except for capital cost allowance on automobiles and airplanes. Therefore, capital equipment required for work, such as cellular phones, computers, and so on, should be leased rather than purchased. The lease cost is then deductible.

IX. Summary and Conclusion

The determination of employment income is governed by a narrow set of rules. These rules require that remuneration—including benefits and allowances—received under a term of employment be taxable. Knowledge of the exceptions to the general rules is vital if one is to understand completely how employment income is taxed. As stated in this chapter, the exceptions are not significant in number, but their value to the employee is significant.

Similarly, deductions from employment income are limited to a very short list of items, which simplifies the process of income determination. One often hears the complaint that employees are at a disadvantage because they are permitted so few deductions. It must be recognized that in most cases employees do not incur many direct expenses for the purpose of earning their employment income. Those that do, appear to be adequately covered by the special deductions that *are* permitted. The deductions attempt to recognize the major types of expenses that employees must incur to earn their income; with the exception of the short-comings of the deduction for supplies consumed, they appear to accomplish this.

Employment income is usually earned from employers who are carrying on a business. Employers determine their income for tax purposes according to the principles of business income (see Chapter 5), which are different from the principles of employment income. It is essential that, while studying the remaining chapters in Part Two of the text, readers compare the general principles for each category; doing so will enable them to understand the full scope of various financial transactions. Employees and employers, while governed by different rules, interact in a way that binds them together in a common decision process. Employers cannot adequately develop compensation packages without understanding their impact on the employee. Chapter 22 is devoted to an examination of specific employee compensation programs.

Reading List

Income Tax Act References

	Section
Income from an office or employment	5(1)
Loss from an office or employment	5(2)
Amounts to be included in income from employment	6
Value of benefits	6(1)(a)
Benefits not taxable	6(1)(a)(i) to (v)
Allowances (personal or living expenses and others)	6(1)(b)
Allowances considered not taxable	6(1)(b)(i) to (ix)
Travel allowances not taxable:	
Salespeople	6(1)(b)(v)
Non-salespeople	6(1)(b)(vii), (vii.1)
Director's fees	6(1)(c)
Standby charge for automobile	6(1)(e), (2)
Goods and services tax	6(7), 8
Employment insurance benefits	6(1)(f)
Reimbursements and awards	6(1)(j)
Payments by employer to employee (inducement payments)	6(3)
Portion of premium under certain group insurance	
policies (life insurance)	6(4)
Employment at a special worksite	6(6)
Interest on employee debt	6(9)
Salary deferral arrangement	6(11)

Forgiveness of employee loans	6(15)
Agreements to issue shares to employees (stock options)	7
Deductions allowed	8(1)
General limitation	8(2)
Legal expenses of employees	8(1)(b)
Salesperson's expenses	8(1)(f)
Travel expenses	8(1)(h)
Motor vehicle travel expenses	8(1)(h.1)
Professional membership dues	8(1)(i)(i)
Office rent or salary to assistant	8(1)(i)(ii)
Cost of supplies consumed	8(1)(i)(iii)
Trade union dues	8(1)(i)(iv)
Automobile and aircraft costs	8(1)(j)
Employee's registered pension plan contribution	8(i)(m)
Meals	8(4)
Work space in home	8(13)
Unpaid remuneration	78(4)
Loans	80.4
Prescribed interest rate	Reg. 4301

Limitations:

Expenses for food, beverages, and entertainment	67.1
Interest on money borrowed for passenger vehicles	67.2
Cost of leasing passenger vehicles	67.3
Capital cost of automobile	13(7)(g), also Regulation (Schedule 2—Class 10.1)

Canada Customs and Revenue Agency Publications

IT-470R	Employee fringe benefits.
IT-63R5	Benefits, including standby charge for an automobile.
IT-377R	Director's, executor's, and juror's fees.
IT-502	Employee benefit plans and employee trusts.
IT-196R2	Payments by employer to employee.
IT-227R	Group term life insurance premiums.
IT-113R4	Benefits to employees—stock options.
IT-522R	Vehicle and other travel expenses—employees.
IT-352R2	Employee's expenses including work space in home expenses.
IT-167R6	Registered pension funds or plans—employee's contributions.
IT-421R2	Benefits to individuals, corporations, and shareholders from loans on debt.
IT-148R3	Recreational properties and club dues.
IT-91R4	Employment at special or remote worksite.
IT-222R	Advances to employees.
IT-168R3	Athletes and players employed by football, hockey, and similar clubs.
IT-109R2	Unpaid amounts.

Major Court Decisions

671122 Ontario Ltd. v. Sagaz Industries Canada Inc. (2001)—Employed v. self-employed.
Wiebe Door Services Ltd. v. MNR, 87 DTC 5025, FCA—Employed v. self-employed.
Mommesteeg et al. v. The Queen, 96 DTC 1011—Frequent flyer plans.
Grant v. MNR, 67 DTC 249—Meaning of remuneration.
Arsens v. MNR, 69 DTC 81—Holiday trips and prizes.
Ransom v. MNR, 67 DTC 5235—Meaning of "allowances."

Other Publications

Tang and Katz, "Automobile Benefits and Expenses: Part I," *Canadian Tax Journal*, Vol. 45, No. 5 (1997), p. 1150. See also Part 2, Vol. 46, No. 1 (1998) and Part 3, Vol. 46, No. 4 (1998).

Magee, J., "Whose Business Is It? Employees or Independent Contractors," *Canadian Tax Journal*, Vol. 45, No. 3 (1997), p. 584.

Roy, J., "Taxing the Virtual Office," Report of Proceedings of the 48th Tax Conference (1996), Canadian Tax Foundation, p. 31.1.

Demonstration Questions

Question One

Carl Collins celebrated his 65th birthday in 20X4. A car accident forced him to quit his job and retire on June 30, 20X4. He received $120,000 from an insurance company for potential loss of earnings. At his retirement party, his employer presented him with an original work of art costing $2,500. He also received a cheque for $40,000 in recognition of his 12 years of valued service. Information relating to his employment activities is presented below.

1. Collins retired on June 30, 20X4. Up to that date he received a salary of $48,000. Collins negotiated contracts for his employer, and was also paid ¼ of 1% of the value of contracts negotiated. As of June 30, 20X4, this amounted to $22,000 and was paid in two instalments of $11,000 each on September 30, 20X4, and January 15, 20X5.

2. To carry out his employment duties, Collins used a company car that was also available for his personal use. He returned the car to the employer on June 30, 20X4. He drove the car 20 000 km for business and 4 000 km for personal use in 20X4.

   The employer's lease cost for the car to June 30, 20X4, was $4,494. In addition, the employer paid operating costs of $3,800. Collins paid the employer $200 as a partial reimbursement for the personal use of the automobile.

3. On June 30, 20X4, Collins paid the employer $20,700. This covered the full principal repayment of an employee loan of $20,000 plus interest of $700 from January 1, 20X4 to June 30, 20X4. CCRA's prescribed interest rate for the period was 9%. Collins had used half of the borrowed funds to repair his home and the other half to help buy an investment in shares of public corporations.

4. As a condition of employment, Collins had worked from an office in his home. A desk was available to him at his employer's place of business, which he used one afternoon a week. He spent the remaining time in his home office or visiting customers. The home office occupied 60 square metres of his 600-square-metre home. His home expenses for the entire year were as follows:

Mortgage interest	$ 4,200
Utilities	2,200
Property taxes	2,600
Insurance	800
Minor repairs and maintenance	1,200
	$11,000

5. After the car accident, Collins received $4,200 ($700 × 6 weeks) from the employer's sickness, accident, and income maintenance insurance plan. In addition, the employer's private medical insurance plan paid hospital expenses of $3,000.

6. Besides Collins's salary, the employer paid the premiums for private medical insurance ($380) and group sickness, accident, and income maintenance insurance ($500). The following amounts were withheld from Collins's salary and remitted to the appropriate parties:

Income tax	$14,000
Registered pension plan	4,000
Share of premiums for group sickness, accident, and income maintenance plan	500
Canada Pension Plan and Employment Insurance	1,915

The group sickness, accident, and income maintenance plan originated in 20X0. By the end of 20X3, Collins had paid $2,000 in premiums, which was matched by the employer.

7. In January 20X4, Collins purchased a computer for $2,000 on time payments. He incurred interest costs of $240. Until his retirement, he used the computer for employment activities 60% of the time. He also obtained a fax machine on a two-year lease arrangement. In 20X4, lease payments were $240. He used the fax entirely for employment until his retirement. The following additional costs were incurred for employment:

Advertising	$300
Entertainment: meals for clients	400
Collins's meals when travelling out of town on occasional 10-hour round trips	200

Required:
Determine Collins's net income from employment for the 20X4 taxation year (ignore GST implications). Comment on any items that have been excluded from the calculation.

Solution:
Note that the standby charge on the next page was reduced from its normal calculation because the number of kilometres driven for employment purposes was greater than 50% of the total kilometres driven (20 000 ÷ 24 000 = 83%). Therefore, the normal standby charge was reduced by the number of personal kilometres driven divided by the arbitrary amount of 1 667 km for each month the automobile was available.

The following amounts were excluded from the calculation of employment income:

• **Deferred commissions** Of the total commissions of $22,000, only $11,000 was received in 20X4. The remaining amount of $11,000 was received in 20X5 and will be included in that year's employment income.

• **Insurance for loss of earnings** The $120,000 of insurance proceeds is not employment income. Also, it does not qualify as "other sources" of income and therefore is not taxable.

Employment income:		
Salary		$48,000
Commissions received in 20X4		11,000
Retirement gift—painting		2,500
Automobile:		
Standby charge (see comment below)		
⅔ × $4,494 = $2,996 × 4 000 km ÷		
(1 667 km × 6 months)	1,918	
Operating benefit—lesser of:		
4 000 km × 17¢ = $680		
50% × $1,918 = $599	599	
	1,797	
Less reimbursement	(200)	1,597
Employee loan—interest benefit:		
Prescribed interest—9% × $20,000 × 6m/12m	900	
Less interest paid	(700)	200
Payments from income maintenance insurance	4,200	
Less premiums paid by Collins ($2,000 + $500)	(2,500)	1,700
		64,997
Employment expenses:		
Home office—($11,000 − $4,200 interest) =		
$6,800 × 60/600 × ½ year		(340)
Registered pension plan		(4,000)
Selling expenses:		
Fax lease payments—$240 × ½ year	120	
Advertising	300	
Entertainment meals—50% × $400	200	(620)
Income from employment		$60,037

- **Retiring allowance**   The retirement payment of $40,000 is a retiring allowance and is not classified as employment income. Instead, it is considered to be other income and is included in a separate part of the aggregating formula for net income for tax purposes.[68]

- **Hospital insurance**   The $3,000 of hospital expenses paid by the employer's insurance plan is not a taxable benefit, unlike the insurance for the lost salary under the sickness, accident, and income maintenance insurance plan.

- **Insurance premiums**   The private medical insurance premium and the group sickness, accident, and income maintenance insurance premium are specifically allowed as non-taxable benefits.

- **Computer**   The computer cost is a capital item and cannot be deducted as selling expenses. Similarly, the interest of $240 on the computer loan is on account of capital.

---

68 ITA 56(1)(a)(ii).

- **Canada Pension Plan and Employment Insurance** The contributions by Collins to the Canada Pension and Employment Insurance plans are not deductible from employment income, as they are not specifically mentioned in section 8 of the *Income Tax Act*, which lists the permitted deductions. The amounts can be used to claim a tax credit when calculating tax (see Chapter 10).

- **Out-of-town meals** The cost of meals while travelling out of town is deductible only if the employee was away for more than 12 hours in the day. Here, Collins was away for only 10 hours.

- **Interest benefit** Note that the employee loan was used by Collins partially to make an investment in shares of public companies. Therefore, one-half of the interest cost paid plus one-half of the low interest benefit on the loan can be deducted when arriving at income from property.

Question Two

Francine Leduc is a senior employee with OM Inc., a public corporation. Information relating to her employment with OM for 20X5 is summarized below.

1. In 20X5 Leduc received a salary of $110,000. From this, deductions of $33,000 for income tax, $2,700 for Canada Pension Plan and Employment Insurance, $6,000 for contributions to a registered pension plan, and $1,200 for charitable donations were made and remitted to the appropriate parties. On November 30, 20X5, Leduc was awarded a $30,000 bonus, receiving $3,000 at the time, and the balance payable on June 30, 20X6.

2. OM provides three of its senior executives with an allowance to attend conventions of their choice. In 20X5, Leduc received $2,000 for this allowance and was not required to account for the costs. Leduc attended one convention and incurred travel costs of $2,200.

3. Leduc's employment contract requires that she use her own car on company business. In 20X5, OM paid Leduc a car allowance of $5,600, being 35¢ for each of 16 000 km driven for employment purposes. Leduc drove her car a total of 24 000 km in 20X5 and incurred the following costs.

Parking—visiting customers	$ 600
Insurance	1,150
Repairs and maintenance	1,400
Fuel	1,800
Interest on car loan	4,200

The undepreciated capital cost of her car at the end of 20X4 was $20,400.

4. On December 20, 20X5, Leduc asked for and received from OM a $6,000 advance against her January 20X6 salary. The funds were needed for a family vacation. OM reduced Leduc's January 20X6 salary for the advance.

5. In June 20X5, OM announced two new employee compensation plans. One plan allowed each employee to purchase 1,000 shares of OM Inc. for $14 per share. At the time of the announcement, OM's shares were trading at $15 per share. Leduc purchased her 1,000 shares for $14 per share in August 20X5. At that time, the shares

were trading for $18 per share. On December 31, 20X5, Leduc sold all the OM shares for $16 per share.

OM also introduced a holiday cruise award for executives who gave special service. Leduc qualified for the award, and in 20X5 she and her spouse enjoyed the five-day cruise. The retail value of the cruise was $3,000 but cost OM $2,150 because of quantity discounts.

Required:
Determine Leduc's net income from employment for the 20X5 taxation year.

Solution:

Employment income			
Salary			$110,000
Bonus—portion received			3,000
Convention allowance—see below			2,000
Car allowance—considered to be unreasonably low			5,600
Salary advance			6,000
Stock option benefit—1,000 × ($18 – $14)			4,000
Holiday cruise award—based on employer's cost			2,150
			132,750
Deduct			
Registered pension plan		6,000	
Parking		600	
Auto:			
Insurance	1,150		
Repairs	1,400		
Fuel	1,800		
Interest ($300 × 12 months—limit)	3,600		
Capital cost allowance $20,400 × 30%	6,120		
16 000/24 000 km × 14,070	14,070	9,380	(15,980)
Employment income			$116,770

Several other items require further explanation. The convention allowance is taxable under the general rule that all allowances are taxable. There is no exception for a convention allowance, unlike a travel allowance, which can be tax-free if it is a reasonable amount. Also, even though the convention allowance is taxable, the actual convention expenses incurred by Leduc cannot be deducted from employment income, because section 8 of the *Income Tax Act* does not list convention expenses as a deductible item. The treatment of travel allowances and travel expenses is unique.

When Leduc exercised the stock option, the related employment income was established as the difference between the market value of the shares at that time ($18) and the cost of the shares ($14). For reasons indicated in this chapter, the cost of the shares for capital gain or capital loss purposes was established at $18. Thus, when Leduc sold the shares for $16 per share on the last day of the year, she incurred a capital loss of $2,000 (1,000 × [$16 – $18]). One-half of this is allowable, though it can be deducted only against other capital gains.

Charitable donations are not deductible from employment income. Instead, they qualify as a tax credit when calculating tax (see Chapter 10).

Review Questions

1. Explain this statement: "It is not the nature of the service that determines whether or not one is employed but rather the relationship which exists between the individual providing the service and the entity receiving the service."

2. Distinguish between
   (a) individual A (a student), who spent the summer painting three houses. The contract for one house provided for a fixed fee; the contracts for the other two provided for a fee per hour and materials costs; and,
   (b) individual B, who worked for a painting company and received a wage of $10 per hour for painting three houses.

3. "Income from employment for tax purposes includes the gross earnings from employment less expenses incurred to earn that income." Is this statement true? Briefly outline the fundamental rules for establishing income from employment.

4. An individual begins employment on December 16, 20X0. The employer pays salaries monthly on the fifteenth day of each month. The individual receives her first salary payment of $3,000 on January 15, 20X1. How much, if any, of the $3,000 is taxable in 20X0? How much in 20X1? Explain.

5. An employer follows the policy of awarding bonuses to employees for their exceptional efforts. Bonuses are awarded on the last day of each calendar year but are not paid until two years later. Does this policy benefit the employer and employee? Explain.

6. In addition to salaries, wages, and commissions, an employer may provide a wide range of benefits to employees. Describe the general tax treatment to the employee of benefits received from an employer, and explain how the value of these benefits is determined for tax purposes. If an employee is permitted to operate an employer's automobile for personal use, does the treatment of this benefit conform to the general treatment of benefits? Explain.

7. From the employee's perspective, what benefits, if any, receive preferential tax treatment? Explain briefly, and compare the tax treatment these different benefits receive.

8. Distinguish between an allowance and a reimbursement.

9. What effect does the receipt of an allowance have on an employee's ability to deduct expenses incurred to earn employment income?

10. With respect to deductions from employment income, compare the general tax treatment of an employee who is a salesperson and earns commissions with that of an employee who earns a fixed salary.

11. Can employees who earn commission income and are required to pay their own expenses to generate that income incur losses from employment for tax purposes? Explain.

12. When an employee is entitled to deduct particular expenses incurred to earn employment income, what restrictions, if any, are placed on the amount of expenses that can be deducted?

CHAPTER FOUR: INCOME FROM EMPLOYMENT ❧ 103

Problems

Problem One

Pasqual Melo is employed by a public corporation. On January 1, 20X0, she was given an option to purchase 1,000 shares of Public Corporation for $8 per share (the option extended for two years).

On December 15, 20X0, she exercised her option and bought 1,000 shares at $8 per share (total = $8,000).

On June 15, 20X3, she sold the 1,000 shares.

The value of the shares at the particular dates was as follows:

Date option granted	$8.50
Date option exercised	10
Date shares sold	14

Required:

1. Determine the amount and type of income received by Melo, and when that income was taxable.

2. How would your answer change if the value of the shares at the date the option was granted was $8.00 rather than $8.50?

3. How would your answer change if the employer were a Canadian-controlled private corporation?

Problem Two

Paul Fenson is employed as a shipping supervisor. In the evenings and on weekends he holds a second job as a real estate salesman for a national real estate firm. His financial information for 20X0 is as follows:

1. His salary from his day job is $30,000 per annum. However, the employer deducts a number of items from his salary, so his net take-home pay is only $20,400. The following amounts were deducted in 20X0:

Income tax	$3,900
Union dues	600
Canada Pension Plan	400
Employment Insurance premiums	300
Registered pension plan contribution	3,000
Reimbursement for personal use of employer's car	600
Charitable donations remitted to United Way	800
	$9,600

The employer paid the following amounts on behalf of Fenson:

Canada Pension Plan	$ 400
Employment Insurance premiums	360
Registered pension plan	3,000
Premiums for a mandatory provincial health insurance plan	600
Group term life insurance premiums ($50,000 coverage)	1,200
	$5,560

Fenson used the employer's summer camp for a one-month holiday and paid the employer $200 rent. When not being used by employees, the summer camp is rented for the normal amount of $600 per month.

Although Fenson owned his own automobile, he was provided with a company car. The car cost the company $23,000. During the year he drove a total of 20 000 km, of which 14 000 was for personal use. The employer also paid all of the operating costs, which amounted to $3,000.

During the year, Fenson attended a shipping conference in Toronto. His wife travelled with him to Toronto at the company's expense ($1,000).

The employer permitted staff to purchase merchandise from its retail outlet at the company's cost. During the year, Fenson purchased, for $800, merchandise with a retail value of $1,200.

2. As a real estate salesman, Fenson earned a base salary of $8,000 and received commissions of $7,000. In relation to his real estate work, he incurred the following expenses:

Dues to a local real estate association	$ 400
Fee for a three-day seminar on how to be an effective salesperson	800
Advertising—calendars and pens	1,700
Automobile operating costs	4,000
Promotion (meals and drinks for clients)	2,800
Personal meals (during in-town business)	400
Purchase of a portable telephone	2,000

Fenson used his own automobile for his real estate activities. The car has an undepreciated capital cost for tax purposes of $10,000. During the year he drove a total of 30 000 km, of which 27 000 was related to selling real estate. His employer provided him with a monthly car allowance of $200 ($2,400 per year).

Required:
Determine Fenson's net income from employment for the particular year. (Assume that the employer's costs include GST/PST where applicable.)

Problem Three
Charles and Cathy are employed by different companies. They earn the same amount of income and share a similar lifestyle. However, each receives a different type of remuneration.

Charles earns a total of $50,000, which is paid in the form of a monthly salary. His annual personal expenses (excluding income tax) are shown in table A, on the next page.

Cathy also earns $50,000 annually. Her remuneration is as shown in table B, next page. Her personal expenses (excluding income tax) are shown in table C.

Both Charles and Cathy pay income tax at a rate of 40%. Both invest any savings in an effort to build up a substantial investment portfolio.

Required:
1. For the current year, compare Cathy's after-tax cash flow with that of Charles, and determine the amount each has available to add to an investment portfolio.

2. What amount of salary would Charles have to receive in order to have the same amount of cash available as Cathy for his investment portfolio?

A. Life insurance ($100,000)	$ 1,000
Lease payments on automobile	6,000
Interest on house mortgage (10% on $70,000)	7,000
Family private medical insurance	1,000
Golf club dues	2,000
Automobile operating expenses	3,000
Other personal living expenses	9,000
	$29,000

B. Salary		$39,000
Private medical insurance		1,000
Group term life insurance ($100,000)		1,000
Lease payments on company automobile used personally by Cathy		6,000
Low-interest (5%) loan of $20,000:		
Prescribed interest rate (10%)	$ 2,000	
Actual interest charged (5%)	(1,000)	1,000
Paid golf club dues		2,000
		$50,000

C. Interest on house mortgage:	
10% of $50,000	$ 5,000
Interest on employee loan used to acquire house:	
5% of $20,000	1,000
Automobile operating costs	3,000
Other personal living expenses	9,000
	$18,000

Problem Four

After a recent staff evaluation, Susan Pearson's employer offered her the following alternative remuneration proposals:

1. A salary increase of $2,500 per annum, from $40,000 to $42,500.

2. A contribution of $2,000 per year to the company's deferred profit sharing plan.

Pearson's living expenses are modest, and if she accepts the salary increase she intends to invest the additional cash flow in secure 10% bonds. Coincidentally, the company's deferred profit sharing plan also achieves an average investment return of 10%.

Pearson plans to retire in 30 years, and her intention is to use the remuneration increase to help fund her retirement. Currently, she pays tax at a marginal rate of 40%.

Required:

Assuming that investment returns and tax rates remain stable at 10% and 40% respectively, which alternative should Pearson prefer? You may also assume that if she accepts the deferred profit sharing plan, it will be paid to her in a lump sum at the end of 30 years.

Problem Five

Jennifer Ratushny is a middle-level manager at a New Brunswick–based advertising agency. Her contract of employment requires her employer to provide her with an automobile for personal use. Two years ago the employer purchased an automobile for her that cost $23,000. All costs to operate the vehicle are paid by Ratushny. She is not required to use the vehicle for any of her employment duties.

The employment contract also stipulates that Ratushny may, if she chooses, purchase the vehicle from the employer at any time for a price equal to the depreciated value of the car. The automobile's depreciated value is now $14,000.

Ratushny is thinking of purchasing the car from her employer. Her bank is willing to loan her the money for it at 10%. The car is in good condition. If she makes the acquisition, she intends to use the car for at least three more years. A friend of hers, who is in the automobile business, has informed her that, subject to any mechanical problems, the car should have a resale value of $8,000 three years from now.

Ratushny earns a high salary; her marginal income tax rate is 50%.

Required:

Should Ratushny purchase the car at this time, or should she continue to use it as an employer-owned vehicle?

Problem Six

Riley Fontaine has requested that you review the calculation of his 20X1 net income for tax purposes. He has provided you with the following information:

1. His salary consists of the following:

Basic salary	$92,000
Bonus	6,000
	$98,000

The bonus of $6,000 was awarded to him on December 31, 20X1, and was paid on January 15, 20X2.

2. His employer deducted the following items from his salary and remitted them to the appropriate party on his behalf:

Canada Pension Plan	$ 660
Employment Insurance premiums	893
Registered pension plan	4,400
Income tax	34,000
Charitable donations (United Way)	3,500

3. Fontaine is employed by Remco, a Canadian public corporation. Two years ago, Remco granted Fontaine an option to purchase 1,000 of its common shares at $16 per share. At the time the option was granted, Remco's shares were trading at the same value of $16 per share. On January 31, 20X1, Fontaine purchased 1,000 shares of Remco (trading value at purchase date—$22 per share). On November 30, 20X1, he sold all of the shares at $24.

4. Remco requires that Fontaine work out of his home from time to time. Remco has supplied him with a computer and modem for this purpose; however, Fontaine must pay for his own supplies. His house is 2,000 square feet and his work station is a room of about 200 square feet. He also uses the room as a den and guest room. Utility costs for his home for 20X1 amounted to $1,200.

5. Fontaine travels out of town from time to time to his employer's manufacturing plant. Remco reimburses him for all travel costs except meal costs. The plant is only 90 km from the head office, and he always returns home the same day after working a normal eight-hour day.

6. Fontaine has calculated his net income for tax purposes as follows:

Employment income		
Salary and bonus		$98,000
Deductions		
Registered pension plan		4,400
Employment expenses:		
Meal costs while out of town: $300 × 50%		150
Office at home:		
Minor repairs		340
Utilities (200/2,000 × $1,200)		120
Office supplies and stationery		410
Computer software (word processor)		220
		92,360
Capital gains (Remco shares)		
Selling price (1,000 × $24)	$24,000	
Cost (1,000 × $16)	16,000	
Gain	8,000	
Taxable ($1/2$ of $8,000)		4,000
Net income		$96,360

Required:
Advise Fontaine whether his calculation of 20X1 net income for tax purposes is correct. If it is not, recalculate a revised 20X1 net income for tax purposes, and briefly explain the changes you made.

Problem Seven
Barry Yuen is district sales manager for a Vancouver-based distribution company. He has requested that you help him establish his employment income for tax purposes for the 20X3 taxation year. He has provided the following information:

1. Yuen's base salary in 20X3 was $78,000. As sales manager, he is entitled to a small commission on the sales made by staff under his supervision. He received $7,200 in such commissions in 20X3, which included $1,000 of commissions earned in late 20X2. The December 20X3 commissions have been computed as $1,800 and were received in January 20X4. The employer deducted the following from his salary in 20X3:

Canada Pension Plan contributions	$1,400
Employment Insurance premiums	900
Private medical plan premiums	300

2. In addition to the above, the employer paid the following to Yuen or on his behalf:

Travel allowance	$2,400
Group term life insurance premiums for $50,000 coverage	600
Premiums for a private medical insuarance plan	300

3. Yuen's wife died in late 20X2, leaving him to support three children. In 20X3 he hired a person at a cost of $9,000 to provide baby-sitting services for the two youngest children. Following his wife's death, Yuen suffered from depression. As a result, his employer paid the cost of $3,000 for counselling services, and also provided him with airline tickets costing $2,400 so that he and the children could attend a relaxation resort.

4. Yuen uses his own vehicle for employment duties. The vehicle (class 10.1) had an undepreciated capital cost of $14,000 at the end of 20X2. Yuen paid $4,000 in 20X3 to operate the car, and used it 70% of the time for employment duties.

5. Yuen incurred the following additional costs relating to his employment:

Promotion (meals)	$ 800
Purchase of a cellular phone	1,200
Lease costs for laptop computer	700
Golf club dues	1,000
Hotel costs—out-of-town travel	4,300

6. When not travelling, Yuen works from an office at his employer's place of business. Increasingly, he has been taking home work to do in the evenings and on weekends. He intends to set aside a specific room in his house that he will use only for this purpose. His house costs include property taxes, insurance, utilities, and mortgage interest. He will also purchase a work desk and chair.

Required:

1. For the 20X3 taxation year, determine Yuen's net income from employment for tax purposes.

2. Briefly explain the tax treatment of the intended home office expenses.

Problem Eight

On January 2, 20X3, Sheldon Bass, a professional engineer, moved from Calgary to Edmonton to commence employment with Acco Ltd., a large public corporation. Because of his new employment contract, Bass requires assistance in determining his employment income for tax purposes. He has provided the following financial information:

1. Bass's salary in 20X3 was $95,000. From this, Acco deducted Employment Insurance of $900, Canada Pension Plan contributions of $1,500, registered pension plan of $6,000, and charitable donations of $1,200.

2. Acco provides its executives with a bonus plan. Bass's 20X3 bonus was $20,000, of which $5,000 was received in December 20X3 and the balance in March 20X4.

3. In November 20X3, Bass asked his employer to loan him $12,000 so that he could acquire an investment. Acco advised him that it was company policy not to make loans to employees. However, they gave him the $12,000, stipulating that it was an advance against his 20X4 salary, which would be reduced accordingly.

4. In 20X3, Bass was provided with a company car, which he drove 12 000 km for employment duties and 8 000 km in personal use. The car was leased for $500 per month. The total operating costs of $7,000 were paid by Acco. The car was available for personal use throughout the year.

5. Bass's moving expenses to transport his belongings to Edmonton were $3,000. Acco paid this cost directly to a moving company on Bass's behalf.

6. Bass travels extensively for Acco. In December 20X3, he and his spouse used some of the travel points he had accumulated from this travel to attend his father's funeral in Toronto. As a result, he saved the normal airfare of $400 per ticket.

7. Acco paid the following additional amounts for Bass:

Allowance ($300 per month) for acquiring executive apparel	$3,600
Investment counsellor fees as part of Acco's counselling program	600
Golf club dues (Bass rarely uses the club to conduct business)	1,500

8. In 20X3 Bass paid for the following:

Dues to the engineers' association	$ 800
Notebook computer and printer	2,200
Computer supplies (paper, etc.)	100

Acco had asked each senior executive to acquire a computer at his or her own expense for work during travel.

9. In 20X3, Bass sold 1,000 shares of Kolex Ltd. (his former employer) for $10 per share. Kolex is a Canadian-controlled private corporation. The shares were purchased under a stock option plan in 20X0 for $3 per share. Appraised value at that time was $5 per share.

Required:
Determine Bass's net income from employment for the 20X3 taxation year. Assume that benefit payments by the employer include GST/PST where applicable.

Problem Nine

Charles Ebo was terminated from his employment with QR Ltd. in July 20X6. In November 20X6, he began work as a commission salesperson for AP Ltd., a Canadian public corporation.

Ebo has asked you to help him prepare his 20X6 tax return. Information regarding his employment is outlined below.

1. Ebo's employment with QR was terminated on July 31, 20X6. His salary to that date was $56,000. Besides income tax, QR had deducted the following amounts from his salary:

Registered pension plan	$4,000
CPP and EI contibutions	1,600
Group sickness and accident insurance plan premium	500
Reimbursement for personal use of employer auto	800

QR also contributed $4,000 to an RPP and $500 to a group sickness and accident insurance plan on Ebo's behalf.

Ebo took a medical stress leave from January 10 to March 15, 20X6. His salary was not paid during the leave. However, he received $4,500 for loss of earnings from the group sickness accident insurance plan. In previous years Ebo had paid a total of $3,000 in premiums to the plan.

2. On July 31, 20X6, Ebo returned the company car to QR, which had been available for his personal use. The car had an original cost of $30,000 and a book value of $24,000. Ebo had driven the car for 20 000 km in 20X6, of which 8 000 km was for employment purposes. QR paid the operating expenses of $2,200.

3. In December 20X6, Ebo sold 4,000 shares of AP Ltd. at $10. He had acquired them in November 20X6 under a stock option plan at $6. At the time of acquisition, the shares were valued at $8. When the option was granted, the shares were valued at $6.

4. When his employment was terminated, Ebo paid a lawyer $800 to settle compensation issues. As a result, he received additional holiday pay of $1,000 and a retiring allowance of $6,000 for his 10 years of service.

5. Ebo collected employment insurance of $5,400 before starting his employment with AP on November 1, 20X6. Besides a base salary of $1,000 per month, Ebo receives commissions on sales.

Ebo's commission is 4% of sales. His first sales were made in late December 20X6 and totalled $150,000. The related commission was received on January 15, 20X7. On December 1, 20X6, AP paid Ebo $1,500 as an advance against commissions.

AP certified that Ebo was required to pay his own car and other expenses. On November 1, 20X6, he leased a car for $750 per month. Operating expenses for November and December were $900. The car was used 70% for employment purposes.

Ebo incurred the following additional expenses:

Entertainment—meal and beverages	$600
Promotion—gift calendars for customers	200
Purchase of a cellular phone	500

Required:

Determine Ebo's net income from employment for the 20X6 taxation year. (Assume that benefit payments by the employer include GST/PST where applicable.)

Problem Ten

Carla Ram is a professional engineer. In 20X1 she sold her consulting business in Hamilton, Ontario, and moved to Vancouver, British Columbia, where she was employed by an equipment-manufacturing business. The following financial information is provided for the 20X1 taxation year:

1. Ram began her employment on February 1, 20X1, and during the year received a salary of $90,000, from which the employer deducted income tax of $30,000 and CPP and EI of $2,400. In addition to her salary, Ram earned a commission of 1% of sales obtained by salespeople under her supervision. At December 31, 20X1, these sales amounted to $1,000,000, for which she had received $6,000 by year end, with the balance received in January 20X2. Ram also received an annual clothing allowance of $1,500 to maintain a professional dress standard. During the year she spent $1,800 on clothing for work.

2. Ram's employer does not have a company pension plan; instead the employer contributed $13,000 directly to her RRSP in 20X1.

3. In December 20X1, Ram received a payroll advance of $3,000 against her January 20X2 salary to help fund a family holiday.

4. Ram is required to use her automobile for employment purposes and to pay certain other employment expenses. In 20X1 she incurred the following costs:

Meals and drinks for customer entertainment	$1,600
Golf club dues used to entertain customers	1,100
Travel—airfares and hotel lodging	3,000
Purchase of a cell phone	800
Monthly telephone bills—cell phone	1,200
Automobile expenses:	
Operating costs	3,800
Parking	100
Interest on car loan	2,200
Purchase of new automobile	37,000

The automobile was used 60% of the time for business.

5. In 20X1, Ram took advantage of her employer's counselling services. She received

personal financial planning advice valued at $400, and her 14-year-old son received mental health counselling valued at $800.

6. Ram purchased a new home in Vancouver in 20X1 and incurred qualified moving expenses of $18,000 to transport her family and household effects to Vancouver. Her new employer reimbursed her for $10,000 of these costs and also paid her $20,000 for the loss incurred on the sale of her former residence.

7. In early 20X2, Ram intends to borrow $20,000 from her employer for the purpose of acquiring shares in the employer's corporation. A low interest rate of 2% per annum will be payable on the loan.

Required:

1. Determine Ram's *minimum net income from employment* for the 20X1 taxation year.

2. Briefly describe the tax implications from the intended employee loan to Ram.

Problem Eleven

Carol Posh is a senior advertising executive with a large Winnipeg company. With winter fast approaching, Posh is seriously considering an offer of employment from Westcoast Promotions Inc. (WPI), a large public company in Vancouver. Although housing costs are high in Vancouver, the climate and opportunities for career advancement would be better.

Posh has received a letter outlining a proposed remuneration package. The package is attractive but she is uncertain of the tax consequences. She has asked you to advise her.

WPI recognizes the problem of housing costs and begins its letter with an offer to loan Posh $150,000, interest-free, to help finance a new house. In addition, WPI will reimburse her for 75% of her moving costs.

In addition to an annual salary of $120,000, WPI has offered the following benefits:

1. Posh will be appointed a director of the company's American subsidiary in California; this will require her to travel to Los Angeles three times a year for board meetings. Posh will be paid a director's fee of $5,000 directly from the American company. Company policy permits spouses to take these trips as well. When a director takes his or her spouse, all travel expenses are paid for by the company.

2. A luxury automobile will be provided for her personal use even though she will never require the car for business. The company will pay all of the operating costs—approximately $3,200 per year—as well as the monthly lease cost of $850. Posh will drive the car approximately 20 000 kilometres per year.

3. WPI will include Posh in its group term life insurance program and pay the premium, which provides $75,000 of coverage. It will also pay the premiums for a private health plan, a dental plan, and a drug plan.

4. The company has a deferred profit sharing plan, for which Posh will qualify. The maximum contribution will be made to this plan only when the company's profit for the year is greater than 12% of the stated balance sheet equity.

5. Posh will be eligible for an annual bonus of up to $40,000, with the actual amount to be based on her productivity. The bonus will be awarded on November 30 of each year (the company's year end) but will not be paid until May 31 of the following year. Of the above-mentioned bonus, 25% will be retained in an employee benefit plan for five years. The investment income earned by the plan will be distributed to Posh each year.

6. WPI will provide Posh with a monthly allowance of $800 to cover any expenses she may incur. In addition, she will be reimbursed for travel costs to attend the annual advertising convention in Paris.

7. All WPI employees are entitled to participate in a stock option plan. The available shares are non-voting but do participate fully in profits. The option price is $12 per share; this price is guaranteed for three years and will then increase to $14 per share. Currently, the shares are trading at $12; they are expected to rise significantly within two years.

8. Posh will be provided with club memberships in the "better" social clubs in the area for relaxation purposes. This will help her to be more productive in her work.

Required:
Prepare a brief report to Posh.

Problem Twelve

John Markowski is a senior mechanic in the logging industry. Because of the specialized nature of his work, he is highly paid. His current employer pays him a basic salary with no special benefits.

Recently, Markowski received an offer of employment from a corporation in the same line of business. The salary offered is lower than what he currently receives but a number of benefits are included in the remuneration package.

Markowski is confused by the offer. He does not like the idea of a reduced salary but realizes that the benefits have some value. He also realizes that what is really important is the level of disposable income that he has for himself and his family.

Markowski has provided you with the pertinent information (see Exhibits 1 and 2) and has asked you to help him make a decision.

Required:

1. Determine what Markowski's net income from employment for tax purposes will be if he remains with his current employer (Exhibit 1). (Assume that the benefit repayments by the employer include GST/PST where applicable.)

2. Determine what Markowski's net income from employment for tax purposes will be if he accepts the offer from the competitor (Exhibit 2). (Assume that the benefit repayments by the employer include GST/PST where applicable.)

3. Assuming that Markowski pays tax at a rate of 40%, determine the amount by which his personal disposable income will increase (or decrease) if he accepts the new offer.

Exhibit 1:
Information Regarding
Current Employment and
Certain Other Expenditures

1. Markowski's gross salary next year will be $70,000. From this, the employer will deduct the required income tax, Canada Pension Plan contributions of $1,400, and Employment Insurance premiums of $900.

2. It is part of Markowski's ordinary duties to work on equipment at locations other than the main repair depot. On average, he is called out of town two or three days each

month. On such trips he must always stay overnight in a hotel. His contract of employment requires that he pay his own automobile expenses. The company reimburses him for his hotel costs (lodging but not meals). No reimbursement is made for the vehicle.

3. Markowski leases his own car for $500 per month. He incurred the following additional travel costs in the current year:

Insurance	$ 800
Repairs and maintenance	600
Gasoline	2,200
Meals (out of town)	200

During the year, Markowski drove a total of 22 000 kilometres, of which 4 000 were for his employer. Markowski anticipates that travel costs in the future will be about the same as they were this year.

4. Markowski is required to purchase and maintain his own small tools. Every year he spends approximately $500 on new tools and to replace lost or stolen tools. He also purchases his own work coveralls and pays for their cleaning, which amounts to another $300 per year.

5. Markowski will take possession of his new home in three months, and he is currently shopping for a mortgage. He expects to obtain a $90,000 mortgage with interest at 10% for a term of five years.

6. Markowski maintains the following insurance policies:

	Premium cost
Term life insurance of $300,000	$1,200
Private medical insurance	600
House fire insurance	1,000

7. Markowski is a golfer and belongs to a private club. His annual membership dues are $1,200.

Exhibit 2:
Information Regarding
Offer of Employment
with Competitor

1. The proposed salary is $60,000 per year. From that amount, the employer will deduct the required income tax, Canada Pension Plan contributions of $945, and Employment Insurance premiums of $1,131.

2. The employer will lease an automobile identical to the one currently used by Markowski. However, the employer's lease cost will be only $450 per month because of a fleet discount. In addition, the employer will pay the annual insurance cost of $800, the repair and maintenance costs, which are estimated to be $600 annually, and the gasoline costs of $2,200.

Markowski will be entitled to operate the car for personal use. The number of business kilometres and personal kilometres driven will be the same as they are now. The employer will pay for all out-of-town meals when an overnight stay is required. The cost of meals is expected to be $200 per year.

3. The employer maintains a good supply of small tools, and mechanics are not required to purchase or use their own. In addition, the employer maintains a complete wardrobe of work coveralls, so Markowski will not have to purchase or clean his own.

4. As a senior mechanic, Markowski will be entitled to a low-interest loan (3%) from the employer of up to five years' duration. Such loans can be renewed at the end of term. The maximum loan amount is $10,000. The prescribed interest rate set by CCRA is currently 11%.

5. The employer maintains a group term life insurance program and a private medical insurance program. At no cost to Markowski, the employer will provide $300,000 of group term life insurance as well as medical coverage equal to what he currently has. The premium costs to the employer will be as follows:

| Life insurance | $900 |
| Medical insurance | 500 |

These amounts are lower than Markowski's current costs because group discounts are available.

6. The employer has agreed to pay Markowski's annual golf club dues of $1,200. As Markowski does not entertain and deal with customers, the employer derives no benefit from Markowski's membership in the club.

Problem Thirteen

Bill Watkins is a chartered accountant. He carried on a professional business as a tax consultant for 12 years. By the end of 20X0, the practice had grown very large. Watkins was overworked and under pressure to hire additional staff or take a partner. Watkins was interested in education and several years earlier had contracted with a publisher to write a book on taxation for university students. Because of the pressures of his practice, this project made little progress.

To rationalize his work life, Watkins decided to close his professional practice and enter into an arrangement with Anthony and Anthony, a national firm of chartered accountants. According to the agreement, he would work a minimum of 600 hours per year for the firm; he would also be free to pursue his writing and other interests. He would provide the 600 hours mainly during the winter months and would not be expected at the office every day of the week.

Anthony and Anthony made a formal announcement in the newspaper that Watkins was now associated with their firm, and provided him with business cards stating both his name and the firm's. The firm did not give him a specific title, though most of its employees had one, whatever their level. The firm did provide him with an office (of the same size as was given to partners) and a secretary at no cost to him.

As a tax consultant, Watkins met with clients of the firm and corresponded with them under the firm's letterhead. Jobs were assigned to him by any partner who required his services. Usually, he charged any time spent on a client directly to the particular partner's account; that partner in turn billed the client and collected the fees.

Anthony and Anthony charged clients for Watkins's time at $150 per hour. The agreement stated that he was to be paid $100 for each hour charged to a client whether the client paid the fee or not. At the end of each month, Watkins prepared an invoice requesting that the firm pay $100 for each hour charged that month.

Throughout the year, Watkins paid for his own parking and for his own subscriptions to several tax services, the latter being necessary for him to carry out his duties.

Whenever the firm held a social function, Watkins was invited. In 20X1 he gave three speeches to various business groups and was always introduced as "Bill Watkins, a tax consultant with Anthony and Anthony."

In 20X1 Watkins worked 820 hours for the firm. He spent the balance of his working time writing his book and giving tax seminars for various professional groups.

Required:

Was Watkins employed or self-employed in 20X1? Give reasons to support your conclusions, and reasons to support the opposing view.

Chapter 5   Income from Business

Income from business encompasses a wide range of financial activity. Businesses vary considerably in size and nature, but they all formulate income for tax purposes in accordance with a common set of principles. The student entrepreneur who paints houses or maintains lawns to finance a university education is subject to the same formula for income determination on those activities as that used by a large Canadian public corporation. The *Income Tax Act* does not attempt to make provision for each type of business activity or transaction. Instead, it contains a set of fundamental rules that are applied to every business transaction regardless of its size or nature but that also make specific provisions for certain exceptional situations. In most cases determinations as to whether an item must be included in income, or is permitted as a deduction, can be made by applying the general principles.

This chapter defines *business income* and develops the broad principles that form the foundation of such income. Specifically, this chapter covers the following major areas:

1. The meaning of the term *business income* and the general scope of the definition.

2. The general rules for determining income from business, and the relationship of those rules to generally accepted accounting concepts.

3. The format for determining the exceptions to the general rules, and a summary of the most commonly used exceptions.

4. A sample calculation of business income utilizing the general rules developed.

I. Business Income Defined

Business income can be earned by all three of the taxable entities within the Canadian tax system—individuals, corporations, and trusts—and each entity determines that income in an identical manner. In order to earn business income or incur a business loss, the taxpayer must, of course, be involved in an undertaking that constitutes a "business."

The term *business* is broadly defined in the *Income Tax Act* to include "a profession, calling, trade, manufacture, or undertaking of any kind whatever and an adventure or concern in the nature of trade."[1] In most circumstances the conduct of a business is readily identifiable by the nature of the activity: such activities as the manufacturing and processing of property for resale; mining, exploration, or drilling for natural resources; construction, logging, farming, or fishing; the selling of property as a retailer or wholesaler; transportation; and the offering of services in a trade or profession are all obvious business activities. As well, enterprises usually maintain identifiable evidence of their existence—a location, a business name, a special telephone listing, and so on.

It is important to note that the definition does not consider size to be a factor; nor does it require that the activity be ongoing, or that it provide evidence of its existence. This means that an individual who, from time to time, provides piano lessons for a fee is considered to be earning business income, even though that activity may be irregular, there is no formal evidence of a business enterprise, and the person may be gainfully employed in another occupation.

In some circumstances an activity may constitute what is referred to as an "*adventure or concern in the nature of trade.*"[2] This occurs when a taxpayer (individual, corporation, or trust) acquires property for the purpose of reselling it at a profit even though it is not the normal business of that person to conduct such an activity.[3] For example, consider the situation of an individual who discovers a used automobile for sale at an apparent bargain price

---

1 ITA 248(1); IT-206R.

2 IT-459.

3 *MNR v. Taylor*, 57 DTC 1125.

and acquires it with the intention of reselling it at a profit. This transaction is similar to those made by an automobile dealer, even though the person does not regularly carry on such an activity. The buying and selling of the automobile is, in this case, considered an adventure in the nature of trade. By definition, this constitutes a business, and the resulting profit or loss on sale is considered income or loss from business, and is treated accordingly for tax purposes.

• **Business income versus capital**   A particular problem arises when a property is sold that, by its nature, had the ability to provide a long-term or enduring benefit to its owner. Depending on the reason for its acquisition and its subsequent use, the gain or loss on the sale of such property can be either a business activity or a capital transaction. The distinction is important, as capital transactions and business transactions are treated differently. While capital gains are not reviewed until Chapter 8, the reader has already learned that only one-half of capital gains are taxable and that one-half of capital losses are available for deduction (though only against other capital gains). At the same time, business income is fully taxable, and business losses can be offset against all other sources of income. As demonstrated in Chapter 3, the impact on cash flow of a transaction being classified as one rather than the other can be substantial.

In making the distinction, one must recognize that the property in question has the *ability* to provide a long-term benefit to its owner but is not always acquired for that purpose. The *intended use* of a property on acquisition is the principal factor in deciding its tax treatment on a subsequent sale.[4] Capital treatment can be distinguished from business treatment by employing the following guidelines:

1. Property acquired for the purpose of providing the owner with a long-term or enduring benefit is *capital property*, and its disposition results in a capital gain or loss.

2. Property acquired for the purpose of reselling it at a profit is *inventory*, and its disposition results in business income or a business loss.

The following examples demonstrate how identical assets receive different tax treatment as a result of their intended use:

• A house constructed for use as a principal residence by its owner is capital property having a long-term benefit. A similar house constructed for resale by a property developer is inventory, as it was constructed with the intention of reselling at a profit.

• Land and buildings acquired by an investor for the purpose of generating a return on investment through rents is capital property, but land and buildings (even though rented out) acquired by a speculator for resale at a profit is inventory.

• Office equipment acquired by an enterprise to assist staff in carrying out their duties is capital property because it has a long-term benefit in that it contributes to the enterprise's earning process. The same equipment acquired for the purpose of resale by a retailer of office equipment constitutes inventory.

• Land acquired by a retail business as a parking area for customers is capital property because it provides a long-term benefit by contributing to the earning process of the owner. However, if the same retailer acquired land for speculative purposes as a side venture from its normal business, the particular land would be inventory. In this case the entity holds two properties of a similar nature, but the tax treatment for each is entirely different.

---

4   *Regal Heights Ltd. v. MNR*, 60 DTC 1270; and *Irrigation Industries Limited v. MNR*, 62 DTC 1131.

- A used car acquired by an individual at a bargain price, if it is used for personal transportation, is capital property providing a long-term benefit. A used car acquired at a bargain price by the same individual for the purpose of resale at a profit is inventory, which means that business income or loss is created when it is resold.

It is sometimes difficult to assess the primary intention of a property acquisition; because of this, several guidelines have been developed in common law to provide an extended definition for determining capital as opposed to business treatment. These guidelines are discussed in Chapter 8, which reviews other aspects of capital transactions.

It is essential that the reader be familiar with the term "business" as it applies to the taxation of income. As previously mentioned, in most cases the existence of a business activity is obvious. However, most individuals and business entities will, at one time or another, enter into transactions that are less obvious. Familiarity with the distinction between capital income and business income is important when it comes to assessing the risks of proposed financial transactions. The degree of risk involved in entering into a transaction is enhanced if the activity may result in a capital loss rather than a business loss, because of the restrictions imposed on the deduction of capital losses against other sources of income.

II. General Rules for Determining Business Income

For income tax purposes, income derived from business activity is determined by computing an entity's net profit (or loss) for the taxation year, having taken into account six general limiting factors. These six general limitations constitute the general rules for determining business income for tax purposes for all entities. They are discussed later in this chapter.

A. Profit Defined

The *Income Tax Act* simply states that, subject to certain exceptions, "a taxpayer's income for a taxation year from a business is the profit therefrom for the year."[5] This very broad statement is the primary rule for business income determination. Interestingly, no attempt is made to define "profit," and as a result this task has been left to the courts.

The courts, in turn, have also failed to specifically define the term; instead they have developed a set of general principles to be used in determining profit for income tax purposes.[6] The main principles are set out below:

1. The determination of profit is a question of law.

2. The profit of a business for a taxation year is determined by setting against the revenues from the business year the expenses incurred to earn that income.[7]

3. The goal in computing profit is to obtain an accurate picture of the taxpayer's profit for the year.

4. In ascertaining profit, the taxpayer is free to adopt any method provided that it is consistent with the provisions of the *Income Tax Act*, established case law principles or "rules of law," and *well-accepted business principles*.

Established case law deals with specific limited issues, and the *Income Tax Act* does not define *profit*. It follows that the above general principles must focus on well-accepted business principles as the fundamental starting point for determining profit. Because of the

---

5   ITA 9(1), (2).

6   *Canderel Limited v. Her Majesty the Queen,* 98 DTC 6100; *Toronto College Park Ltd. v. Her Majesty the Queen,* 98 DTC 6088.

7   *M.N.R. v. Irwin,* supra; *Associated Investors,* supra.

wide variety of commercial enterprises, it is impossible to identify a specific set of business principles. Most businesses determine profit in accordance with generally accepted accounting principles (GAAP). In fact, the courts have stated that well-accepted business principles include but are not limited to GAAP. They have also indicated that GAAP are not rules of law but rather significant interpretive aids for establishing well-accepted business principles. For many years the courts have given considerable consideration to GAAP when dealing with conflicts between taxpayers and CCRA.[8]

Accounting principles are readily identifiable. The CICA (Canadian Institute of Chartered Accountants), with other professional accounting bodies, has developed a specific code of generally accepted accounting principles that guide its members in the determination of profits. These guidelines have been accepted by commercial enterprises, financial institutions, and government bodies and now constitute the most important interpretive aid in establishing profit. This profit is then modified according to the *Income Tax Act,* established case law, and well-established business principles.

Simply stated, business income for tax purposes is the *profit* determined in accordance with well-established business principles using GAAP as an interpretive aid; it *comprises the revenues earned in a taxation year less the expenses incurred for the purpose of earning such revenues.* While there are some limitations as to what expenses can be deducted for tax purposes, it is generally understood that all expenses incurred in an attempt to generate revenues are deductible for tax purposes.

B. Generally Accepted Accounting Principles

As related previously, GAAP is the primary interpretive aid for determining well-established business principles and profit. The CICA's formal guidelines, which are published in the *CICA Handbook*, are too extensive to review fully within the scope of this text. They cover a broad range of general accounting areas as well as issues relating to specific industries and business transactions. However, all of the guidelines are rooted in a short list of fundamental concepts that have guided the development of the specific accounting standards. A few of the major concepts are reviewed below to help the reader understand the meaning of the accounting concept of net profit or loss. As mentioned previously, net profit or loss consists of two basic parts.

Revenues	$XXX
minus	
Expenses	XXX
equals	
Net profit (loss)	$ XX

1. Revenue Recognition

Revenues are derived from the sales value of products sold, or the fees charged for services rendered, before the deduction of expenses. For accounting purposes, and therefore for tax purposes, revenues are recognized at the point in time when the earning process is substantially complete. Normally the earning process is substantially complete when title to the property passes to the purchaser or, in the case of services, when the service contracted for has been provided.

The implication of this concept is that the recognition of revenue is not associated with the receipt of cash. When property is sold on credit, the full sales value is included in revenue even though payment occurs at a later date. In some circumstances cash is received in advance of delivery of the product or the rendering of the service, in which case the realization of revenue is delayed until the service is rendered or the goods are delivered.

---

8 *The Queen v. Metropolitan Properties Co. Ltd.*, 85 DTC 5128.

2. Concept of Accrual

The accrual concept requires that expenses be recognized and recorded for accounting purposes when they are incurred rather than when they are paid. Expenses such as wages, utilities, interest, and so on that are unpaid at the end of an accounting period must be recognized and deducted from revenues even if the actual payment occurs in the following accounting period. In other words, the occurrence and recognition of expenses is not associated with the payment of cash.

3. Concept of Matching

The concept of matching requires that expenses incurred be deducted in the time period in which they contribute to the earning of revenue. This means that expenses incurred in one period that will have a benefit in future periods must be apportioned and allocated in some reasonable manner against those revenues to which they contribute. Almost all business enterprises are subject to this principle, which is the cause of considerable confusion when it comes to understanding the accounting concept of profit.

Consider, for example, the treatment of inventory in a retail or wholesale business. Normally, an entity acquires and stores a supply of product for resale (inventory), which results in a cost at the time the goods are acquired. Even though an expenditure has occurred, the expense of each item held in inventory is recognized only when the product is sold—this way, the expense can be *matched* against the revenue associated with its sale. Often there is a significant gap between the time a product is purchased and the time it is sold. This process is significantly more complex in manufacturing organizations, because the cost of a finished product includes many types of expenses, including raw materials, direct labour costs, indirect labour costs for support staff, and a reasonable allocation of overhead expenses such as depreciation on the manufacturing equipment and buildings that contribute to the creation of a new product. All of these costs must be accumulated, assigned to a particular product, and then held in abeyance until such time as the finished product is sold.

All costs of a capital nature that have a long-term or enduring benefit are treated in a manner similar to the one described above. Many items—buildings, equipment, vehicles, furniture, patents, franchises, licences, and so on—contribute to the revenue-earning process for a number of years. The matching principle requires that the cost of all these items be apportioned and deducted over those future years. For example, the cost of a $500,000 building with an expected life of 20 years may be expensed against the revenues of those years at $25,000 per year.

Consider the costs incurred in researching and developing a product and introducing it into the marketplace. All of these costs will contribute to revenues over a period of future years and must be allocated in some reasonable manner.

It can be seen that compliance with the matching principle requires considerable judgment on the part of those responsible for the allocations. In order to allocate the costs of *fixed* assets, such as buildings and equipment, or *intangible* assets, such as goodwill and the development costs of new products, one must estimate the extent of their useful life, their contribution to the revenue-earning process in future years, and their value (if any) at the end of their useful life. This process offers leeway for a wide range of opinions; as a consequence, businesses with similar financial results may present significantly different annual-profit determinations, even though in the long run of several years, the cumulative results will be the same.

4. Concept of Conservatism

Under this concept, the determination of accounting profit or loss must take a conservative approach. In effect, this means that an enterprise must recognize all losses when they are anticipated rather than when they occur, while delaying the recognition of gains or revenues until they are actually earned. Any errors made should not result in the overstatement of profit. To a certain extent, the concept of conservatism conflicts with the matching principle—for example, in the case of research and development costs. Regarding these costs, the conservative approach takes precedence when there is insufficient evidence that the item will contribute to future revenues.

This concept has led to the use of reserves in such a way that expenses are recognized before costs are incurred. For example, a manufacturer may anticipate that certain warranty costs on defective products will be incurred at some future time. The company makes a reasonable prediction of such costs, and expenses them in the year in which the product is sold. Errors in the estimate, whether too high or too low, are corrected in future years as warranty claims are actually made.

This brief review of some of the fundamental concepts makes it clear that "profit" in accordance with the interpretive aid of accounting principles is by no means precisely determinable, and that there is considerable room for unintended or intended misjudgment. The general limitations and specific exceptions detailed within the *Income Tax Act*, discussed below, are an attempt to provide a more uniform standard in the areas that are most flexible under the accounting guidelines.

C. General Limitations to Business Profit Determination

The determination of income from business for tax purposes is constrained by the imposition of six general limitations that apply to the deduction of expenses. In some cases the limitations are in complete conflict with well-established business principles and generally accepted accounting principles; in such cases the limitations imposed by the *Income Tax Act* take precedence. In order for any expense to be deductible in arriving at business income, the following conditions must be satisfied.

1. Income-Earning-Purpose Test

In order for an expense to be deductible for tax purposes, it must be incurred for the purpose of gaining, producing, or maintaining income from business.[9]

It is not necessary that an expense have a direct relationship to the generating of income; it must, however, have been inspired by and incurred as part of the process of carrying on a business activity with an expectation to profit. The fact that no income is generated from an incurred expense is irrelevant if the expense arose from an attempt to achieve, enhance, or maintain income.[10]

This test can be considered the primary test for the deductibility of expenses in arriving at business income, as it defines the concept of "allowable expense." At the same time, it broadly eliminates those expenses that have no real business value, such as extravagant expenditures that primarily benefit the person incurring them rather than the income-earning process. This test is CCRA's main tool in its attempts to eliminate abusive deductions for tax purposes. The business sector is often accused of having an unfair advantage when it comes to the types of deductions permitted; however, the accusations usually focus on those deductions that are actually restricted by the income-earning-purpose test.

Sometimes individuals carry on activities that create revenue but have no reasonable expectation of earning a profit. For example, raising pets as a hobby may incur a large amount of expenses but earn only small revenues to help offset the costs. If the nature of the enterprise suggests that there is no reasonable expectation of earning a profit, then the expenses are deductible only to the extent of the related revenue, and any loss is considered a personal loss and denied for income tax purposes.[11]

2. Capital Test

Even if an expenditure was incurred for the purpose of earning income, it must also pass the capital test in order to be directly deductible for tax purposes. The capital test dictates that no item is deductible in arriving at business income if it was incurred "on account of capital," or is an allowance in respect of "depreciation obsolescence or depletion," unless it is specifically permitted within the *Income Tax Act*.[12]

---

9 ITA 18(1)(a); IT-104R2, -487; *Royal Trust Company v. MNR*, 57 DTC 1055.

10 *Booth v. MNR*, 79 DTC 595; *Speck v. MNR*, 88 DTC 1518.

11 *Livergrant v. M.N.R.*, 89 DTC.

12 ITA 18(1)(b).

An expenditure on account of capital is one that results in a long-term or enduring benefit to the entity.[13] Such items as the cost of buildings, equipment, vehicles, land, patents, licences, and goodwill all contribute to revenues over a period of years and are therefore not deductible in accordance with the general limitation. In addition, the depreciation or amortization of these items is also not deductible.

The term "capital" must be liberally interpreted and applied to expenditures other than the obvious ones listed above. For example, the interest paid on a loan used to fund the acquisition of a capital asset is incurred on the account of capital and therefore falls within the general limitation. The major renovation of a delivery vehicle that extends its useful life beyond the original expectation is a capital outlay because its benefit is long-term. Legal expenses to register the ownership of a building, or to provide advice and execute the purchase documents on a business takeover, have a long-term benefit and are not deductible. Such legal expenses are simply added to the cost of the building or of the business assets acquired, as the case may be.

The main reason for limiting expenditures of a capital nature is to remove from the calculation of accounting profit those items that are most flexible under accounting principles. The result of this limitation is that expense items such as the depreciation and amortization of fixed assets and intangible assets, which can vary considerably with the owner's procedures for matching expense to revenues, are removed from the normal determination of profit. Instead, most of these items are dealt with specifically as exceptions to the general limitation, and a uniform system of allocation is utilized that applies to all business entities. These exceptions are reviewed later in this chapter.

3. Exempt-Income Test

Under this limitation an expense is not deductible even though it was incurred to earn income, if the income that is expected to be generated is itself not taxable revenue.[14] For example, the life insurance premiums paid by a business to insure its key executives are not deductible because any life insurance proceeds the business later received would not constitute taxable revenue. Similarly, as an extreme example, the purchase of a lottery ticket by a business is not deductible under this limitation because the possible lottery winnings are not subject to tax.

4. Reserve Test

While the process of determining accounting profit permits the deduction of reserves in accordance with the principle of conservatism, the *Income Tax Act* on a general basis disallows as a deduction an amount transferred or credited to a reserve, contingent account, or sinking fund, except as expressly permitted.[15] Therefore, as a general test, *no reserves are deductible* for tax purposes. Again, it is important to note that exceptions are permitted and that some but not all reserves can be deducted within certain guidelines. (This will be reviewed later.)

5. Personal-Expense Test

Under this general limitation no deductions are permitted for a taxpayer's personal or living expenses *except* for those travel expenses incurred away from home in the course of carrying on business.[16] Travel expenses include the amounts expended for meals and lodging. In effect, this limitation is an expansion of the income-earning-purpose test described earlier.

Personal or living expenses encompass the expenses of properties that are maintained by individuals for personal or family use and that are not maintained in connection with a business carried on for profit or with a reasonable expectation of profit. The cost of travel from home to work by a person carrying on a business, by virtue of this general limitation, is not deductible.

---

13 *British Insulated and Helsby Cables Ltd. v. Atherton* (United Kingdom—1926).

14 ITA 18(1)(c); IT-467R.

15 ITA 18(1)(e); IT-215R.

16 ITA 18(1)(h), 248(1); *Cumming v. MNR*, 67 DTC 5312.

6. Reasonableness Test   The final general limitation that applies to the computation of business income—it also applies to deductions from all other sources of income—requires that an outlay or expense be deductible only to the extent that the outlay or expense is *reasonable in the circumstances*.[17] This means that even when the type of expense meets the other general criteria for deductibility, the amount that can be deducted is limited to a reasonable amount. For example, a salary paid to a spouse or child of the owner of a business is deductible if it is for the purpose of earning income, but the amount is limited to what would be reasonable considering the nature and extent of the work provided.

In many cases reasonableness is difficult to establish, but the term implies that an amount would be unreasonable if it were significantly in excess of what other taxpayers in similar situations would incur.

This limitation is designed to combat the abuse of permitted business deductions and to confine business expenses to those that are legitimately incurred as part of the income-earning process.

Income from business is arrived at by first establishing the profit or loss in accordance with well-established business principles, taking into account generally accepted accounting principles. Each item of deduction must pass the six general limitation tests before it can be included in the calculation of profit. Notwithstanding these broad general principles, there are a number of specific exceptions that are designed primarily to create uniformity among taxpayers and to prevent abuse when the general rules described above are being applied.

III. Exceptions to the General Rules

The *Income Tax Act* responds to the general rules by listing specific exceptions. If a particular item is not listed as a specific exception, the general rules determine the outcome. The specific list of exceptions establishes the final parameters of the calculation, and so completes the process of determining business income.

The vast majority of exceptions to the general rules are listed in sections 12, 13, 14, 18, 19, and 20 of the *Income Tax Act*. Sections 12, 13, and 14 deal with items that increase income; sections 18, 19, and 20 outline the expense exceptions. The income tax system also permits inventory costing methods that may deviate from well-established business principles and generally accepted accounting principles.

A. Specific Income and Expense Exceptions

Sections 13 and 14 deal with income earned on the sale of depreciable property and other intangible assets such as goodwill, patents, and licences. These items will be dealt with at length in the next chapter. Many of the items included in section 12 will also be discussed later, as most of them either relate to investment activities (see Chapter 6) or simply restate the treatment of business items provided by well-established business principles and generally accepted accounting principles.

However, three items in section 12 deserve special mention at this time—inducement payments, insurance proceeds, and payments based on production or use.

• **Inducement payments**   It is not uncommon for a business to receive an inducement from another party to carry out some activity. For example, a prospective tenant of a building may receive an inducement from a landlord as part of the lease agreement. Such an inducement may simply take the form of reduced future rents, in which case the tax impact to the tenant is recognized by a lower rent deduction for tax purposes. However, the inducement may be a cash grant or a cash reimbursement for all or a portion of the costs

---

17 ITA 67; *Mulder Bros. Sand and Gravel Ltd. v. MNR*, 67 DTC 475.

incurred by the tenant to improve the property (see leasehold improvements, Chapter 6). In such cases the payments are treated as taxable business income and are included in income in the year of receipt.[18] As an alternative, the taxpayer can elect to apply the inducement payment as a reduction of the cost of the property acquired.[19] In other words, instead of including that payment in income, the tenant can use it to reduce the cost for tax purposes of the leasehold improvements. This means that future deductions for capital cost allowance (amortization) on those improvements will be lower as a result of the reduced cost base. In the event that an inducement payment has to be repaid, a deduction is permitted at that time.[20]

An inducement payment may be a grant, a subsidy, or a forgivable loan, and may come from another business or from a government. The tax treatment for all of these is the same. In most cases the taxpayer will choose to delay the recognition of income by electing to treat the payment as a reduction of the cost of the asset. However, this may not always be the case, especially when it is anticipated that tax rates will increase in the future or when the business is currently not taxable because of excessive losses.

• **Insurance proceeds** When depreciable property is damaged or destroyed, insurance proceeds are likely to be received. When the property is destroyed (as opposed to damaged), the insurance proceeds are treated for tax purposes as proceeds from the disposition of the property. In other words, the insurance proceeds are the same as what the selling price would have been if the property had been sold. The amount of taxable income, if any, depends on the property's tax cost (see Chapter 6).

When the property is only damaged, the proceeds from an insurance policy are treated as taxable income, but only to the extent of the cost of the repairs made to the property.[21] For example, assume that the insurance proceeds are $12,000 but the subsequent actual repair costs amount to only $9,000. In this case $9,000 of the insurance proceeds must be included in income, which effectively offsets the repair expenses. The remaining insurance proceeds of $3,000 are treated as proceeds of a disposition of the depreciable property, much as if they were destroyed property (see Chapter 6).[22]

• **Payments based on production or use** A payment received that is based on the production or use of property, even when it is an instalment payment from the sale of a property, is considered to be business or property income.[23] An example of such a payment is the receipt of a franchise royalty that has been calculated as a percentage of sales volume.

The provisions may also apply when a property is sold and the selling price consists of both a fixed price and an additional amount that is based on the future income from that property. Consider a situation where the owner of an insurance business sells that business for a price equal to the value of the tangible assets (equipment, etc.) *plus* a further amount that is equal to the sum of the commission revenue earned by the new owner for the next three years. The payments based upon the future commissions actually represent the capital value of the business (or the goodwill—see Chapter 6). However, because the variable amount is based upon future production, it may be considered as business income to the vendor.[24] When part of the price of a property is based upon production or use, then only

---

18 ITA 12(1)(x), 12(2.2).

19 ITA 13(7.4), 53(2)(s).

20 ITA 20(1)(hh).

21 ITA 12(1)(f).

22 ITA 13(21)(d)(c).

23 ITA 12(1)(g).

24 *Gault v. MNR*, 65 DTC 5157.

that variable portion is considered to be business income, and the fixed amount represents the normal proceeds from the disposition of property.[25]

Each of the above exceptions relates to items of income. There are also exceptions that deal with expenses. These can be divided into two basic categories:

- expenses denied
- expenses permitted

I. Expenses Denied

Sections 18 and 19 of the *Income Tax Act* list specific expenses that are not permitted as deductions even though they would otherwise qualify under the general rules. The list is not extensive. Several of the expenses denied are reviewed here.

- **Use of recreational facilities and club dues**   Under this restriction, no business entity is permitted to deduct the expenses incurred for the use or maintenance of a yacht, a camp, a lodge, or a golf course, unless such property is part of the entity's normal business (for example, the selling or leasing of yachts).[26] This restriction also denies the deduction of all expenses incurred as membership fees or dues in any club, the main purpose of which is to provide dining, recreational, or sporting facilities to its members.

    This restriction is designed to forestall the abuse of the general rule that permits the deduction of expenses if they are for the purpose of earning income. Facilities and clubs may provide a high degree of personal enjoyment, and in that sense enhance a person's ability to generate revenue; still, they are simply denied altogether as a business expense in order to avoid the difficult task of sorting out the legitimate from the non-legitimate.

- **Political contributions**   No political contributions are deductible for tax purposes even though they may have an income-earning purpose.[27] While such contributions are not deductible in arriving at net income, they do create a tax credit that permits the amount of tax payable to be reduced within certain limits (see Chapter 10).

- **Advertising expenses**   In conflict with the general rules, the cost of advertising in a non-Canadian newspaper or broadcasting undertaking cannot be deducted *if* the advertisement is directed primarily at a Canadian market.[28] For example, advertising placed with an American-border television station to appeal to viewers in Canada is not deductible, but advertising on the same station to attract foreign customers is deductible. This exception is designed to provide assistance to Canadian media enterprises.

- **Allowance for an automobile**   As discussed in Chapter 4, employees often receive a travel allowance from their employers. Such allowances are tax-free to the employee as long as they are reasonable in the circumstances. When the allowance relates to the use of an automobile, the employer who pays the allowance faces limits as to the amount that can be deducted for tax purposes.[29] The maximum allowance that can be deducted by an employer is 42¢ for each of the first 5 000 kilometres in a year, and 36¢ for each additional kilometre (an additional 4¢ is permitted in the Yukon and the Northwest Territories).[30] These deductible rates are modified periodically. This limitation applies only if the allowance is tax-free to the employee. If the allowance is taxable to the employee, the employer can deduct the full amount, provided that it is reasonable.

---

25 IT-462, -426.

26 ITA 18(1)(l); IT-148R3.

27 ITA 18(1)(n).

28 ITA 19.

29 ITA 18(1)(r); Regulation 7306.

30 Regulation 7306 (effective September 1989).

• **Interest and property taxes on vacant land**   Even though interest costs and property taxes are normally tax-deductible (see below), a restriction applies when they relate to idle land. Land is considered to be idle if it is vacant and is not being used primarily to generate income, or if it is being held primarily for resale or development.

In such circumstances, the related interest costs and property taxes are deductible, but *only* to the extent that income is generated from that land.[31] For example, if vacant land generates temporary income of $8,000 (e.g., from rents) but incurs interest and property tax expenses of $11,000, the tax deduction is limited to $8,000. The unclaimed balance of $3,000 is added to the cost of the land. Therefore, the amount initially denied as a deduction ($3,000 in this case) can be deducted against the sale proceeds when the land is sold.[32] Keep in mind that the land may be classified as either inventory or capital property depending on the purpose of its acquisition. The above limitation may not apply if the entity's principal business is the leasing, rental, sale, or development of real property.[33]

• **Certain costs during construction period**   While a building is being constructed or altered, certain costs may be denied as deductions even though they would normally qualify.[34] Such costs include legal and accounting fees, interest costs, mortgage costs, property taxes, and promotional expenses that relate to the construction project. These costs are instead considered part of the cost of the building and as such are eligible for a capital cost allowance deduction over a period of years (see Chapter 6).

• **Work space in a home**   Individuals who operate a business may conduct all or part of that activity from a space in their home. The expenses applicable to that space are not permitted as a deduction for tax purposes unless one of the following conditions is met:[35]

• The space in the home is "the individual's principal place of business."

• The space is "used exclusively for the purpose of earning income from business and used on a regular or continuous basis for meeting clients, customers or patients of the individual."

If either of these conditions is met, the permitted expenses include a proportionate amount of the home's common expenses (mortgage interest, property taxes, utilities, insurance, and so on), in addition to any expenses that relate specifically to the work space. However, the total expenses cannot exceed the business income for the year. If they do, the excess is considered to be an expense of the following year. Notice that these expenses are more generous than those permitted to employees who use a home office (see Chapter 4).

• **Meals and entertainment**   Although entertainment and out-of-town meal expenses are deductible if incurred for the purpose of earning income, the amount permitted as a deduction is limited to 50% of actual costs incurred. This limitation was established in response to significant taxpayer abuses; even so, it arbitrarily eliminates a portion (50%) of all legitimate expenditures incurred for this purpose. It should be pointed out that this rule is not found in sections 18 and 19 of the *Income Tax Act*, with the other denied expenses; rather, it is a general rule that affects all types of income.[36]   One of the exceptions to this rule (which permits a 100% deduction) is the cost of food, beverage, and entertainment for

---

31 ITA 18(2), (3).

32 ITA 53(1)(h), ITA 10(1.1).

33 ITA 18(2).

34 ITA 18(3.1) to (3.7).

35 ITA 18(12); IT-514.

36 ITA 67.1; IT-518R.

events generally available to all employees. This exception is limited to six "occasional events" per year.

- **Costs of an automobile**   As with meals and entertainment costs, arbitrary limitations are placed on certain costs relating to a passenger vehicle used to earn business income.[37] These include the following:

  - Whatever the actual cost of an automobile, its cost for the purposes of claiming a deduction for capital cost allowance cannot exceed $30,000 (exclusive of any GST and PST).[38]

  - The interest cost on money borrowed to acquire a vehicle cannot exceed $300 per month.[39]

  - The deduction for a leased automobile cannot exceed $800 per month.[40]

  The dollar limitations described above change from time to time, so the relevant sections should be examined in the applicable year.

2. Expenses Permitted

Section 20 of the *Income Tax Act* lists approximately 40 specific items that are permitted as deductions even though, according to the six general limitations, they do not normally qualify. Most of these exceptions modify either expenditures of a capital nature that have a long-term or enduring benefit, or reserves put aside in recognition of certain anticipated expenses. Some but not all of these exceptions are identified and discussed below.

- **Capital cost allowance and amortization**   The general rules prohibit the deduction of all depreciation and amortization of capital assets, because their determination is subject to considerable variation by individual businesses and industries. However, the exception rules do permit the gradual expensing, in a controlled and uniform manner, of certain fixed assets and intangible capital property over a period of time.[41] The result is that all business entities are subject to the same application with respect to these items. This area is reviewed in detail in Chapter 6.

- **Interest**   Interest incurred on loans used to acquire long-term assets is considered to be on the account of capital and is therefore denied by the general rules. However, section 20 permits interest of this nature to be deducted provided that the long-term asset to which it relates is used to assist in the income process.[42]

  In addition, interest can, at the taxpayer's option, be deducted on a cash basis when paid, rather than by the accrual method required by generally accepted accounting principles.

  Two special options exist when money is borrowed to purchase depreciable property. Interest can be deducted as it is incurred; or it can be added to the cost of the depreciable property acquired, in which case it becomes eligible for a deduction over time in the form of capital cost allowance (see Chapter 6).[43]

- **Expenses of borrowing money or issuing shares**   Expenses of this nature, even though they have a long-term benefit, are permitted as a deduction in equal proportions

---

37 IT-521R.

38 ITA 13(7)(g).

39 ITA 67.2; Regulation 7307(2).

40 ITA 67.3. A further limitation based on a formula tied to the suggested list price of the car and $26,000 may also apply. See IT-521R.

41 ITA 20(1)(a), (b).

42 ITA 20(1)(c).

43 ITA 21; IT-121R3.

over five years (one-fifth per year).[44] Such items as the cost of registering a mortgage, appraisal fees for financing, selling commissions, and finder's fees are all deductible over five years. Life insurance premiums also may qualify as an expense of borrowing money. Normally, life insurance premiums are considered not deductible under the general rules because the income earned (life insurance) is not taxable revenue. However, if the insurance is required as loan collateral, it becomes a cost of borrowing money and an exception is permitted.[45] In addition, because the life insurance premium is an annual cost, it can be fully deducted each year when incurred rather than amortized over five years.

• **Landscaping of grounds**   Expenses incurred for the landscaping of property around a building or other structure that is used for the purpose of gaining or producing income are deductible when paid (not when incurred), even though such expenditure provides a long-term benefit through land enhancement.[46]

• **Reserves for doubtful debts**   Amounts receivable by a business entity, if it is anticipated that they won't be collected, are deductible as a reserve provided that this reserve is reasonable and that the debt, when established, created income for the taxpayer.[47] Debts such as accounts receivable for the sale of inventory or the rendering of services are entitled to use this reserve. Entities whose business includes the loaning of money qualify for the reserve; this is the case even when such loans did not create income when first established. The tax treatment of reserves is discussed in detail beginning on page 136.

• **Reserve for delayed payment revenues**   A reserve may be deducted from income when inventory has been sold and all or part of the payment is not due until after two years from the date of sale.[48] This means that income from the sale of items that have a long-term payment schedule can be recognized for tax purposes over a period of time. However, such a reserve can be utilized for no more than three years, even though payments may extend beyond that time.

When the inventory sold is land, a reserve can be utilized to reduce profits in proportion to any deferred proceeds beyond the taxation year in which the sale was made, for a maximum of three years. For example, assume that a profit of $40,000 is earned on land inventory that was sold for $100,000 in 20X1. The payment terms include $10,000 cash in 20X1 and the balance of $90,000 payable in 20X5. In 20X1, the profit of $40,000 can be reduced by a reserve of $36,000 ($90,000/$100,000 × $40,000), this being the portion of the sales proceeds that has been deferred. In 20X2 and 20X3, no income is realized because no further proceeds are received. The deferred profit of $36,000 must be recognized for tax purposes in 20X4 (the three-year reserve limit), even though the remaining proceeds are not received until 20X5. Further sample reserve calculations can be found in IT-154R, available from CCRA.

• **Expenses of representation**   Sometimes a business must make a representation to a government body, with long-term implications. For example, a business may present suggestions or concerns to a regulatory body relating to its industry. Or the business may be applying for a permit, franchise, patent, trademark, or broadcast licence. While such expenses are capital in nature, a full deduction is permitted in the year that they are paid.[49] As an alternative, the taxpayer can elect to deduct the amount at the rate of one-tenth per year over 10 years.[50]

44 ITA 20(1)(e); IT-341R3.
45 ITA 20(1)(e.2); IT-309R2.
46 ITA 20(1)(aa); IT-296.
47 ITA 20(1)(l); IT-442R.
48 ITA 20(1)(n), 20(8)(b); IT-152R3, -154R, -345R.
49 ITA 20(1)(cc).
50 ITA 20(9).

- **Investigation of a site**   A deduction is permitted for the cost of investigating a suitable site for a building to be used in a business. The deduction is allowed whether or not the site is actually acquired.[51]

- **Convention expenses**   Usually, attending a convention or conference provides a long-term benefit for the taxpayer and therefore is a capital expenditure. Regardless, a deduction is permitted for the costs of attending up to two conventions in a year provided that the location of the convention is within the territorial scope of the organization holding the convention.[52]

  Convention expenses must be distinguished from expenses of training. Training costs are treated according to the common rules and are denied if they are capital in nature. For example, if an individual pays for a training program in order to *acquire* a new trade or profession, the cost is a capital item and cannot be deducted. However, a course taken to *maintain* or *upgrade* an existing skill is deductible. It should be noted that costs incurred by employers to train or retrain employees are usually considered to be fully deductible as they are incurred.[53]

- **Utilities service connection**   A deduction is permitted for the cost of making a service connection to the taxpayer's place of business for the supply of electricity, gas, telephone service, and water or sewers, even though such costs are normally capital items.[54]

- **Private health services plans**   Businesses often compensate employees with certain fringe benefits in addition to salaries. Private health services plan (PHSP) coverage is one such benefit. As was shown in Chapter 4, this benefit is deductible as an expense to the employer but is not taxable to the employee. An individual who is self-employed and is operating a business as a proprietor cannot employ himself or herself (as could be the case if the business was a corporation) and normally will not be able to deduct such premiums. A special rule covers this anomaly: Individuals can deduct the amounts paid for their PHSP coverage in computing business income provided they are actively engaged alone or as a partner in a business, and either self-employment is their primary source of income in the year (more than 50%) *or* their income from other sources does not exceed $10,000. The deduction applies only if coverage is provided to all permanent full-time employees (other than employees who are related to the owner). Such coverage is deductible to a maximum of $1,500 each for the individual and spouse, and $750 per child. No limit applies to arm's-length employees.[55]

- **Expenses deductible on a cash basis**   As previously described, expenses are normally deducted on an accrual basis when incurred rather than when paid. However, certain expenses must actually be paid in order to obtain a deduction for tax purposes. These include convention expenses, landscaping, representation fees, site investigation fees, utility service connections, and investment counsel fees (see Chapter 7).

- **Contributions to the Canada Pension Plan (CPP)**   These are legally required in Canada. The contribution cost is shared by the employer and the employee. The employer's share of such contributions is, of course, deductible in arriving at business income. When an individual operates a business as a sole proprietor he or she cannot be employed by themselves. Consequently the individual is required to contribute both the employer's and the employee's share of the contributions. When this occurs, the individual can deduct the employer's share of the contribution in arriving at business income. The remaining employee's share is claimed as a tax credit by the individual. This division allows the

---

51 ITA 20(1)(dd); IT-350R.

52 ITA 20(10); IT-131R2.

53 IT-357R2.

54 ITA 20(1)(ee), IT-452.

55 ITA 20.01.

employer's share to reduce income and save tax at the individual's top marginal tax rate. The employee's share, as a tax credit, reduces tax at the individual's lowest tax-bracket rate.

The above exceptions to the general rules do not constitute a complete list. It is extremely important that any entity conducting a business activity make the simple effort to obtain a full list from their tax advisor, with explanations of the 40 or so exceptions to the general rules, so that it can apply the general rules with certainty.

B. Treatment of Inventories

The cost of items sold in the business process normally constitutes a formidable expense in the calculation of profit. As previously explained, the process of recognizing this expense involves holding the costs of products acquired or manufactured in abeyance until they are sold, at which time the expense is matched to the sale. While the use of computer technology has simplified this task considerably, the process is still predicated on the accumulating, throughout the year, of all costs of products available for sale and on deducting from that total the cost of products unsold at the close of the fiscal period. The remainder, after deductions are made for the cost of unsold merchandise (inventory), is the cost of the product sold during the period. For example, the cost may be determined as follows:

Cost of products available to be sold:	
Inventory on hand at beginning of the year	$200,000
Product purchased or manufactured during the year	700,000
Total cost of goods available for sale	900,000
Cost of products unsold:	
Inventory on hand at the end of the year	(150,000)
Cost of products sold and matched to revenues	$750,000

It is obvious that the value assigned to the inventory at the end of the year has a major impact on the cost of goods sold and therefore on the profits.

The *Income Tax Act* specifically permits the closing inventory to be valued using one of two methods:

1. Value *each* item of inventory at the lower of its cost or market value.[56]

2. Value *all* items of inventory at their market value.[57]

Each of these methods is likely to produce a different ending inventory value and, as a result, a different profit for tax purposes. Keep in mind that this variance is only temporary, since ultimately a business must expense its full costs.

The reader must understand the terms "cost" and "market" in order to appreciate the extent of the impact on profits of the above alternatives.[58] When possible, *cost* refers to the actual cost of each specific item unsold at the end of the period (the specific identification method). Often it is not practical or possible to identify the actual cost of each product because the cost of such items has varied throughout the year. In these circumstances it is acceptable to cost each item of inventory at its most current cost, making the assumption that the inventory consists of the most recent purchases and that the first goods purchased were the first goods sold (FIFO—first-in, first-out method). Alternatively, each item may be valued at the average of its costs during the year (average-cost method). It is not acceptable to assume that inventory consists of the older items and that new products acquired are the first sold (LIFO—last-in, first-out method), although this may be acceptable under generally accepted accounting principles.

---

56 ITA 10(1).

57 Regulation 1801; IT-473R.

58 IT-473R.

The term *market* normally reflects the realization value of the inventory, in that it is the expected selling price after the deduction of direct selling costs such as sales commissions. In manufacturing concerns, inventory consists of finished goods ready for sale, unfinished goods (work in process), and raw materials. The selling price of finished goods can be reasonably estimated but is difficult to obtain for unfinished goods and raw materials. For these items it is acceptable to use the replacement cost as a reasonable estimate of market.

Consider the following inventory, which consists of three automobiles held by a car dealer, and the impact on profits of the different valuation alternatives.

Car model	Cost	Market net realizable value	Lower of cost or market
A	$12,000	$14,000	$12,000
B	14,000	11,000	11,000
C	18,000	21,000	18,000
Total	$44,000	$46,000	$41,000

Each of the two permitted inventory valuation methods—all at market, and each item at the lower of cost or market—results in a different inventory value and therefore a different profit determination. When all inventory is finally sold, however, the accumulated profit over the time period is identical for each method.

In addition to the acceptable methods of inventory valuation, profit can also be altered as a result of errors—intended or unintended—during that part of the compilation process which involves the physical counting, the costing, and the determination of the market value of each item.

While there are several options available for valuing inventory, the ability to change from one method to the other is somewhat restricted. First of all, the opening inventory of a new period must be valued in the same manner as the closing inventory of the previous period. Also, a further restriction requires that the closing inventory of a business be valued using the same method as for the closing inventory for the previous taxation year, unless a change is approved by CCRA.[59] This means that the choice of the initial valuation method for a new business is an important one, as it will have an impact on future years as well.

From a management perspective, the acceptable alternatives for valuating inventory must be viewed as tools to enhance cash flow by deferring the realization of income for tax purposes. This means that the information process must be capable of providing relevant information on a timely basis, so that managers can take advantage of the flexibility the tax system provides. The function of inventory costing and control has to be expanded so that alternative inventory valuations for tax purposes can be examined, and the best one chosen.

C. Taxation Year and the Individual Taxpayer

In Chapter 3 it was established that the taxation year for the corporation is the fiscal year and for the individual is the calendar year. This means that a corporation's taxation year can end on any day of the year, whereas an individual operating a proprietorship business must end his or her taxation year on December 31.

For certain businesses, having a year end on December 31 may create an administrative hardship; this is especially true for seasonal businesses that do high volumes of business during the months surrounding December. In recognition of this, individuals can elect to use an alternative fiscal period other than December 31.[60] If this election is made, a complex formula is applied to the fiscal period earnings to arbitrarily adjust the income for tax purposes to approximate the calendar-year income. Consider the following situation and analysis:

---

59 ITA 10(2), (2.1).
60 ITA 11(1), 249.1.

Situation: A taxpayer who is an individual starts a new business on March 1, 20X6. Normally, her first taxation year for the business would be December 31, 20X6, and would include the income earned from March 1 to December 31, 20X6. However, she wishes to close the first business cycle on February 28, 20X7, exactly 12 months from the opening date. Profits from the business for the first two years are as follows:

Year ended February 28, 20X7	$40,000
Year ended February 28, 20X8	$50,000

Analysis: This woman must file a tax return for the 20X6 calendar year that includes income from all sources. However, her first business year end does not arrive until February 28, 20X7, and therefore no income from the business is included in her 20X6 calendar year tax return. Effectively, 10 months (March 1 to December 31, 20X6) of her first year's business profits have been deferred to 20X7. The deferred amount is estimated to be $33,333 ($40,000 × 10 months/12 months).[61] This is a prorated estimate based on time and does not consider that profits may vary each month.

For the 20X7 calendar year for which a tax return must be filed, this woman's income for tax purposes will include the business profit of $40,000 for the fiscal year end February 28, 20X7. In addition, a further amount is included that represents an arbitrary estimate of the profit earned from March 1 to December 31, 20X7. The 20X7 and 20X8 incomes from business are as follows:

20X7	
Year ended February 28, 20X7	$ 40,000
Deduct portion included in 20X6	–0–
	40,000
Add estimated income from March 1 to December 31, 20X7	
$40,000 × 10 months/12 months	33,333
Total 20X7 income from business	$ 73,333
20X8	
Year ended February 28, 20X8	$ 50,000
Deduct portion included in 20X7 above	(33,333)
	16,667
Add estimated income from March 1 to December 31, 20X8	
$50,000 × 10 months/12 months	41,667
Total 20X8 income from business	$ 58,334

Notice that this election puts no business income in 20X6 but creates excessive income in 20X7, likely causing a higher tax rate. To avoid this outcome, this woman can choose a further election to include the 10 months of 20X6 business income ($40,000 × 10/12 = $33,333) in her 20X6 income for tax purposes. Doing this would create the following business incomes in 20X6, 20X7, and 20X8:

---

61 The actual proration is based on the number of days rather than months.

20X6	
Elected amount above	$ 33,333
20X7	
Year ended February 28, 20X7	$ 40,000
Less portion included in 20X6 above	(33,333)
	6,667
Add estimated income from March 1 to December 31, 20X7	
$40,000 × 10 months/12 months	33,333
Total 20X7 income from business	$ 40,000
20X8	
Year ended February 28, 20X8	$ 50,000
Less portion included in 20X7 above	(33,333)
	16,667
Add estimated income from March 1 to December 31, 20X8	
$50,000 × 10 months/12 months	41,667
Total 20X8 income from business	$ 58,334

The above situation and analysis shows that the arbitrary formula that attempts to convert fiscal-year earnings to calendar-year earnings is complex and may create undesirable results. It appears that if annual profits are constant, the calendar-year method and the alternative method should produce similar results for an ongoing business. When profits are rising, the calendar method offers the best timing, whereas when profits are declining, the alternative method is preferable. Note that the two methods produce only a timing difference; over time, the identical amount of profits will be recognized. Predicting future profits is difficult, so most taxpayers choose the calendar-year format for simplicity.[62]

The requirement to use a calendar year rather than a fiscal year also applies to partnerships that include individual partners, and to a special category of corporations called "professional corporations," which are used exclusively by six professions—medical doctors, dentists, accountants, lawyers, veterinarians, and chiropractors.

D. Scientific Research and Experimental Development

Expenditures for scientific research and experimental development (SR&ED) are usually incurred to provide a long-term benefit to the entity. Consequently, the general rules would deny a deduction, on the basis that they are capital expenditures. However, SR&ED activity by the business community is important to the long-term strength and competitiveness of the Canadian economy, so the federal government has put in place special tax provisions that apply to SR&ED outlays, with the goal of encouraging such activity.

To the extent that SR&ED is carried on within Canada, the following special provisions apply:[63]

- Ongoing expenditures, even those that contribute to the long-term benefit of the project, can be deducted in full in the year incurred. These expenditures include salaries and wages, supplies, payments to approved universities or other business entities for research work, and so on.

---

62 Prior to 1995, individuals were permitted to use a fiscal period without adjustments. Individuals were required to convert to the new rules in 1995 by increasing their income for the deferred portion, but were given the option to include the adjustment in income over a 10-year period.

63 ITA 37(1); IT-151R4.

- The cost of tangible assets, such as equipment, that are used all or substantially all of the time in the SR&ED process can be fully deducted in the year of acquisition. This eliminates the normal requirement that such costs be deducted over several years as capital cost allowance. Usually this exception does not apply to buildings.

- The business can choose not to deduct any of the above items when incurred, but instead carry them forward indefinitely as a deduction for any future year.

The above provisions improve cash flow because the SR&ED costs can be deducted immediately to create a tax saving. In addition, the indefinite carry-over period for unused deductions means that companies have a greater chance for such costs eventually resulting in tax savings.

These benefits are significantly reduced when the SR&ED activity is carried on *outside* Canada. In these circumstances, for example, the costs of tangible assets cannot be deducted in full in the year acquired, and unused deductions cannot be carried over indefinitely.[64]

For a taxpayer to take advantage of these special rules, the expenditures must qualify as an SR&ED activity. In general terms, this activity includes "experimental development of new products and processes in addition to applied research." Apparently, it is not intended to "include routine engineering or routine product development."[65] It is important to establish whether proposed activities qualify as SR&ED before embarking on new projects.[66]

Some SR&ED expenditures may also qualify for an investment tax credit. This results in a direct reduction of tax payable and an immediate cash saving. In such cases the expense deduction is reduced by the amount of the tax credit received.

E. Professionals

Individuals and corporations that provide professional services often perform these services over a long period of time before billing for the work. In most businesses, income is not recognized until the customer has an obligation to pay—that is, until the amount is billed and an account receivable is created. For professionals, work carried out before a bill is sent is referred to as "work in progress." Accounting principles require that the work in progress of professionals be included in income so that it can be matched with the related expenses in the year. As a general rule, this is also the case for tax purposes.[67]

An exception is made for accountants, lawyers, medical doctors, dentists, chiropractors, and veterinarians. These professionals can choose to exclude work in progress and recognize income only after an actual billing for services has been made.[68] However, once this election has been made, it must be continued in future years unless a change is approved by CCRA.

Choosing not to recognize work in progress delays the payment of tax until a future time period. This, of course, improves cash flow for the professional unless future tax rates will be significantly higher.

F. Treatment of Reserves

As stated earlier in this chapter, an important general limitation in the determining of business income is that, with a few exceptions, no reserves are permitted as a deduction. For example, a reserve for anticipated warranty costs on products sold cannot be deducted for tax purposes even though it is deducted for accounting purposes. However,

---

64 ITA 37(2).

65 *Tax Principles To Remember*, CICA, 2000, pp. 5–32.

66 IC 86-4R3.

67 ITA 12(1)(b).

68 ITA 34; IT-457R, IT-189R2.

the *actual* warranty costs incurred in the year can be deducted in the year that they occur.

Two important exceptions to this general limitation were discussed earlier: reserves for doubtful debts and reserves to delay the recognition of income when the sale agreement calls for extended payment terms. Whenever a reserve is allowed (including a capital gain reserve—see Chapter 8), the deduction must be added back to income in the year immediately following.[69] At that time a new reserve can be deducted if it can still be justified.

It is important to note that a permitted reserve does not have to be claimed; rather, it is a discretionary reserve. Clearly, reserves are an important tool in that they enable the taxpayer to shift income from one period to another. Consider this situation.

Assume that a business deducted a reserve for doubtful debts of $75,000 in the previous year (20X0). Also assume that for the current year (20X1), the estimated uncollectible debts amount to $90,000, and that the business profit before the reserve is $110,000. If the taxpayer has chosen to claim the full available reserve in 20X1, income for tax purposes is $95,000, as follows:

20X1 income	$110,000
Add last year's reserve	75,000
	185,000
Deduct current year's reserve	(90,000)
20X1 income for tax purposes	$ 95,000

Alternatively, the business can choose not to claim any reserve in 20X1, in which case the income increases to $185,000. This means that no addition will have to be made to the following year's income (20X2), and that if a reserve is claimed in 20X2, that year's income will be significantly lower than it otherwise would have been. When the reserve is not claimed, the 20X1 income is higher and the 20X2 income is lower; in effect, income has been shifted from one period to another. As pointed out in Chapter 2, the shifting of income, even to an earlier year, is an important tax planning technique.

G. Unpaid Remuneration

Business income is determined on an accrual basis. This means that salaries are usually deductible by the employer when they are incurred, even if they have not been paid. However, employment income is included by the employee in income for tax purposes only when received (see Chapter 4).

In order to prevent the unwarranted delay of taxable remuneration payments, a special rule has been established limiting the employer's scope for deducting unpaid remuneration. This can be deducted by an employer for tax purposes only if it is paid within 180 days of its taxation year. If payment is delayed beyond that period, the employer can deduct the remuneration only in the subsequent year in which it is paid (see Chapter 9).[70]

H. Farming

Farming is a business and is subject to the normal rules for calculating income from business for tax purposes. One result is that, as a general rule, farming income is calculated on an accrual basis. However, taxpayers carrying on a farming business can, if they so elect, determine farming income using a cash basis of accounting.[71] In other words, they can recognize income when it is received and deduct expenses when they are paid. This applies to all items except capital expenditures, which are subject to their normal treatment (capital

---

69 ITA 12(1)(d), (e), others.

70 ITA 78(4); IT-109R2.

71 ITA 28(1); IT-433, -427R.

cost allowance on depreciable property, and so on).

When the cash basis is used, inventory costs are deducted at the time of payment and not when the inventory is sold. As a result, it is not unusual for farmers to experience extreme income fluctuations from year to year. Farmers can, at their option, choose to increase their income in a given year by an amount up to the inventory that would have been recorded if the accrual basis had been used. That increase is then deducted in a later year. This option permits them to "smooth" their income and escape the higher tax rates that might result from income surges. In fact, if a farming business incurs a loss in a year, an inventory adjustment to reduce the loss is mandatory. (This adjustment applies only to inventory that has been purchased.)

If a taxpayer's major occupation is not farming (that is, if operating a farm is a secondary activity to the taxpayer's main occupation),[72] the amount of loss that can be deducted against other sources of income in the year may be restricted.[73] In such cases, the farming loss deducted cannot exceed $8,750 in any year. It is further restricted to an amount equal to $2,500 plus one-half of the amount by which the actual loss exceeds $2,500. For example, an actual farming loss of $18,000 results in a maximum deduction for tax purposes of only $8,750, as follows:

$$\$2,500 + \frac{1}{2} (\$18,000 - \$2,500) = \$10,250$$
or
the limit of **$8,750**

The unused amount (in this case, $18,000 − $8,750 = $9,250) can be applied against farming income earned in the previous 3 years or the 10 subsequent years. This carry-over forms part of the taxable income calculation after net income has been calculated for tax purposes (see Chapter 10).[74]

I. Partnerships

A partnership is not a taxable entity and bears no responsibility for tax on income generated within its sphere of operations. Rather, income earned or losses incurred by the partnership are allocated to the partners, in accordance with the agreed sharing ratio, for inclusion in each partner's income for tax purposes.[75] The income shared by the partners is allocated for tax purposes regardless of whether such profits have actually been distributed to the partners. Thus, it is conceivable that a partner may bear the full tax liability on its share of income even though the income remains in the partnership for reinvestment.

It is significant that losses incurred by a partnership are allocated to the partners as well, and included in their separate determinations of taxable income.[76] This means that losses can be offset against the partners' other income, provided that other income exists.

All partnership income or loss allocated retains its source and characteristics when included in each partner's income. Business income of the partnership is business income to each partner and is treated accordingly for tax purposes. Capital gains and losses of the partnership become capital gains and losses of each partner. In this sense, the partnership is a conduit—it earns income like any other entity, but then passes it on to the participants as if it had been earned directly by them. A detailed examination of partnerships is provided in Chapter 15.

---

72 *Moldowan v. The Queen*, 77 DTC 5213.
73 ITA 31; IT-322R.
74 ITA 111(1)(c); IT-232R2.
75 ITA 96(1); IT-138R.
76 ITA 96(1); IT-232R2.

IV. Business Income and the GST

It was indicated in Chapter 3 that most business entities are entitled to a full GST rebate on all items purchased, provided that those purchases are for business purposes. This chapter has shown that a number of expenses cannot be deducted from business income for income tax purposes, in which case neither is a rebate allowed for the related GST on those expenses. There is a close relationship between the denial of an expense for income tax purposes and the denial of a GST rebate.

Some of the expenses that are disallowed or are restricted for income tax purposes are listed here:

- The cost of leasing an automobile in excess of $800 per month.
- Personal and living expenses.
- Club memberships.
- 50% of all food, beverage, and entertainment costs.
- Expenses that are considered to be unreasonable in the circumstances.

In each of the above situations, the GST on the good or service acquired is not eligible for a rebate (or input credit) against the GST collected on goods or services sold.

A similar treatment applies to certain capital assets acquired (e.g., automobiles, which have a restricted cost of $30,000 for tax purposes). This treatment is discussed at greater length in subsequent chapters.

V. Sample Calculation of Business Income

Outlined below is a simplified calculation of income from business for tax purposes. The format used applies the general rules to the accounting profit and then examines the specific list of exceptions. A financial statement for the company is shown at the top of the next page.

Additional Information

1. Closing inventory, in addition to being valued at the lower of cost or market, has been reduced by a reserve of $6,000 for anticipated further declines in value.

2. Insurance expenses include a $2,000 premium for life insurance on the company president, the proceeds of which are payable to the company. The remaining insurance costs relate to insurance for property damage and public liability.

3. Amortization has been computed in accordance with reasonable estimates of each asset's useful life.

4. Legal expenses of $10,000 are made up of the following items:

Registration of a patent	$ 1,000
Collection of delinquent accounts receivable	5,000
Finder's fee for procuring mortgage funds	4,000

5. Research expenses of $15,000 relate to the apportionment of past and current research costs to several years, in accordance with their anticipated contribution to revenue. For the current year, actual research costs amount to $22,000, a substantial portion of which will be allocated to future years for accounting purposes.

6. Advertising and promotion includes television and newspaper advertising for products, as well as $4,000 for club memberships in sports-related facilities for the purpose of enhancing business contacts.

Condor Enterprises Ltd.
Statement of Income
Year ended June 30, 20X1

Revenue:		
Sales		$800,000
Service-contract fees		150,000
		950,000
Cost of goods sold:		
Inventory, beginning of year	$250,000	
Goods purchased during the year	550,000	
Goods available for sale	800,000	
Deduct inventory, end of year	200,000	600,000
Gross profit		350,000
Expenses:		
Selling commissions	22,000	
Insurance	8,000	
Amortization (depreciation) of building and equipment	15,000	
Amortization of goodwill	5,000	
Legal expenses	10,000	
Interest	5,000	
Research costs	15,000	
Advertising and promotion	30,000	
Salaries and wages	100,000	
Employee benefits	22,000	
Donations	5,000	
Repairs and maintenance	20,000	
Warranty costs	8,000	
Bad-debt expense	15,000	280,000
Income before income taxes		$ 70,000

7. Donations consist of the following items:

To registered charities	$3,000
To registered political parties	2,000

8. Warranty costs are recorded annually, in the form of an estimated reserve, as 1% of the sales value of products sold (1% of $800,000 = $8,000). During the year, actual warranty costs paid on defective equipment amounted to $6,000, which was charged against the reserve account.

9. Bad-debt expense is also based on a reserve system, under which outstanding accounts receivable are reviewed and expected losses are forecast.

Calculation of Income for Tax Purposes
The reported accounting profit of $70,000 is assumed to be consistent with accepted accounting principles and, therefore, is the starting point for calculating income for tax purposes. Each item is now examined to determine whether it contravenes one of the six general limitations. The specific exceptions to the general rules are then scrutinized. (References to the *Income Tax Act* are provided for each item.)

Income for Tax Purposes

Income for accounting purposes	$70,000
Analysis and adjustments (expenses disallowed are added back to increase income; additional expenses reduce accounting income):	
1. The reduction of inventory for anticipated future-value declines is a reserve disallowed by the general rules (18(1)(e)). No specific exception is provided in the exception list.	6,000
2. The life insurance premium of $2,000 would earn income that is not taxable, and therefore the general rules negate this deduction (18(1)(c)). No exception is provided.	20,000
3. Amortization on capital items is prohibited by the general rules (18(1)(b)). (15,000 + 5,000)	20,000
However, capital cost allowance for buildings and equipment, and a similar write-off for tax purposes for goodwill, can be deducted (20(1)(a) and (b)). In the absence of specific information, this is assumed to be:	(23,000)
4. Legal expenses for patent registration are on account of capital because they have a long-term benefit (18(1)(b)). However, capital cost allowance for patents can be deducted and is part of the assumed deduction of $23,000 in item 3 above.	1,000
Collection of delinquent accounts is for the purpose of earning income and is acceptable.	—
A finder's fee for a mortgage has a long-term benefit and is disallowed by the general rules. However, a specific exception is provided for costs incurred to borrow money; one-fifth can be written off annually over five years (20(1)(e)). Therefore, add back four-fifths of $4,000.	3,200
5. Research is on the account of capital and its write-off over a period of years is not permitted (18(1)(b)).	15,000
The exception list permits research costs to be written off when incurred (37(1)). This year's actual cost is:	(22,000)
6. Promotion expenses in the form of club dues, while passing all of the general limitation tests, are specifically disallowed as an exception (18(1)(l)).	4,000
7. Donations to charities are not for the purpose of earning income and are disallowed under the general rules (18(1)(a)). No exception for donations is made in calculating business income, although a deduction is permitted for corporations converting net income to taxable income (see Chapter 11). Individual taxpayers are permitted a tax credit for donations (see Chapter 10).	3,000
Political donations are specifically disallowed by the exception list (18(1)(n)). Individuals and corporations are permitted to claim a limited tax credit for political contributions (see Chapters 10 and 11).	2,000
8. Warranty reserves for expected costs are eliminated by the general rule that no reserves are permitted (18(1)(e)). A review of the specific exceptions provides no relief.	8,000
Actual warranty costs incurred for the year are deductible, in accordance with the general rules.	(6,000)
9. Bad debt reserves are disallowed by the general reserve limitation but are specifically permitted by the exception list (20(1)(l)).	—
Income from business for tax purposes	$83,200

VI. Tax Planning Checklist

The category of business income provides a number of tax planning opportunities. Some of these are listed below.

1. The sale of property may be treated as a business transaction or a capital transaction. When acquiring property, anticipate its tax treatment and plan for the best possible outcome in the event the property is sold.

2. Individuals starting a new business should choose its fiscal period carefully. Normally it will be the calendar year. However, if a non-calendar fiscal period is desired for administrative purposes, the effects of the arbitrary alternative-method formula should be anticipated before a decision is made.

3. A business should regularly identify those items of expense and revenue over which it has some discretion as to when they are included in income for tax purposes. Some of those items are listed here:

   - Reserve for doubtful debts.
   - Reserve for sales whose payments extend over future years.
   - Capital cost allowance.
   - Expenses that qualify as scientific research and experimental development (SR&ED).
   - Interest on money borrowed to acquire depreciable property (which can be capitalized or not).

   These items must be considered when losses occur that cannot be offset against other sources of income. Because they are discretionary, their deduction can be delayed, resulting in a reduced loss for the current period. They can also be used as a means of shifting income to another period to take advantage of a preferential tax rate.

4. A business may be permitted to divide its income among family members. For example, when a salary is paid to a spouse or child, business income is reduced, and the salary to the family member may be taxed at a lower rate. However, such remuneration must be for genuine services, and the related salary must be reasonable. Opportunities for splitting income also exist when family members participate as partners (in an unincorporated business) or shareholders (in an incorporated business).

5. An incorporated business can employ its shareholder/manager. This means that the business can compensate the owner, in part, by providing all of the tax-free benefits permitted, such as private health insurance and disability insurance.

6. There are several accepted ways to value inventory—lower of cost or market, all at market, average cost, specific identification, and first-in, first-out (FIFO). Also, manufactured inventory can utilize either the absorption cost method (which allocates both fixed and variable overhead costs) or the direct cost method (which allocates only variable costs to inventory).[77] Every method recognizes the same amount of income but in a different time period. Because it may be difficult to switch to another option once a choice has been made, consider the alternatives carefully when organizing a new business.

---

77 IT-473.

7. Consider when SR&ED expenditures should be deducted. Since this must involve long-range forecasting of results, an element of uncertainty cannot be avoided.

8. Owing to the restrictions on passenger vehicles and to the related tax complexities when employees operate those vehicles for personal use, consider carefully whether to own or lease the vehicles and how to remunerate employees. While every business is different, an efficient outcome can be ensured by examining the special requirements of the business and its employees.

VII. Summary, Conclusion, and Management Perspective

A. Business Income —The Process

The determination of business income for tax purposes follows three basic steps.

1. As a general rule, business income for tax purposes is equivalent to accounting income determined in accordance with generally accepted accounting principles, which interpret well-accepted business principles.

2. Accounting income is modified by established case law and by the application of six general limitations found in the *Income Tax Act*. These limitations define the extent to which income for tax purposes can vary from accounting income.

3. Notwithstanding the general rule and general limitations, the amount of business income may be modified further by reference to two lists of specific exceptions; one of these denies the deduction of items otherwise permitted, while the other permits the deduction of items otherwise denied.

The process is fundamentally simple, in that it starts with the broad definition of business income, establishes the general parameters of that definition, and provides a specific list of exceptions designed to deal with special problems, abuses, and political requirements.

It is vital to accept and utilize the three-step process described in this chapter, since it applies to every business transaction. The *Income Tax Act* does not attempt to deal with the multitude of various business activities; however, in the vast majority of cases, business income for tax purposes can be established by the general rules and limitations. Exhibit 5-1 diagrams the three-step process for dealing with business transactions.

B. Business Income versus Employment Income

It would now be useful to compare the two types of income for tax purposes that have been reviewed to this point. Both employment income and business income play a major part in the management decision processes of a business enterprise.

One can simply compare the brief list of general rules presented above with those outlined in Chapter 4. This comparison indicates that there are three key differences between employment income and business income:

- method of accounting
- deductions permitted
- income excluded

• **Method of accounting** Employment income is accounted for on a cash basis, which means that income is recognized when received and expenses are deducted when paid. Business income, on the other hand, determines income *annually*, in accordance with accounting and business principles, and uses the accrual method, which requires that income be recognized when earned rather than when received, and that expenses be deducted when incurred rather than when paid.

Exhibit 5-1:
The Decision Process
—Business Income

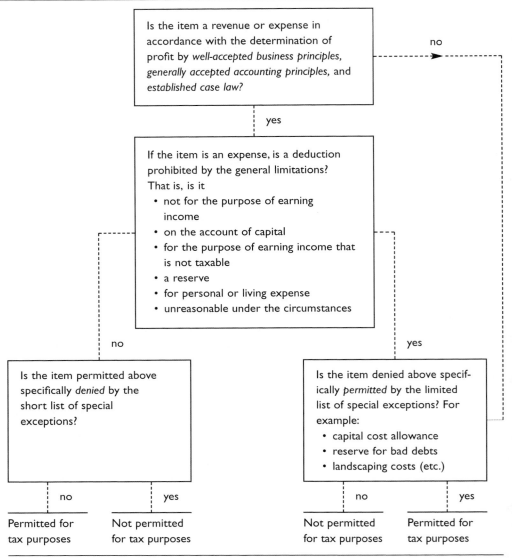

• **Deductions permitted**   The employment income calculation permits no deductions except those specifically allowed in the *Income Tax Act*. The business income calculation, however, permits the deduction of all expenses incurred for the purpose of generating income from business *except those that are specifically denied or restricted.*

• **Income excluded**   Employees can earn, by virtue of their employment, a specified number of benefits that are not included in taxable income. The provisions for determining business income, on the other hand, contain no specific list of income that is tax-free.

The above fundamental differences are useful to remember when it comes to understanding the employer/employee relationship. For example, an employer determines the deductibility of all compensation costs in terms of whether or not they are incurred for the purpose of earning income from a business, and uses the deduction to reduce business income when it is incurred. On the other hand, the employee who receives the benefit as employment income follows the employment income guidelines regardless of how the employer must treat the benefit. The fact that a specific benefit may be tax-free to the employee is irrelevant when its deductibility to the employer is being determined.

C. Business Income and the Management Process

It is obvious that a business enterprise's primary source of taxable income is business activity, as opposed to property income and capital gains. Simple logic dictates that management must be familiar with the process of determining business income for tax purposes; this familiarity ensures that no more tax is paid than what is required, and that the payment of tax occurs at the latest possible time. While external tax consultants can enhance this process, it is of little value if the business entity does not have an information system with the ability to highlight those items that are relevant to the tax process.

Familiarization with the general rules, and with the specific exceptions that apply to the particular business, is a strong catalyst that stimulates managers to recognize the need to expand their enterprise's information systems beyond the normal accounting function. Knowing, for example, that the tax provisions permit inventory to be valued all at market or at the lower of cost or market, for each item of inventory, is of no value unless information is generated that demonstrates how much difference the choice of one over the other would make.

In addition, familiarization with the business income rules permits managers to compare such income with other types of income, and to use the resulting knowledge to their advantage. Often, by understanding the tax treatment to the other party in a transaction, managers have the opportunity to structure their activities to provide an advantage to that other party, which may in turn create cost efficiencies. For example, knowing how an investor is taxed on property income allows management to seek and review alternative methods of raising capital that provide the maximum tax advantage to that investor, which in turn enhances the value of the security offered.

The process of determining business income for tax purposes affects a very wide range of financial transactions but is not overly complex when viewed in terms of the three steps developed in this chapter. Any manager can understand and apply the process and, in so doing, systematically control the tax cost to the business enterprise.

Reading List

Income Tax Act **References**

	Section
Business (defined)	248(1)
Income (loss) from business or property	9(1),(2)
Valuation of inventory	10(1)
Method of valuation (inventory) to be the same	10(2), (2.1)
Proprietor of a business—fiscal period	11(1), 249.1
Amounts to be included in income	12(1)(a) to (2.5)
Inducement payments	12(1)(x), (2.2)
Payments based on production or use	12(1)(g)
Insurance proceeds	12(1)(f)
Reserve for doubtful accounts	12(1)(d)
General limitation (purpose of earning income)	18(1)(a)
Capital outlay	18(1)(b)
Expenses to earn exempt income	18(1)(c)
Reserves	18(1)(e)
Personal and living expenses	18(1)(h)
Reasonableness test for expenses	67
Political contributions	18(1)(n)

Advertising (foreign)	19
Maximum allowance paid for automobile	Regulation 7306
Interest and property taxes—vacant land	18(2), (3)
Certain costs during construction (soft costs)	18(3.1) to (3.7)
Work space in home	18(12)
Meals, beverages, and entertainment costs	67.1
Limitation—cost of automobile	13(7)(g)
Interest cost on automobile	67.2
Limitation—cost of leasing automobile	67.3
Capital cost allowance and amortization of intangibles (goodwill, etc.)	20(1)(a), (b)
Interest expense	20(1)(c)
Costs incurred to borrow money and issue shares	20(1)(e), (e.2)
Landscaping	20(1)(aa)
Reserve for doubtful debts	20(1)(l)
Bad debt expense	20(1)(p)
Capitalization of borrowing costs	21
Reserve for amount not due until later year	20(1)(n)
Cost of representation	20(1)(cc)
Investigation of site	20(1)(dd)
Convention expenses	20(10)
Private health services plan	20.01
Disposal of proprietorship business (year end)	25(1)
Scientific research and experimental development	37(1), (2)
Work in progress—professionals	34, 10(4), 12(1)(b)
Unpaid remuneration	78(4)
Farming—cash basis	28(1)
Restricted farm loss	31

Canada Customs and Revenue Agency Publications

IT-459	Adventure or concern in the nature of trade.
IT-454	Business transactions prior to incorporation.
IT-364	Commencement of business operations.
IT-462	Payments based on production or use.
IT-426	Shares sold subject to an earn-out agreement.
IT-92R2	Income of contractors.
IT-487	General limitation on deduction of expenses.
IT-521R	Motor vehicle expenses for self-employed individuals.
IT-442R	Bad debts and reserve for doubtful debts.
IT-215R	Reserves and contingent accounts.
IT-154R	Special reserves.
IT-152R3	Special reserves—sale of land.
IT-518R	Food, beverages, and entertainment expenses.
IT-473R	Inventory valuation.
IT-151R4	Scientific research and experimental development.
IT-148R3	Recreational facilities and club dues.
IT-514	Work space in a home.
IT-104R2	Deductibility of fines and penalties.
IT-467R	Damage settlements and similar payments.
IT-490	Barter transactions.
IT-457R	Election by professionals to exclude work in progress from income.
IT-433	Farming—use of the cash method.
IT-322R	Farm losses.

Major Court Decisions

MNR v. Taylor, 57 DTC 1125—Adventure or concern in the nature of trade.

Regal Heights v. MNR, 60 DTC 1270—Capital gain versus business income (intention).

Canderel Limited v. The Queen, 98 DTC 6100—Meaning of profit.

Toronto College Park Ltd. v. The Queen, 98 DTC 6088—Meaning of profit.

The Queen v. Metropolitan Properties Co. Ltd., 85 DTC 5128—Meaning of profit; generally accepted accounting principles.

Royal Trust Company v. MNR, 57 DTC 1055—Purpose of earning income.

Booth v. MNR, 79 DTC 595; also, *Speck v. MNR*, 88 DTC 1518—Purpose of earning income.

British Insulated and Helsby Cables Ltd. v. Atherton (United Kingdom—1926)— Meaning of capital expenditure.

Mulder Bros. Sand and Gravel Ltd. v. MNR, 67 DTC 475—Reasonableness of an expense.

Tonn et al. v. The Queen, 96 DTC 6001—Reasonable expectation of profit.

Other Publications

Carr, B., "Current Receipts and Disbursements After Canderel, Toronto College Park, and Ikea," *Canadian Tax Journal,* Vol. 46, No. 5 (1998), p. 953.

Chow, G., "Old Wine in New Bottles— Adventure in the Nature of Trade," Report of Proceedings of the 48th Tax Conference (1996), Canadian Tax Foundation, p. 26.1.

Starkman, "Reasonable Expectation of Profit," *CA Magazine*, Jan./Feb. 1997.

Roy, J., "Taxing the Virtual Office," Report of Proceedings of the 48th Tax Conference (1996), Canadian Tax Foundation, p. 31.1.

Katz and Morgan, "The New Provisions Regarding Business Year Ends," *Canadian Tax Journal*, Vol. 45, No. 1 (1997), p. 146.

Webb, G., "GAAP and the Canadian Income Tax Act," Report of Proceedings of the 49th Tax Conference (1997), Canadian Tax Foundation, p. 10.1.

Demonstration Questions

Question One

TR Ltd. is a Canadian-controlled private corporation operating a franchised retail and mail order business in Vancouver. Denver Chan, the company's president, owns 100% of the corporation's share capital. The corporation was created on December 1, 20X7. For the year ended November 30, 20X8, TR earned a profit before income taxes of $126,000.

You have been retained to help prepare the company's first tax return and to advise on other tax-related matters. Financial information relating to the 20X8 taxation year is summarized below.

1. The following properties were purchased for the new business:

Franchise	$40,000
Land	30,000
Building	270,000
Delivery truck	40,000

The above items were recorded as assets on the balance sheet. The franchise, purchased on December 1, 20X7, permits the corporation to operate under the TR name for a period of 15 years.

The land cost of $30,000 consists of the purchase price of $20,000 plus $7,000 for permanent landscaping and $3,000 for water and sewer connections.

Depreciation and amortization expense of $28,000 has been deducted from income.

2. Legal fees include the following costs:

Preparing annual corporate minutes	$ 300
Incorporation costs for TR Ltd.	1,500
Negotiation of franchise agreement	2,000
Preparing and registering a mortgage loan	1,000

3. Repairs and maintenance expense includes the following items:

Paving the parking lot	$8,000
Cleaning and supplies	1,400
Replacing a broken window	1,000

4. Advertising expense includes a cost of $7,000 to acquire a permanent mailing list for the mail order business. The list has an expected life of six years. Other advertising items are listed below:

Cost of making a television commercial	$25,000
Travel costs for Chan to attend a franchiser convention.	
Chan's spouse travelled with him and attended	
social functions (her expenses were $1,500).	3,000
Charitable donations	2,000
Meals and beverage costs for entertaining suppliers	1,800
Costs of leasing and maintaining a pleasure boat to entertain	
suppliers and employees	2,600
Television advertising:	
Vancouver station	11,000
Seattle station (directed at the Vancouver market)	6,000

5. A contingent reserve for possible defective products of $5,000 was recorded as a charge against cost of sales. During the year, $3,000 of products were returned.

6. On May 31, 20X8, TR invested $40,000 in a one-year bank certificate earning annual interest of 7%. TR intends to recognize the interest revenue upon receipt at its one-year anniversary date.

7. Interest expense includes $14,000 on the building mortgage and $700 from a temporary bank loan of $12,000. The bank loan funds were in turn loaned, without interest, to Y Ltd., a corporation owned by Chan's brother. Y Ltd. used all of its assets to operate an active business but in November 20X8 declared bankruptcy. The loss has been deducted from income as a bad debt.

8. Capital cost allowance for tax purposes has been correctly calculated to be $22,000.

9. Salary expense includes the following:

Wages to employees	$130,000
Year-end bonus to Chan—$5,000 was paid on	
November 30, 20X8, $4,000 is payable on January 31, 20X9,	
and $6,000 is payable on June 30, 20X9	15,000
Automobile allowance paid to an employee	
(10 000 kilometres × 45¢)	4,500

Required:

Determine TR Ltd.'s *income from business* for tax purposes for the 20X8 taxation year. In addition, identify any other types of income or loss that occurred in the year.

Solution:

Income per financial statement	$126,000
Landscaping cost is a capital item but is specifically allowed as a deduction—20(1)(aa).	(7,000)
Utility connection is a capital item but is specifically allowed as a deduction—20(1)(ee).	(3,000)
Depreciation and amortization is not deductible under the general rule—18(1)(b).	28,000
Legal fee for incorporation is a capital item—18(1)(b)—but it qualifies as an eligible capital expenditure to be deducted over a period of years (see Chapter 6).	1,500
Legal fee for negotiating franchise agreement is a capital item—18(1)(b)—but qualifies for capital cost allowance.	2,000
Legal fee for preparing mortgage is a capital item but is specifically allowed to be deducted over five years as an expense of borrowing money—20(1)(e), ⅕ × $1,000.	800
Paving a parking lot is a capital item but qualifies for capital cost allowance.	8,000
Mailing list is a capital item but qualifies as an eligible capital expenditure to be deducted over a period of years (see Chapter 6).	7,000
Cost of making a television commercial is a capital item but qualifies for capital cost allowance.	25,000
Spouse travel is a personal item—18(1)(h).	1,500
Charitable donations are not for the purpose of earning income—18(1)(a)—but a deduction will be allowed when calculating taxable income for the corporation (see Chapter 11).	2,000
Meals and beverage expenses are limited to 50% of the actual cost—67.1—50% × $1,800.	900
Boat lease and maintenance is specifically disallowed even though it is for the purpose of earning income—18(1)(l)	2,600
Television advertising on a foreign station and directed to the Canadian market is specifically disallowed—19.	6,000
Contingent reserve for defective products is not allowed under the general rule that disallows reserves—18(1)(e).	5,000
Actual costs for replacing defective products are permitted.	(3,000)
Interest expense on the bank loan used to make an interest-free loan is not for the purpose of earning income—18(1)(a).	700
The loss on the loan to Chan's brother cannot be claimed as a business bad debt because the loss is a capital loss (see Chapter 8 for tax treatment).	12,000
Capital cost allowance is deductible—20(1)(a).	(22,000)
The bonus payable is unpaid remuneration and cannot be deducted on an accrual basis if it is not paid before 180 days of the taxation year. In this case, $6,000 is beyond the limit—78(4).	6,000
Automobile allowances are limited 42¢ on the first 5 000 km and 36¢ on the excess, assuming that the allowance is not taxable to the employee. Adjustment is $4,500—(5 000 km × 42¢—36¢ × 5 000 km) =	600
Income from business	$200,600

Other sources of income and loss:

The interest income on the bank certificate is classified as property income (see Chapter 7). No income was recorded in the 20X8 taxation year; however, corporations are required to include interest income on an accrual basis, and therefore taxable property income of $1,800 ($40,000 × 7% × 6 months/12 months) must be included in the current taxation year.

The loss of the $12,000 loan to Chan's brother is a capital loss. It qualifies as an allowable business investment loss because the loan was made to a small business corporation that used all of its assets in an active business. The loss for tax purposes is $6,000 (½ × $12,000) and is deductible against all sources of income.

Question Two

In 20X7, HP Ltd. acquired two parcels of land. Parcel 1 was located adjacent to HP Ltd.'s retail store and was purchased for the purpose of providing additional parking for its customers.

Parcel 2 was located three blocks away from the retail store. It was acquired after the president of HP obtained information that a new bridge would be built nearby connecting two populated areas of the city. The president was certain that the property's value would rise and that it could be sold at a profit, giving the company increased funds to help retire a debt.

In 20X8, both properties were sold. Parcel 1 was sold when a public parking facility opened across the street, thereby removing the need for HP to expand its own lot. Parcel 2 was sold to a land developer. Details of the land transactions are as follows:

	Parcel 1	Parcel 2
Original cost	$70,000	$100,000
Selling price	60,000	250,000

Parcel 1 was sold for cash. Parcel 2 sold for $25,000 cash in 20X8 with the balance to be paid over the next five years at the rate of $45,000 per year plus an agreed interest rate. HP Ltd.'s only other income in 20X8 was the profit from the retail store of $100,000.

Required:

Determine the minimum net income for tax purposes for the 20X8 taxation year for HP Ltd. Ignore the tax implications of interest on the deferred proceeds from the land.

Solution:

First, it is necessary to determine the type of income earned from each of the land sales. Parcel 1 was acquired for the purpose of providing a long-term benefit to the retail business by improving the parking facilities. It was sold only after the need for parking was removed by the fortuitous construction of a public parking facility close by. The sale of parcel 1 is, therefore, a capital transaction, and the resulting loss on sale is a capital loss, of which one-half is allowable for tax purposes. HP Ltd. does not have any taxable capital gains in 20X8; therefore, the capital loss cannot be deducted in 20X8 in accordance with the formula for net income determination established in Chapter 3.

On the other hand, parcel 2 was purchased with the intention of reselling it at a profit. The land is considered to be inventory, and the resulting gain is business income. Because $225,000 of the proceeds ($250,000 − $25,000) is deferred to future years, a reserve can be deducted from the gain in 20X8. However, the full gain must be included in income by the end of the third taxation year following the taxation year in which the sale was made.

The net income for tax purposes in 20X8 is $115,000, calculated as follows:

Business income:		
Profit from retail store		$100,000
Sale of parcel 2		
Selling price	$250,000	
Cost	(100,000)	
	150,000	
Less reserve for deferred proceeds:		
$225,000/$250,000 × $150,000 =	(135,000)	15,000
Income from business		115,000
Taxable capital gains:	–0–	
Allowable capital loss:		
½ ($60,000 – $70,000)	(5,000)	–0–
Income for tax purposes		$115,000

Review Questions

1. In order to earn business income, a taxpayer must be involved in an undertaking that constitutes a business. For tax purposes, briefly define "business."

2. Explain the term "adventure or concern in the nature of trade," and provide an example of such an activity.

3. Can an item of property (such as land) that has the potential to provide a long-term benefit to its owner create business income or a business loss when it is sold? Explain.

4. To what extent, if any, does the tax treatment of property that is classified as inventory rather than as capital property affect a taxpayer's financial risk in acquiring such property?

5. A taxpayer's income from business for tax purposes is defined simply as "the profit therefrom." Explain what is meant by this.

6. What impact do the accounting concepts of revenue recognition, accrual, and matching have on the determination of business income for tax purposes?

7. To what extent, if any, does the definition of business income for tax purposes deviate from the general definition of profit? (Note: this relates to the answer to question 5.)

8. Explain why the following expenditures are not deductible in arriving at business income for tax purposes, even though they may be consistent with the general definition of profit.

   (a) Small donations to a large number of charitable organizations.
   (b) A fee paid to a real estate consultant for finding an appropriate building for storing the inventory of a wholesale business.

(c) A reserve for the anticipated cost of product guarantees relating to products sold in the current year.

(d) The cost of entertaining business clients at the wedding of the daughter of the owner of the business.

(e) Fees paid to an architect to draw a set of plans for the expansion of a company's head office building.

(f) Office rent of $40,000 annually, when the building is valued at $100,000 and is owned by the spouse of the corporation's primary shareholder.

9. Explain why a business, in determining net income from business for tax purposes, can deduct a reserve for potentially uncollectible accounts receivable but cannot deduct a reserve for anticipated sales returns.

10. What is the significance of sections 18 and 20 of the *Income Tax Act*?

11. A business maintains a policy of providing memberships for senior employees at social clubs and clubs with sporting facilities. In some circumstances such memberships are provided mainly to improve the business contacts of the employers; in others they are provided solely as compensation. Explain the tax treatment of this kind of expense. In your answer, refer to the general rules for determining income from business.

12. What is the tax treatment when an item of inventory is sold in a particular year but the customer is required to pay for the item in equal annual instalments over four years?

13. At the end of its taxation year, a business has two unsold items of inventory. Item A has a cost of $10,000 and a market value of $15,000. Item B has a cost of $7,000 and a market value of $4,000. For tax purposes, what valuation methods can be used to determine ending inventory? Determine these amounts based on the information provided.

14. One often hears the comment "A business keeps two sets of records—one for the bank and one for tax purposes." While this comment has sinister connotations, to what extent is it not sinister? Explain how the failure to maintain separate records for tax purposes may reduce a company's rate of return on business activities.

15. Briefly compare and contrast the general treatment for tax purposes of employment income and business income.

Problems

Problem One

X, Y, and Z each purchased an identical piece of land at a cost of $4,000.

- X constructed a restaurant on her land and operated it profitably for several years.
- Y did nothing with her land. It simply remained unused for several years.
- Z rented out his land for a number of uses—car parking, summer carnivals, and so on. Reasonable returns were achieved.

Four years later, X, Y, and Z each sold their land for $12,000. X sold the land as part of the sale of the restaurant business. Y subdivided the land into three separate parcels and sold each for $4,000. Z had no intention of selling the land but received an offer that he felt he could not refuse.

Required:

Is the gain on sale of the land ($12,000 – $4,000 = $8,000) income from business for X, Y, and Z? Explain.

Problem Two

Shirley Jensen terminated her employment on May 31, 20X0, after earning taxable employment income of $20,000. On June 1, 20X0, she opened a proprietorship retail store. She has been informed that the taxation year for the business should be the calendar year. However, she is aware that an election can be made that permits her to use a non-calendar fiscal year. She has indicated that for administrative reasons, the desirable fiscal year end is May 31 of each year. Before she makes a decision, Jensen wants to know the tax implications of choosing one method over the other.

Her profits from the retail store for the next few years are estimated to be as follows:

	December 31	May 31
20X0—seven months	$50,000	–0–
20X1	85,000	85,000
20X2	90,000	90,000

Income tax rates for each year are assumed to be 30% on the first $30,000 of income, 40% on the next $30,000, and 50% on income over $60,000. Jensen will have no other sources of income in each of the years except the employment income of $20,000 in 20X0.

Required:

With the information provided, outline the tax consequences to Jensen for each alternative method of determining business income for each of the three taxation years. Which method will you recommend?

Problem Three

P.Q. Enterprises operates a wholesale business. Most of its sales are made on credit. Accounts receivable, therefore, make up a large portion of the company's balance sheet. At year end, the accounts receivable totalled $450,000. Of this amount, management estimates that $25,000 might not be collectible because no payments on account have been made for over 90 days.

In addition, the company loaned $15,000 to a former friend of the owner, charging 13% interest. This loan is also considered to be doubtful, as the friend refuses to acknowledge the existence of the debt.

Required:

1. What amount, if any, can be deducted from income in this particular year?

2. Assume that in the next year the doubtful accounts of $25,000 are re-analyzed, with the following results:

Still doubtful	$15,000
Considered good	4,000
Legally bankrupt	6,000
	$25,000

What is the tax impact in this second year?

Problem Four

Carl Fenson of Winnipeg owned three taxicabs that operated for 24 hours a day (two shifts of 12 hours). Fenson worked one shift himself and hired drivers for the other shifts. At the time, in addition to the normal taxi licence, a special licence was required to deliver passengers to Winnipeg International Airport. This special licence was referred to as a "one way" licence because it could be used to deliver passengers to the airport but not to pick up customers there. The licences were issued for 10-year renewable terms.

In 20X1 Fenson purchased three additional airport licences for $10,000 each, even though he did not have vehicles for their use. He immediately resold two of the licences for $18,000 each to a relative. Shortly thereafter, he purchased a mini-van, assigned the third new licence to that vehicle, and rented the van with the licence to a third party.

In 20X3 Transport Canada converted all one-way licences to two-way licences. In response to an unsolicited offer, Fenson cancelled the van lease and sold the third licence for $45,000.

Required:

What type of income did Fenson earn from the licence sales? Explain.

Problem Five

Demo Ltd., a Canadian-controlled private corporation, sold two parcels of land during its 20X0 taxation year. Details of each transaction are as follows:

1. A one-hectare site in Winnipeg was sold for $200,000. The full price was received in cash. The land had been purchased five years before for $160,000. Demo had intended to construct a warehouse on the land for the purpose of storing inventory for its 12 retail stores. Subsequently, it was decided that the warehouse should be located in Saskatoon; for this reason, the Winnipeg site was sold.

2. A two-hectare site in Calgary was sold for $600,000. The land had been purchased two years previously for $320,000, with the intention that it would be sold after property values increased. Demo received a $90,000 down payment in 20X0. The full balance of the purchase price is due and payable in 20X4.

Required:

1. Determine the minimum increase to the 20X0 income for tax purposes of Demo Ltd. as a result of the two property sales (ignore interest considerations on any unpaid balance).

2. In what year will the entire taxable gain, if any, be recognized for the Calgary property?

Problem Six

The controller of Mead Pipes Ltd. is completing the preparation of the corporation's 20X1 tax return but is uncertain about the tax treatment of the following eight expense items:

1. Finder's fee to obtain a mortgage on the company's buildings. — $6,000

2. Property taxes on the company's new fishing lodge, which is used by employees. — 1,200

3. Interest for late payment of municipal property taxes for the warehouse. — 600

4. Brokers' fees for the purchase of publicly traded shares.   1,400

5. Permanent landscaping of land around the head office buildings.   4,800

6. Cost of investigating a site for a proposed warehouse, when the site
   was rejected.   2,000

7. Hockey tickets to entertain customers.   1,800

8. Reserve for the possible costs for guarantees of products sold in the year.   8,000

Required:
Determine the amount by which the preceding items will reduce the net income for tax purposes of Mead Pipes Ltd. for 20X1. When an item has been totally excluded from your calculation, provide a brief reason why.

Problem Seven

Sharon Cloutier is semi-retired and sits on the board of directors of several Canadian public corporations. A summary of her 20X0 financial activity is presented below.

Interest on long-term bonds.	$20,000
Gain on sale of farmland. Cloutier acquired the farmland three years ago with the intention of subdividing it into building lots for resale, but sold it in 20X0 after losing a rezoning application.	13,000
Director's fees from public corporations.	22,000
Gain on sale of public corporations shares.	16,000
Legal fees paid to collect a bonus on a former employment contract.	2,000
Legal fees paid to dispute an income tax reassessment.	1,500
Loss on sale of shares of a Canadian-controlled private corporation that qualifies as a small business corporation.	8,000
Loss on sale of public corporation shares.	20,000
Share of the operating loss from a partnership that operates a small grain farm with hired help.	18,000
Qualified moving expenses.	1,000

Required:
Determine Cloutier's income for tax purposes in accordance with section 3 of the *Income Tax Act*.

Problem Eight

Central Products Ltd. is in the process of completing its 20X0 financial statements and tax return. A junior accountant has given you a list of items that he does not know how to treat for tax purposes. The list includes the following eight items:

1. Purchase price of a patent giving the company exclusive rights to
   manufacture a product. $120,000

2. Cost of annual dues to a golf club for three senior salespeople to
   entertain existing and potential customers.   8,000

3. The union contract expired four months before the year end and
   bargaining is still in process. A 3% wage increase is expected, and the
   company has recorded a reserve to cover the four-month period.   60,000

4. Legal fees paid for making a representation to a provincial government against a proposal to introduce a payroll tax.   15,000

5. Donations paid to a registered federal political party that advocates more international trade incentives.   10,000

6. Advertising in a foreign trade newspaper that was distributed to Canadian customers.   4,000

7. Travel costs (airfare and lodging) for a senior executive to visit a foreign supplier to inspect and sign a purchase agreement for a new manufacturing machine. The machine was delivered and used in 20X0.   3,000

8. Legal, accounting, and printing costs to prepare a prospectus offering common shares for sale to the public.   32,000

Required:

Describe how each of the above items will be treated for tax purposes for the 20X0 taxation year.

Problem Nine

Simone Cherniak has just completed the second year of operating her own veterinary clinic. You have been retained by Cherniak for tax assistance and advice. At a recent meeting, you gathered information on her practice, which is presented below.

For the year ended December 31, 20X2, the clinic showed a profit of $123,700, as follows:

Professional service	$321,000
Gross profit from surgical instrument sales	28,000
	349,000
Administration and other expenses	228,300
	120,700
Interest income	3,000
Net income	$123,700

Included in the above is depreciation/amortization expense of $23,000 on fixed assets and amortization of development costs of $4,400. Additional information is outlined below.

1. On February 28, 20X2, Cherniak purchased a competitor's business and merged it with her own. The following assets were acquired:

Truck	$ 18,000
Equipment	50,000

2. During the year, Cherniak designed and patented a new surgical instrument. On July 1, 20X2, a legal fee of $4,000 was paid for the patent (life of 17 years) registration; this amount is included in administration expenses. In October, $16,000 was spent on consultants to research metal alloys, and this cost is being amortized as development costs in the financial statement.

3. Professional services revenue includes the value of unbilled services compiled from a work-in-progress file. At December 31, 20X2, unbilled services amounted to $27,000, compared to $18,000 at the same time last year. In 20X1, Cherniak had made an election under section 34 of the *Income Tax Act* to exclude work in process from income.

4. Some of the items included under administrative and other expenses are as follows:

Group life insurance for office staff	$1,100
Christmas gifts to staff (under $200 each)	1,400
Dues to golf club (for employee)	1,200
Meals and drinks for clients	400
Books (15-volume set on veterinary medicine)	3,000
Interest on car loan (six months)	2,100
Finder's fee for a loan to finance equipment	1,000

5. The income statement includes a cost of $3,150 for attending three conventions during the year. Convention #1 ($750) was in July 20X2. Conventions #2 ($1,350) and #3 ($1,050) were both in December 20X2. Each convention includes a cost of $100 for meals. For each of the December conventions, the airfare of $200 was included in accounts payable at the end of the year.

6. Vehicle costs include operating costs of $2,400 for the automobile (including $400 for car parking). The automobile was driven 20 000 km. Of this, 12 000 km was for customer travel, 2 000 km was for travel between home and the clinic, and 6 000 km was for personal travel.

7. Cherniak expects that a number of the new manufactured surgical instruments will be returned for modification, which she will do at no extra cost to the customer. The income statement includes a $2,000 deduction based on her estimate of the returns. As of December 31, 20X2, $800 of costs were incurred for returned items.

8. Cherniak moved from rented premises to new rented premises on February 28, 20X2, with 20 months remaining on the old lease. The landlord accepted a payment of $8,000 in exchange for cancelling the lease. The accounting records have amortized this cost over the remainder of the lease term, and accordingly have deducted $4,000 ($8,000 × 10m/20m) as rent expense.

9. Capital cost allowance for tax purposes has been correctly calculated as $15,000.

Required:
Determine Cherniak's income from business for tax purposes for the 20X2 taxation year. Identify any other sources of income that are taxable in the year.

Problem Ten
The financial information shown in the table at the top of the next page was presented for Massive Enterprises Ltd. for the year ending May 31, 20X1.

Statement of Income

Sales		$1,700,000
Cost of sales		930,000
Gross profits		770,000
Expenses:		
Salaries and wages	$135,000	
Management bonuses	50,000	
Employee benefits	30,000	
Interest expenses	9,000	
Insurance	7,000	
Appraisal costs	8,000	
Legal and accounting	12,000	
Repairs and maintenance	22,000	
Travel	8,000	
Advertising and promotion	10,000	
Bad debts	36,000	
Provision for sales returns	17,000	
Depreciation/amortization	16,000	
Donations	4,000	
Loss on sale of marketable securities	6,000	370,000
		400,000
Other income:		
Interest on government bonds	$ 10,000	
Net gains on sales of land	40,000	50,000
Net income		$ 450,000

Additional Information:*

1. Cost of sales:

Opening inventory (at cost)	$ 280,000
Purchases	970,000
	1,250,000
Closing inventory (at lower of cost or market)	320,000
Cost of sales	$ 930,000

The closing inventory at the end of the previous year was valued at the lower of cost or market, which amounted to $270,000.

2. The salaries and wages of $135,000 included salaries of $45,000 to the president, $30,000 to the president's spouse (who worked as a full-time manager), and $15,000 to a full-time housekeeper, who looked after the children so that the president's spouse could work full-time in the business.

* All relates to the statement of income.

3. Management bonuses:

Bonuses awarded and paid during the current year	$10,000
Bonuses awarded at the end of the current year, to be paid (with interest) at the end of the following fiscal year	30,000
Bonuses awarded at the end of the current year and paid on June 30, 20X1	10,000
	$50,000

4. Employee benefits:

Canada Pension Plan and Employment Insurance	$ 5,000
Lump sum past service contribution to the company pension plan for one particular employee	10,000
Contributions to the company's pension plan for several employees (maximum contribution for each employee was $3,000)	9,000
Annual club dues to three golf clubs for senior managers	6,000
	$30,000

5. Interest expense included interest of $8,000 on a bank loan that was used to purchase new equipment during the previous year. In addition, $1,000 of interest arising from deficient income tax instalments was paid to CCRA.

6. Insurance expenses:

Public liability insurance for the current year	$ 2,000
Three-year fire and theft insurance premium beginning the first day of the current taxation year	3,000
Life insurance on the president of the company (required as collateral for a bank loan)	2,000
	$ 7,000

7. Appraisal costs:

To determine the replacement cost of business assets to establish the current year's fire and theft insurance requirements	$ 5,500
To value the assets of the business in order to establish the company's share value so that the shareholder could use the shares as collateral for a personal bank loan	2,500
	$ 8,000

8. Legal and accounting expenses:

Legal fees:	
To collect an account receivable	$ 400
Cost of amending the Articles of Incorporation	1,000
Costs of issuing a new class of preference shares and debentures	3,000
Accounting:	
Tax consultations for a submission to a federal government task force on sales tax reform	2,000
Annual audit fees	5,600
	$12,000

9. Repair and maintenance costs:

Office cleaning, snow removal, lawn care	$ 2,000
Cost of landscaping grounds	1,000
Repainting several offices	4,000
Engine replacement for four delivery trucks	15,000
	$22,000

10. Travel costs (incurred for sales personnel):

Airfares	$ 5,000
Meals and beverages while travelling	3,000
	$ 8,000

11. Advertising and promotion costs:

Catalogues	$ 6,000
Meals and beverages for employees entertaining customers	3,000
Promotional pens	1,000
	$10,000

12. Bad debts expense of $36,000 represented an increase in the reserve for doubtful accounts receivable arising from the sale of merchandise.

13. As a result of past experience, the company began a new policy of providing a reserve of 1% of sales for expected future returns of defective merchandise sold. Although the year's provision was $17,000, only $12,000 of merchandise was returned.

14. The depreciation/amortization expense of $16,000 was based on the estimated useful life of depreciable property owned (equipment and vehicles). The related capital cost allowance amount was $19,000.

15. The loss on sale of securities resulted from the sale of shares in public corporations. These were acquired several years earlier using excess funds not needed for the business.

16. The net gain on the sale of land of $40,000 consisted of the following:

- *Property 1*, which was acquired three years earlier at a cost of $100,000 as a potential site for a new head office building. However, new leased space became available, thus eliminating the need for a new building. Because of this the land has been sold at the market price of $160,000.

- *Property 2*, which was purchased four years earlier with excess corporate funds after it was learned that a new shopping centre was being planned for the area. The company believed that the new shopping centre would enhance property values, and purchased the land at a cost of $90,000 in the hope that it could be sold at a substantial profit. But the shopping centre proposal was cancelled, and the land was sold in the current year for $70,000.

Required:

1. For the year ended May 31, 20X1, determine the company's net income from business for tax purposes.

2. Also, determine the company's overall net income for tax purposes in accordance with the aggregating formula.

Problem Eleven

At a recent executive meeting of H Co., the president complained, "Our compensation program is unimaginative because we pay our employees by salary or commission only. Surely there are other forms of compensation which would make our company more attractive to employees."

Required:

As the personnel manager of H Co., prepare a list of compensation alternatives. For each, briefly describe the tax consequences to both the employee and the employer.

Problem Twelve

Carlson Electronics Ltd. is a Canadian-controlled private corporation that wholesales electronics equipment. The company also manufactures a small switching device and has begun a research program to improve the product.

The controller has just completed the first draft of the financial statements for the year ended December 31, 20X1. A profit of $100,000 is indicated. The company has recently secured some new major customers, and next year's profits are expected to be $470,000. The current year's income statement and next year's projected income statement are as in the table at the top of the next page.

	20X1 actual	20X2 projected
Sales	$1,280,000	$1,950,000
Cost of sales	810,000	1,108,000
Gross profit	470,000	842,000
Other expenses:		
Selling	146,000	162,000
Administrative	170,000	164,000
Research and development	62,000	54,000
	378,000	380,000
	92,000	462,000
Other income:		
Gain on sale of land	8,000	8,000
Net income	100,000	470,000

As a Canadian-controlled private corporation, the company pays tax at an assumed rate of 20% on its first $300,000 of annual active business income and at 40% on income in excess of $300,000.

At a meeting with the company president, the controller provides the following additional information:

• As a result of improved administration and a revised credit policy, the amount of uncollectible receivables has declined. In fact, the 20X1 administrative expenses include a reserve for doubtful accounts of only $21,000; the previous year's reserve was $70,000.

• The research and development expense of $62,000 in 20X1 includes direct costs (wages and materials) for designing and testing an improved switching device. Of these costs, 90% qualify as scientific research and experimental development costs for income tax purposes.

• In 20X1 the corporation sold a parcel of land for $216,000. The land, which is next to a proposed real estate development, was acquired the previous year for $200,000. Carlson had hoped to turn a quick profit by holding the land until a public announcement about the project was made. The selling price of $216,000 consisted of cash of $108,000, with the remaining amount of $108,000 payable (with interest) in 20X2. In accordance with the income tax provisions, the gain of $16,000 is being recognized as income over two years ($8,000 per year), and this is reflected in the financial statements.

Whenever possible, the company takes advantage of purchase discounts offered by its suppliers. Most suppliers offer a purchase discount of 2% of the merchandise cost if payment is made within 10 days; otherwise, the full purchase price is payable at the end of 30 days, with substantial interest charged thereafter. Owing to the anticipated sales volume increase for 20X2, the company's purchases will be heavy during the early part of the new year. Carlson has a line of credit at the local bank and usually pays interest at 12% on its loans. Currently, it has used up all of its approved line of credit.

Required:

1. Based on the financial statements provided, what amount of tax will the company be required to pay in 20X1 and in 20X2?

2. What actions can be taken to reduce the amount of tax payable over the two-year period? Calculate the tax savings, if any, that can be achieved by these actions.

3. Should the company take the actions suggested in question 2? Why or why not?

Chapter 6   The Acquisition, Use, and Disposal of Depreciable Property

In many businesses the most significant portion of capital is invested in long-term assets such as machinery, equipment, buildings, and vehicles. Intuitively, it makes sense that, because these assets contribute to the revenue-earning process over a long period of time, the cost should be allocated to and deducted from income for tax purposes gradually. The timing of such deductions is critical, because they increase cash flow by reducing the amount of tax paid in the particular year. This enhancement of cash flow in turn makes it easier to fund the purchase of the asset by external financing.

The *Income Tax Act* departs dramatically from generally accepted accounting principles in the way it treats depreciable property. As a result, it is a source of confusion for decision makers whose task it is to acquire and dispose of a wide range of assets. It is also a source of confusion to those who examine financial statements, when they find that the amount of tax paid on business income may not conform to the known rates of tax because of the way that the deductions have been timed for accounting purposes (as opposed to tax purposes).

Although the tax method of dealing with depreciable property deviates from accounting methods, it is not overly complex. It is vital for any businessperson to understand this area of tax law, for it is not possible to contemplate the acquisition or disposal of individual assets—or an entire business—without considering it.

This chapter explains the fundamentals of the tax factors pertaining to the acquisition, use, disposition, and replacement of long-term assets by

(a) examining the rationale for a standardized format for dealing with depreciable property;
(b) outlining the general rules (and their exceptions) of the capital cost allowance system, and of the treatment of eligible capital property; and,
(c) discussing the types of business decisions that may be affected.

I. A Standardized System for Depreciable Property

Business income was defined in the previous chapter as the profit determined in accordance with well-accepted business principles and generally accepted accounting principles, subject to certain general limitations. One of the general limitations denies the deduction of any expenditure of a capital nature and, as well, denies the deduction of depreciation and amortization.[1]

Depreciation and amortization is the process of allocating the cost of a productive asset over its useful life in order to match its cost against the income that it helps to generate. (Recently, the Canadian accounting professions have dropped the term "depreciation" and now simply use the term *amortization* for all cost allocations.) The amortization/depreciation process is difficult, because it requires that the owner estimate three things with regard to the asset:

- useful life
- salvage value at the end of the useful life
- contribution to the business in each year of the useful life

As this process requires judgment, similar businesses acquiring similar assets may reach different estimates of these things and, therefore, arrive at different incomes in each of the years that the asset is used. However, over time, the total cost deducted will be the same, because the maximum deducted cannot exceed the original cost of the asset. As an example, following is the amortization expense on a $10,000 asset for business A and for business B, where A assumes a useful life of four years and an equal annual contribution to revenues, and B assumes a life of six years with a variable contribution to annual revenues. Both A and B assume no salvage value at the end of the asset's useful life.

---

1 ITA 18(1)(b).

	A Amortization	B Amortization
Year 1	$ 2,500	$ 1,000
2	2,500	2,000
3	2,500	3,000
4	2,500	2,000
5	–0–	1,000
6	–0–	1,000
	$10,000	$10,000

If A and B were permitted to use the above for tax purposes, the timing of the respective tax reductions would vary. Considering that a tax saving today is worth more than a tax saving tomorrow, the net after-tax cost of acquiring the asset would be different for each business. If we further assumed that both A and B paid tax at a rate of 40% and could invest their cash at an after-tax return of 15%, the tax savings and net after-tax cost of the asset to each business would be as shown in the table below.

	A Tax saving 40% of amortization	B Tax saving 40% of amortization
Year 1	$ 1,000	$ 400
2	1,000	800
3	1,000	1,200
4	1,000	800
5	–0–	400
6	–0–	400
Total cash saved	$ 4,000	$ 4,000
Net present value @ 15%	$ 2,855	$ 2,571
Cost of asset	$10,000	$10,000
Less net present value of tax savings	2,855	2,571
Net after-tax cost of asset	$ 7,145	$ 7,429

In this simple example, A is better off than B simply because it chose a faster amortization stream. For this reason, accounting amortization/depreciation is disallowed, and a uniform and arbitrary allocation of the asset's cost is imposed for tax purposes. The result is that all businesses have similar results relating to the purchase of similar assets.

The uniform system divides capital assets into two general categories. The first category is referred to as *depreciable capital property* and includes, primarily, tangible assets such as equipment.[2] The allocation of the capital cost of the asset is given the term "capital cost allowance." The second category is referred to as *eligible capital property* and includes only intangible assets.[3] Examples of assets in the second category are purchased goodwill, incorporation costs, and unlimited life franchises and licences. Each of these categories is discussed separately below.

---

2   ITA 13(21), 20(1)(a).

3   ITA 14(5), 20(1)(b).

II. Depreciable Property and Capital Cost Allowance

In general, the calculation of capital cost allowance (CCA) consists of a few basic steps. One starts with the opening balance, then adds additional purchases and deducts any disposals. The appropriate CCA rate is then applied to obtain the deduction for tax purposes for the current year. However, in order to use this simple calculation, it is necessary to establish who qualifies for CCA, which assets qualify, which rates of CCA apply to particular assets, and when gains or losses on disposal of individual assets are recognized. As usual, there are some exceptions to the standard format.

A. Who Qualifies for CCA? and What Assets?

Both individuals and corporations qualify for capital cost allowance, provided that they acquire particular capital assets that are used for the purpose of producing income. The guidelines for determining whether or not an expenditure is of a capital nature were introduced briefly in the previous chapter and are discussed further in Chapter 8. Taxpayers who carry on a business or use assets to earn investment income can claim CCA on a number of different types of assets. Also, individuals who are employed are entitled to claim CCA on automobiles and aircraft they are required to use in the course of their employment duties.[4]

Business entities and investors can claim CCA on all tangible assets other than land. CCA can also be claimed on some but not all intangible assets (discussed below). To be eligible for CCA

(a) the taxpayer must have legal title to the property or have all the incidents of title, such as possession, use, and risk;[5] and,

(b) the asset must be available for use for the purpose of earning income from business or investments.[6]

This means that a building under construction, or equipment not assembled, does not qualify for CCA until construction or assembly is complete.

The total dollar amount available for allocation as CCA is referred to as the "capital cost" of the asset. The capital cost amount consists of the original purchase price plus all costs incurred to bring the asset to a state of working order.[7] Costs for delivery, taxes and duties, installation, and legal fees, as well as financing costs during a construction period and employee costs to bring the asset to a working state, are all part of the capital cost. Subsequent major renovations to an asset that improve that asset beyond its original condition are of a capital nature and also become part of the capital cost.[8]

B. Rates of Capital Cost Allowance

The most difficult aspect of the capital cost allowance system involves how to determine what rate of CCA applies to a particular asset. The *Income Tax Act* assigns various types of assets to specific classes.[9] Each class has a specific rate attached to it.[10] For example, automotive equipment, general-purpose electronic data processing equipment, and systems software are all included in class 10, which has been assigned a rate of 30%.

---

4   ITA 8(1)(j); IT-522R; -272R.
5   IT-285R2.
6   ITA 13(27), (28), (29).
7   IT-285R2.
8   IT-128R.
9   Income Tax Regulations—Schedule II (classes 1–44).
10 Regulation 1100(1).

This rate signifies the *maximum* that can be applied in any year.[11] There is no require-ment that the taxpayer claim this maximum—the taxpayer can choose to claim any amount it wishes to in any year up to the maximum. If the maximum is not claimed in a given year, the unclaimed portion is simply carried forward and is available in future years. Often, tax-payers who have incurred a loss will not claim CCA unless they are certain that other sources of income will be available for offset. The deduction of CCA is thus preserved for when it is needed in the future.

The system of classes ensures that different entities using similar assets will allocate the costs of those assets in a like manner. In some respects this can be inequitable; for example, a business that uses its equipment 24 hours a day must claim the same rate of CCA as one that uses similar equipment for only eight hours a day.

Since currently there are over 40 separate classes of capital assets, it is often difficult to match a specific asset with its appropriate class. Several tax services publish alphabetical lists of assets, with corresponding classifications.[12] The most common classes are listed below, together with a description of some of the assets in each class.

Class 1 (4%)	Buildings or other structures, including component parts such as plumbing, air-conditioning/heating equipment, and elevators and escalators acquired after 1987.[13]
Class 3 (5%)	Buildings, as above, acquired before 1988.
Class 8 (20%)	Equipment and machinery not included in another class, furniture, photocopiers, and facsimile machines.
Class 10 (30%)	Automotive equipment, general-purpose electronic data processing equipment and systems software, and moveable equipment.
Class 10.1 (30%)	Passenger vehicle (automobile) that has a cost greater than the prescribed amount (currently $30,000). The prescribed amount is changed periodically.
Class 12 (100%)	Small tools and kitchen utensils costing less than $200, uniforms, tableware, linens, computer software other than systems software, and videotapes.[14]
Class 13	Improvements made to leased premises.[15]
Class 14	Franchises, concessions, and licences having a limited legal life.[16] Also, patents if a choice is made to exclude them from class 44 below.
Class 17 (8%)	Parking area, including paving.
Class 24 (50%)	Pollution control equipment.
Class 43 (30%)	Property such as machinery and equipment used directly or indirectly in the manufacture or processing of goods for sale or lease.[17]
Class 44 (25%)	Patents and rights to use patents acquired after April 26, 1993.

Notice that classes 13 and 14 do not have specific rates attached to them. Both of these classes have rates that vary according to the nature of the particular asset. This will be discussed later in the chapter.

---

11 Regulation 1100(1)(a).

12 *Canadian Tax Reporter*, CCH Canadian, paragraph 5049.

13 IT-79R3.

14 IT-283R2.

15 IT-464R.

16 IT-477.

17 IT-147R3.

C. The Declining Balance Method

With a few exceptions, the capital cost allowance system uses the declining balance method of allocating capital cost over future years.[18] This method annually applies a constant percentage to the remaining undepreciated portion of the original capital cost. The percentage applied is the designated CCA rate for the class to which the asset is attached. For most classes the amount of CCA that can be claimed in the first year of an asset's acquisition is restricted to one-half the normal rate.[19] Below is a simple demonstration of this method.

Situation: In 20X0 business A, which previously occupied leased premises, purchased a small warehouse building at a cost of $200,000.

Analysis: In accordance with the summary of classes shown above, the building qualifies as a class 1 asset and must use a CCA rate of no higher than 4% annually. The results are shown in the table below.

Class 1	
(20X0)	
Capital cost building #1	$200,000
CCA: 4% × $200,000 × ½*	4,000
Undepreciated capital cost	$196,000
(20X1)	
Undepreciated capital cost	$196,000
CCA: 4% × $196,000	7,840
Undepreciated capital cost	$188,160
(20X2)	
Undepreciated capital cost	$188,160
CCA: 4% × $188,160	7,526
Undepreciated capital cost	$180,634

* One-half the normal rate in year of acquisition or when put to use.

When the constant rate of 4% is applied to the reduced balance every year, the amount of CCA declines each subsequent year. Consequently, this method of allocation results in greater tax deductions in the earlier years of an asset's life, which in turn creates higher after-tax cash flow.

Notice that this example did not provide the particular date in 20X0 when the building was acquired. This is because the date is not relevant, as the CCA rate is applied to the balance at the end of the year. The rule that permits only one-half of the normal rate to be applied in the year of acquisition reflects the fact that an asset may be acquired at any time throughout the year.

It is important to note that the one-half rule does not apply to all of the items in class 14 (discussed later in the chapter) or to certain specific items in class 12 (e.g., small tools, kitchen utensils, and linens).[20] In addition, the amount of CCA that can be claimed may

18 Regulation 1100(1)(a); ITA 13(21).
19 Regulation 1100(2); IT-285R2.
20 Regulation 1100(2).

be further limited when the taxpayer has a taxation year that is less than 365 days (for example, the first taxation year of a new corporation or proprietorship). In such cases the CCA that would otherwise apply (including the amount resulting from the application of the one-half rule) is prorated by the number of days in the taxation year divided by 365.[21]

For example, an individual starts a new business on September 1, 20X0, and purchases class 8 equipment costing $10,000. The first fiscal period ends on December 31, 20X0, and includes 122 days (September 1 to December 31). Capital cost allowance for the period is $334, calculated as follows:

$$\$10,000 \times 20\% \times \tfrac{1}{2} \times 122/365 = \$334$$

D. Pooling Assets of the Same Class

The above example dealt with the acquisition of a single asset. In most cases a business will have many assets of the same class, such as a fleet of delivery vehicles or many items of furniture and equipment. The capital cost allowance system places all assets of the same class in a common pool, provided that those assets are all used in the same business.[22] As a result, each asset loses its individual identity as it gets added to the pool of its class.

The concept of pooling assets of a similar class is demonstrated in the situation/analysis at the bottom of this page, which incorporates the previous example.

In the same way that the purchase of a new asset will add that asset to the pool, the sale of a particular asset will remove that asset from the pool. For an example, see the situation/analysis at the top of the next page.

At this point some further clarifications are needed. With respect to the application of the one-half rule in the year of acquisition, the examples provided in the situation/analysis are limited because they do not demonstrate what happens when additions and disposals occur in the same year. When this occurs, the one-half rule for CCA applies only to the extent that the additions exceed the disposals. For example, in the calculation for class 8 on the next page, the additions exceed the disposals by $10,000, so the CCA rate of 20% is reduced by one-half only on that amount.

Situation: In 20X3 business A acquired a second small warehouse building at a cost of $250,000.

Analysis:

Class 1 (4%)

(20X3)		
Undepreciated capital cost (above)		$180,634
Purchase:		
Building #2		250,000
		430,634
CCA:		
4% × $180,634	$7,225	
4% × $250,000 × ½	5,000	(12,225)
Undepreciated capital cost		$418,409

---

21 Regulation 1100(3) (does not apply to classes 14 and 15).
22 Regulation 1101(1); IT-206R.

Situation: In 20X4 building #1 was sold for $150,000 and was not replaced.

Analysis:

Class 1		
(20X4)		
Undepreciated capital cost		$418,409
Purchases		–0–
Disposals:		
Sale of building #1		(150,000)
		268,409
Capital cost allowance:		
4% × $268,409		(10,736)
Undepreciated capital cost		$257,673

Class 8 (20%)		
Undepreciated capital cost at beginning of year		$70,000
Purchases	$60,000	
Disposals	(50,000)	10,000
		80,000
Capital cost allowance:		
20% × $70,000	14,000	
20% × $10,000 × ½	1,000	(15,000)
Undepreciated capital cost		$65,000

If, in the above example, the disposals had exceeded the purchases, there would have been no requirement to apply the one-half rule.[23]

When assets are sold, the CCA pool is reduced only up to a maximum of the original capital cost of the asset disposed.[24] In the previous demonstration, building #1 was sold for $150,000 (the selling price) and the pool was reduced by that amount because it was less than the building's original cost of $200,000. If building #1 had been sold for $210,000, the class 1 pool would have been reduced by only $200,000. The excess of $10,000 would have constituted a capital gain on disposition (see Chapter 8).

E. Gains and Losses on Disposal of Depreciable Property

It is easy to compute the gain or loss on the disposition of a single asset. Consider an asset that originally cost $10,000 and that, as a result of capital cost allowance, has an undepreciated capital cost of $4,000. If the asset is sold for $5,000, a gain of $1,000 is evident; if it is sold for $3,500, a loss of $500 occurs.

However, when multiple assets are pooled in a single class under the CCA system, no gain or loss is recognized on the sale of individual assets unless the sale price is greater than the asset's original cost. When building #1 in the previous demonstration was sold for $150,000, the amount was actually less than its undepreciated balance and, therefore, a loss actually occurred. However, this loss simply remained in the pool, along with building #2, to be deducted as an expense at 4% per year over a period of time.

---

23 The one-half rule may not apply in certain circumstances when the purchaser does not deal at arm's length with the vendor.

24 TA 13(21)(d), (f)(iv); IT-220R2.

The pool concept recognizes that some assets in a given pool will be sold at less than their depreciated value and others at more. The result is that gains and losses are averaged over the life of the pool.

For tax purposes, gains and losses on depreciable property can occur at three particular points.

1. A loss has occurred if, at the end of a fiscal year, *all* assets in a class have been disposed of but a balance remains in the pool. This balance is written off in full against business or property income as a "terminal loss."[25] In effect, this loss reflects the net losses and gains accumulated over several years.

2. A gain has occurred if, at the end of any particular fiscal year, the balance of a class pool is negative, even if some assets still remain in the pool. This gain is fully taxable as business or property income and is referred to as a "recapture" or "recovery" of CCA.[26]

3. If, at any time, the selling price of a depreciable property exceeds the original cost of the specific property sold, the excess is recognized in the year as a capital gain (see Chapter 8).

Examples of these gains and losses are demonstrated below.

Situation:

In 20X1, business X acquired two items of equipment. Item A cost $10,000 and item B cost $15,000. At the end of 20X2 the undepreciated capital cost of the class was $18,000. In 20X3 items A and B were sold for $6,000 and $7,000 respectively.

Analysis:

Class 8		
(20X3)		
Opening undepreciated capital cost		$18,000
Purchases:		–0–
Disposals:		
Item A	$6,000	
Item B	7,000	(13,000)
		5,000
Terminal loss		(5,000)
Undepreciated capital cost		–0–

As no assets were left in the pool at the end of the year, the full balance of $5,000 was deducted for tax purposes in 20X3.

Consider the tax impact if business X had purchased a $300 piece of equipment on the last day of the company's fiscal year. This very small acquisition would have eliminated its ability to claim a terminal loss, because there would have been an asset left in the pool at the end of the year. If the $300 purchase had been made, the 20X3 deduction for tax purposes would have been only $1,060, as calculated at the top of the next page.

If the company had delayed the purchase of the $300 piece of equipment until the first day after the fiscal year end, the terminal loss of $5,000 would have been permitted in 20X3 and a new pool of $300 would have begun in 20X4.

---

25 ITA 13(21), (21.1), 20(16); IT-478R. A capital loss cannot occur on depreciable property (see Chapter 8).
26 ITA 13(1); IT-478R.

Class 8		
Opening undepreciated capital cost		$18,000
Purchases		300
Disposals:		
Item A	(6,000)	
Item B	(7,000)	(12,700)
		5,300
CCA: 20% × $5,300		(1,060)
Undepreciated capital cost		$ 4,240

Situation: Business X has several pieces of equipment in its class 8 pool. The undepreciated capital cost of the pool at the end of 20X0 was $16,000. In 20X1 the company sold two large pieces of equipment for a total of $20,000. The equipment sold originally cost $22,000.

Analysis:

Class 8		
Opening undepreciated capital cost		$16,000
Purchases	–0–	
Disposals		(20,000)
		(4,000)
Recapture of CCA		4,000
Undepreciated capital cost		–0–

In the above situation a recapture of CCA of $4,000 will be added to business income for tax purposes, because the pool had a negative balance at year end. The gain is recognized even though there are assets remaining in the pool. No further CCA is available on the remaining assets; when those are sold, a further recapture will occur.

Consider, also, the tax impact if the company had purchased additional equipment for $1,000 on the last day of the fiscal year. This would have reduced the amount of taxable income from the recapture from $4,000 to $3,000 as demonstrated below.

Class 8		
Opening undepreciated capital cost		$16,000
Purchases	1,000	
Disposals	(20,000)	19,000
		(3,000)
Recapture of CCA		3,000
Undepreciated capital cost		–0–

In this situation, the company knew that a recapture of $4,000 was about to occur. By purchasing additional equipment before the year end, it reduced its taxable income by the full amount of the purchase. Effectively, the new equipment of $1,000 was fully written off in the year of purchase through the elimination of recaptured CCA. It is advantageous to acquire assets before year end when a recapture is expected.

Situation:

Business X owns a building included in class 1. The undepreciated capital cost of the pool was $215,000 at the end of 20X0. The building, which originally cost $230,000, was sold in 20X1 for $235,000.

Analysis:

Class 1 (4%)	
Opening undepreciated capital cost	$215,000
Purchases	–0–
Disposals—reduction limited to original cost	(230,000)
	(15,000)
Recapture of CCA	15,000
Undepreciated capital cost	–0–
Capital gain calculation:	
Proceeds of disposition	$235,000
Cost	(230,000)
Capital gain	$ 5,000

Notice that in this situation the pool was reduced by $230,000, even though the building was sold for $235,000. This results from the rule that the pool cannot be reduced by an amount greater than the original cost of the asset sold. Therefore, in this situation the sale of the building resulted in a recapture of CCA of $15,000, which is classified as business income, plus a $5,000 capital gain, of which, as will be explained in Chapter 8, only $2,500 (½ of $5,000) is taxable.

Capital gains and recapture of CCA do not always occur at the same time, as happened in this example. Recapture depends on the pool becoming negative, and this may not occur after every sale. A capital gain, on the other hand, occurs whenever the selling price of an asset exceeds its cost amount.

F. Special Treatment of Passenger Vehicles

As previously indicated, passenger vehicles that cost more than $30,000 are considered class 10.1 assets rather than class 10. Class 10.1 was established to limit the tax deduction for luxury cars. The treatment of these vehicles is summarized below.

- CCA can be claimed on only $30,000, even though the vehicle may have cost more.[27]

- Each car is placed in its own class, and CCA is calculated on each car separately. In other words, class 10.1 assets are not pooled.[28]

- When a vehicle is sold, neither a recapture of CCA nor a terminal loss is permitted.[29]

- CCA in the first year is limited to 15%. Also, CCA of 15% is allowed in the year of sale (i.e., the terminal year). This unusual treatment is designed to provide relief from the fact that terminal losses are denied.

Note that vehicles which cost less than $30,000 qualify as regular class 10 assets and are subject to the normal treatment for depreciable property.

27 ITA 13(7)(g).
28 Regulation 1101(1af).
29 ITA 13(2), 20(16.1).

G. Special Treatment of Computers, Faxes, Photocopiers, and Manufacturing Assets

Certain types of equipment have rapid obsolescence due to rapid advances in technology. These include computers, systems software, and ancillary data processing equipment, which are pooled in class 10, as well as photocopiers, facsimile machines, and telephone equipment, which are pooled in class 8. Normally, when the equipment is sold (usually for a nominal value) or junked the undepreciated balance remains in the pool along with other assets of the class, to be depreciated at 30% or 20%, as the case may be. To address this inequity, a special rule permits the taxpayer to elect to set up a separate class of class 10 or class 8 for *each* property costing more than $1,000.[30] This means that when the equipment is sold or junked, the loss will be fully recognized for tax purposes as a terminal loss of that separate class. This rule recognizes the fact that such equipment depreciates at rates that far exceed the permitted capital cost allowance rates. However, if the asset in the separate class has not been disposed of by the beginning of the fifth taxation year from the year it was acquired, the remaining amount is transferred to the general pool of class 10 or 8, as the case may be.

Similarly, taxpayers are permitted to elect to place eligible manufacturing assets costing more than $1,000 in a separate CCA class of class 43 property: a terminal loss will then occur on disposition.

H. Exceptions to the Declining Balance Method

Several classes of assets, by their nature, do not lend themselves to the establishing of an average rate of CCA. For example, the life of improvements made to leased premises depends on the life of the particular lease contract. Similarly, the legal right to a franchise or licence is greatly affected by the agreement between the franchiser and the franchisee. These two exceptions are discussed below.

1. Leasehold Improvements

Contracts for leasing premises vary considerably. In many cases the tenants are responsible for the cost of making the space suitable to their needs. It may be necessary to install internal walls, flooring, light fixtures, and wall coverings. These expenditures represent tangible improvements to the landlord's building and, at the end of the lease, cannot be removed. Costs of this nature qualify as depreciable property and are grouped in class 13.

Under class 13 the cost of improvements for each separate lease is allocated on a straight-line basis over a period equal to the life of that particular lease plus one renewable-option period.[31] However, a minimum allocation period of five years and a maximum allocation of 40 years is imposed.

Situation:

A taxpayer in need of warehouse space enters a six-year lease agreement. The contract gives the tenant the option of renewing the lease for two additional four-year periods. If both options are exercised the tenant will have use of the building for 14 years. In year 1 the tenant spends $30,000 on leasehold improvements. At the beginning of year 4 additional improvements of $7,000 are made.

Analysis:

Under class 13, annual CCA, on a straight-line basis, is $3,000, calculated as follows:

$$\frac{\$30,000 \text{ (capital cost)}}{6 \text{ (lease term)} + 4 \text{ (1st option term)}} = \$3,000$$

In year 4 the additional capital improvements will increase CCA by $1,000 annually, calculated as follows:

$$\frac{\$7,000 \text{ (capital cost)}}{3 \text{ (remaining lease term)} + 4 \text{ (1st option term)}} = \$1,000$$

The one-half rule applies to this class. Therefore, in year 1 the deduction is reduced from $3,000 to $1,500, and in year 4 the deduction of $1,000 is reduced to $500.

---

30 Regulation 1101(5p).

31 Regulation 1100(1)(b); Regulations—Schedule III; IT-464R.

In the above example, the taxpayer has the right to use the premises for a total of 14 years (6 + 4 + 4); however, the initial cost of improvements is allocated and deducted for tax purposes over a 10-year period (6 + 4). The initial lease period and first option period are critical in determining the speed of the deductions for tax purposes. For example, the premises could be tied up for the same 14 years by having an initial lease term of four years plus three option periods of one year, five years, and four years. While this still totals 14 years, the initial improvements would be written off at $6,000 per year over five years, calculated as follows:

$$\frac{\$30,000 \text{ (capital cost)}}{4 \text{ (lease term)} + 1 \text{ (1st option term)}} = \$6,000$$

Under this arrangement the net after-tax cost of the lease would be reduced, as cash flow from the deduction of CCA in the early years would be increased and available for further investment. Normally, the granting of option periods by the landlord also calls for an adjustment to the rent, and this possibility must be examined before lease terms are negotiated.

It may be necessary to make additional improvements some years after the original lease is signed. CCA on the cost of those additional improvements is calculated separately from the CCA on the original improvements. The additional CCA is based on the number of years *remaining* in the lease plus one option period, and the one-half rule applies.

When a tenant enters into a short-term lease (less than five years), it is important to recognize the minimum write-off period of five years under the class 13 formula. For example, leasehold improvements costing $8,000 for a lease of four years (with no option to renew) result in annual capital cost allowance of $1,600, except in the first year, when the one-half rule is applied. This is calculated as follows:

Annual CCA = lesser of:

$$\frac{\$8,000}{4 \text{ (lease term)}} = \$2,000$$

$$\frac{\$8,000}{5 \text{ (minimum)}} = \$1,600$$

The undepreciated balance at the end of year 4 when the lease expires is deducted in full as a terminal loss provided that there are no other leases in the class 13 pool.

In some situations a landlord will persuade a prospective tenant to sign a lease by providing an inducement payment. The tenant can treat the inducement payment in one of two ways. The first is to include its full amount in business income in the year received. The second is to apply it as a reduction of the cost of the leasehold improvements in class 13 (see Chapter 5).[32] When the second option is chosen, the result is reduced CCA over the write-off period, which in turn creates higher taxable income (and tax) in those years. If tax rates in the future are likely to remain the same, this is usually the better option, as the income is then recognized over several future years consistent with the term of the lease.

However, if future tax rates are expected to increase, it may be better to take the first option—that is, to treat the inducement payment as income in the year of receipt. This requires an earlier payment of tax but the overall amount of tax is likely to be lower. Consider that a significant increase in tax rates often occurs in a Canadian-controlled private corporation when its business income goes beyond an annual limit of $200,000 (see Chapters 11 and 13). In such situations, paying tax in an earlier year at a lower rate may be cheaper than paying the tax over several future years at a higher rate. To make an accurate assessment, one must determine the current value of the tax cost for both options. (See the

32 ITA 12(1)(x), 13(7.4).

discussion on capital expansion and cash flow later in this chapter.) The first option may also be wise when the taxpayer has losses and no tax will result.

2. Franchises, Concessions, and Licences

Another class that has special CCA treatment is Class 14. In order to qualify under Class 14, franchises, concessions, and licences must have a *limited legal life*. If the asset has an indefinite life, it does not constitute class 14 depreciable property. Instead it is classified as eligible capital property, which is discussed later in this chapter.

The CCA is determined separately for each item in this class, as is the case with class 13 items. The annual CCA for each asset is normally calculated on the straight-line basis by multiplying the original capital cost by the number of days the property was owned in the year divided by the total number of days in the life of the asset.[33] As an alternative to the straight-line method, CCRA will accept an apportionment of the cost of the asset over its useful life on *any reasonable basis* that reflects *economic value*.

Situation:

A company with a December 31 fiscal year end acquires a limited-life 10-year franchise on October 1, 20X0, at a cost of $50,000.

Analysis:

Class 14

(20X0)
   CCA:

$$\$50,000 \times \frac{92 \text{ (\# of days owned in 20X0)}}{3,650 \text{ (\# of days in life of franchise)}} = \$1,260$$

(20X1 and subsequent years)
   CCA:

$$\$50,000 \times \frac{365 \text{ (\# of days owned in 20X1)}}{3,650 \text{ (\# of days in life of franchise)}} = \$5,000$$

Note that in 20X0, the first year of ownership, the one-half rule was not applied. It is not necessary to apply this rule for class 14 items, as in the year of acquisition any CCA is automatically prorated for the period in the year that it was owned. Similarly, CCA is not prorated when the taxation year is less than 365 days.

In some circumstances, *patents* may be classified as class 14 property. As shown earlier in this chapter, a patent is normally classified as a class 44 property with capital cost allowance at 25% (diminishing-balance method subject to the one-half rule). A taxpayer can elect to treat a new patent acquisition as a class 14 property using the straight-line method described above.[34] This election may be beneficial if the patent acquired has a short life, in which case the write-off time may be faster.

I. Involuntary and Voluntary Dispositions

The requirement that a negative balance in a CCA class result in the recapture of CCA is often a burden when assets are disposed of and there isn't enough time available to replace them before year end. This is especially the case when the disposition is not voluntary. If assets are destroyed, lost, stolen, or expropriated, the receipt of insurance or compensation causes a disposition to occur.[35] When the disposition is forced and a recapture occurs, the taxpayer is permitted to defer recognition of the recapture if property with a similar use is

---

33 Regulation 1100(1)(c); IT-477.

34 Regulation 1103(2h).

35 ITA 13(21).

acquired within two taxation years of the year of forced disposition.[36] This two-year replacement applies to all classes of depreciable property.

A similar opportunity applies to dispositions that are voluntary. However, voluntary dispositions are provided only a one-year extension, and this extension applies only to property that is either a building or a leasehold interest in a building that is used for the purpose of earning business income.[37] The one-year extension, for example, would not apply to the voluntary disposition of a building that was used to earn property (investment) income in the form of rents. The recapture of CCA is included in income in the year of disposition but is subsequently eliminated by filing an amended tax return in the year of replacement.

J. Change in Use

Small enterprises will often use assets for business purposes that the owner had previously used for personal purposes. For example, a personal truck may be converted to business use for making deliveries, or a personal desk or business library may be converted to use in a consulting business. A change of use from personal use to business use causes a deemed disposition for tax purposes.[38] In other words, the individual is deemed to have sold and bought the asset from himself or herself at a value equal to the asset's market value at that time. If the fair market value of the asset is lower than its original cost, then the fair market value becomes the cost for tax purposes and CCA can be claimed on that amount. However, when the fair market value of the asset is *greater* than its original cost, then the amount on which CCA can be claimed is equal to the original cost plus the amount of the taxable capital gain included in income from the change in use deemed disposition (one-half of the excess of deemed proceeds over the original cost). A similar rule applies when depreciable property is sold to a non–arm's length party.

Similarly, a change in use from business use to personal use causes a disposition at fair market value.[39] This may, depending on the value and whether or not there are other assets in the class, cause a recapture of CCA or a terminal loss.

III. The Treatment of Eligible Capital Property

Many capital expenditures do not fall within the definitions of the CCA classes. Normally these items are intangible in nature and have no specific legal life. As a result it is extremely difficult to develop a logical method of allocating their cost over a time period that relates to the asset's usefulness.

Assets that fall into this category are referred to as "eligible capital property." For tax purposes all of these various types of assets are grouped together in a single pool and allocated as a deduction from income over a common, arbitrary time period.

A. Eligible Capital Property Defined

Eligible capital property can generally be defined as a capital expenditure of an intangible nature for which no other provision of the act exists that permits or specifically denies its deduction from income.[40] In effect, it is a catch-all definition that has been arrived at by the process of elimination. Some of the common types of expenditures that qualify in this category are listed below:

- goodwill
- franchises, licences, and concessions that *do not have a specific legal limited life*
- trademarks
- customer lists
- incorporation costs

---

36 ITA 13(4); IT-271R, -259R2.
37 ITA 13(4)(b); IT-259R2, -491.
38 ITA 13(7)(b).
39 ITA 13(7)(a).
40 ITA 14(5); IT-143R2, -386R.

A patent with an unlimited life normally qualifies as class 44 property with CCA at 25% (diminishing balance), but can, by election, be treated as eligible capital property.

Although the above capital expenditures have nothing in common with each other, they are, nevertheless, treated for tax purposes in a like manner. Such treatment may—as is the case with depreciable property—be significantly different from the accounting treatment under generally accepted accounting principles.

B. Goodwill Defined

The most common item of eligible capital property is goodwill. Though often encountered, its nature is often misunderstood, so it is appropriate that the meaning of goodwill be discussed in this chapter.

Goodwill is the value that is attributed to a business in excess of the sum of the values of all other, more specific assets. Consider the following list of a business's specific identifiable assets.

	Fair market value
Cash	$ 20,000
Accounts receivable	120,000
Inventory	400,000
Equipment	300,000
Land	80,000
Building	430,000
Franchise	50,000
	$1,400,000

If each of the assets listed above were sold separately, a total value of $1,400,000 would be realized. However, for an established business that is secure in the marketplace, and has a high degree of profitability, sound product lines, and good management, a buyer of the entire business may be willing to pay more than $1,400,000. If, for example, a buyer pays $1,800,000 to acquire the assets of this business in order to operate the business as a going concern, then the value attributed to the asset referred to as goodwill is as follows:

Value paid for the assets	$1,800,000
less	
Value attributed to specific assets	1,400,000
Goodwill	$ 400,000

The purchase price of $400,000 for goodwill would qualify, to the buyer, as an eligible capital expenditure for tax purposes. To qualify as eligible capital property, the goodwill must be purchased. It cannot be imputed.

C. Basic Rules for Eligible Capital Property

The deduction for eligible capital property is calculated, like capital cost allowance, using the declining-balance method. The amount available for deduction, however, is extremely low. The annual rate of write-off is 7%, and this rate is applied on a starting amount of only 75% of the original cost of the property. Individual gains and losses are not recognized at the time of sale, but rather, as with the CCA system, are averaged and recognized when the pool becomes negative or there are no assets left in the pool.[41]

---

41 IT-123R4.

There are some variations between the two systems and for this reason the eligible capital property system is summarized below.

1. 75% of the cost of all eligible capital property is added to a common pool referred to as "cumulative eligible capital."[42]

2. 75% of the selling price of any item, *even if that price is greater than the original cost*, is deducted from the common pool.[43]

3. If the pool is negative, the full amount is added to business income but only to the extent that it represents the recapture of amounts previously deducted.[44]

4. If the pool is negative and exceeds the amount that represents the recapture of amounts previously deducted (item 3 above), two-thirds ($2/3$) of that excess is added to business income (reviewed later in this section).

5. If, at year end, the pool is positive and the business is continuing, the undepreciated balance is amortized at 7% using the declining-balance method.[45]

6. If the pool is positive at the end of the year but the business has discontinued, the full balance is deducted from income as a terminal loss.[46]

7. The one-half rule does not apply in the year of acquisition. However, if the taxation year has less than 365 days, the deduction is prorated by days.

Situation: In 20X0 a corporation purchases an existing business and acquires, among other assets, a franchise (unlimited life) for $10,000 and goodwill for $50,000. In 20X2 the franchise is sold for $12,000 but the business continues.

Analysis:

Cumulative Eligible Capital	
(20X0)	
Additions:	
Franchise (75% of $10,000)	$ 7,500
Goodwill (75% of $50,000)	37,500
	45,000
20X0 amortization (7% × $45,000)	3,150
Unamortized balance	41,850
(20X1)	
Additions and disposals	–0–
	41,850
20X1 amortization (7% × $41,850)	2,930
Unamortized balance	38,920
(20X2)	
Disposal:	
Sale of franchise (75% of $12,000)	(9,000)
	29,920
20X2 amortization (7% of $29,920)	(2,094)
Unamortized balance	$27,826

42 ITA 14(5).

43 ITA 14(5).

44 ITA 14(1).

45 ITA 20(1)(b).

46 ITA 24.

Notice that although the franchise was sold for $12,000 and had a cost of $10,000 that was partly amortized, no gain on the sale was recognized. The actual gain simply reduced the pool, thereby diminishing the extent of amortization in future years.

An explanation is needed for the treatment of a negative balance to the cumulative deduction account. The treatment described previously is designed to first fully recapture the amounts previously deducted as annual write-offs of the cumulative deduction account. This is similar to the recapture of capital cost allowance. Adjusting any remaining negative amount by two-thirds ($\frac{2}{3}$) is designed to treat that portion of the gain similar to the treatment of a capital gain. To demonstrate, consider a situation where a business purchases goodwill in year 1 for $10,000 and sells it in year 2 for $12,000. The cumulative eligible capital account and income for tax purposes is calculated as follows:

Cumulative eligible capital account:	
Year 1	
Purchase of goodwill – ¾ × $10,000	$7,500
Deduction for the year – 7% × $7,500	(525)
	6,975
Year 2	
Sale of goodwill – 75% × $12,000	(9,000)
Negative balance end of year 2	($2,025)
Business income for tax purposes:	
Recapture of amounts previously deducted	$ 525
Taxable portion of excess – ⅔ × ($2,025 – $525)	1,000
Business income for tax purposes	$1,525

Notice that the goodwill was sold for $2,000 more than its original cost and only one-half ($\frac{1}{2}$) or $1,000 of this amount was included in income. Although this is considered to be business income, the treatment is similar to that of a capital gain which also includes one-half of the gain in income.

In some circumstances, when eligible capital property is sold some or all of the price is paid over a period of years. Even though the proceeds of the sale are deferred, no reserve is permitted, and three-quarters of the full selling price must be credited to the cumulative eligible capital account in the year of sale.[47] However, if it is later established that some or all of the unpaid amount is uncollectible, a deduction is allowed for three-quarters of that amount (or two-thirds of three-quarters to the extent the income exceeded the recapture of amounts previously deducted).[48]

IV. Accounting Rules versus Tax Rules

Now that the tax treatment of depreciable property has been examined, it is important to highlight how it differs from the *accounting* treatment of similar property.

• **Cost allocation**   Generally accepted accounting principles attempt to allocate the capital cost of an asset over its useful life in relation to its contribution to the revenue-earning process. The life expectancy of similar types of assets will vary considerably from taxpayer to taxpayer depending on the manner in which the assets are used. Even within the same entity, similar assets may be used in different ways. For example, the useful life of automobiles used by travelling sales personnel may be three years, but the life of similar automobiles used for light messenger service within a city may be five years.

---

47 ITA 14(5).
48 ITA 20(4.2).

Despite this, the tax system arbitrarily sets the rate and the method of amortization/ depreciation (capital cost allowance) for similar assets. Automobiles, for example, must use a rate of 30% applied to the declining balance whether the normal use of that automobile is three years or five years. And a franchise cost must be allocated over its legal life even if it has ceased contributing to income generation.

The arbitrary CCA rates imposed by the *Income Tax Act* usually are determined on the basis of the average normal use of particular types of assets, but in some cases they are chosen to implement certain fiscal and economic policies. For example, for a period of time the act permitted manufacturing equipment to be allocated over two years on a straight-line basis. The purpose of this fast write-off was to stimulate expansion of the manufacturing sector in order to create a broader base of permanent jobs.

• **Gains and losses** Normal accounting rules recognize a gain or a loss on the sale of property in the year in which the sale is made. For tax purposes, as a result of averaging under the class pool concept, only capital gains (proceeds in excess of original cost) are recognized in the year of sale. Proceeds above or below the depreciated value remain in the pool and are recognized either when the pool becomes negative or when all assets have been disposed of.

In Chapter 5 a sample calculation of business income for tax purposes was demonstrated. This example was incomplete to the extent that it did not provide detailed information on the taxpayer's depreciable property. In order to complete the conversion of accounting income—as described in the financial statements—to income for tax purposes, these additional procedures are followed.

1. The amortization/depreciation expense relating to tangible fixed assets is removed from accounting income. In manufacturing concerns, a certain amount of amortization/ depreciation will be allocated to product costs and inventory. These amounts must also be removed.

2. The amortization of intangible assets is removed from accounting income.

3. Any gain or loss realized for accounting purposes on the sale of depreciable property, and of eligible capital property, is eliminated.

4. CCA, the amortization of eligible capital property, and terminal losses, if any, are deducted.

5. Taxable capital gains and any recapture of CCA are added to income.

These procedures are demonstrated in the demonstration questions and solutions at the end of this chapter.

V. Impact on Management Decisions

The tax treatment of depreciable capital property and eligible capital property has a significant impact on management decisions. First, the way that capital costs are allocated and gains and losses are treated influences the amount and timing of income tax, which in turn affects all decisions relating to capital expansion. Second, the tax method of dealing with depreciable property, however arbitrary it may be, still influences managers who must complete the difficult task of determining accounting amortization/depreciation. This in turn affects a wide range of business decisions relating to capital expansion.

A. Influence on Accounting Amortization/Depreciation

Although the tax system of dealing with depreciable property is quite different from the accounting system, this question arises: Does the arbitrary tax formula for capital cost allowance and eligible capital property influence the depreciation policies of the business community? When one considers how much judgment is required to determine how much and for how long a specific capital asset will contribute to the generation of business revenue, it is easy to understand why a decision maker may attach undue influence to the published and recognized tax rates.

The fact is, the tax system does influence the rates and method of amortization/depreciation chosen by Canadian businesses. This influence is most dramatic in the small-business sector, but big business is not immune. When in doubt, the normal human response is to rely as much as possible on hard data. The *Income Tax Act*'s list of CCA classes is one of the few available sources of independent hard data relating to the allocation of capital property costs.

To the extent that the tax system influences accounting amortization/depreciation, and therefore profits, it will, in turn, affect a number of areas such as pricing decisions, labour negotiations, and financing costs.

• **Pricing** While competition is the main influence on pricing decisions, perfect competition does not always exist. Prices also respond to costs. If inaccurate amortization/depreciation (i.e., too high or too low) forms part of the product cost, then the decision to respond to such costs by a pricing adjustment may weaken the entity's competitive position in the marketplace.

On a broader scale, this influence may have an impact on international expansion. The Canadian tax rules are different from those of other countries. For example, the tax treatment of depreciable property in the United States is different than in Canada. The American tax system influences American accounting-depreciation methods, which in turn have an impact on American companies' pricing policies. Canadian businesses must cope with this impact when pricing their products to compete in the U.S. market.

• **Financing costs** A company's ability to sell an equity issue or a bond issue to finance its expansion plans depends not only on its existing financial structure but also on its earnings per share. Again, inaccurate amortization/depreciation—especially if it is too high in the early years—will alter the earnings-per-share balance and as a result raise the cost of arranging new sources of financing.

It is vital that a business enterprise develop a system that establishes amortization/depreciation policies which reflect the realities of its specific situation. Too often the tax rules are a dominating influence, and are used as an excuse to maintain an unreliable system for allocating capital costs.

B. Capital Expansion and Cash Flow It is important to understand that the criteria used to evaluate capital expansion decisions differ from those used to evaluate a company's performance. Company performance is evaluated by examining profits according to accepted accounting rules. Capital expansion, on the other hand, is evaluated by examining its impact on future cash flow. This analysis is referred to as "capital budgeting" and should be performed for all capital expansion decisions, including those that involve the acquisition of a complete business.

Cash flow will be influenced whenever a capital asset is purchased or sold. It will also be influenced by the resulting tax consequences with respect to the gain or loss on sale and the write-off rate of the new asset acquired. Capital budgeting is completely irrelevant unless the accounting consequences of the transaction are ignored and the tax rules, described in this chapter, are considered instead.

Cash-flow analysis is premised on the fact that it is more desirable to receive cash today than sometime in the future, because that cash can be used to generate more income or reduce the cost of debt. For example, the real cost of a piece of equipment is not its purchase price, but rather the purchase price *less* the tax savings that can be achieved by claiming capital cost allowance in future years. As the tax savings will be received gradually over future years, their value is translated into a current value by discounting the future cash receipt at some accepted rate of return.

The present value of the tax savings arising from capital cost allowance based on the declining balance method can be determined by using this formula:

$$\frac{C \times T \times R}{R + I}$$

Where:
C = cost of the asset
T = tax rate
R = maximum rate of CCA
I = appropriate interest rate (usually expressed on an after-tax basis)

This formula does not take into account the one-half rule for the first year of an acquisition; however, the impact of that rule is normally not material and will seldom influence the decision.[49]

For example, assume that a business is contemplating the purchase of manufacturing equipment at a cost of $100,000. If the corporate tax rate is 45%, and if the company usually can invest its funds in business activities to generate an after-tax return of 10%, the net cost of the acquisition, in terms of current value, is only $66,250, calculated as follows:

Current purchase price	$100,000
less	
Present value of future tax savings from CCA:	
$100,000 × .45 × .30 =	$ 33,750
.30 + .10	
Net after-tax cost	$ 66,250

Further assume that the new equipment will generate after-tax profits of $12,000 per year for 10 years as a result of reduced labour costs and greater capacity. The present value of $12,000 per year discounted at 10% is $73,735. The decision to acquire the equipment is favourable because the net present cost ($66,250) is less than the present value of its future benefits ($73,735), even after allowance for an after-tax return of 10%. If the one-half rule is incorporated into the formula, the net after-tax cost is $67,784 rather than $66,250. In this case, the difference does not materially affect the outcome.

Remember that the formula does not apply when CCA is calculated on a straight-line basis. In such cases the tax saving is the same amount each year, and the net tax saving can be calculated as the present value of an annuity (except for the first year, if the one-half rule applies).

Examining capital acquisitions on an after-tax basis enables the decision maker to

(a) establish the real cash cost of the investment and its viability, as demonstrated above;
(b) determine the length of time required to recover the investment and thereby establish some sense of the risk attached to the acquisition; and,
(c) present an accurate picture of the financing requirements and the ability to repay.

The previous example presented the simple acquisition of a single asset. There are many other decisions that must take into account the tax system for depreciable property as well as capital-budgeting techniques. Decisions involving lease-or-buy, sale-and-leaseback, expansion of operations to new locations, and acquisitions of new businesses are but a few of these. While analyses for such decisions are more complex than the one in the example provided, the basic tax factors are applied in a similar manner. The tax implications of a complete business acquisition are examined in detail in Chapter 17.

---

49 The impact of the one-half rule can be included by using this formula:

$$\frac{C \times T \times R(1 + I/2)}{(R + 1) \times (I + 1)}$$

It is important to recognize that the rate of CCA has a significant impact on the after-tax cost of asset acquisitions. Higher CCA rates provide faster deductions, and thereby increase the present value of future tax savings.

Sometimes a taxpayer acquires a group of assets for a single price. It is then necessary to allocate the total price among the individual assets. This must be done with care to ensure that the assets with the higher CCA rates are allocated the maximum portion that is reasonable in the circumstances. An unreasonable allocation may be revised by CCRA (see Chapter 9).[50]

VI. Tax Planning Checklist

The following tax planning items relate to the capital cost allowance system. Some of the items listed are discussed in more detail in later chapters.

1. Deductions for CCA are discretionary. This means that the taxpayer can shift income from one period to another. Consider delaying the CCA deduction when a loss occurs or accumulated losses from other years are at the risk of expiring (see Chapters 10 and 11).

2. The recapture of CCA and the recovery of eligible capital amounts must be included in income at the time of occurrence even when the related proceeds from the sale are deferred for several years. In contrast, deferred proceeds that relate to capital gains (see Chapter 8) and inventory gains (see Chapter 5) can delay the recognition of that income and the payment of tax.

   Often, several assets are sold as a group. For example, the sale of real estate may include both land and buildings; or the sale of a business may include inventory, land, buildings, equipment, goodwill, and so on. In these situations it may be prudent to write the sale agreement so that it allocates the deferred proceeds first to those assets that will have only a capital gain, with any remaining amount assigned to the other assets. In this way, the assets that can defer tax will be sold for deferred proceeds and little or no cash, with the other assets being sold for cash and little or no deferred proceeds. This will create the maximum tax deferral.

3. When acquiring depreciable property with borrowed funds, consider capitalizing the borrowing costs. These costs, which are added to the cost of the property, can then be deducted as CCA over a period of time. This may be beneficial if losses are at risk of being unused owing to insufficient income.

4. Be sure to properly consider the options when it comes to recognizing any inducement payments received while signing a lease (see Chapter 5). This will ensure that the maximum tax savings will occur.

5. When negotiating a lease, try to combine the initial lease period and the subsequent option periods in a manner that will speed up the deduction of CCA on any leasehold improvements (see "Leasehold Improvements," page 175 ff.). However, take care not to compromise the associated rent costs.

6. Consider speeding up the purchase of new assets when a particular class of depreciable property is about to generate a recapture of CCA. Similarly, consider delaying the purchase of new assets until after the year end if a particular class is about to generate a terminal loss for tax purposes.

7. When purchasing a group of assets for a total price, carefully consider how to allocate that price among the various assets. Try to maximize (within reason) the amounts allocated to depreciable properties that have a high CCA rate. Remember, however, that CCRA has the right to revise unreasonable allocations.

50 ITA 68; IT-220R2.

8. Remember that the right to use an asset is what makes it valuable. Therefore, when acquiring an asset, be sure to consider leasing rather than owning, comparing not just the cost but the amount and timing of any related tax savings (see Chapter 21).

9. Carefully analyze class 14 property in an attempt to justify a CCA rate that is faster than the traditional straight-line method. This may be difficult as it is often hard to determine economic value.

VII. Summary and Conclusion

This chapter has developed the fundamental tax rules that are applicable when the cost of capital property is allocated over a future period of time. This system can be summarized as follows:

1. Assets of a tangible nature, as well as intangible assets that have a limited legal life, are defined as depreciable property, and their capital cost is allocated over future years as capital cost allowance.

2. Various types of assets are grouped together in classes that define the maximum rate of CCA that may be claimed in each year. It is the taxpayer's right to claim any amount of CCA, in any year, up to the maximum permitted for the class.

3. All assets of a particular class are pooled together and averaged according to the following basic procedures:

   • All purchases are added to the undepreciated capital cost of the class.

   • When assets are sold, the class is reduced by the selling price up to a maximum of the original cost of the asset sold. Any proceeds in excess of the original cost are recognized as a capital gain.

   • If, at the end of the year, the balance of the class is positive and there is at least one asset remaining in the pool, the CCA rate is applied to that balance.

   • If, at the end of the year, the balance of the class is positive but there are no assets remaining, the full balance is deducted as a terminal loss.

   • The year end closing balance, if negative, is taken into income as a recapture of CCA, even if assets remain in the pool.

4. Intangible assets that do not have a specific legal life are classified as eligible capital property. Seventy-five percent of the cost of all such assets is placed in a common pool referred to as cumulative eligible capital, and amortized at 7% on a declining-balance basis.

The above rules significantly influence all types of business decisions relating to the acquisition, use, disposition, and replacement of capital assets. Such decisions involve the examination of cash flow through the capital-budgeting process. This process can be applied only when the above tax rules are incorporated into the analysis.

Reading List

Income Tax Act References

	Section
Capital outlay—depreciation denied	18(1)(b)
Capital cost of property—CCA permitted	20(1)(a)
Cumulative eligible capital amount—deduction	20(1)(b)
Depreciable property	13(21)

Available for use	13(27)
Capital cost allowance—rates	Regulation 1100(1)(a)
Capital cost allowance—class 13	Regulation 1100(1)(b), Schedule III
Capital cost allowance—class 14	Regulation 1100(1)(c)
Capital cost allowance—one-half rule	Regulation 1100(2)
Capital cost allowance—asset classifications	Regulations, Schedule II
Capital cost allowance—short taxation year	Regulation 1100(3)
Separate class—each business	Regulation 1101(1)
Separate class—passenger vehicle	Regulation 1101(1af)
Undepreciated capital cost	13(21)
Disposition of property	13(21), (21.1)
Proceeds of disposition	13(21)
Terminal loss	20(16)
Recapture of capital cost allowance	13(1)
Cost of passenger vehicle	13(7)(g)
Passenger vehicle—no terminal loss	20(16.1)
Passenger vehicle—no recapture	13(2)
Deemed capital cost of certain property:	
Inducement payments	13(7.4)
Grants, etc.	13(7.1)
Exchanges of property	13(4),(4.1)
Change of use	13(7)(a), (b)
Non–arm's length transaction	13(7)(e)
Eligible capital expenditure	14(5)
Cumulative eligible capital	14(5)
Income from business (eligible capital property)	14(1)
Ceasing to carry on business (terminal loss)	24
Allocation of amounts in consideration for disposition of property	68

Canada Customs and Revenue Agency Publications

IT-285R2	Capital cost allowance, general comments.
IT-128R	Depreciable property.
IT-50R	Date of acquisition of depreciable property.
IT-478R2	Recapture and terminal loss.
IT-220R2	Proceeds of disposition of depreciable property.
IT-79R3	Buildings and other structures.
IT-522R	Vehicles and other travel expenses—employees.
IT-464R	Leasehold improvements.
IT-477	Patents, franchises, concessions, and licences (class 14).
IT-147R3	Manufacturing and processing equipment (qualified).
IT-172R	Taxation year of individuals (CCA).
IT-121R3	Election to capitalize cost of borrowed money.
IT-259R2	Exchanges of property.
IT-271R	Expropriations.
IT-505	Mortgage foreclosures.
IT-233R	Lease-option agreements; sale-leaseback agreements.
IT-143R2	Meaning of "eligible capital expenditure."
IT-123R4	Dispositions of and transactions involving eligible capital property.
IT-386R	Eligible capital amounts.

Other Publication

Welch and Hanrahan, "Deriving a General Expression for the CCA Tax Shield," *CGA Magazine*, May 1990, pp. 59–62.

Demonstration Questions

Question One

Palay Ltd. is a Canadian-controlled private corporation located in Windsor, Ontario, and operating four retail electronics stores. You, Palay's treasurer, have just reported to the president that the pretax profit for the year ended June 30, 20X5, is $214,000.

As preparation for the upcoming management meeting, you are estimating this year's tax liability and preparing advice on certain tax-related matters. Your assistant has summarized the following information:

1. The reported profit of $214,000 consists of the following items:

Income from retail operations	$192,000
Net gain on sale of land, building, equipment, and goodwill	22,000
	$214,000

2. The previous year's income tax return shows the following account balances:

Depreciable property—undepreciated capital cost:	
Class 1	$420,000
Class 8	70,000
Class 10	40,000
Class 12	4,200
Cumulative eligible capital	28,000

3. The income from retail operations includes the following deductions:

Amortization/depreciation of tangible assets	$ 32,000
Salary and wages	380,000
Rent	26,000
Travel	11,000
Advertising	22,000
Amortization of goodwill	2,000

4. On July 1, 20X4, store 2 was sold. A new store, in leased premises, was opened on the same date. Information on the sale of store 2 is given below.

	Selling price	Original cost
Assets sold:		
Land	$ 28,000	$ 4,000
Building	170,000	162,000
Fixtures and equipment	18,000	28,000
Goodwill	40,000	32,000

All of the assets were sold for cash.

5. The new store is located in leased premises. The purchase price included the following assets:

Franchise—unlimited life	$20,000
Fixtures and equipment	22,000
Leasehold improvements	36,000

The acquired lease had three years remaining in its term at the date of purchase. The lease contract provides for two renewable option periods of one year each.

6. "Other expense" includes the following items:

Site investigation for new store	$ 3,000
Attending two electronics conventions	4,200
Cost of new computer application software	2,000
Other	2,200
	$11,400

7. Advertising expense consists of the following items:

Radio and television commercials	$16,000
Promotion—meals and drinks for suppliers	1,000
Charitable donations	4,000
Contributions to a registered federal political party	1,000
	$22,000

8. On June 30, 20X5, Palay sold its delivery truck for $43,000 and leased a new vehicle. The original cost of the truck was $49,000.

Required:
Determine the net income for tax purposes for Palay Ltd. for the 20X5 taxation year.

Solution:
Beginning with the net income from the financial statement of $214,000, adjustments are made for expenses that are not deductible, for the applicable capital cost allowance and cumulative eligible capital deductions, and for any taxable gains or losses on the sale of property. These are summarized below.

Net income per financial statement	$214,000
Accounting gain on sale of land, building, equipment, and goodwill	(22,000)
Amortization/depreciation of tangible assets	32,000
Amortization of goodwill	2,000
Promotion—meals—50% × $1,000	500
Charitable donations	4,000
Political contributions	1,000
Computer software—is a depreciable item (class 12)—note 1	2,000
Recapture of capital cost allowance—note 1	3,000
Capital cost allowance—note 1	(33,520)
Cumulative eligible capital deduction—note 2	(910)
Taxable capital gain on land— ½ ($28,000 − $4,000)	12,000
Taxable capital gain on building— ½ ($170,000 − $162,000)	4,000
Net income for tax purposes	$218,070

Note 1:

Class (rate)	1 (4%)	8 (20%)	10 (30%)	12 (100%)	13 (st. line)
Opening	$420,000	70,000	40,000	4,200	–0–
Additions		22,000		2,000	36,000
Disposals	(162,000)	(18,000)	(43,000)		
	258,000	74,000	(3,000)	6,200	36,000
Recapture			3,000		
CCA	*(10,320)	**(14,400)		***(5,200)	****(3,600)
Closing	$247,680	59,600	–0–	1,000	32,400

*　$258,000 × 4% = $10,320
**　($70,000 × 20% = $14,000) + ($22,000 – $18,000 = $4,000 × 20% × 1/2 = $400) = $14,400
***　($4,200 × 100% = $4,200) + ($2,000 × 100% × 1/2 = $1,000) = $5,200
**** Lesser of:
　　1/5 × $36,000 × 1/2 = $3,600; or
　　$36,000 ÷ (3 years + 1 year option) × 1/2 = $4,500

Total CCA = $33,520

Note 2:

Cumulative eligible capital:	
Opening	$28,000
Addition—franchise (unlimited life)	
purchased—3/4 × $20,000	15,000
Disposal—goodwill sold—3/4 × $40,000	(30,000)
	13,000
Deduction—7% × $13,000	(910)
Closing	$12,090

Question Two

PX Industries Ltd. operates a wholesale business in Ontario. On October 1, 20X2, the company acquired the assets of a manufacturing business in order to produce some of its existing product lines. The net profit for the year ended December 31, 20X2, is $200,000, as follows:

	Income (loss)
Wholesale division	$335,000
Manufacturing division	(40,000)
Other	38,000
Provision for income taxes	(133,000)
Net income	$200,000

Information relating to the above income statement is summarized below.

1. Other income includes the following:

Gain on sale of furniture	$ 9,000
Interest	29,000
	$38,000

2. Included in the expenses are the following:

• Installation costs for a new computer system	$ 1,200
• Amortization/depreciation of tangible assets	58,000
• Reserve for bad debts	24,000
• Reserve on a potential loss from a lawsuit against the company by a customer for late product delivery	12,000
• Advertising and promotion includes the following:	
Memberships at recreational clubs	4,800
Newspaper advertisements	6,400
• Amortization of manufacturing licence	8,000
• Amortization of research and development costs	5,600
• Legal fees for revising manufacturing licence agreement (see #5 below)	2,000

3. After acquiring the manufacturing business, PX paid an engineering firm $22,000 to research and develop a new product. The cost is being amortized over several years.

4. At December 31, 20X1, the following properties had undepreciated capital cost:

Class 8	$ 80,000
Class 10	120,000
Class 12	1,000

The balance in the cumulative eligible capital account was $23,000.

5. On October 1, 20X2, the manufacturing business was acquired, and the following assets were included:

Manufacturing equipment	$80,000
Goodwill	100,000
Licence	50,000

The licence permitted PX to produce a patented product in exchange for a royalty. The licence had 10 years remaining.

6. On December 31, 20X2, PX sold all of its office furniture to a leasing company for $70,000 under a sale/leaseback arrangement. The furniture originally cost $130,000. The CCA class to which the furniture belongs has no other assets in it.

7. On September 1, 20X2, PX purchased a computer and some accounting software. The price was $28,000, as follows:

Computer	$24,000
Accounting software	4,000
	$28,000

Required:
Determine PX's net income for tax purposes for the 20X2 taxation year.

Solution:
Regarding capital cost allowance issues, it is important to note that two items deducted as expenses should have been added to the cost of depreciable property. The installation costs of the new computer must be eliminated as a full deduction and added to the capital cost of the computer and included in class 10. Similarly, the legal fee for revising the licence agreement is a capital item and must be added to the acquisition cost of the licence and included in class 14. Also note that the new computer, which cost more than $1,000, can be included in a separate class 10 if PX chooses to do so. This would be advisable, as it will ensure a full terminal loss if the computer is sold for a low price or junked in the future. (If the computer is not disposed of by the beginning of the fifth subsequent taxation year, it is transferred from the separate class to the "regular" class 10 pool.)

The net income for tax purposes is calculated as follows:

Income per financial statement	$200,000
Provision for income taxes	133,000
Gain on sale of furniture	(9,000)
Installation cost of new computer	1,200
Legal fee for revising licence agreement	2,000
Amortization/depreciation of tangible assets	58,000
Reserve for potential loss from lawsuit	12,000
Club memberships	4,800
Amortization of licence	8,000
Amortization of research and development	5,600
Research and development costs—actual	(22,000)
Terminal loss from sale of office furniture—note 1	(10,000)
Capital cost allowance—note 1	(56,090)
Cumulative eligible capital deduction:	
7% × ($23,000 + ¾ ($100,000 goodwill))	(6,860)
Net income for tax purposes	$320,650

Note 1:

Class (rate)	8(20%)	10(30%)	10(30%)	12(100%)	14(st. line)	43(30%)
UCC 20X1	$80,000	120,000	–0–	1,000	–0–	–0–
Additions:						
Computer			24,000			
Computer						
installation			1,200			
Software				4,000		
Licence					50,000	
Legal for licence					2,000	
Manufacturing						
equipment						80,000
Disposal:						
Furniture	(70,000)					
	10,000	120,000	25,200	5,000	52,000	80,000
Terminal loss	(10,000)					
CCA		(36,000)	(3,780)	(3,000)	(1,310)*	(12,000)
UCC 20X2	$ –0–	84,000	21,420	2,000	50,690	68,000

Capital cost allowance calculations:
Class 10—$120,000 × 30% = $36,000
Class 10 (computer)—$25,200 × 30% × ½ = $3,780
Class 12—($1,000 × 100%) + ($4,000 × 100% × ½) = $3,000
Class 14—92 days ÷ 3,650 days × $52,000 = $1,310 (note: the one-half rule does not apply)
Class 43—$80,000 × 30% × ½ = $12,000
*Note: The Class 14 CCA could have a different rate if it relates to the asset's economic value.

Review Questions

1. Under the income tax system, neither capital expenditures nor amortization/depreciation can be deducted when income for tax purposes is being calculated. The same system imposes an arbitrary and uniform method of cost allocation based on the type of asset used. Explain the reason for this significant departure from generally accepted accounting principles in arriving at income for tax purposes.

2. The cost allocation system divides capital assets into two general categories. Identify these categories and briefly state, in general terms, what types of assets are included in each category.

3. Can an individual who earns employment income claim a deduction for capital cost allowance in arriving at income from employment? If the answer is yes, are any restrictions imposed?

4. A business acquires land for a customer parking lot and incurs the following costs:

Land	$50,000
Legal fees to complete purchase agreement	2,000
Legal fees in connection with obtaining a mortgage loan for the land	1,000
Small building for attendant	10,000
Exterior landscaping	2,000
	$65,000

Briefly explain the tax treatment of these costs.

5. A business can obtain the right to use property through ownership or leasing. Briefly compare the tax treatment of purchasing land and building with that of leasing land and building. Refer to both the amount and timing of the related deductions for tax purposes.

6. What is the meaning and significance of the term "capital cost" of an asset?

7. Explain why the deduction of capital cost allowance is a "discretionary" deduction.

8. Depreciable properties are divided into a number of different classes, and a specific allocation rate (capital cost allowance rate) is assigned to each class. Explain why this system is fair for some taxpayers, unfair for others, and more than fair for others.

9. Briefly explain what is meant by the "pool concept" in the capital cost allowance system.

10. "In all cases, the acquisition of a new asset in a particular class will result in the reduction of the normal maximum rate of capital cost allowance by one-half in the year of purchase." Is this statement true? Explain.

11. To what extent, if any, does the pooling concept inherent in the capital cost allowance system affect the tax treatment of any gains and losses that occur on the disposition of depreciable property? In general terms, explain when a gain or loss will occur.

12. Describe the possible ramifications of purchasing new depreciable property on the last day of the current taxation year as opposed to the first day of the next taxation year (that is, one day later).

13. What is a leasehold improvement, and how does its tax treatment vary from the normal capital cost allowance treatment?

14. Taxpayer A leases a building for 15 years. Taxpayer B secures the right to lease a building for 15 years by signing a three-year lease with two renewable option periods—one for 2 additional years and a second for 10 years. Both A and B incur leasehold improvement costs at the beginning of the lease. Explain the tax treatment of the leasehold improvements to both A and B. Which taxpayer has signed the better lease? Explain.

15. If the sale of an asset results in income from a recapture of capital cost allowance, is it necessary to acquire another asset in the same year in order to avoid the recapture? Explain.

16. Explain the tax consequences, if any, when an individual proprietor of a new business transfers personal-use office furniture to the business for use in the business.

17. Describe two alternative tax treatments that may apply when a business purchases a franchise.

18. How does the treatment given eligible capital property differ from that given depreciable property?

19. Explain why a businessperson might view the cost of a $100,000 building as being significantly higher than the cost of a $100,000 delivery truck. Make a cost comparison, assuming the taxpayer is subject to a 45% tax rate and can invest funds to generate an after-tax cash return of 9%.

Problems

Problem One

A wholesale business with a December 31 year end purchased new equipment on November 25, 20X0, for $10,000. Before 20X0 the business owned no other equipment.

Required:

1. What are the tax consequences if in 20X2 the business sells the equipment for (a) $3,000? (b) $8,000? (c) $12,000?

2. How would your answer to (a) and (b) change if on December 31, 20X2 the business acquired new equipment costing $1,000? Would it be advisable to delay the purchase by one day (that is, until January 1, 20X3)?

Problem Two

Maple Enterprises Ltd. has always claimed maximum capital cost allowance. The following information relates to the corporation's capital transactions:

1. The undepreciated capital cost of certain capital cost allowance classes at the end of the previous taxation year was as follows:

Class 1	$200,000 (one building in class)
Class 8	190,000

2. In 20X1 (the current year), the company expanded into the manufacturing business by purchasing the following assets:

Equipment (manufacturing)	$30,000
Product licence for an indefinite period	10,000

3. The building was sold in 20X1 for $260,000 (original cost—$230,000).

4. During 20X1 the company purchased office furniture for $14,000.

Required:

1. Calculate the net increase or decrease in the corporation's net income for tax purposes for the 20X1 taxation year.

2. Given that the 20X1 taxation year has passed, can any action be taken in the 20X2 taxation year to reduce the net income for tax purposes of year 20X1? Explain.

Problem Three

Wai Yeung is a self-employed insurance saleswoman. She started her business on July 1, 20X1, and ended her first taxation year on December 31, 20X1. On July 1, 20X1, she purchased a car for $32,000. The car is financed with a bank loan. From July 1, 20X1 to December 31, 20X1, interest costs amounted to $1,960. Yeung incurred the following additional expenses relating to her automobile:

Repairs and maintenance	$ 300
Insurance	1,100
Gasoline	1,700
Parking while on business	420

During the period, Yeung drove 15 000 kilometres, of which 12 000 were for business.

Required:

1. Determine the maximum amount that Yeung can deduct from her business income for tax purposes in 20X1.

2. Calculate the maximum capital cost allowance that Yeung can deduct in 20X2 and 20X3, assuming that business kilometres driven and total kilometres driven both remain constant and that Yeung's car is sold in 20X3 for $21,000 and replaced with a new car costing $34,000.

3. Would your answers to 1 and 2 above change if Yeung were employed as an insurance saleswoman rather than self-employed? Explain.

Problem Four

Window Shine Ltd. was incorporated on July 1, 20X1, and purchased an existing business on the same date. The purchase included the following assets:

Delivery trucks	$30,000
Goodwill	12,000
Franchise	10,000

Immediately after incorporation, the company moved into leased premises, having signed a lease for three years with an option to renew for an additional three. Rental payments of $2,000 per month began in July 20X1. The premises required alterations, and in July 20X1 the company incurred costs of $15,000 for these.

The franchise that was purchased for $10,000 has a legal life remaining of five years. At the end of the five-year period, the franchise may be renewed at a nominal cost only if the franchiser is satisfied with the performance of the franchisee.

The company's fiscal year end is June 30, 20X2. A brief financial statement is presented at the top of the next page for this first year of operations.

Revenue		$120,000
Expenses:		
Wages	$26,000	
Office	4,000	
Building improvements	15,000	
Rent	24,000	
Delivery expense	3,000	
Amortization/depreciation (truck)	6,000	
Amortization of goodwill	2,000	
Amortization of franchise	2,000	
Other	12,000	94,000
Net income for the year		$ 26,000

Required:

Determine the corporation's net income from business for tax purposes for the 20X2 taxation year.

Problem Five

In late 20X0, Conrad Petry retired from his job of 30 years and began receiving a pension of $4,000 per month. Unable to cope with full retirement, he purchased a small retail business on January 1, 20X1. At that time he moved into rented premises under a seven-year lease that included an option to renew for another three years. He immediately spent $12,000 to improve the premises. The business incurred a small loss in 20X1, but 20X2 was profitable. Information relating to the 20X2 business activity is provided below.

In addition, in 20X2 Petry disposed of an investment that he had owned for several years: shares of a small business corporation. He sold the shares, which originally cost $20,000, for $12,000.

Additional information concerning retail business (20X2)

1. The financial statements indicate a profit of $9,500 for the year ended December 20X2.

2. During the year, Petry withdrew $1,000 each month from the business for personal use. However, in order to reflect the proper economic costs of the business, he insisted that the accountant deduct a fair salary for his own efforts in the business. Accordingly, salary expense was increased by $38,000, and Petry's equity was credited with an equal amount.

3. The profit includes a deduction for amortization/depreciation of $3,500.

4. On February 28, 20X2, additional improvements costing $18,000 were made to the leased premises. This amount appears on the balance sheet as a fixed asset.

5. On June 30, 20X2, Petry purchased the land beside the leased premises. This land is to provide extra parking space for customers but can also be used to build a company-owned store building when the current lease expires. The costs relating to the land totalled $58,200, determined as follows:

Land price	$40,000
Cost of paving parking area	12,000
Permanent landscaping costs paid	4,000
Legal fees to prepare purchase agreement	1,000
Legal and registration fees for first mortgage financing of the land	1,200
	$58,200

The land and the paving of the parking lot are recorded as fixed assets. The other costs have been deducted as 20X2 expenses.

6. In January 20X2 Petry purchased an automobile for $34,000. All of the operating expenses (gas, oil, repairs, insurance, and so on) of $4,300 were paid by the business and included in travel costs. No amortization/depreciation was deducted. The car was used for the following purposes:

Travel to and from work	20%
Travel to Vancouver to see suppliers	25
Personal travel	55
	100%

7. Sales revenue has been reduced by $10,000 for a reserve for anticipated post-Christmas returns.

Required:
Determine Petry's net income from business and his overall net income for tax purposes for the 20X2 taxation year.

Problem Six
Harley Krane purchased a side-by-side duplex in 20X0 for $120,000 (land $20,000, building $100,000). The units were designed for residential use but Krane used them for his business. Both units were used to conduct his law practice; one unit housed a small group of paralegals in his employ, who processed most of the real estate transactions for his clients.

In 20X2 Krane stopped practising real estate law in order to concentrate on family law, and terminated the staff positions of all paralegals. Krane then occupied the freed-up duplex unit as his personal residence, which meant he no longer had to commute.

At the end of 20X1 the duplex building had an undepreciated capital cost of $94,000. Recently, a duplex of similar size across the street was sold for $150,000.

Required:
How will Krane's net income for tax purposes for 20X2 be affected by the above activity?

Problem Seven

State the class number for each of the following 13 items, and briefly describe the method and rate of cost allocation:

1. Furniture and fixtures.
2. Tools (each costing less than $200).
3. Printing press used by a publisher of paperback books.
4. Paving of a parking lot.
5. Concession licence for a 10-year time period.
6. Franchise for an unlimited life.
7. Computer application software.
8. Computer hardware.
9. Customer list.
10. Glasses and cutlery used in the operation of a restaurant.
11. Sprinkler system in a building.
12. Television commercial used to promote company products.
13. Cost of reorganizing a corporation's share capital.

Problem Eight

Photo Tonight, a film-developing and camera-repair franchise, began business on January 1, 20X1. In the process of beginning operations, it incurred the following capital expenditures:

Developing equipment	$80,000
Furniture and fixtures	30,000
Small tools (under $200)	15,000
Franchise (expires in 20 years)	75,000
Incorporation costs	5,000
Pick-up truck	12,000
Leasehold improvements (10-year lease)	30,000

The business was immediately successful and generated substantial profits for the years ended December 31, 20X1 and 20X2.

In 20X2 the truck was traded in for a larger unit costing $20,000. A value of $7,000 was assigned to the old truck when it was traded in.

In 20X3 the owner was forced to leave the business due to illness. As a result, the assets were valued and sold on December 31, 20X3, for the following values:

Developing equipment	$ 60,000
Furniture and fixtures	15,000
Small tools	10,000
Franchise	85,000
Incorporation costs	–0–
Pick-up truck	15,000
Leasehold improvements	15,000
Goodwill	50,000
	$250,000

Required:
Determine the effect of all these transactions on net income for tax purposes for the 20X1, 20X2, and 20X3 taxation years.

Problem Nine

KC Restaurants Ltd., a Canadian-controlled private corporation, was incorporated on July 1, 20X0, and began operations immediately. By December 31, 20X0 (the corporation's first year end), three new restaurants had been opened, two of which were franchises.

During the first few months of operations, the following expenditures were made by KCR:

Legal fees for the cost of incorporation	$ 4,000
Cooking equipment, including food processors, ovens, and hot plates	320,000
Franchise #1	40,000
Franchise #2	80,000
Cutlery, plates, glasses, and cups	115,000
Computer programs for restaurant accounting	3,000
Building	220,000

Franchise #1 was purchased on October 1, 20X0, and will expire after 120 months. Franchise #2, which was acquired on July 1, 20X0, has no expiry date and will continue indefinitely provided that the terms of the franchise agreement are met. Other equipment, such as tables and chairs, was leased.

For the taxation year ending December 31, 20X0, KCR claimed a deduction for the maximum available capital cost allowance and cumulative eligible capital account. For tax purposes, after these deductions were made, the company lost $40,000 in 20X0.

The company became profitable in 20X1. A summary of the income statement prepared for accounting purposes for the year ended December 31, 20X1, with additional information, is provided below.

20X1 financial statement (summarized) and other information

Sales		$1,845,000
Cost of sales		1,211,000
Gross profit		634,000
Occupancy costs	$ 72,000	
Salaries and wages	275,000	
General overhead	101,000	
Advertising and other	96,000	544,000
		90,000
Gain on sale of goodwill		60,000
Net losses on sale of fixed assets		(22,000)
Net income		$ 128,000

The following additional information relates to the above 20X1 financial statements:

1. On December 1, 20X1, KCR sold the non-franchised restaurant. The sale price included these proceeds:

	Proceeds	Original cost
Goodwill	$ 60,000	–0–
Land	15,000	12,000
Building	230,000	220,000
Cooking equipment	40,000	72,000
Cutlery, plates, glasses	26,000	37,000

2. Included in advertising expenses is $2,000 of donations made to a registered charity.

3. Salaries include an accrued bonus of $12,000 awarded on December 31, 20X1 to a manager. The bonus will be paid in three equal instalments of $4,000 on April 30, 20X2, August 31, 20X2, and December 31, 20X2.

4. Expenses include accounting amortization/depreciation of $102,000.

Required:

1. Calculate the undepreciated capital cost for tax purposes for each class of depreciable property at the end of the 20X0 taxation year after capital cost allowance claims for that year.

2. Calculate the balance in the cumulative eligible capital account at the end of the 20X0 taxation year after the deduction for that year.

3. For the taxation year ended December 31, 20X1, calculate KCR's net income for tax purposes. Begin your answer with net income per the financial statement, and add or subtract adjustments.

Problem Ten

Samson Enterprises Ltd. achieved a profit in 20X1 of $120,000. The income statement is summarized below.

Sales	$1,300,000
Cost of sales	780,000
Gross profit	520,000
Administrative and selling expenses	451,000
	69,000
Other income (expenses)	51,000
Net income before tax	$ 120,000

Certain details of the summarized income statement are provided below.

1. Administrative and selling expenses include the following:

   (a) Political donations to a federal political party   3,000

   (b) Amortization/depreciation of tangible assets   12,000

Note 1 At the end of the previous year the undepreciated capital cost of certain asset classes was as follows:

Class 1	$80,000
Class 8	32,000
Class 10	50,000

Note 2 During the current year, the company sold its land and building for $150,000 (land $40,000, building $110,000) and moved into leased premises. The original cost of the property was $130,000 (land $30,000, building $100,000). The building had an accounting book value of $70,000 at the time of sale.

Note 3 The company owns several pieces of equipment. During the year, one unit that originally cost $10,000 and had a book value of $6,000 was sold for $8,000.

(c) Legal fees:
- Settling a dispute relating to the purchase of defective merchandise for sale ... 4,000
- Reorganizing the corporation's share capital ... 8,000

(d) Amortization ... 9,000

Note: The current year's amortization expense applies to a number of intangible assets.
- During the previous year (20X0), the company took over a competitor and purchased goodwill for $40,000 and a franchise (unlimited life) for $10,000.
- During the current year, the franchise was sold for $8,000 when its book value for accounting purposes was $9,000. In addition, the company purchased an existing patent from a competitor for $20,000. The patent has a legal life of 10 years remaining and was purchased on the first day of the current year.

2. Other income (expenses) includes the following:

Gain on sale of land	$10,000
Gain on sale of building	40,000
Gain on sale of equipment	2,000
Loss on sale of franchise	(1,000)
	$51,000

Required:
Determine the net income for tax purposes of Samson Enterprises for the 20X1 taxation year.

Problem Eleven
Alpha Ltd. is a Canadian-controlled private corporation operating a small land-development business. In June 20X8 it acquired a licence to manufacture pre-fab homes and began operations immediately. Financial information for the 20X8 taxation year is outlined on the next page.

1. Alpha's profit before income taxes for the year ended November 30, 20X8, was $245,000 as follows:

Income from land development and pre-fab home manufacturing	$248,000
Loss on sale of properties	(3,000)
	$245,000

2. The loss on sale of property results from two transactions. On October 1, 20X8, Alpha sold all of its shares of Q Ltd., a 100% subsidiary, for $100,000. The shares were acquired in 20X1 for $80,000. Also, during the year Alpha sold some of its vehicles for $25,000. The vehicles originally cost $50,000 and had a book value of $48,000 at the time of sale. New vehicles were obtained under a lease arrangement.

3. The 20X7 corporate tax return shows the following undepreciated capital cost allowance balances:

Undepreciated capital cost:	
Class 8	30,000
Class 10	120,000
Class 13	41,000

   Alpha occupies leased premises under a seven-year lease agreement that began December 1, 20X5. At the time, Alpha spent $60,000 to improve the premises. The lease agreement gives Alpha the option to renew the lease for two three-year periods.
   Alpha began manufacturing pre-fab homes on June 1, 20X8. At that time it acquired the following:

Licence: right to manufacture for 10 years	90,000
Manufacturing equipment	105,000
Trucks	60,000

Accounting amortization in 20X8 amounted to $60,000.

4. Alpha normally acquires raw land, which it then develops into building lots for resale to individuals or housing contractors. In 20X8 it sold part of its undeveloped land inventory to another developer for $400,000. The sale realized a profit of $80,000, which is included in the land-development income above. The proceeds consisted of $40,000 in cash, with the balance payable in five annual instalments beginning in 20X9.

5. Travel and entertainment expense includes the following:

Professional hockey tickets for suppliers and staff	$7,000
Hotel and airfare	9,000
Charitable donations	4,000

6. Legal and accounting expense includes the following:

Revising the corporation's articles of association to conduct business in all provinces	2,000
Collection of bad debts	1,500
Reviewing the terms of a collateral agreement on a long-term bank loan	3,000
Annual audit	8,000

Required:

Calculate Alpha's net income for tax purposes for the 20X8 taxation year.

Problem Twelve

East Side Products Ltd. (ESP) recently expanded its business by acquiring the operations of a competitor. As a result of the expansion, additional office space was needed. On the first day of the current fiscal year, ESP rented additional premises under a five-year lease agreement with two three-year renewal options. As an inducement to sign the lease, the landlord paid ESP $20,000 to cover part of the cost of improving the offices. Before occupying the premises, ESP spent $38,000 for necessary renovations.

Profits from business operations for the current year are expected to be $175,000. Because of the expansion, future years' profits are expected to exceed $350,000 annually.

For several years, ESP had invested its excess cash from annual profits in secure bonds. The proceeds from all of these bonds were used to acquire the competitor's business. For the next several years the company will again invest excess cash in secure bonds; it expects to earn an average yield of 13%.

ESP is a Canadian-controlled private corporation. The first $300,000 of annual business profits are subject to a 20% tax rate. Annual business profits over $300,000 are taxed at 40%.

Required:

Describe the alternative tax treatments for the inducement payment. Which treatment should ESP use? Show a detailed calculation that compares the tax cost of each alternative.

Cases

Case One   Patterson Traders Inc.

Patterson Traders Inc. has developed substantial cash reserves after several successive years of profitable operations. The company intends to use those reserves to diversify and has targeted two businesses for possible acquisition. Both target businesses are corporations. Patterson has stated that it wants to acquire only the individual assets of any business it acquires rather than the shares of the corporation that owns the assets. In addition, Patterson has a strong cash position, and so has no desire to incur debt.

Information relating to the two target businesses is as follows:

Assets	1	2
Land	$ 50,000	$ 40,000
Building	300,000	310,000
Equipment (manufacturing)	500,000	200,000
Goodwill	–0–	450,000
Licence	150,000	–0–
	$1,000,000	$1,000,000

Both target companies are manufacturers, though their products are different. Both are expected to generate annual profits of $300,000 before amortization/depreciation and income taxes.

One of the products of business 1 is manufactured under licence. The licence agreement extends for 15 years and stipulates payment of a royalty based on sales volume. The licensee has an option to renew the licence at the end of the 15-year period subject to a renegotiation of the royalty percentage.

Currently, the cash reserves are invested in secure bonds, which earn interest at 12% annually. These cash reserves are not sufficient to acquire both businesses, so Patterson will acquire only one of them. The company intends to use the profits of the acquired business to again build up a cash reserve, which will be invested in secure bonds. The corporate tax rate is 40%.

Required:
Advise Patterson Traders whether it should purchase business 1 or business 2.

Case Two   Platt Enterprises Ltd.

Platt Enterprises started a wholesale business two years ago and has made a profit from the beginning. To date, the company has been storing merchandise inventory in a public warehouse, but the business has grown to a point where this policy is now cumbersome.

The company expects to enjoy unusually rapid growth for the next five years until it achieves a steady market share. Platt is seeking to acquire warehouse space for its exclusive use that will carry it through the growth period. After five years, it intends to obtain a more permanent space designed and built for its own specific needs.

A suitable site has been found that will meet Platt's needs for the next five years. The owner of the property has given Platt two options. Under the first of these, Platt would purchase the land and building for $200,000 ($50,000 for land, $150,000 for the building). Under the second, Platt would lease the land and building for five years at an annual rent equal to 11% of the property's current value ($200,000). The lease would be a net lease requiring Platt to pay for all operating costs associated with the property, including property taxes, insurance, utilities, and maintenance.

The company is having difficulty choosing between the two options. The rental rate of 11% of the property's value does not seem excessive, considering that the company can borrow funds at 10% (it currently has no major debt). In fact, there are sufficient cash resources to purchase the property for cash. The purchase option also appears attractive even though the land and building will have to be sold at the end of five years. In particular, the company is aware that recent studies of the local real estate market predict that warehouse properties will increase in value at the rate of 5% annually for the next eight years.

Platt realizes that the same issue will have to be examined again in five years. A local real estate developer who is planning a long-term industrial real estate development is aware of Platt's five-year plan. The developer has indicated that it is prepared to design and construct a building for Platt that will be ready by the end of the five-year period. The developer has also indicated that a group of investors wants to own the proposed property and lease it to Platt under a long-term lease arrangement. Of course, Platt could also choose to own the future property. Platt Enterprises is subject to a 40% tax rate.

Required:

1. Prepare an analysis and advise Platt Enterprises as to which option is most advantageous. You may assume that the future property needed after five years will be obtained through the lease arrangement suggested by the developer.

2. To what extent, if any, would your decision be affected if it were assumed that the future property needed after five years will be purchased by Platt rather than leased?

Chapter 7   Income from Property

Most individual and corporate taxpayers find themselves, at one time or another, in the enviable position of having excess cash flow available for investment. The marketplace abounds with investment opportunities in bonds, debentures, mortgages, bank certificates, shares of public and private corporations, life insurance, and real estate. The method by which the investment's income or loss is taxed will affect the ultimate returns that can be achieved on each type of investment.

This chapter will define and discuss the term "property income for tax purposes" and establish the basic rules that affect its determination. Specifically, this chapter covers the following areas:

1. It defines the term "property income" and gives the general scope of that definition.

2. It examines the basic rules for determining all types of property income.

3. It highlights the unique aspects of the primary types of investment income.

4. It reviews the impact that the taxation of property income has on investment and management decisions.

I. Income from Property Defined

As is the case with other significant terms, the *Income Tax Act* does not provide a specific definition of property income. However, a series of common-law court decisions has established that income from property can generally be defined as the return on invested capital where little or no time, labour, or attention has been expended by the investor in producing the return.[1] In this context income from property includes the following:

1. The return of *dividend income* on the investment in shares of the capital stock of public and private corporations.

2. The return of *interest income* on investments in bank deposits, loans, mortgages, bonds, and debentures.

3. The return of *rental income* on the ownership of real estate or other tangible property.

4. The *royalty income* on the ownership of properties such as patents and mineral rights.

In each case, property income is the annual or regular return received for allowing another party to use one's property. It does *not* include the gain or loss that may result from the sale of that property. The gain or loss on the sale of shares, for example, is normally classified as a capital gain or loss (see Chapter 8). Similarly, if rental real estate is sold, the sale may result in a gain in excess of the property's original cost as well as a recapture of capital cost allowance or a terminal loss. In this case the gain in excess of the original cost is a capital gain rather than property income. However, because capital cost allowance was originally deducted to determine the property income earned from rents, any recapture of the capital cost allowance is property income, and any terminal loss is a property loss.

Further, it must be noted that the nature of the income does not, in itself, qualify the item as property income. To qualify as property income, interest must be earned in a relatively passive way, without the commitment of significant time, labour, and attention by the owner. Interest income earned by a small or large financial institution is not property income but *business* income, because the taxpayer must expend significant effort in order to generate that income.

---

1 *Ginsberg v. MNR*, 53 DTC 445; IT-434R.

Having the income classified as business income rather than property income will not, in most cases, alter the method by which the income is calculated. However, there are a few circumstances in which a difference *will* occur; some of these will be referred to in this chapter.

II. General Rules for Determining Property Income

The general rules for establishing a taxpayer's property (investment) income are the same as those used for determining income from business. The *Income Tax Act* simply states that a taxpayer's income from property for the year is "the profit therefrom."[2] The term *property income* reflects the *net* property income; that is, it takes into account not only the revenues from such sources but also the related expenses incurred to earn those revenues.

Taxpayers generally understand what types of expenses are deductible from their business income; many are not so informed with respect to their investment income. The tax return that individuals must file does not directly indicate that property income is determined net of expenses. It does require that gross income from interest and dividends be included as a separate item; later in the return, certain undescribed deductions can be made. This unusual format, which is not used for business or rental income, confuses many individuals, who wonder how they can deduct expenses from property income.

In the chapter on business income, it was stated that profit is first determined in accordance with well-accepted business principles as interpreted by the courts and with generally accepted accounting principles; this income is further modified by applying certain general limitations to the deduction of expenses; these in turn may be affected by two lists of specific exceptions. The same process is used to determine income from property. Using the guidelines established in Chapter 5, it can be said that, in general terms, expenses incurred to earn property income can be deducted for tax purposes provided that

(a) they are incurred for the purpose of earning income that is taxable;

(b) they are not an expenditure of a capital nature, or an expenditure on the account of capital, or depreciation and amortization;

(c) they are not a reserve;

(d) they are not a personal or living expense; and,

(e) they are reasonable under the circumstances.

Before continuing with this chapter, the reader may find it useful to review parts of Chapter 5 on business income—especially the area that describes the major exceptions to the above general rules—and apply them to the determination of property income.

Two further items require comment before the unique aspects of the various types of property income are examined.

A. Property Income and the Taxation Year

The taxation year for an individual is the calendar year; for a corporation, it is the fiscal year. You will recall that an individual who earns business income may, by exception, determine that income on a fiscal year that does not coincide with the calendar year.[3] It is important to note that this exception is *not* permitted for an individual's property income.

All of an individual's property income must be determined annually on a taxation year coinciding with the calendar year. Corporations, of course, would use the fiscal period, as is generally required.

---

2   ITA 9(1).

3   ITA 11(1), 249.1.

B. The Deduction of Interest Expense

Although interest expense incurred on a loan used to acquire an investment is on the account of capital, an exception to this general limitation permits the deduction of interest expense if the loan was incurred to acquire property that is used to generate property income.[4] This means that interest on loans used to purchase investments such as bonds, bank certificates, shares of corporations, and real estate is deductible against the interest, dividends, and rental income earned.

It is important that the taxpayer establish, through documentation, that a specific loan was used for the purpose of making an investment, since this ensures that interest can be deducted from income.[5] Consider, for example, a taxpayer Mr. L, who intends to purchase a $10,000 personal automobile and, at the same time, invest $10,000 in shares. However, because Mr. L has only $13,000 of cash available, he must arrange a loan of $7,000 to fund the total cost. If the bank loan funds were added to the cash balance of $13,000 before the two purchases were made, it would be difficult to establish whether the loan was used entirely for the investment, or entirely for the personal automobile, or for both. Obviously, in this situation Mr. L wants the loan to be used for the acquisition of shares; that way, the interest on it can be deducted from property income. However, unless he can prove that the loan was used for this purpose, the best that the tax authorities would accept would be that the loan was allocated to both purchases.

Establishing the purpose for which funds are used is best done by maintaining a separate bank account for investment activities. In the above example, if the loan is first deposited in an investment bank account and the only disbursements from that account are for investments, there is no question as to the use of the loan.

Individual taxpayers can borrow money for investments by increasing the mortgage on their personal residence. When this is done, the portion of the mortgage interest that was used to make the investment is deductible for tax purposes. Again, when using this source of financing it must be shown that the mortgage funds were used to purchase the investment; also again, a separate bank account is useful.

When individuals are in a position to acquire both personal assets and investment assets, they should apply the following principles with respect to loan financing in order to maximize their after-tax cash flow:

1. Personal assets should, to the extent possible, be acquired with excess cash. Such assets—cars, a house, a cottage, and the like—can then be used as collateral to obtain loans for investment purposes.

2. When individuals have both personal and investment loans, excess cash should first be used to repay the personal loans that are incurring non-deductible interest. It is important that separate loans be arranged for personal use and investment use.

It is not uncommon for an individual to have a personal loan outstanding while at the same time owning, clear title, investments yielding taxable income. Consider the situation where an individual has a personal loan outstanding of $10,000 (to acquire a cottage) but also owns bonds of $10,000. If both the loan and the investment bear interest at 10% and the rate of personal tax is 45%, the after-tax return to the individual is minus $450 annually, calculated as shown at the top of the next page.

This individual, by cashing in the bonds and paying off the loan, would at least be breaking even, as there would be no interest income and no interest expense.

4 ITA 20(1)(c).

5 *The Queen v. Bronfman Trust*, 87 DTC 5097.

Cash in:	
Interest income on bond at 10%	$1,000
Less tax at 45%	(450)
Net income	550
Cash out:	
Interest paid on personal loan (not deductible)	(1,000)
Net cash cost	$ (450)

The above example demonstrates that it is worthwhile to use excess cash to reduce personal loans that are incurring non-deductible interest. It is important to realize that using excess cash in this manner does not prevent the taxpayer from making other investments when opportunities arise. A reduced personal debt makes for an expanded borrowing capacity, which in turn makes loans for investment purposes easier to obtain.

In summary, individuals who are in a position to acquire both personal-use and investment assets must take care to plan the related loans in a manner that will generate the greatest after-tax cash flow.

III. The Unique Features of Property Income

A. Interest Income

All of the major types of property income—interest, dividends, rentals—have distinguishing features, which are reviewed below.

"Interest income" is defined as the compensation received for the use of borrowed funds. In most circumstances the amount of interest income earned on a debt obligation is readily identifiable from the stated interest rate attached to the obligation. However, in some situations a loan is made without interest, or at a low rate of interest, but with the requirement that the debtor repay an amount greater than the original principal of the loan. To the extent that the additional payment of principal reflects the normal rate of interest that would have been charged on the particular transaction, that extra amount is treated as interest income. If, however, the extra principal amounts to more than normal interest, such amount is usually treated as a capital gain.[6]

• **Recognition of income**   Different types of debt obligations require the payment of interest to the creditor at different times. Some debt obligations require that regular interest payments be made on a monthly, quarterly, semi-annual, or annual basis over the term of the loan. Others permit interest to be compounded, and paid only at the end of the term of the loan. The timing of income recognition for tax purposes is important, because it affects the net after-tax cash flow and, by extension, the yield on a particular investment.

All *corporations*, private and public, must recognize income according to the normal rules for profit determination, and do so on an accrual basis.[7] This means that a corporation must include interest as income as it is earned on a daily basis, even though the interest may not have been received and may not be receivable until some future time.

Situation:

A corporation that has a December 31 taxation year end loans $10,000 on October 1, 20X1. The debtor is to repay the loan in two years. Interest is charged at the rate of 10% compounded annually and is payable in full at the end of the two-year period.

---

6   IT-396R, paragraph 12; ITA 16(1).

7   ITA 12(1)(c), (3); IT-396R.

Analysis:

Total interest on loan:

Year 1—10% × $10,000	$1,000
Year 2—10% × ($10,000 + $1,000)	1,100
	$2,100

Recognition of income by taxation year:

(20X1)

$$\frac{92 \text{ days}}{365 \text{ days}} \times \$1,000 = \qquad \$\ 252$$

(20X2)

$$\frac{273}{365} \times \$1,000 = \qquad \$\ 748$$

plus

$$\frac{92}{365} \times \$1,100 = \qquad 277$$

$$\$1,025$$

(20X3)

$$\frac{273}{365} \times \$1,100 = \qquad \$\ 823$$

Total interest (20X1 + 20X2 + 20X3) $2,100

It can be onerous to pay tax in advance of the receipt of interest income when interest is compounded and payment is delayed over a long period of time.

Individuals, unlike corporations, have at their disposal, within a certain time limitation, the following three options for recognizing interest income:[8]

- the receivable method
- the cash method
- the annual accrual method

Individuals are entitled to choose any one of the above three methods for a given investment, provided that the method chosen is then used consistently for that investment. For example, one may choose to use the cash method for investment A and the annual accrual method for investment B.

Under the *receivable* method, interest is included in income only when the amount is legally due and payable. For example, a corporate bond may require interest to be paid semi-annually on June 15 and December 15 of each year. If at the end of the taxation year (December 31) the December 15 payment has not been received, it must still be included in that year's income, because it is legally due and receivable.

Under the *cash* method, interest income is taken into income for tax purposes only if it has been received by the individual in the year.

When an investment requires that interest be paid after a long period of time (longer than one year), it appears that choosing the cash method or the receivable method would delay the payment of tax until the interest is received or becomes receivable. In fact, that is not the case. Even though the individual may choose either the cash or the receivable method, a supplementary rule referred to as the *annual accrual method* requires that interest income be recognized for every 12-month period from the date the investment was made.[9] This means that interest-income recognition can be deferred for only a limited

8 ITA 12(1)(c), (4); IT-396R.
9 ITA 12(11), (4); IT-396R, paragraph 19.

period. Notice that individuals cannot use the normal accrual method of accruing interest on a daily basis, as can corporations and partnerships. Consider the following situation:

Situation: An individual loans $100,000 on February 1, 20X1. The loan is to be repaid by the debtor in two years, on January 31, 20X3. Interest is charged at the rate of 12%, compounded annually, and is payable in full at the end of two years.

Analysis: Total interest earned on the loan is as follows:

Year 1: (12% × $100,000)	$12,000
Year 2: (12% × [$100,000 + $12,000])	13,440
	$25,440

Individuals determine income on a calendar-year basis. In this situation, the daily accrual method cannot be used and no income is recognized in 20X1. The cash method and the receivable method would delay the recognition of interest income until the 20X3 taxation year. However, because of the special annual accrual method requirement, neither of these methods can be used. Under the special annual accrual method, interest must be recognized every 12 months from February 1, 20X1, until the end of the term of the loan. The income under this method is recognized as follows:

(20X1)	NIL
(20X2)	
February 1, 20X1, to January 31, 20X2	$12,000
(20X3)	
February 1, 20X2, to January 31, 20X3	$13,440
Total interest	$25,440

• **Foreign interest**   Interest earned on investments in a foreign country is recognized in terms of Canadian dollars under the same rules described above. In most cases the foreign payer withholds an amount as payment of foreign tax. When foreign taxes are withheld from the payment, the full amount of interest, before the amount withheld, must be included in property income. However, Canadian tax on this foreign income can be reduced through a foreign tax credit.[10]

The foreign tax credit, which is described in a later chapter, reduces Canadian tax only to the extent that Canadian taxes are paid in the same year. This means that taxpayers who are forced to use the accrual method for recognizing foreign interest may pay Canadian taxes in years before the interest is paid and the foreign tax is withheld. This would preclude the use of the foreign tax credit. In such circumstances the taxpayer can, as an alternative, treat the foreign tax as an expense against property income. While this alleviates the problem somewhat, it does result in an element of double taxation. If foreign investments are contemplated, it is important that the payment of interest income coincide with its inclusion in income for tax purposes.

• **Life insurance policies**   Certain life insurance policies include both a savings component and a life insurance component (whole life insurance). Other policies are designed solely to provide life insurance protection (term life insurance). When a life insurance

---

10 ITA 126(1), (2).

policy includes a savings element that accumulates interest returns, special rules govern the tax treatment of those returns. With respect to policies issued after 1989, the tax treatment of earnings is similar to that for other investment vehicles—income must be reported annually.[11] However, certain policies are exempt from these rules. When the exemption applies, the combination of life insurance and savings can amount to a significant long-term tax deferral. The rules governing life insurance policies are complex and beyond the scope of this text. Before acquiring a new policy, a taxpayer should thoroughly investigate the tax treatment of its related investment returns.

• **Deductions from interest income** Because property income is the "profit therefrom," interest income from property is calculated on a net basis—that is, as the revenue less the expenses incurred to earn the revenue. The types of expenses permitted can be determined by referring to the general rules and list of specific exceptions outlined in Chapter 5. For convenience, some of the typical expenses incurred to earn interest income are listed below.

- Interest expense on loans used to acquire interest-bearing investments.[12]

- Investment counselling fees.[13]

- Costs incurred to obtain a loan such as legal fees, mortgage appraisal fees, and registration fees (amortized over five years at the rate of one-fifth per year).[14]

- Fees paid to managers of investment portfolios.

- Safe-custody costs, such as safety-deposit-box fees or fees paid to a financial institution for holding securities.

- Accounting fees for record-keeping and determination of income from property.

- Reserves or complete deductions for interest income that has been accrued but is not collectible because of the debtor's inability to pay.[15]

If the expenses incurred exceed the interest income, a loss from property occurs that can be offset against the taxpayer's other sources of income, in accordance with the general aggregating formula described in Chapter 3.

B. Dividend Income

Dividends are the returns provided on the investment in shares of a corporation; they reflect the distribution of a portion of the corporation's profits to the shareholders. Ultimately, shareholders of corporations are individuals, but individuals can own shares in a corporation that, in turn, owns shares of other corporations. In other words, dividend income can be received by both individuals and corporations.

Exhibit 7-1 shows two basic structures of corporate ownership and dividend flows. Structure A consists of a single Corporation X, which is owned directly by an individual shareholder. In this situation Corporation X earns income that is subject to tax.

The after-tax profits, which are referred to as retained earnings for accounting purposes, can be either retained by the corporation or distributed in whole or in part to the shareholder. If the earnings are retained, the value of the corporation, and therefore of its shares,

---

11 ITA 12.2(1); IT-87R2.

12 ITA 20(1)(c).

13 ITA 20(1)(bb).

14 ITA 20(1)(e), (e.1).

15 ITA 20(1)(l).

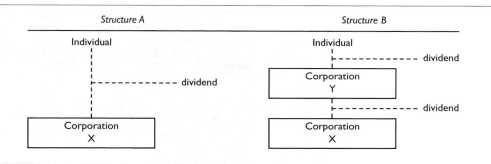

Exhibit 7-1:
Simple Structure of
Corporate Ownership

will rise, increasing the potential for a capital gain when the shares are ultimately sold. Correspondingly, if the earnings are distributed as dividends, the share value will decline, eliminating the capital gain potential and substituting it with dividend income to the shareholder. In summary, corporate earnings are taxed in the hands of the shareholder, either as dividends (property income) or as capital gains depending on whether or not the corporate profits are distributed.

Under structure A the profits of Corporation X are subject to tax, and those after-tax profits are subject to a second level of tax when received as a dividend by the individual shareholder.

In comparison, structure B consists of Corporation X, whose shareholder is Corporation Y. The shareholder of Corporation Y is the individual. Under this structure the after-tax profits earned by Corporation X are distributed, and received as dividend income (property income) by Corporation Y. This increases the earnings of Corporation Y, which can either retain those earnings or distribute them as dividends to its shareholder (the individual). In this case the after-tax profits of Corporation X are received as dividend income for tax purposes by both Corporation Y and the individual.

It would appear from the above discussion that the corporate profits in structure A are subject to double taxation, and those in structure B to triple taxation. The methods by which dividends are included in income for individuals and corporations are designed to deal with the problem of multiple taxation. In some situations multiple taxation of corporate profits is eliminated; in other situations there remains a significant element of double taxation.

• **Dividends received by corporations** Dividends paid by one corporation to another are included in the recipient's net income for tax purposes when they are received.[16] You will recall that the rate of corporate tax is applied to a base referred to as the corporation's taxable income. As described in Chapter 3, the taxable income of a corporation is determined by reducing net income for tax purposes by certain specific items, one of which is dividends received from other taxable Canadian corporations.[17] The result of this in-and-out calculation is that the dividends received by one Canadian corporation from another Canadian corporation are excluded from taxable income and are therefore not subject to normal tax. When Canadian dividends are excluded from taxable income, the possibility of multiple taxation from the flow of after-tax profits between corporations is eliminated. In Exhibit 7-1, for example, the dividends paid by Corporation X are not taxable to the shareholder, Corporation Y. (See Chapter 13 for certain exceptions.)

On the other hand, dividends received by a Canadian corporation from a *foreign* corporation are excluded from taxable income only if the foreign corporation qualifies as a

16 ITA 12(1)(j), (k), 82(1)(a); IT-67R3.
17 ITA 112(1).

foreign affiliate.[18] A foreign corporation qualifies as a foreign affiliate of a Canadian corporation if the owner's equity percentage in the foreign corporation is not less than 10%.

The subject of intercorporate dividends has important tax planning implications. A more detailed analysis of intercorporate dividends is carried out in Part Three of this text, which examines the complete corporate structure.

• **Dividends received by individuals**   Dividends earned by an individual on investments in taxable Canadian corporate shares are included in the individual's net income for tax purposes when received. The amount that must be included in the individual's income is not the actual amount received, but rather an amount equal to 125% of the dividend received.[19] While this gross-up of the dividend appears unfair, it must be viewed as part of an overall scheme to reduce the impact of double taxation when after-tax corporate profits are distributed and taxed a second time in the hands of individual shareholders. This scheme is summarized below.

1. Dividends received by individuals are grossed up by 125% when included in income. The gross-up supposedly reflects the corporate taxes already paid by the corporation on its income. In theory, the grossed-up dividend represents the pre-tax income earned by the corporation that has been distributed as a dividend.

2. The individual shareholders determine their tax on the same corporate earnings reflected in the grossed-up dividend by applying the individual tax rate to income. At this point the corporate profits have been taxed twice.

3. The individual tax on the grossed-up dividend is then reduced by the amount of corporate tax that has already been paid on the same income. This is referred to as a "dividend tax credit." The dividend tax credit is more or less equal (depending on the provincial tax rate) to the gross-up, because the gross-up, at least in theory, reflects the corporate taxes that have been paid.

Supposedly, this system eliminates double taxation by taxing the corporate income twice and then reducing personal taxes by the corporate taxes paid. However, the fixed gross-up rate of 125% makes the assumption that corporate taxes are always 20%. This, as has already been shown, is not always the case. The example on the next page demonstrates how the system works when the corporate tax rate is 20% and the individual tax rate is 45%.

Notice that in this example the total tax paid by the corporation and the individual together is $45 on $100 of corporate profits. This is equal to the personal rate of tax of 45% and is what the individual would have paid if the corporation had not existed and the profits had been earned directly by the individual. The elimination of double taxation works in this example only because the corporate tax rate is assumed to be 20%, which is consistent with the gross-up and dividend tax credit calculation. But when corporate taxes are greater than 20%, which they often are, the dividend tax credit is not sufficient and double taxation occurs.

Individuals receiving dividends from *foreign* corporations are not subject to the gross-up and dividend tax credit treatment described here. Instead, the actual amount of dividends from foreign corporations (before any withholding taxes) is included in income in the year received.[20] In effect, this tax treatment is identical to the treatment given foreign-interest income described earlier in this chapter.

---

18 ITA 113(1), 95(1).

19 ITA 12(1)(j), 82(1)(b); IT-67R3.

20 ITA 12(1)(k), 90.

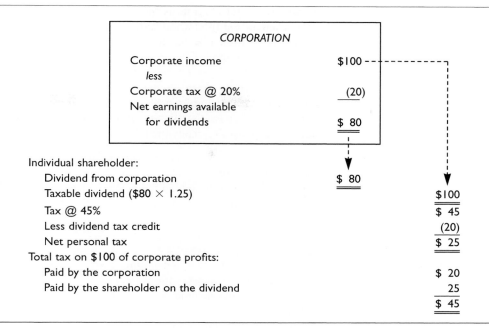

The tax treatment of dividends must also be examined in the context of its relationship to corporate finance and individual investment strategies. This is done in greater detail in several subsequent chapters.

• **Stock dividends** When a corporation issues additional shares in lieu of a cash dividend, the individual shareholders are considered to be receiving stock dividends. From the corporation's perspective, a stock dividend simply transfers a dollar amount from its retained earnings to its permanent capital account. From the shareholder's perspective, the amount transferred to the capital account is deemed to be a taxable dividend; if the shareholder is an individual, this amount is subject to the normal treatment, which includes a gross-up and dividend tax credit.[21]

In effect, a stock dividend is a forced reinvestment of dividend returns in the capital shares of the corporation, although no cash has traded hands. If shareholders wish to receive a cash return on the investment, they are free to sell all or a portion of the stock dividend shares. Because the value of the shares has already been included in income as a dividend, the stock dividend shares are considered to have been acquired at a cost equal to the increase in the paid-up capital of the shares of the issuing corporation (this is often equal to the trading value of shares at the issue date), and any gain or loss on their disposition is determined according to the normal capital gain treatment reviewed in Chapter 8.

C. Rental Income
Rental income is the compensation received for allowing another party to use one's tangible property. In most cases rental income is derived from the ownership of real estate (land and buildings). It is not uncommon for taxpayers to derive rental income from other tangible assets such as equipment, even though they are not in the leasing business. However, this chapter emphasizes the return of rental income from real estate.

• **Recognition of income** Of the three general types of property income discussed in this chapter, rental income most conforms to the normal rules of profit determination.

---

21 ITA 248(1), IT-88R2.

Accordingly, rental revenue is included in income for tax purposes on the accrual basis when earned, rather than when actually received. If rent payments are received in advance, revenue recognition can be delayed and included in the particular year to which the advance payment applies.

• **Deductions from rental income** As with other types of property income, the permitted deductions from rental revenue are in accordance with the normal rules of profit determination for business that were outlined in Chapter 5. The following are some of the deductible expenses typically incurred to earn rental revenue:

- interest expenses incurred on loans used to acquire the rental property or to fund repairs and improvements
- costs incurred to obtain loan financing, such as mortgage fees, legal fees, and appraisal fees (amortized over five years at one-fifth of the cost per year)
- insurance expense
- property taxes
- repairs to the property of a non-capital nature
- maintenance costs such as cleaning, lawn care, and snow and garbage removal
- utility costs (heat, power, and water)
- landscaping costs around a building, even though such costs may be of a capital nature
- capital cost allowance on the building as well as on other related tangible assets such as furniture and equipment
- salaries and wages paid to employees who supervise and/or maintain the property
- property management fees paid to an independent property management organization
- accounting costs for record-keeping and income determination
- costs incurred to collect rents
- advertising

Whether or not an owner incurs such expenses depends on the nature of the property and also on the nature of the lease arrangements. Rental income is derived under two basic types of leases: the gross lease and the net lease. A gross rental agreement requires that the tenant pay only a specific rent; the owner (landlord) is responsible for all expenses associated with the property. A complete net lease, on the other hand, requires that the tenant pay a basic rent as well as all of the costs associated with the running of the property with the exception of financing costs. The gross lease and the complete net lease are the extremes; many lease arrangements fall somewhere between the two.

When the total expenses incurred by an owner exceed the annual rental revenue, a loss from property occurs. In accordance with the aggregating formula for determining a taxpayer's net income for tax purposes, the property loss from rentals can be offset against all other sources of income such as employment income, business income, and capital gains (subject to the restriction discussed below).

• **Special rules for capital cost allowance** Capital cost allowance, terminal losses, and recapture of capital cost allowance all form part of the net income calculation for rental properties. There are two special rules that apply only to rental properties; together, they limit the treatment of capital cost allowance.

1. Capital cost allowance on rental properties can be deducted only to the extent that it does not create or increase a net loss from all rental properties combined.[22]

---

22 Regulation 1100(11); IT-195R4.

2. Each rental building having a cost of $50,000 or more must be held in a separate capital cost allowance class. This is contrary to the normal requirement that assets of a similar class be pooled.[23]

The above exceptions do not change the total capital cost allowance deductions or the income recognized over the full life of the rental property, but they can be a limiting factor on an annual basis, as demonstrated below.

Situation: A taxpayer owns two rental properties. The original cost of the buildings (exclusive of land) was $100,000 for building A and $200,000 for building B. In 20X1 these properties generated the following income or loss:

	Building A	Building B
Gross rental revenue	$ 20,000	$ 30,000
less		
Expenses, other than capital cost allowance	(12,000)	(32,000)
Income (loss) before capital cost allowance	$ 8,000	$ (2,000)

Analysis: Both buildings qualify as class 1 properties and have a maximum capital cost allowance rate of 4% annually. However, because each building cost more than $50,000, each falls into a separate pool. Assuming that buildings A and B have an undepreciated capital cost allowance balance of $90,000 and $170,000 respectively, the maximum capital cost allowance available for 20X1 is as follows:

	Class 1 A	Class 1 B	Total
Undepreciated capital	$90,000	$170,000	$260,000
Maximum capital cost allowance available (4%)	$ 3,600	$ 6,800	$ 10,400

Although a maximum of $10,400 of capital cost allowance is available, the actual capital cost allowance that can be claimed in 20X1 is $6,000, calculated as follows:

Net rental income (before capital cost allowance) on property A	$ 8,000
Net rental loss (before capital cost allowance) on property B	(2,000)
Combined rental income	6,000
Capital cost allowance allowed	6,000
Net rental income for tax purposes	NIL

In this example the $6,000 of capital cost allowance can be claimed partly from the building A class and partly from the building B class, in any proportion up to the maximum available for each class. Alternatively, because the building B class has a $6,800 maximum available, the full $6,000 could be claimed from it.

23 Regulation 1101(1ac); IT-274R.

If the calculation of rental income *before* capital cost allowance results in a combined loss, no capital cost allowance can be claimed in that year. The combined *loss before capital cost allowance can be offset against other sources of income.*

The requirement that each building costing $50,000 or more be placed in its own separate class has a significant impact when the property is sold. Because there is only one asset in each pool, any sale will always trigger the recognition of either a recapture of capital cost allowance or a terminal loss; which one depends on whether the selling price is greater than or less than the undepreciated balance of the building. In most cases the selling price is greater than the undepreciated balance. This means that the sale of a rental building normally results in a recapture even when a new building is acquired in the same year. This, of course, diminishes the amount of after-tax proceeds available for investment—a factor that must be considered in any capital budgeting analysis.

Often, certain furnishings such as stoves, refrigerators, dishwashers, washers, and dryers are part of the premises rented to a tenant. When this is the case, part of the rental income is for those furnishings. The amount of capital cost allowance that can be claimed on the furnishings cannot exceed the net rental income from the property.[24] However, assets of this nature are pooled together under the same class.

In some circumstances an investor will acquire only part ownership in a building along with other owners under tenancy in common. If the cost of the shared building is less than $50,000, it can be pooled with other acquisitions in the same class. From a tax point of view it is advantageous to acquire several partial ownerships under $50,000 rather than a lesser number of wholly owned buildings over $50,000, because sales and acquisitions can then be pooled to avoid recapture of capital cost allowance. Similarly, condominiums purchased in separate complexes can be pooled together if each costs less than $50,000. However, condominium units purchased in the same complex cannot be pooled together if their aggregate cost is over $50,000.[25]

The rules that limit the amount of capital cost allowance and create separate classifications for rental properties do not apply to a corporation or partnership of corporations "whose *principal business* [is] the leasing, rental, development or sale of real property owned by it."[26]

It should also be noted that the amount of capital cost allowance may be restricted on properties other than real estate. When other types of property (leasing property—equipment, vehicles, and so on) are leased, the amount of capital cost allowance in any year is limited to net rental income except for corporations whose principal business is the leasing or sale of such property.[27] This means that taxpayers who invest in leasing properties cannot create a loss by claiming capital cost allowance.

IV. Impact on Investment Decisions

This chapter has examined the tax treatment of the basic types of investment returns—dividends, and rentals. It is readily apparent that the amount of tax on each of these basic types is different, as is the timing of that tax. Consequently, the ultimate after-tax yields vary considerably. The tax treatment of the basic investments can be summarized as follows:

24 Regulation 1100(15).
25 IT-274R.
26 Regulation 1100(12); IT-371.
27 Regulations 1100(15) to (20); IT-443.

A. Cash Flow and Return on Investment

• **Interest-bearing securities**   The return of interest is fully taxed when earned or, for individuals, at least every 12 months from the date the investment is made.

• **Investments in corporate shares**   In most cases such investments present a combined annual yield in the form of both dividend payments and a growth in value of the shares. The dividend is taxed when received; however, for individuals the dividend tax credit reduces the effective rate of tax. For example, as was previously demonstrated, an individual in a 45% tax bracket pays tax of $25, net of the dividend tax credit, on a cash dividend of $80 (grossed up to $100). Therefore, the effective tax rate on dividends for this taxpayer is only 31% ($^{25}/_{80}$ = 31%).

To the extent that common share investments grow in value, the resulting profit normally will be a capital gain for tax purposes. As described in the next chapter, only one-half of the capital gain is taxable, and the gain is taxed when the investment is sold rather than when the growth in value occurs. Therefore, the effective rate of tax on capital growth for a person in a 45% tax bracket is 23% ($\frac{1}{2} \times$ 45% = 22.5%; say 23%), and tax is delayed until the gain is realized.

• **Real estate investments**   Investments in this type of property yield both rental income, which is fully taxable annually when earned, and capital growth, which is taxed as a capital gain only when the property is sold.

A distinguishing feature of this type of investment is that the cost of the building can be deducted as capital cost allowance against rental income over future years. This deduction is valuable because it is permitted even though most rental buildings do not decline in value, but rather appreciate in value. Of course, when the property is sold, the prior capital cost allowance may be recaptured and taxed at that time. The result is that rental income, due to the shelter of capital cost allowance, is not fully taxed until the property is sold. This delay enhances after-tax yields.

Further, to the extent that the property appreciates beyond the original cost, the gain is a capital gain and is not fully taxed until realized.

The dramatic impact of all this is demonstrated in the following situation:

Situation:

An individual has the opportunity to invest $100,000 in one of three separate investments, each of which provides an annual pre-tax yield of 12%.

Investment 1
A bond paying annual interest of 12%.

Investment 2
Common shares of a public corporation that is expected to have an annual yield of 12%, broken down as follows:

Dividends	4%
Capital growth	8%
	12%

Investment 3

A rental property consisting of land ($10,000) and building ($90,000) yielding 12% as follows:

Net rents (before capital cost allowance)	7%
Capital growth	5%
	12%

The investment funds are available for only five years, at which time the investment will be sold and the funds used for other purposes. The individual is in a personal marginal tax bracket of 45%. All annual cash returns can be reinvested in an interest account yielding 12% annually.

Analysis: When analyzing the alternatives it is first necessary to determine the after-tax yield for each type of return. The individual is in a 45% tax bracket. The tax rate and after-tax yield for each income type is as follows:

	(a) Tax rate	(b) After-tax amount 100% − (a)	(c) Pre-tax yield	(d) After-tax yield (b) × (c)
Interest	45%	55%	12%	6.60%
Rent	45%	55%	7%	3.85%
Dividends	31%	69%	4%	2.76%
Capital gain				
Shares	23%	77%	8%	6.16%
Real estate	23%	77%	5%	3.85%

Bond

At the end of five years the $100,000 bond investment will have grown to $137,653, calculated as follows:

Original investment	$100,000
Interest accumulated after-tax:	
$100,000 × 6.6% (compounded) × 5 y	37,653
	$137,653

Common shares

The common share investment will grow in value to $151,883, calculated as shown in table A, next page.

Real estate

Over a period of five years the real estate investment will grow to a value of $144,113, calculated as shown in table B, next page.

A. *Common Shares*

Original investment			$100,000

Dividends:

Annual after-tax dividend is
$100,000 × 2.76% = $2,760.

At the end of each year the after-tax dividend is
deposited in an interest-bearing account yielding
6.6% after tax. After five years this accumulates to: 15,745

Capital growth:

As capital growth is taxed only when the asset is
sold, the investment will compound at the pre-tax
return of 8% annually.

$100,000 × 8% (compounded) × 5 y =	46,933	
Less tax in year 5 @ 23%	(10.795)	36,138
		$151,883

B. *Real Estate*

Original investment			$100,000

Rental returns:

Year	(a) Pre-tax rent	(b) Capital cost allowance	(c) Taxable income (a) – (b)	(d) Tax 45%(c)	(e) After-tax rent (a) – (d)
1	$ 7,000	(1,800)	5,200	2,340	$ 4,660
2	7,000	(3,528)	3,472	1,562	5,438
3	7,000	(3,387)	3,613	1,626	5,374
4	7,000	(3,251)	3,749	1,687	5,313
5	7,000	11,966*	18,966	8,535	(1,535)
	$35,000	–0–	35,000	15,750	19,250

* recapture

Returns of 6.6% on the deposit of annual rents to an interest-bearing account			3,589

Capital growth:

Capital growth, taxed only when the property
is sold, will compound at a pre-tax return
of 5% annually.

$100,000 × 5% (compounded) × 5 y	27,628	
Less tax @ 23%	(6,354)	21,274
		$144,113

In summary, the net after-tax returns of the above three investments indicate that there is a considerable difference in the percentage yields, compared as follows:

	Bond	Shares	Real estate
Original investment	$100,000	$100,000	$100,000
Value at the end of five years	$137,653	$151,883	$144,113
Effective after-tax yield to maturity	6.6%	8.7%	7.6%

The impact of the tax factor on these investments is better exhibited by comparing the differential yields over a longer term. For example, if the bond and share investments described above were extended over a 25-year period, the share investment would compound to a value of approximately $715,000, whereas the bond would grow to a value of only $494,000. The difference of $221,000 is due solely to the tax treatment applied to each investment. Certainly, in choosing between the two investments, the relative risks must be examined and compared in conjunction with the expected returns. But such a comparison is not relevant unless the risks are judged in the context of the *after-tax* yields rather than the pre-tax yields.

B. Business Organization Structure

The special rules and definitions relating to property income can have an impact on corporate structures. For example, it is not uncommon for a business entity to separate the ownership of appreciating assets, such as real estate, from that of other business assets.

Consider Exhibit 7-2, where the shareholders of a business have placed the land and buildings used by the business in a separate corporation. Under this structure Corporation A conducts the business operations and pays rent to Corporation B for the use of its land and buildings.

Exhibit 7-2:
Business Structure
Separating
Appreciating Assets

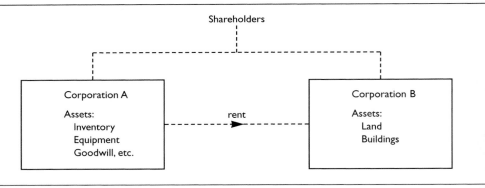

The purpose of this structure may be to shield the appreciating assets from the risk of business failure. Or the owner may want the employees to be able to share the profits from business operations, but not the fortuitous gains that result from the appreciation of the real estate.

Because the land and buildings held in Corporation B earn rental income, they are classified for tax purposes as rental properties, not business properties. As a consequence, each building in Corporation B falls into a separate capital cost allowance pool; as a result of this, the normal business activity of disposing of a small warehouse building and acquiring a larger warehouse will cause the recapture of capital cost allowance. The resulting tax on the recapture will diminish cash available to finance the new acquisition, thereby increasing financing costs. If the land and buildings were held in Corporation A along with the other business assets, the buildings would be pooled in a single class, and no recapture would occur on the disposal and new acquisition.

C. Corporate Financing

The tax treatment of property income has an impact on the cost of corporate financing. The managers of public corporations must have an intimate knowledge of how investment returns will be taxed in the hands of the investors who provide funds for business expansion.

Investors provide debt and equity capital and also lease equipment to businesses to assist in the funding of expansion opportunities. Clearly, the varying tax treatments of property income have an effect on the investor's after-tax rate of return. A corporation that issues securities should attempt to design them in a manner that takes into account the tax sensitivity of the investor who provides the funds. The tax aspects of property income and corporate financing are examined in detail in Chapter 21.

V. Tax Planning Checklist

Many of the tax planning activities relating to property income have been fully discussed in this chapter. Certain others will be reviewed in more detail in later chapters. Below is a brief list of the main tax planning items.

1. Property income is determined using the same rules as for business income. This means that most expenses incurred for the purpose of earning investment income are deductible. Since this is not made clear on the annual tax form, individuals must take special care to gather together all costs related to the investment process.

2. Interest costs often form a large part of investment expenses, so one must be able to establish that borrowed funds were used for investment rather than personal activities.

3. When possible, and as opposed to the reverse, individuals should pay cash for personal assets and then use those assets as collateral when borrowing to make investments.

4. In most cases it is a good investment to use excess funds to repay personal loans that incur non-deductible interest.

5. Securities that compound and delay interest payments may provide higher returns; but they also require that income be recognized annually. This creates an annual tax cost. When possible, reserve such investments for tax-sheltered entities such as RRSPs (see Chapter 9).

6. The rate of corporate tax on interest income is significantly higher than on Canadian dividend income. Therefore, corporations should always compare investment returns on an after-tax basis and then adjust those returns for risk variations (see Chapters 11 and 13).

7. Tax rates for individuals also vary according to whether the income is from interest or Canadian dividends (although not as dramatically as for corporations). In addition, the amount of the variance may differ with the individual's tax bracket (depending on surtaxes and special provincial taxes—see Chapter 10). While the pre-tax rate of return is usually lower from dividends than from interest, the after-tax amounts draw closer together and should be reviewed carefully.

8. The deduction of capital cost allowance on rental properties is restricted to the amount of net rental income. However, the tax deferral that can be achieved from these investments is significant. Again, remember that it is the after-tax return and the difference in the timing of tax that is most relevant.

9. When making real estate investments, consider acquiring a group of partially owned building properties that cost less than $50,000 each, because these can be pooled in the same class for capital cost allowance purposes. This way, recapture of capital cost allowance can be avoided to the maximum extent possible. However, it may be more difficult to sell a part-ownership than one that is 100% owned.

10. Entities that pay investment returns (interest, rents, and dividends) to various types of investors (individuals, corporations, pension funds, and so on) should try to understand the tax treatment that is applied to those investors so that they can design and market cost-efficient securities.

VI. Summary and Conclusion

Income from property is the passive return on investments and primarily includes interest, dividends, and rental income. Income from property for tax purposes is determined under the same rules used to determine income from business. The *Income Tax Act* defines property income as, simply, the profit therefrom; as such, the amount is determined by applying well-accepted business principles and generally accepted accounting principles to ascertain the revenues, and subtracting the expenses incurred to earn those revenues. The accounting rules are modified by six general limitations and a specific list of exceptions, as outlined in Chapter 5.

The concepts of this chapter are not new. The key to understanding property income is to dwell on the unique treatment of interest, dividends, and rental income as highlighted by the exceptions, without losing sight of the general rules for profit determination.

The exceptions that give property income its unique features are summarized as follows:

1. Interest income
   - Corporations recognize interest income only on the accrual basis in accordance with accounting principles.
   - Individuals can recognize interest income when it is received, when it becomes receivable, or by the annual accrual method. The choice of method is the individual's provided that the income from each investment is fully recognized at least every 12 months from the date the investment was made.

2. Dividend income
   - Individuals include in income the dividend received plus 25% of the amount received. The gross-up must be viewed in relation to the dividend tax credit, which reduces individual taxes payable in recognition of corporate taxes that have already been paid on the same income.
   - Corporations are generally not taxed on dividends from other Canadian corporations; the dividend income is first included in net income for tax purposes, but is later deducted when arriving at taxable income.

3. Rental income
   - Both individuals and corporations determine rental income on the accrual basis, in accordance with accounting principles.
   - Capital cost allowance on rental property cannot be used to create a loss from rentals but can be deducted to reduce net rental income to nil.
   - Each rental building costing $50,000 or more is placed in a separate capital cost allowance class, which forces automatic recapture on the sale of each building.

The marketplace offers a wide range of investment opportunities in each category of property income. The terms and conditions imposed on the returns from interest-bearing securities, shares, and real estate can vary considerably. A thorough assessment of each investment and how it compares with others cannot be made unless the returns are expressed on an after-tax basis.

It is essential, especially in public corporations, that managers understand how the investment community is taxed on property income, in order that the corporation can achieve debt, equity, and leasing capital at the most efficient cost. Lease arrangements and public offerings of securities must reflect the realities of the tax system and attempt to take advantage of its unique aspects.

Reading List

Income Tax Act References

	Section
Income from business or property	9(1)
Proprietor of a business	11(1)
Interest (income)	12(1)(c), (3), (4)
Investment contract (annual anniversary)	12(11)
Interest expense	20(1)(c)
Fees paid to investment counsellor	20(1)(bb)
Costs incurred to borrow money	20(1)(e), (e.1)
Reserve for doubtful debts	20(1)(1)
Amounts to be included (life insurance policy)	12.2
Dividends from corporations resident in Canada	12(1)(j)
Taxable dividends received	82(1)
Dividends from other corporations (foreign)	12(1)(k)
Deduction of dividends received by corporations resident in Canada	112(1)
Dividends received from non-resident corporations	90, 112(2)
Dividend and stock dividend (defined)	248(1)
Dividends received by spouse	89(1)
Rental properties	Regulation 1100(11)
Rental properties (principal business)	Regulation 1100(12)
Rental properties (separate class for costs over $50,000)	Regulation 1100(1ac)
Leasing properties (other than real estate)	Regulation 1100(15) to (20)
Rental properties (exclusion of MURBs)	Regulation 1101(56)

Canada Customs and Revenue Agency Publications

IT-434R	Rental of real property by an individual.
IT-396R	Interest income.
IT-87R2	Policyholder's income from life insurance policies.
IT-67R3	Taxable dividends from Canadian resident corporations.
IT-88R2	Stock dividends.
IT-195R4	Rental property—capital cost allowance restrictions.
IT-274R	Rental properties—capital cost of $50,000 or more.
IT-371	Rental property—meaning of "principal business."
IT-443	Leasing property—capital cost allowance restrictions.

Major Court Decisions

Ginsberg v. MNR, 53 DTC 445—Property income distinguished from business income.

The Queen v. Bronfman Trust, 87 DTC 5097—Deductibility of interest—use of borrowed funds.

Demonstration Question

George Chan lives in Brandon, Manitoba. As an employee and minority shareholder of GG Ltd., a private corporation, his income has allowed him to accumulate a modest investment portfolio that includes rental properties.

In 20X4, he had several transactions relating to the rental properties and has requested your tax advice. These transactions and other information are provided below.

Information Relating to Rental Properties

1. Chan first acquired rental properties in 20X2, as follows:

	Land	Building	Total
Property A	$40,000	$220,000	$260,000
Property B	12,000	48,000	60,000
	$52,000	$268,000	$320,000

Subsequently, Chan realized that the properties were located in an undesirable area. He sold both of them in 20X4 for the following proceeds:

	Land	Building	Total
Property A	$36,000	$212,000	$248,000
Property B	10,000	44,000	54,000
	$46,000	$256,000	$302,000

2. In 20X4, Chan purchased rental property C for $70,000 (land $30,000; building $40,000). He also constructed rental property D, which was completed on October 31, 20X4, and included the following costs.

Land	$ 50,000
Building	300,000
Landscaping	6,000
Architect's fees	10,000
Paving (parking lot)	8,000
Heating system	12,000

3. The accounting statement for the year ended December 31, 20X4 for all properties showed a net loss of $40,400. The loss includes deductions for $3,200 of amortization/depreciation, as well as a $31,000 loss from the sale of rental properties.

4. At the end of 20X3, the undepreciated capital costs were $209,376 for property A and $45,696 for property B.

5. A review of the statement of loss includes the following:

   • An amount of $800 was received in 20X4 from a tenant who failed to pay three months' rent in 20X3 and was evicted. The amount was credited to the rent receivable account. The former tenant still owes $400, which will not be collected. A reserve for unpaid rents of $1,200 had been deducted for tax purposes in 20X3. In June 20X4, Chan requested that new tenants pay the last month's rent of a 12-month lease at the time of signing. Included in rental income is $1,000 of these payments.

   • Repairs and maintenance expense includes the following:

Painting interior suites	$2,300
Snow removal and lawn care	2,100
Installation of vinyl siding on the existing walls of building B before sale	5,200

   • "Other expenses" includes land transfer taxes of $1,200 to acquire the new properties.

   • Interest expense is made up of the following:

Mortgage interest paid (all properties)	$7,800
Bank interest on temporary loan to finance construction of property D.	10,000

   • Legal fees include $1,500 to prepare the mortgage documents on property D, and $500 to collect unpaid rents.

Other Financial Information

1. The year end of GG Ltd. is June 30. On May 1, 20X3, GG Ltd. loaned Chan $18,000 to assist him with the purchase of shares in GG Ltd. No interest was charged on the loan. On August 31, 20X4, GG Ltd. declared a dividend of which Chan's share was $22,000. He received $4,000 in cash, and the remaining $18,000 cancelled his debt to the company. CCRA's prescribed interest rate for 20X4 was 7%.

2. Chan received a salary from GG Ltd. of $90,000 in 20X4.

3. On July 1, 20X3, Chan purchased a four-year guaranteed investment certificate for $40,000. The interest compounds at 8% the first year, 9% the second year, and 10% for the last two years. The entire interest will be paid on June 30, 20X7. Chan did not include any of the interest in his 20X3 income for tax purposes.

4. Chan's other receipts and disbursements in 20X4 included the following:

Receipts:	
Dividends from foreign corporations (after 10% withholding tax)	$9,000
Proceeds from the sale of public corporation shares:	
A Ltd. (original cost—$42,000)	50,000
B Ltd. (original cost—$30,000)	20,000

Disbursements:	
Investment counsel fees	500
Life insurance premium on policy required as collateral for a	
loan used to purchase shares in GG Ltd.	1,000
Interest paid on the mortgage on his home. The mortgage is	
$120,000, of which $80,000 was used to acquire the home and	
the balance was used to purchase public corporation shares.	12,000
Donations to registered charity	4,000

Required:
1. Determine Chan's minimum net rental income for tax purposes for 20X4.
2. Determine Chan's overall net income for tax purposes for 20X4.

Solution:
Before we calculate the rental income, we explain certain items. Rental properties A and B acquired in 20X2 are both class 1 properties but are required to be put in separate classes because property A cost more than $50,000. The building of property B, which originally cost $48,000, can be pooled with the new building of property C, which has a cost of $40,000 in 20X4. The building of property D has a cost greater than $50,000 and therefore must be included in a separate class. The result of this is that the sale of property A will incur a recapture of capital cost allowance on its sale, whereas a recapture on the sale of property B is avoided because of the addition of property C to the class.

The construction of the building of property D must include in its cost all of the costs necessary to bring the building to a usable state, such as the architect's fees and interest during the construction period. Also, the cost of the heating system is part of the building cost.

The cost of paving the parking lot qualifies as class 17, which has a capital cost allowance rate of 8% (diminishing balance). The landscaping cost of $6,000 is fully deductible under section 20(1)(aa), even though it is a capital item. The cost of $5,200 for vinyl siding included as a repair expense is a capital item and must be added to the cost of building B before its sale.

Remember that capital cost allowance can be claimed only to the extent of the net rental income. The recapture of capital cost allowance resulting from the sale of property A is included as rental income and therefore increases the net rental income for the purposes of determining the maximum capital cost allowance that can be claimed.

Chan must include a deemed interest benefit on the loan from his employer. The amount is included in employment income. However, because the loan was used to acquire shares that can earn property income, the amount of the benefit can be considered as interest expenses and deducted in arriving at net income from property.

Calculation of rental income

Rental loss per financial statement	$(40,400)
Amortization/depreciation	3,200
Loss on sale of properties	31,000
Landscaping	(6,000)
20X3 reserve for uncollectible rents	1,200
Unpaid rent established to be a bad debt	(400)
Prepaid rent	(1,000)
Vinyl siding—capital item—add to cost of building B	5,200
Land transfer tax—capital item—add to cost of land	1,200
Interest during construction—add to cost of building D	10,000
Legal, financing cost (deductible at $\frac{1}{5}$ per year)—$\frac{4}{5}$ × 1,500	1,200
	5,200
Recapture of capital cost allowance on property A	
($212,000 − $209,376)	2,624
Income before capital cost allowance	7,824
Capital cost allowance—limited to rental income	(7,824)
Net rental income	–0–

Capital cost allowance:

	Property A Class 1	Properties BC Class 1	Property D Class 1	Class 17
UCC—20X3	$209,376	$45,696		
Dispositions (A and B)	(212,000)	(44,000)		
Additions:				
B—Vinyl siding		5,200		
C—Building		40,000		
D—Building			$300,000	
D—Paving				$8,000
D—Architect fees			10,000	
D—Heating system			12,000	
D—Interest (construction)			10,000	
	(2,624)	46,896	332,000	8,000
Recapture	2,624			
Available CCA		*1,852	**6,640	***320

Total CCA available—$8,812 ($1,852 + $6,640 + $320)

* (45,696 × 4%) + ([40,000 + 5,200 − 44,000] × 4% × ½) = $1,852
** 332,000 × 4% × ½ = $6,640
*** 8,000 × 8% × ½ = $320

Net income for tax purposes

Employment income:		
Salary		$90,000
Interest benefit—$18,000 × 7% × 8 months/12 months		840
		90,840
Property income:		
Rental income (above)	–0–	
Canadian dividend—$22,000 × 1.25	27,500	
Foreign dividend ($9,000 + $1,000)	10,000	
Interest, GIC—$40,000 × 8% – interest from		
July 1, 20X3 to June 30, 20X4 (annual accrual)	3,200	
	40,700	
Investment counsel fees	(500)	
Life insurance premium	(1,000)	
Deemed interest expense on employee loan (above)	(840)	
Interest on house mortgage—		
$12,000 × $40,000/$120,000	(4,000)	34,360
		125,200
Taxable capital gains:		
Land—properties A and B—½ ($52,000 – $46,000)	3,000	
Shares of A Ltd.—½ ($50,000 – $42,000)	4,000	
	7,000	
Allowable capital loss—½ ($30,000 – $20,000)	(5,000)	2,000
Net income for tax purposes		$127,200

Review Questions

1. Although the *Income Tax Act* specifically refers to property income as a separate type of income, it does not provide a specific definition of the term. Identify the source from which the definition of property income is derived, briefly explain the term's meaning, and provide examples of income from property.

2. Distinguish between income from property and the gains or losses that may occur from the sale of property.

3. Interest income earned on loans by a financial institution may, for tax purposes, be classified in a different way from interest income earned on loans by taxpayers who are investing their savings. Explain why.

4. Briefly explain how income from property is determined for tax purposes.

5. Compare and contrast the taxation year of an individual with that of a corporation with respect to the determination of business income and property income.

6. "An individual can deduct for tax purposes the interest expense incurred on the mortgage loan attached to his or her personal residence." Is this statement true? Explain.

7. A taxpayer has sold property (land) for $200,000 that was originally purchased for $70,000. The property was sold to an arm's-length party (not related). The terms of sale involve a cash payment of $100,000 on closing, with the balance to be paid at $20,000 per year for five years, with no interest charged on the unpaid balance. For tax purposes, what types of income may result for the vendor from this transaction?

8. An individual invests in a bank term deposit on July 1, 20X0. When does the individual recognize the interest income for tax purposes if the investment has a term of three years, with interest compounded annually but paid only at the end of the three-year term? Would your answer be different if the taxpayer were a corporation? Explain.

9. Can a taxpayer deduct a reserve for unpaid interest on a loan if the interest appears not to be collectible? Explain. How does the treatment of unpaid interest compare with the treatment of the loan principal when its repayment is in doubt?

10. Briefly explain why an individual who receives dividends from a Canadian corporation must include 125% of the dividend received in income for tax purposes, while a corporation receiving the same dividend includes only the actual amount of the dividend.

11. "If a loss occurs from the renting of real estate (that is, if annual expenses exceed rental income), the loss is not recognized in determining a taxpayer's overall net income for tax purposes." Is this statement true? Explain.

12. A building that costs $200,000 and is rental property will always create a terminal loss or a recapture of capital cost allowance when it is sold. The same result may not occur if the building is used directly in a business activity. Explain this.

13. An investor in real estate may achieve a higher rate of return by acquiring a small portion (part ownership) of several properties rather than a lesser number of whole properties. Explain this.

14. Why is the purchase of rental real estate often referred to as a "tax sheltered" investment?

15. Often an enterprise conducting an active business will separate its business operations from its appreciating assets (such as real estate) by establishing a separate corporation for each. How may this type of structure impair future expansion activities?

Problems

Problem One

On April 1, 20X0, a corporation with a December 31 taxation year purchased a three-year investment certificate for $20,000. The certificate pays interest only at the end of the three-year term but is compounded annually at the rate of 10%. Currently, the corporation's marginal tax rate is 40%. However, in 20X1 the marginal tax rate will increase to 43%.

An individual makes the identical investment on April 1, 20X0. The individual's marginal tax rate in 20X0 is also 40% and is expected to rise to 43% in 20X1.

Required:

Calculate and compare the tax on the interest income for the three-year period for the individual and the corporation.

Problem Two

Ken Potman is the sole shareholder in Brickbase Enterprises Ltd., a Regina-based construction company. In addition, Potman is a 25% partner in a retail kitchenware store, although he does not actively participate in its management. The following information relates to Potman's financial affairs for the year 20X1:

1. Brickbase was organized three years ago. For its year ending May 31, 20X1, the company earned a profit of $88,000. Potman originally contributed $200,000 to the corporation, using $50,000 of his own savings and funding the balance with a bank loan. In return, the corporation issued Potman $1,000 worth of common shares and $199,000 of preferred shares. In 20X1 the company declared a dividend of $12,000 on the preferred shares.

2. During the year, Potman sold a warehouse property for $180,000 (land $15,000, building $165,000). The building was used by Brickbase to store construction equipment, and the company paid Potman a fair rental for use of the property. The property was originally purchased at a cost of $140,000 (land $10,000, building $130,000). At the end of 20X0 the building had an undepreciated capital cost of $110,000.

   Simultaneously with the sale, Potman purchased a larger warehouse property, which was also rented to Brickbase. The new property cost $400,000 (land $50,000, building $350,000). During the year, the company paid Potman net rents of $30,000 for both properties. The new property was financed with the proceeds from the sale of the old building as well as mortgage financing.

3. The retail store partnership earned $40,000 for its year ending December 31, 20X1. The profit consisted of a $32,000 profit from operations and $8,000 of interest income earned on excess undistributed cash deposits.

4. Potman's other cash receipts and disbursements for 20X1 are shown in the table below.

5. On July 1 of the previous year, Potman purchased a four-year guaranteed investment certificate for $30,000 that bears interest at 10%. The interest compounds annually but is not payable until the end of the four-year term. Potman did not include any amount of interest in his previous year's income.

6. During the year, one of the Canadian public corporations of which Potman is a shareholder issued him 100 additional shares as a stock dividend. The shares had a stated value of $40 per share. Potman placed the shares in his safety deposit box along with his other securities.

Receipts:	
Salary from Brickbase	$62,000
Dividends from Canadian public corporations	6,000
Dividends from foreign public corporations (net of 10% foreign withholding tax)	9,000
Winnings from provincial lottery	2,000
Interest on a loan to his daughter	1,000

Disbursements:

Contribution to Brickbase employee pension plan	3,000
Investment counsel fees	1,000
Legal fees for registering mortgage on new warehouse	5,000
Life insurance premium on policy required as collateral for the bank loan used to purchase Brickbase shares	1,000
Interest on warehouse building mortgage	21,000
Interest paid on house mortgage. (The house mortgage is $100,000, of which $70,000 was used to acquire the house. The balance was used to purchase public corporation shares.)	10,000
Interest on bank loan (re: Brickbase shares)	15,000
Donations to local charity	4,000
Safety deposit box fees	100

Required:
Determine separately, for the year 20X1, Potman's income for tax purposes from employment, business, and property.

Problem Three
Anne Osinski acquired a townhouse unit in 20X0 for $120,000 (land $10,000, building $110,000). She bought the unit in order to rent it. By the end of 20X2, the undepreciated capital cost of the building was $103,500. In August 20X3, Osinski decided to live in the unit herself. At that time, similar townhouses were selling for $136,000 (land $12,000, building $124,000). Prior to August, her 20X3 net rental income before capital cost allowance was $1,000.

In September 20X3, Osinski purchased, for rental purposes, a condominium unit for $145,000 (land $15,000, building $130,000). Between September and the end of the taxation year, the condo earned net rentals of $900 before capital cost allowance.

Required:
Determine the change to Osinski's 20X3 net income for tax purposes as a result of the above activity.

Problem Four
After receiving an inheritance, Sandra Yaworski decided to invest her newly acquired funds in real estate. In 20X1 she purchased the following properties:

	Land	Building	Total
Property 1	$10,000	$ 40,000	$ 50,000
2	12,000	45,000	57,000
3	20,000	80,000	100,000
4	30,000	100,000	130,000

Each of the properties is a residential condominium unit, and each unit is part of a separate condominium high-rise project. Not all of the units were fully rented during the year of acquisition, and Yaworski determined that her net rental position (before capital cost allowance) for each of the properties was as follows for 20X1:

Property	1	2	3	4	Total
Rent revenue	$4,000	$5,000	$7,000	$12,000	$28,000
Expenses*	(6,000)	(3,000)	(6,000)	(9,000)	(24,000)
Income (loss)	($2,000)	$2,000	$1,000	$ 3,000	$ 4,000

* Property taxes, insurance, interest, maintenance.

In 20X2 one of Yaworski's close relatives ran into financial difficulty, and she was forced to sell two of the properties in order to provide financial assistance. She sold property 1 for $52,000 (land $12,000, building $40,000) and property 3 for $110,000 (land $24,000, building $86,000). In 20X2 the four properties (including the two sold properties to the date of sale) earned net rental income of $7,000.

Required:
Determine Yaworski's net income from property from the rental properties for 20X1 and 20X2.

Problem Five
Toshiaki Minamiyama is a successful business executive. Over the years, he has allocated a portion of his large salary to the building of an investment portfolio. He currently has a net worth of $800,000 (exclusive of retirement plans), as follows:

Personal assets:	
Automobiles	$ 30,000
Sailboat	29,000
House	220,000
Investment assets:	
Corporate and government bonds (average interest return—10%)	200,000
Common shares of public corporations	306,000
Rental real estate	360,000
	1,145,000
Liabilities:	
First mortgage on house (interest at 9%)	(150,000)
Term financing on sailboat (12%)	(15,000)
First mortgage on rental real estate (10%)	(180,000)
Net worth	$ 800,000

Minamiyama seldom trades his investments, as his strategy is to hold various types of investments for a long time in order to delay any tax that may occur on their disposition. (He is in a 45% tax bracket.) In fact, he chose not to dispose of any investments when he needed money to purchase his house and sailboat.

Required:
From a tax planning perspective, what would you recommend he do in order to enhance his wealth accumulation? If possible, quantify how he would benefit from your recommendations, assuming a five-year time period.

Problem Six

Quantro Enterprises Ltd. and Baizley Holdings Ltd. (BHL) are both 100% owned by Harold Baizley. Both companies are Canadian-controlled private corporations. Quantro operates a wholesale business and pays rent to BHL for the use of a warehouse property.

BHL owns only one asset—the warehouse building and related land that is rented by Quantro for $36,000 per year. The property was originally owned by Quantro but was sold to BHL several years ago as a means to reduce the risk exposure of this appreciating asset.

On December 31, 20X1 (the year end of both companies), BHL sold the warehouse property to a third party for $370,000 (land $40,000, building $330,000). The property originally cost $320,000 (land $25,000, building $295,000). The undepreciated capital cost of the building at December 31, 20X0, was $254,000.

One month before selling the warehouse property, BHL purchased a larger warehouse property for $480,000 (land $50,000, building $430,000).

Required:

Determine BHL's net income for tax purposes for 20X1.

Problem Seven

Sally Corbet is the sole shareholder of Corbet Holdings Ltd. (CHL), a Canadian-controlled private corporation. The corporation holds investments in shares, bonds, and real estate. You have been retained to complete CHL's tax return for the year ended December 31, 20X2, and provide certain other tax advice.

It is now February 15, 20X3, and you have gathered the information outlined below.

1. The draft income statement for the year ended December 31, 20X2, is as follows:

Income		
Interest on bonds and certificates		$ 78,000
Dividends from Canadian corporations		32,000
Net loss from real estate rentals		(19,000)
Gain on sale of land (Pelican Lake)		170,000
Share of profits of Pantry Products Ltd.		120,000
		381,000
Expenses		
Legal fees for general corporate affairs	$ 1,000	
Director's fees	21,000	
Donations—charitable	8,000	(30,000)
Income before income tax		$351,000

2. CHL owns a 40% interest in Delroy (a partnership), which has a June 30, 20X2 year end. The partnership's profit for the year was $200,000, which consisted of dividends from taxable Canadian corporations of $80,000 and royalties from mineral rights of $120,000.

   On December 31, 20X2, CHL received $100,000 as its share of a partnership cash distribution. The partnership's results are not reflected in the above income statement.

3. On September 30, 20X2, CHL purchased a $100,000 guaranteed investment certificate bearing 9% interest. The company intends to record the interest of $9,000 on September 30, 20X3, its one-year anniversary date.

4. The dividend income of $34,000 consists of the following:

Public corporations	$16,000
Turner Inc.—an American corporation—net of a 10% U.S. withholding tax	18,000

   Not included in the above is a dividend received from Pantry Products Ltd. of $25,000. CHL owns 50% of its voting shares and records the investment using the equity method of accounting. Pantry earned business income of $240,000 in the current year.

5. During the year, CHL received 100 shares of Mustang Ltd. (a public corporation) as a stock dividend. Mustang increased its paid-up capital by $30 for each stock dividend share issued. CHL did not record the receipt of the stock dividend.

6. In January 20X2, CHL purchased three hectares of land at Pelican Lake for $130,000. The land was then rezoned and subdivided into six building lots. The entire subdivision was immediately sold to a building contractor for $300,000. The payment terms called for no cash down, but payments of $50,000 are required as the contractor completes construction on each lot. By December 31, 20X2, one payment of $50,000 had been received.

7. In 20X1, CHL had purchased two rental properties as follows:

	Land	Building	Total
Fourplex	$50,000	$150,000	$200,000
Townhouse 1	20,000	40,000	60,000
	$70,000	$190,000	$260,000

   Maximum capital cost allowance was claimed in 20X1.
   In 20X2, townhouse 1 was sold for $75,000 (land $25,000, building $50,000).
   On December 1, 20X2, CHL purchased townhouse 2 for $50,000 (land $11,000, building $39,000). Also in 20X2, CHL constructed a sixplex rental unit for $437,000, as follows:

Land	$ 80,000
Permanent landscaping	8,000
Labour and materials	300,000
Air-conditioning and heating equipment	49,000
	$437,000

All of the properties resulted in a net rental loss of $19,000 (as shown on the financial statement). The following items are included in the net loss calculation:

Cost of surveying land (new sixplex)	$ 2,400
Amortization/depreciation	28,000
Legal fees for mortgage (new sixplex)	2,000
Advertising for new tenants	4,000

Required:

Determine CHL's net income for tax purposes for the 20X2 taxation year. Also, prepare a breakdown of the net income for tax purposes showing the net income from property and any other sources of income.

Problem Eight

Carol Wong is the president and major shareholder of CW Ltd., a Canadian-controlled private corporation that operates a construction business in Regina, Saskatchewan.

In 20X7 she had a number of financial transactions. She has asked you to help her prepare her 20X7 tax return and provide advice on other tax matters. The following additional financial information is provided:

1. Wong's 20X7 gross salary was $90,000, from which CW Ltd. deducted the following amounts:

Income tax	$30,000
CPP and EI premiums	2,076
Private health insurance premiums	600
Group sickness and accident insurance premiums	400

In addition to her salary, CW Ltd. paid $2,000 to a deferred profit sharing plan, $600 of private health insurance premiums, and $400 of group sickness and accident insurance premiums on Wong's behalf.

2. Wong is required to use her own automobile for company business. For this, CW Ltd. pays her an annual allowance of $3,600. In 20X7, Wong incurred automobile operating costs of $5,200. Also in 20X7 she purchased a new automobile for $34,000 and received $18,000 as a trade on her old car. At the end of the previous year, the old car had an undepreciated capital cost allowance balance of $15,000 (class 10.1). Of the 20 000 kilometres driven in 20X7, 12 000 were for employment purposes.

3. For three months in 20X7, Wong was sick and could not attend work. She received $9,000 from the company's group sickness and accident insurance plan. Since the plan's inception, Wong had paid premiums totalling $2,000.

4. During 20X7, Wong purchased a warehouse property and leased it to CW Ltd. to store construction equipment. The property cost $250,000 (land 30,000, building 220,000). The price for the land includes $2,000 of permanent landscaping completed just after acquisition. The 20X7 rental income is summarized below.

Rent received		$20,000
Expenses:		
Insurance	1,200	
Property taxes	4,000	
Interest	10,000	
Repairs:		
General maintenance	800	
Storage shed addition	3,000	(19,000)
Income		$1,000

5. Wong is a 30% partner in a computer software business but is not active in its management. The partnership financial statement shows a profit of $40,000 for the year ended December 31, 20X7. The profit consists of $32,000 from software sales and $8,000 from interest earned.

6. On July 1, 20X6, Wong purchased a three-year guaranteed investment certificate for $20,000 with interest at 10%. The interest compounds annually but is not payable until July 1, 20X9.

7. Wong received (made) the following additional receipts (disbursements) in 20X7:

Receipts:	
Dividends from Canadian public corporations	$2,000
Dividends from CW Ltd.	3,000
Dividends from foreign corporations (net of 10% foreign withholding tax)	900
Winnings from a provincial lottery	12,000
Disbursements:	
Contribution to RRSP (within allowable limits)	10,000
Dental expenses for children	3,500
Donation to a charity	2,000
Safety deposit box	100
Life insurance premium used as collateral for personal bank loan	800
Investment counsel fees	1,000

Required:

Determine Wong's minimum net income for tax purposes in accordance with the aggregating formula of section 3 of the *Income Tax Act*.

Problem Nine

CB Ltd. is a Canadian-controlled private corporation owning a portfolio of investments including stocks, bonds, and rental properties. The financial statements for the year ended June 30, 20X1 show a profit of $104,300, summarized as follows:

Bond interest	$50,000
Taxable dividends from Canadian corporations	20,000
Gain on sale of assets	40,000
Rental loss	(5,700)
Income before income taxes	$104,300

Additional financial information is outlined below.

1. The previous year's corporation tax return includes the following tax account balances:

Undepreciated capital cost:	
Class 1—building A	$125,000
Class 1—building B	35,000
Class 1—building C	46,000

2. Taxable Canadian dividends totalling $20,000 include $8,000 from public corporations and $12,000 from X Ltd., a Canadian-controlled private corporation. CB Ltd. owns 30% of X Ltd.'s common shares.

3. The rental properties were purchased in prior years as follows:

	A	B	C
Land cost	$ 20,000	$35,000	$21,000
Building cost	130,000	40,000	49,000
	$150,000	$75,000	$70,000

On February 28, 20X1, property A was sold for $170,000 (land 30,000, building 140,000) and property B was sold for $77,000 (land 40,000, building 37,000).

The combined rentals resulted in a loss of $5,700 after deducting amortization/depreciation of $3,000 for the year ended June 30, 20X1. The rental revenue includes a $1,000 rental deposit applying to the last two months' rent on a lease expiring December 31, 20X2.

For the year ended June 30, 20X0, CB Ltd. deducted a reserve for unpaid rents of $2,000. In January 20X1, $1,000 of the unpaid rents was received and credited to the reserve account. No reserve has been claimed at June 30, 20X1; however, $1,200 of the current year's rents remain unpaid.

Required:

Determine CB's minimum net income for tax purposes for the 20X1 taxation year.

Case

Helen Chapman

Helen Chapman is 56 years old and intends to retire in four years. Most of her investment funds are tied up in her employer's pension plan and in her personal registered retirement savings plan. In addition, she has managed to accumulate a personal investment fund of $100,000, which currently is invested in government treasury bills earning interest at 9%.

Immediately before retirement, Chapman intends to use her personal investments and her pension plans to acquire a life annuity that will provide her with a guaranteed monthly income. She is looking for an investment for the $100,000 currently invested in treasury bills that will maximize the value of the annuity. Her investment counsellor has proposed two secure investment options, as follows:

- *Option 1* is a corporate bond yielding annual interest of 13%. The counsellor has advised that Chapman could fund a purchase of $200,000 of the bonds with $100,000 of cash (from the treasury bills) and $100,000 of borrowed funds. Because her house is debt-free, her bank has offered to provide her with a term loan secured by a mortgage on the house. The loan interest rate would be 10%, and no principal payments would be required until the end of the term of the loan.

- *Option 2* is a real estate investment. A small, single-tenant commercial building is currently under construction and will be completed in six weeks. A prospective tenant has already agreed to a 12-year lease. The lease calls for rent payments of $40,000 annually for four years, at which time the annual rent will increase by 12% and then remain fixed for the remaining eight years of the lease. The tenant will be responsible for all costs associated with the property, including property taxes and insurance.

The developer is prepared to finance up to $300,000 of the project with a 10-year first mortgage that includes a requirement to pay only interest (no principal) at the rate of 9% per annum. The full principal balance is due at the end of 10 years. At the closing date the property will be ready for tenant occupation, except that the landscaping will have to be arranged and paid for separately by Chapman. The total cost of the investment and the related funding is as follows:

Cost:	
Land	$ 40,000
Building	350,000
Landscaping	8,000
Legal fees to register first mortgage	2,000
	$400,000
Funding:	
Cash	$100,000
Mortgage (9%)	300,000
	$400,000

Whichever investment she chooses, Chapman intends to liquidate the investment at the end of four years and use the funds to acquire a life annuity for retirement. Her marginal tax rate is 45%.

Required:
Advise Chapman which investment will best meet her objectives.

Chapter 8   Gains and Losses on the Disposition of Capital Property—Capital Gains

Capital gains (or capital losses) refer to the gain (or loss) realized on the disposal of capital property. Capital property, by definition, is property that provides a long-term and enduring benefit to its owners; consequently, disposals of such property tend to occur irregularly and infrequently over a taxpayer's lifetime. Properties that are held for personal use and enjoyment, or for investment purposes, or for the purpose of assisting in generating business activity, all have the potential for capital gains. Calculating a capital gain or loss for tax purposes is a very simple matter; however, it will become readily apparent that this calculation departs radically from the one used to determine other types of income with respect to the timing of income recognition, the amount of income subject to tax, and the utilization of losses when they occur. Some people regard the tax treatment of capital gains as preferential, and the treatment of capital losses as unfair. In either case, their tax treatment is a significant factor to consider when an investment in capital assets is being contemplated.

Of primary importance is the ability to recognize when a gain or loss on the sale of property is classified as a capital gain or loss as opposed to income or loss from business. Because the *Income Tax Act* does not provide specific guidelines, establishing whether a transaction is a capital one is the most complex aspect of the study of capital gains and losses.

This chapter develops a definition of capital gains for tax purposes, presents the basic rules for determining the amount and timing of gains and losses, and examines certain unique types of properties. In addition, the broad impact of the tax treatment of capital transactions on investment and business decisions is examined.

I. Capital Gain and Capital Loss Defined

A capital gain (or capital loss) is the gain (or loss) realized on the disposition of capital property. For a property to be classified as capital property, it must have been acquired and used for the purpose of providing the owner with a long-term or enduring benefit.

Notice that the definition does not indicate that the property must be held for a long time, or that it must provide a benefit; instead, it is enough that the *intended purpose* of the acquisition was to achieve benefits over a long period of time. Whether or not the property actually achieves its intended purpose is governed by future events that may or may not be controllable by the owner. The key to understanding the concept of capital gains (or losses) lies in focussing on the intended purpose of acquisition. Unfortunately, the ultimate results do not always provide proof of this intended purpose, and consequently, there are frequent disputes between CCRA and taxpayers as to what was in fact the original intention.

It is necessary to clarify the term "benefit." In the context of capital property, *benefit* refers to both direct and indirect benefits achieved from the use of the property. These benefits need not be financial in nature. The acquisition of a rental building will result in direct financial benefits in the form of rent receipts. The purchase of a warehouse building for use in a business will result in indirect financial benefits by creating the ability to store merchandise held for resale. The purchase of a summer cottage will result in a non-financial benefit in the form of personal enjoyment. Each of these items is capital property and is subject to capital gains treatment for tax purposes.

The general definition of capital gains and losses is subjective, because it is based upon the intended purpose of the property acquisition rather than on the actual results achieved. Because the circumstances surrounding each acquisition are different, each property must be assessed in the context of its unique position. Because the *Income Tax Act* does not provide definitive guidelines, it has been left to the common-law process to establish some general considerations. In order to fill out the overall definition of capital property subject to capital gains treatment, it is useful to do the following:

(a) compare the definitions of capital income and business income;

(b) review the principles established by common law for assessing intended purpose; and,

(c) examine the categories of capital property established by the *Income Tax Act*.

A. Capital versus Business Income

The sale of property by any taxpayer can be classified as a business activity or as a capital transaction—it depends on the intended purpose of acquiring the property. The following points were made in Chapter 5:

1. Property acquired for the purpose of resale at a profit is classified as inventory. Its disposition results in business income or a business loss.

2. Property acquired for the purpose of providing the owner with a long-term or enduring benefit is classified as capital property. Its disposition results in a capital gain or loss.

Obviously, the above comparison does not mean that one cannot realize a profit on the sale of capital property. It does, however, hinge on the way in which that profit was generated. The profit on capital property (capital gain) arises from the mere enhancement of the capital value of an asset that was acquired for some other purpose.[1] The profit on other property (business income) results from a scheme of profit making that was the owner's intended purpose.

As stated in Chapter 5, the nature of the asset is not relevant. The same property may be capital property to one taxpayer but inventory to another. A truck that makes product deliveries provides a long-term benefit to the owner and is capital property, but a truck purchased by an automobile dealer for resale at a profit is inventory. Even within the same entity, similar assets may be classified differently. Land acquired to provide parking for customers is capital property. If that same business acquired other land for speculative purposes, it would be classified as inventory. The tax treatment on each land sale would be different.

It is recommended that the reader review the first few pages of Chapter 5, which provide a more detailed comparison of business income and capital gains on similar properties.

In some cases the nature of the transaction is more complex, and the distinction between business income and capital gains is not so apparent. Consider the following example:

Situation: A Canadian corporation that was previously not active in business purchased a 40-year franchise permitting it to operate particular hardware stores across Canada. Subsequently, the corporation sold subfranchises (one for each province) to separate buyers in return for a cash amount and continued royalties based on sales. After seven years the corporation sold the master national franchise at a substantial profit and ceased all operations in the hardware business. The purchaser of the national franchise obtained the rights to all future royalties from the subfranchises.

Analysis: The national franchise is capital property, because it is an income source that brings an enduring benefit to the corporation in the form of continued royalties from the subfranchises. Because of its limited life of 40 years, the master franchise also qualifies as depreciable property under class 14 and can be amortized over 40 years against the royalty income (see Chapter 6).

---

1 *California Copper Syndicate Ltd. v. Harris* (1904), 5 DTC 159.

> The sale of subfranchises constitutes business income. The right to subfranchise the master franchise is property that was acquired for the intended purpose of resale. It is therefore inventory, and the sale to 10 separate buyers constitutes income from business.
>
> The sale of the master national franchise is a sale of capital property that has appreciated in value. To the extent that the selling price is in excess of the original cost, a capital gain results. A recapture of capital cost allowance (business income) also occurs if capital cost allowance is claimed on the original cost.

The above example highlights the issue of "intended purpose" in a complex situation. The situation assumed that the taxpayer meant to obtain long-term benefits from the master franchise by selling royalty-based subfranchises. The corporation's original intention may have been to acquire the master franchise in order to sell it at a profit; if this had been the intention, the gain would have been classified as business income. But the facts were that the master franchise was held for seven years, and that the corporation went through the process of selling subfranchises; neither fact is consistent with this intention.

B. Intention

Because the history of a transaction does not always reflect its original intention, numerous disputes between CCRA and taxpayers have been heard by the courts. These hearings attempt to determine the intended purpose by examining the manner in which the owner dealt with property.[2] While the facts surrounding each case are always different, the courts have consistently taken certain factors into account when establishing the original intention. These factors, which are outlined below, are not ranked, as the importance of each depends on the relative strength and weakness of the others in a particular case.

• **Period of ownership**   That a property is held for a long period of time substantiates the claim that it is capital property which was purchased to provide a long-term and enduring benefit. That a property is held for a short period of time speaks against such a claim, in that it is evidence that the property may have been purchased for resale. Obviously, property purchased for a long-term benefit may, owing to special factors, be sold after a brief ownership period, and property purchased for resale may be held for a long period of time; so period of ownership by itself does not provide compelling evidence of intention. It is, however, a factor when examined in conjunction with the other factors discussed below.

• **Nature of the transaction**   The courts will examine the entity's course of conduct over the ownership of the property, dwelling on the point of acquisition, the use of the property during its ownership, and the reasons for and nature of its disposition.[3] The sale of raw land, even when it is held for a period of 15 years, may be regarded as business income if the owner cannot provide evidence of enduring benefit through rental or personal use and enjoyment. On the other hand, an individual who purchased vacation land with the intention of building a summer cottage, but sold the raw land for a profit after a brief ownership period, may be considered to have achieved a capital gain if the reason for the sale was that the original intention was frustrated by a sudden need for money, an inability to finance the cottage, a job transfer, or the like.

---

2   *Regal Heights Ltd. v. MNR*, 60 DTC 1270; IT-459, IT-218R.

3   *MNR v. Taylor*, 56 DTC 1125.

- **Number and frequency of transactions** A historical pattern of frequent buying and selling supports the premise that the intended purpose of acquisition was to resell at a profit.[4] This factor may be significant even though the property generated benefits during the ownership period. The frequent acquisition and sale of rental real estate properties may be considered as resulting in business income even though those properties were held for a respectable time period and reasonable rental profits were achieved. In some cases the courts have decided that an individual has earned business income on the sale of his or her home when a historical pattern of acquisition, renovation, and sale has emerged, even though the home was used as a residence during the ownership period.

  It should be pointed out that while a history of frequent transactions in similar property is strong evidence that the gains or losses are business income, the reverse is not true. The courts will consider, but have not given significant weight to, the argument that an isolated transaction suggests a capital transaction.

- **Relation of transaction to taxpayer's business** If the property sold is similar in nature to property normally dealt with as part of the owner's trade or occupation, it is difficult to establish that the ownership of such property was of a capital nature.[5] A person who makes his or her living by selling real estate is normally considered to have generated business income by selling a unit of rental real estate even when the property was held for a reasonable period of time and generated normal rental returns. Similarly, a lawyer whose practice consists extensively of real estate transactions will have a more difficult time proving that real estate was acquired for the purpose of providing a long-term and enduring benefit.

The above factors indicate that even when the reason for acquiring a property is clear to the purchaser, it may not be so clear to the tax assessor. It is important that taxpayers, when possible, document their course of conduct relating to the acquisition, period of use, and sale of property. Evidence such as copies of correspondence, internal memos, and the like is invaluable, especially when the original intention was thwarted by external factors.

It is important to remember that the above factors are only guidelines that assist in establishing the primary intention. Each factor by itself is not significant; it is when *all* are considered together that a course of conduct becomes evident. Each transaction must be judged on its own merits. Do not lose sight of the fact that the process of establishing that a transaction was of a capital nature begins with establishing the original purpose of acquisition—i.e., that it was to obtain a long-term or enduring benefit from its use.

There are two areas with respect to intention that require special mention. First, sometimes the intended purpose of ownership changes, so that the property is held for a period of time for one purpose and for a period of time for another purpose. Second, certain properties—marketable securities in particular—are often acquired for the dual purpose of providing annual benefits *as well as* a profit on sale. Each of these situations has a special tax treatment, which is discussed shortly.

Worth noting first is that the issue of intention may be further confused when a taxpayer enters into a transaction with both a primary and a secondary intention. In other words, the taxpayer has considered that if one objective fails, a fall-back plan is available and viable. In such circumstances there must be evidence that the taxpayer had the secondary objective in mind when acquiring the property.[6]

---

4 *Brown v. MNR*, 50 DTC 200.

5 *McDonough v. MNR*, 49 DTC 621.

6 *Racine v. MNR*, 65 DTC 5098.

1. Change in Purpose

Property that was acquired to provide a long-term benefit and has been used for that purpose may, at some point, be converted into inventory and held for the purpose of resale. For example, farmland that has been used to produce farm revenue, or a parking lot used for customer parking, may cease to be used for such purpose and be subdivided and held for property development and resale. Such a change of purpose does not constitute a disposition for tax purposes. Similarly, property that was acquired as inventory for resale, such as a piece of equipment, may, if not sold, be converted to capital property and used to produce income. In both situations, when the property is ultimately sold, this question arises: Is the gain a capital gain, a business gain, or a combination of the two?

While the *Income Tax Act* provides no rules for such situations, CCRA has developed a policy which requires that the gain or loss be allocated between capital and business income in accordance with the property's value at the time the purpose changed.[7] In the land example above, the capital gain would be set at the difference between the property's market value at the time of change and the original cost. Any further gain would be business income. Both gains are recognized only at the time of the actual sale. In such circumstances it is important that the owner attempt to establish the property's value at the time of the change in use, in order to take maximum advantage of the allocation.

2. Canadian Securities

Investments in marketable securities almost always have a dual purpose: to generate annual returns and to realize a profit on resale. Historically, CCRA has applied the common-law principles described previously in a lenient manner; that is partly in recognition of the dual purpose but also a reflection of the government's desire to promote investment in equity securities. With respect to the investment in *Canadian* securities only, the *Income Tax Act* permits taxpayers (other than security dealers) to remove themselves from the common-law rules of intention and simply elect to have all sales of Canadian securities treated as capital transactions.[8] A Canadian security is considered to be (with some minor exceptions) a share of the capital stock of a resident Canadian corporation, a unit of a mutual fund, or a bond, debenture, bill, note, mortgage, or other similar obligation issued by a resident of Canada.

While choosing this election ensures capital treatment of all security transactions, it also locks the investor into using this method indefinitely. This may not always be desirable, especially considering the limitations on the use of capital losses when they occur. Many investors choose not to make the election, and subject themselves to the lenient application of the common-law rules. This gives them the option of treating substantial trading losses as business losses (if the facts support that position), which can readily be offset against other sources of income.

C. Categories of Capital Property

In order to understand which properties are subject to capital gains treatment for tax purposes, it is useful to outline the categories of capital property. The *Income Tax Act*, directly or indirectly, defines three categories of capital property:

- personal-use property
- listed personal property
- financial property

---

7 IT-102R2, IT-218R; *Armstrong v. The Queen*, 85 DTC 5396.
8 ITA 39(4) to (6); IT-479R.

Of the above, only personal-use property and listed personal property are specifically defined in the *Income Tax Act*. After these two specific definitions have been examined, the third definition—for financial property—will be clear.

• **Personal-use property** Personal-use property is property owned by the taxpayer that is used primarily for the personal use or enjoyment of the taxpayer, or persons related to the taxpayer, and that does not generate financial returns.[9] All personal property such as a car, a boat, land, a house, a cottage, furniture, a piano, and so on is personal-use property and subject to capital gains treatment.

• **Listed personal property** Property in this category includes items that are for personal use but also have some element of investment value. This category is limited to several specific items, which are listed in the *Income Tax Act* as follows: [10]

- a print, etching, drawing, painting, or sculpture, or other similar works of art
- jewellery
- a rare folio, rare manuscript, or rare book
- a stamp
- a coin

Any property not listed above that is for personal use and enjoyment is personal-use property.

• **Financial property** In this category is included all capital property that was acquired primarily to generate a benefit through a financial reward. It includes such items as shares, bonds, loans, land, buildings, equipment, patents, licences, franchises, and vehicles. Only a few capital properties are excluded from this category, the main one being property that qualifies as eligible capital property, as described in Chapter 6.

Clearly, the capital gains provisions encompass a wide range of properties. When examining the disposition of a capital property, it is important to establish it in one of the above categories because, as will be described later in the chapter, certain aspects of transactions are treated differently in each category.

II. Determining Capital Gains and Losses— General Rules

Capital gains and losses were introduced in Chapter 3 as one of the five income categories. You will recall that the aggregating formula, which combines all the types of income to arrive at a taxpayer's net income for tax purposes, includes only the amount by which the total taxable capital gains for the year exceed the total allowable capital losses for the year.[11] Hence, the principle is established that capital losses can be offset only against capital gains, and cannot be used to offset other sources of income earned by a taxpayer. (The same restriction is not placed on other sources of income; business losses and property losses can be offset against any other source of income for tax purposes.) The cash-flow implications of this special treatment were discussed in Chapter 3 and are reviewed again later in this chapter; this section restricts itself to establishing the format for calculating the capital gain or loss on each individual asset sold. However, it is important to relate the individual calculation to the aggregating formula in order to establish its effect on the amount of tax payable.

9 ITA 54; IT-332R.
10 ITA 54.
11 ITA 3(b).

A. General
Calculation

The capital gain or loss on the disposition of a given capital property is calculated by completing the following simple procedure:[12]

Proceeds of disposition		xxx
less		
Adjusted cost base (ACB)	xx	
Expenses of disposition	x	xx
Capital gain or capital loss		xx

Only *one-half* of the above capital gain is included in net income for tax purposes; it is referred to as the "taxable capital gain."[13] Similarly, only one-half of a capital loss is included in the calculation of net income for tax purposes; it is referred to as the "allowable capital loss." At the end of each taxation year the taxable capital gains and the allowable capital losses on all properties are totalled separately and included in the aggregating formula.

Notice that the terminology used in the above calculation is different from the normal accounting terminology used in the disposal of long-term assets. The taxation terms "proceeds of disposition" and "adjusted cost base" are much broader than the accounting terms and require special examination.

B. Disposition and
Proceeds of
Disposition

Capital gains and losses are recognized for tax purposes only when a disposition of the property occurs.[14] If an investment in shares of a public corporation increases in value during the year, no capital gain is recognized. Similarly, if the investment declines in value, a capital loss does not occur. In comparison, when a bond compounds interest annually but pays none for 10 years, the investor who purchased it must recognize accrued interest annually.

Normally a disposition of property occurs when[15]

(a) property is sold;
(b) property is involuntarily eliminated by theft, destruction, or expropriation;
(c) a share, bond, debenture, note, or similar property is cancelled, redeemed, or settled; or,
(d) a share owned by a taxpayer is converted by amalgamation or merger (see Chapter 14).

When property is sold, the proceeds of disposition is the selling price, whether it is received in cash or is payable at some future time. Property that is sold in exchange for other property has proceeds of disposition equal to the fair market value of the property received in exchange. The proceeds of disposition for an involuntary disposition is the compensation received for stolen, destroyed, or expropriated property.

In some circumstances property is *deemed* to be disposed even though no proceeds of disposition are received. A deemed disposition of property occurs in the following circumstances:

1. When property is transferred by way of a gift to another party, the taxpayer is deemed to have sold the property at its fair market value at that time (see Chapter 9).[16]

---

12 ITA 40(1)(a)(i).

13 ITA 38.

14 ITA 39(1).

15 ITA 54, "disposition" and "proceeds of disposition."

16 ITA 69(1)(b).

2. When the use of property changes from personal use to business or investment use, or when it is changed from business or investment use to personal use, the property is deemed to have been sold at its fair market value.[17]

3. Property is deemed to have been sold at fair market value when a taxpayer ceases to be a resident of Canada for tax purposes.[18] Certain properties, such as real estate situated in Canada, and inventory, eligible capital property, and capital property from a business in Canada, are excepted. However, if adequate security is posted, the tax payment can be delayed until the property is sold.

4. On the death of an individual, all of that person's capital property is deemed to have been sold immediately prior to death (see Chapter 9).[19]

The definitions of *disposition* and *proceeds of disposition* are very broad when the concepts of actual disposition and deemed disposition are combined.

C. Adjusted Cost Base

Normally the adjusted cost base of a property is the original purchase price plus other costs incurred to make the acquisition, such as brokerage fees, installation costs, and legal fees. Sometimes the original cost is expanded, as described in Chapter 6, when the original cost of depreciable property is increased by the cost of substantial repairs and alterations. There are, however, a number of adjustments to cost for tax purposes that may or may not also be accepted for accounting purposes.[20]

The *Income Tax Act* lists, in section 53, a number of specific additions to and deductions from cost that can be made to arrive at the adjusted cost base of a property. For example, when a taxpayer receives a government grant or subsidy to acquire an asset, the purchase price of the asset is reduced by the amount of the grant to arrive at the adjusted cost base for tax purposes. If the asset is subsequently sold, the capital gain will be determined as the difference between the selling price and the lower cost base rather than between the selling price and the original cost. The adjustment to the cost base ensures that the grant or subsidy will be taxable as a capital gain if and when it is recovered through an asset sale. The taxable benefits received when shares are purchased under an employee stock option arrangement are added to the cost of the shares to ensure that the same income is not counted twice (see Chapter 4). These examples demonstrate that the adjustments to cost base are technical and specialized in nature. A detailed review is beyond the scope of this text.

In some cases it is possible for the accumulated cost base reductions to be greater than the cost of the asset. When this occurs the negative balance is considered a capital gain and is recognized in the year in which it occurs.[21] By exception, a negative adjusted cost base of an interest in a partnership normally does not create a capital gain (see Chapter 15).

Special provisions apply to the adjusted cost base of a property that was acquired before 1972 and is still owned by the taxpayer.[22] Before 1972, capital gains were not taxable; to reflect this, the adjusted cost base of property acquired before that year is tied to its fair market value at December 31, 1971.

---

17 ITA 45(1).

18 ITA 128.1; IT-451R.

19 ITA 70(5).

20 ITA 52, 53, 54.

21 ITA 40(3).

22 ITAR 26(3), 26(7), 20; IT-84, IT-139R.

In some circumstances property may be acquired without a cost. A person who receives a gift of property has no actual cost. However, as described above, the person who made the gift is deemed to have sold the property at fair market value, and consequently the recipient of the gift is deemed to have an adjusted cost base of the same amount.[23]

D. Expenses of Disposition

Because of the nature of capital property, the owner often requires assistance to complete the sale transaction. All costs incurred to complete the disposition are deductible when arriving at the capital gain or loss; such costs include legal fees to complete the sale agreement, brokerage fees or commissions to agents, advertising, and mortgage discharge fees.[24]

E. Deferred Proceeds

Capital property, by its nature, often commands a relatively high selling price; this often means that the buyer must fund the purchase with a combination of cash reserves and debt financing. In order to facilitate a sale, a vendor may act as the financer for the purchaser by accepting payment in the form of an immediate down payment in cash, with the balance, with interest, to be paid over some future time period. When this occurs, the capital gain rules permit the vendor, subject to a time limitation, to recognize the taxable capital gain over a period of years in proportion to the receipt of the proceeds of disposition.[25] The deferred recognition of capital gains is restricted to a maximum of five years, and a minimum of 20% of the capital gain must be recognized, on a cumulative basis, for each of the five years. This method for recognizing capital gains is optional for each property sold.

It should be noted that the time limit of 5 years is extended to 10 years when the sale is made to a child of the taxpayer *and* the property sold is shares of a small business corporation, farm property, or an interest in a family farm partnership.[26]

If the taxpayer chooses to use this method, the capital gain calculation referred to previously must be modified, as demonstrated next.

Situation:

A taxpayer sold property in 20X0 for $200,000. The property had an adjusted cost base of $130,000, and selling costs of $20,000 were incurred. The selling price of $200,000 is to be paid to the vendor as follows:

Cash on sale (20X0)	$ 80,000
20X1	30,000
20X2	–0–
20X3	90,000
	$200,000

23 ITA 69(1)(c).
24 ITA 40(1).
25 ITA 40(1)(a)(iii); IT-236R3, IT-436R.
26 ITA 40(1.1).

Analysis:

Capital gain:

Proceeds of disposition		$200,000
less		
Adjusted cost base	130,000	
Expenses of disposition	20,000	(150,000)
Capital gain		$ 50,000
Taxable capital gain (½ × $50,000)		$ 25,000

(20X0)

Taxable capital gain		$ 25,000
Less deferred portion:		
$\dfrac{\$120{,}000 \text{ (deferred proceeds)}}{\$200{,}000 \text{ (total proceeds)}} \times \$25{,}000 =$		(15,000)
Taxable capital gain recognized		$ 10,000

Notice that the deferred portion of the gain is in the proportion of the unpaid price to the total price. The gain recognized for tax purposes of $10,000 is 40% of the total gain, as 40% of the total proceeds (40% of $200,000 = $80,000) was received in 20X0. Because 40% of the gain is recognized in 20X0, the requirement to recognize at least 20% per year has been satisfied for both 20X0 and 20X1.

(20X1)

Unrecognized capital gain	$15,000
Less deferred portion:	
$\dfrac{\$90{,}000}{\$200{,}000} \times \$25{,}000$	11,250
Taxable capital gain recognized	$ 3,750

(20X2)

In 20X2, no additional payment is received. However, a portion of the gain must be recognized because the cumulative 20% minimum has not been met. By the end of 20X2 only 55% of the price has been received ($110,000/200,000 = 55%), but a minimum of 60% (20% × 3 y) must be included in income.

Taxable capital gain recognized: 5% × $25,000 =	$1,250

(20X3)

In 20X3, the full balance of the proceeds is received, and therefore the balance of the gain must be recognized.

Total taxable gain		$25,000
Less previously recognized:		
20X0	$10,000	
20X1	3,750	
20X2	1,250	(15,000)
Taxable gain recognized in 20X3		$10,000

Deferring the recognition of the capital gain to future years in proportion to the receipt of the proceeds is referred to as a reserve. The reserve is deducted from the taxable capital gain in the year to arrive at the taxable amount. It is important to recognize that claiming the reserve is *discretionary*, and that the taxpayer can choose not to defer the recognition of the gain. This may be desirable if the taxpayer has a capital loss in the year to offset the gain, or if it is anticipated that tax rates will be higher in the future years. When the reserve is claimed, a formula exists to ensure that the reserve will not exceed the requirement that at least 20% of the gain be included in income on an accumulated basis. The formula states that the maximum reserve in any year is equal to the lesser of

(a) deferred proceeds/total proceeds $\times$ taxable gain (as demonstrated above),
   or
(b) 80% of the gain in year 1, 60% in year 2, 40% in year 3, 20% in year 4, and zero in year 5.

An alternative formula for calculating the deferred portion of a capital gain is permitted when the property being sold is already encumbered with a debt and when the buyer assumes that debt as part of the purchase obligation.[27] In such cases the taxpayer can recognize the gain in proportion to receipt of the equity in the property. For example, if capital property has a value of $100,000 but is encumbered by a first mortgage of $40,000, the owner's equity interest is $60,000. If that owner sold the property for $100,000 and the purchaser settled the price by assuming the first mortgage of $40,000, paying cash of $10,000 and owing the balance of $50,000, the deferred taxable capital gain would be calculated as follows:

$$\frac{\$50,000 \text{ (deferred proceeds)}}{\$60,000 \text{ (equity in property)}} \times \text{gain}$$

This method permits a greater deferral than the method previously demonstrated, provided that the 20% rule does not limit its application. The obvious benefit of deferring the proceeds of disposition, and thereby the related tax, is that it permits the owner to reinvest a greater amount of the proceeds on a pre-tax basis by charging interest to the purchaser on the unpaid portion.

This section has developed the general rules for computing the capital gain or loss on the disposal of a single capital asset. With the exception of the rules relating to deferred proceeds, the principles are straightforward and easy to apply. Before examining how the taxation of capital property affects investment and management decisions, it is necessary to review some unique aspects of capital losses and the treatment of special types of property.

III. Unique Aspects of Capital Losses

In accordance with the general rules established in the previous section of the chapter, capital losses are recognized only when a disposition occurs; and as a result of the aggregating formula outlined in Chapter 3, they can be deducted for tax purposes only to the extent that capital gains were realized in the same year. Because of this restriction, a taxpayer who has incurred a capital loss should consider disposing of other capital property that has appreciated in value. Conversely, a taxpayer who is facing a capital gain should consider disposing of property that has declined in value in order to create an offsetting loss.

If a capital loss cannot be used in the current year, it can be carried forward indefinitely and used in the future when a capital gain occurs; or it can be carried *back* to the previous three years provided that capital gains were incurred in those years. This carry-forward and carry-back procedure is not part of the overall net income calculation; rather, it is applied

---

27 IT-236R3, paragraph 8.

when the net income for the year is reduced to taxable income. This topic will be discussed in detail in Chapter 10.

Normal rules do not apply to certain types of capital losses, some of which are discussed below.

A. Allowable Business Investment Losses

An allowable business investment loss (ABIL) is the allowable capital loss (one-half of the actual loss) incurred on the disposition of a loan to a small business corporation, or on a sale of that corporation's shares (provided that sale is made to an arm's-length party).[28] In general terms, a small business corporation is a *private* corporation that is Canadian-controlled and that uses all or substantially all of its assets (valued at fair market value) to conduct an active business.[29] CCRA holds the view that "substantially all" means at least 90% of the assets.

When such a loss occurs, the aggregating formula permits it to be offset against all other sources of income derived by the taxpayer, as an exception to the normal capital loss rules. In this way, the after-tax risk of investing in small business corporations is reduced relative to other capital investments, because the tax savings on a loss, if one should occur, are readily usable.[30]

B. Deemed Disposition on Loans and Shares

The rule that a capital loss can be recognized only when the property is disposed of is a burden to taxpayers when a market is not available for the sale of the property. In particular, when an investment in shares of a corporation has declined in value because the corporation has suffered extreme financial problems, or when an outstanding loan is uncollectible due to the debtor's inability to pay, the owner may be unable to sell the property and trigger the disposition. In recognition of this problem, property that is a loan or a share of capital stock of a corporation is subject to deemed-disposition rules that permit the loss to be recognized before an actual disposition occurs, as follows:[31]

1. An outstanding debt is deemed to be disposed of for a value of nil at the time it is established that it is a bad debt.

2. A share of the capital stock of a corporation is deemed to be disposed of for a value of nil at the time the corporation has become legally bankrupt. If the corporation is not legally bankrupt, a deemed disposition may still be permitted if, at the end of the year, the corporation is insolvent, it has ceased operating its business (with no intention to resume), the value of its shares is nil, and the corporation is expected to be dissolved.

It is clear from all this that it is easier to recognize a loss on a bad loan than on a share, because in the case of a loan it need only be established that the loan is uncollectible, whereas with a share the owner must wait for legal bankruptcy or other specified conditions to occur. Also, the loss from the deemed disposition may be classified as an allowable business investment loss if the loan or the shares are from a small business corporation, as discussed previously.

---

28 ITA 38(c), 39(1)(c), 251(1); IT-484R2.

29 ITA 248(1).

30 Also, when an ABIL is incurred, an individual is restricted from claiming the capital gain deduction (see Chapter 10) in future years until taxable capital gains of an equal amount have been included in income. Conversely, if a capital gain deduction has been claimed in a prior year, the ABIL may be restricted.

31 ITA 50(1), (2), 40(2)(g); IT-159R3.

C. Depreciable Property

Under no circumstances can a capital loss occur on the disposition of capital property that is also classified as depreciable property. As described in Chapter 6, the original cost of depreciable property is written off through the capital cost allowance system. Therefore, any actual loss arising when property is sold for a price less than its original cost is automatically reflected in the annual capital cost allowance calculation or the terminal loss or recapture, if any.

For example, say that all of the depreciable property of a class originally cost $10,000 and has an undepreciated capital cost of $8,000. If it is sold for $7,000, a terminal loss of $1,000 occurs at the time of sale. The selling price of $7,000 is $3,000 less than the original cost of $10,000; this loss is fully recognized for tax purposes as follows:

Capital cost allowance in previous years	$2,000
Terminal loss on sale	1,000
	$3,000

D. Superficial Losses

When property has declined in value, a taxpayer who has no real intention of ridding himself or herself of the property may dispose of it in an attempt to trigger the recognition of a capital loss; subsequently, or before the sale, that person may reacquire the same property. In such circumstances, when the reacquisition occurs within 30 days of the sale of the original property, the resulting loss is classified as a superficial loss and is deemed to be nil for tax purposes.[32] The actual loss is not permanently denied, but rather is added to the adjusted cost base of the new identical property and will be recognized when the new property is sold.[33]

Situation: On December 31, 20X0, a taxpayer sold 500 shares of Corporation X for $8,000 that originally cost $10,000. On January 5, 20X1, the taxpayer reacquired 500 shares of Corporation X for $7,500.

Analysis:

(20X0)

Proceeds of disposition	$ 8,000
less	
Adjusted cost base	(10,000)
Actual capital loss	$ 2,000
Superficial loss deemed to be—	NIL

(20X1)

Cost of new shares:	
Actual cost of 500 shares	$ 7,500
plus	
Loss previously denied	2,000
Adjusted cost base of new shares	$ 9,500

When the new shares are ultimately sold, the original loss of $2,000 is deducted from the selling price as part of the cost of the new shares sold.

---

32 ITA 54, 40(2)(g).
33 ITA 53(1)(f).

The same treatment applies when a taxpayer incurs a loss from the sale of property to his or her own corporation or to a corporation controlled by a spouse. In these circumstances the loss is deemed to be zero.[34] A capital loss is also denied when it results from the transfer of property by an individual to an RRSP.

E. Personal-Use Property

As previously mentioned, personal-use property is capital property from which the owner derives a long-term benefit—that is, personal use and enjoyment.[35] For tax purposes, any loss suffered on the sale of personal-use property is deemed to be nil, even though gains on such property are taxable.[36] Presumably, this policy reflects the fact that the loss on sale is equivalent to the enjoyment received from the use of the property.

This restriction is applied to each item of personal property, which means that the capital loss on one item of personal-use property cannot be offset against a capital gain realized on the sale of another personal-use property.

Personal-use property is further distinguished from other capital property by having a deemed minimum cost for tax purposes of $1,000 and deemed minimum proceeds of $1,000.[37] Therefore, small items of personal-use property will be subject to capital gains treatment only to the extent that the proceeds of disposition exceed the minimum amount of $1,000.

F. Listed Personal Property

Listed personal property was defined previously as personal-use property that has personal value as well as investment value; it is restricted by definition to specific items such as works of art, rare books, jewellery, stamps, and coins.[38]

Listed personal property is different from personal-use property in this way: a loss from the sale of listed personal property is recognized for tax purposes. However, capital losses from listed personal property can be offset only against capital gains from listed personal property; they cannot be offset against other capital gains or other forms of income.[39] To the extent that capital losses on listed personal property cannot be used in the current year (because there are not sufficient capital gains from listed personal property), the unused loss can be carried back three years or forward seven years and deducted against listed personal property gains, if any, in those years. These carry-overs form part of the calculation of annual net income for tax purposes (see Chapter 3, also Exhibit 10-1 in Chapter 10).

As is the case with personal-use property, each item of listed personal property that costs less than $1,000 is deemed to have a minimum cost for tax purposes of $1,000. Each property also has a deemed minimum proceeds of $1,000.

IV. Unique Aspects of Specific Capital Properties

Certain specific types of property require special mention either because the tax treatment deviates from the general principles of capital gains or because it is difficult to establish whether or not the property is capital property. Several of these items are discussed briefly in this section of the chapter.

---

34 ITA 54. Technically, the superficial-loss rules apply where the property is repurchased by the taxpayer, or his or her spouse, or an "affiliated" person, 30 days before or after the sale of property on which the loss has occurred.

35 ITA 54; IT-332R.

36 ITA 40(2)(g).

37 ITA 46(1) to (3).

38 ITA 54.

39 ITA 41(1), (2).

A. Identical Properties

Often several properties of an identical nature are acquired over a period of time and at different costs. For example, an investor may acquire shares of the same corporation over a period of years, with the per-share price different at each time of acquisition. It is difficult in this situation to distinguish one share from another; if some but not all of the shares are sold, this question arises: What is the adjusted base of the shares sold?

The adjusted cost base of each identical property acquired is the weighted average cost of all the identical properties acquired up to the point of sale.[40] This calculation is demonstrated below.

Situation: An investor acquired shares of X Corporation as follows:

Year	No. of shares	Cost per share	Total cost
20X0	100	$ 6	$ 600
20X1	200	8	1,600
20X2	80	10	800
	380		$3,000

In 20X2 the investor sold 150 shares of Corporation X for $9 per share.

Analysis:

Proceeds of disposition (150 × $9)	$1,350
Adjusted cost base of one share: $3,000/380 = $7.89	
Cost base of all shares sold: 150 × $7.89	1,183
Capital gain	$ 167
Taxable capital gain (½ × 167)	$ 84

In the above example, if additional shares are subsequently purchased, they are added to the cost base of the 230 shares (380 – 150) remaining, which now have a total average cost of $1,815 (230 × $7.89).

Shares acquired under an employer stock option arrangement after February 27, 2000, that are *eligible to defer* the employment benefit to the year the shares are sold (see Chapter 4), are *not* treated as identical properties.

B. Convertible Securities

Normally the exchange of one property for another will result in a disposition for tax purposes. However, when securities such as shares, bonds, and debentures are issued, and the owner has the right to convert or exchange them for shares of the same corporation, and the owner makes use of that right, a disposition is not considered to have occurred. Instead, the adjusted cost base of the old security becomes the cost base of the new security, and a gain or loss is recognized when the new security is eventually sold.[41]

C. Options and Warrants

In order to secure the opportunity to acquire property at some future time, a taxpayer may pay an amount that grants him or her the right or option to purchase property at a specified price over some limited time period.

---

40 ITA 47(1), (2); IT-387R2. (Also see proposed ITA 47(3)).
41 ITA 51(1), (2).

From the payer's perspective this type of transaction has no tax consequences at the time of payment. If, at a subsequent time, the payer exercises the option and purchases the property, the cost of the option is added to the adjusted cost base of the property acquired. On the other hand, if the payer allows the option to expire, and does not purchase the property, the full cost of the option is considered a capital loss in the year of expiry.[42]

The tax treatment to the taxpayer who granted the option and received the payment is somewhat different. In this case the amount received for granting the option is considered a capital gain in the year in which it is received. If, in a subsequent year, the option is exercised, the original option amount received is included as part of the proceeds of disposition in that year, and the original option amount reported as a capital gain in the earlier year is reversed through the filing of an amended tax return.[43]

D. Commodities and Futures Transactions

Commodities and commodity futures cannot, by definition, be classified as capital property because no long-term or enduring benefit can result from their acquisition. Commodities are acquired solely for the purpose of obtaining a gain on resale and are therefore inventory of trade. But in spite of the obvious position of commodity transactions, CCRA has set a policy that allows taxpayers to choose between capital treatment and business-income treatment, provided that the chosen method is used consistently in future years.[44] However, this option is not permitted for taxpayers who are associated with the commodity business or who are taking commodity positions as part of their normal business or trade. For example, farmers who grow wheat must treat commodity transactions in wheat as part of their business income.

E. Goodwill and Eligible Capital Property

The tax treatment of eligible capital property was described in Chapter 6. Eligible capital property includes goodwill as well as other intangible assets, such as franchises and licences that do not have a limited legal life. It is important to note that although such properties are capital in nature, they are not usually subject to capital gains treatment for tax purposes. Gains or losses on the sale of eligible capital property are determined as described in Chapter 6 and are treated as business income or business losses.

In comparison, depreciable properties such as buildings, equipment, and franchises of a limited legal life (class 14) are both depreciable property *and* capital property and, therefore, may have a capital element as well as a business element (see Chapter 6).

F. Principal Residence

A principal residence (which is specifically defined in the *Income Tax Act*) can generally be regarded as a housing unit owned, either directly or through a cooperative, by the taxpayer and ordinarily inhabited for personal use.[45] A principal residence is personal-use property, as previously defined; as such, it may be subject to a capital gain on sale, but it cannot realize a capital loss.

The capital gain realized on the sale of a principal residence is reduced by the following formula:[46]

$$\frac{1 + \text{Number of years designated as principal residence}}{\text{Number of years owned}} \times \text{Gain}$$

---

42 ITA 54 (disposition).

43 ITA 49(1) to (5).

44 IT-346R.

45 ITA 54.

46 ITA 40(2)(b), 40(6).

If a taxpayer owns more than one personal residence—for example, a house as well as a summer cottage—only one can be designated for any particular year. Further, only one property can be designated for each family (husband and wife). It is clear from the above formula that if one residence is designated as the principal residence for each year of ownership, the reduction is equal to the full capital gain.

The "+ 1" is included in the formula to cover the year in which two houses are owned as a result of the normal process of selling one house and acquiring a new one.

It is easy to make the principal residence calculation when the individual owns a single residence. However, when more than one residence is owned, the problem of designation is complex because of the nature of the formula. The decision to designate a particular property is made at the time of sale, not when the property is acquired. This is demonstrated below.

Situation: A taxpayer acquired a house in 20X1 for $100,000. In 20X3 the same taxpayer acquired a vacation home for $50,000. In 20X5 both properties were sold: the house for $150,000 and the vacation home for $95,000.

Analysis:

Vacation home:

Capital gain ($95,000 − $50,000)	$45,000
Exemption:	
$\frac{2+1}{3} \times \$45,000 =$	45,000
Net capital gain	–0–

House:

Capital gain ($150,000 − $100,000)	$50,000
Exemption:	
$\frac{3+1}{5} \times \$50,000 =$	40,000
Net capital gain	$10,000
Taxable capital gain ($\frac{1}{2} \times \$10,000$)	$ 5,000

In this example the house realized a capital gain of $50,000 over five years, or $10,000 for each year of ownership. The vacation home had a capital gain of $45,000 over three years, or $15,000 for each year of ownership.

Because the exemption formula is based on both the period of ownership and the amount of the gain, the summer home will receive an exemption of $15,000 for each year designated, whereas the house exemption will be only $10,000 per year. Therefore, even though the total gain on the house is greater, it is better to emphasize the vacation home. Because of the "+ 1" in the formula, one only needs to designate the vacation home for two years in order to receive the full exemption. This in turn permits the house to be designated for three years.

It was mentioned previously that a deemed disposition occurs (at fair market value) when property that has a personal use is altered so that it has a business or investment use. This rule also applies when a principal residence is converted into a rental property. However, an individual can elect to have this rule not apply to a former principal residence for a maximum of four years.[47] This is particularly valuable when that individual rents the home and later resumes using it as a principal residence. In order to qualify for this exception, the owner cannot claim capital cost allowance on the property while renting it.[48]

Transactions relating to a principal residence are very common and affect a large number of taxpayers. It is unfortunate that the tax rules relating to such transactions are exceedingly complex. This area has been reviewed in a very superficial manner; the more detailed rules are significantly more complex and should be consulted if more than one residence is owned.[49]

G. Real Estate Used to Carry on a Business

Special treatment is provided for the recognition of capital gains on the disposition of real estate (land and buildings) that is used to conduct a business. In such cases the recognition of the capital gain can be deferred provided that replacement property is acquired in the same year the property is sold, or within one taxation year of the year it is sold.[50] The replacement property must be used for a similar purpose as the original property. The capital gain that would normally have been recognized is used instead to reduce the adjusted cost base of the replacement property acquired; in this way it is deferred until the replacement property is sold without being similarly replaced. Similar treatment is available for the recapture of capital cost allowance (see Chapter 6).

It should be noted that this exception does not apply to real estate that is used to earn property income from rentals. Nor does it apply to personal-use real estate.

A similar treatment applies to property that has been lost, stolen, destroyed, or expropriated, and for which compensation has been received. In such cases the capital gain can be deferred if replacement property is acquired within two years of the end of the taxation year in which the disposition occurred. The opportunity to defer the recognition of the capital gain is not restricted to business real estate. It also applies to rental properties as well as machinery and equipment.

H. Mutual Funds

It is common for individuals to invest in mutual funds. When the investment is owned directly by the individual, and not through an RRSP, there are a number of possible tax consequences. These are reviewed below.

An investor acquires units of a particular mutual fund at a specified cost. As the units are capital property, the purchase price represents the units' adjusted cost base for tax purposes. The money is pooled with that of other investors and is used to purchase a variety of publicly traded securities such as shares, bonds, mortgages, treasury bills, and commercial paper. On a regular basis—usually quarterly—the mutual fund distributes its gains to the unit holders. For tax purposes, these distributions retain the source and characteristics of the income earned by the mutual fund—capital gains, dividends, interest, and ordinary income—and are included in each unit holder's income for tax purposes in the taxation year of the distribution. Often, investors choose to reinvest the distribution by acquiring additional units of the mutual fund. When they do, the distribution is still taxable to the unit holder as capital gains, dividends, interest, or ordinary income (as the case may be), and the total amount of the distribution is added to the adjusted cost base of the investment (see the discussion on identical properties on page 258).

---

47 ITA 45(2), (3).
48 ITA 45(4).
49 IT-120R4.
50 ITA 44(1), (2); IT-259R2.

A disposition for tax purposes occurs whenever all or some of the units are redeemed for cash or transferred to another mutual fund. The disposition will result in a capital gain or loss to the extent that the redemption price or transfer value varies from the adjusted cost base of the units at the time.

l. Eligible Small Business Investments

To improve access to capital for small business corporations, *individuals* who dispose of a small business investment can *defer* the recognition of a limited amount of the related capital gain if the proceeds from the sale are used to make other small business investments.[51] There are a number of qualifications that must be met to be eligible for the deferral. An important qualification is that the new investment be in newly issued *treasury* common shares of a replacement entity. Purchasing shares from an existing shareholder does not qualify for the deferral. This means that the replacement entity is strengthened by the receipt of additional capital resources that can be used to support its growth. The eligible capital gain is deferred until the new investment is eventually sold or the proceeds of its sale are again reinvested in another qualified replacement investment. The concept of the deferral is demonstrated in the following situation:

Situation: In 20X2 an individual sells her shares in Corporation X for $1,000,000. The shares are eligible small business investments having an adjusted cost base of $400,000. Within the qualifying time period she reinvests $900,000 of the sale proceeds in Corporation Y treasury shares, which are new small business investments. In 20X5 she sells the shares of Corporation Y for $1,200,000.

Analysis: The sale of the Corporation X shares in 20X2 results in a capital gain of $600,000 ($1,000,000 − $400,000). However, because 90% of the proceeds from the sale of Corporation X ($900,000/$1,000,000 = 90%) are reinvested in Corporation Y (a qualified small business investment), she can defer only 90% of the capital gain. Her capital gain recognized in 20X2 is $60,000 as follows:

Capital gain from sale of Corporation X	$600,000
Less amount deferred − 90% × $600,000	(540,000)
Capital gain in 20X2	$ 60,000

The deferred portion of the capital gain ($540,000) reduces the adjusted cost base of the new investment in Corporation Y shares from $900,000 to $360,000 ($900,000 − $540,000). Therefore, when the shares of Corporation Y are sold in 20X5 a capital gain of $840,000 is recognized as follows:

Proceeds of disposition	$1,200,000
Adjusted cost base	
($900,000 − $540,000 deferred from 20X2)	(360,000)
Capital gain in 20X5	$840,000

Notice that the 20X5 capital gain of $840,000 includes the deferred gain from 20X2 of $540,000 plus the actual gain of $300,000 from the sale of the corporation Y shares ($1,200,000 − $900,000).

---

51 ITA 44.1.

Some further qualifications that must be met to be eligible for the deferral are outlined below:

- The deferral is available to individuals only.

- The deferral applies to the capital gains realized from the sale of shares in an eligible small business corporation. Normally, this refers to a Canadian-controlled private corporation with at least 90% of its assets used in active business carried on primarily in Canada. In addition, the corporation's total assets cannot be greater than $50 million immediately after the investment.[52] Corporations that do *not* qualify include professional corporations, specified financial institutions, corporations whose net real estate assets exceed 50% of their total asset value, and corporations whose principal business is the leasing, rental, development, or sale of real property.

- The replacement eligible investment must be purchased at any time during the year of sale of the former shares or 120 days after the end of the taxation year.[53]

V. The Aggregating Formula Revisited

Because the aggregating formula (described in Chapter 3) for determining a taxpayer's net income from all sources imposes special restrictions on capital losses, it would be useful to examine how the various items reviewed in this chapter relate to that formula.

Situation:

A taxpayer, in addition to earning business income of $50,000, property income of $18,000, and other sources of income of $4,000, had the following capital transactions in the year:

Property	Proceeds of disposition	Cost base and selling costs	Gain or (loss)
Shares of company X	$60,000	$40,000	$20,000
Shares of company P	17,000	41,000	(24,000)
Art	8,000	6,000	2,000
Boat	9,000	12,000	(3,000)
Grand piano	11,000	10,000	1,000
Stamp collection	18,000	21,000	(3,000)
Shares of small business corporation	8,000	20,000	(12,000)

Analysis:

This taxpayer sold property of all three general types—financial property, personal-use property, and listed personal property.

• **Listed personal property** The art incurred a capital gain of $2,000, the stamp collection a loss of $3,000. Because losses from listed personal property can be offset only against gains from listed personal property, the net gain from this type of property is zero.

---

52 Applies to transactions after October 17, 2000. A different limit applied to transactions between February 28, 2000 and October 18, 2000.

53 Prior to February 19, 2003 there were restrictions of $2,000,000 for the cost of the shares sold and the amount reinvested.

• **Personal-use property** The loss on the boat is deemed to be zero. The piano had a gain of $1,000, of which $500 (½ of $1,000) is taxable.

• **Financial property** Shares of company X have a taxable capital gain of $10,000 (½ of $20,000).
 Shares of company P have an allowable capital loss of $12,000 (½ of $24,000).
 Shares of the small business corporation are a business investment loss, of which $6,000 (½ of $12,000) is allowable.

Aggregating formula:

(a) Business income		$50,000
Property income		18,000
Other income		4,000
		72,000
(b) Taxable capital gains:		
Listed personal property	$ –0–	
Piano	500	
Shares of company X	10,000	
	10,500	
Allowable capital loss:		
Shares of company P	$(12,000)	–0–
		72,000
(c) Other deductions		–0–
		72,000
(d) Allowable business investment loss on shares of small business corporation		(6,000)
Net income for tax purposes		$66,000

Notice that in part (b) of the formula the net effect of the capital gains and losses is zero even though the capital losses exceed the capital gains. The excess net capital loss of $1,500 can be carried back three years and forward indefinitely when *taxable income* is computed provided that sufficient capital gains are available. In addition, the unused listed personal property loss ($3,000 – $2,000 = $1,000 × ½ = $500) can be carried back three years and forward seven years and used in arriving at *net income* provided that listed personal property gains are available.

Also notice that the allowable business investment loss on the shares of the small business corporation is included in part (d) of the formula and, as a result, is deducted from all other sources of income for the year.

As stated previously, it is important that when applying the normal rules for determining individual gains and losses on capital property, those rules be approached in the context of the aggregating formula. This way, that formula's effect on the tax payable for the particular year can be more readily understood.

VI. Impact on Investment and Management Decisions

The influence of the tax treatment of capital properties on investment and management decisions centres on the fact that *preferential* treatment is given to capital gains, regarding the amount taxable and the timing of income recognition; whereas *restricted* treatment is given to the utilization of capital losses. Managers must build these fundamental variables into the decision process when forecasting the returns on alternative investment opportunities, and also when considering the downside risk if a particular investment is not successful and results in a loss.

A. Return on Investment

The fact that only one-half of a capital gain is taxable at the time of disposition substantially increases the after-tax yield over other forms of investment returns. For example, for a taxpayer in a 45% tax bracket, a $100,000, 20-year investment in a property that will increase in value by 12% annually will provide $411,000 more in after-tax returns over the life of the investment than would an investment of the same amount in property yielding 12% in annual interest.

Capital growth:
    Gross value at end of 20 y:
        $100,000 + (12% × 20 y)   **$965,000**
    Less tax payable in year 20:
        45% × (½) ($965,000 − $100,000)   195,000
           Future value after tax   **$770,000**
Annual interest return:
    The 12% return is taxed annually at 45%, resulting in an
    after-tax yield of 6.6%. Future value of investment, after tax:
        $100,000 + (6.6% × 20 y)   **$359,000**
        Difference in after-tax yield   **$411,000**

In most cases, achieving a return by capital growth involves greater risk (example—shares) or greater effort (example—real estate) than is the case with interest-bearing securities. However, one cannot properly assess the importance of additional risk or effort without examining the after-tax yield potential. In the above example the after-tax returns are so substantial that the concept of risk takes on a different meaning.

The above example compared the decision to invest in property that yields a capital gain with the decision to invest in a venture yielding property income. The impact of tax on capital gains is also relevant when a decision is being made whether to sell one capital property and replace it with another. Because tax must be paid on the sale of the first property, there will be less after-tax value to invest in the second property.

Assume that a taxpayer in a 45% tax bracket owns investment A, which originally cost $10,000 but is now worth $100,000. The taxpayer is contemplating the sale of investment A in order to acquire investment B. If investment A were sold, a tax of $20,250 (45% × ½ [$100,000 − $10,000]) would be payable, leaving only $79,750 for reinvestment in investment B. When a sale of property A to acquire property B is being considered, this question must be asked: Is an investment of $79,750 in property B equivalent in value to the investment of $100,000 in property A? In order to justify acquiring property B, that property would have to be significantly more attractive in terms of its future potential than property A.

The above examples again emphasize the need to examine investment and asset-replacement decisions on an after-tax cash flow basis.

B. Downside Risk

In addition to considering the tax impact of a given investment, it is important to consider the potential loss in the event that the investment must be sold at a loss. While it is difficult to assess the real risk of an investment, the investor should at least know the potential magnitude of the loss. The real loss is the after-tax loss; therefore, the amount of the loss and the timing of the loss utilization to reduce taxes payable are both vital considerations.

For example, an investment of $100,000 in a capital property by a taxpayer in a 45% tax bracket may incur a loss of only $77,500, calculated as follows:

Maximum loss	$100,000
Less tax saving on utilization of the loss:	
45% × (½) ($100,000)	(22,500)
Net loss after tax	$ 77,500

In this situation, an investment of $100,000 can result in a maximum cash loss of only $77,500; this knowledge may well alter the investor's attitude toward the risk. Unfortunately, in most cases the ability to utilize capital losses is uncertain because such losses can be offset only against capital gains. This means that a taxpayer who is able to realize capital gains when capital losses occur is at less risk from an investment than an investor who cannot readily utilize the loss.

You will recall that the restrictions on the use of capital losses are relaxed for certain types of property. When this is the case, the downside risk of such an investment is reduced owing to the enhanced ability to generate tax savings through the utilization of losses if they occur. Consider a loan to, or an investment in shares of, a small business corporation. If a capital loss occurs on disposition, one-half of the loss is classified as an allowable business investment loss and can be offset against the investor's other sources of income such as business income, property income, and employment income. Notice that a loss on a loan to the corporation is realized for tax purposes when it is established to be uncollectible, whereas a loss on the shares can be realized only when the corporation is legally bankrupt. Therefore, there is less downside risk if the investors in a small business corporation contribute capital to the company primarily by way of loans and less by way of share capital (see Chapter 12).

VII. Tax Planning Checklist

The following tax planning opportunities were touched on in this chapter:

1. When contemplating an investment opportunity, anticipate the potential tax treatment (capital gain versus business income, capital loss versus business investment loss, and so on). This way, the ultimate after-tax position can be assessed in relation to the risks associated with that investment.

2. Remember that achieving a return via a capital gain delays tax until the property is sold, and even then only one-half of the gain is taxable. So, be sure to carefully compare investments that have capital growth potential with other types of investments on an after-tax basis rather than on a pre-tax basis.

3. Review capital properties regularly throughout the year. Consider selling those that will result in a loss in order to offset capital gains that have occurred. As well, consider selling properties that have appreciated in value to trigger a capital gain that can utilize an existing unused loss.

4. When selling one property to obtain funds to acquire a new, higher-yield property, bear in mind that the tax on the sale of the first property will reduce the amount

available for reinvestment, and that the actual overall return on investment may thus be lower than it was previously.

5. When investing in private corporations, attempt to minimize investments in share capital and maximize shareholder loans. This may speed up any loss recognition if the company should fail or run into severe financial difficulty.

6. Whenever possible, take advantage of the available reserve for deferred proceeds on capital properties in order to delay the recognition of taxable income. Keep in mind that it may sometimes be better not to use the reserve if a tax advantage can be gained by recognizing income earlier (e.g., if current tax rates are lower than those expected in future years, or if the taxpayer has accumulated losses). However, before accepting an agreement to defer proceeds on a sale, be sure there is sufficient cash available to meet the tax obligations as they come due.

7. Capital gain reserves are optional, which means that the reserve provisions constitute an opportunity to shift income from one time period to another within specified limits.

8. When selling a security for a loss, remember to consider the superficial loss rules if contemplating a reinvestment in that property.

9. When investing in Canadian securities, consider electing capital gains treatment on those and future properties. However, keep in mind that capital losses can be offset only against capital gains. A similar decision must be made when investing in commodity futures.

10. When replacing properties in order to defer the related capital gain, be aware of the time limits—one year for business real estate after a voluntary disposition and two years for assets destroyed, stolen, or expropriated. Eligible small business share replacements also have time limits.

11. When investing in shares of a private corporation, regularly review its dividend policy. When a corporation does not declare a dividend, the value of its shares increases and so does the potential capital gain. The greater the dividend a corporation declares, the lower the share value and potential capital gain.

VIII. Summary and Conclusion

Capital gains and losses occur when property is disposed of that was acquired for the purpose of providing the owner with a long-term or enduring benefit. It is the *intended purpose* of acquisition that establishes its capital nature, not the nature of the asset itself. The tax authorities, in an attempt to determine "purpose," examine the owner's course of conduct with the property over the period of ownership; this process may or may not substantiate the owner's claims regarding intended purpose. Owners should be aware of the subjective nature of the definition and look on this as part of the overall risk when making investment decisions.

In relation to the overall scheme of income determination for tax purposes, capital gains have preferential treatment because

(a) only one-half of the gain is taxable; and,
(b) the gain is included in income only when a disposition of the property occurs.

Because capital gains are given preferential treatment, capital losses are treated in a restrictive manner compared with other types of losses.

A capital gain or loss on a property is calculated as the difference between the proceeds of disposition and the sum of its adjusted cost base and selling expenses. This formula is simple but also limited. Notice that no deductions are available for the costs associated with maintaining the property or financing its acquisition. If the property is of a financial nature and provides long-term benefits from business revenues, interest, dividends, or rent, expenses associated with the property can be deducted against those sources of income. However, if the property is personal-use property, the related expenses are ignored for tax purposes.

The reader may be aware that individuals, but not corporations, are exempt from a certain amount of capital gains through the capital gain deduction. This deduction, which applies in limited situations for individuals, forms part of the calculation that converts net income for tax purposes to taxable income, and will be discussed in Chapter 10.

The impact of capital gains and losses on decisions involving investment and—for businesses—capital expansion and replacement is tied to the special tax treatment afforded to capital property transactions. Investors and business managers faced with long-term investment decisions should recognize that these tax preferences are continually being debated in the political arena. There are those who argue that capital gains should not be taxable at all, especially if the proceeds of disposition are reinvested in capital expansion. (This concept already applies, in a limited manner, to real estate used to conduct an active business.) Others argue that it is unfair to tax only a portion of capital gains, which are earned by a small minority of taxpayers, when the great majority of low- and middle-income taxpayers, who are unable to invest in capital property, are fully taxable on their normal sources of income. Because investment in capital properties is a long-term process, decision makers must be cognizant of the debate and consider its possible outcome. Capital gains were not taxable at all before 1972. Beginning that year, 50% of capital gains were taxable. In 1990 this was increased to 75%. In 2000 the inclusion rate was reduced to 50%. What may it be in the future?

Reading List

Income Tax Act References

	Section
Income for taxation year (capital gains)	3(b)
Adjusted cost base	54
Capital property	54
Disposition of property	54
Listed personal property	54, 41(1) to (3)
Personal-use property	54, 46(1) to (3), 40(2)(g)
Principal residence	54, 40(6), 40(2)(b)
Proceeds of disposition	54
Superficial loss	54, 40(2)(g), 53(1)(f)
Election: disposition of Canadian securities	39(4) to (6)

General rules (calculation of capital gain)	40(1)(a)
Taxable capital gain	38(1)(a)
Allowable capital loss	38(1)(b)
Allowable business investment loss	38(1)(c), 39(1)(c)
Small business corporation	248(1)
Meaning of capital gain or loss	39(1)
Gifts	69(1)(b)
Property with more than one use	45(1) to (4)
Deemed disposition—ceased to be resident	128.1
Death of a taxpayer	70(5)
Negative adjusted cost base	40(3)
Assets owned in 1971	ITAR 26(3), (7)
Deemed cost of property received as gift	69(1)(c)
Deferred proceeds—reserve	40(1)(a)(iii)
Deferred proceeds—reserve (property to child)	40(1.1)
Arm's length	251(1)
Bad debts and shares of bankrupt corporations	50(1)
Identical properties	47(1), (2)
Convertible property	51(1), (2)
Options	49(1) to (4), 54
Exchanges of property	44(1), (2)

Canada Customs and Revenue Agency Publications

IT-459	Adventure or concern in the nature of trade.
IT-218R	Profit, capital gains, and losses from the sale of real estate, including farmland and *conversion* of real estate from capital property to inventory and vice versa.
IT-102R2	Conversion of property (other than real estate) for or to inventory.
IT-479R	Transactions in securities.
IT-95R	Foreign-exchange gains or losses.
IT-236R4	Reserves—disposition of capital property.
IT-259R2	Exchanges of property.
IT-461	Forfeited deposits.
IT-332R	Personal-use property.
IT-84	Capital property owned at December 31, 1971—median rule.
IT-139R	Capital property owned at December 31, 1971—fair market value.
IT-484R2	Allowable business investment losses.
IT-159R3	Capital debts established to be bad debts.
IT-239R2	Deductibility of capital losses from guaranteeing loans.
IT-387R2	Meaning of "identical properties."
IT-451R	Deemed disposition and acquisition on ceasing to be or becoming a Canadian resident.
IT-346R	Commodity futures and certain commodities.
IT-120R4	Principal residence.
IT-264R	Part dispositions.

Major Court Decisions

California Copper Syndicate Ltd. v. Harris (1904), 5 DTC 159—Business income v. capital gain.

Regina Shoppers Mall Ltd. v. The Queen, 89 DTC 5483—Establishing a taxpayer's intention.

Regal Heights Ltd. v. MNR, 60 DTC 1270—Intention.

Racine v. MNR, 65 DTC 5098—Secondary intention.

Gairdner Securities v. MNR, 54 DTC 1015—Relationship of transaction to taxpayer's business.

Demonstration Questions

Question One

Teresa Sereti, a resident of Halifax, Nova Scotia, has requested your tax advice regarding a number of financial transactions that occurred in 20X5. Information relating to these transactions is outlined below.

1. In 20X0, Sereti purchased shares of Pluto Inc., a Canadian-controlled private corporation, for $20,000. After several years of financial problems, the corporation recently ceased operations and is insolvent. When operations ceased, all of Pluto's assets were being used in an active business.

2. In 20X3, Sereti purchased, for $30,000, a three-hectare parcel of land in a rural area. In 20X5, two of the three hectares were sold separately for $20,000 per hectare. She used the proceeds to construct a greenhouse on the remaining land. She will use the greenhouse to grow and sell vegetables in her spare time. Sereti could have acquired a one-hectare site in 20X3, but opted for the larger property in the hope that she could sell part of the property at an increased value and raise funds to help pay for the cost of constructing the greenhouse. Sereti paid property taxes of $500 per year on the three-hectare site.

3. Sereti's previous employer, Seaco Ltd., a public corporation, provided her with options to acquire shares. Information relating to these options is outlined below.

	1st option	2nd option
# of shares	1,000	1,000
Date option granted	May 20X1	June 20X2
Option price	$12.00	$13.00
Value at date granted	$12.40	$13.20
Date acquired by Sereti	September 20X3	July 20X4
Value at date acquired	$13	$16

In December 20X5, Sereti sold 500 of the Seaco shares for $20 per share.

4. In 20X4, Sereti invented a board game and incurred $6,000 in legal fees to obtain a patent. She had intended to manufacture and market the game herself, but a feasibility study showed that she did not have the necessary financial resources or management expertise. As a result, she sold the patent and the distribution rights to a marketing company in 20X5 for $36,000 plus an annual royalty on sales. Her 20X5 royalty receipts totalled $12,000.

5. Sereti's mother died several years ago, and left her a house valued at $90,000 and a gold bracelet worth $600. Sereti's brother is using the house until it is sold.

   In 20X5, a land developer paid Sereti $6,000 for an option to purchase the house. As of December 31, 20X5, the option had not been exercised. Also in 20X5, Sereti sold the gold bracelet for $2,000. Sereti's 20X4 tax return shows an unused listed personal property loss of $400 carried forward from the previous year.

6. Sereti sold the following other properties in 20X5:

1937 classic automobile	$25,000
Camper trailer	7,000
Shares of Tex Inc., a public corporation	6,000

   Sereti purchased the classic automobile, which she drove only on warm summer days, in 20X0 for $8,000; restoration costs for it were $6,000. She acquired the camper trailer in 20X1 for $16,000, and the Tex Inc. shares that same year for $60,000.

7. In 20X5, Sereti earned a salary of $85,000. She contributed $2,000 to her employer's registered pension plan and also made an allowable contribution of $7,000 to her RRSP.

Required:
Determine Sereti's net income for tax purposes for the 20X5 taxation year.

Solution:
Each transaction is discussed below before net income is calculated for tax purposes.

The shares of Pluto Inc. are deemed to have been sold for nil because the corporation has ceased to carry on business and is insolvent. The result is a capital loss of $20,000. The shares are qualified small business corporation shares, because the company was a Canadian-controlled private corporation that used all of its assets in an active business. Consequently, the capital loss is also classified as an allowable business investment loss.

   Part of the farmland was purchased with the intention of selling it at a profit; therefore, the profit is considered to be income from business. The property taxes on the two hectares of vacant land that were sold cannot be deducted from annual income except to the extent of any incidental income earned on the property. The property taxes are, however, added to the cost of the land (see Chapter 5—interest and property taxes on vacant land).

   When Sereti acquired the shares of Seaco Ltd. under the stock option agreement, she earned employment income equal to the difference between the value of the shares at the date of acquisition and the purchase price. The recognition of the stock option employment benefit could not be deferred to the year when the shares are sold because the value of the shares was greater than the option price at the date the options were granted (see Chapter 4—stock options). The adjusted cost base of the shares is increased by the amount of employment income, resulting in the ACB being equal to the shares' market value at the acquisition date. The two acquisitions in 20X3 and 20X4 are identical properties, and therefore the ACB is determined as the weighted average of the two purchases.

   The patent on the board game is a capital property because it was developed with the intention of generating a long-term benefit. Its adjusted cost base is the cost of registering the patent.

The house is a capital property having an ACB of $90,000 (the market value at the time of her mother's death). It does not qualify as Sereti's principal residence because she does not occupy it. The receipt of the option results in a capital gain in the year of receipt. If the option is subsequently exercised, the capital gain will be the amount by which the selling price plus the option proceeds of $6,000 exceed the ACB of $90,000. The capital gain from the option received in 20X5 can then be eliminated by filing an amended tax return for that year. If the option expires, the capital gain of $6,000 in 20X5 stands.

The gold bracelet that Sereti received from her mother's estate is listed personal property (jewellery). Its ACB would normally be $600, but as listed personal property it has a deemed minimum ACB of $1,000. The unused listed personal property loss from her 20X4 tax return must have occurred because an LPP loss exceeded the LPP gain in a previous year. Unused LPP losses can be carried back three years and forward seven years, and can be deducted from LPP gains only. This carry-over is deducted in arriving at net income for tax purposes, unlike other types of losses (net capital losses and non-capital losses), which are deductible after net income for tax purposes in arriving at taxable income (see Chapter 10).

The classic automobile and the camper trailer are both personal-use properties. The ACB of the automobile is $14,000 (original cost of $8,000 plus the $6,000 for restoration). The camper trailer incurred a loss, but as personal-use property the loss is deemed to be nil.

Net income for tax purposes:
(a) Employment income:

Salary			$ 85,000
Registered pension plan			(2,000)
			83,000
Business income:			
Sale of farm land—proceeds	$ 40,000		
Less—cost (²/₃ × $30,000)	(20,000)		
—property taxes on vacant land ²/₃ ($500 × 3 y)	(1,000)		19,000
Property income—royalties			12,000
			114,000

(b) Taxable capital gains:
Seaco shares:

Proceeds—500 × $20		10,000
ACB 1,000 @ $13 = $13,000		
1,000 @ $16 = 16,000		
2,000 $29,000		
Average—$29,000 ÷ 2,000 = $14.50 × 500 shares	(7,250)	
	2,750	
Taxable—¹/₂ × $2,750	1,375	
Patent—¹/₂ ($36,000 − $6,000)	15,000	
Option—¹/₂ ($6,000)	3,000	
Classic automobile—¹/₂ ($25,000 − [$8,000 + $6,000])	5,500	
Camper trailer—loss deemed to be nil	−0−	
Net gain on listed personal property:		
Bracelet—¹/₂ ($2,000 − deemed cost of $1,000) − loss carry-over of ¹/₂ ($400)	300	
	25,175	

Allowable capital loss:
  Tex Inc.—½ ($6,000 – $60,000) = $27,000
    Limited to taxable capital gains   (25,175)   –0–
                                                                     114,000
(c) Other deduction:
  RRSP contribution   (7,000)
                                                                     107,000
(d) Loss:
  Pluto shares—allowable business investment loss
    ½ ($20,000)   (10,000)
  Net income for tax purposes $ 97,000

Question Two

In 20X3, in anticipation of retirement, Philip Portnoy sold several properties. Information relating to these transactions is outlined below.

1. In 20X1, Portnoy purchased a recreational parcel of land for $20,000 near a mountain resort, with the intention of building a cottage for personal use. The cottage was never built because of Portnoy's declining health. The land was sold in 20X3 for $21,000. A commission of 10% of the selling price was paid to a real estate broker.

2. On November 30, 20X3, he sold all of his 1,000 shares of TR Ltd. (original cost—$21,000) for $18,000. He also sold a bond for $62,000 (including accrued interest of $200) that he had purchased in January 20X3 for $64,000 (including $600 accrued interest). Prior to these sales, he had received bond interest of $2,800. On December 15, 20X3, on the advice of his broker, he purchased another 500 shares of TR Ltd. for $8,000.

3. In 20X0 Portnoy had sold shares of Hazel Ltd. (a Canadian-controlled private corporation) for $50,000, with the proceeds payable over several years. The original cost of the shares was $10,000. By the end of 20X3, $15,000 of the $50,000 selling price remained unpaid. Portnoy's 20X2 tax return shows that he claimed a capital gain reserve of $12,000.

4. On December 31, 20X3, Portnoy sold a rental property for $120,000 (land $50,000, building $70,000). He had acquired the property seven years earlier for $90,000 (land $10,000, building $80,000). At the end of the previous year the building had an undepreciated capital cost of $58,000. A net rental loss of $6,000 was incurred in 20X3 after a deduction of $2,000 for amortization/depreciation. Portnoy intends to purchase a new rental property in early 20X4 for $300,000.

5. Portnoy bought and sold commodity futures in 20X3 and made a profit of $15,000. He first traded commodities in 20X2, incurring a loss of $23,000, which he fully deducted against his employment earnings for that year.

6. During 20X3, Portnoy sold shares of PC Ltd., a Canadian-controlled private corporation operating a small manufacturing business, for $30,000. He had acquired the shares in 20X0 for $40,000. He paid legal fees of $1,000 to draw up the sale agreement. At the time of the sale, PC Ltd.'s balance sheet had total assets of $600,000 (equal to their fair market value) as follows:

Current assets	$220,000
Manufacturing equipment	215,000
Government of Canada bonds	165,000
	$600,000

7. Portnoy's only other income in 20X3 was his salary of $80,000.

Required:

Calculate Portnoy's net income for tax purposes for the 20X3 taxation year. Also, what are the tax implications if Portnoy purchases a new rental property in 20X4?

Solution:

Each transaction is discussed before the net income is calculated for tax purposes.

The cottage property results in a capital loss of $1,100 (proceeds of $21,000 less the adjusted cost base of $20,000 and the selling commission of $2,100 [10% × $21,000]). However, for tax purposes the property is classified as personal-use property and the loss is deemed to be nil.

The sale of the TR Ltd. shares would normally result in a capital loss of $3,000 ($18,000 − $21,000). However, because 1,000 shares were sold on November 30, 20X3, and 500 shares were repurchased within 30 days on December 15, 20X3, a superficial loss results with respect to the 500 shares replaced. The allowable capital loss for 20X3 is, therefore, $750, calculated as follows:

Proceeds of disposition	$18,000
Adjusted cost base	(21,000)
	3,000
Deemed superficial loss:	
500 shares/1,000 shares × $3,000	(1,500)
Capital loss	$1,500
Allowable capital loss—½ ($1,500)	$ 750

The superficial loss of $1,500 that was denied recognition in 20X3 is added to the adjusted cost base of the newly acquired shares, giving them a total adjusted cost base of $9,500 ($8,000 + $1,500). The loss will be recognized when the new shares are eventually sold.

The bond proceeds include accrued interest of $200, which must be included in property income. Similarly, the purchase price of the bond includes accrued interest of $600, which must be deducted from property income. The allowable capital loss on the bond is $800 (½ × ([$62,000 − $200] − [$64,000 − $600])). Property income from the bond is $2,400 ($2,800 plus the sale of accrued interest of $200 minus the purchase of accrued interest of $600).

The shares of Hazel Ltd. were sold in 20X0, resulting in a taxable capital gain of $20,000 (½ × [$50,000 − $10,000]). Because some of the proceeds are being paid over several years, Portnoy has been claiming a capital gain reserve and deferring the recognition of the gain. In 20X2, a reserve of $12,000 was claimed, and this amount must be included as a 20X3 taxable capital gain, from which a new reserve can be deducted. As

20X3 is the fourth year from the date of sale, this year's reserve cannot exceed 20% of the taxable gain (a minimum of 20% of the gain must be recognized each year, which means that 80% must be recognized by the end of 20X3). The taxable capital gain for 20X3 is $8,000, calculated as follows:

Inclusion of 20X2 reserve	$12,000
Less 20X3 reserve—lesser of:	
20% × $20,000 = $4,000	
$15,000/$50,000 × $20,000 = $6,000	(4,000)
Taxable capital gain	$ 8,000

The rental property income of $8,000 is calculated as follows:

Net rental loss	$(6,000)
Amortization/depreciation not deductible	2,000
Recapture of capital cost allowance on the building	
($70,000 − $58,000)	12,000
	$ 8,000

The disposition of land results in a taxable capital gain of $20,000 (½ × [$50,000 − $10,000]). Notice that there is no capital loss on the building even though it was sold for $70,000, which is less than its original cost of $80,000. This loss of $10,000 has been fully deducted as capital cost allowance in prior years. The undepreciated capital cost of the building at the end of 20X2 was $58,000, indicating that $22,000 of capital cost allowance had been deducted to that time. The sale for $70,000 resulted in income from the recapture of capital cost allowance of $12,000 ($70,000 − $58,000); this left a net deduction over the years of $10,000 ($22,000 − $12,000).

The gain of $15,000 from the trading of commodity futures appears to be business income. In the previous year, a loss of $23,000 was fully deducted against employment income, indicating that a choice was made not to treat the transaction as a capital item. Therefore, Portnoy's tax treatment for the 20X3 transaction must be treated in the same manner.

The sale of shares of PC Ltd. results in an allowable capital loss of $5,500 (½ × [$30,000 − $40,000 − 1,000]). The shares are not qualified small business corporation shares because all or substantially all of the corporation's assets at the time of the sale were not used in an active business. The corporation does carry on an active business, but 28% of its assets ($165,000/$600,000) are invested in bonds. Therefore, the loss cannot be classified as an allowable business investment loss. Here it is of no consequence because there are sufficient taxable capital gains from which the capital loss can be deducted.

Net income for tax purposes:		
(a) Employment income—salary		$ 80,000
Business income—commodity trading		15,000
Property income:		
Net rentals	8,000	
Interest on bond	2,400	10,400
		105,400

(b) Taxable capital gains:		
Rental property land	20,000	
Shares of Hazel Ltd.	8,000	
	28,000	
Allowable capital losses:		
Shares of TR Ltd.	(750)	
Bond	(800)	
Shares of PC Ltd.	(5,500)	25,950
Net income for tax purposes		$126,350

The purchase of a new rental property in 20X4 will have no tax effect on Portnoy's 20X3 income. If the land and building sold in 20X3 had been used for business purposes rather than to earn income from property, the capital gain and recapture of capital cost allowance realized in 20X3 could have been deferred if a replacement property had been acquired within one taxation year from the end of the 20X3 taxation year.

Review Questions

1. A capital gain or capital loss is the gain or loss realized from the disposition of capital property. What is meant by the term "capital property," and how is it different from other types of property?

2. Is it necessary for property to provide a long-term benefit to its owners in order for the gain or loss on sale to be considered a capital gain or capital loss?

3. When it is unclear whether a gain or loss on a sale of property is of a capital nature, what factors are considered when judging the transaction?

4. An investor acquired a residential high-rise apartment as an investment. The property has now been owned for 11 years and annually has provided reasonable net rental income. This net rental income has been reinvested in other types of properties as well as in improvements to the apartment building. The owner is considering either selling the property to another investor, or dividing the property into separate condominium units that will be marketed to existing tenants and to the public. Explain how a gain on sale will be treated for tax purposes under each alternative.

5. Distinguish among financial property, personal-use property, and listed personal property. Which of these three categories is (are) subject to capital gains treatment?

6. Distinguish between a capital gain and a taxable capital gain, and a capital loss and an allowable capital loss.

7. Explain why the tax treatment of capital gains is often described as preferential, while the treatment of capital losses is often considered unfair.

8. "A capital gain or loss can be recognized for tax purposes only when capital property is sold." Is this statement true? Explain.

9. A corporation acquires a licence that permits it to manufacture a patented product for 10 years in exchange for the payment of a royalty. Describe the tax treatment that will occur if the taxpayer sells the licence for more than its cost or less than its cost to another party before the 10-year term expires. Would the tax treatment be the same if the licence had an unlimited life?

10. What advantage can a taxpayer achieve by incurring a capital gain on property and permitting the purchaser to pay for the property over a number of years?

11. Because of the tax treatment, an investment in shares of a small business corporation may present less risk than an investment in shares of a public corporation. Explain why.

12. What difference does it make when the sole shareholder of a corporation provides $10,000 of additional capital to the corporation as a loan (shareholder's loan) rather than in return for additional share capital?

13. "The sale of a warehouse building used by a taxpayer to operate a business can result in a capital gain but not a capital loss." Is this statement true? Explain.

14. Explain how the tax treatment of personal-use property deviates from the normal tax treatment of capital property.

15. When an investor buys some shares of a corporation at one price and later buys more shares of the same corporation at another price, how does the investor determine the cost for tax purposes when some, but not all, of the shares are eventually sold?

16. When an investor acquires a commodity or a contract to purchase a commodity in the future, what type of property does that investor own? Can a gain or loss on the sale of commodities or futures contracts result in a capital gain or loss?

17. An investment in capital property that appreciates in value at 10% per year is more valuable than an investment in capital property that provides an annual return, such as interest, of 10%. Explain why.

Problems

Problem One

Jennifer Farmer farmed for 36 years. She has recently sold her farm assets. Her primary crop was asparagus, and 20 of Jennifer's 25 hectares of land were devoted to growing this vegetable.

The land cost her $10,000 in 1967. She has sold it for an all-inclusive price of $175,000 that includes an unharvested asparagus crop that is 70% mature.

Asparagus is a perennial plant consisting of a strong root stock which, when planted, remains in the soil for many years and requires little annual maintenance. Every year the root stock provides two or three asparagus crops, which are harvested at little cost and sold directly to a food wholesaler.

The sale agreement for $175,000 included a cash down payment of $35,000 and a first mortgage of $140,000, held by Farmer. The mortgage is to be paid in seven annual instalments of $20,000. Interest of 12% will be charged on the unpaid balance.

Farmer has sought your advice concerning the tax implications of the sale.

Required:

1. Describe to Farmer how the preceding transaction will be treated for tax purposes.

2. What additional information will you require to determine the actual amount of income for tax purposes created by the transaction?

Problem Two

Murray George is a professional musician and composer. For 15 years he has made a good living from this profession. He derives his income from concert appearances (for substantial fees) and from royalties on original musical compositions.

As of 20X0 George was internationally famous in the classical music field. In 20X1 the Canadian National Music Library agreed to purchase a number of documents from him. These documents included

(a) 26 of George's original manuscripts, in his own hand;
(b) a box containing 15 of his youthful works, including first drafts and final versions; and,
(c) a copy of George's personal diary, to be exhibited to the public only after his death.

For these items he received $50,000, to be paid in the amount of $30,000 in 20X1 and $20,000 in 20X2. Over the years, the compositions (other than his youthful works) had generated income from royalties, which George had declared as professional income for tax purposes.

The Canadian National Music Library is not a commercial enterprise. It is a registered charitable foundation.

Before filing his 20X1 tax return, George obtained CCRA's advice on how the receipt of $50,000 should be handled. Their response was that the $50,000 clearly represents business revenue and should be added to his professional earnings in 20X1.

Required:
State whether you agree or disagree with CCRA's advice, and provide reasons for and against your position.

Problem Three*

R.M. Inc. (RMI) manufactures earth-moving and excavation equipment. RMI is owned and managed by Ross Meister.

It is now February 15, 20X2. Meister has asked you to help the company deal with a tax problem. CCRA is questioning the capital gains treatment of a 20X1 sale of land by RMI; it believes that the full amount of the gain should have been included in income. Meister wants to know what arguments CCRA will likely present and how RMI can counter them. Also, he wants to know what the tax consequences will be if CCRA succeeds in making an adjustment. Details of the land transaction are offered below.

RMI purchased 50 hectares of vacant land in an industrial park on December 2, 20X0, for $1.35 million. The purchase was financed in part by a five-year first mortgage of $500,000 with interest at 12%. At first, Meister intended to move RMI from its current location to the new location just north of Toronto. He knew that even if he decided later not to move from his current premises, he had purchased the land at a bargain price and would be able to make a profit if he sold it.

On April 1, 20X1, RMI accepted an offer of $3.68 million for 40 hectares of the vacant land. RMI took back a $685,000 first mortgage, repayable at $30,000 per year, with the balance due in 20X6. In RMI's 20X1 corporate tax return, the land disposition was recorded as a capital gain. The remaining 10 hectares of land were retained by RMI. Meister decided to build RMI's new warehouse on the 10-hectare site. RMI will retain its current location as a garage for storing and servicing construction equipment.

RMI is subject to a 45% tax rate on all of its income.

* Adapted, with permission, from the 1991 Uniform Final Examination ©1991 of the Canadian Institute of Chartered Accountants, Toronto, Canada. Any changes to the original material are the sole responsibility of W.J. Buckwold and have not been reviewed or endorsed by the CICA.

Required:
Prepare a brief report that answers Meister's questions.

Problem Four
In 20X0, Kiranjit Dhillon acquired 1,000 shares of Pluton Ltd. (a Canadian public corporation) at a cost of $21,000 plus a brokerage commission of $600. During 20X0 she received cash dividends of $1,200. In 20X1, Pluton failed to pay the cash dividend owing to a cash-flow shortage; instead, it issued a stock dividend, whereby Dhillon received an additional 100 shares. At the time of the stock dividend, the share value was $18 per share.

On December 15, 20X1, with the company's financial position continuing to decline, Dhillon sold all of her shares of Pluton for $15,000. She felt relieved when the share values declined further over the next two weeks. She incurred brokerage fees of $300 on the sale.

Early in the new year, Pluton apparently solved its financial crisis by selling an unprofitable subsidiary. Dhillon's broker recommended that she again invest in Pluton's shares. On January 11, 20X2, she purchased 1,000 shares at a cost of $12,000 plus brokerage fees of $200.

In June 20X2 she gifted all of her shares in Pluton to her son, who was about to attend university. At that time the shares were valued at $20,000.

Required:
Calculate the amount by which Dhillon's net income for tax purposes will be affected by the above transactions for the years 20X1 and 20X2.

Problem Five
For the year ended August 31, 20X0, Zefer Ltd., a Canadian-controlled private corporation, reported a net income before income taxes of $485,000. The statement of income is summarized as follows:

Income from operations	$380,000
Other income:	
Interest	5,000
Net gain on sale of assets	100,000
	$485,000

The net gain on the sale of assets consists of the following amounts:

• **Gain on sale of franchise—$40,000** The franchise to operate a retail store was acquired seven years previous at a cost of $110,000. It was sold in 20X0 for $140,000. The sale proceeds included a cash down payment of $20,000, with the balance payable in seven annual instalments of $20,000 plus interest beginning in 20X1. The franchise, which qualified as a class 14 asset, had an undepreciated capital cost of $92,000 at the time of the sale and was the only asset in its class.

• **Gain on sale of warehouse property—$80,000** In July 20X0, a warehouse property was sold for cash proceeds of $430,000 (land $180,000, building $250,000). The property had an original cost of $370,000 (land $60,000, building $310,000). The building, which was the only asset in class 1, had an undepreciated capital cost of $290,000. After the sale of the warehouse, temporary premises were leased until a new, larger warehouse is constructed. New land was purchased in January 20X1 for $200,000. Construction of the new warehouse will be completed by July 20X1.

- **Loss on sale of shares of subsidiary—$20,000** Zefer sold shares of a subsidiary corporation for cash proceeds of $450,000. The shares were acquired five years ago for $470,000. Legal fees of $2,000 were paid to draw up the sale agreement and were charged to the legal expense account.

Required:

1. Calculate Zefer's net income for tax purposes for the 20X0 taxation year.

2. What are the tax implications relating to the construction of the new warehouse in 20X1?

Problem Six

Charles Bartello intends to leave Canada and start a new life in southern Florida. Before leaving, he intends to dispose of all his property so that he will have sufficient capital to acquire a business in the United States.

Bartello has provided the following information:

1. He currently owns 40% of the shares of a Canadian small business corporation, which are valued at $70,000. The shares were purchased four years ago for $100,000. Bartello is employed by the corporation and anticipates that his salary up to the date of departure will be $75,000.

2. At the beginning of the current year, he purchased a rental property as an investment. To date, the property has provided rental revenue of $14,000; however, Bartello has incurred cash expenses for property taxes, maintenance, interest, and insurance of $17,000. At the same time, the property has appreciated in value by $12,000. When he purchased the property, Bartello was not yet thinking of leaving Canada.

3. Three years ago, Bartello loaned $10,000 to a small business corporation owned by a friend. The business has suffered serious losses, and he has little hope of being repaid. In addition, no interest has been paid on the loan, although in the past two years Bartello has included interest in income for tax purposes on the anniversary dates. The total interest included is $2,000.

4. His home is worth $180,000 (original cost, $150,000.) He has owned the home for eight years and has lived in it all that time.

5. Bartello owns the following additional properties:

	Cost	Value
Motorboat	$ 14,000	$ 10,000
Furniture	21,000	6,000
Shares of public corporation X	10,000	14,000
Shares of public corporation Y	50,000	15,000
Corporate bond	100,000	102,000
Art collection	15,000	17,000
Stamp collection	20,000	16,000
Grand piano	10,000	14,000

Required:

Determine Bartello's net income for tax purposes for the year in which he leaves Canada.

Problem Seven

The following financial information is provided for the 20X0 taxation year of Virginia Couture:

Interest income	$20,000
Net loss from retail store for the year ended December 31, 20X0	(7,000)
Gain on sale of public corporation shares	8,000
Loss on sale of shares of a CCPC qualified as a small business corporation	(10,000)
Dividends from foreign corporations, net of $300 withholding tax	2,700
Loss on sale of land that was originally purchased to build a rental property. The project was cancelled after a rezoning application was lost.	(38,000)
Gain on sale of an oil painting	4,000
Director's fees for attendance at corporate meetings	6,000
Loss on sale of personal jewellery	(5,000)

In 20X0, Couture gifted shares of a Canadian public corporation to her 16-year-old son. The shares, which originally cost $8,000, had a value of $10,000 at the time of the gift.

Also in 20X0, Couture had a rental loss of $3,000 (before amortization/depreciation and capital cost allowance). The property was originally purchased for $70,000 (land $9,000, building $61,000). The class 1 building had an unamortized capital cost of $50,000 at the end of the previous year. On the last day of 20X0, Couture sold the property for $100,000 (land $12,000, building $88,000). She intends to purchase a new rental property in early 20X1 for $200,000 (land $20,000, building $180,000).

In the previous year, by agreement, Couture obtained the exclusive licence to distribute a certain product in Canada. In 20X0 she divided the country into six sales territories and sold 10-year sub-licences to individuals in each territory. Total proceeds were $24,000.

Required:

1. Calculate Couture's income for tax purposes for the 20X0 taxation year in accordance with the aggregating formula of section 3 of the *Income Tax Act*.

2. What are the tax implications if Couture acquires the new rental property in 20X1?

Problem Eight

Cindy Tse retired in April 20X9 and moved from Thunder Bay to Vancouver Island. During her retirement she plans to accept the occasional small consulting contract. Her financial transactions for 20X9 are summarized below.

1. Tse sold her home in Thunder Bay for $240,000. She paid a real estate commission of $8,000 and legal fees of $2,000 to complete the sale. Tse had purchased the home in 20X3 for $110,000.

    In 20X6, she purchased a summer cottage for $74,000. She sold it in 20X9 for $175,000. She paid a legal fee of $1,000 to draw up the sale agreement. Tse had used the summer cottage regularly for summer vacations.

2. Tse's gross salary from January 1, 20X9, to her date of retirement was $30,000.

3. Three years ago, Tse purchased 20% of the shares of T Ltd. and 15% of the shares of Q Ltd. Both are Canadian-controlled private corporations. T's assets consist entirely of

investment properties, including shares, bonds, and rental properties. All of Q's assets are used to operate an active business. Tse sold her shares in both corporations in 20X9. Details of the transactions are outlined below.

	T Ltd.	Q Ltd.
Cost	$30,000	$40,000
Selling price	63,000	28,000

Tse received $9,000 in cash for the T Ltd. shares, with the balance payable at the rate of $9,000 annually for the next six years. The Q Ltd. shares were sold for cash.

4. A local farmer has been trying to purchase Tse's hobby farm land. Tse purchased the land in 20X2 for $69,000. In July 20X9, Tse received $2,000 from the farmer, for which she granted him an option to purchase the land. The option is open for two years and allows the farmer to purchase the land for $100,000.

5. In February 20X9, Tse paid an investment counsellor $300 for investment advice. The same month, she purchased 5,000 units of ABC mutual fund for $10 per unit. An additional 3,000 units were purchased in April 20X9, for $14 per unit. On October 31, 20X9, ABC fund distributed $1,500 of taxable Canadian dividends, which Tse reinvested in the fund, thereby acquiring another 100 units. On December 3, 20X9, Tse sold 2,000 units of ABC for $16 per unit. At year end the fund units were valued at $18.

6. To obtain the funds to complete the purchase of the ABC mutual fund units, Tse increased the mortgage on her house by $20,000. She incurred interest of $500 on this amount before paying off the mortgage when the house was sold.

7. In 20X8, Tse invested in a real estate project with her friend, a real estate agent and part-time developer. Together they purchased a parcel of land and constructed four town homes at a cost of $500,000. In 20X9, the four town homes were sold for $580,000 to a single buyer, who planned to use them as rental properties. Tse's share of the gain was 40%. No cash was invested in the project, which was funded entirely with bank financing.

8. Tse sold shares of X Ltd. (a public corporation) for $18,000 during the year. She had acquired the shares in 20X4 for $25,000.

9. Most of Tse's investments have been in blue-chip shares that pay dividends. Recently she has decided to invest and trade in speculative Canadian mining shares and commodity futures. Before she does so, she wants to know the tax implications of gains and losses on such trading.

Required:
1. Calculate Tse's minimum net income for tax purposes for the 20X9 taxation year in accordance with the aggregating formula of section 3 of the *Income Tax Act*.

2. Explain to Tse the potential tax consequences of gains and losses realized on trading speculative Canadian mining shares and commodity futures.

3. What will be the tax consequences to Tse if the option on the farmland is exercised the following taxation year?

Problem Nine

Sheila Ram is a professional engineer. In 20X7 she sold her consulting business and retired. Her financial information for the year 20X7 is outlined below.

1. On January 1, 20X7, Ram sold her engineering consulting business to a senior employee. The business had been operated as a franchised proprietorship with a December 31 fiscal year end. The following assets were sold:

	Original cost	Price
Goodwill	38,000	40,000
Franchise	40,000	50,000
Library	2,000	1,000
Office equipment	12,000	4,000

The sale agreement called for cash proceeds for all assets except the franchise, which required a down payment of $20,000 at closing, with the balance payable on June 30, 20X8.

The accounts receivable of $90,000 were not sold but were retained by Ram for collection. During 20X7, Ram collected $82,000 of the receivables. The remainder is uncollectible.

On August 15, 20X7, Ram paid $4,000 to a former employee for a bonus awarded on December 31, 20X6.

A review of Ram's 20X6 income tax return showed the following:

Undepreciated capital cost:	
Class 8	$ 6,800
Class 14	24,000
Cumulative eligible capital	20,460
Reserve for bad debts	10,000
Unused listed personal property loss	800

2. In January 20X7, Ram sold her home for $230,000. She had acquired the house in 20X0 for $200,000. In May 20X7 she sold her Ontario vacation home, which she had acquired in 20X3 for $50,000, for $140,000. She also sold an oil painting for $1,400 that originally cost $600.

3. Also in 20X7, she received $30,000 from the sale of her 10% interest in Q Ltd., a Canadian-controlled private corporation. She had purchased the shares in 20X0 for $50,000. Q operates a small manufacturing business, and at the time of sale its assets were appraised as follows:

Working capital	$200,000
Manufacturing assets	300,000
Goodwill	100,000
Government bonds (three-year term)	200,000

4. In 20X7, Ram withdrew $45,000 from her RRSP.

Required:
Determine Ram's net income for tax purposes for the 20X7 taxation year.

Problem Ten

Simon Shansky is about to sell his shares in a private corporation for $100,000. He has owned the shares for many years, having originally acquired them at a cost of $20,000. Shansky intends to invest the proceeds from the sale in interest-bearing securities yielding 10%.

Two potential purchasers have made offers on the shares. One purchaser has offered to pay the full purchase price in cash. The other has offered to pay $40,000 at the date of sale and the balance of $60,000 in three annual instalments of $20,000, plus interest of 10% on the unpaid balance. The unpaid balance would be secured with adequate collateral. Shansky is subject to a 45% tax rate.

Required:

1. Which option should Shansky accept?

2. Calculate the amount of funds that Shansky will have after three years under each option.

3. What rate of return would have to be earned on the invested proceeds of sale under the full cash payment option to provide the same capital value as under the deferred payment option after three years?

4. Indicate, without providing detailed calculations, whether your answer to question 2 would be different if Shansky were selling a building for $100,000 that originally cost $80,000 and had an unamortized capital cost of $35,000.

Problem Eleven

Jordana Lea has accumulated a substantial portfolio of investments in bonds and shares of public corporations. She selects shares that provide low dividends and maximum long-term growth, but is risk averse and will purchase only shares of corporations in secure industries. Currently, all of her investments are achieving capital growth but her investment in shares of Cory Corporation is providing the lowest yield. This year her share value in Cory increased to $50,000, a 10% increase (i.e., from $45,000) over the previous year. Cory has consistently maintained this growth rate. The shares were purchased several years ago at a cost of $20,000.

Lea's investment counsellor has recommended that she sell her shares in Cory and use the proceeds to purchase shares in J2 Industries Ltd. J2 is in the same industry as Cory but has recently achieved industry dominance. There is strong evidence that the shares of J2 will maintain a growth rate of 13% annually for the next five years.

Lea has high earnings from her annual salary, and her marginal tax rate is 45%.

Required:

1. Should Lea dispose of the Cory shares and use the proceeds to acquire the J2 shares?

2. What rate of return on the J2 shares is required to justify the exchange of securities?

Cases

Case One   The Concorde Theatre Ltd.

The Concorde Theatre Ltd., a local company owned by J. Bleet, operates a small neighbourhood cinema. The business is usually profitable, but this year, because of unusual events, a net loss has occurred. The income statement for the year ended December 31, 20X1, is summarized in the table below.

The company does not usually invest in real estate. The land and building that was sold for a gain of $70,000 was acquired seven months before its sale. An acquaintance of Bleet who ran into some serious financial difficulties required immediate cash to stop bankruptcy proceedings and asked Bleet to purchase his real estate. Bleet had no money to invest in real estate and was not in the market for such an investment. However, the acquaintance pleaded with Bleet to help him out and kept reducing the purchase price to provoke an immediate cash sale.

Bleet, watching the price drop to below what he felt was the fair market value, finally gave in. Concorde Theatre borrowed 100% of the purchase price and bought the property. The loan from the bank was payable on demand.

Sales	$ 600,000
Cost of sales	400,000
Gross profit	200,000
Operating expenses	170,000
Operating income	30,000
Other:	
Gain on sale of land and building	70,000
Loss on sale of land	(110,000)
Net loss	$ (10,000)

Four months later, the company received an offer from a local real estate investor to buy the property for $65,000 above the original purchase price. The same day, the original owner, who had improved his financial situation, asked if he could buy the property back. He was upset when Bleet agreed only if the price was $70,000 above the original price. Reluctantly, the acquaintance agreed to pay that much provided that the closing date was delayed to three months hence.

The land that resulted in a $110,000 loss on sale had been purchased three years earlier. The land was across the road from the theatre, and Bleet had intended to turn it into a parking lot for theatre patrons. However, because of the traffic patterns on the street, the city refused to grant vehicle access for the property. After a long battle, Bleet gave up and posted the land for sale. After six months without an offer, he finally accepted a reduced price to free up needed cash.

Bleet has just met with his accountant, who has informed him that the company will have to pay income tax of $45,000 for the year ended December 31, 20X1. Bleet knows that the corporate tax rate is 45% on income but cannot believe that a tax of $45,000 is payable on a net loss of $10,000.

Bleet asks his accountant to explain how such a result is possible, and asks whether there is any possibility of a more logical result.

Required:

As the accountant, outline your response to Bleet.

Case Two   Pan Li Ltd.

Pan Li Ltd. is a Canadian private corporation owned 100% by David Benjamin. The corporation operates an active business. Its most recent statement of financial position is summarized in the table below.

PAN LI LTD.

Statement of Financial Position

Assets:		
Current assets		$ 100,000
Land		50,000
Building	400,000	
Equipment	700,000	
	1,100,000	
Accumulated depreciation	(400,000)	700,000
Goodwill, at cost		200,000
		$1,050,000
Liabilities and shareholders' equity:		
Liabilities		$ 600,000
Common shares	20,000	
Retained earnings	430,000	450,000
		$1,050,000

Benjamin purchased the shares of Pan Li seven years ago from the previous shareholders at a cost of $100,000. He is considering retirement and has let it be known that the business is for sale. Recently he received an offer of $700,000 for the shares of the corporation.

A second potential group of buyers has indicated that it would like to buy the business but does not want to buy the shares of the corporation. Instead, it wants to purchase the individual assets (current assets, land, building, equipment, and goodwill). Benjamin knows that certain of the corporate assets are worth more than their stated value on the financial statement and has asked his advisor to provide an appraisal. If he sold to the asset-buying group, the buyers would assume the corporation's liabilities of $600,000 as part of the purchase price.

Both potential buyers have indicated that they have sufficient cash resources to pay only 70% of the purchase price, and that the remaining 30% will have to be paid over three years, with appropriate interest.

Benjamin does not understand the tax implications of selling the shares rather than the assets. Once the business is sold, he intends to use the funds to buy investments that will provide an annual return to supplement his retirement income.

Required:

1. Keeping in mind Benjamin's objectives, explain to him the general tax implications of selling the shares of Pan Li rather than the company's individual assets.

2. What difference does it make to the purchasers whether they acquire the shares from Benjamin or the individual assets from Pan Li?

Chapter 9   Other Income, Other Deductions, and Special Rules for Completing Net Income for Tax Purposes

The previous chapters introduced and developed the primary sources of income in the Canadian income tax system—employment income, business income, property income, and capital gains. In order to complete the process of determining a taxpayer's overall net income for tax purposes, it is necessary to examine the treatment of transactions that do not fall into one of the four primary income sources. Transactions of this nature are grouped together and referred to as "other sources of income" and "other deductions." The items in this category have little in common with each other; consequently, there are no general rules that apply to this classification.

In terms of the aggregating formula described in Chapter 3, the total of other sources of income is separated from the total of other deductions and included at a different part of the formula.

Other sources of income and *other deductions* apply primarily to individuals. With the exception of retirement savings plans, they normally do not have a significant impact on investment strategies or management decisions. For this reason, this text will give these areas only brief consideration; this chapter will concentrate on how they fit into the overall scheme of income determination.

The *Income Tax Act* has a list of special rules relating to the computation of income from all sources. These rules cover unusual aspects of transactions and usually override the standard rules developed for each of the income categories described previously.

This chapter will finish explaining how to calculate net income for tax purposes for both individuals and corporations. By the end of this chapter the full scope of income for tax purposes under the *Income Tax Act* will be apparent.

Specifically, this chapter will

(a) highlight the process for determining other sources of income and other deductions;
(b) examine the list of special rules for overall income determination and, where applicable, their impact on investment and management decisions; and,
(c) revisit the aggregating formula outlined in Chapter 3 and provide a sample calculation of net income for tax purposes.

I. Other Sources of Income

"Other sources of income" is a catch-all category that captures taxable income which does not qualify as one of the primary sources. It is important to recognize that the items classified as other sources of income are *all* from a specific list found in sections 56 through 59.1 of the *Income Tax Act*. The scope of this category, therefore, is very limited. The major types of income that are taxable as other sources of income are as follows:[1]

- Benefits received from a registered retirement savings plan, either as a lump sum or over a period of time in the form of an annuity.

- Benefits received from a registered retirement income fund created from a registered retirement savings plan.

- Pension benefits received from an employer's pension plan either as a lump sum or by way of regular payments over a period of time.

- Old-age security payments from the government of Canada.

- Benefits from the Canada and Quebec pensions plans.

- Benefits received from an employer's deferred profit sharing plan.

- Foreign pension benefits.

---

1   ITA 56(1)(a) to (c), (h), (i), (n), (o), (q), 146, 147.

- Retiring allowances received from an employer in recognition of a period of service as an employee.

- Employment benefits received from the government's employment insurance plan.

- Income from a registered education savings plan.

- Amounts received by a student as scholarships, fellowships, or bursaries, to the extent that such payments exceed $3,000. The $3,000 exemption applies only to amounts received by a student enrolled in a program entitling the student to claim the education tax credit (see Chapter 10). Otherwise such receipts, including prizes for achievement in a field of endeavour, are exempt only to the extent of $500 annually.

- Research grants received in excess of expenses incurred to conduct the related research activity.

- Payments received from a former spouse as alimony or maintenance, provided that they are received as periodic payments (not in a lump sum) and are pursuant to a court order or written agreement. Note that maintenance payments are taxable only to the extent that they are for the support of a former spouse. Maintenance payments received that are for the support of a child are not taxable.[2]

The above list is not complete and does not describe particular details that may apply to specific items.

Notice that several of the above items relate to transactions that originally pertained to an employment activity. For example, in Chapter 4 it was determined that a contribution by an employer to a registered pension plan or deferred profit sharing plan is *not* included in the employment income of the employee as a benefit received. When these contributions, plus the related investment returns, are paid from the plans to the employee, the income is not recognized as employment income but is included, as mentioned above, with other sources of income.

The total of a taxpayer's other items of income is included in the first part of the aggregating formula for overall net income determination, along with employment income, business income, and property income. This positioning is important in that other deductions and losses from employment, business, and property, and allowable business investment losses, are deducted subsequently. As a result, losses from, for example, business or investments can be offset against the taxpayer's other sources of income such as pension income and alimony.

In reviewing other sources of income, it is important to be familiar with the items included, but it is equally important to think in terms of which items are *not* included. Doing so provides an answer to this question: What items are not subject to tax under the Canadian tax system? Consider, for example, the receipt of lottery winnings. To determine whether such a gain is taxable, one must first determine its nature. It is not employment income earned from providing services; it is not business income earned from trading property or providing services; it is not property income earned as a return on investment; and it is not a capital gain from the disposition of property acquired to provide a long-term or enduring benefit. The only remaining category is other sources of income, which may be a logical home for lottery winnings. However, lottery winnings are not specifically included in the list of other sources of income; therefore, they are not subject to income tax. Similarly, such items as those listed next are not taxable, because they are excluded from the list of other sources of income:

---

2   The exclusion of child support payments applies to agreements made or modified after April 30, 1997. IT-530, Support Payments.

- The receipt of a gift.

- The receipt of an inheritance.

- Life insurance proceeds on the death of an individual.

- Profits from betting or gambling, when conducted for pleasure or enjoyment (as opposed to a gambling business enterprise).

- Proceeds from accident, disability, sickness, or income maintenance insurance policies. However, if an employer has paid all or part of the premiums for such policies (see Chapter 4), a different treatment applies: the insurance proceeds received from a claim are taxable as employment income to the extent that they exceed any premiums paid in past years by the employee.[3]

II. Other Deductions

"Other deductions," like "other sources of income," is a catch-all category that permits the deduction of items that do not qualify under the four primary sources of income. Deductions in this category must come from a specific list of items found in sections 60 through 66.8 of the *Income Tax Act*. Some of the major items included in this list are as follows:

- Contributions to an individual's private registered retirement savings plan.[4]

- Alimony and maintenance payments to a former spouse, provided that such payments are paid on a regular, periodic basis (not in lump sum) and are pursuant to a written agreement or court order.[5] Maintenance payments are deductible only to the extent that they are for the support of a former spouse. Maintenance payments for the support of a child are not deductible.[6]

- Amounts paid by a taxpayer as fees or expenses to conduct an objection or appeal in relation to an assessment under the *Income Tax Act*.[7]

- Moving expenses incurred by an individual for relocation to commence a business or employment in another part of Canada, or to attend a university or other post-secondary school, to the extent of income earned in the new location. Deductible moving expenses include travel costs (including meals and lodging and automobile expenses) incurred while moving, transportation and storage of belongings, temporary board and lodging near the new or old residence (up to 15 days), costs of cancelling a lease for the old residence, selling costs of the old residence (commission, legal fees, and mortgage prepayment fees), and legal fees and land transfer taxes for the purchase of a new residence if an old residence is sold.[8] Also included is the cost of maintaining a vacant former residence for a period of three months to a maximum of $5,000. Such maintenance costs include mortgage interest, property taxes, insurance, heat, and power. In addition, eligible moving expenses will include the cost of revising legal documents to reflect a change of address, replacing driver's licences, and obtaining utility connections and disconnections.

  Moving expenses are eligible for a deduction only if the new residence location is at least 40 kilometres closer to the new work location than the previous residence. Also, if a person is employed or self-employed, the deduction is limited to the amount

---

3   ITA 6(1)(f); IT-54.

4   ITA 60(i), 146; IT-124R6.

5   ITA 60(b); IT-118R3; IT-530: Support Payments.

6   Applies to agreements made or modified after April 30, 1997; IT-530: Support Payments.

7   ITA 60(o).

8   ITA 62; IT-178R3.

of employment income or business income earned at the new location. If all or a portion of the expenses cannot be deducted in the year of the move because of insufficient income at the new location, the unclaimed portion can be carried forward and deducted in the following year. An example of a moving expense calculation is shown in the demonstration question at the end of this chapter.

- Child-care expenses (within certain limits) such as baby-sitting, day care, or lodging at a boarding school, for children 16 years of age or less, provided that the expenses were incurred so that the taxpayer could pursue employment, business, or research activities. The actual child-care expenses are deductible only to the extent that they do not exceed $4,000 per child ($7,000 if the child is under seven years of age at year end, or $10,000 if the child has a serious physical or mental disability and is eligible for the disability tax credit [see Chapter 10]), or two-thirds of the taxpayer's "earned" income for the year. The term *earned income* means the total of the individual's employment income, business income, research grants, bursaries and scholarships, and a government disability pension. If more than one person supports a child, the deduction usually must be claimed by the person with the least amount of income for tax purposes.[9]

The category of other deductions also houses extensive provisions relating to exploration and development in the specialized resource industries—oil and gas, mining, and timber. While exploration and development expenses are of a capital nature (because they may provide a long-term benefit), they are permitted a quick write-off in recognition of the high risk and cost of such activity.

In terms of the aggregating formula for determining net income for tax purposes, the total of other deductions is included *after* income from employment, business, property, and other sources, and capital gains, but *before* the deduction of losses from those sources. For example, alimony and maintenance expense, because of its position in the formula, can be deducted against all sources of income for that year; the deduction, however, must be claimed to reduce net income before a deduction is made for business losses or a loss from property.

The other-deductions category is important because it is the last test in the income tax scheme for determining the deductibility of an expenditure. If an expenditure cannot be deducted in accordance with the rules for determining employment income, business income, property income, or capital gains, the only remaining area for examination is other deductions. If the expenditure is not specifically listed in this category, it is simply not deductible when arriving at net income for tax purposes.

III. Registered Retirement Savings Plans

The other-deductions category permits individuals to deduct contributions to a registered retirement savings plan (RRSP). As such plans are used by many taxpayers, their general principles are reviewed in this section of the chapter.

An RRSP is a private, tax-sheltered retirement savings program initiated and controlled by the individual taxpayer for his or her exclusive use. It is different from a registered pension plan, which is initiated and controlled by the employer for the benefit of a number of employees. An RRSP can be an individual's primary retirement vehicle or it can be used to supplement the retirement program provided by the employer.

9 ITA 63; IT-495R2. Certain other limits are also available where the higher-income spouse makes a claim because the other spouse is disabled or pursuing full-time or part-time education.

A. Benefits of
Investing in
an RRSP

Investments made through an RRSP have a substantially higher return. This is because they permit the investment of pre-tax earnings (from employment, business, and certain other sources) to generate returns that are not taxed until they are required for personal use. Specifically, this is achieved as a result of the following:

1. Contributions to an RRSP are deductible from income, which reduces the amount of tax that would otherwise be payable. The tax reduction increases the amount of funds available for investment.

   Normally, to make an investment, an individual must first pay tax on earnings and then invest some portion of the after-tax amount. Consider an individual who, after paying tax and personal expenses, has $3,300 for investment purposes. An individual in a 45% tax bracket could afford to invest $6,000 through an RRSP as follows:

Contribution to the RRSP	$6,000
Tax savings generated:	
(45% × $6,000)	(2,700)
Net cost of investment	$3,300

   Obviously, if you have $3,300 available for an investment, it is better to acquire one that provides a return on $6,000 rather than on $3,300. Effectively, through an RRSP, taxpayers are permitted to delay the payment of tax and invest those funds for their own benefit.

2. Investment returns accumulated on funds contributed to the plan are not subject to annual taxation, which means that investments compound on a pre-tax basis rather than on an after-tax basis. In the previous example, if the invested funds generate a 10% annual return, an investment in an RRSP will provide 10% on $6,000, compounded annually; an investment outside the plan would provide only 5.5% (10% – tax @ 45%) on $3,300, compounded annually.

3. Funds accumulated within the plan, from contributions and investment returns, are subject to tax only when removed from the plan. Usually, funds are removed from the plan on retirement in the form of a regular pension payment, although all or a portion of the funds can be removed if the investor wishes.[10]

The significance of this tax deferral can be more easily seen by examining its impact over a long period of time. For example, if the individual in the situation above had after-tax cash flow of $3,300 available for investment every year for 30 years, the results would be as shown at the top of the next page.

The difference between $1,086,000 and $252,000 is dramatic, although it must be remembered that the $1,086,000 is fully taxable once removed from the plan. However, even the worst-case scenario, where the funds are withdrawn in a lump sum after 30 years and taxed at a rate of 45%, would still leave $597,000 in after-tax value. An individual who invested $3,300 annually without using an RRSP, in order to achieve an after-tax value of $597,000 after 30 years, would have to find an investment yielding 18% annually instead of 10%.

---

10 Individuals are able to make tax-free RRSP withdrawals of up to $10,000 per year over a four-year period (provided that the total withdrawals do not exceed $20,000) to finance full-time education or training for the plan holder or his or her spouse. Amounts withdrawn must be repaid (without interest) in equal instalments over a 10-year period. If the withdrawals are not repaid, they will be included in income. Also, first-time home buyers can withdraw funds up to $20,000 on a tax-free basis to purchase a home. Up to 15 years are allowed for repayment; otherwise, any unpaid portion will be taxable.

Investment through an RRSP

Annual investments in RRSP	$ 6,000
Tax savings @ 45%	(2,700)
Net annual cost	$ 3,300
Total cost ($3,300 × 30 y)	$ 99,000
Future value of investment:	
$6,000 × 30 y × 10% (compounded)	$1,086,000

Investment outside an RRSP

Total cost ($3,300 × 30 y)	$ 99,000
Future value of investment:	
$3,300 × 30 y × 5.5% (compounded)	$ 252,000

The impact of the tax factors on RRSP investments is so substantial that one cannot afford to exclude such plans from one's investment strategy.

B. Contribution Limits

The amount of the contribution to an RRSP that can be deducted for tax purposes is subject to an annual limit.[11]

If an individual *does not belong* to an employer's registered pension plan or deferred profit sharing plan, the annual RRSP contribution limit is equal to 18% of the individual's prior year's "earned income," up to a maximum as shown here:

2003	$14,500
2004	15,500
2005	16,500
2006 (and thereafter)[12]	18,000

For example, the most an individual can contribute to an RRSP in 2004 is 18% of the 2003 earned income, to a maximum of $15,500. When an individual chooses not to contribute the maximum, the unused portion can be carried forward indefinitely and contributed as a deductible contribution in any future year.[13] While it is advantageous to make the contribution as early as possible, the carry-forward provides flexibility to individuals in terms of their particular cash-flow requirements.

When individuals also *belong* to an employer's pension plan or deferred profit sharing plan, the RRSP contribution limit is integrated with those plans. For example, an individual with earned income of $50,000 has a normal contribution limit of $9,000 (18% of $50,000). However, if the individual's employer contributes $3,000 to a deferred profit sharing plan, the RRSP contribution limit is reduced to $6,000.

As a further example, consider a situation where in 20X3 an employer has contributed $3,300 to the company's registered pension plan (RPP) and the employee has contributed an equal amount. Assume that the RPP is a money purchase type of plan (i.e., that will acquire a pension with whatever funds the employee has available in the plan) rather than a defined benefit plan (i.e., that must provide a pension based on an established formula). Also assume that the individual's earned income in 20X3 was $60,000. Based on these assumptions, the maximum contribution that the individual can make to an RRSP in 20X4 is $4,200, as follows:

11 ITA 60(i), 146; IT-124R6.

12 Beginning in 2006, the contribution limit will be indexed to increases in the average industrial wage.

13 ITA 146(1)(1).

Total limit—18% of $60,000	$10,800
RPP contributions—employer	(3,300)
—employee	(3,300)
	$ 4,200

In the above example, if the employee's salary was $110,000, the total limit for the year would be the maximum of $15,500 (using the 2004 limit) rather than 18% of the earned income (18% of $110,000 is $19,800 and is in excess of the absolute limit). The contribution limit for 20X4 would then be $8,900 ($15,500 − [$3,300 + $3,300]).

The value of the contributions to the RPP ($3,300 + $3,300 = $6,600) is technically referred to as the pension adjustment (PA). When the employer's RPP is a defined benefit plan, the value of this pension adjustment may be different from the actual pension contributions because it is based on a formula related to the defined pension benefit. As noted earlier, the pension adjustment also includes contributions by an employer to a deferred profit sharing plan. Employees cannot contribute to an employer's deferred profit sharing plan.

Keep in mind that the RRSP contribution limit as calculated in the above example is further increased by any unused contribution limits carried forward from previous years.

The calculation of the maximum deductible RRSP contribution for the current year can be summarized as follows:

Prescribed dollar limit (current year)	$15,500 (A)†
18% × earned income of the *previous year*	$ xx,xxx (B)
Lesser of A and B above	$ xx,xxx
Add:	
Accumulated unused RRSP contribution limit at the end of the *previous year*, if any	x,xxx
Deduct:	
Pension adjustment from the *previous year*,* if any	(x,xxx)
Maximum deduction for the *current year*	$ xx,xxx

† Using the 2004 limit.

*A further reduction may occur if the employer makes a past-service contribution to the pension plan.

It should also be noted that the contribution limit of 18% applies to "earned income," which is determined by a special calculation, the details of which are easily found in the tax guide accompanying the annual tax return. In general terms, earned income includes employment income (excluding the deduction for contributions to a registered pension plan), rental income, royalty income, alimony and maintenance income, and research grants net of related expenses.[14] This amount must be reduced by negative amounts of a similar nature—business losses, rental losses, and deductible alimony payments. Notice that the calculation of earned income excludes certain passive types of income such as interest, dividends, and capital gains.

Usually, all contributions that exceed the annual limit are subject to a penalty tax of 1% per month on part of that excess until the overcontribution is removed.[15] However, an individual is permitted to overcontribute up to $2,000 during his or her lifetime without penalty. This overcontribution can be carried forward and deducted from income in a future year when sufficient earned income is available.

---

14 ITA 146(1)(c); IT-124R6.

15 ITA 146(8.2); IC 77-18.

An example of an RRSP contribution limit calculation is provided in the demonstration question at the end of this chapter.

C. RRSP Investment Opportunities

RRSP funds are restricted to certain types of investments. The list of qualified investments includes most of the common securities such as cash deposits in banks or other financial institutions, term deposits, government-insured or guaranteed bonds, bonds and debentures of public corporations, shares of public corporations, mutual funds, and mortgages on real estate (including one's own mortgage). Also, investments in foreign securities cannot exceed 30% of the value of all investments in the plan.

RRSP investments are normally managed by banks, trust companies, insurance companies, and other similar financial institutions. Alternatively, an individual can create a self-administered RRSP and manage his or her own investment portfolio.

Special attention should be given to the type of investment, and to the amount of returns that can be achieved within the plan. Too often, the attractiveness of the tax savings from the deductible contribution overshadows, in the investor's mind, the importance of maximizing the return on investments. Because the return on the investment compounds on a pre-tax basis, a slight variation in the rate of return can significantly alter the wealth accumulation—and the ultimate retirement benefits.

Exhibit 9-1 demonstrates the ultimate value of investing $6,000 per year at various rates of return. Increasing the return from 8% to 10% will increase the ultimate value from $734,000 to $1,086,000, providing an extra $352,000 in retirement benefits. Notice that, because of the compounding factor, each successive yield increase of 2% affects the final total by a greater amount. For example, expanding the return from 10% to 12% will increase the ultimate value by $536,000 ($1,622,000 – $1,086,000), compared with an increase of only $352,000 when the return is increased from 8% to 10%. Also notice that doubling the return from 8% to 16% increases the ultimate value fivefold, from $734,000 to $3,691,000.

Of course, with increased returns comes increased risk, and it is unwise to expose retirement funds to excessive risk. However, by regularly reviewing RRSP investments, maximum returns can be achieved within the acceptable boundaries of risk.

In addition to the amount of expected returns, consideration should be given to the *type* of investment return earned by the RRSP. Capital gains, for example, receive preferential treatment, as only one-half of the gain is taxable. Capital gains that are realized in an RRSP are not taxable while they remain in the plan; however, they are *fully* taxable as pension income when paid out of the plan. This means that an individual who invests in common shares through an RRSP is converting otherwise tax-free gains into taxable pension income. This consequence is important for those individuals who hold a variety of investments both inside and outside an RRSP. It is prudent for those investors to hold investments yielding capital gains outside the plan, and interest-bearing securities (which do not have preferential tax treatment) within the plan.

Exhibit 9-1: *Value of $6,000 Invested* *Annually for 30 Years*	*Return on* *investment*	*Value after* *30 years*	*Impact of* *2% increase*
	8%	$ 734,000	–0–
	10	1,086,000	352,000
	12	1,622,000	536,000
	14	2,440,000	818,000
	16	3,691,000	1,251,000

D. Retirement Options

Funds accumulated in an RRSP can be paid out in a lump sum or gradually over a period of time in the form of a pension, depending on the individual's particular requirements. If those funds are paid out gradually in the form of a pension, the funds remaining in the plan continue to generate investment returns without tax consequences. In order to receive regular payments from an RRSP, the plan must be formally converted into a pension vehicle. Financial institutions offer these. Three general types of pension vehicles are available, each of which is described briefly below.

- **Life annuity** Under this option the accumulated RRSP funds are used to purchase an annuity that provides a monthly payment for the life of the owner. The amount of the payment depends on the age of the individual and on the prevailing interest rates at the date of purchase. This option is considered to be a risk vehicle, because if the annuitant dies before his or her normal life expectancy, the payments cease, and the remaining funds in the plan accrue to the benefit of the financial institution that issued the annuity. Because of this risk, life annuities usually provide the highest pension income. The risk of life annuities can be tempered by arranging a guaranteed payment term (e.g., a life annuity with payments guaranteed for 10 years, or a life annuity for the life of the annuitant and his or her spouse), but reducing the risk this way also reduces the regular pension payments.

- **Guaranteed fixed-term annuity** This option guarantees that the full RRSP funds will be paid out over a period of time to the owner or any designated beneficiaries. Regular payments are made over a term that begins with the date of purchase and ends when the annuitant or his or her spouse reaches the age of 90. For example, an annuity purchased at age 65 will be paid over 25 years (90 – 65) whether or not the annuitant lives to age 90. This type of annuity usually consists of fixed, equal payments; however, arrangements can be made to have regular payments tied to specific investment returns.

- **Registered retirement income fund (RRIF)** Under this option the RRSP funds are invested and guaranteed to be fully paid out over the remaining lifetime of the holder (or the holder's spouse). However, the regular payment is fixed at a low minimum, with the annuitant having the right to withdraw any additional amount desired in any particular year. This option provides the greatest flexibility by permitting the owner to alter the payments in accordance with his or her needs.

When must an individual convert his or her RRSP to one of the above-mentioned retirement options? It is mandatory to convert all of the accumulated RRSP funds to a retirement income vehicle by December 31 of the year in which the individual reaches 69 years of age. Retirement income can begin in the following calendar year. It is not necessary to wait until age 69 to make the conversion; retirement income can begin earlier than age 69 if desired. It should be noted that failure to convert by age 69 will result in the automatic cancellation of the RRSP at the beginning of the following year, in which case the full amount of the plan will be taxable.

E. Spousal RRSP

An additional important tax planning opportunity is available to taxpayers who are married and contribute to an RRSP. Once an individual's total contribution limit has been established, that individual can contribute all or any part of that limit to the RRSP of a spouse. The person who makes the contribution is entitled to claim the related tax deduction. This does not affect the normal contribution limit of the spouse.[16] This type of contribution does not create any immediate tax advantage because the maximum deduction for the contributor remains the same. However, the long-term benefits may be substantial.

---

16 ITA 146(5.1), 146(8.3).

The point of designating contributions to a spouse's plan is that it allows the future pay-out—usually in the form of an annuity—to be included in the spouse's taxable income rather than that of the contributor. If a wife and husband can equalize their RRSP funds, future withdrawals can be divided between them upon retirement. This will usually result in lower annual taxes than would have been levied if all of the withdrawals had been included in one person's income. This form of income splitting between spouses is specific-ally permitted; other types of income splitting between spouses are usually discouraged (as is discussed later in this chapter).

In order to prevent abuses of this program, there is an anti-avoidance rule stating that any contributions withdrawn from such a plan by the spouse within two taxation years of the contribution year must be included in the contributor's income. However, once the two-year period (for any contribution) passes, the amounts are taxable only to the spouse.

In conclusion, the RRSP is an important tool for maximizing wealth accumulation through the use of tax-sheltered funds.

IV. Special Rules for Net Income Determination

The parameters of net income for tax purposes have been established to include five sources of income. Each source, with the exception of "other income," is calculated in accordance with its own set of fundamental principles. Within each source of income unusual transactions may occur, the treatment of which is not clearly answered by the established general principles. In addition, taxpayers may attempt to structure transactions in such a way as to avoid the application of the general principles. Consequently, the *Income Tax Act* includes a set of special rules for determining net income; these provide greater cer-tainty when the established general rules are applied in unusual transactions, and also fore-stall certain tax-avoidance schemes.

The special rules are grouped together in sections 67 through 81 of the *Income Tax Act*. In some cases these rules are in conflict with the previously established principles; when they are, the special rules take precedence. Although the special rules are presented sepa-rately, they apply to all of the five sources of income. For example, when business income is being determined, the special rules must be viewed in terms of their application to business transactions. In other words, the special rules outlined in this section of the chapter should be thought of as an extension of the rules that have been established for each source of income.

The fundamental application of several of the special rules is described briefly below.

A. The Reasonableness Test

All items that are deductible from any source of income are deductible only to the extent that the expenditure is considered reasonable in the particular circumstances.[17] The ques-tion of what is "reasonable" is a difficult one; the answer depends on the nature of the trans-action. For example, a portion of automobile expenses incurred to earn business income or employment income may be denied when the cost of the automobile is too high for the par-ticular purpose. Similarly, overly extravagant entertainment expenses may be deemed unnecessary for the intended purpose.

The denial of a deduction for unreasonable salaries paid to related parties is extremely punitive. A small business owner may be denied the deduction of all or a portion of the salary paid to a spouse or child if the payment is excessive in relation to the services pro-vided; but the actual salary paid to the spouse or child remains as taxable employment income in their hands. Effectively, this creates double taxation within the family unit.

The general reasonableness test was reviewed in several previous chapters, especially Chapter 5, which dealt with the determination of business income. It is important to recog-

---

17 ITA 67; *No. 511 v. MNR*, 58 DTC 307.

nize that the reasonableness test applies to deductions for *all* types of income. In addition to the general reasonableness test, there are several more specific reasonableness tests that apply to various categories of income. One of these limits the deduction for meals, beverages, and entertainment expenses to 50% of the actual costs (provided that those costs meet the general reasonableness test). Another places limits on the deduction of interest, lease costs, and the capital cost of a passenger vehicle (see Chapters 4, 5, and 6).[18]

B. Allocation of Purchase Price for Multiple Assets

In some cases a number of different properties may be acquired or sold as a group. This is most common when the assets of an entire business are sold. The total price may include such items as inventory, land, buildings, equipment, and goodwill. Similarly, when real estate is sold, the price includes the land and the building(s). While the total price is obvious, it may be difficult to allocate that price among the various assets included in the transaction.

A conflict often arises between the purchaser and the vendor. It is in the buyer's interest to allocate a greater amount to assets that are permitted a faster write-off rate for tax purposes. For example, the buyer achieves greater tax benefits if, in a real estate purchase, a greater amount is allocated to the building and a lesser amount to the land. Similarly, when a complete business is purchased it is to the buyer's advantage to increase the value of equipment and reduce the value of goodwill, which has a slower write-off rate. On the other hand, it is in the vendor's interest to reduce the amount of tax on the sale. A vendor will often try to enhance the value of properties yielding capital gains (land, for example), because only one-half of such gains are taxable, and reduce the value of properties that create a recapture of capital cost allowance, which is fully taxable.

The special rules permit CCRA to allocate or reallocate the total price for both parties, in accordance with the apparent fair market values of individual properties.[19] CCRA is permitted to do so irrespective of the legal agreement of sale. It should be pointed out, however, that when the parties are dealing at arm's length (i.e., are not related), an agreed allocation in the legal agreement of sale carries considerable weight in the absence of evidence of a sham or scheme to reduce taxes.

It is important that decision makers, when they are about to acquire or sell a group of assets, give reasonable consideration to how the total price is allocated in order that they can forecast both the related tax consequences and the impact on cash flow of the proposed transaction.

C. Transactions with Inadequate Consideration

When taxpayers enter into a transaction with non-arm's-length (related) parties, special rules apply that prevent the elimination or reduction of tax by selling at a price other than fair market value. Taxpayers are considered *not* to be dealing at arm's length if they are related to each other. The term "related" has a specific limited definition within the *Income Tax Act* and can apply to both individuals and corporations, as discussed later in this section.

The following rules apply to taxpayers not dealing at arm's length:[20]

1. Property sold at a legal price less than its fair market value is deemed to have been sold by the vendor at fair market value. No adjustment is made to the purchaser, for whom the cost of the property for tax purposes remains the actual price paid.

2. Property sold at a price higher than its fair market value is not adjusted to the vendor, and the selling price constitutes the proceeds of disposition. However, the cost to the purchaser is deemed to be equal to the fair market value, not the actual purchase price.

---

18 ITA 67.2 to 67.4; IT-521R.

19 ITA 68; *Schellenberg v. MNR*, 86 DTC 1463.

20 ITA 69(1)(a) to (c); IT-405.

3. Property transferred by way of a gift is deemed to have been sold at fair market value by the person making the gift. The recipient of the gift is deemed, for tax purposes, to have purchased the property at a cost equal to its fair market value. This particular rule applies even when the gift is made to an arm's-length party.

Notice that the first two of the above rules apply to only one party in the transaction. As a result, the application of those rules is extremely punitive, as demonstrated in the following situation:

Situation: Corporation X, a manufacturer, has inventory on hand that was produced at a cost of $10,000. The inventory if sold direct to retail stores is worth $18,000, and if sold on the wholesale market is worth $13,000. Corporation Y is a sister corporation of X, as it is owned by the same shareholders.

Corporation Y is a wholesale enterprise that buys manufactured products for resale to retail stores. Corporation X sells the above inventory to its sister corporation for $10,000, which is its cost amount. Subsequently, Corporation Y sells the inventory to retail stores for the going price of $18,000.

Analysis: Corporation X and Corporation Y are related, and do not deal at arm's length, because they have common ownership.

Impact on Corporation X (seller):	
Deemed selling price at fair market value	$13,000
Cost	(10,000)
Business income for tax purposes	$ 3,000
Impact on Corporation Y (purchaser):	
Actual selling price to retail stores	$18,000
Actual cost paid to X	(10,000)
Business income for tax purposes	$ 8,000

In the above example the combined taxable income of Corporation X and Corporation Y was $11,000 ($3,000 + $8,000) on the sale of inventory, even though a real profit of only $8,000 had been realized. The impact of these rules is severely punitive; managers *must* take great care in their transfer-pricing decisions in a related group of companies.

The punitive provisions may apply even when the parties have intended to deal at fair market value but have erred while estimating that value. In such cases, the related parties can protect themselves with a covering written agreement which indicates that the established price is a reasonable estimate of fair market value and that, if found to be in error, the price charged and paid will be altered accordingly.[21] Usually the existence of such an agreement will cause CCRA to adjust both sides of the transaction, thereby eliminating the punitive result, which is double taxation.

Similar provisions also apply for the sale of property and services between a Canadian taxpayer and a non-arm's-length foreign entity. This means that transactions between a Canadian subsidiary and its foreign parent corporation cannot unduly shift the burden of tax from one jurisdiction to another by means of transactions at other than reasonable values (see Chapter 20).[22]

21 IT-405.
22 ITA 69(2), (3); IT-486R.

D. Non-Arm's Length Defined

Normally, the values placed on financial transactions are determined by the free market forces of supply and demand. In such circumstances, the parties to the transaction are said to be dealing at *arm's length*. Sometimes, however, supply and demand are *not* the motivating factors, in which case the parties are considered not to be dealing at arm's length. For tax purposes, the *Income Tax Act* deems parties not to be dealing with each other at arm's length if they are *related*[23] and their transactions may be subject to scrutiny, as was shown in section C above. Non-arm's-length transactions can occur between

- an individual and another individual
- an individual and a corporation
- a corporation and another corporation

The rules that deem the above parties to be related are extremely complex and may require interpretation by an expert. Outlined below are some of the most *common* relationships.

• **Transactions between individuals** For tax purposes, individuals are related to each other if they are direct-line descendants (grandparents, parents, children, grandchildren, and so on) or if they are brothers, sisters, spouses, or in-laws.[24] Excluded from the definition are cousins, aunts, uncles, nieces, and nephews.

• **Transactions between individuals and corporations** An individual is related to a corporation if he or she controls the corporation, or is a member of a related group that controls the corporation, or is related to an individual who controls the corporation. Control in this context usually means the ownership of a majority of the corporation's voting shares. Consider the following ownership structures:

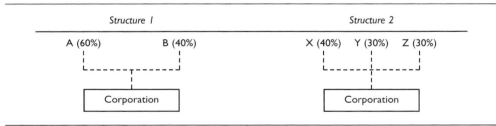

In structure 1, the corporation is controlled by individual A (60%), and therefore individual A and the corporation are related and do not deal at arm's length. Individual B (40%) is not related to the corporation unless he or she is also related to individual A (e.g., is the sister, child, or parent of individual A). In structure 2, none of the individual shareholders are related to the corporation because none of them has control. However, if individual X (40%) and individual Y (30%) were themselves related, they would together control the corporation (70%), and each would be considered related to the corporation.

• **Transactions between corporations** Two corporations are related if one corporation controls the other corporation, or if both corporations are controlled by the same person, or if one corporation is controlled by one person who is related to the person who controls the other corporation. Consider the following ownership structures:

---

23 ITA 251(1)(a); IT-419R.
24 ITA 251(2); 252(1), (2).

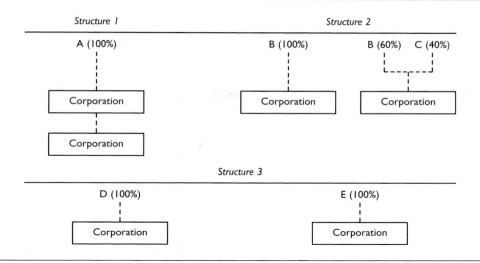

In structure 1, the two corporations are related because one controls the other. In structure 2, both corporations are controlled by individual B (100% and 60%), which means that the two corporations are related. In structure 3, the two corporations are not related because they are controlled by different shareholders. However, if shareholders D and E are related to each other, the two corporations will also be related, because one corporation is controlled by a person who is related to a person who controls the other corporation.

Note that even when parties are *not related*, it is a question of fact whether they are dealing at arm's length for a particular transaction.[25] Where there is sufficient cause, CCRA can deem two unrelated parties not to be dealing at arm's length.

E. Property Transferred to a Spouse or Child

Property transferred to a child, whether by gift or by sale, is deemed for tax purposes to have been sold at fair market value in accordance with the rules described earlier in this chapter. By exception, farm property transferred to children is permitted to be sold at less than fair market value.[26]

Property transferred to a spouse, however, is not subject to the rules regarding fair market value. Instead, any property sold or gifted to a spouse is automatically deemed, for tax purposes, to have been sold and acquired at its cost amount.[27] As a result, capital property is deemed to have been sold at its adjusted cost base (see Chapter 8) and depreciable property at its undepreciated capital cost (see Chapter 6). The result is that no taxable income is created on the transfer of property between spouses.

Alternatively, a taxpayer can choose to recognize a gain on a spousal transfer. This may be attractive when losses are available that can be offset against the resulting income.

F. Future Income on Property Transferred to a Spouse or Child

The above section described the tax treatment resulting from the actual transfer of property to a spouse or child. Additional special rules govern the treatment of income that may be earned on the property after it has been transferred. For example, the property may generate interest, dividends, or rents, or may incur a gain or loss when it is subsequently resold.

Subsequent income received by the *spouse* on transferred property must be included in the net income for tax purposes of the original owner for as long as the couple remains

---

25 ITA 251(1)(b).

26 ITA 73(3).

27 ITA 73(1), (2); IT-258R2.

married.[28] This rule prevents a taxpayer from transferring his or her income to a spouse, who may be in a lower tax bracket. The process of allocating subsequent income back to the original owner is referred to as "attribution." Similarly, if interest-free loans are made to a spouse, any income earned by the spouse on the loaned funds is attributed to the lender.

The attribution rules do not apply if property is transferred to a spouse in a manner equivalent to an arm's-length transfer.[29] This means that a loan to a spouse must have a reasonable interest rate, and that property sold to a spouse must be paid for in normal commercial terms. In addition, the spouse who made the transfer must recognize the related gain on the transfer if the transfer value is greater than the cost amount (see discussion in section D above).

Similarly, income on property transferred to a child under the age of 18 is attributed to the parent until the child's 18th birthday.[30] However, in the case of children, subsequent capital gains or losses are not subject to attribution. Usually, transfers of property occur between parents and children. However, these attribution rules are not restricted to children; they may also apply when property is transferred to other minors, such as a niece or nephew.

In the past, tax planners have found creative ways to avoid the attribution rules for dividend distributions from private corporations to minor children. To counter this, a new anti-avoidance rule is now in force.[31] Dividends received by *minor* children (directly or through a trust) from a *private* Canadian or foreign corporation are not subject to the attribution rules described in the above paragraph. Instead, those specific dividends are subject to tax at the top marginal tax rate (less any applicable dividend tax credit). Because the dividends are taxed at the top rate, the benefit of splitting dividend income from private corporations is eliminated. Dividend income from shares of public corporations continues to be subject to the attribution rules mentioned previously. Also, note that the new rule applies to *dividends* from private corporations and *not to capital gains* (or losses) realized from the disposition of private corporation shares. For minors, this type of income remains not subject to the attribution rules; therefore, it is taxed in the hands of the minor at whatever tax rate is applicable to that person in the year.

G. Unpaid Remuneration

In Chapter 5 it was established that business income is determined on an accrual basis. This means that salaries are normally deductible by the employer, as are other forms of remuneration that have been incurred but not paid to an employee. However, employment income is included by the employee in income for tax purposes only when received (see Chapter 4). In order to prevent the undue delay of taxable remuneration payments, the special rules limit the deductibility of unpaid remuneration.[32] The employer can deduct unpaid remuneration for tax purposes only if it is paid within 180 days of its taxation year. If payment is delayed beyond that period, the employer can deduct the remuneration in a subsequent year when it is paid.

H. Mortgage Foreclosures and Default Sales

Property is often acquired with borrowed funds (e.g., through a mortgage on real estate) and then pledged as collateral security to the lender. A debtor who is faced with financial difficulty may decide to default on the loan payments, thereby allowing the creditor to take ownership of the secured property. The tax treatment of this unusual type of transaction is specifically provided for in the *Income Tax Act*.

From the debtor's perspective, a foreclosure means that a debt has been extinguished and that a property has been disposed of in satisfaction of the debt. For tax purposes, the

---

28 ITA 74.1, 74.2(1), (2).

29 ITA 74.5(1), (2).

30 ITA 74.1(2).

31 ITA 120.4. The special tax may also apply to certain income derived from the sale of goods or services to a business carried on by a relative of the child.

32 ITA 78(4); IT-109R2.

taxpayer is deemed to have sold the property for a price equal to the principal amount of the debt owing. As a result, depending on the amount of the deemed proceeds, the transaction may result in a recapture of capital cost allowance and/or a capital gain.[33]

From the creditor's perspective, a foreclosure means that an amount receivable has been satisfied. For tax purposes, the creditor is deemed to have acquired the property at a cost equal to the principal amount of the debt outstanding, less any reserves that were previously claimed. The creditor may eventually recognize a gain or loss for tax purposes when the acquired property is eventually sold.

I. Gain on Settlement of Debt

An individual or a corporation may be in a position to settle an outstanding debt for less than the amount of principal owing. Often this situation arises under conditions of extreme financial difficulty. It may also occur when the creditor offers a discount as an inducement for early payment and the debtor utilizes this inducement, or when a debt is forgiven. In effect, the debtor achieves a gain from the transaction. The treatment of that gain for tax purposes is unusual.[34]

When this type of gain occurs, it is not directly included in taxable income. Instead, it is first applied to reduce any losses that have been carried over from other years, in the following order (see Chapter 10 for a discussion of these loss carry-overs):

- non-capital losses (business and property losses, but excluding allowable business investment losses)
- farm losses
- restricted farm losses (when farming is not the chief source of income)
- allowable business investment losses
- net capital losses

When a taxpayer has such unused losses, a reduction in their amount results in an increase in future taxable income. In effect, the gain is taxed but in some future year. Often, however, the taxpayer does not have any of these losses available. When that is the case, the gain is applied to reduce the capital cost or the adjusted cost base of the following types of assets, in any order:

- depreciable property
- capital property (non-depreciable)
- cumulative eligible capital
- certain other properties

When the cost of these assets is reduced, any subsequent sale results in either a greater gain or a lesser loss for tax purposes. This in turn means that the gain on debt settlement is delayed for tax purposes until the particular asset is sold. It should be pointed out that within each of the preceding asset categories, the taxpayer has the right to choose which asset's cost will be reduced, and so should make an attempt to reduce the cost of an asset that will not be sold in the near future.

If all of the forgiven debt is not consumed by applying it to the above items, three-quarters of the remaining amount will be included in the taxpayer's income in that year.

J. Death of a Taxpayer

Unfortunately, although life ceases, financial matters—including imposition of tax—continue. Below is a brief summary of the tax implications triggered by the death of an individual taxpayer.

1. Income from all sources is accrued up to the date of death.

---

33 ITA 79; IT-505.
34 ITA 80(1) to (18); Regulations 5400, 5401; IT-293R.

2. All capital property that was owned by the deceased is deemed to have been sold.[35] Capital property, including depreciable property, is deemed to have been sold at a fair market value. Usually this results in the recognition of capital gains and a recapture of capital cost allowance. However, if the above assets are left to a spouse or spouse trust, they are deemed to have been sold at their cost amount, and no taxable gains occur.

3. Representatives of the deceased, referred to as "executors," are given control of the assets. After all liabilities have been satisfied, the assets are either sold or transferred to beneficiaries, or to trusts for the benefit of beneficiaries, in accordance with the terms of a will. During the period that assets are held by the executors, they may generate income; this income, for tax purposes, constitutes income of the executor's trust. Thereafter, income from the assets is included in the income of the beneficiaries, or of the trusts that have been established for the beneficiaries.

Exhibit 9-2 diagrams the flow of income for tax purposes of the deceased taxpayer and the beneficiaries.

Exhibit 9-2: Death of a Taxpayer

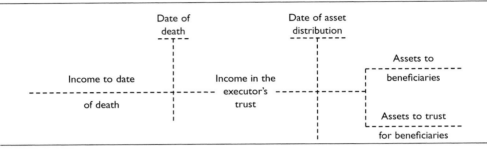

Tax on death can be significant. Individuals should consider acquiring life insurance so that properties do not have to be sold to pay the tax on the deemed disposition.

K. Amounts Not Included in Income

A number of items are given preferential treatment and excluded from income for tax purposes even though they fall within the normal sources of income. These items are unusual in nature and are specifically listed in section 81 of the *Income Tax Act*. For example, allowances received from employers are taxable in accordance with the principles of employment income, but the special rules exempt allowances received by members of a provincial legislature, municipality, or school board. Similarly, pension income is taxable as other sources of income, but special pensions received by members of the RCMP for injury or disability are exempt.

The special rules for determining net income for tax purposes described above are not all-inclusive and have been examined in a superficial manner. Even so, it is important to recognize that they form an integral part of the overall process of determining income for tax purposes, and that they are the source for determining the treatment of unusual transactions that may occur within one of the primary sources of income.

V . Review of Net Income for Tax Purposes

A. The Scope of Income Tax in Canada

The apparent complexity of the Canadian income tax system is significantly diminished when its parameters are understood. The preceding chapters have shown these parameters and developed a fundamental framework that can be used to apply the income tax to both personal and business financial activities.

This framework, which was outlined in Chapter 3, established that any individual, corporation, or trust that is resident in Canada is subject to tax on world income in each

35 ITA 70(1) to (5).

taxation year. In addition, it established that nonresidents are taxed on certain income earned in Canada. Fundamental to the tax system is the process for determining the amount of the income to which the tax applies. This process is reviewed below.

1. Each of the primary entities is required to pay tax on its taxable income. Taxable income is the taxpayer's net income for tax purposes less special reductions. (These special reductions, which are few in number, will be reviewed in two subsequent chapters.)

2. Individuals and corporations determine their net income for tax purposes in the same manner. There are five potential sources of income: employment income, business income, property income, capital gains, and other sources of income and deductions. These sources are summarized below.

A *Employment income*　Employment income, which takes the form of a wage, salary, or other benefits, is derived from the providing of personal services under a contract of employment. Such income is determined in accordance with the following basic rules:

- Remuneration is included in income on a cash basis—that is, when received.

- All benefits (subject to specific exceptions) received or enjoyed by virtue of employment are taxable.

- All amounts received as allowances (subject to specific exceptions) are taxable.

- No deductions are permitted from employment income except those indicated in a specific, limited list.

B *Business income*　Business income encompasses a wide range of activities, but is generally considered to be income from an enterprise that sells goods or services with the intention to profit. Business income is determined as follows:

- Business income is the profit therefrom and is determined in accordance with well-accepted business principles, which are normally interpreted through generally accepted accounting principles and case law.

- The accounting rules are modified by six general limitations specified in the *Income Tax Act*.

- The accounting income, subject to the six general limitations, may be further modified by two lists of specific exceptions. One of these lists denies the deduction of specific items, the other permits the deduction of items denied by the general rules.

C *Property income*　Income from property is the return on invested capital in the form of interest, dividends, rents, and the like. Property income is determined in accordance with the same basic rules as govern business income.

D *Capital gains*　Capital gains are the profits realized on the disposition of property that was acquired to provide a long-term or enduring benefit to the owner. Capital gains or losses are determined by the following basic rules:

- A gain or loss is recognized only when a disposition occurs or is deemed to occur.

- One-half of the gain or loss is applicable.

- The gain or loss is calculated as the proceeds of disposition less the sum of the adjusted cost base of the property and the expenses of disposition.

- The recognition of capital gains can be deferred (within limits) in relation to the receipt of the proceeds of disposition.

E *Other sources of income and deductions*   "Other sources of income" includes items of income that cannot otherwise be placed in one of the above four primary categories. Similarly, "other deductions" includes items that do not fall within the definition of the primary sources. Items in this category are limited to a specific short list—a list that constitutes the final parameter of income sources. There are no general rules for determining income in this category.

3. The normal income determination methods for each of the primary income sources may be modified by the special rules for income determination. These rules are grouped together in the *Income Tax Act* and deal with unusual transactions for each of the primary income sources.

4. The net income from each source is combined by means of an aggregating formula, which is used by both individuals and corporations. The formula establishes that losses from employment, business, and property, and allowable business investment losses, can be offset against any of the five types of income earned by the entity. Allowable capital losses, however, can be offset only against taxable capital gains. The total of the aggregating formula is referred to as the taxpayer's net income for tax purposes (see Exhibit 3-4, Chapter 3, and Exhibit 10-1, Chapter 10).

In order to understand the tax treatment of a particular transaction, managers must first assign that transaction to one of the five sources of income. Once this has been done, they can determine the amount and timing of the tax payment from the general principles of income determination for that specific source. They can then assess the impact of that tax treatment on cash flow. If a transaction does not fall within one of the five sources of income, it is outside the fundamental framework and not subject to income tax.

In the following section is a sample calculation of net income for tax purposes. The example uses, as the taxpayer, an individual who has income from several sources. The information that follows is presented randomly. Each income item is assigned a source; net income is then determined for each source. Finally, the aggregating formula is used to arrive at net income for tax purposes.

B. Sample Calculation of Net Income for Tax Purposes

Summary of Information

Carla Fenson is employed as a financial executive. In addition, she is a partner in a retail store and maintains a portfolio of investments. Information with respect to these activities for 20X5 is given below.

1. Carla's job as an executive provided a gross annual salary of $50,000. In addition, her employer contributed $3,000 to the company pension plan in her name. Carla made an equal contribution of $3,000 to the plan. In the summer of 20X5, Carla used the company's vacation home for a one-month personal holiday at no cost to her. When the vacation home is not used by employees, the company rents it out for $2,000 per month.

    Also, Carla received a bonus of $10,000 in 20X5, which was awarded for her special efforts in 20X4.

2. The retail store in which Carla is a partner suffered a loss of $40,000 for the fiscal period ending December 31, 20X5. Her share of the loss amounted to $10,000 and was calculated by an accountant in accordance with the required tax rules.

3. In 20X0 Carla purchased three rental properties. Financial information on each property is as follows:

	Property 1	Property 2	Property 3
Land cost	$10,000	$ 4,000	$ 8,000
Building cost	60,000	40,000	45,000
Undepreciated capital cost (20X4)	52,000	37,000	40,000
20X5 net rental income (loss) before capital cost allowance	4,000	(5,000)	4,000

In 20X5, Carla sold property 1 for $80,000 (12,000 for the land, 68,000 for the building).

4. In 20X5, Carla gifted shares of a *public* corporation to her 16-year-old son. The shares had cost her $10,000 and were worth $13,000 at the time of the gift. After receiving the gift, the son received dividends of $1,000 on the shares. Also in 20X5, Carla gifted shares of a public corporation to her husband. The shares, which had a value of $15,000 at the time of the gift, had originally cost $9,000. No dividends were received.

5. In 20X1, Carla purchased some shares of a Canadian-controlled private corporation (a qualified small business corporation) that was set up to start a new business venture. She recently sold the shares, which cost $30,000, for $20,000.

6. Carla also sold the following assets in 20X5:

	Cost	Proceeds
Shares of public corporation X	$22,000	$27,000
Shares of public corporation Y	40,000	18,000
Grand piano	14,000	9,000

7. She also received the following additional items:

Dividends from public corporations	$4,000
Lottery winnings	6,000
Lump-sum payment from a former employer's registered pension plan	1,500

8. Carla paid out the following in 20X5:

Interest on a bank loan to purchase shares	$2,000
Interest on a loan to acquire a personal automobile	1,200
Contribution to a registered retirement savings plan	1,000
Donations to charitable organizations	3,000

Calculation of Net Income for Tax Purposes (20X5)

Employment income:		
Gross salary		$ 50,000
20X4 bonus received in 20X5		10,000
Employment benefit—use of vacation home		2,000
		62,000
Contribution to company pension plan		(3,000)
Net income from employment		$ 59,000
Business income (loss):		
Share of loss from partnership		$(10,000)
Property income:		
Dividends received ($4,000 × 1.25)		$ 5,000
Dividends received by son, attributed to Carla		
($1,000 × 1.25)		1,250
		6,250
Interest on loan to acquire shares		(2,000)
Net dividend income		4,250
Real estate:		
Rental income before capital cost allowance:		
Property 1	4,000	
Property 2	(5,000)	
Property 3	4,000	
	3,000	
Recapture of capital cost allowance (below)	8,000	
	11,000	
Capital cost allowance (below)	(3,080)	7,920
Net income from property		$ 12,170

Capital cost allowance:

	Class 1 Property 1	Class 1 Property 2 & 3
Undepreciated capital cost	$52,000	$ 77,000*
Disposal (to maximum of cost)	(60,000)	–0–
	(8,000)	77,000
Recapture	8,000	
Capital cost allowance (4%)	–0–	(3,080)
Undepreciated capital cost	–0–	$ 73,920

* Note: Properties 2 and 3 are combined, as the original cost of each building was less than $50,000.

Capital gains:

	Proceeds	Cost	Gain
Property 1:			
Land	$12,000	$10,000	$ 2,000
Building	68,000	60,000	8,000
Gift to son	13,000	10,000	3,000
Shares of Corporation X	27,000	22,000	5,000
			$18,000
Taxable capital gains—$18,000 × ½			$ 9,000

Note: The gift of shares to spouse is deemed to have been sold at the adjusted cost base, and therefore no gain occurs.

Capital losses:

Shares of Corporation Y

Proceeds	$ 18,000	
Adjusted cost base	(40,000)	
	$(22,000)	
Allowable capital loss: $22,000 × ½		$(11,000)

Note: The loss on the sale of the piano is deemed to be nil, as it is personal-use property.

Allowable business investment loss:

Shares of private small business corporation:

Proceeds	$ 20,000	
Adjusted cost base	(30,000)	
	$(10,000)	
Allowable loss: $10,000 × ½		$(5,000)

Other sources of income:

Receipt of pension income	$ 1,500

Other deductions:

Contribution to RRSP	$(1,000)

Items excluded from calculation:

- The contribution of $3,000 by the employer to the registered pension plan is excluded as a taxable benefit.

- Lottery winnings do not conform to any of the five sources of income and therefore are not taxable.

- Interest paid on the loan for the personal automobile does not conform to the primary sources of income and is not specifically listed in other deductions; therefore, it is not deductible.

- Charitable donations are not specifically listed as other deductions and consequently are not deductible when arriving at net income for tax purposes.

The aggregating formula:

(a) Employment income		$59,000
Business income		–0–
Property income		12,170
Other sources of income		1,500
		72,670
(b) Taxable capital gains	9,000	
Allowable capital losses		
($11,000) to a maximum of	(9,000)	–0–
		72,670
(c) Other deductions		(1,000)
		71,670
(d) Business loss	(10,000)	
Allowable business investment loss	(5,000)	(15,000)
Net income for tax purposes		$56,670

VI. Tax Planning Checklist

The items discussed in this chapter affect a number of tax planning opportunities. As can be expected, many of them relate to investing in an RRSP. Some of the items are reviewed below.

1. When acquiring a group of assets for a single purchase price, carefully consider how to allocate the total price among the assets. Remember that CCRA has the power to revise the allocations. Within reason, allocate the price to properties that can be deducted quickly for tax purposes. Be prepared to justify the method used to the tax authorities.

2. When a taxpayer dies, assets that are left to beneficiaries, other than a spouse, usually are deemed to have been disposed of for tax purposes at fair market value. Knowing this, individuals can take steps to transfer assets during their lifetime to the intended beneficiaries. This allows future value increases to accrue to those beneficiaries and minimizes taxes on death. Often, such transfers can be achieved on a tax-deferred basis. This activity is referred to as an "estate freeze" (see Chapter 18).

3. Upon separation or divorce, carefully negotiate alimony or maintenance agreements to ensure the best possible tax treatment for both parties.

4. Taxpayers can split income with children who are 18 years of age or older by gifting them property that will earn investment income. This may take advantage of their lower tax rate while ensuring that they can use all available deductions and tax credits.

5. Attribution does not apply when property is transferred to children who are under 18 years of age when the income is a capital gain. Therefore, consider loaning funds to children and using those funds to obtain capital growth investments. Keep in mind that capital losses will also remain with the child.

6. In some families the income of one spouse is higher than that of the other. When this is the case, family expenses should first be paid with income earned by the high-income spouse. The result will be that all or most of the family savings available for investment purposes will belong to the lower-income spouse and will be taxed at a lower rate.

7. Be certain to equalize the retirement funds of each spouse by utilizing spousal RRSP contributions. This will result in income splitting on retirement.

8. An RRSP contribution can be made within 60 days after the year for which it will be deducted. However, taxpayers can and should contribute the funds as early as possible in the applicable year to increase the amount of income that will be sheltered from tax.

9. RRSP funds must be carefully monitored and managed. As previously shown, a small increase in the percentage return on investment can significantly increase the retirement balance in the long term. However, keep in mind that increased returns may involve an increased risk.

10. If funds are available, consider making the permitted $2,000 overcontribution to an RRSP. This will increase the amount of tax-sheltered earnings and in the long term compound to a substantial sum. The excess contribution can be deducted from income in a later year. This action should also be considered for a spouse and children who are not under the age of 19.

11. Remember that all amounts removed from an RRSP are fully taxable. This means that incomes which have preferential tax treatment such as capital gains (one-half taxable or fully exempt) and dividends (dividend tax credit) become fully taxable when distributed from an RRSP. Some individuals have both an RRSP and a personal investment portfolio, and invest in shares as well as interest-bearing securities. These individuals should place the interest-bearing securities in the RRSP and the investments that have preferential tax treatment in the personal portfolio.

12. Individuals who are employed by their own corporation should attempt to receive sufficient annual salary to meet the "earned income" requirements for maximum RRSP deductions. Dividends from the corporation do not qualify as "earned income."

13. Carefully consider the RRSP retirement options and attempt to choose a vehicle that will balance the payouts with the need for funds. A registered retirement income fund (RRIF) may provide more flexibility but may also require more fund management.

VII. Summary and Conclusion

This chapter has finished establishing the parameters that limit the types of income subject to Canadian income tax. "Other sources of income" and "other deductions" are catch-all categories in that they define the extent to which income items or deductions that fall outside the four primary categories are included in net income for tax purposes.

This chapter has also identified and discussed the list of special rules that deal with the treatment of unusual transactions within each of the main sources of income. These special rules should be included as an "appendix" to the principles previously established for each of the five sources of income.

The process of establishing net income for tax purposes for individuals and corporations is now complete. This process can be summarized as follows:

1. Define the nature of a transaction to determine which of the five income sources it relates to.

2. Apply the principles of income determination attached to that specific source of income.

3. Ascertain whether any of the special rules of income determination may override the established principles.

4. Relate the income to the aggregating formula.

The fundamental principles all taxpayers use to establish net income are not overly complex. Nor is the basic process. Even when transactions are extremely complicated, the general tax impact can usually be ascertained by analyzing them in terms of the basic principles developed in Chapters 3 through 9. Applying these principles enhances the effectiveness of financial decision making by allowing managers to locate the points along the cash-flow path where the tax factor is relevant.

The process for determining net income for tax purposes is now fully explained. The next step is to convert net income into taxable income and establish the method of calculating tax. At this point the common ground between individual and corporate taxpayers disappears. The unique issues involved in determining taxable income and tax for each type of entity are examined in the next two chapters.

Reading List

Income Tax Act References

	Section
Pension benefits, unemployment benefits, old-age security	56(1)(a)
Alimony and maintenance (received)	56(1)(b)
Annuity payments	56(1)(d)
Registered retirement savings plan	56(1)(h), 146
Deferred profit sharing plan	56(1)(i), 147
Scholarships and bursaries	56(1)(n)
Research grants	56(1)(o)
Education savings plan payments	56(1)(q)
Capital element of annuity payment	60(a)
Alimony and maintenance payments	60(b)
Transfer of superannuation payments	60(j)
Transfer of retiring allowances	60(j.1)
Transfer of RRSP	60(1)
Expense of objection or appeal	60(o)
Moving expenses	62
Child-care expenses	63
Reasonableness—general limitation	67
Expenses of food, etc.	67.1(1) to (4)
Interest on money borrowed for passenger vehicles	67.2
Limitation re: cost of leasing passenger vehicles	67.3, .4
Inadequate consideration	69(1)(a) to (c)

Unreasonable consideration	69(2), (3)
Death of a taxpayer	70(1) to (5)
Inter vivos transfer of property to spouse	73(1), (2)
Inter vivos transfer of farm property to children	73(3), (4)
Transfers and loans to spouse	74.1(1)
Transfers and loans to minors	74.1(2)
Gain or loss deemed that of lender or transferor	74.2
Definition of excluded consideration	74.4
Transfers for fair market consideration	74.5
Unpaid amounts	78(1)
Unpaid remuneration	78(4)
Mortgage foreclosures	79
Debtor's gain on settlement of debt	80(1)
Amounts not included in income	81
Tax on split income	120.4

Canada Customs and Revenue Agency Publications

IT-178R3	Moving expenses.
IT-495R2	Child-care expenses.
IT-54	Wage loss replacement plans.
IT-124R6	Contributions to registered retirement savings plan.
IT-530	Support payments.
IT-118R3	Alimony and maintenance.
IT-405	Inadequate considerations—acquisitions and dispositions.
IT-419R	Meaning of arm's length.
IT-258R2	Transfer of property to a spouse.
IT-109R	Unpaid amounts.
IT-518R	Food, beverages, and entertainment expenses.
IT-505	Mortgage foreclosures and conditional sales repossessions.
IT-293R	Debtor's gain on settlement of debt.

Major Court Decisions

No. 511 v. MNR, 58 DTC 307—Reasonable expense.
Schellenberg v. MNR, 86 DTC 1463—Allocation of proceeds.

Demonstration Question

In November 20X5, Walter Spink's employer transferred him from Winnipeg to Edmonton. His financial information for the 20X5 taxation year is provided below.

1. Spink received a salary in 20X5 of $80,000, of which $7,000 was earned at his new location in Edmonton. His employer contributed $3,000 to a money-purchase registered pension plan on Spink's behalf. Spink also contributed $3,000 to the plan. The employer also contributed $1,000 to a deferred profit sharing plan. Spink is required to use his own automobile for employment purposes, and in 20X5 incurred allowable costs for tax purposes of $3,600.

2. On January 2, 20X5, Spink sold a rental property to his wife for $150,000 (land $20,000, building $130,000). Payment consisted of a non–interest-bearing demand loan of $150,000. The original cost of the property was $100,000 (land $10,000, building

$90,000), and at the end of 20X4, the undepreciated capital cost of the building was $72,000. In 20X5, the rental property incurred a net loss of $4,000 before capital cost allowance.

3. On June 1, 20X5, Spink gifted cash of $30,000 to his 19-year-old son, who attends university. The son invested the funds and in 20X5 earned interest income of $1,200, which was used to support his education. At the same time, Spink gifted shares of a public corporation to his 17-year-old daughter. The shares, which originally cost $10,000, were valued at $12,000 at the time of the gift. During the year the daughter received a dividend of $600 and then sold the shares for $15,000.

4. The following costs were incurred to move Spink and his family to Edmonton:

Real estate commission on the sale of his former residence	$ 7,000
Interest, property taxes, and utility costs for maintaining former residences for two months prior to sale	6,000
Transportation of household effects	6,000
Automobile expenses—travelling to Edmonton	300
Hotel accommodation and meals for 20 days in Edmonton	4,000
Land transfer tax on purchase of new residence	2,000
Legal fees to sell former residence	800
Legal fees to purchase new residence	1,000
	$27,100

5. In his spare time, Spink operates a small consulting business. He earned $6,000 in 20X5 prior to arriving in Edmonton.

6. During the year, Spink received interest income of $5,000 and dividends from taxable Canadian corporations of $1,000.

7. In 20X5, Spink contributed $4,000 to his registered retirement savings plan, which was the maximum allowed for the year.

8. In 20X5, Spink's wife, Sally, earned a salary of $30,000, consulting income of $15,000, and interest income of $3,000. She paid child-care expenses of $5,000 relating to their nine-year-old daughter.

Required:

1. Determine Spink's net income for tax purposes for the 20X5 taxation year.

2. What is the maximum allowable RRSP contribution that Spink can make in 20X6?

3. Determine the net income for tax purposes of Sally Spink for the 20X5 taxation year.

Solution:

Before we answer the above questions, we provide the following comments on several of the transactions:

• **Rental property sale** The sale of the rental property to his wife is a non–arm's-length transaction that would normally be subject to the fair market value rules described in this chapter. However, because the transfer is to a spouse, Spink is deemed to have sold the land at its adjusted cost base and the building at its undepreciated capital cost. There-fore, no income is generated on the sale. The rental loss of $4,000 on the property, which occurred after the transfer, must be attributed to Spink and included in the calculation of his income for the year. If his spouse subsequently sells the property, any capital gain or recapture of capital cost allowance will also be attributed to Spink. The attribution rules could have been avoided if the transaction had been subject to normal commercial terms (a reasonable interest rate on the loan and specific repayment terms) and if Spink had elected to recognize the taxable gain and the recapture of capital cost allowance that would result if the property were sold at fair market value.

• **Cash gift to the son**   The gift of the cash has no tax effect. The future income earned on the investment made is taxable to the son. It is not attributed to Spink because the son is over seventeen.

• **Gift of shares to the daughter**   The gift results in a deemed disposition of the shares at fair market value, resulting in a taxable capital gain to Spink of $1,000 ($\frac{1}{2} \times$ [$12,000 − $10,000]). The daughter is deemed to have acquired the shares at a cost of $12,000. The dividend of $600 must be attributed to Spink and included in his taxable income because the daughter is under eighteen. The sale of the shares by the daughter results in a taxable capital gain of $1,500 ($\frac{1}{2} \times$ [$15,000 − $12,000]). This gain is taxable to the daughter and is not attributed to Spink. This treatment is different from a capital gain or loss that may occur on property that has been transferred to a spouse.

• **Moving expenses**   All of the various types of moving expenses are eligible for deduc-tion. However, three restrictions apply. First, the cost of accommodation and meals in a hotel at the new location is limited to expenses for 15 days. Therefore, the eligible mov-ing expenses must be reduced by $1,000 ($4,000 × 5 days/20 days), from $27,100 to $26,100. Second, the costs of maintaining the former residence are limited to a maximum of $5,000. Therefore, $1,000 of these costs do not qualify for a deduction, and the quali-fied moving expenses are further reduced to $25,100 ($26,100 − $1,000). Third, moving expenses in 20X5 can be deducted only to the extent of the earned income at the new location, which is $7,000. The unused expenses from 20X5 of $18,100 ($25,100 − $7,000) can be carried forward and deducted in 20X6.

• **Child-care expenses**   Normally, child-care expenses must be deducted from the spouse with the lower income. In this situation, the expense is deducted by Sally Spink. The deductible amount is limited to the least of these: the actual expense of $5,000; the prescribed limit of $4,000 for children who are seven years of age or older; and two-thirds of Sally Spink's earned income of $45,000 (this includes the salary of $30,000 and the consulting income of $15,000 but excludes interest income of $3,000). Thus, the deduction is limited to $4,000.

1. Net income for tax purposes—Spink

Employment income—salary	$80,000
Automobile expenses	(3,600)
Registered pension plan contribution	(3,000)
	73,400

Business income—consulting		6,000
Property income		
Daughter's dividend attributed—$600 × 1.25	750	
Other dividends—$1,000 × 1.25	1,250	
Interest income	5,000	7,000
		86,400
Taxable capital gain		
Gift of shares to daughter—½ ($12,000 – $10,000)		1,000
		87,000
Other deductions		
RRSP	4,000	
Moving expenses—above	7,000	(11,000)
		76,400
Loss—rental loss attributed from spouse		(4,000)
Net income for tax purposes		$72,400

2. Allowable RRSP deduction for 20X6

Calculation of earned income for 20X5		
Employment income—above		$73,400
Add back registered pension plan deduction		3,000
Adjusted employment income		76,400
Business income		6,000
Rental loss		(4,000)
Earned income for 20X5		$78,400

Notice that the earned income does not include the property income (other than rentals), the taxable capital gain, and the other deductions.

Allowable 20X6 deduction is the least of:		
18% of 20X5 earned income—18% × $78,400 = $14,112; *or*		
the prescribed limit for the year—$15,500 (2004 limit)		$14,112
Less the pension adjustment for 20X5:		
Employer's contribution to the registered pension plan	3,000	
Spink's contribution to the registered pension plan	3,000	
Employer's contribution to the deferred profit		
sharing plan	1,000	(7,000)
20X6 allowable RRSP deduction		$7,112

3. Net income for tax purposes—Sally Spink

Employment income—salary	$30,000
Business income—consulting	15,000
Property income—interest	3,000
	48,000
Other deduction—child care (determined above)	(4,000)
Net income for tax purposes	$44,000

Review Questions

1. In addition to income from employment, business, property, and capital gains, taxpayers must include income from "other sources" when determining their income for tax purposes. How does the *Income Tax Act* limit the scope of "other sources of income"?

2. Explain why the receipt of property from an inheritance is not included in net income for tax purposes.

3. Can an individual deduct for tax purposes the amount of regular alimony payments to a former spouse? Would it matter if that individual's only source of income were from interest on bond investments? Explain.

4. Why is the category "other deductions" considered to be the last test for determining the deductibility of an expenditure?

5. Briefly explain why an RRSP is an attractive investment.

6. If you hold investments both inside and outside an RRSP and usually invest in both corporate bonds and corporate shares, which type of investment would you prefer to hold within the RRSP? Explain.

7. What is the significance of the special rules for net income determination, and how do they relate to the five categories of income that are taxable?

8. "When in doubt, it is always best to claim a deduction for an expenditure because the worst possible result is that CCRA will simply deny the deduction." Is this statement true? Explain.

9. If a group of business assets is being sold for a total agreed price, is it important that the vendor and the purchaser seriously consider how the total price will be allocated to the separate assets in the group? Explain.

10. What are the tax consequences if a parent sells property to a child at a price that is less than the actual value of the property? What difference would it make if the property were simply gifted to the child?

11. What are the tax consequences if an individual sells property to his or her spouse at a price that is less than the property's market value but more than its cost?

12. How are property income (losses) and capital gains (losses) treated for tax purposes if the funds used to acquire the property were provided by the taxpayer's spouse? How does the tax treatment differ if the funds are provided by the taxpayer's parent?

13. What is the implication to the employer and to the employee if the employer delays the payment of remuneration to the employee?

14. What difference does it make for tax purposes when an individual's last will and testament bequeaths property to a spouse rather than to a child?

15. The scope of the income tax system is defined by five specific types of income—employment, business, property, capital gains, and other sources. This being so, why is it necessary for the *Income Tax Act* to specifically list a number of items that are not included in income?

16. Briefly outline the process that can be used to establish the tax treatment of a particular transaction.

Problems

Problem One

Harvey Caseman died on July 15, 20X1. At the time of his death he owned the assets listed in the table below.

	Cost	Value
Land	$10,000	$15,000
Building	40,000	60,000
Piano	5,000	8,000

The building is a rental property, and over the years Caseman had claimed capital cost allowance. Its undepreciated capital cost is $28,000.

In his last will and testament, Caseman directed his executors to transfer the rental property to his two children and the piano to his spouse.

Required:

1. Determine to what extent, if any, Caseman's net income for tax purposes for 20X1 will be affected by his death.

2. What are the tax implications to the spouse and children if they sell the property immediately after they receive ownership?

Problem Two

Blue Ltd. is a Canadian corporation owned 100% by Karen Samson. Blue manufactures hockey sticks that are marketed to retail sporting goods stores across Canada and Europe. Green Ltd. is a Canadian corporation also owned 100% by Samson. Green operates a retail sporting goods store. It purchases hockey sticks from Blue.

Blue charges $10 a stick to all of its customers in Canada except Green, which pays only $8 a stick. Each stick costs Blue $4 to manufacture. Last week Green purchased 1,000 sticks from Blue and sold them to retail customers for $14 each.

Required:

1. With respect to the 1,000 sticks, determine the income for tax purposes of both Blue and Green.

2. How would your answer to question 1 change if Blue charged Green $12 per stick?

Problem Three

For each of the following independent transactions, determine the amount of net income or loss for tax purposes, and the taxpayer to which it applies.

1. A parent purchased a $10,000 bond for her 15-year-old daughter. During the year, the bond paid interest of $1,000.

2. A student who is 20 years old borrowed $20,000 from his parent and used the funds to purchase shares in a public corporation. After receiving a dividend of $1,000, the student sold the shares for $24,000. (How would your answer change if the student were 17 years old?)

3. A woman gifted shares of a public corporation, for which she had paid $15,000, to her husband. At the time of the gift, the shares had a value of $30,000. After receiving the gift, the husband received a dividend of $1,000 and then sold the shares for $26,000.

4. A man loaned money to his wife, who used the borrowed funds to purchase a rental property. During the year, the rental property earned net rentals of $7,000. The amount of the loan, which is interest-free, is $60,000. (How would your answer change if the loan were subject to a reasonable interest rate of 10% and was secured by a mortgage on the rental property?)

5. A man gifted common shares of a Canadian-controlled private corporation to his 16-year-old daughter. At the time of the gift, the shares were valued at $10,000. Their original cost was $6,000. During the year, the daughter received a dividend of $1,000 from the shares and then sold them for $15,000.

Problem Four

Health Kicks Ltd. is a Canadian-controlled private corporation owned 100% by Wally Bose. The company's year end is December 31, and its 20X1 fiscal period has just come to a close.

Following is certain information in the accounting records of the company for the year ended December 31, 20X1:

- **Rent expense ($22,000)** The company rents a warehouse building for $2,000 per month from Joe Holy. As of December 31, 20X1, the December rent had not been paid owing to an employee error. Holy, a schoolteacher, purchased the building as an investment several years ago for $180,000. During 20X1 he incurred operating expenses for the building (taxes, insurance, interest, and the like) totalling $20,000. The UCC of the building is $120,000.

- **Repairs and maintenance expense ($70,000)** This account includes snow removal and lawn-care costs, in addition to $62,000 for building improvements: the installation of an air-conditioning system and three additional loading docks (ramps and doors). The $62,000 was paid to a warehouse contractor that is an American corporation operating a branch office in Winnipeg.

- **Accounting and legal expense ($16,000)** This amount was paid to a law firm for the following services:
  — Registering of a debenture against the company's assets on a loan from the bank ($4,000).
  — Drawing up of a legal agreement to purchase all of the common shares of Dash Ltd., which now operates as a wholly-owned subsidiary ($9,000).
  — Preparing of articles of amendment to revise the company's articles of incorporation ($3,000).

- **Interest expense ($22,000)** Several years ago the company purchased a small warehouse in Winnipeg. The previous owner, a resident of England, permitted Health Kicks to pay a small amount down and the balance over eight years, with interest at 11%. Of the above interest, $7,000 represents interest paid on this obligation. The remaining interest of $15,000 was paid to the shareholder, Bose, on a loan he made to his own company.

- *Land cost ($19,000)*   This represents the cost of landscaping the grounds around the company's office building (trees, shrubs, and flower beds), and was added to the capital cost of the land. The $19,000 was paid to Wesley Perkins, a management student who operates a summer lawn service.

- *Salary and remuneration expense ($290,000)*   This account is made up of the following items:

Salaries	$238,000
Sales commissions accrued but not paid until 20X2	30,000
Retirement gift to the sales manager	1,000
Clothing allowance to senior executives so that they can acquire expensive wardrobes to maintain their image	21,000
	$290,000

- *Licence cost ($120,000)*   Health Kicks purchased a licence to manufacture a health product that was patent protected by another company. The licence permitted Health Kicks to manufacture and sell the product for six years. The licence was acquired from Bobo Enterprises Ltd., which sold several licences for this product to other companies in certain geographic areas. Health Kicks can sell the product only in western Canada.

Required:

Discuss, in point form, the tax implications of the preceding transactions from the point of view of (a) Health Kicks and (b) the other party to each transaction.

Problem Five

The following information relates to Perry Somer's financial affairs in 20X1:

1. Somer is employed as a salesman and is remunerated by commissions. He must pay all his own expenses. During 20X1 he earned commissions of $28,000. His expenses were as follows:

Automobile (operating costs)	$3,000
Entertainment	1,000
Convention (related to his employment)	500
Donations	500
Telephone long-distance charges (personal use was 80%)	1,000

   The personal-use portion of his automobile expense is 20%. The UCC of his automobile at the end of the previous year was $5,000.

2. He made the following capital transactions:

	Gain (loss)
Shares of public corporation A	$10,000
Shares of public corporation B	(18,000)
Shares of Canadian-controlled private corporation C (a small business corporation)	(6,000)

3. In 20X0 Somer acquired two rental properties.

	Property X	Property Y
Land	$10,000	$15,000
Building	70,000	60,000
	$80,000	$75,000

Maximum capital cost allowance was claimed in 20X0.

In 20X1 the city expropriated property Y for $77,000 (land $17,000, building $60,000). Perry was pleased because property Y was vacant for part of the year after a tenant vacated unexpectedly.

In 20X1 net rental income from both properties (after all expenses but before capital cost allowance) was $1,000.

4. Somer's other income and expenses are as follows:

Income:	
Taxable dividends—Canadian corporations	$2,000
Interest on foreign bonds (net of 15% withholding tax)	1,700
Expenses:	
Interest on a loan used to acquire the foreign bonds	1,300
Investment counsel fee	800

5. During the year, he made a contribution to a registered pension plan of $1,000, which was matched by his employer. In addition, Somer contributed $2,000 to his RRSP.

6. Somer currently lives in rented premises but is considering moving into rental property X and occupying one-half of the building sometime in 20X2.

Required:

1. Calculate Somer's minimum 20X1 net income in accordance with the aggregating formula for determining net income for tax purposes.

2. What would be the tax consequences, if any, if Somer occupied rental property X?

Problem Six

Peter Carletti is a professional architect employed by a Halifax-based architectural firm. He is 58 years old and married, and has a 22-year-old son. Peter's wife, Carla, recently returned to university and will complete a law degree in three or four years. Their son, who lives with them, also attends university and will continue to do so for at least three years.

Peter has asked you to review his family's financial position and tell him what tax planning opportunities are available. Also, he does not have a will and would like you to tell him what tax consequences may occur at the time of his death. He provides you with the following information:

1. The Carlettis' home in Halifax is owned by Carla. She acquired the property five years ago for $200,000 with funds received from her father's estate. The home is now worth $230,000 and has no mortgage. She has no other assets.

2. Last year Peter purchased a vacation home on the Atlantic coast. The property cost $150,000 and has already increased in value to $180,000. Upon purchase, Peter assumed the mortgage of $70,000, which has an interest rate of 10%.

3. Peter owns a term life insurance policy that will pay $400,000 upon his death.

4. Peter's annual salary is over $100,000. Carla currently has no income. Annually, Peter contributes to an RRSP, which is now worth $200,000. The plan invests primarily in secure common shares and earns capital gains and dividends.

5. Peter owns a rental property, for which he paid $240,000 (land $40,000, building $200,000) five years ago. It is debt-free and currently worth $300,000 (land $50,000, building $250,000). The undepreciated capital cost of the building is $166,000.

6. Peter owns the following other investments:
   • $50,000 of Nova Scotia Hydro Bonds, which earn interest of 12%.
   • Bank term deposits (one-year terms) of $140,000, which earn 11% interest.
   • Common shares of a Canadian public corporation that are valued at $90,000. He purchased the shares two years ago for $40,000. Peter has not sold any capital property in the past 10 years.

Required:
Prepare a brief report for Peter Carletti outlining the tax consequences that may occur on his death. The report should also suggest what he might do now to minimize annual taxes during his lifetime.

Problem Seven
In 20X3 Carol Fortier was transferred by her employer to Vancouver from Toronto. She has made a number of financial transactions related to the move. Fortier has asked you for help in determining her 20X3 income for tax purposes. She has provided the following information:

1. Fortier is divorced and supports her two children, Lise (age 17) and Randy (age 19). In the summer of 20X3, Randy earned net profits of $4,000 as a street vendor. Lise's only source of income was from an investment purchased for her by her mother. The investment, in bonds of a Canadian public corporation, paid interest of $1,000 during the year.

2. Fortier began work in Vancouver in February 20X3, as a senior saleswoman for a clothing manufacturer. During 20X3, she received a gross salary of $110,000 as well as selling commissions of $6,000. In addition, on June 30, 20X3, her employer's year end, she was awarded a bonus of $12,000 payable in 12 monthly instalments of $1,000 beginning July 31, 20X3. During 20X3 she contributed $3,700 to the company's registered pension plan, and her employer contributed the same amount. She also paid $1,500 to the Canada Pension Plan and made Employment Insurance contributions of $920.

3. Fortier's employer has certified that she is required to pay some of her own expenses as part of her selling duties. In 20X3 she incurred the following costs:

Purchase of computer		$ 3,000
Advertising and promotion		1,800
Entertainment:		
Meals and drinks	2,000	
Golf club dues	2,400	4,400
Automobile—gas, repairs, and insurance		4,200
		$13,400

Fortier uses her own car for business activities. At the end of 20X2 the car had an unamortized capital cost of $20,000 (original cost in 20X2, $22,000). In 20X3 she drove the car 30 000 kilometres, of which approximately 12 000 was for personal use. In 20X3 she acquired a computer (see table), which she uses at home to maintain customer files and industry information. She estimates that 90% of her 20X3 computer time was employment-related.

4. On January 15, 20X4, Fortier contributed $7,000 to an RRSP. For the 20X2 taxation year her earned income was $63,889. In 20X2 the combined (employer and employee) contribution to her employer RPP was $6,400.

5. In relocating to Vancouver from Toronto, Fortier incurred the following costs:

Real estate commission on sale of former home	$19,000
Moving furniture	14,000
Legal fees to purchase new home	2,000
Legal fees on sale of former home	2,500
Temporary lodging and meals, in Toronto after the sale of the former home and in Vancouver before taking possession of the new home (30 days)	6,000
	$43,500

Her employer, in accordance with company policy, paid her the maximum $10,000 as a partial reimbursement for transporting furniture to Vancouver.

6. Fortier wrote an article on selling strategies in the fashion industry. It was published in a national trade journal. The article received wide acclaim. In September 20X3 she was awarded a $2,000 prize for the best article of the year.

7. In January 20X3 Fortier sold her home in Toronto for $300,000. She acquired the home in 20X0 for $180,000 and had occupied it until the move to Vancouver.

8. Five years ago, Fortier purchased 5% of the common shares of Prentice Ltd. for $20,000. Prentice is a Canadian-controlled private corporation manufacturing specialized furniture. In June 20X0, when the company had cash-flow problems, Fortier lent Prentice $10,000. The loan was unsecured and payable on demand. Although Fortier has received no interest to date, in 20X1 and 20X2 she included in her taxable income on each anniversary date interest of $1,500 ($750 x 2 y = $1,500) based on the agreed 7½% interest rate. In 20X3 she demanded payment of the loan and accrued

interest, but the company was unable to pay. The company's only assets, other than the leased manufacturing equipment, were inventory and receivables, which were pledged on a bank loan; these were insufficient to meet even that obligation. In January 20X4, Prentice closed operations and declared bankruptcy.

9. Fortier sold the following properties in 20X3:

	Original cost	Selling price net of disposal costs
4,000 shares of Teulon Ltd. (a public corporation)	$22,000	$114,000
Oil painting	800	4,000
Commodity futures contract	16,000	28,000

The sale of the commodity futures contract was Fortier's second commodity transaction. In 20X1 she purchased and sold a similar contract but lost $14,000. She deducted the full $14,000 in computing her 20X1 taxable income.

10. Fortier owns a rental property in Toronto. She acquired the property in 20X2 for $414,000 (land $54,000, building $360,000). She incurred a substantial loss in 20X2 as a result of an unexpected vacancy. She found a new tenant in 20X3. She received gross rents of $46,000 in 20X3. Expenses for utilities, taxes, insurance, interest, and maintenance were $47,100 that year. One of the tenants failed to pay its December 20X3 rent of $2,000. However, she received that payment on January 20, 20X4.

11. Fortier received the following additional amounts in 20X3:

Dividends from taxable Canadian corporations	$6,000
Interest on bank deposits	7,000
Winnings from a provincial lottery	800

12. Fortier hired an investment counsellor in 20X3. On his recommendation, she used $40,000 of the $200,000 mortgage loan on her new home to acquire Canadian public securities. Her mortgage interest payments in 20X3 totalled $22,000. She paid the investment counsellor $2,000 for his advice.

13. In 20X3 Fortier made donations to registered charities of $4,000.

14. During 20X3 Fortier's 20X1 tax return was reassessed. She hired a lawyer to prepare an appeal. The legal fee was $1,200. The appeal was not successful.

Required:
For the 20X3 taxation year, calculate Fortier's net income for tax purposes. Prepare the calculation in accordance with the net income formula, and organize the items of income by the categories described in that formula.

Problem Eight
A Review of Net Income for Tax Purposes
Mr. Active holds a job, operates a small farm, and makes numerous investments. A description of his financial activities for 20X1 is given below.

1. Active is a lawyer and is employed in the legal department of a large public corporation. In 20X1 he received a gross salary of $72,000. In addition, the corporation provided the following items of remuneration:

   - A car allowance of $400 a month to cover costs of travel in the performance of his duties. During 20X1, Active used his own car to travel from his home to work and back. Rarely was the car used during working hours on company business.
   - A contribution of $3,000 to a deferred profit sharing plan.
   - A group term life insurance policy for $100,000 (premium cost, $800).
   - A cash bonus of $3,000 that was awarded to him in the previous year and that he received in the current year.

2. Active's employer gives all senior executives the option to acquire a certain number of shares of the corporation at a price that is guaranteed for two years. In 20X0 the employer granted Active an option to purchase up to 5,000 of its shares for a price of $10 per share. At the time the option was granted, the shares were valued at $10.75 per share. During 20X1, Active purchased 500 shares at a cost of $10 per share. At the date of purchase, the corporation's shares were trading at $14 per share.

3. Active purchased a small parcel of land (20 hectares) in 20X1 and began raising goats. In 20X1 he lost $1,000 from this operation.

4. In 20X1, Active purchased 1,000 shares of public corporation X for $20 per share and received a stock dividend of 100 additional shares of the same class. During the year, he sold the 100 shares for $21 per share, which was the same value of those 100 shares as on their date of issue.

5. Three years ago Active purchased three rental properties and has provided you with the following information:

	Property 1	Property 2	Property 3
Land cost	$10,000	$ 4,000	$ 8,000
Building cost	60,000	40,000	45,000
Building UCC (31/12/20X0)	52,000	37,000	40,000
20X1 net rents (before CCA)	3,000	(5,000)	4,000

   In 20X1, Active sold property 1 for $80,000 (land $12,000, building $68,000), and property 2 for $50,000 (land $6,000, building $44,000). Also in 20X1, he purchased property 4 for $90,000 (land $30,000, building $60,000). In 20X1 property 4 had net rentals before capital cost allowance of $1,000.

6. During the year, Active gifted 1,000 shares of Shell Canada Ltd. (a public corporation) to his daughter. The shares had cost him $10 each and had a value at the time of the gift of $12 each. In 20X1 his daughter (16 years old) received dividends of $1,000; she then sold the shares for $30 each.

7. In 20X1, Active gifted 2,000 shares of Exxon Ltd. (a public corporation) to his wife. The shares had a value of $40 each at the time of the gift. He had paid $30 per share several years before. His wife sold the shares in 20X1 for $28 per share during a market slump.

8. Active's mother died in 20X0 and left him her house. The house cost $40,000 at time of purchase and had a value in 20X0 of $60,000. Active sold the house in 20X1 for $66,000.

9. Three years ago, Active purchased 15% of the shares of two private corporations. Each carried on an active business. He sold the shares of both corporations in 20X1. Information relating to the shares is as follows:

	PC 1	PC 2
Cost	$40,000	$35,000
Proceeds of sale	56,000	20,000
Terms of payment	8,000 per y for 7 y	All cash

10. In 20X1, during a market slump, Active sold 500 shares of public corporation A for $30,000; the shares had cost him $40,000. Two weeks later, as the market began to strengthen, he purchased 500 shares of the same corporation for $29,000.

11. Active also sold the following assets in 20X1:

	Cost	Proceeds
Public corporation B shares	$10,000	$12,000
Public corporation C shares	47,500	20,000
Stamp collection	8,000	12,000
Jewellery	6,000	1,000
Boat	5,000	2,000
Stereo set	800	900

12. Active had the following additional receipts in 20X1:

Dividends from public companies	$4,000
Interest on bonds	1,000
Lottery winnings	6,000

13. Active paid out the following in 20X1:

To purchase a Dictaphone for use at home when working on his employer's business	$ 700
Interest on bank loan to purchase shares of public corporation	2,000
Interest on house mortgage (mortgage funds of $60,000 were used —$40,000 for the purchase of the house, $20,000 for the purchase of shares)	6,000
Lump-sum alimony settlement to ex-wife	9,000
Tuition fees for attending university	1,000
Donations	4,000
Gift to the Liberal Party of Canada	1,000
Contribution to an RRSP	2,800
Annual dues to the provincial law society	1,000

Required:

Calculate Active's net income for tax purposes for 20X1.

Case **Trans-Am Suppliers Ltd.**

Trans-Am Suppliers Ltd. is just completing negotiations to sell its manufacturing division to a competitor. The purchaser has agreed to purchase the inventory, manufacturing equipment, licence, and goodwill for $1,200,000.

The payment terms require that the purchaser pay $900,000 on the closing date, with the balance of $300,000 deferred for two years. The unpaid balance is subject to annual interest of 10%. Trans-Am intends to use the proceeds from the sale to expand its wholesale division, which is expected to generate returns of 24% annually before tax. The company's tax rate is 40%.

Although the total price and payment terms have been agreed to, a conflict has arisen between Trans-Am and the purchaser regarding the price of each asset sold. The sources of the dispute are as follows:

- **Inventory** Trans-Am's accounting records indicate that the inventory amounts to $300,000, valued at the lower of cost or market. Traditionally, the company has been conservative in establishing the market value. The purchaser, after examining the merchandise, feels that the proper value is $340,000 and expects that it could all be sold within one year.

- **Equipment** The manufacturing equipment, which originally cost $600,000, has a book value for accounting purposes of $300,000. The undepreciated capital cost is $320,000. Trans-Am has valued the equipment at $400,000 but the purchaser's appraiser is confident that the equipment has a value of $450,000 in the used-equipment market.

- **Licence** One of Trans-Am's products is manufactured under licence from a company that holds the patent. The licence, which has a life of 10 years, was purchased only six months earlier for $100,000. Shortly after the purchase, the product gained wide recognition; the company that holds the patent rights now sells licences in other geographic areas at a price of $300,000. Both Trans-Am and the purchaser agree on this value.

- **Goodwill** No discussion was held with respect to the goodwill, as both parties acknowledge that its value reflects the difference between the total purchase price of $1,200,000 and the combined values of the other specific assets.

The president of Trans-Am is concerned that the negotiation process will be stalled if the above issues are not settled. He is prepared to make some concessions but feels that before doing so he must understand what the differences mean to Trans-Am. Also, the president thinks it would be useful to know the impact of his own stance on the purchaser, as this will suggest how rigid he should appear at the next round of discussions.

The president has asked you to report to him and provide the information requested. In addition, he has asked you to separately examine the tax implications of the deferred payment terms and determine whether the agreement should state the terms of payment for each asset as opposed to the total package.

Required:
Prepare an outline of the report, including any necessary calculations.

Chapter 10   Individuals: Determination of Taxable Income and Taxes Payable

So far in the text, the structure of the tax system has treated all taxable entities (individuals, corporations, and trusts) according to a common set of principles. It has been established that an individual who earns business income, property income, and capital gains determines his or her net income for tax purposes in exactly the same manner as a corporation that earns the same types of income.

A taxpayer's net income for tax purposes must be converted to taxable income before tax can be calculated. It is important to recognize that individuals determine their taxable income and tax payable by a different method than corporations. Even so, because the ultimate shareholder of a corporation is the individual, the different tax treatments of the two entities must, in the final analysis, be viewed together. The relationship between a corporation and its shareholders is reviewed briefly in Chapter 11 and more extensively in Part Three of the text, which deals exclusively with corporations.

For individuals, the process of converting net income for tax purposes to taxable income focusses largely on two areas: the utilization of losses and the lifetime capital gain deduction. The influence of this process on the individual's finances is, therefore, limited.

The calculation of tax for individuals follows a basic format. However, parts of the calculation are subject to frequent changes as the government alters its fiscal and social policies. While these areas of frequent change affect an individual's tax cost, they seldom have a major impact on decision making for investment and business purposes. In most cases it is the basic format and the comparative marginal rates of tax that are relevant to the decision maker.

This chapter examines the two main areas that affect the determination of taxable income for individuals, and highlights their importance to investment and business decision making. Also discussed is the framework for the calculation of tax.

I. Determination of Taxable Income

It was established earlier that a taxpayer's taxable income for a taxation year is determined by the following simple formula:

$$\text{Taxable income} = \text{Net income} - \text{Special reductions}$$

In this formula, net income consists of the aggregate of the five sources of income established in Chapters 4 through 9. The special reductions are grouped together in Division C of the *Income Tax Act*. Several of these reductions apply to individuals; the most important of these are the loss carry-over provisions and the lifetime capital gain deduction. A third important reduction relates to employment income derived from stock options; this was reviewed in Chapter 4 and will not be commented on in this chapter.

The above simple formula can be expanded to show how overall taxable income is calculated for an individual. This is done in Exhibit 10-1. The formula represents the complete framework for establishing the base to which tax is applied.

Notice that in part 1 of this formula, (b) includes the item "net taxable gains from listed personal property." This item was excluded from the formula when it was first described in Chapter 3. It requires that only net *gains* be included in the formula.[1] Net taxable gains in this context are the taxable gains for the year in excess of the allowable losses. If the losses exceed the gains, the amount entered into the formula is zero. As described in Chapter 8, losses from listed personal property can be offset only against gains from listed

---

1   ITA 3(b)(i)(B).

Exhibit 10-1:	1. *Net income for tax purposes:*	
The Taxable Income	(a) The aggregate of:	
Formula for an	Employment income	+
Individual	Business income	+
	Property income	+
	Other items of income	+
		+ or 0

plus

(b) The amount by which:		
Taxable capital gains	+	
Net taxable gains from listed personal property	+	
	+ or 0	

exceed

Allowable capital losses	−	+ or 0
		+ or 0

less (to the maximum of above)

(c) Other items of deduction		−
		+ or 0

less (to the maximum of above)

(d) The aggregate of:		
Employment losses	−	
Business losses	−	
Property losses	−	
Allowable business investment losses	−	− or 0
Net income for tax purposes		+ or 0

2. Special reductions:		
(a) Stock options[a]	−	
(b) Losses not utilized in other years[b]	−	
(c) Lifetime capital gain deduction[c]	−	− or 0
Taxable income		+ or 0

a   ITA 110(1)(d), (d.1); IT-113R4.
b   ITA 111.
c   ITA 110.6

personal property. However, a loss that cannot be used in a given year can be carried back three years or forward seven years for use against a listed personal property gain in those years. This carry-over forms part of the net income calculation. In other words, the net taxable gain for the year is the amount by which the current year's taxable gains exceed the allowable losses from the current year *plus* those from a carry-over year, if any. This treatment differs from that for other carry-over losses, which are described later in the chapter.

The items in the formula must be included in the order in which they appear. The special reductions applied to arrive at taxable income should not be merged with the net income calculation, since in some cases the special reductions depend on the amount of net income otherwise determined. The net income portion of the formula is reserved exclusively (except for listed personal property loss carry-overs) for transactions of the current year. The special-reduction portion of the formula deals with transactions of other years, or modifies the treatment of certain items in the net income portion.

II. Loss Carry-Overs

Losses incurred in a particular taxation year can be offset against other sources of income provided they follow the restrictions of the aggregating formula for determining net income for tax purposes. Capital losses can be deducted only to the extent that capital gains were realized in the year. Losses from business, employment, and property, and allowable business investment losses, can be offset against all other sources of income; however, they too may be restricted if the losses are greater than the combined total of other income sources.

In previous chapters it was indicated that losses incurred in a year, if they are restricted by the aggregating formula, are available for carry-over to other years. Such carry-overs have limited application, and because of this their use is not certain. As indicated in Exhibit 10-1, loss carry-overs are deducted as special reductions after the taxpayer has determined net income for that particular year. This means that losses incurred in the particular year must be deducted first, as part of net income, before losses of other years can be applied.

The fundamental principles for applying loss carry-overs are different for capital losses than for other types of losses.[2] This is discussed below.

A. Net Capital Losses

Allowable capital losses incurred in a current year, if they cannot be utilized in arriving at net income (because there are insufficient taxable capital gains), are reclassified as *net capital losses*. These can be carried back three years and forward indefinitely.[3] During this carry-over period, the net capital losses can be deducted only to the extent that the taxpayer has realized net capital gains (gains minus losses) for that year. In other words, capital losses carried back or forward continue to have restricted use, in that they can be used only to offset capital gains. However, upon the *death* of an individual, the unused losses may be utilized as a deduction against any other type of income earned in the year of death or in the preceding year.[4]

B. Non-Capital Losses

Most other losses incurred in a year, if they cannot be used, are reclassified as *non-capital losses*. In effect, employment losses, business losses, and property losses, as well as allowable business investment losses, if they cannot be used because there is insufficient income in the year, discard their identity and become lumped together as non-capital losses.

Non-capital losses can be carried back three years and forward for seven years. Such losses can be deducted in arriving at taxable income regardless of the type of income earned in those other years.[5]

There is one exception to the seven-year carry-forward limit. When a non-capital loss that was created by an allowable business investment loss is unused after the seven-year carry-forward period, that unused loss is reclassified as a net capital loss and can be carried forward indefinitely to be used against future capital gains. This does not apply to non-capital losses that are derived from business, property, or employment losses.

C. Farm Losses and Restricted Farm Losses

There are two further categories of loss carry-overs—farm losses and restricted farm losses. *Farm losses* concern taxpayers whose chief source of income is farming or fishing. These losses are actually business losses and are created in the same way as the non-capital losses described above. However, they can be carried back three years and forward *ten* years (as opposed to seven).[6]

---

2 IT-232R3.

3 ITA 111(1)(b).

4 ITA 111(2).

5 ITA 111(1)(a).

6 ITA 111(1)(d).

Restricted farm losses are losses from a "hobby farm" (see Chapter 5). The annual deductible loss from a hobby farm can be no more than $2,500 plus one-half of the next $12,500 (i.e., $8,750 annually). To the extent that losses are limited by the formula, they are classified as restricted farm losses. These unused losses can be carried back three years and forward ten years but can only be deducted to the extent that farming income was earned in those years.[7]

D. Sample Calculation of Loss Carry-Overs

A simple application of loss carry-overs for capital losses and other types of losses is demonstrated below.

Situation:

An individual taxpayer has the following sources of income and losses in 20X0 and 20X1:

	20X0	20X1
Employment income	$12,000	$18,000
Business income (enterprise A)	20,000	–0–
Business loss (enterprise B)	(50,000)	–0–
Other items of income	4,000	–0–
Taxable capital gains	8,000	4,000
Allowable capital losses	(14,000)	(1,000)
Allowable business investment losses	(6,000)	–0–
Other deductions	(2,000)	–0–

The individual had no income or losses in the preceding years.

Analysis:

(20X0)
Net income:

(a) Employment income		$12,000
Business income (enterprise A)		20,000
Other sources		4,000
		36,000
(b) Taxable capital gains	8,000	
Allowable capital losses	(14,000)	–0–
		36,000
(c) Other deductions		(2,000)
		34,000
(d) Business loss (enterprise B)	50,000	
Allowable business investment loss	6,000	(34,000)
Net income for tax purposes		–0–
Special reductions		–0–
Taxable income		–0–

---

7   ITA 111(1)(c).

The unused losses available for carry-over are as follows:

Net capital losses:		
$14,000 – $8,000 =		$ 6,000
Non-capital losses:		
Business loss		$50,000
Allowable business investment loss		6,000
		56,000
Used in 20X0		(34,000)
Available for carry-over		$22,000
(20X1)		
Net income:		
(a) Employment income		$18,000
(b) Taxable capital gains	4,000	
Allowable capital losses	(1,000)	3,000
		21,000
(c) Other deductions		–0–
(d) Losses in 20X1		–0–
Net income for tax purposes		21,000
Special reductions:		
Net capital losses forward	(3,000)	
Non-capital losses forward	(18,000)	(21,000)*
Taxable income		–0–
Net capital losses:		
Amount in 20X0		$ 6,000
Used in 20X1		(3,000)
Carried forward		$ 3,000
Non-capital losses:		
Amount in 20X0		$22,000
Used in 20X1		(18,000)
Carried forward		$ 4,000

*Because of a tax credit available to all individuals, there is no federal tax on approximately the first $8,000 (in 2004) of taxable income. Consequently, in this example the taxpayer should reduce the loss carry-over claim by that amount.

In the preceding example the remaining net capital losses can be carried forward indefinitely, but the non-capital losses remaining can be carried forward for only six more years. A taxpayer who had income and taxes in the years before 20X0 could carry back the losses to those years and receive a tax refund.

The timing of the loss carry-overs is up to the taxpayer. Obviously, the faster they are utilized, the faster any after-tax cash flow will be increased. However, consideration must also be given to the rates of tax applicable in particular years. For example, in the above situation the 20X1 income was relatively low ($21,000) and would have been subject to the lowest tax rate for individuals. Taxpayers who anticipate that their 20X2 income will be much higher, and therefore subject to the higher rate of tax, may prefer to delay utilizing the non-capital loss until 20X2. However, the reduced 20X1 cash flow and the degree of certainty regarding the 20X2 income must also be considered. Also, taxpayers must remember that there is a limited time period available for using the loss carry-over.

A second alternative is available in the above example. The taxpayer could have chosen to claim the maximum non-capital loss of $21,000 to reduce the net income to zero, thereby leaving the entire net capital loss for future years. This may be prudent if there is a possibility that the non-capital loss will expire before it can be used. The net capital loss can then be carried forward indefinitely, awaiting a taxable capital gain.

It should be pointed out that the losses incurred in a given year *must* be used to the extent possible in that year when determining net income for tax purposes. Only the unused loss carry-over can be utilized in other years at the taxpayer's discretion.

III. Loss Utilization —Impact on Decision Making

The previous chapters have regularly demonstrated the extent to which increased returns on investments are created by delaying recognition of income for tax purposes. The reverse is true when it comes to recognizing losses: the sooner losses are utilized, the sooner cash flow will be increased as a result of reduced taxes. However, losses have this added dimension: the taxpayer must utilize them against sources of income within a specified time period. Consider the timing of the following incomes and losses of a business venture:

Year 1	$ 50,000 profit
2	100,000 profit
3	–0–
4	–0–
5	–0–
6	(150,000) loss (business operations cease)

In the above situation the business earned total profits of $150,000 in years 1 and 2, broke even for the next three years, and then lost $150,000 in year 6 before ceasing operations. Over the six-year period the business has zero income ($150,000 of profits minus $150,000 of losses). However, it is subject to tax on $150,000, because the loss in year 6 can be carried back only three years and, therefore, is not available for offset against the profits of the first two years. If the taxpayer was in a 40% tax bracket in the first two years, the after-tax cost of breaking even on the venture is $60,000 ($150,000 profits – $150,000 loss – $60,000 tax). While the loss of $150,000 in year 6 can be carried forward for seven years and used against other sources of income if they should arise, the time differential between the payment of tax in years 1 and 2, and the tax recovery from the loss, is considerable.

Similarly, a taxpayer who realizes a capital gain of $200,000 in year 1, then suffers a capital loss of $200,000 in year 5, and has no further capital transactions, will not be able to utilize the loss, as it can be carried back only three years.

Obviously, when investing in an active business or making a passive investment, the taxpayer must consider the method in which potential losses can be utilized, in order to assess the overall after-tax risk if the investment should result in a loss.

A. Forms of Business Organization

The organizational structure chosen to carry on an active business has an influence on loss utilization. Exhibit 10-2 outlines two basic structures that are being contemplated to conduct a business venture.

Under structure A the individual carries on the business as a proprietorship. A proprietorship is not a taxable entity; instead, any profits it realizes or losses it incurs belong directly to the individual proprietor and are merged by the aggregating formula with all other sources of income generated by the taxpayer. This means that if losses occur in the proprietorship, they can be offset against the owner's other income sources in the year of loss, or carried over to other years, also against all other sources of income.

Exhibit 10-2:
Two Basic Business
Structures

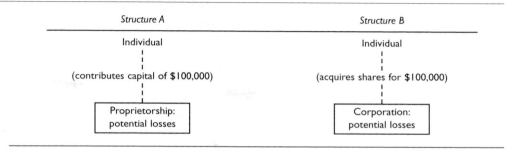

Under structure B the business is operated as a corporation. For tax purposes the individual and the corporation are two separate taxable entities. The individual's only tie with the corporation is the investment in share capital of $100,000, which may or may not generate dividend income. If the business suffers losses, the share value will decline, but such a loss can be recognized only by the shareholder when the shares are sold or if the corporation becomes legally bankrupt or is insolvent. The business losses of the corporation are separate from the shareholder, and can be offset only against the corporation's own income. Therefore, a business loss in the corporation must be carried over to years in which that corporation generates income. This is true even though the individual shareholder may have substantial other sources of income.

In the above example, choosing the corporate structure diminishes the taxpayer's opportunity to use the losses as quickly as possible and, in so doing, reduces the annual cash flow and after-tax return on investment.

Consideration should also be given to the possibility of a complete business failure and the cessation of operations. Under structure B the losses incurred from operations and the disposal of assets would remain in the corporation and would not be available for use by the shareholder. Thus there is an increased risk that losses may expire, owing to the restricted carry-over period. Indirectly, the individual shareholder would recognize the business losses when the shares were disposed of at a loss. However, this loss would be a capital loss, of which only one-half would be available for use against other capital gains. If the share loss qualified as an allowable business investment loss, one-half of the loss would be available for carry-over against other sources of income.

Exhibit 10-2 considered the situation of a single individual choosing an organization structure for a business activity. Although choosing a corporate structure increases the risk that any losses will be unusable, the individual who controls the company can at least take whatever steps are at his or her disposal to utilize the losses as quickly as possible and before they expire. This flexibility is reduced when an investment is made jointly with other parties.

An individual who is contemplating investing in a venture with other parties must weigh the risks of a partnership structure of several partners against those of a corporate structure of several shareholders. The partnership structure, like the proprietorship, is not a taxable entity, and therefore losses are allocated directly to the individual partners. Such business losses can be immediately offset against the individual's other sources of income, or carried over to other years against all other income sources. On the other hand, if a corporate structure with several shareholders is used, the corporation's losses are locked into the corporation and the individual shareholder's ability to utilize those losses is diminished. The risk of using a corporate structure is increased further when the shareholder making the investment does not control the actions of the corporation and is unable to take the necessary steps to utilize corporate losses. In addition, there is less flexibility in triggering a capital loss on the shares if the corporation is in serious financial difficulty. A detailed comparison of the partnership and corporate structures is made in Chapter 15.

In summary, when an individual chooses a corporate structure over a proprietorship or partnership, the risk of not being able to use a loss for tax purposes is increased. Creating two taxable entities rather than one effectively doubles the restrictions that apply to loss carry-overs. There may be other reasons for choosing a corporate structure. For example, when there is a risk of losses, the limited-liability features of a corporation may be more important than any loss utilization features. As well, the corporate structure is often chosen to take advantage of special tax rates on business income, without regard to the treatment of losses, should those occur (see Chapter 11). It should be pointed out that business structures are not permanent, and that a proprietorship or partnership can later be converted into a corporation after losses have been incurred and the operations become profitable.

B. Preserving Tax Losses

The restrictions placed on the use of loss carry-overs are onerous. The risk of loss expiration can be minimized by making decisions that create taxable income or reduce deductible expenses, thereby permitting a greater amount of the loss carry-over to be used. While this statement sounds trite, it does not mean that an individual should stimulate new income by entering new ventures, or cut actual expenses that are necessary to earn income. Rather, it means that actual expenses should be deferred for tax purposes when possible, and that accrued gains should be realized sooner than later.

• **Reducing expenses** There are a number of expenses which can be claimed at a time that is at the discretion of the taxpayer. If the expenses are not claimed in a particular year, they can be deducted in a subsequent year. For example, a taxpayer can choose not to claim the full amount of capital cost allowance in a year, thereby increasing the amount of taxable income available to be offset against a loss carry-over that may expire. Or a business may choose not to claim capital cost allowance when it is regularly incurring losses; this would diminish the loss that is subject to the time restriction. By not claiming capital cost allowance, the undepreciated capital cost of the asset's class would remain at a higher amount; the capital cost allowance deduction would thus be preserved for future years.

Similarly, it is not necessary to claim a reserve for accounts receivable that may be uncollectible. If the receivables still remain doubtful in future years, they can be deducted at that time, after the loss carry-overs have been utilized.

• **Creating income** There are a number of ways that taxable income can be created at the individual's discretion. Often an individual owns business assets, investments, or personal-use assets that have appreciated in value. These gains can be realized for tax purposes by triggering a disposition. An individual who does not wish to actually dispose of a property can sell it to a spouse or to a corporation owned by the individual; in doing so, that individual retains the ownership in another form. The sale of such property can create capital gains and/or recapture of capital cost allowance, which can be used to offset the losses carried over. Because the property has been sold and reacquired, its cost base for tax purposes is increased by the gain. Effectively, this activity transfers the loss carry-over to the cost of the asset(s), preserving it for a deduction when the property is ultimately sold to a third party.

Similarly, a financially troubled business may want to dispose of appreciating assets but still retain their use through a sale-and-lease-back arrangement. This process creates much-needed cash and uses up losses before they expire, yet still keeps the assets(s) available for use.

C. Future Investment Strategies

The existence of loss carry-overs, especially of capital losses that can be offset only against future capital gains, can change investment strategies with respect to the redeployment of capital investments. In Chapter 8 on capital gains, a situation was considered where the taxpayer was contemplating selling investment A and replacing it with investment B. In that example, the proceeds on the sale of investment A were reduced from $100,000 to $79,750 as a result of the tax on the capital gain realized. This meant that only $79,750 was available for investment B. It was indicated that in order to justify the disposal of a $100,000 investment in property A, property B would have to be significantly more attractive than company A in terms of future potential.

The availability of a capital loss carry-over would completely change the return-on-investment requirements in the above example. The disposal of property A would generate $100,000 of cash for investment in property B because there would be no tax on the sale. Therefore, this transaction could be justified if the potential return on property B were only marginally better than on property A.

Clearly, it is important to re-examine strategies relating to investment and business-asset replacement decisions when loss carry-overs are available.

IV. The Capital Gain Deduction

The final step in arriving at the taxable income of an individual is to apply the capital gain deduction. The deduction applies *only* to gains realized on two specific types of property—qualified small business corporation shares and qualified farm property. All individuals who are resident in Canada are permitted to reduce their taxable income by the net capital gains realized on these properties over their lifetime to a maximum of $500,000. As only one-half of capital gains are included for tax purposes, the maximum deduction is $250,000 of net taxable capital gains.[8]

As described in Chapter 8, a small business corporation is a Canadian-controlled private corporation that uses all or substantially all of its assets to conduct an active business in Canada.[9] Qualified farm property includes real property, eligible capital property (such as farm quotas) used in the business of farming, a share of a family farm corporation, and an interest in a farm partnership.

The deduction is discretionary, and in some circumstances it may be desirable to forgo its use until a later year. For example, some individuals may not want to claim the deduction in a year of low income if they are reasonably certain that further capital gains on the specified properties will be realized in future years, when their tax rate will be substantially higher.

The ability to claim the capital gain deduction is limited by two items—capital losses incurred (including allowable business investment losses), and accumulated investment losses, which are referred to as the cumulative net investment loss.[10] Each item is reviewed briefly below.

To demonstrate the first item, consider this situation. Assume that an individual has, in the current year, a taxable capital gain of $40,000 from the sale of qualified small business corporation shares, allowable capital losses of $10,000, and an allowable business investment loss of $4,000. In addition, she has unused net capital losses of $12,000 carried over from a previous year. Assuming that she has a capital gain deduction available (i.e., that has not been previously used), the maximum deduction she can claim in this particular year is $14,000, as follows:

---

8 ITA 110.6(4).

9 There are two further requirements to be met. The shares of the SBC sold must not have been acquired by another non-related person in the past 24 months, and, during the same period, more than 50% of the fair market value of the SBC's assets must have been used in an active business.

10 ITA 110.6(1).

Net income:	
Taxable capital gain	$40,000
Allowable capital losses	(10,000)
Net gain for the year	30,000
Allowable business investment loss	(4,000)
Increase to net income	26,000
Taxable income:	
Net capital losses of other years	(12,000)
Available for capital gain deduction	$14,000

If, in the above example, the taxpayer had chosen not to claim the $12,000 loss carry-over, the available capital gain deduction would have been $26,000. The purpose of this calculation is clear: it is to provide a deduction only to the extent that lifetime capital gains exceed capital losses. However, timing is an important factor. For example, if an individual with no previous capital losses (since 1984, when the capital gain deduction began) achieves a qualified capital gain of $500,000 ($250,000 taxable), a full capital gain deduction is available. If in a subsequent year a capital loss occurs, it will not affect the original deduction.

The second limiting item, the cumulative net investment loss (CNIL), is more difficult to understand. It is based on the premise that an investment in capital property normally results in two types of returns—the annual net income (loss) from rents, dividends, or interest (property income), *and* the change in the value of the investment itself (capital gain or loss). Consider the following extreme example:

An individual invests $20,000 in qualified small business corporation shares. After one year, interest expense of $5,000 is incurred on a loan used to buy the shares. The property is then sold for $25,000, resulting in a capital gain of $5,000. If the capital gain deduction were permitted for the $5,000 capital gain and the interest expense were deducted against other income, as is permitted, a tax saving would occur even though no real profit had been achieved. The actual gain from the investment would be as follows:

Capital gain on sale	$5,000
Interest expense	(5,000)
Net gain to investor	–0–

Assuming a 45% tax rate, the investor's tax position would be this:

Tax on capital gain (if deduction is allowed)	–0–
Tax saving from interest expense (45% of $5,000)	2,250
Overall tax reduction	$2,250

Because of this apparent inequity, the CNIL was introduced in 1988. Under its provisions, a capital gain deduction cannot be claimed to the extent that the accumulated annual investment returns (from *all* types of property) from 1988 to the year in question are in a negative position. In other words, if property expenses exceed property incomes on a cumulative basis, the capital gain deduction is reduced by that amount. For example, assume that an individual has a taxable capital gain from qualified small business corporation shares of $20,000 in a particular year. In addition, she has a cumulative net investment loss of $14,000, as follows:

Investment income (interest, rents) from 1988 to the present	$ 39,000
Expenses incurred to earn the above income	(53,000)
Accumulated loss	$ (14,000)

Assuming that a capital gain deduction is available, the maximum deduction that can be claimed in that year is $6,000 ($20,000 – $14,000). It is important to note that the CNIL does not eliminate or reduce an individual's total available capital gain exemption; it simply delays its use until a later year.

An example of the capital gain deduction rules is presented in the following situation and analysis:

Situation: In 20X6, an individual sold all of her shares of ABC Ltd., a Canadian-controlled private corporation, realizing a gain of $280,000. ABC operates a retail business, and all of its assets are used to operate the active business. Also in 20X6, this individual sold shares of a public corporation—a move that resulted in a loss of $40,000—and had a rental loss of $4,000. In 20X5 the individual had claimed her first capital gain deduction of $120,000. At the end of 20X5, her cumulative net investment loss (CNIL) was $31,000. No net capital losses are being carried forward.

Analysis: The shares of ABC Ltd. are qualified small business corporation shares because all of the corporation's assets are being used in an active business. The unused capital gain deduction at the end of 20X6 is $130,000 (maximum allowable $250,000 – used in prior years $120,000). The accumulated property losses (CNIL) at the end of 20X6 are $35,000 (balance at 20X5 $31,000 + current-year loss of $4,000). The capital gain deduction for 20X6 is $85,000, calculated as follows:

Taxable capital gain—ABC Ltd.—$280,000 × ½	$140,000
Allowable capital loss—public corporation shares—$40,000 × ½	(20,000)
Net gain qualified for the deduction	$120,000
Deduct the cumulative net investment loss (CNIL) at the end of 20X6	(35,000)
Capital gain deduction for 20X6	$ 85,000

The unused capital gain deduction at the end of 20X6 is $45,000 ($130,000 – $85,000). Notice that the qualified deduction in 20X6 of $140,000 was reduced by the allowable capital loss on the public corporation shares. If the individual had additional taxable capital gains in the year from other sources, the allowable capital loss would first reduce those gains before reducing the qualified gain from the qualified small business corporation shares.

The capital gain deduction must be built into the overall decision process described in Chapter 8. The deduction was originally introduced to the tax system as a means to stimulate investment in capital property. Whether this objective was achieved is questionable. Most investors realize that the decision to invest carries an inherent risk, and that diminished risk stimulates greater investment. From a tax perspective, the risk in capital investments is reduced if potential losses can easily be utilized to gain a tax recovery. The restrictions on the use of capital losses serve to increase the risk inherent in capital investments, whereas the capital gain deduction may have little if any impact. The capital gain deduction, like other preferences given to capital gains, is a continuing source of contention. The chances of its being removed are, therefore, high, and this should be considered with all the other factors when investment decisions are being made.

V. Calculation of Tax for Individuals

Income tax is imposed by the federal government and all 10 provinces. Federal tax is expressed in terms of a tax rate applied to the individual's taxable income. In all provinces and territories, taxes for individuals are expressed as a *percentage of the taxpayer's taxable income*. Non-residents do not pay provincial tax but instead pay an additional tax (48%) that is a percentage of the federal basic tax.

The rates of federal tax are reasonably stable. Provincial tax rates vary considerably from province to province and are subject to regular changes based on provincial budget demands. The federal and provincial governments attempt to implement certain social and economic policies by reducing the tax otherwise payable for certain individuals or types of transactions. These reductions are provided in the form of tax credits. There are many federal and provincial tax credits, which are subject to frequent changes in amount.

While the existence of numerous tax credits increases the complexity of the overall tax calculation, this is seldom relevant to the decision-making process for business and investment activities. From a business and investment perspective, decision makers want to know when and how much additional tax (federal and provincial) they will have to pay from potential income on contemplated transactions. Conversely, they wish to know when and how much tax they may save if they incur certain expenses or if proposed activities result in a loss instead of a profit. Therefore, what is relevant is the marginal tax rate that will apply to each additional dollar earned or lost in new activities.

This part of the chapter attempts to develop the relevant marginal rates of tax that apply to decision making. It is recognized that these particular rates may change from time to time as federal and provincial policies evolve. Even so, while the specific rates developed in the following examples may not be current, the process for determining them does not change. *It is important that the reader update the specific rates at the time they are needed for a particular decision.* Keep in mind that the rates in effect at the time the decision is being made may have changed by the time the income or loss from the transaction is realized. In an attempt to project rates of tax in the future, consideration must also be given to the government's fiscal position at the time.

While this chapter does describe the overall tax calculation for individuals, it should be recognized that this is done for the purpose of showing the overall process rather than to provide a detailed tax calculation guide. Such information can be obtained from a number of other sources, including the personal tax return guide and forms.

A. Overall Tax Calculation

The overall calculation for determining federal and provincial tax for an individual is outlined in Exhibit 10-3.

Notice that the federal tax is reduced by tax credits, which have been divided into two categories. Each of these categories will be discussed later. The first category of tax credits reduces the primary federal tax to an amount referred to as the "basic federal tax."

Each segment of the overall tax calculation outlined in Exhibit 10-3 is examined below. An accompanying sample tax calculation is also provided.

Exhibit 10-3:
Determination of Tax
for an Individual

(a) Federal tax:

Primary federal tax (rate × *taxable income*)		xx
First-category tax credits		(x)
Basic federal tax		xx
Second-category tax credits		(x)
Total federal tax		xx
(b) Provincial tax:		
Primary provincial tax*		
(graduated rates × taxable income)	xx	
Provincial surtax	x	
Specific provincial tax credits	(x)	xx
(c) Combined federal and provincial tax		xx

* Non-residents do not pay provincial tax. Instead, non-residents pay an additional tax of 48% of the *basic federal tax*.

B. Primary Federal Tax

The primary federal tax is determined by applying progressively higher tax rates to higher levels of annual income.[11] Exhibit 10-4 outlines the rates of tax applicable to each range of taxable income.

Exhibit 10-4:
Primary Federal
Tax Rates

Taxable income range 2003* (with minimum 2004 brackets)	Rate
Up to $32,183 (minimum $35,000 in 2004)	16%
$32,184–$64,364 (minimum $70,000 in 2004)	22%
$64,365–$104,648 (minimum $113,804 in 2004)	26%
Over $104,648 (minimum $113,804 in 2004)	29%

* The taxable income range is adjusted regularly by a cost-of-living factor.

Each rate of tax is applied separately to the portion of the individual's income that falls within the applicable range. For example, an individual who has taxable income of $70,000 would calculate primary federal tax as follows:

On the first $32,183 of income:	
16% × $32,183	$5,149
On income between $32,183 and $64,364:	
22% × $32,181	7,080
On income between $64,364 and $104,648:	
26% × $5,636	1,465
Total primary federal tax	$13,694

The overall effective rate of tax for this individual is 20% ($13,694/$70,000); however, each additional dollar earned by the taxpayer over $70,000 is subject to tax at the marginal rate of 26% until $104,648 of income is reached, and then 29% on income over $104,648. It is these rates, combined with provincial taxes, that are most relevant to the decision-making process.

---

11 ITA 117(2), 117.1(1)(d).

C. First Category
of Federal
Tax Credits

Before reviewing the tax credits that fall within this category, it is worthwhile to explain the difference between a tax credit and a tax deduction.

A tax credit is a specific reduction of the tax otherwise payable and has a value equal to its stated amount. For example, a tax credit of $150 reduces the tax otherwise payable by $150, whatever the individual's tax bracket.

A tax deduction, on the other hand, reduces taxable income; the related amount of tax saving is based on the marginal tax bracket of the individual for that particular year. Thus, a tax deduction of $150 would reduce federal taxes by $44 for taxpayers in the 29% tax bracket, and by $24 for taxpayers in the 16% tax bracket. Tax credits benefit all individuals equally, whereas tax deductions provide a greater benefit to those in higher tax brackets.

• **Dividend tax credit**   From a decision-making perspective, the most important tax credit in the first category is the *dividend tax credit*, which is equal to 13⅓% of the taxable amount of dividends received from Canadian corporations.[12] In Chapter 7 it was indicated that a Canadian dividend is included in income for tax purposes at 125% of the actual dividend received. As explained in that chapter, this increase is part of a scheme to diminish the impact of double taxation when after-tax corporate income is distributed as dividends.

The receipt of a $1,000 cash dividend reduces federal taxes by a tax credit amount of $167, as shown below.

Cash dividend received	$1,000
Dividend included in taxable income and subject to primary federal tax: $1,000 × 1.25	$1,250
Dividend tax credit: 13⅓% × $1,250	$ 167

The tax credit of $167 is received whatever the individual's tax bracket; in other words, a taxpayer in the 16% bracket will receive the same $167 credit as a taxpayer in the 26% or 29% bracket.

• **Other first-category tax credits**   There are several other first-category tax credits available to individuals. These are described below. The amounts relate to the *2003* taxation year and are subject to change periodically. These credits *reduce the basic federal tax*. The credits are normally established as 16% (the lowest federal tax bracket rate) multiplied by a designated amount of income.

Basic   All individuals receive a basic credit of *$1,241*, which is equivalent to $7,756 of taxable income (16% × $7,756).[13] This means that income below $7,756 is not subject to federal tax (minimum in 2004 is $8,000).

Spouse or equivalent to spouse   Individuals supporting a spouse (including a common-law spouse) receive an additional credit of *$1,054,* which is equivalent to taxable income of $6,586 (16% × $6,586).[14] The credit is reduced by 16% of the spouse's *net income* in excess of $659. If, for example, a supported spouse has net income of $2,000, the credit to the supporting spouse is $839 ($1,054 − 16%[$2,000 − $659]). The credit is fully eliminated when

---

12 ITA 121.

13 ITA 118(1)(c).

14 ITA 118(1)(a), (b).

the supported spouse's income reaches $7,245 ($1,054 – 16%[$7,245 – $659]). The married credit is not available when support payments are being made to a spouse who is separated and living apart.

In some cases an individual is unmarried but supports another person who lives with him or her, such as a child or other relative. A credit referred to as the "equivalent to spouse" credit is available and is exactly the same as the spouse credit described earlier. This normally applies to a dependent child who is under the age of 18 at any time in the year, or who is over the age of 18 and dependent by reason of physical or mental infirmity. The dependant could also be a parent or grandparent (regardless of age) or another related individual (subject to the same age restrictions as children). The equivalent-to-spouse credit is not available for a person for whom periodic payments of support are being provided as a consequence of marriage breakdown.

Infirm dependants   A credit of *$586,* which is equivalent to $3,663 of taxable income (16% × $3,663), is available for supporting a related person who is over the age of 18 and is dependent by reason of physical or mental infirmity.[15] The credit is reduced by 16% of the dependant's net income in excess of $5,197. It is not necessary that the dependant be living with the supporting individual. However, dependants, other than children, must be resident in Canada.

Caregiver   Individuals who provide in-home care for a parent or grandparent who is 65 years of age or over, *or* for a dependent relative who is infirm, are entitled to a $586 tax credit against federal tax. The credit is reduced by 16% of the dependant's income in excess of $12,509. The credit is completely eliminated when the dependant's income exceeds $16,172.[16]

Age amount   Individuals who are 65 years of age or older can claim an additional credit of *$606,* which is equivalent to taxable income of $3,787 (16% × $3,787).[17] The limit of $3,787 is reduced by 15% of the taxpayer's net income in excess of $28,193. The 16% credit is then applied to this reduced amount. This reduction is more complicated than the others because of the added 15% feature. For example, a taxpayer with net income of $40,000 is entitled to a credit of $322 (16% × [$3,787 – 15% [$40,000 – $28,193]). The credit is completely eliminated when net income reaches $53,440.

Disability   An individual with a severe and prolonged mental or physical impairment can claim an additional credit of *$1,004,* which is equivalent to taxable income of $6,279 (16% × $6,279).[18] To the extent that the credit exceeds the tax payable of the disabled person, the unused amount can be transferred to a spouse, parent, or grandparent.

Pension   Individuals can claim a credit of 16% of the first $1,000 of qualified pension income received in a year.[19] If the taxpayer is 65 years of age or older, the credit applies to a wide range of retirement income, including annuity payments from a superannuation or pension fund, RRSP, RRIF, or DPSP. When the annuitant is under 65 years of age, annuities from an RRSP, RRIF, or DPSP do not qualify for the credit. Canada Pension Plan and Old Age Security payments do not qualify at any time.

CPP and EI   Individuals are required to make contributions to the Canada Pension Plan and the Employment Insurance plan. Taxpayers can claim a tax credit of 16% of their maximum allowable CPP and EI contributions in any year.[20]

Charitable donations   Gifts to charities receive a credit of 16% on the first $200 of annual

---

15 ITA 118(1)(d),(e).

16 ITA 118(1)(b.1)

17 ITA 118(2).

18 ITA 118.3(1).

19 ITA 118(3).

20 ITA 118.7.

contributions and 29% on the remainder.[21] Annual donations cannot exceed 75% of the individual's net income for the year. Donations in excess of the limit can be carried forward for five of the subsequent taxation years. Qualified donations include gifts to registered charities, to Canadian amateur athletic organizations, to Canadian universities (and certain foreign universities), to the United Nations, and to Canada and the provinces. Special rules may apply for gifts of property, gifts of cultural property, and gifts of ecologically sensitive land.

Medical expenses   The tax credit for medical expenses is 16% of the qualified medical expenses that exceed either 3% of the taxpayer's net income for the year, or $1,756, whichever is less.[22] For example, if a taxpayer has net income for tax purposes of $40,000, the 16% credit can be applied only on medical expenses above $1,200 (3% × $40,000). The $1,756 threshold occurs at net income of $58,533 (3% × $ 58,533). Taxpayers with net income above $58,533 can deduct all medical expenses above $1,756. The credit is available for medical expenses paid on behalf of the taxpayer, a spouse, or a dependant.

Education amount and tuition fees   Individuals who attend a university, college, or other certified post-secondary institution can claim a credit of 16% of tuition fees paid.[23] Also, an individual is entitled to deduct 16% of the interest portion of *student loan payments*. The credit applies to interest payments (not principal payments) on outstanding loans under the Canada Student Loan Program and provincial student loan programs. The credit may be claimed in the year it is earned (the year of interest payment) *or* in any of the following five years. The optional five-year carry-over provides a greater opportunity to use the full credit to reduce tax. In addition, when the student is in full-time attendance at the qualified institution, an additional credit is available equal to 16% of $400 for each month of full-time attendance.[24] This amounts to $64 per month (16% × $400). Also, a *part-time* education credit of 16% × $120 ($19.20) is available for each month of attendance. To qualify, the student has to be enrolled at an educational institution in Canada, in an eligible program lasting at least three weeks and involving a minimum of 12 hours of courses each month. Students cannot claim both full-time and part-time credits.

The student may not have sufficient income to utilize the above credits. In this situation, the unused portion is transferable (within limits) to a spouse, parent, or grandparent. Alternatively, the student may keep the unused credit and carry it forward indefinitely until such time as he or she has sufficient income to use the credit.[25] The maximum credit that may be transferred to a spouse or parent is $800 annually (16% × $5,000). The unused deduction is determined after the individual first applies the basic credit of $1,221 and the CPP/EI and disability credits. Consider the following situation:

A student has taxable income of $10,000, and CPP/EI contributions of $300, and has paid tuition fees of $5,000 to attend university for eight months. The unused tuition and education credit for the year is $981, as calculated at the top of the next page.

The student can carry forward the $981 unused credit for use in the future or transfer the amount to a supporting spouse, parent, or grandparent.

D. Second Category of Federal Tax Credits   The most important tax credit in the second category of federal tax credits is the *foreign tax credit*. Individuals who earn income in a foreign country may be subject to tax on that income both in the foreign country and in Canada. To avoid the full impact of double taxation, Canadian taxpayers can reduce their Canadian taxes through the foreign tax

21 ITA 118.1(3).
22 ITA 118.2(1).
23 ITA 118.5; IT-516.
24 ITA 118.6(2).
25 ITA 118.9.

Federal tax—16% × $10,000	$1,600
Basic credit	(1,221)
CPP/EI credit—16% × $300	(48)
Federal tax before education and tuition credit	331
Tuition credit—16% × $5,000	(800)
Education credit (2003)—$64 × 8 months	(512)
Unused credit	$ (981)

credit.[26] Separate credits are provided for foreign investment income and foreign business income. In both cases the foreign tax credit is based on the amount of foreign tax paid on income that is also taxable in Canada; this amount, however, cannot exceed the equivalent amount of Canadian tax on that income. The credit for foreign investment income is further limited to 15% of the foreign income earned; however, any unused amount can be used as a deduction from income rather than a credit.[27] Unused foreign tax credits from foreign business income can be carried back three years and forward seven years. A more detailed review of business foreign tax credits is made in a later chapter on international business expansion.

Other tax credits in the second category include the following:[28]

- political contributions
- investment tax credits for the purchase of certain equipment in designated regions of Canada
- logging tax credit
- labour-sponsored fund credit

The tax credit for *federal political contributions* is based on a graduated scale. The annual credit is 75% of the first $200, 50% of the next $350, and 33⅓% of contributions over $550. However, the total annual political contribution credit cannot exceed $500. This figure is reached when contributions total $1,075.

The tax credits mentioned in the first and second categories can be used only to the extent of the taxes otherwise payable by the individual.

E. Provincial Taxes

The majority of provinces and territories determine their primary tax by applying specified tax *rates* to the *federal taxable income*. The rates of tax and income brackets to which they apply vary widely from province to province. These provinces also specify their own tax credits similar in nature to the federal non-refundable tax credits described earlier in the chapter. For example, in 2003, British Columbia applied the following tax rates to the federal taxable income:

$0 to $31,653	6.05%
$31,653 to $63,308	9.15%
$63,308 to $72,685	11.7%
$72,685 to $88,260	13.7%
Over $88,260	14.7%

Notice that the above income ranges do not correspond with the federal income ranges for particular tax rates. They are also not the same as those of other provinces. As a further example, some of British Columbia's non-refundable tax credits are as follows:

---

26 ITA 126; IT-270R2.

27 ITA 20(11).

28 ITA 127(1) to (26), 127.1 to .4, 127(3).

Dividend tax credit – 5.1% × grossed-up dividend
Basic personal credit – 6.05% × $8,307 = $503
Charitable donations – 6.05% on first $200 plus 14.7% on amounts over $200

*Information on various provincial tax rates and credits can be obtained by accessing links on this text's Web site at **www.mcgrawhill.ca/college/buckwold7**.*

Individuals are subject to tax in a particular provincial jurisdiction if they resided in that province on the last day of the calendar year—December 31. An exception to this rule requires that an individual who resides in a particular province but carries on business from permanent establishments in other provinces must allocate business income to those provinces.[29] This allocation is based on an arbitrary formula relating to sales and salaries, and does not necessarily reflect the actual business profits in a particular province. The allocation procedure is demonstrated in the following situation:

Situation:
An individual resides in Manitoba. In 20X0 she earned net income of $140,000 consisting of property income of $40,000 and net income from a business of $100,000. The head office of the business is in Manitoba, but a branch location is maintained in Ontario that has staff and inventory. An analysis of the business operations provides the following information:

	Manitoba	*Ontario*	*Total*
Sales	$600,000 (75%)	$200,000 (25%)	$800,000 (100%)
Salaries	200,000 (80%)	50,000 (20%)	250,000 (100%)
Actual profits	$ 70,000	$ 30,000	$100,000

Analysis:
The allocation of the business income to each province is based on the average of sales and salaries in each province, as follows:

Manitoba:		
Sales	75%	
Salaries	80%	
Average	(80% + 75%)/2 =	78%
Ontario		
Sales	25%	
Salaries	20%	
Average	(25% + 20%)/2 =	22%
		100%

Allocation of business income to Ontario is

22% × $100,000 =	$22,000

All remaining income is allocated to Manitoba.

---

29 ITA Regulations 2600 to 2607.

Notice that in the example situation, the amount of income allocated to Ontario was $22,000, even though the actual profits earned in that province were $30,000. The allocation formula, which is tied to sales and wages, arbitrarily shifted Ontario profits to Manitoba, which has a different provincial tax rate. If the mixture of sales and salaries had been different, the opposite might have occurred, resulting in a higher profit allocated to Ontario. It should also be pointed out that this formula applies only because a permanent establishment exists in Ontario. If sales had been made to Ontario directly from Manitoba, no allocation would have been made, and all business activity in Ontario would have been taxed in Manitoba.

F. Sample Calculation of Tax

A sample calculation of taxable income and of the related federal and provincial income tax is performed below. The purpose of the demonstration is to highlight the *form* of the calculation rather than its technical accuracy. The federal tax brackets, certain tax credits, and the rates of provincial tax may have changed since publication. A more detailed tax calculation is shown in the demonstration question at the end of this chapter.

Summary of Facts

An individual who resides in British Columbia has net employment income of $96,000 for a particular year. He maintains a small portfolio of investments that resulted in a taxable capital gain of $5,000 from the sale of qualified small business corporation shares (the lifetime capital gain deduction is available). The investments also generated dividends from Canadian corporations of $8,000, and interest income from the United States of $2,000. From the $2,000 of American interest income, he paid $200 (10% of $2,000) on account of American taxes. During the year, this taxpayer made payments of $2,000 to charitable organizations. He is single.

Calculation of Tax

Before calculating tax for the year, one must determine the taxable income.

Net income:		
(a) Employment		$ 96,000
Property:		
Dividends ($8,000 × 1.25)	10,000	
Foreign interest	2,000	12,000
		108,000
(b) Net taxable capital gains		5,000
Net income for tax purposes		113,000
Special reductions:		
Capital gain deduction		(5,000)
Taxable income		$108,000

Tax can then be calculated on the basis of taxable income of $108,000, as shown on the next page.

G. Tax Calculation— Impact on Decision Making

As was mentioned at the beginning of this section, the impact of the tax calculation on investment and business decisions centres on how the marginal tax rates will be applied to cash flows generated from proposed financial activities. For every proposed transaction it is necessary to project the following:

(a) the nature of the expected income or potential loss that may occur;
(b) when the particular income or loss will be recognized for tax purposes;
(c) the tax bracket that the income or loss will fall into, considering expected other sources of income; and,
(d) the combined federal and provincial tax that will apply.

In order to determine the marginal tax rate for each bracket of income, it is necessary to combine the federal and provincial tax calculations. This can be confusing because the tax rates and the income brackets to which those rates apply differ from province to province.

Federal tax:
    Primary federal tax (2003)

16% on first	32,183	$ 5,149
22% on next	32,181	7,080
26% on next	40,284	10,474
29% on balance	3,352	972
	$108,000	23,675

First-category tax credits:

Dividend tax credit: 13⅓% × $10,000		(1,333)
Individual tax credit (2003 rate)		(1,241)
Donation tax credit:		
On first $200 of donations		
($200 × 16%)	32	
On donations over $200		
($1,800 × 29%)	522	(554)
Basic federal tax		20,547

Second-category tax credits:

Foreign tax credit		(200)
Total federal tax		$20,347

Provincial tax (British Columbia):

6.05% on first	31,653	$ 1,915
9.15% on next	31,655	2,896
11.7% on next	9,377	1,097
13.7% on next	15,575	2,134
14.7% on balance over $88,260	19,740	2,862
	$108,000	10,904

Tax credits:

Dividend tax credit: 5.1% × $10,000		(510)
Basic individual credit (2003)		(503)
Donation tax credit:		
On first $200 of donations		
($200 × 6.05%)	12	
On donations over $200		
($1,800 × 14.70%)	265	(277)
Total provincial tax		$ 9,614
Total federal and provincial tax		$29,961

Exhibit 10-5 calculates the combined federal and provincial tax rates for an *unspecified* province, using arbitrary provincial tax rates of 10%, 12%, 14%, and 16% that correspond to each of the four federal income brackets. The calculations for the actual provinces and territories would be similar, except that the particular provincial rates would have to be substituted.

Exhibit 10-5 indicates that any income on a proposed financial activity in this province would incur a tax cost of either 26%, 34%, 40%, or 45%, depending on the amount of income from other sources that would be earned in the applicable years. Similarly, any loss would generate tax savings of the same magnitudes. ***Most sample calculations throughout the text use tax rates based on Exhibit 10-5 for demonstration purposes.***

Exhibit 10-5: *Combined Federal and Provincial Marginal Tax Rates*		INCOME RANGE (2003)			
		Up to *$32,183*	*$32,183 to* *$64,364*	*$64,364 to* *$104,648*	*Over* *$104,648*
	Primary federal tax rate	16	22	26	29
	Add provincial tax	10	12	14	16
	Combined tax rate	26%	34%	40%	45%

When applying the marginal rates of tax, remember that the actual amount of income or loss is not always the same as the amount that must be included for tax purposes. For example, an actual capital gain of $100 results in only $50 ($\frac{1}{2}$ of $100) of taxable income. In this case, the marginal tax rates that are applicable to an *actual* capital gain are as follows:

First bracket	$26\% \times \frac{1}{2} = 13\%$
Second bracket	$34\% \times \frac{1}{2} = 17\%$
Third bracket	$40\% \times \frac{1}{2} = 20\%$
Fourth bracket	$45\% \times \frac{1}{2} = 23\%$ (rounded)

Similarly, an actual dividend of $100 requires that $125 be included in taxable income. In this situation the calculation of the marginal rate of tax is complicated by the dividend tax credit, which reduces federal tax by the same amount for each tax bracket. Also, most provinces have a separate fixed dividend tax credit. To demonstrate, we assume a provincial dividend tax credit rate of 7% for an *unspecified* province. A cash dividend of $100 (for which $125 is included in income) will generate a combined federal and provincial dividend tax credit in this province of $26, calculated as follows:

Actual dividend received	$100
Federal dividend tax credit:	
$13\frac{1}{3}\% \times \$125$	$17 (rounded)
Provincial dividend tax credit:	
$7\% \times \$125$	$ 9 (rounded)
Total tax reduction	$26

In other words, every $100 of *cash* dividends received will reduce federal and provincial taxes by approximately $26. With this information, the marginal rate of tax on dividends earned in the unspecified province can be calculated as follows:

Normal combined tax rates	26%	34%	40%	45%
Cash dividend received	$100	$100	$100	$100
Taxable income ($100 × 1.25)	$125	$125	$125	$125
Tax (rate × $125)	$33	$43	$50	$56
Combined dividend tax credit	(26)	(26)	(26)	(26)
Net tax on a $100 dividend	$ 7	$17	$ 24	$ 30
Marginal rate of tax	7%	17%	24%	30%

In applying the rates of tax to investment and business decisions, it is important to relate the rate of tax to the amount of cash income or loss rather than to the special amount that is included in income for tax purposes. The preceding calculations are summarized and presented in Exhibit 10-6, which highlights the marginal tax rates of various types of income. Keep in mind that these rates were calculated using provincial tax rates from a fictitious province. Notice, for example, that for a person in the lowest bracket, the tax rate on dividends is 6% lower than on capital gains (13% versus 7%). Since an investment in shares of a corporation may provide both dividends and capital growth, a person in the lower bracket may seek out shares that provide higher dividends and lower capital growth rather than the reverse. On the other hand, in the two middle tax brackets the rates of tax on capital gains and dividends are much closer together and at the top tax bracket capital gains are preferential to dividends.. This analysis must be tempered by the fact that dividends are taxed when received, whereas capital gains are taxed only when a disposition occurs and, further, may be exempt under the lifetime capital gain deduction.

The marginal rates shown in Exhibit 10-6 also permit decision makers to compare the after-tax yields on various types of investments. For example, a person in the highest tax bracket who earns interest income at 10% will receive an after-tax yield of 5.5% (10% – [45% of 10%] = 5.5%). The same after-tax yield can be earned on a share investment yielding dividends of 7.8% (7.8% – [30% of 7.8%] = 5.5%), or on an investment yielding a capital gain of 7.1% (7.1% – [23% of 7.1%] = 5.5%). Although the timing of the related tax for each type of investment may vary, the comparative after-tax yields are relevant when the relative risk is examined for each type of investment.

Exhibit 10-6: Marginal Tax Rates by Type of Income (excluding provincial surtaxes)	Income range (2003)	Capital gains	Canadian dividends	Ordinary income
	Up to $32,183	13%	7%	26%
	$32,183 to $64,364	17	17	34
	$64,364 to $104,648	20	24	40
	Over $104,648	23	30	45

The marginal tax rates developed in Exhibit 10-6 are fundamental to decision making; but the overall tax calculation should also be examined for unusual aspects that may affect certain business decisions. For example, the arbitrary formula for allocating business income to various provinces has an impact on business expansion decisions. Expansion to other provinces can be carried out by selling directly from the home province or by establishing a more formal structure, such as branch locations in the other provinces. Each of these basic alternatives involves certain costs and benefits from a marketing perspective. As well, each has a different effect on the amount of tax payable. The decision to establish a branch location has a big impact on the amount of provincial tax, and so does the location of the branch.

The effect of the arbitrary tax formula must be factored into the cost/benefit analysis of the expansion decision if the complete costs of each alternative are to be known (see Chapter 20).

• **Actual marginal tax rates**   As previously indicated, the marginal tax rates developed in Exhibit 10-6 were based on fictitious provincial rates. *Throughout the text, the marginal rates in Exhibit 10-6 are used for demonstration purposes.* Exhibit 10-7 shows the *actual* top marginal tax rates for each province and territory. These rates relate to the *2003* taxation year. *It is important that the reader update the rates at the time they are needed for a particular decision.* A complete set of marginal tax rates for all provinces and territories is available by accessing the Web links shown on this text's Web site at **www.mcgrawhill.ca/college/ buckwold7.**

Exhibit 10-7: Actual 2003 Marginal Tax Rates—Top Income Bracket Only	Top Income Bracket	Ordinary Income & Interest	Capital Gains	Canadian Dividends
	Alberta	39%	20%	24%
	British Columbia	44%	22%	32%
	Manitoba	46%	23%	35%
	New Brunswick	47%	23%	37%
	Newfoundland and Labrador	49%	24%	37%
	Nova Scotia	47%	24%	32%
	Ontario	46%	23%	31%
	Prince Edward Island	47%	24%	32%
	Quebec	48%	24%	33%
	Saskatchewan	44%	22%	28%
	NWT	42%	21%	28%
	Nunavut	41%	20%	29%
	Yukon	42%	21%	29%
	Non-resident	43%	21%	29%

Note: All percentages are rounded. The rates assume the provinces and territories will also choose to use a 50% inclusion rate for capital gains. The rates are based on information available in March 2003 and may be altered by provincial budgets occurring after the date of this publication. See **www.mcgrawhill.ca/college/buckwold7** for updated marginal tax rates.

VI. Special Adjustments to the Tax Calculation

In certain circumstances, special rules apply that increase the amount of tax payable beyond the normal amount. To a great extent these rules are politically motivated and are a response to public and media pressures, which are often based on misconceptions. For example, the media often report how many individual and corporate taxpayers earn high incomes but do not pay income tax. For obvious reasons, such statements upset many taxpayers, most of whom are struggling along under the normal tax burden. The problem is that many of the statistics quoted in the media are misleading. For example, an individual who earns business income of $100,000 in 20X1, but who then reduces that income by applying a large loss carry-over from the previous year, may well be reported as having income in 20X1 of $100,000 and no tax payable. Many CCRA statistics report net income and the related tax figure rather than *taxable* income and its related tax.

There are two basic areas where the normal tax calculation may be adjusted to a higher amount. These areas relate to what are sometimes called the "give and take-back rules." One is the alternative minimum tax; the other is the special tax on old-age security benefits. Both are discussed next.

A. The Alternative Minimum Tax

The alternative minimum tax rules are designed to impose a minimum level of tax on individuals when the normal amount of tax has been reduced as a result of certain "tax preference" items being included in income.[30] It is important to establish at the outset that this additional tax is not a permanent tax. Any additional minimum tax that is paid in one year can be carried forward for up to seven years to reduce the normal tax of a future year to the extent that the minimum tax rules do not apply. For example, consider the following information:

	20X1 Income reduced by tax preference items	20X2 Normal income (no tax preference)	Total
Taxable income	$20,000	$100,000	$120,000
Normal tax	$ 4,000	$ 40,000	$ 44,000
Tax increase (decrease) due to minimum tax	7,000	(7,000)	–0–
Actual taxes paid	$11,000	$ 33,000	$ 44,000

For 20X1 the income was reduced by a number of tax preferences so that the actual tax increased from $4,000 to $11,000. However, there were no tax preference items in the 20X2 income, so the tax for that year was reduced by the previous year's increase. Consequently, the total tax for the two years was the same ($44,000) but the years in which the tax was paid was adjusted.

When the alternative minimum tax is calculated, taxable income is revised to exclude certain tax preference items to the extent that they exceed a base amount of $40,000. The entire income is then subject to a federal tax rate of 16% rather than the graduated rates that normally apply (16%, 22%, 26%, and 29%). The dividend tax credit is also excluded (as a result of the elimination of the gross-up described above). If the revised federal tax is greater than the normal federal tax, the former applies. Provincial taxes are then calculated on the revised amount.

Some of the tax preference items referred to here are now listed. Taxable income is increased by the following:

• The non-taxable portion of net capital gains earned (i.e., ½ of net capital gains).

• Deductions claimed from certain specified tax-shelter investments, including Canadian exploration expenses, Canadian oil and gas property expenses, and capital cost allowance on film investments, to the extent that any of these create losses.

• Employee stock option deduction.

And taxable income is reduced by the following:

• The gross-up on Canadian dividends (see Chapter 7).

• A basic exemption of $40,000.

It will be clear from the next sample calculation that the increases to taxable income are offset, to a large degree, by both the $40,000 exemption and the lower tax rate of 16%. Unless a taxpayer has major losses from a tax-shelter investment, the minimum tax will often not apply. It should also be noted that under the current tax regime, very few tax-shelter investments are available.

---

30 ITA 127.5 to .55.

To demonstrate, consider a taxpayer who in a particular year received a salary of $140,000, and a capital gain of $400,000 (taxable – $200,000), of which $75,000 was eligible for the capital gain deduction on qualified small business corporation shares. She also received Canadian dividends of $4,000 ($5,000 after the gross-up). This taxpayer is single.

The normal taxable income and the revised (alternative minimum tax) taxable income are calculated and compared in the first table below. The normal tax payable for the year (assuming provincial taxes of a fictitious province as used in Exhibit 10-5) would be $107,923, calculated as shown in the second table.

The alternative minimum tax does not apply unless its federal tax calculation is greater than the normal federal tax amount. In this case the federal tax under the AMT calculation is $67,399 (16% of $429,000 = $68,640, less the personal tax credit of $1,241 = $67,399; notice that the dividend tax credit was ignored). The normal federal tax is greater— $70,655. Therefore, in spite of the tax preferences, the alternative minimum tax has no effect on this taxpayer.

It should be noted that the alternative minimum tax applies only to individuals.

	Normal taxable income	Taxable income for AMT	Increase (decrease)
Salary	$140,000	$140,000	–0–
Dividends	5,000	4,000	(1,000)
Capital gain	200,000	400,000	200,000
Net income	345,000	544,000	199,000
Capital gain deduction	(75,000)	(75,000)	–0–
AMT exemption	–0–	(40,000)	(40,000)
	$270,000	$429,000	$159,000

Federal tax (2003 rates):
First	$ 32,183 @ 16%	$ 5,149
Next	32,181 @ 22%	7,080
Next	40,284 @ 26%	10,474
Remaining	165,352 @ 29%	47,952
	$270,000	70,655

Dividend tax credit (13 1/3% of $5,000)	(667)
Personal credit (2003 rate)	(1,241)
Basic federal tax	68,747
Provincial tax	39,176
	$107,923

B. Special Tax on Old Age Security Benefits

The federal government provides monthly old-age security payments on a universal basis. These payments are taxable (see Chapter 9).

As a challenge to the concept of universal social services, the income tax system imposes a special tax on individuals who receive old-age security benefits and also earn more than $57,174 (indexed) in net income for tax purposes.[31] The special tax is equal to 15% of net

31 This amount is indexed and adjusted periodically.

income (i.e., not taxable income) in excess of $57,174, up to a maximum of the old-age security payments.[32] For example, an individual who earns $86,000 of property income plus $5,000 of old-age security (total income—$90,000) pays an additional tax of $5,000 (15% of [$91,000 – $57,174] = $5,074, but the maximum is $5,000). Notice that in this case, the tax is 100% of the old-age security benefits.

As compensation for the fact that old-age security benefits have already been included in income, the amount of the special tax can be deducted in arriving at net income for the year. Effectively, this removes the regular tax cost on that income in favour of a higher special tax. Because the tax on these benefits can equal 100% of the income, the special tax is referred to as a "clawback"—that is, what is given is fully returned. The only result is higher administration costs for both the government and each taxpayer to whom it applies. A similar clawback tax applies to employment insurance benefits, but with a different threshold amount.

VII. Tax Planning Checklist

Below are the primary tax planning items relating to the major topics discussed in this chapter.

1. Always remember the definition of a small business corporation, and plan for the opportunity to use the capital gain deduction of $500,000. Steps can be taken to ensure that the shares of the corporation qualify for the higher deduction.

2. Try to minimize the cumulative net investment loss (CNIL) whenever possible, in order to retain the option of utilizing the full capital gain deduction. For example, if funds are borrowed, try to use the loans for business purposes and any available cash for investment acquisitions. This shifts expenses to the business activities and reduces investment borrowing costs. Also, a taxpayer who owns shares of a private corporation can declare dividends to increase investment income and offset the CNIL.

3. Charitable donations in excess of $200 have a higher tax credit, so a greater tax saving will occur if family donations are claimed by only one spouse.

4. A taxpayer who wishes to reduce taxable income, and who can choose between a capital gain deduction and a net capital loss carry-over, should opt for the former, because of the risk that it may be repealed.

5. The capital gain deduction does not apply to proprietorships. Consequently, consider incorporating the business so that it qualifies as a small business corporation.

6. Political donations should be divided among family members so that the highest-rate tax credit can be enjoyed as many times as possible.

7. The deduction of loss carry-overs is optional. Consider delaying this deduction if income in future years is likely to be taxed at a higher rate.

8. Non-capital losses have a limited carry-over period. Be sure to use the discretionary provisions of the *Income Tax Act* to delay expenses (or create income) when there is a risk those losses may expire.

9. Always consider alternative business structures (proprietorship, corporation, partnership, and so on) before consummating a new venture. While doing so, anticipate the tax treatment of possible losses and consider choosing the structure that will allow the greatest use of those losses at the earliest time possible. Remember that it is more difficult to use the losses when the entity is controlled by other parties (see Chapters 15 and 16).

---

32 ITA 180.2(1) to (3).

10. If net capital losses are available for carry-over, future investment strategies should be reviewed. It may be possible to dispose of one investment without incurring tax on the gain (by using the loss carry-over), and to replace it with a higher-yield investment. Previously, this may not have been possible, if the situation was such that the potential tax on sale of the first asset overcame the advantage of the higher yield on the proposed new investment.

11. Always apply the marginal tax rates of the various types of income when making investment decisions so that after-tax returns, and the potential after-tax losses if those should occur, can be compared.

VIII. Summary and Conclusion

This chapter has completed the tax framework for individuals by examining the conversion of net income for tax purposes to taxable income, and the structure for the calculation of tax. The reader is reminded that this chapter applies only to taxpayers who are individuals—previous chapters applied to *all* taxpayers.

An individual's taxable income is determined by reducing net income for tax purposes by a limited number of special reductions. The most important special reduction is the one that allows the deduction of losses from other years that could not be used in the year incurred because of a lack of income in those years. Loss carry-overs of a capital nature can be used only to the extent that capital gains were achieved; all other types of loss carry-overs can be utilized against any source of income. Because of the restrictions placed on the use of such losses, the taxpayer must give them special attention in order to ensure that they will be utilized so as to maximize after-tax cash flow.

To reduce the risk of loss expiration, an individual can delay the deduction of certain discretionary expenses such as capital cost allowance, and can also trigger the realization of gains attached to assets that have appreciated in value. Before embarking on business activities, taxpayers should examine the possibility of future losses with an eye to considering which organization structures would speed up their utilization and reduce the risk of their expiring. In addition, unused losses must be factored into future investment strategies so that accurate after-tax returns can be projected.

The calculation of tax is affected by both provincial and federal tax jurisdictions. Federal tax has four specific rates, which apply to different levels of the individual's taxable income. All provinces and territories also have multiple rates that apply to various levels of income. Of primary importance to the decision-making process is the combined federal and provincial rate of tax that will apply to future returns on investment. The individual must not only understand the current marginal rates, but also anticipate future marginal rates in light of economic trends. While the fundamental principles of income determination rarely change, the rates of tax applicable to income (especially provincial rates) are subject to frequent changes. It is the reader's responsibility to impose these rate changes on the framework developed in this chapter.

Reading List

Income Tax Act References

	Section
Employee stock options	110(d), (d.1)
Capital gain deduction—small business corporation shares	110.6(2.1)
Capital gain deduction—qualified farm property	110.6(2)
Non-capital losses	111(1)(a)

Net capital losses	111(1)(b), (1.1)
Restricted farm losses	111(1)(c)
Farm losses	111(1)(d)
Year of death	111(2)
Losses—definitions	111(8)(a) to (b.2)
Ordering of applying provisions	111.1
Federal tax	117(2), (6)
Federal tax—indexing	117.1(1)(d)
Individual surtax	180.1
Dividend tax credit	121
Tax credits—personal	118(1)
Foreign tax credits	126
Donations credit	118.1(1) to (3)
Medical expense credit	118.2(1)
Tuition credit	118.5(1)(a), (b)
Mental or physical impairment credit	118.3, .4
CPP and EIC credit	118.7
Transfer of unused credits	118.8, .9
Ordering of credits	118.92
Goods and services tax credit	122.5
Political contributions	127(3)
Other tax credits	127(1) to (10)
Alternative minimum tax	127.5 to .55
Allocation of provincial income	Regulations 2600 to 2607
Tax on family allowances and old-age security benefits	180.2(1), (2)

Canada Customs and Revenue Agency Publications

IT-113R4	Benefits to employees—stock options.
IT-232R3	Non-capital losses, net capital losses, restricted farm losses, farm losses, and limited partnership losses—their composition and deductibility in arriving at taxable income.
IT-523	Order of provisions applicable in computing an individual's taxable income and tax payable.
IT-513	Personal tax credits.
IT-515R	Tuition tax credits.
IT-519R	Medical expense tax credit.
IT-270R2	Foreign tax credit.
IT-520	Unused foreign tax credits—carry-forward and carry-back.

Other Publications

Bernstein, J., "Loss Utilization by Individuals and Corporations," Proceedings of the 48th Tax Conference, Canadian Tax Foundation, p. 51.1.

Demonstration Question

Carol Tse is employed as a marketing manager for TX Ltd., a Canadian-controlled private corporation. She is divorced and supports her two children. In September 20X5, Tse was transferred from Regina to TX Ltd.'s head office in Calgary, Alberta. Her 20X5 financial information is summarized on the following page.

1. Tse received a salary of $90,000. From this, TX deducted Canada Pension Plan (CPP) and Employment Insurance (EI) of $2,400 and income tax of $27,000. During 20X5, Tse sold shares of TX Ltd. for $30,000. She had acquired the shares in 20X1 under a stock option arrangement for $12,000. At the time of purchase the shares were valued at $14,000. TX Ltd. has indicated that all of its assets are being used in an active business. In 20X5, Tse received taxable dividends of $3,000 from TX Ltd.

2. Tse incurred moving expenses in 20X5 of $7,000, which qualified as allowable deductions for tax purposes.

3. In 20X3, Tse inherited a small farm acreage. The farm is operated by a neighbour, who assumes 25% of the farm's revenues and expenses. In 20X5, Tse's share of the profits was $6,000.

4. During the year, Tse sold a work of art for $3,000 that originally cost $2,000.

5. Tse's 19-year-old daughter attended university for eight months in 20X5 and paid tuition fees of $3,000. She earned a salary of $6,000, from which the employer deducted CPP/EI of $250. Tse's son is 14 years old and earned income of $1,000 from a bond inherited from his grandmother. During 20X5, Tse paid dental fees of $2,500 on behalf of the son.

6. In 20X5, Tse contributed $500 to a registered political party, and $2,000 to registered charities.

7. A review of Tse's 20X4 tax return shows the following amounts carried forward to 20X5:

Net capital loss	$ 4,000
Listed personal property loss	2,000
Restricted farm loss	8,000
Unused capital gain deduction	210,000
Cumulative net investment loss (CNIL)	5,000

Required:
For the 20X5 taxation year, calculate Tse's *net income for tax purposes, taxable income,* and *federal income tax.*

Solution:
Before we complete the calculation, a few items require comment. Tse earned income in two provinces in 20X5. However, she will be subject to provincial tax in Alberta because it is the location of her residence on the last day of the taxation year (the Alberta tax is excluded from the calculations). The TX Ltd. shares sold in 20X5 are qualified small business corporation shares and therefore eligible for the capital gain deduction, provided that it has not been used to this point. Also, the shares were part of a stock option arrangement from 20X1. This means that the employment income from the exercise of the option in 20X1 is taxable in 20X5 (the year of sale) rather than in the year of acquisition, as might be the case if the shares were from a public corporation (see Chapter 4). There are some items in the calculation that can be claimed at the option of the taxpayer. These were claimed in 20X5 and are discussed in the solution.

Net income for tax purposes and taxable income:

Employment income:			
Salary			$ 90,000
Stock option (TX shares)—$14,000 – $12,000			2,000
			92,000
Business income—farming			6,000
Property income—Canadian dividends			
$3,000 × 1.25			3,750
			101,750
Taxable capital gains:			
TX shares— ½ ($30,000 – $14,000)		8,000	
Net gains from listed personal property:			
Work of art— ½ ($3,000 – $2,000)	500		
Listed personal property loss			
carried forward from 20X4	(500)	–0–	8,000
			109,750
Other deduction—moving expenses			(7,000)
Net income for tax purposes			102,750
Deduct:			
Stock option reduction— ½ × $2,000			
(employment benefit)			(1,000)
Net capital loss forward			(4,000)
Restricted farm loss (to the limit of 20X5			
farming income)			(6,000)
Capital gain deduction (note below)			(2,750)
Taxable income			$ 89,000

Note:

As indicated, the gain on the TX shares of $8,000 is eligible for the capital gain deduction, and there is a sufficient amount of unused lifetime deduction available ($210,000). However, the eligible gain of $8,000 must be reduced by the net capital loss claimed in 20X5 and the CNIL at the end of the year. The capital gain deduction is therefore reduced to $2,750, as follows:

Qualified gain for the year		$8,000
Deduct:		
Net capital loss claimed		(4,000)
CNIL:		
Balance at end of 20X4	5,000	
20X5 property income—dividends	(3,750)	(1,250)
		$2,750

It is important to remember that the deduction of the net capital loss in the current year is optional. If it is not claimed in the current year, it can be carried forward indefinitely. This would increase the amount available for the capital gain deduction in the current year by $4,000. It may be prudent to do this, as there is always a possibility that the capital gain deduction will be cancelled in a future year.

Federal and provincial income tax:
  Federal tax:
  Primary tax:

16% × $32,183	$ 5,149
22% × $32,181	7,080
26% × $24,636	6,405
$89,000	18,634

Deduct first-category tax credits:

Dividend tax credit—13⅓% × $3,750	(500)
Basic	(1,241)
Equivalent to spouse (son has lowest income)	
$1,054 – 16% ($1,000 – $659)	(999)
CPP/EI—16% × $2,400	(384)
Tuition and education credit transferred from daughter (note below)	(992)
Charitable donations—(16% × $200) + (29% × $1,800)	(554)
Medical expenses—16% × ($2,500 – $1,756)	(119)
Basic federal tax	13,845

Deduct second-category credit:

Political contribution—(75% × $200) + (50% × $300)	(300)
Total federal tax	13,545

Note:

Transfer of education and tuition credits from daughter:

Daughter's taxable income	$ 6,000
Federal tax—16% × $6,000	$ 960
Deduct:	
Basic credit	(1,241)
CPP/EI credit—16% × $250	(40)
Tax before education and tuition credit	–0–
Tuition credit—16% × $3,000	(480)
Education credit (*2003* rate)—16% × $400 × 8 months	(512)
Unused credit available for transfer	$ 992

Remember, the transfer of the unused education and tuition credits is optional. The daughter can choose to retain the credits and carry them forward (indefinitely), to be used by her in a future year when she earns sufficient income.

Review Questions

1. Briefly explain the difference, for individuals, between net income for tax purposes and taxable income.

2. Explain the difference between an allowable capital loss and a net capital loss.

3. Describe the tax treatment of net capital losses.

4. Explain how a non-capital loss is created, and how it is treated for tax purposes.

5. Is it always worthwhile to utilize a net capital loss or a non-capital loss as soon as the opportunity arises? Explain.

6. Is it possible for taxpayers to pay tax on more income than they actually earned over a period of years? Explain.

7. How does the risk of not being able to utilize a business loss for tax purposes vary for each of the following individuals?

   • *Individual A* operates the business as a proprietorship.
   • *Individual B* is the sole shareholder of a corporation that owns the business.
   • *Individual C* is a 30% shareholder of a corporation that operates the business.
   • *Individual D* is a 30% partner of a business partnership.

8. What can a taxpayer do to reduce the risk of not being able to utilize a net capital loss or a non-capital loss?

9. Two separate taxpayers are considering investing in shares of the same public corporation. How is it possible that the risk associated with that investment may be greater for one taxpayer than for the other?

10. If an individual has a net taxable capital gain in a year that qualifies for a capital gain deduction, is there any advantage to not claiming the applicable portion of the deduction in that year? Explain.

11. If an individual is considering selling his business to a daughter, does it make any difference to him whether that business is a proprietorship or is housed within a corporation?

12. What is the difference between the basic federal tax and the total federal tax?

13. What is the difference between a tax deduction and a tax credit?

14. An individual usually has taxable income in a year of $60,000 and pays federal and provincial taxes totalling $20,000. Would this information be relevant when the implications of investing in a partnership that operates a small retail business are considered?

15. Does an individual who lives in Alberta and receives a $100 dividend obtain the same tax reduction from the dividend tax credit as an individual who resides in New Brunswick? Explain.

16. In what circumstances may an individual be subject to provincial tax in more than one province in a particular year?

17. An individual resides in Manitoba and operates a business that has no profit from its Alberta operations. Is it possible for that person to have a tax liability in Alberta in a particular year?

Problems

Problem One

The financial results of an individual are outlined below for three years.

	20X1	20X2	20X3
Employment income	$22,000	$27,000	$40,000
Taxable capital gains:			
Listed personal property	–0–	–0–	5,000
Other capital property	20,000	–0–	6,000
Allowable capital losses:			
Listed personal property	–0–	(9,000)	–0–
Shares of a small business corporation	–0–	(20,000)	–0–
Other capital property	–0–	(24,000)	–0–
Share of a business partnership's			
income (loss)	7,000	(57,000)	–0–
Actual dividends from			
Canadian corporations	12,000	4,000	–0–
RRSP contributions	4,000	–0–	–0–

Required:

1. Determine the individual's net capital losses, non-capital losses, and unused listed personal property losses for 20X2.

2. Determine the individual's minimum taxable income for 20X1 and 20X3.

Problem Two

Barbara Legault operates a full-time law practice in southwestern Ontario. In her spare time she maintains a small rural acreage for the purpose of growing and selling Christmas trees. In addition, she derives income from various investments and is an art collector.

Below are her financial results for 20X1.

Net income from law practice	$ 97,000
Loss on tree farm operation	(12,500)
Gross rents received on rental property	28,000
Operating expenses on rental property before capital cost allowance	37,000
Gain on sale of shares of public corporations	80,000
Loss on sale of summer cottage	4,000
Gain on sale of oil painting	8,000
Gain on sale of shares of a small business corporation	20,000
Lump-sum payment to ex-husband as part of divorce settlement	40,000
Loss on sale of shares of a public corporation	14,000

At the end of 20X0, the following tax accounts existed:

Net listed personal property losses forward from 20X0 (represents the actual loss)	$ 4,000
Undepreciated capital cost allowance on rental property	160,000
Net capital losses	7,000
Cumulative net investment loss	14,000

Legault had not previously used any of her lifetime capital gain deduction.

Required:
What is Legault's taxable income for 20X1?

Problem Three

In 20X1, Gary Kwok, who is single, earned the following income and incurred the following losses: employment income, $16,000; business loss, $4,000; taxable capital gains, $7,000; property income (interest), $18,000; allowable capital loss from the sale of shares of public corporations, $9,000; allowable capital loss from the sale of shares of a Canadian-controlled private corporation that qualifies as a small business corporation, $2,000.

At the end of 20X0, Kwok had unused net capital losses of $16,000 and unused non-capital losses of $37,000. Kwok does not want to pay any federal tax in 20X1. For 20X1, Kwok is entitled to a basic personal tax credit of $1,241.

Required:
Assuming Kwok's wishes are met, what is the maximum amount of non-capital losses remaining for carry-forward after 20X1?

Problem Four

Abra Swan is 30 years old and single. She is employed as a middle-level manager with a national Canadian company. After living and working for five years in Regina, Saskatchewan, she was transferred to her employer's office in Winnipeg on December 15, 20X1.

Her financial transactions for the 20X1 taxation year are shown below.

1. Swan received an annual salary of $50,000, but her take-home pay for the year was only $36,800 (see top of next page).

2. During the current year, Swan purchased 1,000 shares of her employer's company (a public corporation) under a stock option program. The shares cost $10 each and at the time of purchase had a market value of $14 per share. When the stock option was granted two years ago, the share price was $11. To fund the purchase, she borrowed $10,000 from her bank. During the year, she paid interest of $800 on the loan.

Gross salary	$50,000
Amounts withheld by employer:	
Income tax	(10,000)
Company pension contribution	(2,000)
Canada Pension Plan	(700)
Employment Insurance	(500)
	$36,800

3. The previous year, Swan had unwisely invested in commodity futures and lost a large portion of her savings. She considered this loss to be a business loss but was unable to use the full amount for tax purposes because her other income was not sufficient. Of the total loss, $6,000 was unused.

4. As well, Swan had the following receipts for 20X1:

Dividends from taxable Canadian corporations	$ 4,000
Dividends from a foreign corporation of $2,000, less foreign taxes of $200	1,800
Cash received from RRSP cancellation	2,000
Proceeds from the sale of public corporation shares (originally purchased for $20,000)	26,000

5. In 20X1 she made the following disbursements:

Mortgage payments on her new home	$1,000
Life insurance	400
Charitable donations	800
Contribution to a federal political party	600
Tuition fees to a university	300

Required:
For the 20X1 taxation year, determine Swan's

(a) net income for tax purposes;
(b) taxable income; and,
(c) federal tax liability.

To which province will Swan pay provincial tax?

Problem Five
Carl Kay is the vice-president of KM Ltd., a Canadian-controlled private corporation located in Halifax, Nova Scotia. KM operates a real estate development business, constructing and selling commercial buildings and residential apartments. Kay's 20X3 financial transactions include the following:

- Kay received a salary of $95,000 from KM. From this amount, KM deducted CPP and EI of $2,100 and income tax of $30,000. The company provided him with a car that cost $40,000 and that has an undepreciated capital cost of $18,000. The operating costs of $3,000 were paid by KM. In 20X3, Kay drove the car 20 000 km, of which

8 000 km was for employment purposes. KM contributed $4,000 on Kay's behalf to a deferred profit sharing plan. Although KM does not have a group life insurance plan, it paid Kay's personal life insurance premium of $1,000 (coverage – $75,000).

- During the year, Kay sold 1,000 shares of KM Ltd. for $10 per share. He had acquired the shares three years earlier for $6 per share as part of a company stock option plan. At the time of purchase, the shares were valued at $7 per share.

- In 20X2, Kay constructed a 10-suite apartment block. He sold the property in 20X3 for $800,000, which was $150,000 more than the original land and building cost. He received $80,000 of the proceeds in cash, with the balance due in five annual instalments beginning in 20X4. The property incurred a net rental loss of $7,000 (before amortization).

- Kay sold his summer cottage for $90,000 after it was announced that a waste disposal site would be developed in the area. He had purchased the cottage six years earlier for $120,000.

- In 20X0, Kay loaned $16,000 to Alloy Ltd., a Canadian-controlled private corporation. All of the company's assets are used in an active business. The 20X2 interest of $1,400, which Kay included in income, has not been received. The company is in severe financial difficulty and may not survive beyond next year.

- Kay sold shares of a public corporation, purchased in 20X1 for $12,000, for $20,000.

- In November, Kay received a legal bill for $2,000 relating to a dispute over a tax reassessment. Kay paid $1,200 in December 20X3, and the balance in January 20X4.

- Kay received dividends of $3,000 from Canadian corporations and $1,800 from a foreign corporation. The foreign corporation remitted a 10% withholding tax to its government.

- Kay celebrated his 65th birthday in December 20X3. He supports his spouse, who is retired. She had investment income of $4,000 in 20X3. During the year, Kay made gifts of $3,000 to a local charity. He paid tuition fees of $300 to attend a three-month evening course at a university.

- Kay has used his entire capital gain deduction. At the end of 20X2 he had unused net capital losses of $12,000 and non-capital losses of $7,000.

Required:
Calculate Kay's minimum 20X3 net income for tax purposes, taxable income, and federal income tax.

Problem Six (comprehensive)
Sandra Dumont is a lawyer. For five years, until June 30, 20X5, she was employed by Calco Ltd., a national restaurant company. On July 1, 20X5, she began to practise law as a sole proprietor from an office in her home.

Dumont has asked you to prepare her 20X5 income tax return. At a recent meeting you gathered the information provided in Exhibits I and II.

Required:
1. Determine Dumont's *minimum income for tax purposes* in accordance with the aggregating formula of section 3 of the *Income Tax Act*, and her *minimum taxable income* for the 20X5 taxation year.

2. Based on your answer to question 1, calculate Dumont's *federal income tax* for the 20X5 taxation year.

3. Why did CCRA deny the deduction of Dumont's 20X3 convention expenses? Can she obtain a deduction for the proposed 20X6 convention? If so, why?

Exhibit I:
Sandra Dumont
Information Regarding
Work at Calco and
Law Practice

1. Dumont's salary to June 30, 20X5, was $51,200. From this, Calco deducted CPP and EI of $2,100, income tax of $16,000, and $300 for Dumont's portion of the private group medical insurance premium. An additional premium of $300 was paid by Calco. Also, Calco paid the $200 premium for Dumont's group term life insurance coverage of $50,000.

2. On June 30, 20X5, Dumont returned the company car that Calco had provided her. The car had a cost of $30,000, and Calco's undepreciated balance was $18,000. Calco also paid the operating costs for the car, which amounted to $2,100. Dumont drove her car 16 000 km, of which 12 000 km were for business use.

3. Dumont travelled by air when working for Calco. In March 20X5, she and her husband used some of her accumulated frequent-flyer points to obtain free airline tickets for a vacation. As a result, they each saved the $800 airfare.

4. In 20X3, Dumont borrowed $20,000 from Calco. She has paid interest at 5% on the loan. Dumont used the borrowed funds for the down payment to purchase a rental property. CCRA's prescribed interest rate was 9% in 20X5. Dumont repaid the loan on June 30, 20X5.

5. On June 30, 20X5, Dumont sold 500 shares of Calco Ltd. for $20 per share to the company's controlling shareholder. Calco had issued the shares to Dumont at $10 in 20X2. At that time, the shares were appraised at $12. Calco Ltd. is a Canadian-controlled private corporation. At the time of the share sale, all of Calco's assets were being used in an active business.

6. Dumont began practising law from her home office on July 1, 20X5. She purchased the client list and files of a retiring lawyer for $50,000. She also purchased a computer for $4,000 and a legal library for $5,600.

7. On July 4, 20X5, Dumont purchased an automobile for $31,000. She used the car 60% of the time for her law practice.

8. For the six months ended December 31, 20X5, the financial statements of Dumont's law practice showed a profit of $41,000. The gross revenue of $88,000 consisted of the following:

Fees billed and received	$47,000
Fees billed but unpaid at the year end	24,000
Work in progress—not billed	17,000
	$88,000

Dumont indicated that she wanted to elect under section 34 of the *Income Tax Act*.

9. Operating expenses for the law practice included the following:

Liability insurance	$ 2,200
Depreciation and amortization	9,100
Reserve for bad debts	1,200
Golf club dues—while attending the club, clients are entertained approximately 30% of the time	1,600
Charitable donations	800
Promotion—client lunches	400
Secretarial services	12,000
Computer software—word processing and billing program	900

10. Dumont uses 12 square metres of her house exclusively as an office for her law practice. Expenses for the entire 80-square-metre home for all of 20X5 consist of the following:

Insurance	$ 700
Mortgage interest	9,000
Property taxes	2,300
Utilities	3,000
	$15,000

The financial statements do not include the home-office costs.

Exhibit II:
Sandra Dumont
Other Financial
Information

1. Dumont owns a rental property, which she purchased in 20X3. Details of the rent and expenses in 20X5 are as follows:

Rental		$6,000
Repairs and maintenance	1,200	
Property tax	900	
Interest on first mortgage	3,300	(5,400)
		$ 600

As of December 31, 20X5, there were no unpaid rents from the tenant.

2. In 20X3, while employed at Calco, Dumont attended a national law convention. She deducted her expenses of $2,300 on her 20X3 tax return. Her employer willingly gave her the time off from work to attend the convention even though it was not directly related to her employment work. In 20X5, Dumont received a reassessment notice from CCRA disallowing the entire convention expense deduction. Now that Dumont is practising law, she will attend the 20X6 convention to upgrade her skills.

3. In 20X5, Dumont contributed $11,000 to her RRSP and another $1,000 to a spousal RRSP. She has contributed the same amount to the spousal plan for the past four years. On December 20, 20X5, her husband withdrew $4,000 from this spousal account.

4. The following additional receipts and disbursements occurred during 20X5:

Paid dental fees	$2,900
Paid contributions to a registered federal political party	1,000
Paid interest on late payment of 20X4 income tax	240
Received cash dividends on Calco shares	1,000
Received proceeds from the sale of a silver tea set (original cost—$1,600)	1,100

5. In 20X5, Dumont received 100 shares of Parla Ltd., a public corporation. The shares were a stock dividend on the 2,000 shares she purchased in 20X1 for $4 per share. At the time of the stock dividend, the shares were at $8. She sold the 100 stock dividend shares in December 20X5, at $7.

6. Dumont's husband earned $110,000 in 20X5.

7. A review of Dumont's 20X4 tax return showed the following:

Maximum RRSP deduction available in 20X5	$10,500
Capital gain deductions claimed in past years	75,000
Net income from real estate rentals (after deducting a reserve for uncollectible rents of $500)	860
Undepreciated capital cost—class 1 (rental property)	52,000
Reserve for unpaid rents	500

Problem Seven

Victor is 63 years old and retired from his employment with Meter Ltd., a Canadian public corporation, on September 30, 20X8.

Victor has asked you to help him prepare his 20X8 tax return and to advise him on certain other tax matters. Information regarding his financial activities for 20X8 is summarized below.

1. Victor's gross salary to September 30, 20X8 was $80,000. From this amount, Meter deducted income tax of $22,000 and CPP and EI of $2,200. In addition to salary, Meter paid $9,000 directly into Victor's RRSP at a local bank. Victor paid the annual RRSP administration fee of $100.

    During the year, until September 30, 20X8, Victor had the use of an employer's automobile. Meter paid the *monthly* lease cost of $400 plus monthly operating expenses of $200. Victor drove the car a total of 16 000 km, of which 4 000 km was for personal use.

2. Victor suffered an illness in 20X8 and was off work for six weeks. During this period, the employer's group sickness and accident insurance policy paid Victor $4,000 for lost salary. The entire premium of $500 was paid by Meter in 20X8. Due to his illness, Victor incurred medical expenses of $3,000 in 20X8.

3. In 20X5, Meter granted Victor an option to acquire up to 5,000 of its shares at $8 per share. At that time the shares were trading at the same price. In January 20X8 he purchased 2,000 shares when they were trading at $10 per share. He purchased an additional 1,000 shares in July 20X8, when they were trading at $15 per share. In

November 20X8, Victor sold 2,000 shares at $20 per share after receiving a cash dividend of $800.

4. In 20X7, as a sideline, Victor began carving wood bowls for resale. He hoped to generate a small profit and keep himself occupied during his retirement. He made his first sales in 20X8, which resulted in a loss of $8,850. This excludes amortization but includes a deduction of $4,000 for the cost of woodworking equipment, which is included in class 43.

5. On January 2, 20X8, Victor gifted his stamp collection to his grandson. He had acquired the collection over the past 15 years at a cost of $7,000. The collection has recently been appraised at $12,000. At the same time, he gifted a convertible bond valued at $20,000 to his wife. The bond had been purchased in 20X3 for $16,000.

6. On November 15, 20X8, Victor received $1,020 from an acquaintance in exchange for an option to purchase a small piece of land he had acquired four years earlier with the intention of constructing a rental property. For financial reasons, the construction plan was terminated.

7. Victor is married and lives with his wife. She retired in 20X7 and will begin receiving her pension in 20X9. During 20X8, she earned interest income of $5,000, which includes $900 from the convertible bond she received from her husband.

8. Victor's tax return from the previous year showed the following balances:

Listed personal property losses forward to 20X8	$ 1,000
Maximum RRSP deduction available in 20X8	11,000

Required:

1. Determine Victor's *minimum net income for tax purposes* in accordance with the format of section 3 of the *Income Tax Act* for the 20X8 taxation year.

2. Based on your answer to question 1, calculate Victor's *minimum federal income tax liability* for the 20X8 taxation year.

3. Now that Victor is retired, can he make a contribution to his RRSP in 20X9? If so, estimate the maximum deduction available.

Problem Eight

Harvey and Walter Bachynski operate a welding supply business as a partnership in Sackville, New Brunswick. Over the years, their sales territory has expanded steadily, as they maintain an efficient, customer-oriented business.

However, their success has created problems. More and more customers are demanding their services, and the time required to reach those customers has increased. The brothers feel that because of this, service to distant areas is suffering from a lack of efficiency. In response, during the current year they opened their first service depot, in Amherst, Nova Scotia, 50 km away, just across the provincial boundary. The new depot is in rented premises. It maintains a supply of inventory and is staffed by two new employees.

Because of the start-up costs, the new depot operation has suffered a loss of $20,000 in the current year. However, the brothers are convinced that they have made the right decision.

A summary of the partnership income statement for the year is provided in the following table:

Sales		$400,000
Cost of sales		100,000
Gross profit		300,000
Expenses:		
Salaries and wages	100,000	
Travel and delivery	20,000	
Rent	12,000	
Advertising and promotion	4,000	
Office and supplies	2,000	
Insurance	4,000	
Utilities	6,000	148,000
		152,000
Net loss from new depot operation		(20,000)
Net income before taxes		$132,000

The brothers are pleased with the profit, although a large portion of it is a result of their own efforts. As the business is a partnership of two individuals, the brothers do not pay themselves salaries. Instead, they simply draw out some of their profits for personal living expenses.

The net loss of $20,000 from the new depot is calculated in the following table:

Sales		$ 70,000
Cost of sales		30,000
Gross profit		40,000
Expenses:		
Rent	7,000	
Salaries	40,000	
Advertising	10,000	
Supplies	2,000	
Insurance	1,000	60,000
Net loss		$ (20,000)

Each brother has other sources of income that generate approximately $30,000 annually.

Required:
For each brother, determine the amount of taxable income that will be subject to provincial income tax in New Brunswick and Nova Scotia for 20X1.

Problem Nine

Sam Collins had been investing for several years. Most of his investments were in the stock market. For several years he made substantial capital gains. As his success grew he began to invest in riskier shares.

Last year, after a serious market downturn, Collins suffered significant losses that left him with cash resources of only $50,000. He was unable to use all of the capital losses for tax purposes and was left with unused net capital losses of $70,000.

The substantial losses have shattered his confidence in the stock market. He has requested that his broker find him a secure bond in which to invest his remaining $50,000. Collins is not destitute, as he has a substantial annual salary of $115,000.

His broker has suggested a five-year corporate bond that will provide an interest return of 13%, and at the same time, he has tried to convince Collins to remain in the stock market but to acquire only high-level blue-chip shares. In this vein, he has suggested, as a possible alternative to the bond, a common-share investment in a utility company that historically provides an annual dividend return of 5% as well as capital growth of 6%.

In addition, the broker has indicated that any annual cash returns can be invested in treasury bills earning 13% annually.

Required:
1. Which investment will best help Collins recover his lost capital? (Use a five-year period for your analysis.)

2. What rate of return must the bond offer in order for it to yield the same return as the share investment?

Problem Ten

Jennifer Jones has decided to open a small business that will be supervised by a hired manager. With her current cash resources, she will be able to acquire the necessary assets for the business and provide basic working capital. However, any losses that occur will have to be funded by an infusion of additional capital.

Jones and the new manager have just finished drawing up a business plan. It projects the following operating results over the next five years:

Year 1	loss	$(20,000)
2	loss	(10,000)
3	break even	–0–
4	profit	10,000
5	profit	20,000
Profit after 5 years		–0–

Although Jones has substantial wealth, all of her capital will be tied up for several years. In addition, all of her after-tax annual income is committed to personal living expenses. Her pre-tax annual income is over $100,000.

Jones has made an arrangement with her bank, which will provide an annual loan to cover any losses from the business. The bank will charge 10% interest. As cash flow is generated from the business, the loan will be repaid. She has yet to decide whether the business will be operated as a proprietorship or a separate corporation owned by her.

Required:

Determine the amount of the outstanding loan at the end of year 5 under both the corporate structure and the proprietorship structure. Assume that any bank loans will be obtained or repaid at the end of each year.

Chapter 11   Corporations—An Introduction

The concept of imposing an income tax on corporations is subject to two extreme points of view. At one extreme, it is argued that a corporation is simply an extension of the individual shareholders, and that any income generated should be allocated to the shareholders for tax purposes. At the other extreme is the argument that corporations control economic power and that they, rather than the individual shareholders, should be subject to full taxation. Canadian tax policy adheres to neither of these extremes, and taxes both the corporation and the individual shareholder on the basis that each is a distinct entity.

To understand the full impact of corporate taxation, one must accept two things: first, that the corporation is separate from its owners; and second, that a relationship between the two exists in which income flows first to the corporation and then to the shareholders. This two-level approach enables decision makers to identify when tax occurs along the cash-flow path and to determine whether, and when, double taxation results.

In isolation, the tax framework for corporations is completed in much the same way as it is for individuals. First, net income for tax purposes is converted to taxable income by the applying of special reductions. The most important special reductions are loss carry-overs and dividends from other corporations. Next comes the calculation of corporate tax, which follows a simple format; however, certain corporations and certain types of income are provided tax preferences.

This chapter completes the basic framework of the Canadian tax system by providing an overview of corporate taxation and establishing the fundamental relationship between the corporation and its shareholders. It also serves as an introduction to Part Three of the text, which examines the corporate structure in greater detail.

I. Relationship between the Corporation and Its Shareholders

A. Corporation Defined

When a company is incorporated, an artificial person is created that is separate from its owner or owners.[1] This artificial person is recognized by law as an entity that has the power to act in its own right and to enter into enforceable legal agreements with individuals or other corporations.

As a separate entity, the corporation can own property. Property owned by a corporation is not considered to be owned by the shareholders. While the shareholders who control the actions of the corporation may have the right to decide on how the corporate property is used, and may ultimately receive the benefits from its use, they are not the legal owners of the property.

This separation between the corporation and its owners also extends to the liability for outstanding debts and losses. Shareholders are liable for the debts of the corporation only to the extent of their contributions to the corporation in the form of share capital. In some cases, however, the net of limited liability is opened when shareholders agree to guarantee the payment of certain debts of the corporation.

In accordance with the above definition, a corporation, separate from its owners, can buy, own, sell, and lease property, and can borrow funds for its own use as well as loan funds to others.

Exhibit 11-1 illustrates which parties can form relationships with a corporation. Shareholders provide equity capital, creditors provide borrowed capital, suppliers provide property and services, customers acquire goods and services, employees provide human resources, and lessors rent property to the corporation.

It is important to recognize that a shareholder may have more than one relationship with the corporation. The shareholder, in addition to providing equity capital to the corporation, can also act as the following:

---

1 IT-343R.

Exhibit 11-1:
The Corporation and Its
Fundamental Relationships

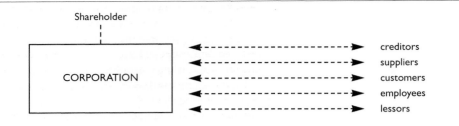

(a) a creditor who loans funds to the corporation;
(b) a supplier who sells property to the corporation such as land, buildings, equipment, goodwill, franchises, and the like;
(c) a customer who buys property or services from the corporation;
(d) an employee who is paid for services provided to the corporation; and,
(e) a lessor who rents property to the corporation.

Each of these relationships has different legal obligations and different financial results. Consequently, the tax status of income generated from each relationship may vary. In order to understand the tax impact on the shareholder and the corporation, it is necessary to compartmentalize the types of transactions that the shareholder and the corporation enter into.

B. Tax Impact of Shareholder/Corporate Relationships

The legal separation of the corporation from its shareholders creates a two-tier system of taxation. The corporation, as a separate entity, is subject to tax on its income, which is calculated in accordance with the principles established in previous chapters. The shareholder is also a separate entity and is subject to a second level of tax, on income derived from the corporation. While the shareholders of a corporation may be other corporations, all corporate income ultimately flows to individuals. Discussions in this section of the chapter relate to the fundamental structure of a corporation owned by a shareholder who is an individual.

The corporation's primary relationship is, of course, with the shareholder as the provider of equity capital to the corporation. The tax consequences of this relationship differ radically from those of the secondary relationships—those in which the shareholder also acts as a creditor, supplier, customer, employee, or lessor to the corporation. The tax consequences of both the primary and the secondary relationships are reviewed separately below.

1. The Primary Relationship

Under the primary relationship the shareholder provides equity capital to the corporation by contributing cash or other property to the corporation in exchange for shares. Shares issued can have various rights attached to them. Most commonly, shares entitle the owner to part of the accumulated earnings of the corporation on a pro rata basis. Some of the earnings may be distributed to the shareholder as dividends; this is at the discretion of the corporation's directors. The undistributed earnings remain in the corporation and will ultimately be distributed to the shareholder upon dissolution of the corporation. Such shares are referred to as "participating shares" or "common shares," and increase in value as corporate earnings are accumulated. Other shares do not participate fully in corporate earnings but rather pay a fixed dividend; any corporate profits in excess of such a dividend accrue to the benefit of the common shareholders. These shares are referred to as "non-participating shares" and usually do not increase in value.

Shareholders who provide share capital to a corporation can realize a return on investment through dividends or through a capital gain when they sell their shares at a profit.

It is important to recognize that dividends and capital gains (or losses) from corporate shares are interconnected. Increased dividends reduce the potential for capital gains; reduced dividends (for earnings retention) increase the potential for capital gains. Exhibit 11-2 diagrams the basic relationship between corporate earnings, dividends, and capital gains.

Exhibit 11-2 can be analyzed as follows:

- Profits earned by the corporation are subject to corporate tax, which is the first level of taxation on corporate income.

- The after-tax profits of the corporation can either be retained for corporate investment or distributed in whole or in part to the shareholders.

- If the corporate profits are retained, no further immediate tax occurs. However, because the undistributed profits belong to the participating shareholders, the value of the shares increases to reflect the undistributed profits. A shareholder has the right to dispose of the shares to a new shareholder, at which point he or she recognizes a capital gain for tax purposes and a second level of tax occurs. Because the capital gain is tied to corporate profits, the second level of tax means that, indirectly, the corporate profits have been taxed a second time.

- If corporate profits are distributed as dividends, the value of the shares declines and, accordingly, the potential for a capital gain also declines. The dividend is included by the individual shareholders in their income for tax purposes. Because the dividend represents the distribution of after-tax corporate profits, the corporate income is taxed a second time, indirectly.

The overall impact of the two levels of tax is diminished somewhat by the dividend tax credit and by the preferential treatment given capital gains, only one-half of which are taxable. In the previous chapter it was shown that, for individuals, the marginal rates of tax on capital gains are different from those for dividends, and that the degree of difference varies in each of the four federal tax brackets.

In summary, corporate profits are taxed a second time at the shareholder level as either dividends or capital gains. The extent to which double taxation occurs depends on the rate of corporate tax. This will be reviewed later in the chapter. The relationship between dividends and capital gains is demonstrated in the following example:

Exhibit 11-2:
Relationship of Corporate
Income, Dividends,
and Capital Gains

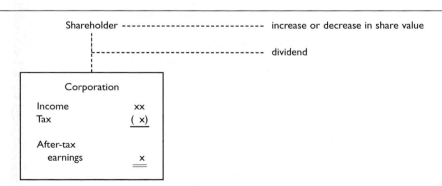

Situation: Individual A established a new corporation by contributing $1,000 as initial share capital in exchange for common shares. In the first year the corporation earned profits of $15,000 and paid corporate tax of $6,000, leaving $9,000 in after-tax retained earnings. The financial position of the corporation at the end of its first year is as follows:

Assets		Shareholders' equity	
Cash	$10,000	Share capital	$ 1,000
		Retained earnings	9,000
	$10,000		$10,000

At the end of the first year the shareholder decided to discontinue the business and to convert his share investment into cash.

Analysis: Assuming individual A is in the highest personal tax bracket, the marginal rate of tax is 30% for dividends and 23% for capital gains (see Chapter 10, Exhibit 10-6).[2]

As the controlling shareholder of the corporation, individual A has two basic options available for converting the share investment into cash: he can sell the shares, which are assumed to have a value of $10,000, to individual B; or he can wind up the corporation and pay out its earnings and share capital to himself. The tax impact for each of these alternatives is as follows:

A sells shares to B	
Proceeds of disposition	$10,000
Adjusted cost base of shares	(1,000)
Capital gain	$ 9,000
Tax @ 23%	$ 2,070
A winds up corporation	
Dividend income	$ 9,000
Tax @ 30%	$ 2,700
Return of share capital:	
Proceeds of disposition	$ 1,000
Adjusted cost base of shares	(1,000)
Capital gain	–0–

In the above situation individual A earned profits from the business venture of $15,000 and paid tax on those profits at two levels at different times. Note that the amount of tax payable varies with the method by which the corporate income is realized by the shareholder. The after-tax effects of the two options are compared in the table below.

	Dividend option	Capital gain option
Corporate profits	$15,000	$15,000
Corporate tax	(6,000)	(6,000)
Shareholder tax	(2,700)	(2,070)
After-tax income	$ 6,300	$ 6,930

2 As indicated in Chapter 10, these rates may vary from province to province.

The primary relationship can be further demonstrated by extending the previous situation one step further.

Situation: Assume that individual A in the above situation chose to sell the shares of the corporation to individual B for $10,000. Immediately after acquiring the shares, B decided that the purchase was a mistake; she now wants to convert the investment in shares into cash for investment in another venture. Individual B is subject to the same rates of marginal tax. The financial position of the corporation immediately after her acquisition is unchanged from the previous situation.

Analysis: Individual B, like individual A, also has two options available for converting the share investment into cash: she can either sell the shares to new shareholder C (for $10,000) or wind up the corporation and distribute the assets. The results are below.

B sells shares to C	
Proceeds of disposition	$10,000
Adjusted cost base of shares	(10,000)
Capital gain	–0–
Tax	–0–
B winds up corporation	
Dividend income	$ 9,000
Tax @ 30%	$ 2,700
Return of share capital:	
Proceeds of disposition	$ 1,000
Adjusted cost base	(10,000)
Capital loss	$ (9,000)
Tax *savings* if capital loss can be utilized:	
$9,000 @ 23%	$ (2,070)

Keep in mind that although the shares have changed ownership at a price of $10,000, the corporation remains unchanged, with $1,000 of share capital and $9,000 of retained earnings.

Notice that in the above situation the investment in shares by B at a cost of $10,000 was not paid to the corporation but rather to the previous shareholder, A. The $10,000 cost is represented in the company by $1,000 (initial share capital) plus $9,000 (retained earnings). Therefore, the wind-up of the corporation that returned B's investment of $10,000 was made up of dividend income of $9,000 and a capital loss of $9,000. While the dividend and capital loss balance out to zero in absolute terms, the capital loss will create tax savings at a different rate than the dividend income will create a tax cost. This greatly affects B's tax treatment. In addition, the capital loss can be offset only against capital gains unless it qualifies as an allowable business investment loss.

2. The Secondary Relationships

Where the shareholder has a secondary relationship with the corporation as a creditor, supplier, employee, customer, or lessor, the resulting tax consequences and cash flows between the parties are significantly different from those in the primary relationship. For example, because the corporation is a separate legal entity, the shareholder can be employed by the corporation and receive salary or other benefits as compensation. The compensation paid can be deducted by the corporation from its pre-tax income and is fully taxable when received by the employee/shareholder. The result of this treatment is that corporate income paid as compensation to the employee/shareholder is converted from corporate income into employment income, and taxed only once within the overall system.

Similarly, when a shareholder loans money to a corporation and receives interest, or leases property to a corporation and receives rents, corporate income is shifted to the individual shareholder and taxed only once.

Consider also the situation where the shareholder acts as a supplier and sells property to the corporation. The sale of property at fair market value may result in taxable gains to the shareholder, but the cost of the asset to the corporation is established by the selling price; this reduces corporate income for tax purposes. The timing of the deduction from corporate income will depend on the nature of the property acquired (that is, whether it is inventory, depreciable property, or something else).

The fundamental difference between the primary relationship and the secondary relationships centres on the tax treatment given to income flows between the corporation and its shareholders. In the primary relationship, *dividends paid* by the corporation are *not deductible* by the corporation for tax purposes, but are taxable to the recipient shareholder. In secondary relationships, payments such as salaries, interest, and rents *are* deductible by the corporation and taxable to the recipient. This difference is particularly important in closely held corporations, which are controlled by a single shareholder or by a relatively small group of shareholders. Decisions by such corporations such as whether the corporation should be capitalized with shareholder debt rather than equity, whether the owners should take salaries rather than dividends, and whether property should be owned by the corporation rather than leased from the shareholders, all relate back to how the corporation and its shareholders are taxed in primary and secondary relationships. In widely held corporations such as public corporations, secondary relationships usually do not exist; however, the two-tier system of tax in the primary relationship affects such corporations' decisions concerning whether to raise capital by debt or by equity. This question is examined in subsequent chapters.

In order to understand the tax impact on cash flow of the two-tier system of tax for corporations, it is first necessary to establish the taxable income and the rates of tax for corporations.

II. Determination of Taxable Income

A corporation's taxable income, like an individual's, is determined by reducing net income for tax purposes by a short list of special reductions.

Exhibit 11-3 outlines the basic framework for converting net income for tax purposes to taxable income. Notice how this framework differs from the one for individuals. The corporation does not have a capital gain deduction. Also, it treats charitable donations as a reduction of taxable income, whereas the individual treats such donations as a tax credit. Of particular importance is the special reduction for dividends received from other Canadian corporations and from foreign affiliate corporations. This reduction and the loss carry-over reductions are reviewed briefly below.

A. Loss Carry-Overs

The loss carry-over provisions for corporations are the same, structurally, as they are for individuals.[3] Net capital losses incurred can be carried back three years and forward indefinitely to the extent of taxable capital gains realized in those years. Non-capital losses (business losses, property losses, and allowable business investment losses) incurred in a year can be carried back three years and forward seven years as a special reduction against any other

---

3   ITA 111; IT-232R2.

Exhibit 11-3:	Net income for tax purposes		xxx
Taxable Income	Special reductions:		
of a Corporation	Donations to charitable organizations*	x	
	Net capital losses	x	
	Non-capital losses	x	
	Dividends from taxable Canadian corporations	x	
	Dividends from foreign affiliates	x	(xx)
	Taxable income		xx

* ITA 110.1(1)(a)

source of income. As the calculation for these items—and its application to investment and business decisions—was examined in Chapter 10 for individuals, it is not repeated in this chapter. However, because of the nature of the corporate structure, there are certain aspects of loss carry-overs that apply to corporations only. These are reviewed below.

• **Change in control**   Although a corporation is a separate legal entity, beneficial ownership of the corporation can change when shares are transferred from one shareholder or group of shareholders to another. This means that the carry-forward of unabsorbed losses may be attractive to acquiring shareholders if they can use those losses against income they can generate in the corporation. Whenever a new shareholder or group of shareholders acquires control of a corporation, the unabsorbed losses being carried forward may be restricted as to use or entirely eliminated.[4] In general terms, a change in control will affect the unabsorbed loss carry-over as follows:

1. The net capital losses that exist in the corporation at the time of change in control are deemed to have expired. This is the case even though the corporation may hold assets that have appreciated in value and that will create capital gains in the future when a disposition occurs.

2. Non-capital losses that resulted from a business operation continue to be carried forward but can be utilized only against income generated from the business that incurred the loss, or against income of a business that is similar to the business that incurred the loss. This is a significant departure from the normal carry-forward rules, which permit non-capital losses to be offset against any other source of income. Further, in order to utilize the unabsorbed business losses, the business that incurred the loss cannot be terminated until the losses are used. Any losses incurred by the corporation after the change in control can be carried forward in the normal manner against any other source of income.

The purpose of the above restrictions is to prevent the transfer of unabsorbed corporate losses to other parties through a change in share ownership. However, the fact that business loss carry-overs can be utilized against income from a similar business opens up a narrow opportunity with respect to business sales and acquisitions. For example, the shareholders of a corporation that has significant unabsorbed business losses may achieve a higher price on their shares by selling them to a party that operates a similar business and can take steps to combine some of its profitable operations with those of the corporation it is acquiring (see Chapter 14). When conducting a search for a possible buyer, it is important to target potential buyers who are in the same or a similar line of business. Similarly,

---

4   ITA 111(4), (5), (5.4); IT-302R2.

profitable businesses that are considering an expansion should seek out corporations in a similar line of business that have substantial unabsorbed business losses which can be merged with their profitable operations. In this context the term "similar business" is subjective. However, it does include vertical-integration acquisitions where, for example, a chain of retail stores acquires a manufacturing operation to produce products sold to the retail operation.[5]

These restrictions relate to the treatment of losses that have already occurred but have not been absorbed by later, profitable operations. When a change in share ownership occurs, the acquired corporation may own certain assets that have declined in value. In such cases, after the ownership change, additional losses will occur if those assets are sold. For example, a corporation may own depreciable property that has an undepreciated capital cost for tax purposes of $500,000 but is actually worth only $400,000. After a change in control, the new owners can sell the asset and create a loss of $100,000; this loss would not fall under the restrictions reviewed earlier.

To ensure that unrealized losses do not escape the restrictions, the corporation's year end is deemed, for tax purposes, to be the date of the control change.[6] This adds any operating losses since the previous year end to the non-capital losses, which makes them subject to the restrictions. Also, depreciable property, eligible capital property, and other capital property are all deemed to have been sold at their market value *if* that value is below the tax cost.[7] This means that in the above example, the depreciable property would be deemed to have been sold for $400,000, the result being a realized loss of $100,000 that is also subject to the restrictions. These further adjustments to the control rules are indicative of the Department of Finance's commitment to placing limits on loss transfers.

It is important to recognize that these restrictions do not apply when control is acquired by a related party (see Chapter 14).[8]

• Loss utilization in corporate groups   Often a shareholder or group of shareholders will control a number of corporations that conduct various separate business activities. Although each corporation in the group is controlled by the same shareholders, each corporation is, nevertheless, a separate entity for tax purposes and determines its income or losses separately. This structure can be onerous when some companies in the group are profitable and subject to tax, while others have unabsorbed losses.

Consider Exhibit 11-4, in which the same shareholder(s) directly or indirectly control three separate corporations, of which two are profitable and one has substantial losses. The combined financial results are as shown in the next table.

Corporation A—profit	$ 100,000
Corporation B—loss	(400,000)
Corporation C—profit	50,000
Net loss for group	$(250,000)

Even though the group as a whole has lost $250,000, both Corporation A and Corporation C will pay tax on their profits of $100,000 and $50,000 respectively, and the loss in Corporation B will remain unused. While Corporation B may be able to absorb its losses in future years, the immediate cash flow of the group is diminished, with the result that it

---

5   IT-206R, IT-259R2.

6   ITA 249(4).

7   ITA 111(5.1), (5.2); IT-302R2 (paragraphs 14–15).

8   ITA 256(7).

Exhibit 11-4:
Corporate Groups
and Loss Utilization

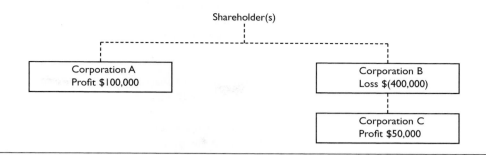

must forgo investment opportunities or, if it is in financial difficulty, face the increasing risk of a business failure.

In this type of situation the profits and losses of the various corporations can be combined *if* the operations of each corporation are formally merged and housed in a single corporate entity. For example, the operations of Corporations B and C can be merged with those of Corporation A. While this will not alter the past year's results, it *will* permit B's losses to be absorbed by the future profits of the other operations. (A number of methods can be used to reorganize corporations. They are examined in Chapter 14.)

The difficulty of combining losses with profits in a corporate group should be remembered when making expansion decisions. For example, a corporation that is contemplating an expansion into new activities can either house the expansion operation as a branch within the existing corporation or establish a subsidiary corporation. If the new venture is going to incur losses in the initial years, a branch structure would permit the losses to be used immediately against the profits of other operations; the subsidiary structure, on the other hand, would separate the profits of the existing operations from the losses incurred by the expansion activity. The increased cash flow from the immediate tax savings under the branch structure can be used to fund the losses of the expansion operation and thus reduce the risk of its failure. It should be remembered, however, that the subsidiary structure provides some protection in the form of limited liability, as well as the opportunity to merge the operations at a later time when it is clear the new operation will succeed (see Chapter 20).

B. Dividends from Other Canadian Corporations

It will be recalled that a corporation includes dividends received from other corporations as property income when determining net income for tax purposes. In order to avoid multiple taxation on the distribution of corporate after-tax income, a corporation's taxable income is reduced by the amount of dividends received from other taxable Canadian corporations.[9] The dividend is first included in net income and then removed in calculating taxable income. This means that dividends can flow tax-free between Canadian corporations and are not subject to a second level of tax until they are received by the ultimate shareholder—the individual. In simpler terms, it can be said that corporate profits, once taxed by the initial corporation, can be shifted to other corporations via dividends without further taxation.

In certain cases private corporations may be subject to a temporary tax on dividends received from other corporations (see Chapter 13). However, for most *business* structures, Canadian intercorporate dividends flow tax-free.

In addition, Canadian corporations that receive dividends from a foreign affiliate corporation are also not taxable on such dividends, as a result of the special reduction in arriving at taxable income.[10] To qualify as a foreign affiliate, the Canadian corporation must have an equity percentage in the foreign corporation that is at least 10%.

9 ITA 89(1)(i), 112(1), 248.

10 ITA 113, 95(1)(d).

This ability to move after-tax retained earnings freely from one corporation to its corporate shareholder has an important impact on the relationship between dividends and capital gains. Consider the alternative tax treatments in the following situation:

Situation: An individual owns all of the shares of Corporation A. Corporation A has used its funds to acquire, at a cost of $100,000, all of the shares of Corporation B, which operates an active business. Corporation B has been profitable and has accumulated after-tax retained earnings of $400,000. Corporation A is contemplating disposing of its investment in Corporation B. The shares of Corporation B have recently been valued at $700,000, and a willing buyer is available.

Analysis: The organization structure in this situation is as follows:

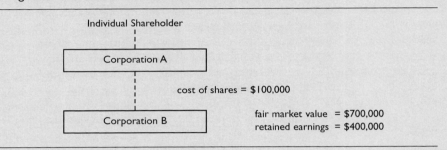

The value of Corporation B's shares is $700,000 even though its retained earnings are only $400,000. This difference in value results from the fact that the corporation has assets such as land, buildings, and goodwill that have appreciated in value but have not been sold.

Corporation A can realize its investment in Corporation B by selling the shares for $700,000 or by selling the shares for a reduced value after declaring a dividend from Corporation B to Corporation A. Keep in mind that the payment of the dividend will reduce the value of the shares by an equivalent amount. The tax treatment of these two alternatives is as follows:

Sale of shares for $700,000	
Proceeds of disposition	$ 700,000
Adjusted cost base	(100,000)
Capital gain	$ 600,000
Combination dividend and sale of shares	
Dividend (equal to retained earnings)	$ 400,000
Amount of dividend taxable	NIL
Sale of shares:	
Proceeds ($700,000 − $400,000)	$ 300,000
Adjusted cost base	(100,000)
Capital gain	$ 200,000

In the above situation both alternatives provide the owner with total proceeds of $700,000. However, in the second alternative, the payment of a tax-free dividend of $400,000 to Corporation A reduces the value of Corporation B's shares by $400,000. In turn, the amount of the capital gain on the sale of the shares is reduced from $600,000 to

$200,000. By arranging for a dividend rather than a capital gain, Corporation A now has a greater amount of after-tax proceeds for reinvestment in another venture. Of course, utilizing the dividend option in this structure results in a tax deferral and not a tax saving, because ultimately a second level of tax will be incurred when dividends flow to the individual who owns Corporation A.

The concept of tax-free intercorporate dividends is fundamental to the relationship between corporations and their shareholders. An investor can interpose a holding corporation between himself or herself and the active corporation, transfer after-tax retained earnings into it, and reinvest those earnings on a tax-deferred basis. This use of holding companies is discussed in greater detail in Chapter 14.

III. Calculation of Corporate Tax

Corporations are divided into two basic categories for tax purposes.

1. *Public corporations*, which are companies that are resident of Canada and whose shares are traded on a stock exchange.[11]

2. *Canadian-controlled private corporations* (*CCPCs*), which are corporations that are resident in Canada, do not qualify as public corporations, and are not controlled by non-residents of Canada.[12]

Although other types of corporations exist, these two are the main corporate structures in the Canadian tax system.[13]

Both of the above types are subject to federal and provincial taxes. The overall format for calculating corporate income tax for all types of corporations is outlined in Exhibit 11-5. Notice that provincial taxes are expressed as a percentage of *taxable income*, and, as a result, it is easy to determine the basic marginal tax rates.

Exhibit 11-5: Determination of Tax for Corporations			
(a) Federal tax:			
Primary federal tax (*rate* × *taxable income*)			xx
Abatement for provincial tax			(x)
			x
Federal surtax (*rate* × *federal tax after abatement*)			x
Refundable tax on investment income			x
			xx
less			
Special reduction		x	
Small-business deduction		x	
Manufacturing and processing deduction		x	
Federal tax credits		x	x
Federal tax			*xx
(b) Provincial tax:			
Primary provincial tax (*rate* × *taxable income*)		x	
Specific provincial tax credits		(x)	x
(c) Combined federal and provincial tax (a + b)			xx

* An additional tax under Part IV of the ITA is applicable on certain dividends received by a private corporation. This tax is reviewed in Chapter 13. Also, the refundable tax on investment income and the small-business deduction do not apply to public corporations.

---

11 ITA 89(1).
12 ITA 89(1), 125(7)(b); IT-458R.
13 ITA 89(1)(f).

A. Federal Tax

The primary federal tax is calculated by applying a flat-rate tax of 38% to the corporation's taxable income. In order to provide room for the provinces to impose a tax, the federal rate of 38% is reduced by 10% as a federal abatement for provincial taxes. So, the basic rate of federal tax is actually 28% (38% – 10%) for all corporations.[14]

The federal rate of tax may be increased or reduced further on specific types of income earned by certain corporations. These are reviewed below.

• **Federal surtax**   A federal surtax applies to corporations. This tax is temporary, and the rate changes from time to time. In 2003 the rate was 4% of the federal tax otherwise payable.[15] Note that this rate is applied as a percentage of federal tax after the provincial abatement is deducted. Therefore, the tax is 4% × (38% – 10%), resulting in an effective rate of 1.12% of taxable income. As already indicated, the surtax is supposed to be temporary and may be withdrawn at any time.

• **Special reduction**   A special tax rate reduction applies to particular types of income earned by corporations. These are listed below.

Public corporations—In 2004 federal tax is reduced by 7% of the corporation's taxable income other than its income from manufacturing and processing activities (M&P), which has a separate reduction described below. (The reduction in 2003 was 5%.)

Canadian-controlled private corporations—In 2004 federal tax is reduced by 7% on active business income (other than income qualifying for the M&P reduction described below) that is above the annual limit to which the small-business deduction applies (see below). This reduction does *not* apply to the tax on its *investment* income.

• **Refundable tax on investment income**   This special tax is applied only to the investment income (not active business income) of Canadian-controlled private corporations. The rate of tax is $6\frac{2}{3}$% of the corporation's investment income and is *fully refundable* to the corporation when dividends are paid to its shareholder(s).[16] This tax, which has a special purpose, is reviewed in Chapter 13.

• **Small-business deduction**   The small-business deduction is available only to Canadian-controlled private corporations. This deduction permits the normal federal tax rate to be reduced by 16%, so that the net federal tax is 12% (28% – 16%); beginning in 2006 this applies only to the first $300,000 of annual active business income of the corporation, or to its taxable income, whichever is lower.[17] Two or more corporations owned by similar shareholders may have to share this $300,000 limit (see Chapter 13). The annual limits in 2004 and 2005 are $250,000 and $275,000 respectively.

Consider this example: A Canadian-controlled private corporation has active business income of $125,000 and taxable income of $110,000 (after deducting a loss carry-over of $10,000 and charitable donations of $5,000). Its small-business deduction for the year is $17,600, calculated as follows:

---

14 ITA 123(1), 124(1).

15 ITA 123.2.

16 ITA 123.3.

17 ITA 125(1); IT-73R5.

16% × the least of:	
Active business income	$125,000
Taxable income	110,000
Annual limit	300,000
16% × $110,000 = $17,600	

The small-business deduction effectively creates a progressive rate structure for Canadian-controlled private corporations. The tax treatment of Canadian-controlled private corporations is examined in greater detail in Chapter 13.

• **Manufacturing and processing deduction**   Profits that result from manufacturing and processing activities are subject to a rate reduction of 7% for all public corporations.[18] Canadian-controlled private corporations are entitled to the same manufacturing reduction, but only on annual manufacturing profits in excess of the $300,000 (in 2006; $275,000 in 2005 and $250,000 in 2004) small-business deduction limit described previously. Therefore, the net federal rate of tax on manufacturing activities (except those eligible for the small-business deduction) is 21% (28% – 7%). Note that the special tax reduction (described above) applicable to other types of income is also 7% in 2004. Therefore, most corporate income will be subject to a net federal tax rate of 21% (excluding the surtax). Prior to 2004, the manufacturing and processing rate reduction was greater than the special reduction on other business income. Certain provincial jurisdictions have special rates for manufacturing and processing income and so the following discussion remains relevant.

The following arbitrary formula is used to determine the manufacturing profits subject to the rate reduction. The result of this formula may be higher or lower than the actual manufacturing profits. The details of this rather complex formula can be obtained from the federal tax return.[19] Its fundamentals are presented below, for use in a later discussion on how it affects business structure and organization.

$$\frac{MC + ML}{TC + TL} \times \text{Total business profits} = \text{Manufacturing profits}$$

Where:

MC = manufacturing capital, determined as the annualized cost of all *depreciable* property used directly in qualified manufacturing activities[20]

TC = total capital, determined as the annualized cost of all depreciable property of the corporation

ML = manufacturing labour, determined as the total wages paid for qualified manufacturing activities[21]

TL = total labour, determined as the total wages and salaries paid by the corporation

Notice that the above formula arbitrarily determines manufacturing profits as a function of the labour and capital employed in such activities. Consider the impact this may have on the corporate structure of an enterprise that carries on both manufacturing and non-manufacturing activities. Exhibit 11-6 diagrams alternative structures for conducting a combined retail/manufacturing operation.

---

18 ITA 125.1(1).

19 IT-145R.

20 The annualized cost is calculated as 10% of the original cost of owned property plus the annual rent for leased property. This sum is grossed up by an arbitrary amount of 100/85. Total capital is calculated in a similar manner, except that the gross-up is not applied.

21 Manufacturing labour is the actual amount grossed up by an arbitrary amount of 100/75. Total labour is not grossed up.

Exhibit 11-6:
Alternative Structures
for Manufacturing and
Other Activities

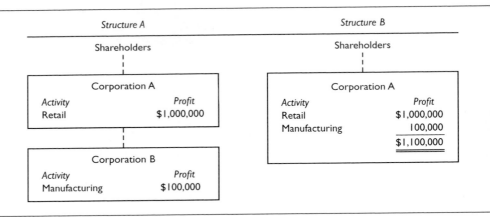

Under structure A the activities are divided between two corporations. Because manufacturing is carried on only in Corporation B, the maximum profit eligible for the 7% manufacturing reduction is $100,000.

However, under structure B the manufacturing and retail operations are combined in one corporation that has a total profit of $1,100,000. The portion of this total profit that is considered to be manufacturing profit is based on the arbitrary formula and is governed by the capital and wages employed in each operation. If, for example, this relationship amounted to 30%, the manufacturing profits eligible for the 7% rate reduction and certain provincial rate reductions would be $330,000, as follows:

$$\frac{MC + ML}{TC + TL} = 30\% \times \$1,100,000 = \$330,000$$

In structure B the overall tax may be lower simply because the operations are combined rather than separated. This, of course, is not always the result; the reverse could happen if the relationships were altered. The organization structure of a business is influenced by a number of factors, one of which is the tax factor. While calculating manufacturing profits may be a complex task, understanding the impact of the result is not; and it is important that a small item like this formula, rather than being tucked away in an accountant's office, instead be remembered and applied to the business activities that it influences.

B. Provincial Tax

As previously mentioned, provincial corporate tax rates are expressed as a percentage of corporate taxable income. Each province and territory imposes a primary flat rate of tax on all corporate income. These rates vary from province to province. Exhibit 11-7 outlines the primary provincial tax rates applicable for 2004 (or 2003 where indicated). They are subject to frequent changes and are presented here merely to show the range of provincial rates. The reader should update these rates to conform to the particular period in question. Information on provincial tax rates can be obtained by accessing this text's Web site at **www.mcgrawhill.ca/college/buckwold7**.

In addition, certain provinces apply a reduced rate of tax to the first $300,000 of active business profits of Canadian-controlled private corporations, and some reduce the rate for manufacturing profits. For example, in Ontario the primary rate of 11% is reduced to 5% for active business profits that qualify for the federal small-business deduction and to 10% (2004) for manufacturing income.

A corporation incorporated or based in a particular province will be taxed entirely in that province *unless* it carries on business in another province through a permanent establishment such as an office, branch, warehouse, or factory. If such a permanent establishment exists, the profits attributable to that location are based on the ratio of *sales* in the province to total sales, and the ratio of *wages* paid in the province to total wages, multiplied by the total business profits of the whole corporation.[22] For example:

(a)

$$\frac{\text{Wages paid in Alberta}}{\text{Total wages paid by corp.}} = 33\%$$

(b)

$$\frac{\text{Sales in Alberta}}{\text{Total sales of corp.}} = 45\%$$

Average of (a) and (b):

$$\frac{33 + 45}{2} = 39\%$$

Therefore, 39% of the total business profits of the corporation are taxed at Alberta rates even though the real profits in Alberta may be higher or lower.

No provincial allocations are made when corporations carry on business in other provinces by way of direct sales from the home province. The use of alternative business-expansion strategies, such as direct sales, branch operations, and separate corporations, significantly alters the rates of corporate tax (see Chapter 20).

Exhibit 11-7:	Alberta	11.5%	(3%)	Nova Scotia	16	(5%)
Primary Provincial	British Columbia	13.5	(4.5)	Nunavut	12	(4)
Tax Rates—2004	Manitoba*	16	(5)	Ontario	11%	(5)
Regular Income:	New Brunswick	13	(3)	P.E.I.*	16	(7.5)
(income subject to the	Newfoundland and			Quebec	16	(9)
small-business deduction)	Labrador	14	(5)	Saskatchewan	17	(5.5)
	Northwest Territories	12	(4)	Yukon	15	(6)

As applicable in March 2003 and subject to change.
Note: Special rates may also apply to manufacturing income.
* 2003.

C. Combined Federal and Provincial Tax

It would be useful to review federal and provincial taxes by establishing the marginal rates of tax for each type of corporation. Exhibit 11-8 combines the federal tax rates with those of an unspecified province to demonstrate how the calculation is made. The exhibit combines the normal federal rates with those of *a fictitious province having a 15% rate on normal income, a 13% rate on M&P income, and a 5% rate on income subject to the small-business deduction.*

Notice the significantly lower tax rate (18%) for the first $300,000 (in 2006) of annual active business income in the Canadian-controlled private corporation. Not only is the rate lower than other rates of corporate tax, but it is also lower than the personal rates of tax described in Chapter 10. (The benefits of incorporating a small business are reviewed in Chapter 13.) Actual marginal rates for this type of income range from 16% to 22% in 2004. It should also be noted that the other corporate tax rates are close to the highest rate of tax for individuals.

Excluded from Exhibit 11-8 is the special rate of tax on investment income earned by Canadian-controlled private corporations. This income is subject to an additional refundable tax of $6^2/_3\%$, and is reviewed in Chapter 13.

Actual combined federal and provincial corporate tax rates may vary from province to province. These actual tax rates can be obtained by accessing links on this text's Web site at **www.mcgrawhill.ca/college/buckwold7**.

---

22 ITA 124(4)(a); Regulations 400–415; IT-177R2.

Exhibit 11-8:
Combined Federal and
Provincial Tax 2004
(fictitious province)

	Public corporations		Canadian-controlled private corporations			
	M&P income	Other income	1st $250,000 (2004) and $275,000 (2005) business income	1st $300,000 of business income in 2006	M&P income in excess of $300,000 (2006), $275,000 (2005), $250,000 (2004)	Other business income
Primary federal tax	38%	38%	38%	38%	38%	38%
Federal abatement	(10)	(10)	(10)	(10)	(10)	(10)
Surtax	1	1	1	1	1	1
Special reduction		(7)				(7)
M&P reduction	(7)				(7)	
Small-business deduction			(16)	(16)		
Federal tax	22	22	13	13	22	22
Provincial tax	13	15	5	5	13	15
Combined rate*	35%	37%	18%	18%	35%	37%

* The tax rate on investment income earned by a Canadian-controlled private corporation has not been calculated (see Chapter 13).

For demonstration purposes, these assumed rates will be used throughout the text, including the $300,000 threshold for the small-business deduction beginning in 2006.

IV. The Integration of Corporate and Individual Taxation

At the beginning of this chapter, a review of the primary relationship between a corporation and its shareholder(s) established that corporations, as separate legal entities, are taxed on their profits separate from the shareholders. The review further established that although after-tax corporate profits can be shifted freely to corporate shareholders, the ultimate shareholder of a corporation is the individual, who is taxed a second time when after-tax corporate profits are distributed as dividends. This two-tier system creates the possibility of double taxation. In order to fully understand the impact of corporate taxation on financial decisions, it is necessary to establish the degree to which double taxation, if any, results from the two-tiered structure.

The effect of double taxation is modified by the dividend tax credit, which the individual can apply to reduce the personal tax on dividends received from Canadian corporations. This reduction represents a credit for all or a portion of the corporate taxes paid on the income represented by the dividend. In Chapter 7 it was established that the dividend tax credit attempts to reduce double taxation by reducing personal taxes, and assumes that the corporate tax rate is approximately 20%. Exhibit 11-8 indicates that the corporate tax rate is not, in fact, always 20%.

By applying the corporate rates in Exhibit 11-8 and the individual tax rates on dividends in Exhibit 10-6 (see Chapter 10), the extent of double taxation on the flow of corporate income to shareholders can be determined. The table on the next page illustrates what happens when a *public corporation* pays its after-tax profits to an individual shareholder who is in the top marginal tax bracket. The same table also demonstrates that business income earned by a public corporation and then transferred to its shareholder will incur a combined tax rate of 56%; whereas if the same business income were earned directly by the individual, a tax rate of only 45% would apply.

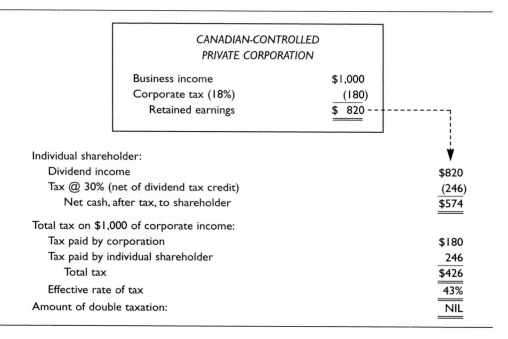

```
                    PUBLIC CORPORATION

        Business income                    $1,000
        Corporate tax (37%)                 (370)
        Retained earnings                  $  630 ----┐
                                                       ↓
Individual shareholder:
   Dividend income                                   $630
   Tax @ 30% (net of dividend tax credit)            (189)
      Net cash, after tax, to shareholder            $441

Total tax on $1,000 of corporate income:
   Tax paid by corporation                           $370
   Tax paid by individual shareholder                 189
                                                     $559

   Effective rate of tax (rounded)                   56%*

Amount of double taxation:
   Combined corporate and shareholder tax            56%
   Maximum personal tax rate on business income       45
      Double taxation                                11%
```

* This rate varies by province.

The same calculation can be applied to a Canadian-controlled private corporation that earns business income subject to the small-business deduction (see table below). In this example, because the corporate tax rate is only 18%, the dividend tax credit eliminates the element of double taxation. However, it should be noted that annual business income in excess of $300,000 (in 2006) is subject to a higher rate of corporate tax; consequently, that income is subject to double taxation, much like income from public corporations.

```
              CANADIAN-CONTROLLED
              PRIVATE CORPORATION

        Business income                    $1,000
        Corporate tax (18%)                 (180)
        Retained earnings                  $  820 ----┐
                                                       ↓
Individual shareholder:
   Dividend income                                   $820
   Tax @ 30% (net of dividend tax credit)            (246)
      Net cash, after tax, to shareholder            $574

Total tax on $1,000 of corporate income:
   Tax paid by corporation                           $180
   Tax paid by individual shareholder                 246
      Total tax                                      $426
   Effective rate of tax                             43%
Amount of double taxation:                           NIL
```

The amount of double taxation is a vital component in the calculation of the long-term return on investment in corporations. So is the timing of that taxation. In a public corporation, double taxation on returns to the owner is automatic; in a Canadian-controlled private corporation, it may or may not occur depending on the nature of the income (see Chapter 13). In either case the combination of corporate tax and tax on distributions to shareholders has a significant impact on dividend policy, capital (debt/equity) structures, and the form of business organization (see Chapters 12 and 13).

Consider, for example, the impact of double taxation on a public corporation that must choose between two alternatives for raising capital: the acquiring of additional debt, or the issuing of preferred shares bearing a fixed dividend rate. If the going interest rate for corporate debt were 10%, an individual investor in the top tax bracket would receive a net return of 5.5% after tax (10% − tax @ 45%). In order to receive an after-tax return of 5.5% on a dividend, the dividend rate would have to be 7.8% (7.8% − tax @ 30% = 5.5%). To provide the same after-tax return to an investor, the corporation can issue debt that bears interest at 10% or preferred shares with a dividend rate of 7.8%. Because the interest is deductible from corporate income, the corporation could invest the borrowed funds at 10% in order to generate enough income to pay out 10% interest. However, for the preferred shares, the dividend is not deductible and an element of double taxation occurs. Therefore, given that the corporate tax rate is 37%, the corporation would have to generate a return of about 12.5% with the equity capital in order to have sufficient funds to pay a dividend of 7.8% (12.5% − tax @ 37% = approximately 7.8%).

The above example demonstrates the effect that double taxation has on the cost of equity capital, and compares it with the cost of debt in public corporations. (A more detailed review of corporate financing is made in Chapter 21.) Similar analyses can be applied to Canadian-controlled private corporations. It must be noted that in private corporations the corporation/shareholder relationship is much stronger because there are only a few shareholders. In such circumstances the shareholder can reduce the impact of double taxation by also acting as creditor, and provide debt capital to the corporation in return for interest, or lease assets to the corporation in return for rents. In such circumstances double taxation is avoided because interest and rents are deducted from corporate income (see Chapter 12).

V. Tax Planning Checklist

As this chapter presents only an *overview* of corporate taxation, an extensive list of tax planning items cannot be drawn from it. The next three chapters examine a number of corporate tax planning issues in more depth. The main tax planning items relating to this chapter are listed below.

1. Shareholders of a closely held corporation should consider maintaining some secondary relationships. By acting as creditors, lessors, and/or employees, they may be able to alter the amount and timing of tax payable so that it is less than would have resulted on a dividend distribution.

2. An increase in the value of shares arising from accumulated corporate profits can be realized in the form of a dividend or a capital gain. A shareholder who controls a corporation should regularly review these two methods and take advantage of the option that results in the minimum amount of tax.

3. When a change in the controlling shareholder(s) is being considered, the treatment of loss carry-overs should be reviewed. Non-capital losses from business operations have restricted use after a control change. These restrictions are less onerous when

control is acquired by an entity in the same or a similar line of business. A vendor may do well to target this type of buyer.

4. Some businesses divide their operations among several corporations. In such structures, it is important for the taxpayer to monitor the potential for losses in each corporation to ensure that steps can be taken to utilize those losses against profits in other operations as soon as possible after they occur.

5. When contemplating expansion activities, the structure (i.e., separate corporations vs. branch of the existing corporation) should be chosen carefully from the perspective of loss utilization as well as liability exposure.

6. Dividends usually flow tax-free from one corporation to another (see Chapter 13 for exceptions). In such circumstances it is worthwhile to realize returns on intercorporate investments by way of dividends rather than capital gains. As well, dividend policies should be reviewed regularly, especially when a disposal of share investments is being contemplated.

7. Corporations that engage in both manufacturing and non-manufacturing activities should examine how the corporate structure affects the arbitrary formula which determines the amount of the manufacturing tax reduction. Depending on the capital and labour input of the two activities, tax savings may be achieved by either separating or combining those activities.

8. When attempting to extend operations into new provinces, the taxpayer is strongly advised to consider the effect on provincial taxes of alternative expansion structures. Different expansion methods such as direct sales, or an out-of-province branch location, or a separate corporation will result in different provincial tax costs.

VI. Summary and Conclusion

This chapter has completed the framework of corporate taxation by showing how net income for tax purposes is converted into taxable income, and by outlining the structure for calculating corporate tax.

Corporate taxable income is determined by reducing net income by a small number of special reductions. As is the case with individuals, the utilization of loss carry-overs has an important effect on cash flow and return on investment. A unique aspect of corporate loss carry-overs is that further restrictions are imposed when shareholder control of the corporation changes. When this occurs, net capital losses cease to exist, and unabsorbed business losses at the time of the change in control can be used in future years only against profits from the business that incurred the losses, or against the profits of a similar business. In addition, the calculation of corporate taxable income permits the deduction of certain intercorporate dividends, which means that corporate after-tax retained earnings can be shifted from one corporation to another without additional tax being incurred.

Corporate tax is determined at both the federal and provincial levels; in each case, the tax payable is expressed as a percentage of taxable income. Public corporations and private corporations are subject to similar rates of tax, although both federal and provincial taxes are reduced for manufacturing profits and for a portion of the business income earned by Canadian-controlled private corporations.

A significant portion of this chapter was devoted to establishing the relationship between the corporation and its shareholder(s). There is a two-tiered system in which income is taxed first in the corporation and then a second time when distributed as a dividend to shareholders. The second level of tax can be avoided when the corporation does not declare dividends, but this increases the share value, which ultimately may be recognized as a capital gain on disposition.

In conclusion, the corporation, although treated as a separate entity within the tax system, cannot be viewed in isolation from the shareholders when the tax impact of investment and management decisions is being considered. What affects the corporation will, at a different time perhaps, also affect the shareholders, because of the fundamental relationship between the two.

VII. Conclusion to Part Two

This chapter brings to a conclusion Part Two of the text, which was designed to provide an overview of the fundamentals of income determination and tax for the two primary entities—individuals and corporations. Chapters 3 through 11 have developed the framework of the Canadian income tax system by establishing who is subject to tax, what income is taxable, and how tax is calculated. This framework can be summarized as follows:

1. Individuals and corporations are the two primary entities subject to tax in Canada.

2. Individuals and corporations that are resident in Canada are taxable on their world income. Non-resident individuals and corporations are taxable only on certain income derived in Canada.

3. Taxable income for the primary entities is the net income for tax purposes less limited special reductions.

4. Net income for tax purposes consists of five specifically defined types of income:
   • employment income
   • business income
   • property income
   • capital gains
   • other specific sources of income

Each of the above income sources is clearly identifiable and is determined in accordance with its own set of fundamental principles.

The overall system, while sometimes complex, has an innate logic and direction. Of primary importance is the statutory scheme, or aggregating formula, which is the foundation of income determination. The tax treatment of most financial transactions can be understood if such transactions are first related to the aggregating formula. The dividend tax credit and the treatment of intercorporate dividends are the ties that bind together the corporation and its shareholders.

As stated in the introductory chapter, one need not be a tax specialist to apply taxation questions to business and investment decisions. In most cases the after-tax cash flows of alternative business opportunities and strategies can be projected by applying the fundamentals of the tax system. Chapters 3 to 11 have attempted to relate the basic principles to business and investment decisions through a number of specific examples. These examples were designed primarily to stimulate the reader to develop an "after-tax" approach to business and investment decisions. Taxation of income cannot be placed in a vacuum, but rather must be included, in a formal way, in all financial decision making.

Reading List

Income Tax Act References

	Section
Deduction for gifts (charitable, the Crown, institutions)	110.1(1)
Losses deductible (non-capital and net capital losses)	111(1)
Acquisition of control (effect on losses)	111(4), (5)
Acquisition of control (other restrictions)	111(5.1) to (5.5)
Net capital loss (defined)	111(8)(a)
Non-capital loss (defined)	111(8)(b)
Year end on change of control	249(4)
Control deemed not to be acquired	256(7)
Deduction of taxable dividends received by corporations resident in Canada	112(1)
Meaning of taxable Canadian corporation	89(1)(i), 248
Dividends received from non-resident corporations	112(2)
Deduction in respect of dividend received from foreign affiliate	113(1)
Foreign affiliate (defined)	95(1)(d)
Private corporation	89(1)(f)
Public corporation	89(1)(g)
Canadian-controlled private corporation	89(1), 125(7)(b)
Tax rate for corporations	123(1)
Corporate surtax	123.2
Deduction from corporate tax	124(1)
Small-business deduction	125(1)
Amount of business limit	125(2)
Deduction re: manufacturing and processing profits	125.1(1)
Canadian manufacturing and processing profits	125.1(3)(a)
Manufacturing and processing	125.1(3)(b)
Taxable income earned in a province (defined)	124(4)(a)
Taxable income earned in a province (tax treatment of)	Regulations 400–415
Permanent establishment	Regulation 400(2)
Foreign tax deduction	110.5, 126
Investment tax credit	127(5) to (26)

Canada Customs and Revenue Agency Publications

IT-343R	Meaning of term "corporation."
IT-232R2	Non-capital losses, net capital losses, etc.; their composition and deductibility in computing taxable income.
IT-302R2	Losses of a corporation—the effect on their deductibility of changes in control, amalgamation, and winding up.
IT-206R	Separate business (includes discussion on the meaning of a similar business).
IT-259R2	Exchange of property (see paragraphs 17–20 for a discussion of the term "Same or similar business").
IT-328R3	Losses on shares from which dividends have been received.
IT-458R	Canadian-controlled private corporation.
IT-73R5	The small-business deduction.
IT-145R	Canadian manufacturing and processing profits—reduced rate of corporate tax.

IT-177R2   Permanent establishment of a corporation in a province and of a foreign enterprise in Canada.

Major Court Decision

MNR v. Panther Oil and Grease Manufacturing Co. of Canada Ltd., 61 DTC 1222—Meaning of permanent establishment.

Other Publications

Bernstein, J., "Loss Utilization by Individuals and Private Corporations," Report of Proceedings of the 48th Tax Conference, Canadian Tax Foundation, p. 58.1.

Kellough, H., and P. McQuillan, "Interpretation Revisited: Coordinating the Corporate and Personal Tax System," Canadian Tax Foundation, 1998 Corporate Management Tax Conference, p. 22.1.

Novis, D.A., "Provisions that Restrict or Deny Losses and Corporate Attribution," Canadian Tax Foundation, 1989 Conference Report—Discussion on "Same or Similar Business Test," pp. 14:28–32.

Demonstration Questions

Question One

Tap Inc., a Canadian-controlled private corporation, was incorporated on January 1, 20X1, and was profitable in its first fiscal period ending December 31, 20X1. Substantial losses were incurred in 20X2, but in 20X3 modest gains were achieved. Tap Inc. sells farm implements. As a sideline, the company operates a small grain farm. The farm is a minor part of the corporation's business activity.

Tap Inc. has asked you to examine the effect of the 20X2 loss on the company's tax position. From the financial statements, you have summarized the following information:

	20X1	20X2	20X3
Business income (loss)	$76,000	$(120,000)	$30,000
Canadian taxable dividends	—	—	10,000
Capital gains	4,000	4,000	8,000
Capital losses	—	(28,000)	—
Farm income (loss)	4,000	—	(15,000)
Charitable donations	(28,000)	—	(2,000)
Income (loss)—financial statements	$56,000	$(144,000)	$31,000

You have noted that the 20X2 capital losses of $28,000 include a loss of $8,000 from the sale of shares of a qualified small business corporation.

Required:

1. Assuming that Tap Inc. wants to use the maximum losses as soon as possible, determine its net income and taxable income for 20X1, 20X2, and 20X3.

2. For each type of unused deduction, determine the carry-forward balance, if any, and briefly explain the time period remaining before it expires.

3. In what circumstances, if any, may it be beneficial for Tap Inc. to delay the use of a loss carry-over beyond a year in which it could be used?

Solution:

1. Calculation of losses available for carry-over.

20X2

Net capital loss

Taxable capital gains—½ ($4,000)	$ 2,000
Allowable capital losses—½ ($28,000 – $8,000 ABIL)	(10,000)
	$ 8,000

Non-capital loss

Business loss	$120,000
ABIL—½ ($8,000)	4,000
	$124,000

20X3

Restricted farm loss

Actual loss	$ 15,000
Allowed in 20X3—$2,500 + ½ ($15,000 – $2,500)	8,750
	$ 6,250

20X1 net income and taxable income

Business income	$ 76,000
Farm income	4,000
Taxable capital gains—½ ($4,000)	2,000
Net income	82,000
Donations (actual—$28,000)—lower than limit of 75% of net income	(28,000)
Net capital loss—from 20X2 (limit to taxable capital gains)	(2,000)
Restricted farm loss—from 20X3 (limit to farm income)	(4,000)
Non-capital loss—from 20X2 (balance)	(48,000)
Taxable income	–0–

20X2 net income and taxable income   –0–

20X3 net income and taxable income

Business income	$ 30,000
Dividends	10,000
Taxable capital gains—½ ($8,000)	4,000
Farm loss—limit (see above)	(8,750)
Net income	35,250
Donations (actual in 20X3—$2,000)	(2,000)
Dividends	(10,000)
Net capital loss—from 20X2 (limit to taxable capital gains)	(4,000)
Non-capital loss—from 20X2 (balance)	(19,250)
Taxable income	–0–

2. Carry-forwards after 20X3.

Net capital loss—$8,000 – ($2,000 + $4,000)	$ 2,000
Carried forward indefinitely against future capital gains.	
Non-capital loss—$126,000 – ($48,000 + $19,250)	$ 58,750
Carried forward for next six years (seven years after 20X2).	
Restricted farm loss—$6,250 – $4,000	$ 2,250
Carried forward for 10 years.	

3. It may be beneficial to delay the use of a non-capital loss when a higher tax rate is anticipated in a future year. For example, a corporation could decline the use of a loss carry-forward when all of its income in the particular year is subject to the small-business deduction, and use it in a year when there is income not subject to the small-business deduction (i.e., ABI over $300,000).

Question Two

Salco Ltd. is a Canadian *public* corporation. The company operates a chain of retail stores and a manufacturing business in Ontario. The financial statement for the year ended May 31, 20X6, is summarized below.

Income from retail operation	$500,000
Income from manufacturing business	240,000
Interest income	40,000
Taxable dividends from Canadian corporations	10,000
Net income before income tax	$790,000

Salco's balance sheet shows that the original cost of all depreciable property is $700,000. Of this amount, $500,000 is used in the manufacturing business. The total payroll for the year is $600,000, of which $200,000 is directly related to the manufacturing business.

Required:

1. Calculate Salco's *net income for tax purposes*, *taxable income*, and *federal and provincial income tax* for the 20X5 taxation year.

2. If Salco Ltd. were a *Canadian-controlled private corporation*, how would its federal and provincial income tax change?

Solution:

1. As there is no detailed information about the revenues and expenses for the year, it can be assumed that the net income for tax purposes is equal to the net income reported on the financial statement.

Net income for tax purposes	$790,000
Deduct:	
Taxable Canadian dividends	(10,000)
Taxable income	$780,000

Before determining the federal income tax, it is necessary to derive the manufacturing and processing (M&P) profit for the M&P deduction calculation. The applicable amounts for this calculation are as follows:

Manufacturing capital (MC)	
Manufacturing depreciable property—	
$500,000 × 10% × 100/85	$ 58,823
Total capital (TC)	
Total depreciable property—$700,000 × 10%	$ 70,000
Manufacturing labour (ML)	
$200,000 × 100/75	$266,667
Total labour (TL)	$600,000
M&P profit:	
$\dfrac{\text{MC } \$58,823 + \text{ML } \$266,667}{\text{TC } \$70,000 + \text{TL } \$600,000} \times (\$500,000 + \$240,000) =$	$359,496

Notice that in this situation, the arbitrary formula creates M&P profit ($359,496) that is greater than the actual profit from the manufacturing business ($240,000).

Federal tax:
Primary federal tax—38% × $780,000 — $296,400
   Less abatement—10% × $780,000 — (78,000)
    218,400
M&P deduction—7% × $359,496 — (25,165)
Federal surtax—4% × $218,400 — 8,736
Special reduction—7% × ($780,000 − $359,496, M&P income) — (29,435)
   Total federal tax — $172,536

Provincial tax:
Ontario—11% × ($780,000 − $359,496, M&P income) — $ 46,365
   —10% × 359,496 (M&P income) — 35,950
    $ 82,315

2. If it is assumed that Salco Ltd. is a Canadian-controlled private corporation, several changes to the tax calculation arise. First, the small-business deduction is applicable. For this purpose the active business income is $740,000, which is the sum of the retail ($500,000) and manufacturing ($240,000) profits. Second, the M&P deduction applies only to the M&P profits that are not subject to the small-business deduction. When the active business income consists of both M&P profit and other business profit, it is always assumed that the small-business deduction applies first to the M&P profit. Any amount remaining is then subject to the M&P deduction. Third, the special refundable tax of 6⅔% applies to the investment income. Here, the investment income is the interest income of $40,000. Fourth, the special tax reduction changes as shown below. The dividend income is excluded because it is deducted in arriving at taxable income. In Chapter 13 it will be shown that taxable capital gains are also subject to the special refundable tax. Finally, the provincial income tax will change, as Ontario has a lower rate (5% in 2004) on income that is subject to the small-business deduction.

Federal tax:
Primary federal tax—38% × $780,000 — $296,400
   less abatement—10% × $780,000 — (78,000)
    218,400
Special refundable tax on investment income
  6⅔% × $40,000 — 2,667
Small business deduction—16% × least of:
  Active business income—$740,000
  Taxable income—$780,000
  Annual limit—$300,000 (2006)
    16% × $300,000 — (48,000)
M&P deduction
  M&P profit — 359,496
  Less amount subject to the small-
    business deduction — (300,000)
        7% ×   59,496 — (4,165)
Special tax reduction (calculated below) — (26,635)
Federal surtax—4% × $218,400 — 8,736
   Total federal tax — $151,003
Provincial tax:
Ontario
  5% × $300,000 (amount eligible for the small-
    business deduction) — $15,000
  11% × ($780,000 − $300,000 − 59,496) — 46,255
  10% × $59,496 (M&P) — 5,950
   Total provincial tax — $ 67,205

The above calculation does not include the possible tax on dividends received by a private corporation (referred to as a *Part IV* tax). This tax, which is fully refundable when dividends are paid to the shareholder(s), is not discussed until Chapter 13.

The special tax reduction of 7% applies to income in excess of income eligible for the small-business deduction, income eligible for the M&P reduction, and investment income, and is calculated below.

Taxable income	$780,000
Deduct:	
Investment income	(40,000)
Income eligible for the small-business deduction	(300,000)
Income eligible for the M&P reduction	(59,496)
Income eligible for the 7% special reduction	$380,504
Special reduction—7% × 380,504	$ 26,635

Review Questions

1. "A corporation is an artificial person separate and distinct from its owners." Briefly explain this statement.

2. Identify the types of relationships that can exist between a corporation and its shareholders.

3. What factors may influence the value of a corporation's common share capital?

4. Identify two ways in which a shareholder can realize a return on a share investment. Describe the relationship between them.

5. "Given the choice, individual shareholders of a corporation prefer to receive their return on investment by way of dividends rather than from the sale of shares at a profit." Is this statement true? Explain.

6. "A shareholder may have a primary relationship as well as secondary relationships with the corporation. The difference between the two relationships relates to the tax treatment of income flows between the corporation and the shareholder." Explain.

7. Corporations and individuals determine their taxable income in different ways. What are the differences?

8. How are the net capital losses and non-capital losses of a corporation affected when voting control of the corporation shifts from one shareholder to another?

9. If the shares of a corporation that has non-capital losses are about to be sold, and if those losses arise from business operations, why is it important for the vendor to consider the nature of the purchaser?

10. An existing corporation that operates a profitable retail business is considering expanding its activities to include manufacturing. The expansion business can be organized in either of two basic ways. Describe them. Also, what factors must be considered when a choice is being made between the two structures?

11. How does the tax treatment of intercorporate dividends affect the relationship between dividends and capital gains when one corporation invests in shares of another corporation? (Assume that both entities are taxable Canadian corporations.)

12. Explain why the federal tax reduction of 7% on manufacturing and processing activities may apply to an amount that is greater than or less than the corporation's actual income from manufacturing. Is it possible for a corporation that earns $500,000 from retail activities and suffers a loss of $50,000 from manufacturing activities to be eligible for the 7% manufacturing reduction?

13. What is the marginal tax rate for a public corporation in Ontario on income derived from a chain of restaurants? Show calculations.

14. Because income earned by a corporation is first subject to corporate tax and then taxed a second time when after-tax profits are distributed to individual shareholders, shareholders are entitled to claim a dividend tax credit. Does the dividend tax credit eliminate the double taxation of corporate profits? Explain.

15. The following statement appeared in the media: "There are 60,000 Canadian corporations that earned a profit for the year but incurred no income tax liability." Is it possible for this statement to be true? If it is, explain the principal reasons why, and state your opinion as to whether changes to the tax system are warranted.

Problems

Problem One

U.P.I. Industries Ltd., a Canadian corporation, has recently been designated a public corporation. Its shares are traded on the Winnipeg Stock Exchange.

Over the past year, the company has pursued an aggressive expansion policy. Sales personnel based at head office have travelled to North Dakota and Minnesota and have achieved moderate success in developing new customers in the United States. In addition, the company has opened a branch location in Alberta by establishing an office and manufacturing plant staffed by new Alberta personnel. The Alberta manufacturing plant is the company's first venture into manufacturing.

Selected financial information for the company's current fiscal period is presented below.

1.

	Head office	Alberta branch
Canadian sales	$7,000,000	$1,300,000
Foreign sales	700,000	–0–
Cost of sales	4,620,000	910,000
Salaries and wages	1,200,000	200,000
Profit from operations	1,200,000	10,000
Dividend income	80,000	–0–
Taxable capital gains	70,000	–0–

2. At the end of the previous year, the company had net capital losses of $90,000 and non-capital losses of $120,000 that were available for carry-forward.

3. The Alberta branch location includes a building and equipment. The company's accountant is in the process of determining the corporation's tax liability, and indicates that the annualized cost of manufacturing capital employed in the Alberta branch is $200,000 and that the corporation's total annualized cost of tangible property used amounts to $800,000. The accountant also indicates that the manufacturing labour in the Alberta branch amounts to $120,000. This amount has been calculated in accordance with the income tax rules for determining manufacturing labour.

4. The assumed provincial corporate income tax rate is 16% in Manitoba and 13% in Alberta.

When organizing the Alberta expansion, management had considered establishing a separate corporation. They decided instead on the branch structure because of anticipated losses in the first year of expansion. As it turned out, the branch generated a small profit of $10,000. Management is now considering converting the branch into a separate subsidiary corporation. U.P.I. already owns two separate subsidiaries in Manitoba that account for the dividend income described earlier.

Required:
1. For the current year, determine U.P.I.'s
   (a) net income for tax purposes;
   (b) taxable income; and,
   (c) federal and provincial tax liability.

2. How would the overall federal and provincial tax liability be different if the Alberta branch had been incorporated from the outset? Show calculations.

Problem Two
During the 20X1 taxation year, K2 Ltd., a Canadian-controlled private corporation located in Nova Scotia, earned $160,000 of active business income. In addition, the company made the following capital transactions:

Gain on sale of shares of a public corporation	$ 48,000
Loss on shares of a public corporation	(12,000)
Gain from settling a long-term debt of $300,000 for a reduced amount of $240,000	60,000

At the end of the previous taxation year, the following unused losses were available for carry-forward:

Net capital losses	$29,000
Non-capital losses	42,000

Required:

For the 20X1 taxation year of K2 Ltd., calculate
(a) net income for income tax purposes;
(b) taxable income; and,
(c) total federal and provincial income tax.

Problem Three

Patrice Dupuis is the sole shareholder of Dupuis Distributors Ltd., a successful Canadian-controlled private corporation that wholesales automobile parts. The corporation's profits are in excess of $450,000.

Inventory for the corporation's business is stored in a warehouse owned by Dupuis. He acquired the building five years ago and began charging his corporation an annual rent of $20,000. At the time the building was acquired, the annual rent of $20,000 was considered realistic in terms of the real estate market at the time.

The lease is renewed annually on an informal basis, but the rental amount has never been adjusted even though rental rates for similar properties have increased substantially. Dupuis has never considered a rental adjustment important because "it would just be transferring money from one pocket to the other."

Both Dupuis and the corporation are located in Winnipeg, where there is little available warehouse space. A leasing agent recently informed Dupuis that the building could be rented to a third party under a five-year lease for $38,000 per year.

Required:

Should Dupuis enter into a five-year lease with Dupuis Distributors, charging an annual rent of $38,000? What tax savings could Dupuis and the company achieve as a result of this adjustment?

Problem Four

MX Manufacturing Ltd. is a Canadian-controlled private corporation located in Saskatchewan. The company regularly earns pre-tax profits of $400,000. These qualify as manufacturing profits for tax purposes.

The common shares of MX Manufacturing are owned 50/50 by Mr. and Mrs. Waldman. Only Mrs. Waldman works for the business, and she is paid a substantial salary for her efforts. Mr. Waldman is a lawyer and earns a large income from his law firm. In addition, the Waldmans receive annual dividends from MX. The company has consistently maintained a policy of distributing half its after-tax profits to the shareholders.

The Waldmans are dismayed at the amount of tax both they and the corporation must pay when corporate profits are distributed. They have asked you to explain to them the tax effect of distributing the corporate profits. In addition, they intend to sell the shares of the company in the next two or three years and want you to explain what the effect would be if they stopped paying dividends from MX.

The provincial income tax rate in Saskatchewan is 17% for corporations. However, the corporate rate is reduced to 5.5% on income eligible for the small-business deduction and 10% on qualified manufacturing income. Both Waldmans have already used up their capital gain exemption. The marginal tax rate the Waldmans personally pay is 43% on regular income and 29% on dividends.

Required:

1. What rate of tax are the Waldmans paying on the profits of MX that are distributed to them annually? Show calculations.

2. Should the Waldmans stop paying dividends? Your answer should indicate how their overall tax rate would be affected.

Problem Five

Hope Enterprises Ltd. is a Canadian-controlled private corporation that operates a jewellery manufacturing business in southwestern Ontario. The company was profitable for a number of years until a serious economic recession (which began three years ago) put the company in financial difficulty.

For the past three years, Hope Enterprises has suffered serious losses. Currently, it has unused non-capital losses of $650,000. Jean Talouse, the president and sole shareholder, has called a meeting of his senior staff to review the company's operations for the year and to plan a survival strategy. The meeting begins with the accountant presenting the current year's financial statements and a projection of operating results for the next three years. Part of this information is outlined in the tables on the following page.

The accountant reports the following additional information:

1. The company realized a gross profit of 20% on sales of $4,000,000, which is considerably lower than normal. However, all of the bad inventory has been cleaned out, and the current inventory can be sold to realize a 25% gross profit.

2. The accounts receivable represents a true evaluation of what can be collected. A reasonable reserve has been taken into account, and the credit policy has been adjusted to reduce the losses on future sales.

3. Both the bank loan and the loan from the shareholders are payable on demand and require interest payments of 12%. The bank is not uncomfortable with the current level of debt and has adequate security in the receivables and inventory.

4. So that only a minor loss will result this year, expenses have been cut to the bone. The projections are that over the next three years, if economic conditions remain basically the same, the company will suffer minor losses or perhaps break even.

5. The $650,000 loss carry-forward for tax purposes is a cause for concern. Most of this loss was incurred three years ago, so there is a possibility that the company will not generate profits in time to meet the time limit for carry-forwards.

The president is pleased that the company has got the losses under control. He instructs the accountant to determine whether any action can be taken to minimize the risk of the losses expiring.

Although he did not say so at the meeting, the president has decided to investigate the possibility of selling the company, as he feels that things may get worse in spite of the accountant's projections.

Required:

1. What steps can be taken to ensure that the loss carry-forward of $650,000 will not expire before profits are generated? Be specific, and indicate the amount of losses that will be preserved by your actions.

2. What can the president do to maximize the value of the shares in the event that he actively solicits a buyer for the company?

Balance Sheet

Assets:		
Cash		$ 20,000
Accounts receivable	1,250,000	
Allowance for doubtful accounts	(310,000)	940,000
Inventory, at lower of cost or market		750,000
Equipment, at cost	400,000	
Accumulated amortization	(250,000)	150,000
		$1,860,000
Liabilities:		
Accounts payable		699,000
Bank loan		500,000
Due to shareholder		400,000
		1,599,000
Shareholder's equity:		
Share capital	1,000	
Retained earnings	260,000	261,000
		$1,860,000

Statement of Income (Loss)

Sales		$4,000,000
Cost of sales		3,200,000
Gross profit		800,000
Expenses		
Selling and administrative salaries	300,000	
Shareholder's salary	60,000	
Delivery	50,000	
Rent	79,000	
Utilities	12,000	
Amortization (equal to CCA)	40,000	
Insurance	9,000	
Legal and accounting	12,000	
Interest	108,000	
Other expenses (including bad debts, office, repairs)	160,000	830,000
Net loss for the year		$ (30,000)

Problem Six

Norex Distributors Inc. is a small Canadian public corporation that derives all of its business income from the wholesale distribution of floor coverings.

Currently, Norex does not manufacture any of its products, and purchases all of its inventory from manufacturers in eastern Canada.

Norex has decided to acquire a small manufacturing plant in Saskatchewan. The following assets will be acquired:

Assets	Cost
Land	$ 80,000
Building	300,000
Manufacturing equipment	600,000
Goodwill	50,000
	$1,030,000

The planned acquisition date is July 1, 20X1, the day after the year end of Norex. The company's vice-president realizes that the manufacturing business can be purchased and operated through a newly created subsidiary corporation, and that the subsidiary's manufacturing profit of $240,000 (see below) can result in a federal manufacturing and processing deduction of $16,800 at the most. The province of Saskatchewan also offers a 7% rate reduction on manufacturing income.

As an alternative, Norex can purchase the assets and operate the manufacturing business as a division. The vice-president has asked you to determine, from a tax perspective, whether this alternative is preferable to the other. Norex has provided you with estimated results for the first year of operations *after the acquisition* (i.e., year ended June 30, 20X2). These results are summarized below.

Information relating to new manufacturing plant

1. Manufacturing activities take up 80% of the building's space. The remaining space is used for storing finished products and for administrative offices.

2. Estimated net income for tax purposes is $240,000, after appropriate deductions for capital cost allowance, eligible capital property, and the following:

Direct labour	$ 320,000
Utilities	14,000
Property taxes	4,000
Raw materials	610,000
Administrative and office salaries allocated from Norex (see below)	80,000
	$1,028,000

Information relating to Norex
(excluding new manufacturing plant)

1. Estimated net income for tax purposes is $4,730,000, including:

Interest income on long-term bonds		$130,000
Administrative salaries	630,000	
Warehouse and sales salaries	340,000	
	970,000	
Salaries allocated to new plant	(80,000)	890,000
Rent for fleet of delivery trucks		80,000

2. In estimating the net income of $4,730,000, an appropriate deduction for CCA was made on the following properties:

	Original cost of assets in class	Undepreciated CC (after CCA)
Class 1	$1,340,000	$ 965,000
Class 8	190,000	75,000
Class 10	360,000	190,000
	$1,890,000	$1,230,000

Required:

Should Norex operate the proposed new manufacturing operation as a separate subsidiary corporation or as a division? Provide calculations to support your answer.

Case   **National Industries Ltd.**

National Industries Ltd. is a Canadian venture corporation that holds investments in several industries. The company owns shares in a number of active business corporations in both Canada and the United States. Its income consists of dividends and management fees from the subsidiaries.

Charles Prokopchuk is a vice-president of National and is responsible for acquiring companies in the transportation industry. Currently, National owns three subsidiary corporations in this industry. Prokopchuk monitors their progress and provides head office management services.

Three months ago Prokopchuk sought a buyer for, and negotiated the sale of, Tri-Lon Transport Ltd. The shares of Tri-Lon were sold for $14,000,000. He is extremely pleased with the sale because he was instrumental in acquiring the shares of Tri-Lon seven years earlier for a price of $2,000,000. At that time, Tri-Lon was in its early growth stages; Prokopchuk is happy that he recognized the company's potential so early on. After acquiring Tri-Lon, Prokopchuk had hired new managers, streamlined the operations, and focussed expansion in the areas where the company was strong. Profits grew rapidly, so that by the time the shares were sold Tri-Lon had retained earnings of $8,000,000.

The president of National Industries congratulates Prokopchuk for a job well done and indicates that the cash generated from the sale of Tri-Lon shares was vital, as the company is facing the termination date of one of its major bond issues. However, even after receiving the additional cash from the Tri-Lon sale, National will still have to restructure its debt and obtain new long-term financing. The president has indicated that it is critical for the company to get a high rating on its bonds in order to secure the lowest possible interest costs. He informs Prokopchuk:

"Your success with Tri-Lon will make a big impact on our bottom line and earnings per share for the current year. Stock prices should improve and our proposed new bond issue will be better accepted in the market. You have carried out your responsibilities perfectly."

Historically, the shares of National Industries have traded on the Toronto Stock Exchange at a price equivalent to 12 times after-tax earnings. The company has 8,000,000 shares outstanding, and the president is certain that the share price will be $60 after the current year's earnings have been released.

Required:

Do you agree with the president's assessment of Prokopchuk's success? Explain.

The Corporate Structure

Business, more than any other occupation, is a continual
calculation, an instinctive exercise in foresight.

Henry Luce ✍

part three

Chapter 12 Organization, Capital Structures, and Income Distributions of Corporations

The basic framework for the taxation of corporations was introduced in Chapter 11. This part of the text expands that framework by examining, in three separate chapters, the organization of corporations, the implications of carrying on business within a Canadian-controlled private corporation, and complex corporate structures and their reorganization.

While the subject matter of each chapter relates to complex provisions of the *Income Tax Act* and other corporate statutes, the information is presented in a simplified and abbreviated form that emphasizes the fundamental concepts that have an impact on business decision making. Having read these chapters, the reader will understand the implications of alternative corporate structures and be able to compare those structures with other forms of business organization, which are discussed in Part Four of the text.

Chapter 12 explains how corporations are formed. It also discusses alternative capital structures and the entry and departure of shareholders. Specifically, this chapter covers three basic areas:

1. The implications of capitalizing a corporation with shareholder debt as opposed to equity.

2. Alternative methods of transferring assets to a corporation.

3. Income distributions to shareholders.

I. Corporate Capitalization— Debt or Equity

It was indicated in previous chapters that a corporation is a separate legal entity distinct from its owners, the shareholders. As such, both private and public corporations are subject to tax on their income, and their shareholders are subject to a second level of tax at the time corporate profits are distributed.

The process of creating a corporation requires that, at a minimum, share capital be issued to the shareholder in return for some consideration. This means that a corporation can be created by issuing some shares to an owner in exchange for a nominal asset such as a cash contribution of $1. In addition to this initial contribution, the corporation, in order to function, must have a capital base for the purposes of acquiring assets and conducting business. This capital base is also contributed by the shareholder(s) and can be in the form of debt or equity. Capital contributed by a shareholder in the form of debt is referred to as a "shareholder loan." Capital contributed in the form of equity consists of additional share capital, which can relate to fixed value shares that do not participate in corporate profits, or to shares that participate in profits and fluctuate in value depending on the extent of corporate earnings.

It should be pointed out that a corporation can obtain capital by borrowing funds from parties that are not shareholders. However, discussion in this chapter relates to capitalization by debt or equity by the shareholder(s).

From the shareholder's perspective, both debt (loans receivable from the corporation) and equity (shares owned in the corporation) constitute capital property for tax purposes, and yield a return on investment in the form of interest or dividends. As capital property, both debt and equity are subject to capital-gains treatment if and when disposed of at a value different from the initial cost.

The value of a shareholder loan may decrease if the assets within the corporation decline in value and are insufficient to satisfy the obligation, or increase in value if the debt bears a long-term interest rate that is high in relation to current economic conditions. The value of shares may change as a result of the following factors:

1. Profits earned or losses incurred by the corporation.

2. Increases or decreases in the value of assets owned by the corporation such as land, buildings, equipment, goodwill, and other intangibles.

3. The distribution of profits by corporate dividends.

The capitalizing of a corporation by a combination of share capital and shareholder debt is most often found in closely held private corporations in which the affairs of the corporation and the shareholders are closely linked. In widely held corporations, such as public corporations, this method is not common. However, this alternative may be used by public corporations to capitalize either a subsidiary corporation or a corporation whose shares are closely held by a small group of public corporations.

Each of these two alternatives—capitalization by share equity, and capitalization by a combination of share equity and shareholder debt—has advantages and disadvantages that are a function of the tax treatment resulting from

(a) the return on the invested capital—interest versus dividends;
(b) any losses that occur when the shares or loans are disposed of; and,
(c) the return of all or a portion of the original capital to the investor.

Both debt and equity capitalization are examined below in terms of the above three elements.

A. Corporate Capitalization by Shareholder Debt

Shareholder debt can take several different forms. The terms attached to the debt instrument can provide security to the lender (shareholder) by attaching specific assets of the corporation, or they can provide no security; they can provide specific repayment terms, or call for payment on demand; and they can provide for interest at normal rates, or no interest at all.

Shareholder debt, by definition, is arranged in conjunction with the ownership of share capital, and the ratio of debt to equity can vary. Exhibit 12-1 shows the initial capitalization of a corporation using a minimum of share capital and a maximum of shareholder debt. The initial capital base provided by the shareholders is $200,000, consisting of a shareholder's loan of $199,999 and share capital of $1.

If the corporation in Exhibit 12-1 wishes to obtain additional credit or loans from outside sources, it may find it necessary to subordinate the shareholder loan of $199,999. For example, a lending institution may advance funds to the corporation only on the condition that its loan takes precedence over the shareholder's loan and, further, that any repayments of the shareholder's loan be made only with the concurrence of the lending institution. Under these conditions the lending institution views the shareholder's loan as part of the equity capital of the corporation, even though in legal terms it constitutes a debt obligation.

The reasons for regarding the shareholder loan as part of the shareholder's equity in Exhibit 12-1 should be readily apparent—they have to do with the extreme ratio of debt to equity. Usually, a corporation capitalized with $1 of equity would have great difficulty acquiring debt funding of $199,999 from an outside source. Therefore, the shareholder's

Exhibit 12-1: Capitalization—Maximum Debt and Minimum Equity		Corporation		
Assets	$200,000		Shareholder loan	$199,999
			Share capital	1
	$200,000			$200,000

willingness to provide the loan reflects a need for additional equity. If the shareholders provided $200,000 to the corporation by way of $150,000 of share capital and a $50,000 shareholder loan, it would be difficult to establish whether or not the loan constituted a true debt rather than part of the equity base. Normally the marketplace, which provides outside debt financing, will establish the real nature of shareholder debt.

For tax purposes, a shareholder loan qualifies as debt regardless of how it may be viewed by the marketplace. However, it is important to recognize that the decision to use shareholder debt for tax reasons may have an impact on other, non–tax-related issues. For example, independent credit reports may indicate unfavourable debt/equity ratios when shareholder capital is included as debt rather than equity. As well, to properly value the equity of a business for acquisitions and divestitures, it is necessary to establish the true nature of the shareholder's capital (see Chapter 19).

• **Return on investment**   As previously mentioned, shareholder loans may bear some rate of interest or be interest-free.

Interest paid by the corporation is deductible for tax purposes; this reduces corporate taxable income and increases the shareholder's taxable income by an equivalent amount. Effectively, the payment of interest converts corporate business income into property income of the shareholder and funnels a certain amount of corporate income directly to the shareholder. This reduces the amount of corporate income that is subject to two levels of taxation.

If the shareholder loan does not bear interest, corporate taxable income will be higher, the result being increased corporate taxes and a further tax when corporate retained earnings are distributed as a dividend.

In the following situation, a shareholder loan that bears interest is compared with one that does not.

Situation: X Corporation is subject to a corporate tax rate of 37% and earns business income of $1,000 before the payment of interest. A shareholder loan of $10,000 to the corporation can bear interest of 10% or be interest-free. The shareholder's personal income is subject to a tax rate of 45%.

Analysis: If the shareholder debt is subject to a 10% interest rate (10% × $10,000 = $1,000), the combined tax to the shareholder and the corporation amounts to $450, calculated as follows:

Corporation:	
Business income	$1,000
Interest paid	(1,000)
Income for tax purposes	–0–
Corporate tax	–0–
Shareholder (individual):	
Interest income	$1,000
Personal tax @ 45%	$ 450
Combined tax ($0 + $450)	$ 450

If the shareholder's debt is interest-free, the combined corporate and shareholder tax will ultimately be $559, calculated as follows:

Corporation:	
Business income	$1,000
Interest paid	–0–
Income for tax purposes	$1,000
Corporate tax @ 37%	$ 370
Shareholder (individual):	
Potential dividend ($1,000 – $370)	$ 630
Tax (net of dividend tax credit)*	$ 189
Combined tax ($370 + $189)	$ 559

* 30% of $630 = $189; see Exhibit 10-6 in Chapter 10.

In the above example the payment of interest eliminated the corporate tax of 37% and shifted the income to the shareholder, who was taxed on it at 45%. While the amount of immediate tax (37%) is higher, the payment of deductible interest eliminates the potential for double taxation that occurs when no interest is paid. This result stems from the fact that when a corporation is subject to a high tax rate, double taxation will occur when the after-tax corporate profits are distributed to the shareholder as dividends at some future time. If the rate of corporate tax were lower—for example, if the corporation were subject to the small business rate of approximately 18%—the tax results of paying or not paying interest would be dramatically different.

Assuming the same facts as in the above situation, except that the corporate rate of tax is reduced to 18% from 37%, the following results would occur.

If the shareholder debt is subject to 10% interest, the combined corporate and shareholder tax remains the same, as follows:

Corporation:	
Corporate income after interest	–0–
Corporate tax	–0–
Shareholder (individual):	
Tax @ 45% on $1,000 of interest income	$450
Combined tax	$450

If the shareholder debt is interest-free, the combined corporate and shareholder tax is ultimately about $426, as calculated below.

Corporation:	
Business income	$1,000
Interest paid	–0–
Income for tax purposes	$1,000
Corporate tax @ 18%	$ 180
Shareholder (individual):	
Potential dividend ($1,000 – $180)	$ 820
Tax (net of dividend tax credit)*	$ 246
Combined tax ($180 + $246)	$ 426

* 30% of $820 = $246.

Notice that in the above example, the combined tax is approximately the same under both alternatives; however, the *immediate* tax to the corporation if no interest is paid is only $180, as opposed to $450 under the interest-paying option. It is important to note that the second level of tax on corporate distributions may occur at some time in the future and that it is necessary to consider not only the ultimate amount of tax payable, but also when that payment must be made.

The results of the previous two analyses are compared in Exhibit 12-2. The exhibit indicates that when corporate taxes are 18%, an interest-free loan is preferable, because even though the total tax will eventually be similar, the immediate tax is substantially lower at $180. However, when the corporate tax rate is 37%, an interest-bearing loan is preferable because, although the immediate tax is the same, the ultimate total tax is lower because double taxation is avoided.

Exhibit 12-2: Interest Versus No Interest on Shareholder Debt	Immediate tax	Future tax on dividend distribution	Total
Corporate tax rate (18%):			
Interest	$450	–0–	$450
No interest	180	246	426
Corporate tax rate (37%):			
Interest	$450	–0–	$450
No interest	370	189	559

In each of the previous examples, the tax impact was calculated on the assumption that the corporation earned income in the particular year. However, when the corporation is incurring losses, the paying of interest on a shareholder loan has a negative impact. In such cases the interest paid out increases the corporate loss, which remains unused until future corporate profits are achieved; the related interest income to the shareholder is fully taxable, however. In effect, although the economic entity has suffered a loss, taxation still occurs in that year. This diminished cash flow reduces the shareholder's ability to provide further contributions to the corporation if those are required to fund the losses and restore the original capital base. This factor is particularly important when the corporation is a new venture that is suffering losses during its start-up years and requires maximum shareholder support.

• **Loss of investment** When providing capital to a corporation, the investor must consider the possibility of ultimately losing all or a portion of the investment if the corporation should encounter financial difficulty. In particular, the investor must determine to what extent, and when, such a loss can be used for tax purposes to generate additional funds through the reduction of tax otherwise payable.

As the shareholder debt is capital property to the shareholder, a loss incurred on it is a capital loss, of which only one-half is available for tax purposes. If the loan is to a small business corporation (see Chapter 8), the capital loss becomes a business investment loss and one-half of the loss can be offset against all other sources of income; otherwise, it can be offset only against other capital gains. While the amount of loss that can be used for tax purposes is the same for share capital and shareholder debt, the timing for recognizing those losses in order to create cash flow by reducing taxes is different.

As indicated in Chapter 8, a loss on a loan is recognized for tax purposes in the year in which it is *established* to be uncollectible, whereas a loss on share capital is recognized only when the shares are actually sold, or the corporation is insolvent and has ceased operations, or the corporation has become legally bankrupt.[1] Therefore, a loss on shareholder loans can normally be recognized for tax purposes before a loss on share capital. This treatment provides an advantage to the shareholder for two reasons:

1. Recognizing the loss earlier rather than later diminishes the real loss, in cash-flow terms, on the initial investment.

2. The shareholder loss can be recognized when a corporation is in extreme financial difficulty but is not yet bankrupt and still has a chance of survival. The cash flow created for the shareholder from the early loss recognition can be used to strengthen the corporation and increase its chances for survival.

For example, a shareholder loan of $200,000 that is established to be a bad debt may generate tax savings to the shareholder in a 45% tax bracket of $45,000 (45% $\times$ ½ of $200,000). The shareholder can choose to keep the $45,000 to reduce the investment loss from $200,000 to $155,000 ($200,000 – $45,000), or can contribute the $45,000 to the corporation to strengthen its capital base. Either way, the tax treatment has diminished the downside risk of the investment.

• **Return of capital**   The capital base contributed to a corporation by its shareholder(s) is not permanent. A corporation may require additional capital for expansion, or its financial strength may be in excess of its capital requirements so that a return of all or a portion of the shareholder's initial capital is appropriate.

Shareholder capital contributed in the form of debt can be returned with relative ease and without tax consequences. Consider the capital structure described in Exhibit 12-3. The structure is based on the initial capital structure outlined in Exhibit 12-1, in which the shareholder contributed $200,000 to the corporation by way of share capital of $1 and a loan of $199,999. Say that the corporation subsequently generated and retained after-tax profits of $200,000, increasing its total equity to $400,000. If the company is able to operate with a capital base of only $200,000, it can return $200,000 to the shareholder.

Exhibit 12-3:	Corporation (before)			
Capital Structure—				
before and after	Assets	$400,000	Shareholder loan	$199,999
Return of Capital			Share capital	1
			Retained earnings	200,000
		$400,000		$400,000
	Corporation (after)			
	Assets	$200,001	Share capital	$ 1
			Retained earnings	200,000
		$200,001		$200,001

The $200,000 can be returned to the shareholder in two ways:

1. The company can declare a dividend from its retained earnings.

2. The company can repay the loan to the shareholder for $199,999.

---

1   ITA 50(1), (2); IT-159R3, IT-239R2.

The dividend payment is taxable to the shareholder; the loan repayment constitutes a return of capital and is not taxable. Obviously the shareholder would prefer that the debt be repaid, because this would delay the tax on a dividend distribution until some future time.

This tax treatment results because the retained earnings are attached to the share capital rather than to the loan. The share capital, which had an original value of $1, has increased in value to $200,001, and in certain circumstances may be taxable if returned to the shareholders, as described in Section B.

B. Corporate Capitalization by Share Capital	A corporation can be capitalized with share capital in several ways. It can issue several different classes of shares under a wide range of terms and conditions. Corporate law does not normally assign labels to the various classes of shares; however, the *Income Tax Act* does make reference to common shares and preferred shares.

For tax purposes, a *common* share is a share that entitles the owner to share in corporate assets and earnings beyond the initial share price plus a fixed premium or dividend rate.[2] A *preferred* share is a share that entitles the owner to participate in corporate assets and earnings *only* up to an amount equal to the initial share price plus a fixed dividend rate, regardless of the extent of corporate earnings.[3] Consequently, common shares increase or decrease in value in relation to the accumulation of corporate earnings or losses; preferred shares seldom increase in value, because the potential return is predetermined and fixed, but can decline in value if corporate assets are depleted.

The initial shareholders can provide base capital to the corporation either by common shares alone or by a combination of common shares and various types of preferred shares.

• **Return on investment**   Share capital provides a return to its owners in the form of dividends. Dividends are not deductible by the corporation and are taxable to the individual shareholder. This treatment imposes the two-tier system of taxation that was described in Chapter 11. The corporation must earn income, pay tax, and use its after-tax earnings to pay dividends. In comparison, a corporation issuing debt can pay interest from pre-tax profits.

As previously mentioned, to the extent that corporate profits are taxed at the high rate of 37%, the combination of corporate tax and the subsequent tax on dividend distributions results in severe double taxation. Corporate profits taxed at the lower rate, however, are not subject to double taxation. When a corporation is subject to the higher corporate rate of tax, it is in the shareholder's interest to provide capital to the corporation with a maximum amount of shareholder loans in order to increase the return in the form of interest and reduce the impact of double taxation. Consider the following situation:

Situation: A corporation that is earning $1,000 of business income and is subject to tax at a rate of 37% requires $10,000 of shareholder capital. The shareholder can provide a loan of $10,000 bearing interest at 10% (10% × $10,000 = $1,000) or provide share capital of $10,000 that provides a dividend equal to the corporation's after-tax profits. The shareholder, an individual, is in a 45% tax bracket.

Analysis: The calculation for this analysis is identical to the previous analysis that compared a shareholder loan paying 10% interest with one that paid no interest. The results are summarized in the following table:

2   ITA 248.
3   ITA 248.

Shareholder debt with interest:	
Corporate tax (owing to deductible interest)	–0–
Shareholder tax on interest	450
Total tax	$450
Share capital with dividends:	
Corporate tax	$370
Shareholder tax on dividend	189
Total tax	$559

If, in the above situation, the corporate tax rate had been 18% the combined tax would have been the same for each alternative, but the share capital option would have been preferred, because in such cases the shareholder can choose to delay the payment of dividends so that the immediate tax is only 18%.

• **Loss of investment**   A loss incurred on a share capital investment is normally a capital loss, of which one-half is recognized for tax purposes. However, unlike losses on shareholder loans, a share capital loss is recognized only in the year in which the shares are disposed of, or the corporation becomes legally bankrupt, or the corporation is insolvent and has ceased operations. From the perspective of downside risk, share capital is inferior to shareholder debt, which usually can be recognized for tax purposes at an earlier time.

• **Return of capital**   Before reviewing how share capital is returned to the corporate shareholder, it would be useful to examine the methods available for acquiring shares in a corporation.

Corporate shares can be acquired in two ways:

1. The prospective shareholder can purchase all or a portion of previously issued shares from other shareholders.

2. The prospective shareholder can purchase, directly from the corporation, new shares issued from the corporate treasury.

Each of these alternatives has different tax and price implications to the parties involved in the transaction.

1. Acquisition of Shares Directly from the Corporation

Under this alternative the new shareholder contributes cash or other assets directly to the corporation in exchange for shares of an equivalent value.

The receipt of assets in exchange for shares in the corporation has no tax consequences to the corporation. In effect, the corporation has acquired property (cash or other assets) and paid for it by issuing new share capital. The stated value of the shares to the corporation is equal to the value of the property exchanged. When the corporation receives equipment valued at $10,000 in exchange for five common shares, the stated value of each share is $2,000 ($2,000 × 5 shares = $10,000). For tax purposes, the stated value of the shares is referred to as "paid-up capital."[4]

From the shareholder's perspective, the receipt of shares represents the acquisition of capital property having an adjusted cost base for tax purposes equal to the value of the

4   ITA 89(1)(c); IT-463R2.

property exchanged. In the above example the adjusted cost base of the five shares received is $10,000 ($2,000 per share), that being the value of the equipment given up in exchange.[5]

When a corporation with existing shareholders admits a new shareholder by issuing additional shares, referred to as "treasury shares," there are no tax consequences to the existing shareholders. Exhibit 12-4 diagrams a change in the share structure of an existing corporation. The "before" diagram indicates that the corporation was originally owned by a single shareholder and had a total value of $100,000. In the "after" diagram a new shareholder has acquired a 50% ownership of the corporation by acquiring shares directly from the corporation. It is important to recognize that the original shareholder did not dispose of any shares even though his/her ownership interest diminished from 100% to 50%. In such cases, there are no tax consequences to the original shareholder.

Exhibit 12-4:
Admitting New
Shareholders by Issuing
Treasury Shares

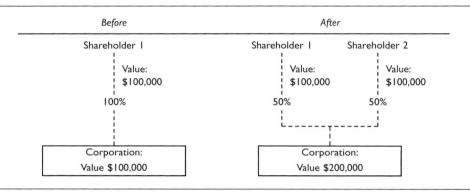

Also notice that in order to acquire a 50% ownership of the corporation, which had an original value of $100,000, the new shareholder contributed $100,000 to the company and not $50,000 (half of $100,000). The result of this transaction is that the value of the company has increased from $100,000 to $200,000. The additional resources are available for business expansion or debt retirement. The original shareholder now has a diluted ownership percentage but still holds shares worth $100,000.

2. Acquisition of Shares from Other Shareholders

Under this alternative the new shareholder buys the shares directly from the other shareholders, and no funds are contributed to the corporation. The original shareholders will have a capital gain or loss on the sale of whatever shares they have sold, whether this involves all their shares or only a fraction of them.

From the buyer's perspective, the shares acquired will have an adjusted cost base for tax purposes equal to the purchase price. However, it should be noted that the paid-up capital value of the shares in the corporation remains unchanged even if the purchaser has acquired the previously issued shares at a price different from the original issued value.

Consider the situation in Exhibit 12-5, in which a corporation with a value of $100,000 is owned 100% by a single shareholder. A new shareholder acquires 50% of the shares by purchasing half the original shareholder's shares. In this situation the purchase price for 50% of a $100,000 company is only $50,000, compared with $100,000 when shares are purchased from the corporation.

Also notice that the resources of the company remain the same after the new shareholder arrives—they consist of share capital of $1,000 plus retained earnings of $99,000 for a total value of $100,000. The new shareholder owns shares that for tax purposes have an adjusted cost base of $50,000 but a paid-up capital value on the corporate balance sheet of only $500 (half of $1,000). The difference ($49,500) has implications if and when share capital is returned to the shareholders.

---

5   ITA 53(1).

Exhibit 12-5:
New Shareholder
Acquires Shares from
Other Shareholders

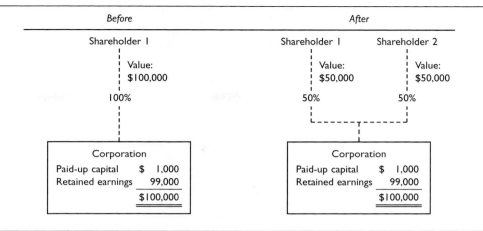

Corporate share capital is divided into a number of units represented by the number of shares held. For example, an owner can contribute $100,000 to a corporation in return for one share or a number of shares. Capital can be returned to the shareholder when that shareholder disposes of all or a portion of the shares. (There is a second method for returning capital—see Section 5.) Common shares, which participate in earnings, change in value over time, and as a result the disposition of shares to provide a return of capital may have tax consequences.

A shareholder can dispose of shares in two ways:

1. The shares can be sold to other shareholders.

2. The shares can be bought back by the corporation for cancellation.

Each alternative has its own tax implications, which are reviewed below.

3. Sale of Shares to Other Shareholders

Under this alternative, the sale of shares creates a capital gain or a capital loss depending on whether the shares have increased or decreased in value. This alternative allows the shareholder to realize a return on the original investment as well as any share appreciation resulting from corporate earnings. It should also be noted that when shares are sold to other shareholders, the vendor's percentage ownership in the corporation is diminished.

Since transactions of this nature are between the shareholders, the corporation's resources and capital base remain unchanged.

4. Sale of Shares Back to the Corporation

This type of transaction is referred to as a "share redemption" or "buy-back." It involves the distribution of corporate assets (normally cash) to the shareholders and a cancellation of all or some of their shares. This alternative automatically diminishes the value and resources of the corporation because it involves the direct return of share equity to the shareholders.

This type of transaction is useful when a corporation wishes to return some of its equity on a proportionate basis to all existing shareholders without changing the ownership ratio. It can also be used to buy the shares of one or a few of the shareholders, thereby automatically expanding the ownership percentage of the remaining shareholders.

Consider the situation in Exhibit 12-6. A corporation with two equal shareholders has a value of $100,000 consisting of $10,000 of common share capital and $90,000 of retained earnings. Shareholder 2 departs by selling shares back to the corporation for $50,000. Notice that after the transaction the corporate resources have diminished from $100,000 to $50,000 as a result of the cancellation of half the entity's shares and a distribution of half its retained earnings. After the share redemption, shareholder 1 is the sole shareholder. The interesting aspect of this transaction is that shareholder 1 has acquired control not by

Exhibit 12-6:
Corporate Redemption
of Shares

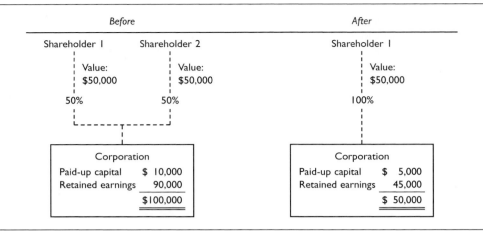

purchasing any additional shares but by removing the other shareholder, thereby depleting the corporation's resources.

The redemption value of corporate shares is the sum of two separate values—the original capital value of the shares, and the change in value resulting from corporate earnings accumulated and attached to those shares. The *tax consequences* to the shareholder when a *redemption* occurs are summarized as follows:

- To the extent that the redemption price exceeds the paid-up capital (original issue price) of the shares, a *dividend* is deemed to have been distributed.[6]

- In addition, the shareholder is deemed to have sold the shares, for the purpose of determining the capital gain or capital loss, at an amount equal to the paid-up capital of the shares.[7]

In other words, a share redemption involves both a dividend payment and a sale of shares.

The tax consequences of this are demonstrated below using the share redemption example in Exhibit 12-6. In order to complete the calculation, an assumption must be made with respect to the adjusted cost base of the shares owned by shareholder 2. If shareholder 2 were an original shareholder who acquired shares directly from the corporate treasury, the adjusted cost base of the shares would be $5,000, which is equal to the paid-up capital. However, if those same shares were purchased from a previous shareholder, they would have a different cost for tax purposes that would not be the same as the paid-up capital. Assuming that shareholder 2 acquired the shares as an original shareholder, the result of the redemption is as follows:

Deemed dividend:	
Redemption price	$50,000
Paid-up capital	(5,000)
Dividend to shareholder 2	$45,000
Capital transaction:	
Deemed proceeds of disposition (selling price of $50,000 minus dividend)	$ 5,000
Adjusted cost base	(5,000)
Capital gain	–0–

---

6   ITA 84(3).

7   ITA 54(h) (redemption value less deemed dividend).

The above indicates that shareholder 2 received the return of original capital without tax consequences. However, any additional value was treated as a dividend and *not* as a capital gain, which would have occurred had the shares been sold to a new shareholder.

It is important to recognize that when redeeming corporate shares, the company cannot simply repay the original share capital but also must distribute the attached retained earnings as a dividend.

5. Reduction of Paid-up Capital

As an alternative, a corporation can return only its paid-up capital to the shareholders without redeeming any of its shares. The tax treatment of this option varies depending on whether the corporation is private or public. If the proper legal steps are taken, a *private* corporation can make a payment to its shareholders that constitutes a return of capital. There are no tax consequences for this transaction provided the payment reduces and does not exceed the paid-up capital value.[8]

Consider the three capital structures shown in Exhibit 12-7. Each includes $100,000 of capital. If each entity is a private corporation, in each case the company can return the original capital to the shareholders without triggering a simultaneous distribution of taxable dividends.

In contrast, a public corporation that executes the same transaction and reduces paid-up capital is considered to have paid a taxable dividend for the entire payment.[9] Therefore, if the entities in Exhibit 12-7 were public corporations, only under structures A and B would the company be permitted to return the original share capital to the shareholder without triggering a taxable dividend.

Exhibit 12-7: Alternative Capital Structures

	A	B	C
Shareholder loans	$ 99,000	–0–	–0–
Preferred shares	–0–	99,000	–0–
Common shares	1,000	1,000	100,000
	100,000	100,000	100,000
Retained earnings	50,000	50,000	50,000
	$150,000	$150,000	$150,000

While the amount of capital a corporation requires in order to function may be clear, the manner in which that capital is provided by the shareholder is not. The opportunity exists for a wide variety of capital formats, including shareholder debt, preferred shares, and common shares. Each format will have a different effect on the amount and timing of future tax costs, and on the resulting cash flows.

Shareholders must determine which capital structure is most appropriate by examining the tax implications of the following: regular returns provided on the capital; the possible loss of the investment; and the return of the original capital.

II. Transferring Assets to a Corporation

It was mentioned earlier that a shareholder may capitalize a corporation by providing assets in exchange for share capital or debt. The assets exchanged can consist of either cash or other assets such as land, buildings, equipment, franchises, and the like. The transfer of assets to the corporation constitutes a sale and disposition for the shareholder. To the extent that those assets appreciated in value before the transfer, there will be tax implications.

8 ITA 84(4); IT-67R3.
9 ITA 84(4.1), 53(2)(a).

A corporation need not acquire assets in order to use them, as the right of use can be achieved by leasing the asset from the shareholder. However, this section of the chapter restricts itself to a discussion of asset transfers.

For tax purposes, an existing or proposed shareholder can transfer an asset to a corporation either at the fair market value or at an elected value, which is normally equal to the asset's cost for tax purposes. Each alternative has different tax implications to the shareholder and to the corporation.

A. Transfer of Assets at Fair Market Value

When assets are transferred at fair market value, any gains on the sale are recognized by the shareholder. Depending on the nature of the asset transferred, the resulting income may be a capital gain, a recapture of capital cost allowance, or normal business income.

The recognition of taxable income is not necessarily a negative consequence. For example, the shareholder can use the income from an asset sale to offset accumulated losses that could not otherwise have been used.

The corporation that acquires the asset at fair market value has an increased cost for tax purposes that may, in turn, reduce the taxes payable by the corporation. Consider the following situation:

Situation: A shareholder who owns equipment that originally cost $100,000 and that has an undepreciated cost of $60,000 sells the equipment to a corporation at the fair market value price of $90,000 in exchange for a combination of shares and debt. The shareholder's tax rate is 45% and the corporation's tax rate is 37%.

Analysis: The sale of the equipment creates taxable income to the shareholder of $30,000 ($90,000 − $60,000 = $30,000).

The cost of the equipment to the corporation that is available for capital cost allowance is $90,000. Since the pre-transfer undepreciated capital cost of the equipment was $60,000, the corporation will have additional capital cost allowance deductions, over a period of time, of $30,000.

While most taxpayers automatically shy away from paying tax up front in return for future reductions in tax, the circumstances should always be considered in real cash-flow terms. For example, a taxpayer in the 45% income bracket may well feel overwhelmed at the prospect of incurring taxable income of $30,000. However, the real cost of transferring the asset at fair market value in the preceding situation is $6,100 (assuming the discount factor for the time value of money is 10%), calculated as follows:

Immediate tax cost on transfer:	
$30,000 × 45%	$13,500
less	
Present value of tax savings from additional capital cost allowance in the corporation (using the formula described in Chapter 6):	
$\dfrac{\$30,000 \times .37 \times .20}{.20 + .10} =$	(7,400)
Net cost in cash-flow terms	$ 6,100

Although the result is still negative, the impact is softened when measured in real cash-flow terms. It should also be pointed out that the tax cost (above) might have been lower if the particular asset had had a higher capital cost allowance rate, or if the personal rate of tax had been lower than the corporate rate of tax.

B. Election to Transfer Assets at Tax Values

The *Income Tax Act* permits assets to be transferred to a corporation at their tax cost provided that certain formal procedures are adhered to. This option is permitted even though the transfer price for legal purposes may be at fair market value. For example, using the facts in the previous situation, the shareholder could legally sell the equipment to the corporation for $90,000 and receive full consideration in exchange, but for tax purposes elect that the equipment's sale price was $60,000 (its undepreciated capital cost). The result of such an election would be that the shareholder had no taxable income from the transfer and that the corporation would incur any taxable income in the event that it ultimately sold the equipment to a third party.

Such an election is often called a "rollover" because the shareholder's potential taxable income is rolled over to the corporation but not eliminated.

• **Election limitations**   The tax provisions that apply to the procedure for electing a transfer price other than fair market value are complex, and managers should seek professional advice. Even so, from a decision-making perspective, the reader must be aware of when the election applies, and of the resulting tax consequences in terms of cash flow to the shareholder and the corporation. The fundamental limitations of the election procedure are presented below.[10]

The corporation acquiring the asset can pay the shareholder in the form of either share consideration or non-share consideration. Share consideration can consist of various types of common or preferred shares. Non-share consideration can consist of cash, a debt owing to the shareholder, the assumption by the corporation of shareholder liabilities, or the exchange of some other corporate asset. For example, a shareholder building valued at $100,000 but encumbered by a $60,000 mortgage can be purchased by the corporation in exchange for assumption of the $60,000 mortgage liability and the issuing of additional preferred shares for $40,000.

The primary limitations of the election procedure relate to the nature of the consideration paid for the asset. In order for the transfer to avoid tax, the consideration must include some shares, although there is no specified amount; as well, the non-share consideration (cash or debts owing to the shareholder) cannot be greater than the elected value of the asset transferred. (The elected value is normally the asset's tax cost.)

The above limitations are demonstrated in the following situation:

Situation: A shareholder owning a building that originally cost $100,000 and that has an undepreciated capital cost of $90,000 and a fair market value of $130,000 transfers the property to a corporation and wishes to avoid tax on the transfer.

Analysis: Notwithstanding that the legal selling price would be $130,000, taxable income can be avoided if the shareholder and the corporation agree that the transfer price for tax purposes is $90,000, which is the building's undepreciated capital cost. In accordance with the preceding limitations, payment must include some shares, but the non-share payment cannot be higher than $90,000. Therefore the legal form of the transfer can be as follows:

Legal selling price	$130,000
Payment consideration:	
Debt owing to shareholder	$ 90,000
Preferred shares	40,000
	$130,000

---

10 ITA 85(1); IT-291R2.

• **Tax implications to the shareholder and the corporation**   In this situation, choosing the elective option avoids tax to the shareholder at the time of the transfer. However, there will be future tax implications, and these should be anticipated before the decision to use the election is made, in order that the real impact on cash flow can be understood. The above situation will have the following implications:

1. The legal purchase price of the building was $130,000, and the corporate accounting balance sheet may reflect this amount. However, the cost of the building to the corporation *for tax purposes* is dramatically different. Because the elected tax value was $90,000, the corporation is deemed to have an undepreciated capital cost of $90,000 and an original cost of $100,000 for the building.

    As a result, if the corporation were to subsequently sell the building for, say, $130,000, no accounting gain would occur, but taxable income would be created as follows:

Recapture ($100,000 − $90,000)	$10,000
Taxable capital gains:	
($130,000 − $100,000 = $30,000) × ½	15,000
	$25,000

   Notice that this is the same amount of taxable income that the shareholder would have incurred upon selling the building for tax purposes at fair market value.

   The after-tax corporate income from the asset sale may ultimately be distributed as a dividend to the shareholder, causing a second level of tax, at which time, if the corporation is subject to the high rate of tax on business income, double taxation will occur. This means that delaying taxation by using the election may create greater taxation in the long run.

2. After the transfer the shareholder will own a note receivable from the corporation of $90,000 and preferred shares of $40,000, both of which are capital property. Because the transfer price was $90,000 for tax purposes, this amount represents the cost base to the shareholder of debt and the shares, with the amount being allocated first to the debt. Thus, the cost base of the loan is $90,000, and the cost base of the shares is zero.

    In addition, the preferred shares are deemed to have a nominal paid-up capital.[11] If those shares are subsequently redeemed, a deemed dividend occurs for the full redemption amount. However, if the loan of $90,000 is paid out to the shareholder, no tax consequences occur. In this way, the elective option permits the shareholder to recover, free of tax, an amount up to the elected tax transfer price.

   The elective option is designed to provide flexibility when assets are incorporated. However, in exchange for this flexibility, other long-term implications may arise that diminish the attractiveness of satisfying immediate tax concerns. While it is usually advantageous to defer tax to a later period, this is not always the case. Therefore it is vital that managers anticipate future events when deciding whether to use the election.

---

11 ITA 85(2.1).

C. Applying the Election Option

A wide range of assets can be transferred to a corporation at the tax cost rather than at fair market value. The following types of assets are eligible for such election:[12]

1. Capital property, both depreciable and non-depreciable, such as land, buildings, equipment, and depreciable intangibles including patents, franchises, and licences of a limited legal life.

2. Inventory.

3. Eligible capital property (see Chapter 6) such as goodwill, and patents, franchises, and licences with an undefined legal life.

4. Resource property.

The above list includes virtually all types of assets. A few exceptions exist; for example, real estate that is being held for resale (in other words, that is not capital property but inventory) is not permitted the rollover election.

The elective option is available to various types of transactions. Its use is most often associated with transactions involving the creation or altering of corporate structures by related parties; however, there is no requirement that its use be restricted to parties that are not at arm's length. The following transactions often make use of the election:

1. The incorporation of a proprietorship where the proprietor becomes the shareholder of the new corporation.

2. The transferring of assets from a parent corporation to a new or existing subsidiary corporation. For example, if a corporation wants to operate one of its divisions as a separate company, the assets of the division can be transferred at tax values to a newly created subsidiary corporation.

3. Shareholders often own several "sister" corporations. The elective option is useful in transferring assets from one sister corporation to another within the corporate group.

4. A corporation or an individual can sell assets to an unrelated third party and defer tax by using the election. For example, Corporation X may want to dispose of its business by selling assets to Corporation Y. The parties can defer tax by opting for transfer at the tax cost, provided that Corporation X (the seller) becomes a shareholder in Corporation Y (the buyer).

Several of the above transactions are examined in greater detail in Chapter 14.

III. Corporate Distributions to Shareholders

Corporate distributions to shareholders consist of either accumulated profits or the return of capital. As indicated previously, any distribution of property from a corporation that relates to share capital is automatically considered to be, first, a distribution of earnings and therefore a dividend, and second, a return of capital. This holds true not only when dividends are declared in the normal fashion but also when a corporation redeems or buys back its own shares.

---

12 ITA 85(1.1).

This section of the chapter briefly examines certain unique forms of corporate distributions as well as the general tax treatment resulting from the wind-up and elimination of a corporation.

A. Stock Dividends

A stock dividend involves the issuing of additional shares in lieu of a cash distribution. From the corporation's perspective, there are no tax or cash implications, as the transaction simply involves making an accounting entry that reduces retained earnings and increases the share capital.

The shareholder who receives additional shares as a result of a stock dividend is deemed, for tax purposes, to have received a normal taxable dividend. The amount of the dividend is equal to the amount the corporation transfers from retained earnings to paid-up capital on the corporate balance sheet.[13] As indicated in Chapter 7, this treatment forces the shareholder to reinvest the dividend in additional share capital of the corporation. In the event that the share is later sold, its cost base for tax purposes is equal to the deemed dividend previously included in income.

B. Special Distributions of Canadian-Controlled Private Corporations

The policy of double taxation is applied fully for public corporations. However, this policy applies to Canadian-controlled private corporations only to the extent that their earnings represent business income in excess of $200,000 annually. For example, it was demonstrated previously that business income taxed at the low corporate rate does not result in double taxation when distributed because the dividend tax credit provides sufficient relief. However, the low rate of tax applies only to business income and not to property income or to the taxable portion of capital gains.

A Canadian-controlled private corporation is taxed on property income (interest, rents, and so on) at the high corporate rate (44% or 45% in most provinces) plus a special refundable tax of $6\frac{2}{3}\%$. In order to avoid double taxation, a portion of this tax is refunded to the corporation when dividends are distributed from this source (see Chapter 13). Any dividend declared is considered to have come first from this source of income, to the extent that it exists.

In addition, certain income earned by corporations is tax-free—for example, life insurance proceeds and one-half of capital gains. In order to eliminate double taxation, these amounts, net of any losses from similar sources, are permitted to be distributed as a tax-free dividend referred to as a "capital dividend." Dividends from this source are not automatic and require a special election.[14]

Both of the above items are examined more closely in Chapter 13.

C. Distributions Other than Cash

While corporate distributions are normally made in the form of cash, a corporation can pay a dividend by transferring ownership of corporate assets to the shareholder. This is referred to as a "dividend in kind."

If the asset distributed has a value greater than the corporation's tax cost, the corporation is deemed to have disposed of the asset at fair market value, which results in taxable income to the corporation. Similarly, the taxable dividend received by the shareholder is equal to the fair market value of the asset received.[15] For example, consider the situation where a corporation transfers land that is capital property, having a fair market value of $100,000 and a cost base of $70,000, to a shareholder as a dividend distribution. The

---

13 ITA 248, 89(1)(c); IT-88R2.
14 ITA 83(2), 89(1)(b); IT-66R6.
15 ITA 52(2).

corporation will incur a taxable capital gain of $15,000 ($100,000 − $70,000 = $30,000 × ½), and the shareholder will receive a dividend of $100,000. The adjusted cost base of the land received from the dividend will be $100,000 for the shareholder, and any gain or loss from a subsequent sale will be measured against that base.

D. Wind-up of a Corporation

A corporation can end its existence by disposing of all its assets, meeting its debt obligations, and distributing all its earnings and capital to the shareholders.

On wind-up, the corporate assets can be converted to cash through a sale on the open market, or the assets can be distributed to the shareholders as part of the distribution of capital and earnings. If assets are first sold on the open market, taxable income will occur to the extent that the proceeds of disposition exceed the tax cost of the various assets. This additional income will, after the tax liability has been satisfied, form part of the earnings distribution on the wind-up.

Similarly, if corporate assets are distributed as part of the wind-up proceedings, the corporation is deemed to have sold them at fair market value, which provides the same tax result as if they had been sold on the open market.[16] It is important to recognize that, except when a 90%-owned subsidiary is being wound up into its parent corporation, there is no opportunity to defer tax through election options when assets are being transferred to the shareholder on wind-up. This, of course, is in complete contrast to the situation where a corporation is being created; at such a time, a shareholder can choose to defer tax on assets transferred into the company. In short, the process of getting into a corporation provides significant flexibility, but the process of getting out of a corporation is very restrictive.

The comments in this section were brief, and were designed to provide an overview of the general treatment of corporate wind-ups. A more detailed examination of wind-ups and their implications is made in Chapter 17. In addition, a review of the procedures for winding up a subsidiary into its parent corporation is made in Chapter 14.

IV. Summary and Conclusion

This chapter has examined the tax factors and implications on cash flow relating to the start-up, maintenance, and wind-up of corporations.

At the outset, shareholders organizing a corporation must decide how to capitalize that corporation—that is, how to use share capital and shareholder debt. Each possible alternative affects the amount and timing of tax with respect to returns received on the capital invested, the treatment resulting from the possible loss of the capital invested, and the repatriation of capital for reinvestment by the shareholders. These areas are compared below.

• **Return on investment**   Capitalization by shareholder debt permits the shareholders to receive part of their return in the form of interest, which is deductible from corporate income. By shifting corporate income to the shareholder, the two-tier system of corporate and shareholder tax is circumvented. To the extent that the corporation is subject to the high rate of tax, interest payments eliminate double taxation.

Capitalization by share capital imposes a return by dividends. This dooms the structure to double taxation unless the corporation is subject to the low rate of corporate tax that is applicable on a portion of a Canadian-controlled private corporation's income.

• **Loss of capital**   To the extent that a shareholder's capital investment is lost, shareholder debt holds a distinct advantage over share capital. A loss on a shareholder debt can be recognized for tax purposes—which may create tax savings—in the year in which it is

---

16 ITA 84(2); IT-149R4.

established to be bad, whereas a loss on share capital can be recognized only when the shares are sold or the corporation becomes legally bankrupt or insolvent and ceases operations. Speeding up the loss recognition enhances cash flow, which in turn reduces the overall risk factor.

• **Repatriation of capital**   Capitalization by shareholder debt permits the repayment of the initial capital to the shareholder at any time without tax consequences and leaves accumulated corporate profits to be distributed at a later time. On the other hand, share capital, unless it consists of preferred shares, can only return the initial capital without tax consequences if the entity is a private corporation.

Where assets are transferred from a shareholder to a corporation, or from a corporation to a shareholder, the transaction automatically is deemed to occur at fair market value. As an alternative, an election is permitted that transfers assets into a corporation at an agreed value for tax purposes; this can delay the tax until the asset is ultimately disposed of by the corporation. No such opportunity exists when assets are transferred from the corporation to the shareholders except during the wind-up of a subsidiary into its parent corporation.

This chapter has demonstrated the need to anticipate the long-term implications of investing in and utilizing the corporate structure. It is important to consider the tax treatment of corporate income (see Chapter 11), and, as well, to recognize that the tax treatment accorded to the different methods of getting into and out of a corporation has a significant impact on the ultimate cash return from the investment.

Reading List

Income Tax Act References

	Section
Debts established to be bad debts and shares of bankrupt corporations	50(1), (2)
Common share (defined)	248
Preferred share (defined)	248
Adjustments to cost base (of shares issued)	53(1)
Paid-up capital (defined)	89(1)(c)
Redemption of shares	84(3)
Proceeds of disposition (on share redemption)	54(h)
Reduction of paid-up capital	84(4)
Deemed dividend on reduction of paid-up capital	84(4.1)
Cost base adjustment—reduction of paid-up capital	53(2)(a)
Transfer of property to corporation by shareholders	85(1)
Property eligible for transfer	85(1.1)
Transfer of property to corporation—computation of paid-up capital	85(2.1)
Stock dividend (defined)	248
Paid-up capital (stock dividend)	89(1)(c)
Capital dividend	83(2)
Capital dividend account	89(1)(b)
Cost of property received as a dividend in kind	52(2)
Distribution on wind-up	84(2)

Canada Customs and Revenue Agency Publications

IT-159R3	Capital debts established to be bad debts.
IT-239R2	Deductibility of capital losses from guaranteeing loans and from non–interest-bearing loans.
IT-463R2	Paid-up capital.
IT-67R3	Taxable dividends from Canadian resident corporations.
IT-291R2	Transfer of property to a corporation under section 85(1).
IT-88R2	Stock dividends.
IT-66R6	Capital dividends.
IT-149R4	Winding-up dividend.

Demonstration Question

Carol Chomsky owns 20% of the common shares of Tindell Ltd., a Canadian-controlled private corporation. She acquired the shares from a former shareholder in 20X2 for $40,000. The corporation's balance sheet indicates that the paid-up capital of her shares is $2,000. In 20X8, Chomsky decided to sell her shares for $100,000. The controlling shareholder has offered to purchase the shares. Alternatively, she can sell the shares back to Tindell Ltd. for cancellation.

Chomsky's personal marginal tax rates are 45% on regular income and 30% on taxable Canadian dividends. In past years, Chomsky had used her entire $500,000 capital gain deduction. The shares of Tindell Ltd. are qualified small business corporation shares.

Required:

Describe the tax treatment to Chomsky if she sells the shares to the controlling shareholder, and if she sells the shares to Tindell Ltd.

Solution:

Sale of shares to controlling shareholder:

Under this option, Chomsky has a taxable capital gain of $30,000 and tax of $13,500, calculated as follows:

Proceeds of disposition	$100,000
Adjusted cost base	(40,000)
Capital gain	$ 60,000
Taxable capital gain—½ × $60,000	$ 30,000
Tax—45% × $30,000	$ 13,500

If Chomsky had not used her entire capital gain deduction in past years, the taxable capital gain would have been eligible for the capital gain deduction and all or a portion of the tax would have been eliminated.

Sale of shares to Tindell Ltd.:

Under this option, Chomsky has a taxable dividend of $98,000 and an allowable capital loss of $19,000. These amounts and the resulting tax are calculated as follows:

Dividend portion:	
Selling price	$100,000
Less paid-up capital of the shares	(2,000)
Deemed dividend	$ 98,000
Tax on dividend—30% × $98,000	$ 29,400
Capital portion:	
Proceeds of disposition	$100,000
Less deemed dividend (above)	(98,000)
Adjusted proceeds (equal to paid-up capital of shares)	2,000
Adjusted cost base	(40,000)
Capital *loss*	$ 38,000
Allowable capital *loss*—½ × $38,000	$ 19,000

Normally, the capital loss of $19,000 is classified as an allowable business investment loss (ABIL), which can be offset against any source of Chomsky's income and saving tax at the rate of 45%. However, because Chomsky has, in the past, used her full capital gain deduction, the ABIL status is denied and the loss is treated as a regular allowable capital loss. This means that the allowable capital loss of $19,000 can be deducted only to the extent that Chomsky has net taxable capital gains in the year. If we assume Chomsky has sufficient taxable capital gains from other sources, a tax saving of $8,550 occurs (45% × $19,000). The net tax under this option is calculated as follows:

Tax on deemed dividend	$29,400
Tax saving from allowable capital loss	(8,550)
Net tax	$20,850

If Chomsky had no taxable capital gains in the year, the tax on the deemed dividend would have been $29,400 and the allowable capital loss would be carried back three years and forward indefinitely until capital gains were obtained.

Clearly, in this situation the sale of shares to the controlling shareholder is preferred even if Chomsky can deduct the allowable capital loss on the sale of shares to the corporation. This result may not always occur, especially in tax brackets where capital gains and dividends are taxed at similar marginal rates.

Review Questions

1. "To function, a corporation must have some capital contributed by its shareholders. When capitalizing a corporation, the shareholder must provide only share capital." Is this statement true? Explain.

2. Why is it that a corporate debt owed to a shareholder may be considered as part of the shareholder's equity of the corporation? How is a shareholder's loan treated for tax purposes?

3. "When a corporation is partly capitalized with shareholder debt, the amount of corporate income subject to double taxation is reduced." Explain. Does it matter whether the shareholder debt pays interest or not?

4. If a corporation that is in financial difficulty has been capitalized with shareholder debt and a small amount of share capital as opposed to the reverse, the shareholder may be at less financial risk and the corporation may have a better chance of surviving. Why is this so?

5. A corporation owned solely by shareholder A has a value of $100,000. Individual B intends to acquire a 50% equity interest in the corporation. The cost to that individual of acquiring 50% of the corporation's shares may be either $100,000 or $50,000. Explain.

6. What is a buy-back of corporate shares?

7. Describe the tax treatment to the shareholder when a corporation buys back its own shares. Is the tax treatment to the shareholder different if that shareholder sells the shares to another party rather than back to the corporation that issued them?

8. "If a corporation no longer requires the initial common share capital provided by the shareholders, all or a portion of it can be returned to the shareholders without any tax consequences to the shareholders." Is this statement true? Explain.

9. Would your answer to question 8 be different if the share capital consisted of non-participating preferred shares? Or if the initial capital had been provided by the shareholders as a shareholder loan?

10. Identify and briefly explain two alternative tax treatments that can apply when assets are transferred to a corporation by a shareholder or a proposed shareholder.

11. When a shareholder sells property to his or her corporation at fair market value for tax purposes, what impact may the sale have on the shareholder and on the corporation?

12. If a shareholder sells property to a corporation at fair market value for legal purposes but elects an alternative price for tax purposes, what are the tax implications to the shareholder and to the corporation acquiring the asset? Why is this election option referred to as a "rollover"?

13. When a shareholder sells property to a corporation, and that property has a value greater than its cost amount, and when the shareholder chooses to use the elective option for tax purposes, what is the maximum amount of non-share consideration that the shareholder can receive from the corporation as payment?

14. A corporation purchases an asset from a shareholder for the market value price of $20,000 and pays the shareholder by issuing preferred shares of $8,000 and a note payable to the shareholder for $12,000. Both the shareholder and the corporation elect that the transfer price for tax purposes is $12,000. What are the tax consequences for the shareholder if the corporation pays the debt and buys back the shareholder's preferred shares? What would the tax consequences be if the shareholder sold the acquired preferred shares to another party?

15. What types of property, if any, are not eligible for the elective option when they are transferred to a corporation?

16. Can the elective option be used when one corporation transfers property to another corporation?

17. What are the tax consequences to a corporation and its shareholder when that corporation declares a dividend but, instead of paying cash, distributes property to the shareholder that has a value greater than the cost amount to the corporation?

Problems

Problem One

Shelter Tent Ltd. is a Canadian-controlled private corporation owned 50/50 by two individual shareholders. The corporation has consistently achieved annual profits of between $300,000 and $400,000.

Recently, the company has experienced a cash shortage as the result of an expansion that added a manufacturing component to the tent and awning business. The bank offered some relief, but the shareholders will have to contribute additional capital to the corporation. Although both shareholders have alternative uses for their personal capital, they are prepared to provide the funds necessary to alleviate the cash squeeze.

The shareholders have approached you for advice on how they should contribute their capital to the corporation. Under its articles of association, the company is permitted to issue both common shares and preferred shares. The preferred shares have a fixed non-cumulative dividend rate of 8%.

Required:

1. Identify three methods by which the shareholders can provide additional capital to the corporation.

2. Outline the tax factors that should be considered in evaluating the three alternatives.

Problem Two

Cynthia Yeung owns 10% of the common shares of Bantam Brokers Ltd. She acquired the shares, which have a stated paid-up capital amount of $1,000, from a previous shareholder in 20X0 at a cost of $20,000. Since 20X0 Yeung has worked for the company as a senior broker earning a salary and commissions. The remaining 90% of Bantam's shares are owned by three other senior executives of the company.

Yeung has decided to leave the company and has agreed to dispose of her Bantam shares, which have a current fair market value of $60,000. A shareholders' agreement stipulates that she must sell her shares either to the other shareholders or back to the corporation for cancellation, with payment terms to be negotiated.

Currently, Bantam does not have substantial cash resources, nor does it have non-business properties that it could sell and convert into cash. Consequently, if the company is going to buy back its shares from Yeung for $60,000, deferred payment terms will have to be established.

Similarly, none of the other shareholders have any cash reserves. Although each earns a high salary, all have committed their income to personal expenditures. In addition, none of them holds any other investments, and each looks to the company as his/her sole source of cash.

After a negotiation, these options are presented to Yeung:

1. Bantam will buy back her shares immediately for $60,000. Payment would involve $20,000 cash, with the balance of $40,000 paid in two annual instalments of $20,000, with interest at 10%.

2. The other shareholders will immediately purchase her shares for $60,000 under terms identical to those in option 1.

The other shareholders realize that if Yeung accepts option 2 they will have to either borrow the money from a bank to make the payments or distribute funds to themselves from the company. Even if they borrow the money, they will have to look to the company for help in repaying the principal.

Bantam is a Canadian-controlled private corporation and has annual profits of approximately $100,000. Yeung, like the other shareholders, usually pays personal tax at the rate of 45%.

Required:

1. Which option should Yeung accept? Your answer should include a comparative analysis of the options listed, and state any assumptions you feel are necessary.

2. If you were one of the other shareholders, which option would you prefer? Explain.

Problem Three

Harvey Malon has decided to incorporate his proprietorship. Certain properties of the business have a current value that is greater than their cost amount for tax purposes. These assets are as follows:

	Fair market value
Land	$ 40,000
Building	180,000
Goodwill	70,000
	$290,000

The original cost of the land and building was $175,000 (land, $25,000; building, $150,000). The building currently has an undepreciated capital cost of $120,000.

The goodwill was purchased from the previous owner for $50,000, and the balance in the cumulative eligible capital account is $30,000.

In addition, the business also has some current assets (primarily inventory), which have not appreciated in value and have a cost of $90,000. The proprietorship's only liabilities are amounts payable to trade creditors totalling $70,000.

Malon is aware that a shareholder can transfer assets to a corporation and defer tax on the transfer by using a special election of the *Income Tax Act*. He finds this option attractive, as his personal tax rate is very high and he needs all the cash flow he can get.

Within the next year or two, Malon intends to sell the land and building and acquire larger premises for the business. At this point, he is uncertain whether he will buy or lease the proposed new premises.

Required:

1. Assuming that Malon will sell the assets to the corporation using the elective option for tax purposes, determine the elected amounts required for tax purposes to avoid recognition of taxable income.

2. Assuming that the corporation will issue debt and preferred shares to Malon in exchange for the properties, determine (a) the maximum amount of debt and (b) the amount of remaining preferred shares that would be issued.

3. What would be the tax consequences to Malon if the corporation later repaid the debt and bought back the preferred shares? Would the result be different if he sold the preferred shares to a third party?

4. Prepare a brief balance sheet for the corporation after the assets are acquired, showing the accounting value for each item. How do the values for accounting purposes of the real estate and goodwill compare with their tax values to the corporation?

5. Since Malon may sell the land and building to a third party within two years, he could choose to retain ownership for two years and lease it to the corporation rather than transfer it to the corporation and then sell it to the third party. Briefly outline the tax factors to consider when making this decision.

Problem Four

Not long ago, Colson and Harmantz formed a corporation to carry on a construction business. Each owned 50% of the common shares, which were issued at a nominal cost. In addition, each shareholder sold certain of his own property to the corporation.

Colson sold construction equipment to the corporation for $60,000 (its fair market value). He originally purchased the equipment for $75,000. At the time of the sale it had an undepreciated capital cost of $40,000. For tax purposes the corporation and Colson elected that the transfer price was $40,000. Consideration for the sale consisted of the following:

Note payable to Colson	$40,000
Preferred shares	20,000
	$60,000

Two months after the incorporation, Harmantz and Colson had a dispute, which they could not resolve. Colson now has decided to leave the company. The departure agreement includes the following terms:

- Colson will buy back his old equipment from the corporation for the current fair market price of $60,000, paying in cash.

- Immediately after the equipment sale, the corporation will use its new cash of $60,000 to pay off its debt of $40,000 to Colson and buy back his preferred shares for $20,000. In addition, the corporation will buy back Colson's common shares for a nominal cost.

Although the corporation has not begun any construction, it expects to earn a large profit in its first year if the contract bid is accepted. Some of the expected profits will be subject to a corporate tax rate of 37%. Colson has significant personal income and is subject to a 45% tax rate.

Required:

1. What are the tax consequences to both the corporation and Colson as a result of the above transactions?

2. Will double taxation occur? If it will, calculate the amount.

3. If you were Harmantz, would you have agreed to have the corporation pay Colson $60,000 for the debt and the preferred shares? Explain.

4. Assume that Colson was the sole shareholder of the corporation and had sold the equipment to the corporation in the same manner as described previously. Assume further that shortly after incorporation, the company sold the equipment to a third party for cash and discontinued its existence by paying off its debt and cancelling its shares. What amount would Colson have received? Calculate the amount of double taxation, if any. Would your calculation be different if the corporate tax rate were 18%?

Chapter 13   The Canadian-Controlled Private Corporation

The Canadian-controlled private corporation (CCPC) is a widely used organization structure in Canadian enterprise. This type of entity is used to house both small and large business operations as well as investment portfolios in bonds, shares, and real estate.

Canadian-controlled private corporations and their shareholders are provided with certain tax incentives and other unique opportunities that distinguish them from other types of corporations. Because the incentives are designed to apply only within certain guidelines, the related tax rules appear to be more complex. This chapter will examine the unique aspects of the taxation system for Canadian-controlled private corporations, and discuss their implications on cash flow and return on investment. In particular, this chapter will

(a) provide a definition of the Canadian-controlled private corporation and state the fundamental principles underlying that definition;
(b) show how various types of corporate income are taxed;
(c) examine the benefits of incorporating business income and investment income;
(d) develop a policy for distributing corporate earnings to the shareholders; and,
(e) develop a complete, detailed tax calculation for the Canadian-controlled private corporation.

I. Definition and Basic Principles

A Canadian-controlled private corporation is a private corporation that is not controlled by a public corporation or a non-resident of Canada.[1] Notice that the definition does *not* say that certain parties have to control,[2] but rather indicates that in order to qualify certain parties *cannot* control. For example, a private corporation whose shares are owned 50% by Canadian residents and 50% by non-residents is considered to be Canadian-controlled because the 50% ownership does not provide control to the non-residents.

Corporations that qualify as Canadian-controlled private corporations are distinguished from other corporations in three basic areas: rates of tax, double taxation, and secondary relationships.

• **Rates of tax**   The same rates of tax do not apply to all types of income earned by the corporation. In particular, the first $300,000 (2006)[3] of annual active business income is subject to a reduced rate of tax (see Chapter 11, Exhibit 11-8). Not only is this reduced rate of tax substantially lower than other corporate rates, but it is also lower than the majority of personal rates of tax that would be applicable if the business income were earned directly by an individual from a proprietorship or partnership.

• **Double taxation**   Except for business income over $300,000 annually, the income generated by Canadian-controlled private corporations is not subject to double taxation. In other words, the combined tax—corporate income tax plus the tax on subsequent dividend distributions to the shareholders—is no greater than what the tax would have been if the income had been earned directly by the individual without the use of a corporation. Therefore, to the extent that double taxation does not occur, there are no long-term adverse consequences arising from utilization of the corporate form of organization. However, because some income is subject to double taxation and some is not, there is more complexity with respect to corporate distributions.

---

1   ITA 125(7)(b), 89(1)(f); IT-458R.
2   ITA 256(5.1).
3   $250,000 in 2004; $275,000 in 2005.

• **Secondary relationships**   In Chapter 11 it was established that shareholders can have both primary and secondary relationships with the corporation. A secondary relationship exists when a shareholder also acts in another capacity, for example as a creditor loaning money to the corporation, or a lessor renting property to the corporation, or an employee providing services to the corporation. Because the shares of a Canadian-controlled private corporation are not traded on a public stock exchange, the number of shareholders is relatively few. Such a corporation is referred to as a "closely held corporation." Often in closely held corporations, the affairs of the corporation and the shareholders are closely associated, and as a result shareholders have the opportunity to form secondary relationships with the corporation.

For example, in an owner-managed corporation, the shareholder is also an employee hired to manage the affairs of the corporation. In such situations that individual can receive a return from the company through a combination of dividends and salary, the ratio of which he or she has a right to establish. This right to establish secondary relationships increases the corporation's flexibility when it comes to transferring corporate income to the individual. By paying its employee–shareholder interest on debt, rent on leases, and salaries for services performed, the corporation can reduce the amount of its income that is subject to double taxation.

The above three principles constitute the base upon which tax planning activities for Canadian-controlled private corporations are built. Together they form a unique framework that puts this type of entity in a class of its own.

II. Taxation of Income Earned by a Canadian-Controlled Private Corporation

In Chapter 11, it was indicated that corporate tax is determined by applying the corporate rate of tax to taxable income. Taxable income has been defined as net income for tax purposes less special reductions. Net income is determined in accordance with the aggregating formula described in Chapter 3 and consists of five basic types of income. Of the five basic types of income, corporations are capable of earning only three—business income, property income, and capital gains. Notwithstanding that corporate tax is based on normal taxable income, its calculation for Canadian-controlled private corporations makes special adjustments relating to certain categories of income. Before those special tax adjustments can be applied, the corporation's net income for tax purposes must be slotted into five separate areas:

- active business income
- specified investment business income
- capital gains
- personal services business income
- dividends

Each of the above categories may receive special tax treatment. This is discussed below.

A. Active Business Income

An active business carried on by a corporation is technically defined as *any business* carried on by the corporation *other than* a specified investment business or a personal services business.[4] Therefore, one must review these two other definitions before one can appreciate the full scope of the term. Effectively, almost all business activity results in active business income, including manufacturing, farming, construction, transportation, fishing, logging,

---

4   ITA 125(7)(a), 129(6); IT-73R5.

mining, the selling of property as a retailer or wholesaler, and the selling of services in a trade or profession.

Notice that the above definition excluded income from a personal services business. This exclusion should not be interpreted to mean that income derived from personal services is not active business income. As will be explained later, the term "personal services business" has an extremely narrow definition and seldom has application. It can be stated here that a corporation that derives income from selling services—for example, a consulting business or a plumbing service business—normally has active business income.

In some circumstances a business may earn property income that is closely related or incidental to its business activities. For example, interest income earned on overdue accounts receivable from product sales is actually property income, but is treated as part of active business income when the special tax adjustments are calculated.[5]

The actual calculation of active business income starts with the corporation's *net income for tax purposes* (not taxable income). This amount is *reduced* by specified business investment income, including net taxable capital gains, taxable Canadian dividends, and personal services business income. The calculation is reviewed in Part VI at the end of this chapter.

- **Tax treatment of active business income**   A Canadian-controlled private corporation that realizes active business income is entitled to reduce its federal taxes otherwise payable by 16% for the first $300,000 (2006)[6] of active business income earned in each taxation year.[7] In addition, most provinces apply a reduced provincial rate of tax on the same income.

This reduction of tax is referred to as the "small-business deduction," and applies to the first $300,000 of annual profits. This annual limit of $300,000 may be reduced or eliminated when the corporation exceeds a certain size (a point that is reviewed later in this chapter). The combined federal and provincial rate on the first $300,000 of active business income is approximately 18% (assuming there is a particular provincial tax rate—see Exhibit 11-8). This is about half the normal rate of 37%. The reader is reminded that the normal tax rates vary from province to province and may change from year to year, and so may require updating. For example, in 2004, combined federal/provincial small business rates (including provincial surtaxes) were as follows:

New Brunswick and Alberta	16%
Nunavut and NWT	17%
British Columbia, Manitoba, Newfoundland, Nova Scotia	18%
Ontario, Saskatchewan, and Yukon	19%
Prince Edward Island	21%
Quebec	22%

It is important to recognize that the $300,000 small-business deduction limit is an annual amount. If the full amount is not used in a given year, the unused portion will not be available for carry-over to other years. Consider the situation in Exhibit 13-1. Both Corporation A and Corporation B earned a total of $600,000 over a two-year period. However, Corporation A earned $200,000 in year 1 and $400,000 in year 2, whereas Corporation B earned $300,000 in each of the two years. While both corporations earned the same total income, Corporation A has a tax liability of $127,000 compared with $108,000 for Corporation B. This is only because each corporation earned its income in different years.

---

5   ITA 125(7)(c).

6   ITA 125(1), (2); 16% applies to net Canadian active business income up to the maximum annual limit or taxable income—whichever is least.

7   $250,000 in 2004; $275,000 in 2005.

Exhibit 13-1:
The Annual Small-
Business Deduction Limit

	Corporation A	Corporation B
Active business income:		
Year 1	$200,000	$300,000
Year 2	400,000	300,000
Total over two years	$600,000	$600,000
Tax payable:		
Year 1	$ 36,000	$ 54,000
Year 2	91,000	54,000
Total over two years	$127,000	$108,000

Corporation A's tax is calculated as follows:

Year 1:		
18% on $200,000		$ 36,000
Year 2:		
18% on first $300,000	54,000	
37% on remaining $100,000	37,000	91,000
Total tax		$127,000

Because Corporation A earned only $200,000 in year 1, it lost a portion of its small-business deduction. Corporation B fully utilized the small-business deduction in both years, incurring tax on all of its income at 18% (18% × $300,000 = $54,000 for each year).

When possible, a corporation should take steps to maximize its use of the small-business deduction. For example, in the previous situation Corporation A could have increased its year 1 income by choosing not to deduct a reserve for doubtful accounts receivable in year 1 and delaying it until year 2 (see Chapter 5). This would have increased income in year 1 and decreased it in year 2. To the extent that the timing of income or expense recognition is discretionary, the taxpayer can shift income from one year to another; this is an important tool that can be used to take fullest advantage of the small-business deduction.

• **Tax treatment of income distributions**   Canadian-controlled private corporations are taxed on active business income at both the low rate and the high rate, which creates a two-tier effect on corporate distributions to shareholders. The tax implications of corporate distributions were reviewed in Chapter 12. Exhibit 13-2 summarizes the tax treatment of a corporation earning active business income, and of a shareholder receiving a distribution from that corporation. The example assumes that the shareholder is in the highest individual tax bracket.

Exhibit 13-2 indicates that *active business income subject to the small-business deduction does not result in double taxation upon distribution.* The combination of corporate tax at 18% and shareholder tax on the dividend totalled only 43%, which left the shareholder with 57% of the active business income earned. A similar result would have occurred if the owner had earned the active business income directly as a proprietor. It should be pointed out that the timing of the dividend distribution is discretionary; that is, the corporation could have chosen not to pay a dividend, with the result that the immediate tax would have been only 18%, and 82% of the income would have been retained in the corporation for business expansion.

Exhibit 13-2: Combined Corporate and Shareholder Tax on Active Business Income	1st $300,000 of active business income	Income in excess of $300,000
Corporate tax rate[a]	18%	37%[c]
Corporate income	$1,000	$1,000
Tax	(180)	(370)
Income available for dividends	$ 820	$ 630
Shareholder income (dividend)	$ 820	$ 630
Tax (net of dividend tax credit)[b]	(246)	(189)
	$ 574	$ 441
Total tax:		
Corporation	$ 180	$ 370
Shareholder	246	189
	$ 426	$ 559
Combined tax rate	43%	56%

a Chapter 11, Exhibit 11-8.
b 30% of dividend—Chapter 10, Exhibit 10-7.
c The same rate applies to eligible manufacturing income.

In the same example, income in excess of $300,000 was subject to an immediate tax of 37% plus an additional tax on distribution that brought the total to 56%. This is significantly greater than the 45% rate that would have been incurred if the owner had earned the business income directly without the use of a corporation. Clearly, the impact of double taxation can be reduced or eliminated if corporate active business income in excess of $300,000 can be shifted from the corporation to the shareholder without being flowed through the corporation as a dividend. This is possible only if the shareholder also has secondary relationships with the corporation. Payments of interest on shareholder debt, rent on assets leased from the shareholder, and salaries or bonuses to shareholder/employees all reduce corporate taxable income by shifting that income directly to the shareholder to be taxed only once. This is discussed in more detail later in this chapter.

B. Specified Investment Business Income

A specified investment business of a Canadian-controlled private corporation is defined as a business the principal purpose of which is to derive income from property.[8] As described in Chapter 7, property income consists of the return on invested capital and includes interest, rents, dividends, and royalties. It was indicated in Chapter 11 that dividends received from other Canadian corporations and from foreign affiliates are not taxable to the recipient corporation. Therefore, the property income referred to in this definition includes only interest, rents, royalties, and dividends from non-affiliated foreign corporations.

Because these items are classified as specified investment business income, they are automatically disqualified as active business income and are not entitled to the small-business deduction or the 7% special reduction when corporate tax is calculated.

It was also indicated in Chapter 7 that property income has been earned when the return on investment was achieved with little attention or labour on the part of the owner—if this were not so, income such as interest, rents, and royalties could be considered business

8   ITA 125(7)(e); IT-73R5.

income. The decision as to whether a given item constitutes property income is very subjective, and for the purposes of the small-business deduction is made on an arbitrary basis. One result is that two arbitrary exceptions are made to the definition of specified investment business income:

1. Rental income that is derived from the leasing of movable property—for example, vehicles and equipment (but not real estate)—is deemed to require sufficient attention and labour to be automatically considered active business income; as such, it is eligible for the low rate of corporate tax.

2. Other property income, such as interest, royalties, and rents from real property, is considered to be active business income only if the corporation employs more than five full-time employees to generate that income.[9]

In many cases the above arbitrary rules appear unfair. For example, a corporation that employs four employees to administer a portfolio of loans earning interest is not eligible for the low rate of tax on that income, but a corporation with six employees is.

• **Tax treatment of specified investment business income**   As indicated above, property income from interest, rents, and royalties, if it is not deemed to be active business income by the two exceptions, is not eligible for the small-business deduction. It is also not eligible for the special reduction (7%) described in Chapter 11. Therefore, the total standard *federal* tax rate for specified business investment income amounts to about 29% [38% – abatement 10% = 28% + surtax 1% (4% × 28%) = 29%]. Using the same provincial rate used in Chapter 11 of 15%, the total standard tax rate is 44%. Provincial tax rates vary; some are below 15%, and others are above 15%. *For discussion and demonstration purposes* in this and other chapters, I have chosen to use a provincial rate of 16% (29% + 16%) which results in a combined standard tax rate of 45% *for specified business investment income*.

In addition to the standard corporate tax rate of 45%, income in this category is subject to a *special refundable tax* of $6^2/_3$%.[10] This means that the combined federal and provincial tax rate (excluding the federal surtax) is $51^2/_3$% (45% + $6^2/_3$%). The special refundable tax was introduced at a time when the top corporate tax rate (45%) was substantially lower than the top tax rate on similar income earned by individuals (after various provincial surtaxes were applied). The purpose of the special refundable tax was to eliminate the tax advantage that used to occur when an individual opted to hold investments in a private corporation. Remember that the $6^2/_3$% tax is fully refundable to the corporation when the income to which it applies is distributed to the shareholder(s) as a dividend. As shown in Chapter 10, personal marginal tax rates are declining and the marginal tax rates in all provinces now vary from 39% to 48%. *This brings into question the need for continuing the imposition of the $6^2/_3$% special refundable tax.*

• **Tax treatment of income distributions**   Dividend distributions of property income from a Canadian-controlled private corporation to its shareholders are not subject to double taxation. The fact that the property income is subject to the high rate of tax implies that double taxation will occur on distribution; however, a portion of the tax paid is refundable to the corporation if and when the corporation decides to distribute the after-tax income as a dividend.

---

9   ITA 125(7).

10   ITA 123.3.

All property income that is subject to the high rate of corporate tax is entitled to a tax refund of $26^2/3\%$ when it is distributed to the shareholders.[11] In a province where the corporate tax rate is $51^2/3\%$ ($45\% + 6^2/3\%$), the refund reduces the effective tax rate to 25% ($45\% + 6^2/3\% - 26^2/3\%$). The impact of this is demonstrated in Exhibit 13-3.

Notice that the calculation in Exhibit 13-3 indicates three separate points of tax activity. First, the corporation pays tax at $51^2/3\%$, leaving $48^1/3\%$ of the income in the corporation for reinvestment. Second, at some future time, when it is decided to distribute corporate earnings, $26^2/3\%$ of the property income is refunded to the corporation.[12] Third, the individual shareholder is taxed on receipt of the dividend. Thus, assuming that the individual shareholder is in the top personal tax bracket, the combined corporate tax and shareholder tax amounts to 47%. This is slightly higher than what would have been paid (45%) if the individual had earned the property income directly rather than passing it through a corporation.

Exhibit 13-3:	Corporate income (from interest, rents, royalties)	$1,000
Combined Corporate	Corporate tax @ 45%	(450)
and Shareholder Tax	Special refundable tax @ 6⅔%	(67)
on Property Income	Net available for the corporation	483
	Potential refund when dividends are paid	
	(26⅔% of $1,000)	267
	Available for dividend	$ 750
	Shareholder income (dividend)	$ 750
	Tax (net of dividend tax credit)*	(225)
		$ 525
	Total tax:	
	Corporation ($450 + 67 − 267)	$ 250
	Shareholder	225
		$ 475
	Combined tax rate	47%

* 30% of $750 = $225

In the above example a negligible amount of double taxation has occurred (2%), and this is mainly a result of the provincial tax rates in the province for which the sample rates were developed (see Chapter 11). In some provinces the combined tax rate is equal to the personal tax rate or slightly less. While these slight variations occur, for all intents and purposes it can be stated that double taxation does not arise when property income is earned by a Canadian-controlled private corporation.

The concept of applying a high rate of tax to investment income, followed by a refund, for the purpose of avoiding double taxation is easy to understand. The actual mechanism to achieve this is more complex. In order to keep track of the amount of tax eligible for a refund as a result of paying dividends, the corporation maintains a running balance referred to as the *refundable dividend tax on hand account (RDTOH)*. When dividends are distributed, the refund is equal to $33^1/3\%$ of the dividend paid or the balance in the RDTOH account, whichever is the least. This mechanism is reviewed later in the chapter.

---

11 ITA 129(3). Referred to as "refundable dividend tax on hand" and usually calculated as $26^2/3\%$ of the *least* of aggregate investment income *or* the taxable income less the income subject to the small-business deduction.

12 ITA 129(1); IT-243R4. Usually the dividend refund is equal to one-third of the dividend paid, or the balance in the refundable dividend tax on hand account.

C. Capital Gains

The tax treatment of capital gains earned by a Canadian-controlled private corporation is *identical* to the tax treatment given specified investment business income (property income). The taxable capital gain (one-half of the capital gain) in excess of the allowable capital loss for a year is taxed at the high corporate rate of 45% plus a special refundable tax of 6²/₃%; however, 26²/₃% of the taxable gain is refunded in the event that the income is distributed to the shareholder. In this way double taxation is avoided. Therefore, the calculations shown in Exhibit 13-3 are also applicable to the taxable portion of capital gains.

In order to fully avoid double taxation on capital gains, a mechanism must be available to distribute the tax-free portion of the gain (one-half of the capital gain) to the shareholders. The non-taxable portion of the capital gain can be distributed by means of a special dividend referred to as a "capital dividend."[13] Capital dividends received by the shareholder are fully exempt from tax. Consequently, capital gains earned by a corporation and flowed through to the shareholder are taxable as if they had been earned by the shareholder directly, without the use of a corporation.

The amount of tax-free capital dividends available for distribution is accumulated in a corporate tax account referred to as the *capital dividend account*. The capital dividend account is a running balance that includes the non-taxable portion of capital gains (one-half of capital gains) less the non-allowable portion of capital losses (one-half of capital losses). The account also includes the non-taxable portion of gains on eligible capital property (see Chapter 6) and the receipt of non-taxable life insurance proceeds.[14]

D. Personal Services Business Income

A personal services business can generally be defined as a business that provides services, when the person providing those services is a specified shareholder of the corporation, even though the relationship between the person providing the services and the entity receiving the services is of an employment nature.[15] For example, consider the situation of an employed executive who resigns her position and returns immediately to offer the same services to the employer in the form of a service contract with a newly created corporation owned by the executive. In such cases the fees earned by the corporation may be classified as personal services business income if the real relationship between the parties remains unchanged and an indirect employer/employee relationship continues to exist.

A Canadian-controlled private corporation earning this type of income is not eligible for the small-business deduction on that income, and faces significant restrictions regarding the types of expenses that can be deducted from income. This category exists to prevent the abuse of the small-business deduction; because of the inherent restrictions, most corporations avoid carrying on activities of this nature.

It is important to recognize that this category does not include income from any type of service where an employee/employer relationship does *not* exist. This means that most corporations which provide services on a fee-for-service basis, even if that work is done by a shareholder, are considered to be earning active business income that is eligible for the low rate of tax.

E. Dividends

It was established in Chapter 11 that dividends received by one corporation from another Canadian corporation are not taxable because, although they are included in net income for tax purposes, they are deducted in arriving at taxable income. The purpose of this exemption is to eliminate multiple taxation on the same income as it flows from one corporation to another via dividends.

---

13 ITA 83(2), 89(1)(b); IT-66R6.

14 Technically, the capital dividend account consists of the following: half of capital gains less half of capital losses; *plus* half of the proceeds of disposition from eligible capital property less half of the cost of eligible capital property; *plus* proceeds from a life insurance policy less the adjusted cost base of the life insurance policy; *plus* capital dividends received from other corporations; *less* capital dividends paid out.

15 ITA 125(7)(d); IT-73R5.

Taxable Canadian dividends received by a Canadian-controlled private corporation are subject to special tax treatment. This special treatment depends on the degree of ownership that the corporation has in the corporation paying the dividend. When a Canadian-controlled private corporation owns *more than 10%* of the voting shares and more than 10% of the fair market value of all the classes of shares issued of another corporation, the two corporations are said to be *connected*.[16] The actual definition of a connected corporation is more technical; but in most situations, owning more than 10% of another corporation's voting shares will cause the two corporations to be connected. On the other hand, if a Canadian-controlled private corporation owns *10% or less* of the voting shares of another corporation, the two are considered to be *non-connected*. For example, a Canadian-controlled private corporation investing in a small number of shares of a public corporation would be non-connected. Similarly, a Canadian-controlled private corporation owning 8% of the voting shares of another Canadian-controlled private corporation would be non-connected with that corporation. The special tax treatment of dividends received from non-connected and connected corporations is reviewed below.

1. Dividends Received from Non-connected Corporations

It would appear that, given the above exemption, an individual who owns a portfolio of public corporation shares paying dividends should find it possible to transfer these shares to his or her own corporation, thereby ensuring that any dividends received can be reinvested on a tax-free basis. In fact, the *Income Tax Act* has rules in place to forestall such transactions—Canadian-controlled private corporations are subject to a special refundable tax on the receipt of dividends from other non-connected Canadian companies. This special tax is referred to as a "Part IV tax" because it is administered under Part IV of the *Income Tax Act*.[17] The rate of tax is 33⅓% of the actual dividend received; this amount, however, is *fully refundable* to the corporation if and when it is distributed to the shareholder as a dividend.[18] Exhibit 13-4 demonstrates the tax treatment of non-connected dividends received by a Canadian-controlled private corporation.

Exhibit 13-4: Refundable Tax on Dividends from Non-connected Corporations

Corporation income:
Dividends from portfolio shares	$1,000
Normal income tax	NIL
Special Part IV tax @ 33⅓%	(333)
Available for reinvestment	$667
Refund of Part IV tax on distribution	333
Dividend to shareholder	$1,000

Shareholder income:
Dividend from corporation	$1,000
Tax (net of dividend tax credit)	(300)
Net to shareholder	$ 700

Total tax:
Corporation ($333 – $333)	$ –0–
Shareholder	300
	$ 300

16 ITA 186(4). Technically, two corporations are connected if one controls the other (owns more than 50% of the voting shares) *or* if one corporation owns more than 10% of the voting shares and more than 10% of the fair market value of all shares of the other corporation.

17 ITA 186(1); IT-269R3.

18 ITA 129(3), 129(1); IT-243R4.

The calculation assumes that the individual shareholder is in a tax bracket of 45% and therefore would incur a tax on dividends, net of the dividend tax credit, of 30% (see Chapter 10, Exhibit 10-6).

Upon receipt of the dividend, the corporation pays a special Part IV tax of $33\frac{1}{3}\%$ that leaves $66\frac{2}{3}\%$ of the dividend available for reinvestment by the corporation. If the corporation decides to distribute these earnings to the shareholder at some future time, the $33\frac{1}{3}\%$ tax is fully refunded to the corporation, effectively eliminating the corporate tax. In this way the dividend paid by the company is equal to the original dividend received from the non-connected corporation. As a consequence, the tax payable by the shareholder is the same as what would have been paid if the portfolio dividends had been received directly rather than via the holding corporation.

It is important to note that in this example, the corporate tax rate is $33\frac{1}{3}\%$, whereas the individual's tax rate on dividends is 30%. This means that it would not be worthwhile to leave the dividend in the corporation for reinvestment. If it were passed on to the shareholder, the corporation would receive a refund of the $33\frac{1}{3}\%$ tax and the individual would pay a 30% tax, leaving a greater amount for reinvestment. This is not always the case. A review of Exhibit 10-7 in Chapter 10 shows that after provincial surtaxes are considered, the tax rate on dividends for individuals in the top tax bracket ranges from 24% to 37%. This means that in some situations the Part IV tax rate of $33\frac{1}{3}\%$ is slightly more attractive than the individual rate. Note also that in the lower tax brackets, the tax rate on dividends is much lower than the Part IV rate for corporations.

2. Dividends Received from Connected Corporations

Dividends received by a Canadian-controlled private corporation from a *connected* corporation are normally *not* subject to the standard Part IV tax of $33\frac{1}{3}\%$.[19] There is one exception: If the connected corporation that pays the dividend obtains a refund of tax (from its RDTOH account), the corporation that receives the dividend must pay a Part IV tax equal to its proportionate share (share percentage) of the paying corporation's refund. Consider the following situation and analysis:

Situation:

A Ltd., a Canadian-controlled private corporation, owns 20% of the voting shares of B Ltd., also a Canadian-controlled private corporation. B earns active business income that is subject to the small-business deduction, and also investment income that is taxed at the high corporate rate, of which a portion is refundable on payment of dividends. At its year end, B paid a dividend of $20,000. The dividend payment triggered a refund to B of $3,000.

Analysis:

A's share of the dividend is $4,000 (20% × $20,000). A and B are connected corporations because A owns more than 10% of B's voting shares. Consequently, the standard Part IV tax of $33\frac{1}{3}\%$ is not applicable. However, because B received a tax refund of $3,000 from the payment of the dividend (referred to as a dividend refund), A must pay a Part IV tax of $600, which is 20% (A's percentage ownership of B) of $3,000 (B's refund). The Part IV tax of $600 is fully refundable to A when it declares a dividend to its shareholder(s).

The above shows that the Part IV tax on dividends received from a connected corporation is applicable only when the dividend triggers a refund to the payer. As explained earlier, such refunds occur only when the payer corporation earns investment income or taxable capital gains, or itself pays Part IV tax on dividends received. To the extent that the payer corporation earns active business income and passes that on as a dividend to the connected shareholder, no Part IV tax is applicable and the dividend flows completely tax-free. Therefore, when investing in a Canadian-controlled private corporation that operates

---

19 ITA 186(1); IT-269R3.

an active business, it may be wise to hold that investment through a holding corporation. This structure would permit dividends from the active business corporation to be received tax-free for reinvestment. The benefits of using a corporation to hold investments in other business corporations are reviewed in detail in Chapter 14.

F. Summary

The tax treatment for Canadian-controlled private corporations presented in this chapter introduces significant complexities to the two-tier system of corporate taxation. The complexities are a result of government policies that provide tax incentives to Canadian small business operations while also providing Canadians with the opportunity to hold their investments within private corporations without long-term adverse consequences.

The tax treatment of the various types of income is summarized for comparison in Exhibit 13-5. Except in the case of business income over $300,000, income earned is not subject to double taxation. Notice that this is achieved in different ways. Active business income is subject to an initial rate of tax that is low enough to provide an immediate tax incentive and eliminate future double taxation. Property income and capital gains are initially taxed at a high rate that provides no incentive; for these types of income, double taxation is avoided by means of a subsequent reduction in corporate taxes.

It is important to remember that the above tax treatments apply only to Canadian-controlled private corporations and not to public corporations.

III. Benefits of Incorporation

The process of deciding whether to operate a business or hold investments within a private corporation involves consideration of both tax and non-tax issues. While non-tax issues such as limited liability are important, this section restricts its discussion to the tax implications of incorporating business or investment income, concentrating on the major tax factors affecting cash flow for the immediate owner. It does not attempt to examine matters involving ownership transfer or estate planning.

While business income incorporation is discussed separately from investment income incorporation, the reader should keep in mind that a single corporation can earn more than one type of income.

Exhibit 13-5: Summary of Tax Treatment by Income Type	Tax treatment to the corporation	Double taxation on distribution
Business income:		
1st $300,000 of income	18%	No
Income in excess of $300,000	37%	Yes
Property income:		
Interest, rents, royalties	51⅔% (45% + 6⅔%)	
	Reduced by 26⅔%	
	on distribution	No
Canadian (non-connected) dividends	33⅓%	
	Fully refunded	
	on distribution	No
Canadian (connected) dividends	–0–	No
Taxable capital gains	51⅔% (45% + 6⅔%)	
	Reduced by 26⅔%	
	on distribution	No

A. Benefits of
Incorporating
a Business

1. Tax Deferral—
The Small-Business
Deduction

The major benefits associated with incorporating a business enterprise are as follows.

The primary advantage of incorporating a business as a Canadian-controlled private corporation is this: it permits the achievement of significantly lower tax rates as a result of the small-business deduction on the first $300,000 of active business profits. As described in Chapters 10 and 11, an individual in the top tax bracket paying tax on business income at a rate of 45% would pay only 18% after incorporating the business, thereby deferring 27% (45% − 18% = 27%) of the income tax.

This benefit is a tax *deferral* rather than a tax *saving* because the lower tax of 18% will ultimately be followed by a second level of tax to the shareholder when after-tax corporate profits are distributed as dividends, or when the shares are sold. It should be pointed out that no tax benefit will be achieved by incorporating business income if the individual shareholder intends to withdraw all of the corporate profits from the corporation for personal use. When the shareholder does this, the combined corporate and personal tax is equal to the tax on a proprietorship.

Deferring tax on business income has two basic advantages:

1. The increased cash flow produced by the reduced tax rate can be reinvested in business expansion or in passive investments that result in greater ultimate returns on investment. By making certain assumptions, this benefit can be quantified.

2. Increased cash flow at the early stages of a business reduces the risk of failure. Such an increase also provides additional resources that can be used to respond to changes in the marketplace requiring asset retooling or new business development. Increased cash flow also makes for greater borrowing capacity, in that it increases an entity's ability to repay debt obligations. This type of benefit is more subjective and hence more difficult to quantify.

The long-term benefits derived from the small-business deduction remain significant provided that the tax deferral is reinvested to generate returns of income that are either subject to the low rate of tax or are in the form of property income, which is not double-taxed on distribution. However, when the increased cash flow is reinvested to generate business income over the $300,000 limit, double taxation will occur that over time may override the benefits of the small-business deduction. This is demonstrated in the two separate scenarios that follow:

Situation: A corporation earning $10,000 of business income annually for 20 years reinvests the after-tax profits to generate an additional *business return* on investment of 20% before tax. After 20 years, all accumulated profits are distributed to the shareholder, who is subject to tax at the rate of 45% (therefore 30% on dividends after the dividend tax credit).

Analysis: The $10,000 of business income generates $8,200 after tax ($10,000 − 18% tax = $8,200), which is reinvested to earn an after-tax return from business expansion of 16% (20% − 18% tax = 16%). If the income were earned by an individual proprietorship, it would generate $5,500 after tax ($10,000 − 45% tax = $5,500), which would be reinvested at an after-tax return of only 11% (20% − 45% tax = 11%). These alternatives would produce the following after 20 years:

As a corporation:	
$8,200 annually × 20 y × 16%	$1,097,000*
Tax on dividend distribution ($1,097,000 × 30%)	(329,000)
Net to owner	$ 768,000
As a proprietorship:	
$5,500 annually × 20 × 11%	$ 392,000
Benefit of incorporation	$ 376,000

* Calculation assumes annuity-due formula.

In the above situation the small-business deduction almost doubled the owner's ultimate return on investment. The after-tax return increased by 96% ($376,000 ÷ $392,000) as a result of incorporation. This is because the increased cash flow was invested to create higher after-tax returns that were not double taxed when paid out to the shareholder.

Dramatically different results occur when the return on the investment of after-tax profits is in the form of business income subject to the highest rate of corporate tax.

Situation: A corporation earning $400,000 of business income annually for 20 years reinvests the after-tax profits in business expansion providing 20% returns.

Analysis: As the annual profits of $400,000 use up the full limit of the small-business deduction ($300,000), all future returns from business expansion are taxed at 37%, and so are ultimately subject to double taxation. The after-tax corporate profits on the first $300,000 of business income is $246,000 ($300,000 − 18% tax = $246,000) and generate after-tax returns of 13% (20% − 37% tax = 13%) compared with 16% in the previous example. If the business were operated as a proprietorship, the after-tax profits from the first $300,000 of business income available for reinvestment would be $165,000 ($300,000 − 45% tax), providing an after-tax return of 11%.

As a corporation:	
$246,000 annually × 20 y × 13%	$22,502,000
Tax on dividend distribution ($22,502,000 × 30%)	(6,750,000)
Net to owner	$15,752,000
As a proprietorship:	
$165,000 annually × 20 y × 11%	$11,759,000
Advantage from incorporation	$ 3,993,000

In the above situation the benefit achieved from increased cash flow due to the small-business deduction is lower than in the previous example because the resulting returns on the cash reinvestment were subject to high corporate tax rates and double taxation on distribution. In this particular example, the after-tax return increased by 34% ($3,993,000 ÷ $11,759,000) as a result of incorporation, compared to 96% in the previous example. However, the results could have varied depending on the time frame used.

It should also be pointed out that the above example did not consider the importance of the corporation achieving increased cash flow on an annual basis. That extra cash flow, although ultimately lost on distribution, might have been vital to the success of the business.

Finally, consider a situation where corporate profits are invested to provide a return in the form of property income.

Situation: A corporation earning business income of $300,000 for 20 years reinvests the after-tax profits of $246,000 ($300,000 − 18% tax = $246,000) in bonds, yielding interest of 10% before tax and 4.833% after tax (10% − 45% − 6⅔% tax = 4.833%). After 20 years all accumulated profits are distributed to the shareholder.

Analysis: In this situation the future returns result from property income, not business expansion. Although those returns are taxed at 51⅔% (45% + 6⅔% refundable tax), the refund on future distributions will eliminate double taxation. The net comparative results are as follows:

As a corporation:	
$246,000 annually × 20 y × 4.833%	$8,378,000
Potential refund of tax on distribution	1,908,000*
Available for distribution	10,286,000
Tax on dividend distribution ($10,286,000 × 30%)	(3,086,000)
Net to owner	$7,200,000
As a proprietorship:	
$110,000 annually × 20 y × 5.5%	$4,046,000
Benefit of incorporation	$3,154,000

* The refund is calculated as follows:

Total income accumulated	$8,378,000
Less earned from business:	
$246,000 × 20 y	4,920,000
After-tax investment income	$3,458,000
Pre-tax investment income:	
$3,458,000 ÷ .4833	$7,155,000
Refund: 26⅔% of $7,155,000	$1,908,000

The preceding four situations demonstrate that the small-business deduction normally results in an increased rate of return over a long period of time. In order to maximize the cash returns of a business operation, it is important to consider not only the immediate tax but also the future tax relating to the distribution of profits to the shareholders.

2. Employment Benefits

In most small-business corporations the shareholder also participates in the management of corporate affairs and is entitled to receive compensation as an employee. The corporation can provide the owner/manager with various types of employment benefits. As described in Chapter 4, a number of these benefits are fully deductible from the employer's income but are not taxable to the employee.[20] For example, the corporation can provide disability insurance as an employee benefit, which is not taxable to the employee/shareholder.

---

20 ITA 6(1)(a); IT-470R.

When a business is operated as a proprietorship, the owner cannot be an employee because the business is not distinct from the owner. Consequently, to acquire the above-mentioned insurance policies the owner must first pay tax on business profits and then acquire the policies with after-tax funds.

While these items do not constitute a significant annual dollar amount, over a period of time their value can be substantial.

A corporation can also provide a registered pension plan that is available to the owner/employee. Under a proprietorship structure the owner cannot participate in such a plan.

3. Flexibility in Family Ownership

Many businesses are family run. The corporate structure allows for the issuing of share capital, which provides flexibility when it comes to bringing family members into ownership positions or changing the percentage ownership of family members.

Also, people who own shares of a qualified small business corporation may be entitled to a $500,000 capital gains deduction when those shares are transferred to their children (see Chapter 8). No such deduction exists when all or part of a proprietorship business is transferred to children. The same $500,000 capital gains deduction may apply when shares of a small business corporation are sold to third parties.

4. Stabilization of Annual Income

The corporate structure, which imposes a two-tier system of taxation, gives the shareholder the right to choose when the second level of tax (on dividend distributions) will occur. While this may in part be governed by the shareholder's need for funds, the payment of dividends can be delayed until such time as they will receive the most favourable tax treatment. For example, in a year in which the shareholder's other sources of income are very low, a dividend distribution can be made that results in a lower rate of tax on that dividend than would normally apply. Similarly, a shareholder may delay the payment of dividends from a private corporation until after retirement, when other sources of income are reduced. This flexibility permits the owner to fully utilize the progressive tax rates imposed on individuals.

5. Primary Disadvantages

The major disadvantage to incorporating a business as a Canadian-controlled private corporation relates to the utilization of losses. As pointed out in previous chapters, losses within a corporation cannot be offset against income earned by the shareholder. This restricts the opportunity to use losses to generate cash flow through reduced taxes on other income.

From a tax perspective, the benefits of incorporation all relate to periods of profitability. Even so, new businesses are often incorporated in the anticipation of profits, without regard to the possibility of losses in the start-up period. Limited liability, while an obvious consideration, must be viewed in the context of after-tax costs before a realistic decision can be made on which entity structure to use (see Chapter 20).

B. Benefits of Incorporating Investments

The incorporation of investment income (interest, rents, and royalties) and capital gains does not result in substantial tax advantages for the individual. Since property income and capital gains are taxed at the high corporate rate (plus the special refundable tax of $6^{2}/_{3}\%$), no substantial tax deferral occurs, as the corporate rate is close to the highest personal tax rate.

Dividends from non-connected Canadian corporations that are received by a Canadian-controlled private corporation are subject to a special (Part IV) refundable tax of $33^{1}/_{3}\%$ and this removes any substantial tax-deferral opportunities. Exhibit 10-7 in Chapter 10 showed that in some provinces the tax rate for individuals on dividend income is 37%; when it is that high, a small deferral of tax can be achieved through incorporation. Incorporating investment in shares of a *connected* corporation that earns active business income would eliminate the Part IV tax of 33⅓% on dividends received. This provides a major tax deferral. However, the incorporation of an investment in shares of a connected active business corporation may have a future disadvantage: If the shares are subsequently sold, any capital gain would not be eligible for the $500,000 capital gain deduction, as the deduction is available only to an individual who sells such shares. The benefits of using a holding corporation to invest in shares of other corporations are examined fully in Chapter 14.

IV. Dividend Policy

Because of the varying tax treatments applied to income earned by Canadian-controlled private corporations, and to the shareholders receiving dividends from such corporations, it is difficult to establish a single policy to govern the method and timing of distributions to owners. Distributions to owners can be in the form of dividends or in the form of compensation for secondary relationships (salaries, interest, rents, and the like). These distributions can be made either sooner or later depending on the shareholder's need for funds and the ultimate tax cost of distribution.

This section of the chapter develops some general guidelines relating to the decision to distribute corporate profits derived from an *active business*.

A. Distributions— Dividends versus Salary

A Canadian-controlled private corporation that is also managed by its shareholder(s) can distribute corporate income by salary payments or by dividends. Salaries reduce the corporate income that accrues to the shareholders but do not disturb the relationship between shareholders if paid out in proportion to the ownership ratio. For example, a corporation owned 60% by one manager/shareholder and 40% by another could pay additional salaries of $60,000 and $40,000 respectively to each shareholder without disturbing the normal share of profits.

As indicated in Chapter 5, salaries paid are deductible from taxable income only if they are reasonable in the circumstances.[21] This means that the salary option cannot be used to distribute corporate income to shareholders who do not perform services for the company. Even when shareholders do participate in management, the salaries or bonuses paid are subject to a reasonableness test. In most cases CCRA is extremely liberal in applying the reasonableness test on salaries paid to shareholders who are fully active in the management of the corporation.[22]

Currently, business income earned by a Canadian-controlled private corporation is taxed at three rates depending on the amount of annual income. These are as follows:

Income subject to the small-business deduction ($300,000)	18%
Income over $300,000 and not eligible for the M&P reduction	37%
Income eligible for the M&P reduction (varies by province)	30%–37%

Consider situations where a corporation is taxed at the above rates on its active business income. The sole shareholder is also the manager, who is in a 45% tax bracket as a result of his base salary from the corporation and other sources of income. In these situations the dividend/salary policy of the corporation could be analyzed as follows:

1. *On income over $300,000* In any particular year the shareholder may or may not need additional funds for personal use. If the shareholder needs them, the corporation should pay an increased salary, as this would reduce corporate income (and save

21 ITA 67.

22 IC 88-2 (paragraph 18); "Revenue Canada Roundtable," Report of Proceedings of the 33rd Tax Conference, 1981, Canadian Tax Foundation, pp. 757–58.

37% tax), and increase the shareholder's personal income (and tax, at the 45% rate and lower in some provinces). If the payment were in the form of a dividend, the combined corporate tax and tax to the shareholder on the dividend would amount to approximately 56%, as shown in previous examples.

If the shareholder does *not* need additional funds, the decision is complicated. Here, in situations where the shareholder does not need immediate funds, a decision to leave the funds in the corporation to gain an 8% tax deferral (45% – 37%) must be weighed against the impact of the double taxation that will occur when funds are distributed to the shareholder in the future.

2. *Income eligible for the M&P reduction*   Income in this category is taxed at a rate of approximately 30% – 37% (depending on provincial incentives) similar to business income over $300,000 (above). The comments in section 1 above are applicable here as well.

3. *On the first $300,000 of income*   In this situation, if the shareholder needs additional funds, the decision whether to pay salary or dividends is not critical. Paying additional salary would shift corporate income to the shareholder, who would be taxed only once, at the rate of 45%. Under the dividend option, corporate income would first be taxed at 18%; a second tax would follow on the dividend, resulting in a combined tax that is close to 45%. The method chosen therefore often makes no difference.

If the shareholder does *not* require additional funds, no payment in either form should be made. Instead, the corporate income should be retained to be taxed at the low rate of 18% and then used for reinvestment, in the knowledge that any further distribution is not subject to double taxation.

The above analysis applied to a structure involving a single shareholder whose rate of tax was specifically defined. Similar analyses can be applied to structures that involve both multiple shareholders and varying tax rates.

B. Loans to Shareholders

In certain circumstances a shareholder may be able to secure temporary use of corporate funds without declaring a taxable dividend or paying a taxable salary.

In particular, a corporation is permitted to advance or loan funds to a shareholder, provided that the shareholder is also an employee and that the loan is advanced due to the employment relationship, for the following purposes:[23]

1. To assist the employee/shareholder in acquiring a personal residence.

2. To permit the employee/shareholder to acquire treasury shares in the corporation.

3. To assist the employee/shareholder in acquiring an automobile to be used in performing employment duties.

Loans for the above purposes have no tax consequences to the shareholder provided that the repayment terms are reasonable. For example, a loan to acquire a house could be repaid over 25 years, as this is reasonable for a house loan. There is no requirement that the loan bear interest; however, to the extent that no interest is charged or interest is less than a prescribed rate, a taxable benefit will occur (see Chapter 4).[24] It is important to recognize that the tax treatment of the loan principal is different from the tax treatment of interest.

---

23 ITA 15(2), (2.2), (2.3), (2.4); IT-119R3. A corporation can also loan funds to a shareholder if the lending of money is part of the corporation's ordinary course of business.

24 ITA 80.4; IT-421R2.

This opportunity is particularly valuable to Canadian-controlled private corporations that have business income taxed at the low corporate rate. For example, a corporation that has earned $100,000 of business income, which leaves $82,000 after tax, could loan the full amount to the shareholder/employee to acquire a home. Although the loan must be repaid over time, the shareholder has immediate access, for personal use, to corporate profits that have been taxed at only 18%. This would not have been the case if the business had been operated as a proprietorship.

A corporation is not precluded from loaning funds to shareholders for reasons other than those mentioned above. However, in such cases the loan must be repaid within one taxation year of the year in which the advance was made;[25] otherwise, the full amount of the loan will be taxable to the shareholder as business income. If these loans are later repaid, a deduction from income is permitted in the year of repayment.[26]

Consider this situation. In February 20X6, a corporation with a May 31 year end loans $50,000 to a shareholder to fund a personal investment. The loan is repaid in August 20X7. In this situation, the loan remains unpaid at the corporation's year end of May 31, 20X7, which is one year following the year the loan was made (20X6). Consequently, the shareholder must include $50,000 in his or her 20X6 income for tax purposes and pay the related income tax. In 20X7, which is the year the loan is repaid, the shareholder can deduct $50,000 from his or her income for tax purposes. Notice the timing in this situation: the shareholder has taxable income in the year the loan is received, and obtains a deduction only in the year the loan is repaid.

Note also that one-year shareholder loan rules will not apply if the shareholder attempts to "extend" the loan by repaying it just prior to the one-year limit and then re-borrowing it immediately after the corporation's year end. This is referred to as a series of loans and repayments. The original loan will be included in the shareholder's income in the year the loan was made, and no deduction will be permitted if and when the loan is repaid.

V. Limitation of the Small-Business Deduction

As shown earlier, a Canadian-controlled private corporation is normally permitted to claim the small-business deduction (resulting in the low tax rate of 18%) on the first $300,000 of annual active business income. There are two situations where this annual limit may be reduced or eliminated. Each of these situations is examined below.

A. Associated Corporations

The fact that the small-business deduction is limited to $300,000 of annual business profits may entice a corporation's shareholders into utilizing a number of corporations to conduct their business activities. The claiming of multiple small-business deductions in this manner is greatly limited, however, by what are referred to as the "associated corporations" rules.

If two or more corporations are found to be *associated*, a single $300,000 income limit on the use of the small-business deduction will apply to all of the associated corporations combined. However, the owners can apportion this limit among those corporations on an annual basis in any proportion desired.[27]

Whether or not two or more corporations are associated is governed by extremely complex definition sections in the *Income Tax Act*.[28] In addition, CCRA can, at its discretion, deem corporations to be associated when it may reasonably be considered that one of the main reasons for the separate existence of those corporations is to reduce taxes.[29] It is beyond the scope of this text to define "associated corporations" except in the roughest

---

25 Except when the corporation's business includes the lending of money.

26 ITA 20(1)(j).

27 ITA 125(3), (4); IT-64R3.

28 ITA 256(1) to (9); IT-64R3.

29 ITA 256(2.1).

terms, and the reader should consult expert advice before embarking on corporate structures with the intention of applying the small-business deduction. Notwithstanding the limitations, expansion of the small-business deduction can be achieved, and this fact plays a vital role in business-expansion decisions (see Chapter 20).

In general terms, corporations are associated when

(a) one corporation controls the other; or,

(b) the corporations are controlled by the same shareholder or the same group of shareholders.

While control normally means having a majority of the voting shares, in this context it also means having indirect control when a shareholder (or group) that does not have a majority of votes can exercise significant influence over other shareholders.[30]

Consider the business-expansion structures in Exhibit 13-6. In both situations Corporation A, which is owned entirely by shareholder Y, has decided to expand a segment of its business by creating a new Corporation B that includes a new participating shareholder X.

Under structure 1, Corporation A controls Corporation B because it holds 60% of the voting shares. Thus, Corporation A and Corporation B are associated and must share the $200,000 limit on the use of the small-business deduction. On the assumption that Corporation A will use the full $300,000 for its income, Corporation B will have all of its income taxed at the high corporate rate.

In structure 2, neither shareholder controls Corporation B. This means that A and B are not associated, so *each* can apply the low rate of tax to its first $300,000 of business income. Corporation A has thus indirectly expanded its small-business deduction: it can apply the full $300,000 limit to itself; at the same time, its 50% ownership of Corporation B entitles it to a half-share of that new corporation's $300,000 limit. Notice that structure 2 has enhanced the after-tax cash flow of B, thereby increasing that entity's chances of success.

Various possible methods of expanding the small-business deduction by means of business expansion are discussed in more detail in Chapter 20 on domestic business expansions.

Exhibit 13-6:
Associated and
Non-Associated Structures

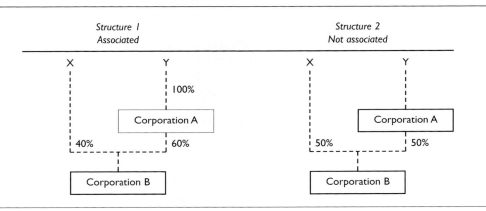

B. Large
Corporations

True to its name, the small-business deduction applies only to Canadian-controlled private corporations (CCPC) that are of a certain size. Beyond that size, the annual small-business deduction limit of $300,000 on active business income is gradually reduced until it is elimi-

---

30 ITA 256(5.1).

nated. For this purpose, the size of a CCPC is measured not by the amount of annual income but rather by the amount of the capital (referred to as taxable capital) it uses in Canada to conduct its operations. Corporations with *taxable capital in excess of $10 million* are considered to be large corporations. For each $1 million of taxable capital in excess of $10 million, the small-business deduction limit of $300,000 is reduced by $60,000.[31] The entire annual limit is eliminated when the taxable capital of the corporation and its associated corporations (discussed earlier) reaches $15 million, as follows:

Taxable capital	Annual limit
$10 million	$300,000
$11 million	$240,000
$12 million	$180,000
$13 million	$120,000
$14 million	$ 60,000
$15 million	–0–

The rules for establishing a corporation's taxable capital are complex, and explaining them is beyond the scope of this text. In general terms, taxable capital consists of the corporation's shareholders' equity (share capital and retained earnings), plus corporate debt, less an allowance for the cost of investments in other corporations. Besides reducing their small-business deduction, large corporations must pay a special tax (referred to as the large-corporation tax) of .200% (in 2004) of the taxable capital they employ in Canada in excess of $50 million.[32] The rate declines to .175% in 2005, .125% in 2006, .0625% in 2007, and then eliminated. This tax is reduced by the corporate surtax, which was discussed in Chapter 11.

VI. Overall Tax Calculation for a Canadian-Controlled Private Corporation

The actual tax calculation for a Canadian-controlled private corporation (CCPC) is more complex than was demonstrated earlier in this chapter and in Chapter 11. The discussions to this point have focussed on the basic tax treatment of the various types of income earned by a CCPC and on how this treatment affects shareholders when after-tax profits are distributed as dividends. This section summarizes the detailed tax calculation and then reviews each of its major parts. A complete tax calculation is provided in a demonstration question at the end of the chapter. The calculation uses the $300,000 annual small-business deduction limit that begins in 2006.

Summary Tax Calculation

Part I tax

Federal basic tax—38% × taxable income	xxx
Less abatement—10% × taxable income	(x)
	xx
Plus surtax—4% × Part I tax after abatement	x

Plus refundable tax on investment income—6⅔% of the least of:

- Aggregate investment income
- Taxable income less amount subject to the small-business deduction (below)   x

---

31 ITA 125(5.1).

32 ITA 181.1(1).

Less *small business deduction*—16% of the least of:
- Active business income (ABI)
- Taxable income (TI) less (10/3 × foreign tax credit)
- Annual business limit ($300,000 less amounts allocated to associated corporations and the large-corporation reduction, if applicable)   (x)

Less *manufacturing and processing (M&P) deduction*—7% of the least of:
- M&P profits less amount subject to the small-business deduction (above)
- Taxable income less:
    - —amount subject to the small-business deduction, plus
    - —aggregate investment income   (x)

Less *special reduction*—7% of the amount by which the taxable income (TI) *exceeds* the *total* of
- Income subject to the 7% M&P deduction, *plus*
- Income subject to the 16% small-business deduction, *plus*
- Aggregate investment income   (x)

Less *foreign tax credit*   (x)

Less *political contribution tax credit*—(75% × first $200) + (50% × next $350) + (33⅓% of excess), maximum $500   (x)

     Federal Part I tax   xx

Provincial tax—Provincial rate × taxable income   x

     Total federal and provincial Part I tax   xx

Part IV tax (federal)

On dividends received from non-connected corporations
   33⅓% of taxable Canadian dividends   xx

On dividends received from connected corporations

$$\text{Dividend refund of the connected corporation} \times \frac{\text{Taxable Canadian dividends received from the connected corporation}}{\text{Total taxable dividends paid by the connected corporation in the year}}$$ xx

     Total Part IV tax   xx

Dividend refund (federal)

Lesser of:
- ⅓ (33⅓%) × dividends paid in the year
- balance in the RDTOH before refund   (xx)

RDTOH (federal)

Balance at beginning of year   xx

Add:
- Part IV tax   x
- The least of:
    - —26⅔% × aggregate investment income
    - —26⅔% × (taxable income – amount subject to the small-business deduction)
    - —Part I federal tax – federal surtax   x

     RDTOH *before current year refund*   xx

Less dividend refund for the current year (above)   (x)

     RDTOH at end of year   xx

Note: Regarding the special reduction, certain limitations relating to resource allowances, credit unions, and specified partnerships have been ignored.

The main parts of the above calculation are reviewed below. For demonstration purposes, a situation with a common set of facts is used. These facts are as follows:

- X Ltd. is a Canadian-controlled private corporation operating a wholesale business and a manufacturing business. Also, X owns 60% of the voting common shares of S Ltd.

- For the year ended December 31, 20X6, X has taxable income of $440,000, as follows:

Net income for tax purposes	$460,000
Less	
Charitable donations	(5,000)
Taxable Canadian dividends from shares of public corporations	(15,000)
Taxable income	$440,000

The net income for tax purposes includes $8,000 of net taxable capital gains and $12,000 of interest income from bonds. It also includes $15,000 of dividends from public corporations (these were deducted in arriving at taxable income above). Manufacturing and processing (M&P) profits qualifying for the M&P deduction are $200,000.

- X's RDTOH at the end of the previous year was $6,000.

- During the year, X paid a dividend of $30,000 to its shareholders.

- S Ltd. and X Ltd. are associated for tax purposes. For the year ended December 31, 20X6, S claimed the small-business deduction on $110,000 of its active business income. S did not pay any dividends in 20X6.

A. Small-Business Deduction

Before calculating the small-business deduction, we must determine the corporation's active business income and its annual business limit. As shown earlier, the *active business income* is determined by reducing *net income for tax purposes* by the corporation's property income (interest, dividends, rents, and royalties) and net taxable capital gains (gains – losses). In the above situation, the active business income is $425,000, calculated as follows:

Net income for tax purposes	$460,000
Less	
Interest income from bonds	(12,000)
Dividends from taxable Canadian corporations	(15,000)
Net taxable capital gains	(8,000)
Active business income	$425,000

Normally, the active business income eligible for the small-business deduction is $300,000 (the annual business limit). However, S, an associated corporation, used $110,000 of this limit. Therefore, the business limit for X is $190,000, as follows:

Total business limit	$300,000
Less amount claimed by associated corporation S	(110,000)
Business limit available to X	$190,000

The small-business deduction for X in 20X6 is $30,400, calculated as follows:

16% of the least of:
- Active business income · $425,000
- Taxable income · $440,000
- Annual limit ($300,000 – $110,000 allocated to associated corporation) · · $190,000

16% × $190,000 = $30,400

B. Refundable Tax on Investment Income

As shown in the summary tax calculation, the refundable tax is $6\frac{2}{3}\%$ of the least of these: investment income, *or* taxable income minus the amount on which the small-business deduction is applied. The latter of these may apply when substantial loss carry-overs or charitable donations are deducted in arriving at taxable income. However, in most situations, the $6\frac{2}{3}\%$ rate is simply applied to aggregate investment income. For this purpose, and other parts of the tax calculation, the term *investment income* has a special meaning.[33] It includes Canadian and foreign net property income (interest, rents, and royalties, less related expenses) as well as net taxable capital gains (gains minus losses) for the current year less any net capital losses from other years claimed in the current year. Notice that dividends from taxable Canadian corporations are excluded from the definition. This is because such dividends were deducted in arriving at taxable income, and are not subject to tax under Part I of the *Income Tax Act*.

In the above situation the investment income is $20,000 (net taxable capital gains of $8,000 + interest income of $12,000). The refundable tax is $1,333, as follows:

$6\frac{2}{3}\%$ of the least of:
- Investment income · $ 20,000
- Taxable income ($440,000) minus income subject to the
  small-business deduction ($190,000) · $250,000

$6\frac{2}{3}\%$ × $20,000 = $1,333

C. Manufacturing and Processing Deduction

Normally, the 7% manufacturing and processing deduction applies only to the M&P profits that are not subject to the small-business deduction. This usually means that the deduction applies to profits over the $300,000 small-business deduction limit. In the above situation, X Ltd. earned M&P profits of $200,000. However, the small-business deduction applied to only $190,000 because an associated corporation used $110,000 of the $300,000 limit. Consequently, the M&P deduction for X Ltd. is $700, calculated as follows:

7% of the least of:
- M&P profits ($200,000) – Income subject to the small-business
  deduction ($190,000) · $ 10,000
- Taxable income ($440,000) – [Income subject to the small-business
  deduction ($190,000) + Investment income, calculated earlier ($20,000)] · · $230,000

7% × $10,000 = $700

Notice the wide spread between the two "least of" items in the calculation. In most situations the 7% M&P deduction will apply to the M&P profits in excess of the income that

---

33 ITA 129(4).

is subject to the small-business deduction. The latter part of the calculation may apply when the corporation deducts significant loss carry-overs or charitable donations in arriving at taxable income.

D. Special Reduction

The special reduction of 7% applies to the corporations' *taxable income other than* income eligible for the M&P and small-business deductions, resource income, and investment income. As a result, the amount of income eligible for the special reduction is $220,000 and the tax reduction is $15,400 calculated as follows:

Taxable income	$440,000
Less	
Income eligible for the M&P deduction	(10,000)
Income eligible for the small-business deduction	(190,000)
Investment income	(20,000)
Income eligible for the second special reduction	$220,000
Second special reduction—7% × $220,000	$ 15,400

E. Refundable Dividend Tax on Hand

The refundable dividend tax on hand (RDTOH) is designed to accumulate the eligible tax refund that occurs when dividends are paid to shareholders. In general terms, the potential refund consists of all Part IV taxes paid by the corporation (these are fully refundable) *plus* $26^{2}/3\%$ of all investment income earned. As shown earlier, the investment income for this purpose includes net Canadian and foreign-property income (excluding taxable Canadian dividends) *plus* net taxable capital gains.

In the above situation, X Ltd. pays Part IV tax of $5,000 on the dividends from public corporations ($33^{1}/3\%$ of $15,000 = $5,000). The RDTOH at the end of its 20X6 taxation year (before the current refund) is $16,333, calculated as follows:

RDTOH at end of previous year		$ 6,000
Add		
Part IV tax paid in the current year		5,000
The least of:		
• $26^{2}/3\%$ × investment income ($20,000)	$ 5,333	
• $26^{2}/3\%$ × [taxable income ($440,000) − income subject to the small business deduction ($190,000)]	$66,675	
Part I tax − surtax	not calculated	
Least of is		5,333
RDTOH before 20X5 refund		$16,333

The last part of the above calculation limits the potential refund to the amount of Part I tax paid in the current year. It normally does not apply unless significant loss carry-overs are deducted in arriving at taxable income. It was not calculated in the above demonstration because it is obvious that the total Part I tax is much greater than the lowest amount, which is $5,333.

F. Dividend Refund

As shown earlier in the chapter, a corporation that has taxes eligible for a refund is provided that refund when dividends are distributed to its shareholder(s). The tax refund (referred to as the "dividend refund") is equal to $33^1/_3\%$ of the dividend paid, but it cannot exceed the balance in the RDTOH. In the situation at hand, X Ltd. paid a dividend of $30,000, and its dividend refund is $10,000, calculated as follows:

Least of:	
• $33^1/_3\%$ of the dividend paid ($30,000)	$10,000
• Balance in the RDTOH	$16,333
Least of is $10,000	

The refund reduces the RDTOH to $6,333 ($16,333 – $10,000) at the end of 20X6, and this amount is carried over to the 20X6 taxation year.

The above calculations are complex. The "least of" calculations tend to confuse the fundamental tax treatment applied to the various types of income earned by Canadian-controlled private corporations. Remember the following fundamentals:

1. The first $300,000 of active business income is taxed at the low rate of 18% (depending on the province) as a result of applying the small-business deduction.

2. M&P profits in excess of the $300,000 small-business deduction limit are subject to a 7% tax reduction.

3. Property income (other than taxable Canadian dividends) is subject to the high rate of tax of $51^2/_3\%$ (standard rate of 45% + refundable tax of $6^2/_3\%$). The tax on this income is reduced by $26^2/_3\%$ when dividends are paid to shareholders.

4. Certain dividend income is subject to a Part IV tax of $33^1/_3\%$, which is fully refundable when dividends are paid to shareholders.

VII. Tax Planning Checklist

Much of this chapter was devoted to describing the tax benefits of operating a business or holding investments in a corporation. These benefits, and some additional tax planning considerations, are summarized below.

1. Consider incorporating a business whenever the annual business profits consistently exceed the funds required for personal use. The low rate of corporate tax on those profits will increase the cash available for use in the business.

2. At the time of incorporation, consider including family members as shareholders to achieve income splitting on future profits. (See Chapter 9 for special rules on dividends paid to minors from private corporations.)

3. If the corporation will be providing services, be sure that the activity does not qualify as a personal services business, as the small-business deduction is not permitted for any income generated by such a business.

4. Before incorporating, consider the problems that might arise if the corporation were to incur losses, and how those losses might be used to reduce future taxes.

5. As a shareholder/manager, be certain to utilize the employment provisions in the *Income Tax Act* that allow employees to receive tax-free benefits. Also, make sure that the owner's salary is sufficient to allow him or her to make the maximum permitted RRSP contributions every year.

6. Consider paying bonuses or increased salaries to shareholders who are active in the business, thus reducing or eliminating double taxation for corporate business income that is in excess of the $300,000 annual small-business deduction limit.

7. Remember that the small-business deduction limit of $300,000 is an *annual* amount and that any unused portion cannot be carried forward to another year. When the current year's business profit is below the limit but the following year's profit is expected to exceed the limit, consider increasing the current profit by not claiming certain discretionary deductions, such as a reserve for bad debts. This shifts income from the following year, which would have been taxed at the high corporate rate, to the current year, where it will be taxed at the low corporate rate.

8. When possible, time the corporation's dividend distributions to obtain a tax deferral and the lowest possible tax rate. For example, wait until a year in which the shareholder has unusually low income.

9. A shareholder/employee who will need funds from the corporation should consider making use of shareholder loans and/or deferred bonuses. This would delay the payment of tax for the longest possible time.

10. When acquiring or creating new corporations that will be owned with other shareholders, be sure to seek advice on the rules governing associated corporations, with the goal of establishing a separate $300,000 small-business deduction limit.

11. A minority shareholder should be aware that the controlling shareholder has the power to allocate the annual business deduction limit of $300,000 to another corporation that he or she controls, leaving the minority shareholder with a higher tax rate. The minority shareholder can avoid this problem by making sure that the deduction's allocation is set out in the shareholders' agreement.

VIII. Summary and Conclusion

The Canadian-controlled private corporation is a commonly used structure designed to house a wide range of business activities and investments. The tax treatment of its income and subsequent distributions to shareholders deviates from the standard principles of corporate taxation. These deviations are designed to provide temporary tax incentives to incorporated small businesses; at the same time, they provide neither advantages nor disadvantages to the incorporation of investment income. Because of the different tax treatments accorded various types of corporate income, additional complexities arise that tend to cloud the decision-making process by making it difficult to estimate the resulting cash-flow impact.

Active business income earned by the corporation receives a significant tax preference through the application of the small-business deduction on the first $300,000 of annual business income. This deduction, combined with similar provincial incentives, reduces corporate tax on such income to approximately 18%. As this rate is significantly lower than the top marginal personal tax rate, incorporation provides increased after-tax cash flow, which enhances returns on investment as well as the chances of business success. Although additional taxes are payable when the business income is distributed to the shareholders, double taxation does not occur because the dividend tax credit is designed to offset the corporate taxes of 18% to 20%.

Active business income in excess of $300,000 is subject to higher rates of corporate tax, the result being substantial double taxation in the future. Depending on the amount of income in this category and when it is paid out, this double taxation may override the benefits achieved from the use of the small-business deduction. In some circumstances double taxation can be avoided by maintaining a salary/dividend policy that shifts income in this category directly to the shareholder.

An entity earning investment income and capital gains derives no substantial tax benefit from incorporation. However, double taxation is avoided through a refund mechanism when investment income or a capital gain is distributed as a dividend to the shareholders.

The relationship between a Canadian-controlled private corporation and its shareholders is closely integrated; this is not the case with public corporations and their shareholders. It is, therefore, essential that decision makers anticipate the effect that corporate decisions will ultimately have on the shareholders.

Reading List

Income Tax Act References

	Section
Small-business deduction	125(1)
Amount of "business limit"	125(2)
Associated corporations	125(3), (4)
Active business income (defined)	125(7)
Canadian-controlled private corporation	125(7)
Personal services business	125(7)
Specified investment business	125(7)
Dividend refund to private corporation	129(1)
Refundable dividend tax on hand	129(3)
Investment income from an associated corporation deemed to be active business income	129(6)
Capital dividend	83(2)
Capital dividend account	89(1)(b)
Tax on certain taxable dividends (Part IV)	186(1)
Shareholder debt	15(2)
Associated corporations (defined)	256(1)
Control, etc.	256(1.2)
Associated with third corporation	256(2)
Anti-avoidance (association)	256(2.1)
Control in fact	256(5.1), (6)

Canada Customs and Revenue Agency Publications

IT-458R	Canadian-controlled private corporation.
IT-73R5	The small-business deduction—income from an active business, a specified investment business, and a personal services business.
IT-189R2	Corporations used by practising members of a profession.
IT-243R4	Dividend refund to private corporations.
IT-269R3	Part IV tax on taxable dividends received by a private corporation.
IT-119R3	Debts of shareholders, certain persons connected with shareholders, etc.
IT-421R2	Benefits to individuals, corporations, and shareholders from loans or debt.
IT-64R3	Corporations: association and control—after 1988.
IC 88-2	General anti-avoidance rule (paragraph 18).

Major Court Decisions

Mayon Investments Inc. v. MNR, (TCC), 91 DTC 364—Business income v. specified investment business income.

533702 Ontario Ltd. v. MNR, 91 DTC 723—Personal service business v. active business income.

La Compagnie Idéal Body Inc. v. The Queen, (FCTD), 89 DTC 5450—Reasonableness of bonuses to shareholders.

Beckerfields Ltd. v. MNR, 64 DTC 5301—Meaning of control (*de jure v. de facto*).

Other Publications

Berglas, R., "Mixing it Up," *CA Magazine*, December 1996.

Cadesky, M., "Planning Considerations in Owner-Manager Remuneration," 1988 Conference Report of Proceedings of the 40th Tax Conference, Canadian Tax Foundation, pp. 9:1–48.

Flexman, B., "Incorporating Investment Income," *Canadian Tax Journal*, Vol. 45, No. 5 (1997), p. 1032.

Teltscher, L., "Loans to Shareholder-Employees: Salary Versus Dividends," Report of Proceedings of the 48th Tax Conference (1996), Canadian Tax Foundation, p. 53.1.

Demonstration Questions

Question One

TL Ltd. is a Canadian-controlled private corporation operating a retail mail-order business and a small manufacturing operation. At December 31, 20X5, the company's year end, all of the outstanding shares were owned by Jason Tallon.

On November 30, 20X5, Tallon informed you, the treasurer, that he wants to declare a dividend of $80,000 on December 31, 20X5. He has asked you for advice on how to minimize tax on the dividend. He also wants to know if there will be sufficient cash to pay the dividend. With this in mind, you have prepared a projected income statement for the year ended December 31, 20X5, and intend to estimate the corporate tax liability.

Information regarding the company's financial transactions is provided below.

TL Ltd.
20X5 Financial Information

1. The projected profit for the year ended December 31, 20X5 is $273,000, as summarized below.

Mail-order profit	$221,000
Loss from the manufacturing operation	(32,000)
Dividends from taxable Canadian corporations	19,000
Interest income on bonds	5,000
Gain on sale of asset	60,000
	$273,000

2. The mail-order profit includes the following expense items:

Advertising	$37,800
Amortization	66,400
Charitable donations	3,000
Legal —Collection of accounts receivable	1,500
—Drafting debenture agreement for bank financing	4,000
Rent	72,600

3. On February 1, 20X5, TL began a policy of providing a warranty on its manufactured products. The manufacturing loss includes the deduction of $8,000 as a reserve for anticipated product returns. In 20X5, the actual returns were $6,000.

4. Dividends from taxable Canadian corporations include $9,000 from public corporations and $10,000 from Q Ltd. (a Canadian-controlled private corporation). TL owns 20% of Q's voting common shares. Q's total dividend paid was $50,000 (TL's share − $10,000). As a result of the dividend, Q received a dividend refund of $6,000.

5. TL's 20X4 tax return shows the following information:

Refundable dividend tax on hand	$ 3,000
Capital dividend account	–0–
Cumulative eligible capital (see comment in next paragraph)	–0–
Undepreciated capital costs:	
Class 8	72,000
Class 43	144,000
Class 14	13,000

During 20X5, TL Ltd. purchased welding equipment costing $60,000 for use in the manufacturing operation. In 20X3, the company acquired a licence for $15,000 to manufacture a patented product. The licence has a legal life of 10 years. No deductions have ever been made from the cumulative eligible capital account.

6. A segment of the mail-order business was sold on October 1, 20X5. The proceeds included $70,000 for inventory and $40,000 for a permanent customer list. TL developed the customer list over the past 10 years. Also, TL sold shares of a public corporation, resulting in a gain of $20,000.

7. The treasurer's assistant analyzed the accounting records and provided the following tax-related information:

Manufacturing capital (MC)	$212,000
Manufacturing labour (ML)	196,000
Total capital (TC)	460,000
Total labour (TL)	323,000

8. Jason Tallon purchased all of his brother's shares in TL Ltd. in January 20X5 for $120,000. His brother had acquired the shares in 20X0 for $150,000. A summary of the assets of TL Ltd. and their fair market values at the time of the sale is provided below.

Current assets—business	$ 700,000
Mail-order assets	340,000
Manufacturing assets	516,000
Investment in shares of public corporations	150,000
	$1,706,000

Excluding the sale of shares, the brother's taxable income in 20X5 was $12,000. His marginal tax rate in 20X4 was 50%.

9. In addition to owning all of the TL Ltd. shares, Jason Tallon owns 60% of the voting shares of PY Ltd., a Canadian-controlled private corporation. PY Ltd. earned active business income of $270,000 for its taxation year ending December 31, 20X5. It claimed the small-business deduction on all of this income.

Required:

1. Under Part I of the *Income Tax Act*, determine the *minimum income for tax purposes* and the *minimum taxable income* for TL Ltd. for the 20X5 taxation year.

2. Based on your answer to part 1, calculate the Part I and Part IV federal income tax for the 20X5 taxation year, before the dividend refund, if any.

3. What is the maximum capital dividend that can be paid in 20X5? Determine the dividend refund for the 20X5 taxation year based on the planned dividend payment.

4. Briefly describe the tax implications for Tallon's brother from his sale of the TL Ltd. shares.

Solution:

This solution assumes the annual small-business deduction limit is $300,000 as applicable in 2006. For 2004 and 2005 the limits would be $250,000 and $275,000, respectively.

Before the solution is completed, two items are explained. First, TL Ltd. and PY Ltd. are associated for tax purposes because both are controlled by Jason Tallon (TL 100%; PY 60%). Therefore, TL and PY must share the small-business limit of $300,000. As PY has already used $270,000 of this limit, TL's business limit for 20X5 is reduced to $30,000 ($300,000 − $270,000). Second, TL Ltd. and Q Ltd. are connected corporations because TL owns more than 10% of Q's voting shares. Therefore, standard Part IV taxes are not applicable on the dividend received by TL from Q. Instead, TL pays a Part IV tax equal to its proportionate share of any dividend refund that Q received as a result of the dividend. This can be calculated as follows:

$$\frac{\text{Dividend received by TL—\$10,000}}{\text{Total dividend paid by Q—\$50,000}} \times \text{Q's dividend refund (\$6,000)} = \$1,200$$

Effectively, TL's Part IV tax is 20% (percentage share ownership) of Q's refund of $6,000 (20% × $6,000 = $1,200). The dividends received from the public corporation (which is not connected) are subject to the full Part IV tax.

1. Income for tax purposes and taxable income

Projected income		$273,000
Gain on sale of assets		(60,000)
Amortization		66,400
Charitable donations		3,000
Legal fees for debenture—$^4/_5$($4,000)		3,200
Warranty reserve		8,000
Actual warranty costs		(6,000)
CCA —Class 8—$72,000 × 20%		(14,400)
—Class 43—[$144,000 × 30%] + [$60,000 × 30% × $^1/_2$]		(52,200)
—Class 14—$15,000 ÷ 10 y		(1,500)
Taxable capital gain—public corporation shares—$^1/_2$ ($20,000)		10,000
Gain on sale of eligible capital property, customer list—$^1/_2$ ($40,000)		20,000
Income for tax purposes		249,500
Deduct		
Donations	3,000	
Dividends	19,000	(22,000)
Taxable income		$227,500

2. PART I FEDERAL TAX

Federal—38% × $227,500		$ 86,450
Abatement—10% × $227,500		(22,750)
		63,700
Surtax—4% × $63,700		2,548

Refundable tax—6⅔% × least of:
- Investment income—interest $5,000 + taxable capital gain $10,000 = $15,000
- Taxable income—$227,500 − $30,000 (amount subject to small-business deduction below) = $197,500

6⅔% × $15,000		1,001

Small-business deduction—16% × lesser of:
- Active business income—$215,500 (see below)
- Taxable income—$227,500
- Annual limit—$30,000 ($300,000 − $270,000 used by PY Ltd.)

16% × $30,000		(4,800)
		62,449

Active business income:

Net income for tax purposes	$249,500	
Less		
Taxable Canadian dividends	(19,000)	
Interest from bonds	(5,000)	
Taxable capital gain	(10,000)	
	$215,500	

M&P deduction:

$$\frac{\$212,000 \ (MC) + \$196,000 \ (ML)}{\$460,000 \ (TC) + \$323,000 \ (TL)} \times \$215,500 \ (ABI) = \$112,291$$

M&P profit		$112,291	
Less amount subject to small-business deduction		(30,000)	
Deduction—	7% ×	82,291	(5,760)
Special reduction (see next paragraph)			(7,015)
			$ 49,674

Notice that the M&P profit determined by the formula is $112,291 even though the manufacturing operation actually lost $32,000. This is so because the formula applies to the total active business income, including the retail income. Also notice that the special tax reduction is very small. The income eligible for the special tax reduction of 7% is $100,209 (taxable income of $227,500 minus [income eligible for the M&P deduction – $82,291; income eligible for the small business deduction – $30,000; investment income – $15,000]). The reduction is $7,015 (7% × $100,209).

PART IV TAX

Dividends from non-connected public corporation—33⅓% × $9,000	$3,000
Dividends from connected corporation, Q Ltd.—above	1,200
	$4,200

3. *Capital dividend account*

Opening	$ –0–
Add the non-taxable portions of:	
Eligible capital property gain—½ ($40,000)	20,000
Capital gain—½ ($20,000)	10,000
	$30,000

The balance in the capital dividend account can be distributed as a tax-free capital dividend if appropriate forms are filed. TL intends to declare a dividend of $80,000 and wants to minimize tax to the shareholder. Therefore, it should pay a capital dividend of $30,000 and the balance of $50,000 ($80,000 – $30,000) as a regular taxable dividend.

RDTOH

Opening	$ 3,000
Part IV tax	4,200
Refundable portion of Part I tax—the least of:	
26⅔% × $15,000 (investment income, above) = $4,000	
26⅔% × $197,500 (taxable income $227,500, minus $30,000	
of income subject to the small-business deduction) = $52,667	
Part I tax $49,674 – surtax $2,548 = $47,126	
Least of	4,000
Balance before 20X5 refund below	$11,200

Dividend refund:
Least of:
   RDTOH, above—$11,200
     33⅓% × taxable dividend paid ($65,000) = $21,664
       Least of   **$11,200**

4. The sale of shares by Tallon's brother results in an allowable business-investment loss of $15,000 [½ ($120,000 − $150,000)]. This is so because over 90% of the company's assets are used in an active business, making the corporation qualify as a small business corporation. As the brother's income in 20X5 is $12,000, the loss of $15,000 creates a non-capital loss in 20X5 of $3,000 ($15,000 − $12,000). This loss can be carried back to 20X4 and recover taxes of $1,500 (50% × $3,000).

Question Two

Karen Toor owns and operates a retail store as a proprietorship. For the past several years the store has earned annual profits of approximately $80,000. Toor is planning an expansion of the store. The expansion cost will be financed with a bank loan. Financial projections for the expanded store show that annual profits will increase to $140,000 annually.

Toor also has substantial income from bond investments. Consequently, her marginal tax rate (federal and provincial) is 50% on regular income and 34% on taxable Canadian dividends.

In past years most of the store profits had been used by Toor for personal spending. She estimates that in the future she will have to withdraw $50,000, after tax, from the business to meet her personal spending requirements.

Because of the anticipated increase in profits from the store expansion, Toor is considering incorporating the business. She wants to increase the after-tax profits so that the expansion bank loan can be paid down as quickly as possible. Toor has heard that incorporation can result in lower income taxes, but is aware that double taxation may occur because of dividend payments to shareholders.

Required:

Will incorporation of the retail store increase the business's after-tax cash flow? If so, by how much? If the store is incorporated, will double taxation occur if dividends are paid to Toor in the future? Explain.

Solution:

If the retail store remains as a proprietorship, the annual after-tax cash flow available for reinvestment in the business (and to pay down the bank loan) will be $20,000, calculated as follows:

Projected business income	$140,000
Income tax @ 50%	(70,000)
Income after tax	70,000
Required by Toor for personal expenses	(50,000)
Available for business reinvestment	$ 20,000

If the business is transferred to a corporation owned by Toor, the first $300,000 of active business income will be taxed at 18% (depending on the provincial tax rate). After incorporation, Toor will have to extract funds from the company to meet her personal spending needs of $50,000 after tax. To achieve this, she can have the corporation pay her a salary of $100,000, which after personal taxes at 50% will leave her with the required $50,000. The salary will reduce corporate profits to $40,000. The annual after-tax cash flow available to the corporation for reinvestment will be $32,000, as follows:

Projected income	$140,000
Less salary to owner	(100,000)
Net income	40,000
Corporate tax @ 18%	(7,200)
Available for business reinvestment	$ 32,800

Thus, incorporating the business will increase after-tax cash flow by $12,800 ($32,800 − $20,000).

If and when dividends are paid by the corporation, double-tax will not occur because the corporation's income is subject to the low corporate tax rate (18%). To demonstrate, assume that all of the after-tax corporate profits above are paid to the shareholder as a dividend. Her total tax on the $140,000 of business income earned is calculated below.

Tax to corporation on $40,000 of business income	$ 7,200
Tax paid by Toor on salary of $100,000	50,000
Tax paid by Toor on dividend—34% × $32,800	11,152
Total tax	$68,352

As a proprietorship, Toor's tax on $140,000 is $70,000 (50% × $140,000), which is very close to the $68,352 of total taxes paid under the corporate option.

Review Questions

1. Explain why a Canadian corporation whose voting share capital is owned 50% by Canadian residents and 50% by non-residents is classified as a Canadian-controlled private corporation.

2. Canadian-controlled private corporations differ from public corporations in the rate of tax, the extent of double taxation, and the degree of secondary relationships with shareholders. Briefly describe these differences.

3. "A business that derives its income from selling personal services (plumbing repairs, for example) cannot be viewed as earning active business income." Is this statement true? Explain. How is a personal services business different from an active business?

4. Why may a Canadian-controlled private corporation that earns business income of $100,000 in year 1 and $300,000 in year 2 (total: $400,000) pay less tax than a corporation earning $50,000 in year 1 and $350,000 in year 2 (total: $400,000)?

5. In question 4, what might the latter corporation be able to do to ensure that it pays the same amount of tax as the first corporation? If these options are in fact available, what other factors must be considered before a decision is made to take such actions?

6. "The use of the small-business deduction by a Canadian-controlled private corporation does not result in a tax saving; rather, it creates a tax deferral." Explain.

7. Interest income and/or rental income earned by one Canadian-controlled private corporation may be treated as specified investment business income. At the same time, income from the same source(s) earned by another Canadian-controlled private corporation may be treated as active business income. Why is this? And to what extent will the rate of tax applied to that income be different for the two corporations?

8. Identify and briefly explain the mechanism that is used to reduce the incidence of double taxation when specified investment business income is distributed by a Canadian-controlled private corporation to its shareholders.

9. Does double taxation occur when a Canadian-controlled private corporation earns capital gains and distributes those gains as dividends to individual shareholders? Explain.

10. "An investor can achieve a tax deferral on portfolio dividends received from public corporation shares if those shares are owned by his or her private corporation." Is this statement true? Explain.

11. There are several advantages to deferring tax by utilizing the small-business deduction. Briefly state two of them.

12. A Canadian-controlled private corporation can obtain a tax deferral from the small-business deduction. Will the corporation's owner always benefit from investing the extra cash flow that results, regardless of the type of return that may be received from the investment? Explain.

13. Briefly state the advantages and disadvantages of earning investment income in a Canadian-controlled private corporation.

14. Why may it be worthwhile for a corporation to pay an additional salary or bonus to its shareholder/manager even though he or she does not require additional funds?

15. Is it possible for a shareholder to obtain personal use of corporate funds without first declaring a dividend or salary? Explain.

16. Individual A is about to acquire 30% of the shares of a new corporation (a Canadian-controlled private corporation) that will carry on an active business. The remaining 70% of the shares will be owned by X Corporation, a company that also owns an active business. What concern should individual A have regarding the tax treatment of the new corporation's income?

Problems

Problem One

John Basler is employed in the transportation industry and earns a substantial salary. His personal marginal tax rate is 45% (federal and provincial).

He also owns 100% of the shares of Truck Ltd. The corporation is a 20% partner in a small trucking business. In 20X1 the partnership earned a net profit of $80,000.

Basler intends to do some consulting work starting in 20X2, while continuing in his present employment. A small trucking company has requested that he provide advice on how to set up a proper accounting system. He would be paid on a fee-for-service basis. The contract, if he accepts it, would likely last for two years and earn him $20,000 per year. It would also use up his entire available consulting time. In the future, he may accept two or three smaller contracts a year.

Basler has requested advice on whether he should incorporate his proposed consulting activities. He has indicated that he will not require the income for personal use and intends to invest the after-tax profits.

Required:

1. What are the tax benefits, if any, to Basler if he incorporates his consulting activities? Provide any appropriate calculations.

2. Would your answer change if Basler required all of the income for personal use? Show calculations.

3. Should Basler incorporate a separate company or simply use his existing company?

Problem Two

Ruth Delaney owns all of the common shares of Delaney Fast Food Services Ltd. In addition, she has several investments that generate reasonable annual cash returns, as follows:

	Income
Corporate bonds	$ 5,000
Land and building	10,000
Shares of public corporations	8,000

The property has the following relevant values:

	Cost	UCC	Fair market value
Land	$30,000	$ –0–	$ 50,000
Building	70,000	50,000	95,000
Shares	75,000	–0–	105,000
Corporate bonds	40,000	–0–	42,000

Delaney has expressed an interest in using a corporation to hold her investments and has sought your advice. She has suggested that the investments could be transferred to Delaney Fast Food Services, which operates three restaurants.

Delaney's marginal tax rate is 46% (federal and provincial) on regular income and 32% on dividends. The provincial corporate tax rate in her province is 16%. To date, she has not used any of her lifetime capital gain deduction.

Required:

1. Advise Delaney on the benefits, if any, of incorporating her investment income. Show sample calculations. Your answer should be specific with respect to (a) interest and rents, (b) capital gains, and (c) dividends.

2. Discuss the implications of Delaney's suggestion re: transferring the investments to her active business corporation.

3. Assuming that she decides to incorporate the investments, outline a plan that will enable the investments to be transferred to the corporation without tax consequences.

Problem Three

Pembroke Realtors Ltd. is a closely held Canadian-controlled private corporation. At the end of 20X2, during which it earned an unusually high profit, the corporation paid additional salaries of $200,000 to its officers, who are also the shareholders. The salaries were paid in proportion to each shareholder's holdings in the corporation.

After reviewing the transaction, CCRA proposed to disallow $60,000 of the $200,000 salaries as an expense for tax purposes.

Required:

1. On what basis may CCRA justify such a proposal?

2. If the $60,000 is properly disallowed, what impact will it have on the shareholders who received the salary? Explain.

Problem Four

Joe Crum is a restaurant consultant and also owns two restaurants. His corporate structure and activities are outlined below.

Crum Restaurants Ltd.
- Owned 100% by Crum.
- Owns and operates Crum Slow Foods.
- Provides consulting services to a large number of small restaurants.
- Provides managerial and administrative services to Hamburger Joint Ltd., a company owned 15% by Joe Crum.
- 20X1 income is as follows:

Consulting services	$10,000
Managerial services (Hamburger Ltd.)	35,000
Crum Slow Foods	40,000
	$85,000

Pecky's Restaurant Ltd.
- Owned 100% by Crum Restaurants Ltd.
- Owns and operates Pecky's Coffee Shop.
- 20X1 income is $240,000.

Real Co. Ltd.
- Owned 51% by Crum and 49% by his wife.
- Owns several commercial and residential real estate properties, including the building occupied by Pecky's.
- 20X1 income is as follows:

Rents:	
Outside parties	$40,000
Pecky's Coffee Shop	10,000
	$50,000

Required:

1. Diagram the organization structure of Crum's financial activities.

2. Describe the type of income each entity earns, and explain the related tax treatment.

3. Identify any problems that the existing structure may present and suggest changes that you feel would be appropriate. If you are suggesting structural changes, briefly explain how they would be accomplished.

Problem Five

CKG Ltd. is a Canadian-controlled private corporation owned equally by Mr. and Mrs. Ducharme. The company has been profitable for several years, largely because of the efforts of the Ducharmes, who both participate actively in the management of the business.

The current year's business profit, before taxes, is expected to be $340,000. This is a record high for the company and is $50,000 higher than in the previous year. Over the past two years the company has built up substantial cash reserves. The Ducharmes are considering using the funds as follows:

- A competitor wants to sell out and has offered to sell its shares to CKG for $500,000. The following summary of the competitor's most recent operating results was provided to the Ducharmes:

Sales	$850,000
Cost of sales	378,000
Gross profit	472,000
Operating expenses	370,000
Income	102,000
Income taxes	(22,400)
Net income	$ 79,600

- The Ducharmes recently agreed to purchase a large new personal residence, which they will take possession of in two months. They have not yet sold their existing home, but when they do, they will need an additional $100,000 to complete the purchase.

The Ducharmes feel that CKG has sufficient resources to fund both of the above transactions. They are particularly interested in purchasing the competitor's business, and feel that the purchase price of $500,000 is reasonable, as it will provide an after-tax return on investment of 16% ($79,600 ÷ $500,000).

Both Ducharmes are paid an annual salary of $70,000.

Required:

1. Comment on the purchase of the competitor's business by CKG.

2. What methods should CKG use to provide funds to the Ducharmes so that they can meet their cash needs in acquiring their new home? Explain.

Problem Six

Carol Stoller is the president and sole shareholder of Modern Floors Ltd., a Canadian-controlled private corporation based in Manitoba. It is one month before the company's year end and Stoller is reviewing the company's financial information. The operating results to date are good, and her accountant has projected the following results to the end of the fiscal year:

Sales		$1,300,000
Cost of sales		840,000
Gross profit		460,000
Expenses:		
Salaries and wages	100,000	
Rent and utilities	19,000	
Amortization	8,000	
Travel and delivery	17,000	
Insurance	3,000	
Reserve for doubtful debts	22,000	
Advertising	15,000	
Charitable donations	5,000	
Other	6,000	195,000
Operating income		265,000
Other income:		
Interest on bonds	15,000	
Dividends from taxable Canadian public corporations	8,000	
Capital gain on the sale of securities	40,000	63,000
Net income before tax		$ 328,000

In preparing the year-end projection, the accountant determined the ending inventory based on an estimated value at the lower of cost or market (which is $20,000 lower than the estimate of the inventories cost). Amortization is equal to CCA for tax purposes.

Stoller has noticed that the financial statement does not provide an estimate of the company's tax liability and has asked her accountant to provide this. Also, the following two developments have taken place that may affect the company's tax position as well as Stoller's personal tax position:

- Modern Floors has signed a long-term contract to supply products to a large national chain organization. The contract will begin early in the new year. Operating profits for next year will increase by approximately $180,000.

- Stoller has decided to sell 30% of her common shares in the company to a senior manager for $400,000. She originally purchased the entire share capital of the company seven years ago for $100,000.

While Stoller is pleased with these developments, she is also concerned about their tax consequences. She understands that corporate tax rates increase when a certain level of income is reached. Stoller has never sold any capital property before but is aware that a friend of hers recently sold the shares of his corporation and was entitled to claim a capital gain deduction of $500,000. Stoller now asks you to address these issues and explain what steps, if any, she can take to minimize the overall tax impact on the company and on herself.

Stoller's personal marginal tax rate is 45%.

Required:

1. For the current taxation year, determine the following for Modern Floors: (a) net income for tax purposes; (b) taxable income; and (c) federal and provincial tax payable.

2. Explain to Stoller the tax impact of the projected higher corporate profits for next year.

3. Identify any actions which the corporation can take this year or next year that will be advantageous for the corporation and/or Stoller.

4. Describe the tax consequences to Stoller arising from the proposed sale of shares. What steps, if any, can she take to minimize any potential tax on the sale?

Problem Seven

Cinder Inc. is a Canadian-controlled private corporation based in Alberta. The company operates a wholesale and manufacturing business. The following information is provided for its year ended May 31, 20X5:

1. Net income for tax purposes is $212,000. Included in this amount is the following:

• Interest income from bonds	$10,000
• Interest income on overdue trade accounts receivable	1,000
• Taxable capital gain on sale of land	12,000
• Dividends from Canadian public corporations	14,000
• Dividends from PQ Ltd. (see item 2 below)	6,000

2. PQ Ltd. is a Canadian-controlled private corporation. Cinder owns 60% of its common voting shares. In 20X5, PQ claimed the small-business deduction on $120,000 of its active business income. PQ paid a dividend of $10,000, of which Cinder's share is $6,000 (60%). As a result of the dividend, PQ received a dividend refund of $1,000.

3. Cinder made contributions of $4,000 to registered charities and $1,000 to a registered federal political party. These amounts have been excluded from the calculation of net income for tax purposes.

4. Manufacturing and processing profits for tax purposes have been determined at $60,000.

5. At the end of 20X4, Cinder had the following tax account balances:

• Non-capital losses	$5,000
• Refundable dividend tax on hand	2,000

6. On May 31, 20X5, Cinder paid a dividend of $20,000 to its shareholders.

Required:
Determine Cinder's federal income tax for the 20X5 taxation year.

Problem Eight

TR Ltd. is a Canadian-controlled private corporation operating a franchised retail and mail-order business in Vancouver. Denver Chan, the company's president, owns 100% of the corporation's share capital. The corporation was created on December 1, 20X5. For the year ended November 30, 20X6, TR Ltd.'s financial statement reported income before income taxes of $126,000.

You have been retained to help prepare the company's first tax return and to advise on other tax-related matters. Financial information relating to the 20X6 taxation year and to the corporation's financial statement is summarized below.

TR Ltd.
Selected Financial Information

1. The following properties were purchased for the new business:

Franchise	$ 40,000
Land	30,000
Building	270,000
Delivery truck	40,000

The franchise, purchased on December 1, 20X5, permits the corporation to operate under the TR name for a period of 15 years. A renewable period of another 15 years is available, subject to satisfactory performance.

The land cost of $30,000 consists of the purchase price of $20,000, $7,000 for permanent landscaping, and $3,000 for water and sewer connections.

On October, 15, 20X6, the truck was involved in an accident. The damage was not repairable, and TR immediately signed an agreement with the insurance company to settle the claim for $31,000. The cash was received on December 10, 20X6. Another truck was obtained under a lease arrangement.

Amortization expense of $28,000 has been deducted from income.

2. Legal expense includes the following costs:

Preparing annual corporate minutes	$ 300
Incorporation costs for TR Ltd.	1,500
Negotiation of franchise agreement	2,000

3. Repairs and maintenance expense includes the following items:

Paving the parking lot	$8,000
Cleaning and supplies	1,400
Replacing a broken window	1,000
Small tools costing less than $200	1,200

4. Advertising expense includes a cost of $7,000 to acquire a permanent mailing list for the mail-order business. The list has an expected life of six years. Other advertising items are listed below.

Cost of making a television commercial	$25,000
Travel costs for Chan to attend a franchiser convention. Chan's spouse travelled with him and attended a social function (her expenses were $1,500)	3,000
Charitable donations	2,000
Meals and beverage costs for entertaining suppliers	1,800
Costs of leasing and maintaining a pleasure boat to entertain suppliers and employees	2,600
Television advertising	
Vancouver station	11,000
Seattle station directed at the Vancouver market	6,000

5. A contingent reserve for possible defective products of $5,000 was recorded as a charge against cost of sales. During the year, $3,000 of products were returned.

6. On May 31, 20X6, TR invested $40,000 in a one-year bank certificate earning annual interest of 7%. TR intends to recognize the interest revenue upon receipt at its one-year anniversary date.

7. Interest expense includes $14,000 on the building mortgage and $700 from a temporary bank loan of $12,000. The bank loan funds were in turn loaned, without interest, to Y Ltd., a corporation owned by Chan's brother. Y Ltd. used all of its assets to operate an active business, but in November 20X6 declared bankruptcy.

8. TR is planning to sell a new product in 20X7—a bracelet featuring a charm depicting a popular cartoon character. The bracelet and charm will be ordered from separate suppliers, and TR's staff will assemble the two pieces and enclose them in a specially designed package.

9. Shortly after incorporation, TR acquired 46% of the voting common shares of Q Ltd., a Canadian-controlled private corporation that supplies certain products to TR and other retailers. On October 31, 20X6, TR received a dividend of $15,000 from Q Ltd. At the time, Q Ltd. had an RDTOH account of $2,000.

   An opportunity exists for TR to purchase an additional 5% of the voting common shares of Q Ltd. early in 20X7. A decision will be made in January 20X7.

10. On November 30, 20X6, TR declared and paid a taxable dividend of $40,000.

Required:

1. Under Part I of the *Income Tax Act*, determine the *minimum income for tax purposes* and *taxable income* for TR Ltd. for the 20X6 taxation year.

2. Based on your answer to 1, calculate TR's *minimum Part I and Part IV federal income tax* for the 20X6 taxation year.

3. Briefly describe the tax consequences, if any, if TR Ltd. purchases the additional 5% of the shares of Q Ltd. in January 20X7.

4. Advise TR Ltd. on the tax implications, if any, of selling its new charm bracelet in the 20X7 taxation year.

Cases

Case One   Hockey Facilities

Don Cameron operates Hockey Facilities as a sole proprietorship. The operations consist of two retail outlets that sell all types of hockey equipment, as well as a separate manufacturing facility that manufactures the famous Slap Shot hockey stick.

Financial information for the most recent 12-month period is outlined in Exhibits I and II.

In addition to the income derived from Hockey Facilities, Cameron has substantial investments that generate high returns. The investment income by itself has put Cameron in the top marginal tax bracket of 45%. That income consists of dividends from shares of public corporations and interest on bonds.

As the proprietor, Cameron draws funds from Hockey Facilities to pay his personal expenses and income taxes. He usually requires $40,000 annually for living expenses exclusive of any income taxes.

You have recently met with Cameron to discuss the possibility of incorporating Hockey Facilities' business operations. At the meeting, Cameron provided you with the following additional information:

1. Expected profits from Hockey Facilities are as follows:

20X2	$275,000
20X3	320,000
20X4	370,000

2. The assets described in the attached balance sheet have the following current fair market values:

Current assets	$300,000
Land	150,000
Buildings	400,000
Equipment	100,000
Licence	120,000
Goodwill	200,000

3. The undepreciated capital cost of depreciable property at December 31, 20X1, after current capital cost allowance, is as follows:

Buildings	$240,000
Equipment	90,000
Licence	70,000

4. The cumulative eligible capital account at December 31, 20X1, amounted to $22,000 after the 20X1 deduction.

5. The financial statements include amortization at an amount equal to the available capital cost allowance.

6. Cameron does not have a detailed breakdown of manufacturing profits and retail profits, although he estimates the retail profits to be $100,000.

You have asked Cameron to provide you with a list of manufacturing assets and manufacturing labour, but to date he has not provided this information, as he has been tied up arranging for a contractor to build his new home.

Cameron is confused about how a corporate structure would be worthwhile and is concerned that according to what he had heard, double taxation might result in certain circumstances.

Cameron's son Eric is 23 years old and is actively involved in the business, earning a salary of $20,000 annually. Eric has spent most of his time at the manufacturing plant but intends to become involved in the retail operations as well. Cameron looks at the manufacturing activity as a separate business from the retail operation.

The meeting ended with you agreeing to provide a report to Cameron on the issues discussed.

Required:

Prepare the report, together with any supporting calculations and analyses you feel are necessary.

Exhibit I
HOCKEY FACILITIES
Balance Sheet
31 December 20X1

Assets		
Current assets		$300,000
Fixed assets (at cost):		
Land	100,000	
Buildings	300,000	
Equipment	200,000	
	600,000	
Accumulated amortization	(220,000)	380,000
Slap Shot manufacturer's licence (at cost)		80,000
Goodwill, at cost		60,000
		$820,000

Liabilities and Equity

Liabilities	$600,000
Proprietor's equity	220,000
	$820,000

Exhibit II
HOCKEY FACILITIES
Statement of Income
Year Ended December 31, 20X1

Sales (retail and manufacturing)		$1,400,000
Cost of sales:		
Opening inventory	$ 300,000	
Purchases and manufacturing costs	800,000	
	1,100,000	
Closing inventory	200,000	900,000
Gross profit		500,000
General administrative and selling expenses		250,000
Net income		$ 250,000

Case Two   Eastern Smallwares Ltd. and Byron Ltd.

Sheila Stekylo is the sole shareholder of Eastern Smallwares Ltd., a Canadian-controlled private corporation based in southwestern Ontario. The company wholesales smallwares to retail variety stores in eastern Canada. Two years ago, ESL purchased 40% of the common shares of Byron Products Ltd., a company in a similar line of business but operating in western Canada. The remaining 60% of BPL's shares are owned by Radjit Dhillon. Dhillon is actively involved in managing BPL's operations.

It is two months before ESL's year end and Stekylo has completed a review of the company's financial information. ESL's operating results to date are good. The company's internal accountant has prepared projections to the end of the year (see Exhibit I). Stekylo notices that the projections do not include an estimate of the current year's taxes, and tells her internal accountant,

"We need an estimate of the current year's tax cost for ESL so we can properly plan our cash flows. Also, there are a lot of planned activities that you and I have discussed that are going to have tax consequences and may require some planning. . . Also, some changes are happening at BPL. For example, BPL has taken out a $200,000 life insurance policy on both me and Dhillon as part of the buy/sell agreement, and I have no idea what the tax implications are if BPL collects on that insurance. And Dhillon is talking about acquiring a separate business in his own name.

"Prepare as much information as you can and send it over to our accountants at Carlson and Kominsky (C&K). Have them estimate this year's tax cost for ESL, then have them explain to us the tax implications of the various planned events and make any planning suggestions."

As a member of C&K, you have been assigned to report to Stekylo. You intend to prepare a preliminary draft report for review based on the information provided in

Exhibits I, II, and III. Your report will include an estimate of ESL's net income for tax purposes, taxable income, and tax cost for the current year.

Required:
Prepare the preliminary draft report for Stekylo.

Exhibit I
EASTERN SMALLWARES LTD.
Projected Year End Statement of Income
with Supplementary Notes

Sales		$1,333,000
Cost of sales		690,000
Gross profit		643,000
Expenses:		
Salaries and wages	320,000	
Rent and utilities	24,000	
Repairs and maintenance	23,000	
Amortization	8,000	
Travel and delivery	17,000	
Interest	26,000	
Insurance	7,000	
Reserve for doubtful debts	37,000	
Advertising	11,000	
Charitable donations	5,000	
Legal and accounting	20,000	
Other	15,000	513,000
Income from operations		130,000
Other income:		
Interest on bonds (13%)	35,000	
Dividends from taxable Canadian public corporations	8,000	
Gain on sale of marketable securities	40,000	
Net gain on land sales	15,000	98,000
Net income before tax		$ 228,000

Supplementary Notes:

1. The insurance expense of $7,000 consists of three separate premiums: fire and theft ($2,500), public liability ($1,500), and term life insurance on Stekylo that has been pledged to the bank as required collateral for a loan ($3,000).

2. Legal fees include $2,700 for the collection of delinquent accounts receivable, $7,000 for preparing a debenture agreement to obtain an expanded line of credit with the bank, and $8,000 for amending the company's articles of association. The remaining costs relate to annual audit fees.

3. Repairs and maintenance include the following:

Office cleaning, snow removal, lawn care	$ 4,500
Engine replacements on two delivery trucks	18,000
Other	500
	$23,000

4. This year, the company began a new policy of establishing a reserve of 1% of sales for future returns of defective merchandise. This reserve, along with several other minor items, is included as a deduction under "other" expenses. During the year, only $9,000 of defective merchandise was returned.

5. On the first day of the current taxation year, the company rented additional premises under a 6-year lease agreement. The agreement includes two 3-year renewal options. Improvements costing $28,000 were made to the premises. As an inducement to sign the lease, the landlord paid ESL $10,000 to cover some of these improvements. This amount was credited to contributed surplus on the balance sheet.

6. The undepreciated capital cost of certain assets at the end of the previous year was as follows:

Class 8	$27,000
Class 10	31,000

   There were no acquisitions or sales of equipment during the current year.

7. At the end of the previous year, the following additional tax accounts existed:

Refundable dividend tax on hand	$ 2,000
Capital dividend account	9,000
Cumulative eligible capital	12,000

8. The net gain on land sales ($15,000) resulted from two transactions. One property was acquired five years ago as a possible site for a warehouse. However, when new leased space became available, ESL sold the land for $40,000 more than it cost. The other property was sold for a loss of $25,000 after being held by ESL for only six months. It had been acquired in the expectation that its value would rise rapidly after a new shopping centre was developed nearby. However, the shopping centre project was cancelled, and land values in the area declined.

9. Not reflected in the projected income statement is an anticipated dividend from BPL. Dhillon has informed Stekylo that BPL intends to declare a dividend of $200,000. The dividend will be received before the current year end.

10. Included in the amount for salaries and wages are estimated bonuses of $30,000 for senior staff. These will be accrued at year end. The bonuses will be paid in three instalments of $10,000 over the next taxation year. The first instalment will be paid 4 months after year end, the remaining two at 8 and 12 months respectively.

Exhibit II
EASTERN SMALLWARES LTD.
Anticipated Developments

1. ESL has just signed a long-term contract to supply products to a large national chain organization. The contract will begin early in the new year. Operating profits for next year will increase by approximately $230,000.

2. Stekylo has agreed to sell 33⅓% of her common shares in the company to a senior manager for $400,000. She had purchased the entire share capital of the company seven years before, for $570,000.

   She intends to use all of the proceeds to pay off what she still owes the previous owner of ESL. Stekylo's personal marginal tax rate is 45% on normal income except dividends, which are subject to a 30% marginal rate (net of the dividend tax credit).

3. Early in the new year, Stekylo will need $300,000 in cash to finish paying for the construction of her new personal residence. Except for her salary of $80,000 per year from ESL, she has no personal cash. She plans to extract $300,000 from ESL and wants to keep her tax bill to a minimum. The following summary of the ESL balance sheet indicates that there are sufficient assets to fund the distribution:

Cash, receivables, inventory	$ 640,000
Equipment and leaseholds	108,000
Goodwill, at cost	100,000
Investment in bonds	320,000
	$1,168,000
Current and long-term liabilities	$ 366,000
Shareholders' equity	802,000
	$1,168,000

Exhibit III
Information Pertaining to Byron Products Ltd.

1. BPL has consistently earned pre-tax profits from operations of between $150,000 and $200,000. It does not earn any investment income. In the taxation year just passed, BPL earned profits from its business operations of $180,000 and paid taxes of $36,000 on that income.

2. Dhillon and Stekylo have recently signed an agreement which states that if one dies, the survivor must purchase the interest of the deceased. The agreement does not specify how the buy-out is to be structured. In conjunction with the agreement, BPL has purchased a $200,000 term life insurance policy on both individuals, with BPL as the beneficiary. The entire shares of BPL were recently valued at $600,000. At the most recent year end, BPL had retained earnings of $480,000. ESL had purchased its 40% interest for $100,000. The paid-up capital of the BPL shares owned by ESL is $1,000.

3. BPL will soon declare a dividend of $200,000 (see Exhibit I). Dhillon has initiated the dividend in order to free up cash so that he can purchase another business. Dhillon has informed Stekylo that he is about to buy 100% of the shares of a highly profitable manufacturing corporation.

Chapter 14   Multiple Corporations and Their Reorganization

Up to this point in the text, the corporate structure has been examined in its simplest form—that of a single corporation owned by shareholders who are individuals. While simple structures are commonplace, far more complex structures are found in the financial community.

Often the business affairs of a group of shareholders are spread among a number of different corporations; those corporations may in turn own subsidiary corporations. While each corporation in the group may be controlled directly or indirectly by the same shareholder(s), and while together those corporations may form a single economic resource, each nevertheless constitutes a separate entity for tax purposes. Over time, the need for placing business activities in one corporation rather than another may disappear, at which time a reorganization of some or all of the activities of the group will be desirable.

This chapter will describe the basic techniques for combining or separating financial activities within an economic group, and the related tax implications. While these techniques are used primarily in reorganization activities, they are also applicable to business acquisitions and divestitures (see Chapter 18). This chapter will also examine the use of holding corporations, and the resulting implications to after-tax cash flow.

I. Corporate Reorganizations

Relocating business activities from one corporation to another involves the transfer of assets. For example, if a corporation decides to close its business it may sell its assets such as land, buildings, and equipment to an arm's-length purchaser. To the extent that the assets' fair market value exceeds their cost, the selling corporation incurs taxable income. In effect, the corporation has changed the substance of its activities by converting business assets into cash or notes receivable. However, when the transfer of the assets is to another corporation owned by the same shareholders, a change in form has occurred but not a change in substance. In other words, the same owners continue to conduct the same business, but from within a different entity. This type of transaction is referred to as a reorganization.

Similarly, two independent corporations owned by different shareholders may decide to combine their operations into a single economic force. For example, a corporation operating a chain of retail stores in eastern Canada may join with a corporation operating a similar chain of stores in western Canada, and do so in such a way that shareholders of both corporations will participate in the larger combined entity. This type of transaction may also be considered a reorganization because both parties have a continuing interest in the combined activity. It is different from a sale, which requires that one party give up its interest by removing itself from the activity in exchange for cash, notes receivable, or other assets that do not include shares in the continuing activity.

All of this means that corporate reorganizations can occur within a related group of companies having similar shareholders, or among independent business entities, in the form of combinations and divestitures.

Current tax policy provides that when a reorganization occurs, the parties, if they so desire, may elect a form of transaction that does not result in the fair market value disposition of assets. By avoiding a transfer of assets at fair market values, the creation of taxable income is deferred. The types of transactions that can be used to execute a reorganization are outlined below. The discussions deal primarily with reorganizations within a related corporate group, but they are also applicable to reorganizations of independent entities.

A. Basic Reorganization Techniques

Before examining the reasons for, and the tax impact of, various reorganization transactions, it would be useful to have a mental picture of the change in structure that results from the reorganization.

Consider the multiple corporate structure presented in Exhibit 14-1. A single shareholder directly owns both Corporation A and Corporation C and indirectly owns Corporation B, which is a subsidiary of Corporation A.

It is assumed that each corporation owns business assets used to conduct a separate business. If the shareholder wishes to combine some or all of the business activities, two basic formats are available:

1. Assets can be transferred directly from one corporation to another.

2. The corporate structure can be altered by combining two or more of the corporations into one corporation.

For example, the activities of Corporations A and C could be combined by having A sell its business assets to C or vice versa. Another alternative is for A and C to combine to form a single legal entity, thereby creating Corporation AC. While both of these basic methods have the same result—combining of the business activities—the longer-term tax implications may differ. Much depends on the reasons for carrying out the reorganization.

Each of the basic reorganization techniques is reviewed below; following this, a simple case study is analyzed that shows the impact of choosing one technique over the others.

Exhibit 14-1:
Multiple Corporate
Structure

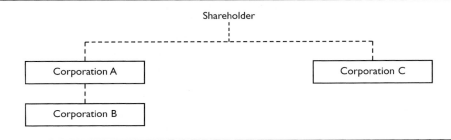

B. Asset Transfers

The transferring of assets from one entity to another is the simplest form of reorganization because it does not involve the restructuring of the corporations themselves. This method provides considerable flexibility in that it permits a corporation to transfer either all of its activities or only a specified part of its activities. For example, a corporation that operates several divisions within its business could transfer the assets of one of the divisions to a separate corporation, leaving the other divisions in the original corporation.

Asset transfers involve an actual sale of property by one corporation to another; for this reason, for legal purposes there must be an established selling price and an equivalent amount of payment. Notwithstanding the established legal selling price, the transfer price for tax purposes can be determined in one of two basic ways:

1. The transfer price of assets can automatically be deemed equal to the fair market value.[1]

2. If the corporations so elect, an agreed transfer price can be chosen that is usually equal to the cost for tax purposes (see Chapter 12).[2]

---

1   ITA 69(1); IT-405.

2   ITA 85(1); IT-291R2.

The above alternatives are available for each asset transferred, which means that when a group of assets is transferred together, some of the assets may be transferred at fair market value and others at an agreed lower value.

The choice of methods depends on the circumstances of the parties and the reasons for the transfer. For example, if the selling corporation has accumulated losses that are about to expire, it may want the transfer price to be at fair market value in order to create taxable income against which those losses can be offset. The corporation acquiring the assets would have a higher cost base for tax purposes, which may create future tax savings from capital cost allowance deductions.

Alternatively, the selling corporation may choose not to create taxable income on the transfer, by electing a transfer price equal to the tax cost. For example, a depreciable asset may be sold with an elected price for tax purposes equal to its undepreciated capital cost. When this is done the selling corporation has no taxable gain on the transfer. The acquiring corporation will use the asset to generate income from business or property and can claim capital cost allowance based on the lower transfer price. If the asset is subsequently sold to a third party at fair market value, the acquiring corporation will incur all of the taxable income associated with that asset even though part of the value increase occurred when the asset was owned by the original corporation. In effect, the tax status of the asset has been transferred from the original corporation to the acquiring corporation.

It should be pointed out that choosing the elected-price method involves certain formalities and restrictions. Some of these were discussed in Chapter 12.

Within a corporate group, assets can be transferred vertically or horizontally. The terms "vertical" and "horizontal" refer to the corporate group's organization chart. A vertical transaction occurs between a parent and its subsidiaries, whereas a horizontal transaction occurs between two corporations that are owned by the same shareholders.

A vertical transfer of assets is diagrammed in Exhibit 14-2, in which Corporation X, consisting of two separate business divisions, transfers the assets of division 2 to a new Corporation Y (the subsidiary). The assets of division 2, which may consist of land, buildings, equipment, inventory, goodwill, and patents, can be transferred to the subsidiary at fair market value or at tax values. The result of the reorganization is that all future business income of division 2 is now taxed separately in Corporation Y. The after-tax profits of Corporation Y can be transferred back up to the parent corporation by way of a dividend distribution, which is not taxable to the parent.

This same reorganization could also have been achieved by a horizontal transfer of assets, as diagrammed in Exhibit 14-3. Under this alternative Corporation X sells the assets of division 2 to Corporation Y. The transfer price can be at fair market value or at tax values. As explained in Chapter 12, in order to use an elected price at tax values, the seller

Exhibit 14-2:
A Vertical Transfer
of Assets

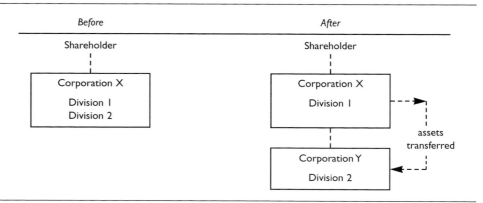

Exhibit 14-3:
A Horizontal
Transfer of Assets

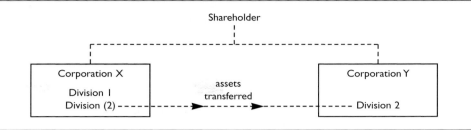

must take back some shares of the buyer as part of the payment. Therefore, in this case, Corporation Y would be owned by both Corporation X and the regular shareholder.

In both of the above examples, the business operations of division 2 could have been transferred to Corporation Y without necessarily transferring all of the assets associated with the division. For example, while it may have been necessary to transfer the inventory and goodwill, Corporation X could have retained ownership of the land, buildings, equipment, and patents and leased them to Corporation Y in return for rents and royalties. This would have avoided any complications associated with the asset transfers; it would also have changed the amount of income being shifted to Corporation Y. This point is made to stress the concept that there is a difference between the right to operate a business and the assets used to maintain those operations. The opportunity of leasing adds another dimension to the reorganization process.

In summary, asset transfers as part of a reorganization can involve some or all of the assets; can be transferred horizontally or vertically; and can be transferred at fair market value or at tax values. This provides a wide range of options and significant flexibility.

C. Amalgamations

An amalgamation involves the complete merging of the assets, liabilities, and shareholdings of two or more corporations.[3] By law, all of the former corporations cease to exist and a new corporation is born.[4] In effect, all of the corporations amalgamated have disposed of their assets to a new corporation, and all of the shareholders have disposed of their shares in the former corporations in exchange for shares of the new corporation. The number and value of shares distributed by the new corporation to the former shareholders depends on the proportionate values of the corporations entering into the merger. This form of reorganization is used to restructure corporations within a related group, and is also used extensively in arm's-length business acquisitions and mergers.

Corporate amalgamations, like asset transfers, can be vertical or horizontal. Consider the vertical amalgamation in Exhibit 14-4: an amalgamation of parent Corporation A and subsidiary Corporation B completely eliminates the former corporations; in their place is a single new corporation, AB, which now houses the combined operations.

Exhibit 14-4 uses a wholly owned subsidiary as an example. However, Corporation A need not own all of the shares of Corporation B in order to enter into an amalgamation. For example, if Corporation A owned only 60% of Corporation B, with the balance of shares owned by a non-related party, an amalgamation would still result in the creation of Corporation AB. However, the other shareholders of the former Corporation B would now be shareholders in the combined operations.

---

3   ITA 87(1).

4   ITA 87(2)(a). The taxation year of the new corporation commences at the date of amalgamation. As with any new corporation, a fiscal year end can be chosen. The former corporations have a deemed year end immediately before the amalgamation.

Exhibit 14-4:
Vertical
Amalgamation

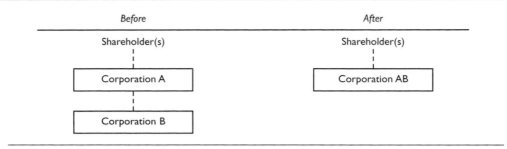

Exhibit 14-5 demonstrates a horizontal amalgamation of two sister corporations owned by the same shareholder. Upon amalgamation, both Corporation A and Corporation B cease to exist, and Corporation AB is created.

- **Tax treatment**   Provided that certain criteria are met, the amalgamation of two or more corporations results in a tax-free merger of the entities. The predecessor corporations are deemed to have sold their assets to the new corporation at their tax values.[5] Similarly, the shareholders are deemed to have sold their former shares at a value equal to their cost base in exchange for shares of the new corporation that have the same cost base.[6] In other words, all former tax positions are preserved in the combined entity.[7]

Exhibit 14-5:
Horizontal
Amalgamation

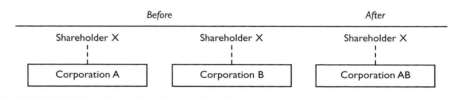

Of major importance is the treatment of any tax losses being carried forward by the predecessor corporations. In most circumstances all losses being carried forward by the former corporations become, upon amalgamation, losses that can be carried forward by the new, combined corporation.[8] Any restrictions that were previously attached, such as limits to the time period for loss carry-forward or to the types of income that losses can be offset against, simply continue as restrictions in the combined corporation.

The tax treatment of corporate losses was examined in Chapter 11. Recall that business loss carry-overs may become restricted, and capital loss carry-overs are eliminated, when a change in control occurs. The amalgamation of corporations within a related corporate group does not result in a change of control for this purpose, so an amalgamation does not normally alter the usual treatment of losses. Indeed, one of the major purposes of amalgamations is to combine the losses of one entity with the profits of another.[9]

Losses may be affected on amalgamation when an unrelated party achieves control of the amalgamated entity. For example, in Exhibit 14-6, Corporation A has losses carried forward and is controlled by shareholder 1. Corporation B is profitable and is controlled

---

5   ITA 87(2)(b) to (j.2); IT-474R.

6   ITA 87(4).

7   Including the capital dividend account—ITA 87(2)(Z.1), and the refundable dividend tax on hand account —ITA 87(2)(aa).

8   ITA 87(2.1); IT-302R2.

9   ITA 256(7).

Exhibit 14-6:
Change in Control
on Amalgamation

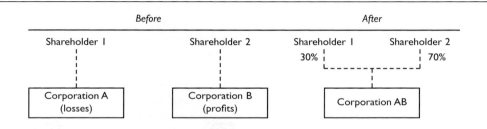

by shareholder 2, who is unrelated to shareholder 1. Upon amalgamation, shareholder 1, who previously controlled the loss company, does not control the new corporation. This constitutes a change in control. As a consequence, any net capital loss carry-overs are eliminated. Business loss carry-overs (non-capital losses) can be offset only against the income from the business that incurred the loss or from a similar business; thus, if Corporations A and B are in a similar line of business, the business loss carry-overs are unaffected.[10]

In order for an amalgamation to result in a tax-free combination, the following conditions must be met:[11]

1. All of the corporations must be Canadian corporations.

2. All assets and liabilities of the old corporations must become assets and liabilities of the new corporation.

3. All of the shareholders of the old corporations must become shareholders of the new corporation.

These conditions follow the basic principle of a reorganization—that owners must maintain a continuing interest in the venture.

D. Wind-up of a Subsidiary

The wind-up of a subsidiary corporation involves the transfer of all of the assets of the subsidiary to its parent corporation, followed by the termination of the subsidiary's existence. Subsidiary wind-ups differ from amalgamations in that they result in the elimination of the subsidiary *only*—the parent corporation continues its normal existence.

The tax treatment of a wind-up is similar to that of an amalgamation. In most cases no tax occurs on the transfer of assets from the subsidiary to the parent, as the transfer price is considered to be equal to the tax values of the assets transferred. In addition, any tax accounts of the subsidiary become available to the parent.[12] For example, accumulated unused losses of the subsidiary are transferred to the parent and continue to be carried forward under the same restrictions, if any, that were imposed on the subsidiary.[13]

In order to utilize the tax-free wind-up provisions, the parent company must own at least 90% of each class of the subsidiary's shares. If the parent owns less than that 90%, it must resort to the amalgamation procedure in order to achieve the desired tax relief.

At least superficially, wind-ups and amalgamations have similar results. However, there are certain differences that may result in one being preferred over the other.[14] As the purpose of this chapter is to provide an awareness of alternative reorganization techniques and their general tax impact, the differences between the two are not discussed.

---

10 ITA 111(4), (5), (5,4).

11 ITA 87(1).

12 ITA 88(1); IT-488R2.

13 ITA 88(1.1), (1.2); IT-302R2.

14 ITA 88(1)(d).

E. Reorganization of Share Capital

Each of the previous reorganization methods involved the transfer of assets from one entity to another. In some circumstances the shareholders may wish to alter the *nature* of their interest in the corporation without changing the *amount* of dollar capital that they have invested in that corporation. For example, shareholders may convert some of their common shares to preferred shares; this will alter the way future profits are apportioned even though the amount of capital invested is the same. When a reorganization of share capital occurs that maintains a continued interest of all parties, the shareholders are permitted to exchange all shares of a particular class for shares of another class on a tax-deferred basis.[15]

Consider the change in ownership structure diagrammed in Exhibit 14-7. Before the reorganization, shareholders 1 and 2 each own 50% of the common shares of a corporation valued at $100,000. A change in this ownership ratio can be achieved by completing the following steps:

1. Both shareholder 1 and shareholder 2 convert their common shares, worth $50,000, into fixed value preferred shares that have a value of $50,000 and bear a fixed dividend rate. At this point the full value of the company is attached to the preferred shares, which will achieve no further growth in value.

2. Because the full value of the company is now tied up in the preferred shares, new common shares can be issued at a nominal value. The corporation therefore issues ten new common shares for $1 each. Shareholder 1 purchases eight of these shares, shareholder 2, the remaining two.

The result of all this is not only that the existing full value of the company ($100,000) is frozen in the form of preferred shares in the former ratio of $50,000 for each shareholder, but also that any future change in the corporation's value will accrue at 80% to shareholder 1 and 20% to shareholder 2.

The above transaction permitted a change in ownership ratio without immediate tax consequences. In normal circumstances a change in ownership ratio would require that one shareholder purchase shares of the other, or that the company buy back some of its shares; both of these alternatives would have tax consequences to the shareholder.

The above example demonstrated how share capital can be reorganized among existing shareholders; the technique is also useful as a means of admitting *new* shareholders without the requirement of a substantial cash contribution. For example, consider the situation

Exhibit 14-7:
Change in Ownership Ratio by Share Reorganization

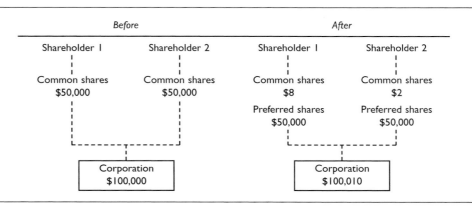

15 ITA 86.

where the sole shareholder of a corporation valued at $100,000 wants to transfer ownership to a group of employees who are capable of managing the company but have no capital with which to make the purchase. Exhibit 14-8 diagrams a share reorganization plan that achieves this goal. Before the reorganization, shareholder 1 owned 100% of the common shares having a value of $100,000. Shareholder 1 exchanges all of the common shares for preferred shares valued at $100,000. The company then issues ten new common shares for $10 to the new employee/shareholders.

Notice that after the reorganization the company is still worth $100,000; however, this full value belongs to shareholder 1 in the form of preferred shares. Over a period of time the company can buy back the preferred shares from shareholder 1, at which time that shareholder will incur taxable income.

Exhibit 14-8:
New Shareholders
and Share Reorganization

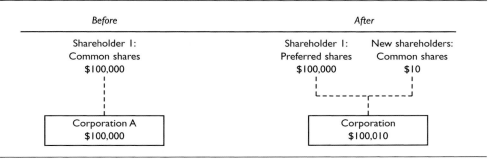

F. Reorganization
Procedures and
Case Analysis

Each of the reorganization methods has the same objective, which is to combine or separate business activities within a group of corporations. However, the choice of method in a particular set of circumstances is not obvious. In addition, to accomplish a particular end it may be necessary to use two or more of the techniques in a sequence. In most cases the methods used to reorganize a corporation are determined by trial and error, by performing the following procedures:

1. Define the problem in the existing structure and the objective to be satisfied by changing that structure.

2. Choose and test one of the reorganization techniques. This involves determining the immediate and future tax implications of the method chosen.

3. Determine whether the immediate and future tax implications satisfy all or a portion of the problem, and also whether any new problems are created by the proposed new structure. This means anticipating possible future activities and considering how they will be treated under the proposed structure.

4. If all of the problems are not solved, and/or if new difficulties are created from the proposed structure, choose another method and perform the analysis again.

In the simple corporate reorganization examined below, the above procedures are used to establish the most appropriate method of completing a corporate reorganization.

Summary of Facts
Blue Ltd., a Canadian corporation, is a successful manufacturer of men's clothing. The current year's pre-tax profits amounted to $700,000, and similar profits are expected in the future. Blue Ltd. has two wholly owned subsidiaries, A Ltd. and B Ltd.

A Ltd. was acquired five years ago and manufactures a line of men's winter clothing. A Ltd. generates a modest profit of approximately $50,000 annually.

Blue Ltd. acquired the shares of B Ltd. two years ago. At the time of acquisition B Ltd. had unused business losses carried forward of $200,000. Since the acquisition, B Ltd. has incurred additional losses of $150,000; it is expected to lose an additional $80,000 in each of the next three years. B Ltd. operates a small retail chain of clothing stores. Although B Ltd. rents most of its locations, it *does* own the land and buildings that house two of its stores. This property has appreciated in value.

The organization structure of the group is as follows:

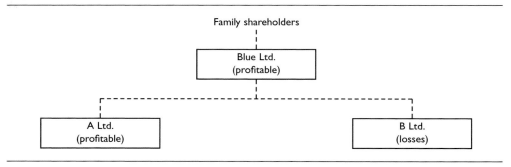

Analysis

The major problem with the existing structure is that Blue Ltd. and A Ltd. are profitable, and taxable on their operations, while B Ltd. has accumulated unused losses. For example, next year the group will have a combined profit of

Blue Ltd.	$700,000
A Ltd.	50,000
B Ltd. (loss)	(80,000)
	$670,000

but will be taxable on $750,000 (profits of Blue Ltd. and A Ltd.).

The accumulated losses of B Ltd. have two limitations that must be dealt with. First of all, the losses that existed at the time of acquisition are restricted and can be offset only against income from that business or a similar business (see Chapter 11). As all three corporations appear to be in a similar line of business, this restriction is not a major problem. Second, all of the losses are subject to a time limitation (each year's loss can be carried forward seven years), and so it must be determined when the losses will expire.

Some, but not all, of the reorganization alternatives are discussed briefly below.

• **B Ltd. sells assets to A Ltd.** This option involves the loss company selling its assets to a company that has continued, though modest, profits. Within this option there are several sub-alternatives: the assets may be sold at fair market value or at tax values; further, all of the assets or only some of the assets may be sold.

One possibility is to sell, at fair market value, only the assets that have appreciated in value. B Ltd. has land and buildings which, if sold, would create taxable income to B Ltd. and use up some or all of the existing losses carried forward. However, this alternative would leave the business operations in B Ltd., which would continue to generate losses over the next few years that would remain unused until the retail stores become profitable.

A second possibility is for B Ltd. to sell not just the land and buildings but the entire business operations to A Ltd. This procedure has two potential advantages: the taxable income on the sale of land and buildings might use up the accumulated losses in B Ltd., thereby preventing their expiration; and also, all future losses ($80,000 annually) will occur in A Ltd., where they can be offset against A Ltd.'s profits ($50,000 annually). While this method addresses the concerns regarding both accumulated and future losses, it nevertheless has two shortcomings:

- The future profits of A Ltd. are less than the future losses from the retail stores. For this reason the issue of future losses is not totally satisfied.

- While the sale of assets at fair market value prevents B's losses from expiring, no immediate tax reductions are achieved. Effectively, the accumulated losses are preserved in the form of a higher cost base of the assets now owned by A Ltd. Therefore, future taxes will be reduced as A Ltd. claims capital cost allowance on the higher building value or when the land is finally sold. Even though the losses are preserved, cash flow is increased later rather than sooner.

- **A Ltd. sells assets to B Ltd.**   This option requires the transfer of A Ltd.'s business operations to B Ltd. In order to avoid tax on the sale, the assets would have to be transferred at tax values in exchange for notes and shares of B Ltd. After the transfer B Ltd. would operate both a manufacturing business (gloves) and a chain of retail stores. The future profits from the manufacturing business ($50,000) would first be offset against the future losses of the retail stores ($80,000).

While this option eliminates the taxes on the $50,000 manufacturing profit, it leaves approximately $30,000 annually of new losses, as well as all of the accumulated unused losses in B Ltd.

- **Amalgamation of A Ltd. and B Ltd.**   This method eliminates both corporations and creates a new corporation, AB Ltd., that combines the operations of A and B. The result would be similar to that from the previous alternative and would not resolve the matter of how to use the annual future losses and the accumulated past losses.

- **Wind-up of B Ltd. into Blue Ltd.**   With this option, all of the assets of the loss company are transferred at tax values to the parent company. B Ltd. would cease to exist; the parent company would operate its clothing manufacturing business as well as the chain of retail stores. In addition, the accumulated losses of B Ltd. would be transferred to the parent company and would be available for use in future years.

As the parent company's profits are $700,000 annually, there would be sufficient income in the first year after the wind-up to absorb all of the accumulated losses of B Ltd. ($200,000 + $150,000 = $350,000) as well as the annual loss of $80,000. This alternative is extremely attractive because the accumulated losses would be used rapidly and the method of utilization (deduction against taxable income) would generate immediate tax savings. This enhanced cash flow could be used for business expansion or to fund the losses from the retail chain.

This result could also have been achieved by amalgamating Blue Ltd. and B Ltd.

The combining of the retail operations with the manufacturing operations may have other tax consequences, which should be anticipated before the decision is made. For example, the amount of profit eligible for the manufacturing and processing tax reduction is determined by an arbitrary formula based on the amount of capital and labour employed in manufacturing activities. Combining the retail and manufacturing operations will alter this calculation, and may either expand the manufacturing base or diminish it depending on the ratio of retail labour and capital to manufacturing labour and capital (see Chapter 11).

It is important to recognize that the above analysis is not complete and that there are other alternatives which could have been explored. In addition, while winding up B Ltd. into Blue Ltd. appears to provide the most favourable outcome in this particular set of circumstances, this may not be the case if the assumed facts are altered. The most satisfactory outcome can only be determined by exploring the consequences of several alternatives and evaluating their immediate tax impact, as well as their impact on anticipated future activities.

II. Holding Corporations and Intercorporate Investments

An individual who owns shares in one or more business corporations can choose to interpose a corporation between himself/herself and the operating corporations. The interposed corporation is referred to as a "holding corporation," as its primary purpose is to own shares of other corporations.

A holding corporation can be a private company that owns shares in other private or public corporations, or a public corporation created for the purpose of investing in other public corporations. The benefits derived from the use of such a structure are tied to the tax treatment given to intercorporate dividends paid by the operating companies to the holding corporation. The tax treatment of intercorporate dividends is examined below. So is the resulting impact on certain business decisions.

A. Tax Treatment of Intercorporate Dividends

It was established in previous chapters that dividends received by a corporation from another Canadian corporation are not included in taxable income.[16] However, it was also indicated that certain dividends received by a Canadian-controlled private corporation are subject to a special 33 1/3% refundable tax (see Chapter 13).

Chapter 13 dealt with the situation where a Canadian-controlled private corporation receives dividends from another Canadian private corporation. When this occurs, the dividends received may, in limited circumstances, be subject to a special refundable tax. These limited circumstances are as follows:

1. When the dividend received is from a corporation that is not substantially owned by the receiving corporation, a special refundable tax of 33 1/3% is applicable to the recipient.[17] One corporation does not have substantial ownership of another if it owns 10% or less of the other corporation.[18] In Chapter 13, it was said that such corporations are non-connected.

2. Notwithstanding the degree of ownership, a special refundable tax is also payable whenever the paying corporation receives a refund as a result of the dividend payment.[19] As explained in Chapter 13, this occurs when a Canadian-controlled private corporation distributes any investment income that it has earned.

The application of the special refundable tax has been described here in general terms. The specific provisions of the *Income Tax Act* are more detailed and complex (see Chapter 13). For the purposes of this text and for the discussion of holding corporations in general, the following generalizations can be made with respect to intercorporate dividends:

---

16 ITA 112(1).

17 ITA 186(1)(a); IT-269R3.

18 ITA 186(2), (4). The recipient usually does not pay Part IV tax when the dividend is paid from a "connected" corporation. A corporation is connected if the receiving corporation owns more than 10% of the payer's voting shares and more than 10% of the fair market value of all shares issued.

19 ITA 186(1)(b); IT-269R3.

1. All Canadian dividends received by a public corporation are tax-free.

2. Dividends from one Canadian-controlled private corporation to another flow tax-free, provided that the dividends are paid from the paying corporation's business income and the recipient owns more than 10% of the paying corporation's shares.

With these generalizations in mind, the benefits of using a holding corporation are reviewed below from the perspective of both public corporations and Canadian-controlled private corporations that hold a substantial interest in another business corporation.

B. Dividend Reinvestment

The primary benefit of establishing a holding corporation is that it permits the shareholder to receive dividends from the operating company, free of tax, for reinvestment.

Consider the two corporate structures outlined in Exhibit 14-9. Under structure A both shareholder 1 and shareholder 2 are individuals and own directly 50% of the shares of a Canadian-controlled private corporation carrying on a business. If the business corporation pays a dividend with its excess funds, both individual shareholders will pay tax on the dividend, leaving the after-tax amount available for investment in another venture.

Under structure B both shareholders own 100% of their own separate holding corporations. Each corporation in turn owns 50% of the shares of the active business corporation. In this case any dividends paid by the business corporation flow tax-free to the holding corporations, which can reinvest the full amount of the dividends. In effect, the tax on the dividends is deferred until either shareholder decides to make a distribution for personal use.

The use of holding corporations under structure B permits maximum flexibility when the operating company has excess cash that is not needed for business expansion. For example, shareholders 1 and 2 may want to be business partners but not investment partners, as the types of investments that each prefers are different. When a holding company is used, the operating company can distribute all of its excess funds on a regular basis without further tax; the shareholders can then invest in ventures of their choice. Similarly, shareholder 1 may want funds for personal use while shareholder 2 does not. If dividends are paid first to the holding companies, shareholder 1 can pass the dividend on to himself or herself for personal use and pay the required tax; shareholder 2 can leave the funds in the holding corporation and continue to defer the tax.

A structure that permits the operating company to maintain a policy of distributing all of its excess cash to the shareholders also has the effect of keeping the operating company at its minimum value. In the long run this makes it easier for the shareholders to sell the shares of the operating company to an independent buyer, or to each other.

Exhibit 14-9:
Business Structure and
Holding Corporations

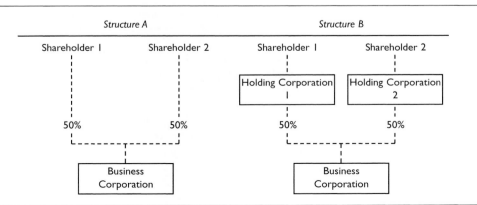

In summary, holding corporations give shareholders access to corporate profits in such a way that they do not immediately have to pay a second level of tax. This second level of tax should have to be paid only when the shareholder requires the funds for personal use.

C. Holding Companies and Corporate Acquisitions

A holding corporation can also be extremely useful as a vehicle for acquiring shares in an active business corporation, especially when the purchaser uses borrowed funds to make the purchase.

Consider the cash-flow requirements for purchasing a corporation in the following situation:

Situation: Ms. X intends to acquire all of the shares of Opco for $400,000. She intends to borrow the full $400,000 to fund the purchase. Opco is a Canadian-controlled private corporation that will earn $100,000 annually. The corporation pays tax at a rate of 18%. Ms. X is in a 45% marginal tax bracket. She intends to use the future profits of Opco to retire the debt of $400,000 as quickly as possible.

Analysis: To make the purchase, Ms. X can borrow the funds and purchase the shares in her own name or, alternatively, create a holding corporation that would borrow the funds and purchase the shares in the corporation's name. In both cases the cash flow generated from future profits will be used to repay the loan. Both alternatives are reviewed below.

• Shares purchased by Ms. X To obtain funds to make payments on the loan, Ms. X will have to extract funds from the corporation by dividend distributions or increased salaries, both of which are taxable. Interest incurred on the loan is deductible from her income, which will reduce the taxes payable on the salary or dividend payments. However, payments on the loan principal are not deductible and must therefore be paid after all taxes have been paid by the corporation and Ms. X.

The after-tax annual profits available for principal repayment are as follows:

Corporate income (Opco)		$100,000
Corporate tax	18,000	
Shareholder tax on dividend	24,000	(42,000)
After-tax annual funds		$ 58,000
Payback period:		
$\frac{\text{Loan (\$400,000)}}{\text{Annual cash (\$58,000)}} =$		7 years*

* Interest on the debt has been excluded from the calculation. A complete cash-flow analysis must consider the after-tax cost of interest to establish a realistic payback period.

As a result, even though the company is entitled to the small-business deduction, the shareholder must pay the second level of tax to obtain the personal funds to repay the debt principal.

• Shares purchased by holding corporation Under this option Ms. X creates a new holding corporation capitalized with a nominal amount of share capital. The corporation borrows $400,000 and purchases the shares of Opco as an intercorporate investment.

To repay the loan's principal, Opco can pay dividends to the holding corporation, which are tax-free. The after-tax funds available for debt repayment are as follows:

Corporate income (Opco)		$100,000
Corporate tax	18,000	
Tax on dividend	–0–	(18,000)
After-tax annual funds		$ 82,000
Payback period:		
$\frac{\text{Loan (\$400,000)}}{\text{Annual cash (\$82,000)}} =$		5 years

In the above example, the use of a holding corporation permitted the loan principal to be repaid in five years rather than seven, because the second level of tax was avoided. While the holding corporation method described above appears preferable, it may also create a problem: the holding corporation will also incur the annual interest cost, which is, of course, deductible from income. However, if the holding company's only source of income is dividends from Opco—which are tax-free—the interest will remain unused in the holding company as losses carried forward.

When the holding corporation has no other sources of taxable income, the problem of unused losses from interest can be solved by applying the reorganization techniques described earlier in this chapter. For example, immediately after the holding corporation acquired the shares of Opco, the two companies could be amalgamated. As a result, Ms. X would own a single corporation that combines the affairs of both original corporations. The new corporation would operate the business and earn $100,000 annually but would also have the loan of $400,000 as its obligation. The interest would be deductible against the business profits, and the remaining after-tax income (taxed at only 18%) would be available to repay the loan principal.

The above situation and analysis is an example of a "leveraged buy-out" whereby the purchaser funds a large portion of the price with borrowed funds and looks to the acquired corporation to provide the cash flow to repay the debt. In effect, the corporation is paying for itself by committing some of its resources not to business expansion but to distributions to the purchaser for the purpose of funding the takeover. In this form of buy-out it is vital to minimize the amount of tax on the distribution of corporate funds. This is achieved by the use of a holding corporation.

In a corporate buy-out, while the expected future profits are a primary source of funding, the purchaser may also use the corporate assets as an immediate source of cash to fund a portion of the purchase price. For example, consider the following balance sheet of a company that is targeted for a purchase of its shares:

Assets		Liabilities and equity	
Working capital	$300,000	Liabilities	$400,000
Equipment	50,000	Share capital and	
Business real estate	200,000	retained earnings	250,000
Marketable securities	100,000		
	$650,000		$650,000

Upon acquiring the shares of the above company, the new owner could cash in the marketable securities of $100,000, which are not needed for the business, and distribute the cash to himself/herself to help fund the share purchase. If the shares were purchased with a holding corporation, the distribution would be tax-free. Similarly, the business real estate may have appreciated in value, in which case it could either be sold and leased back or remortgaged to create additional cash resources for distribution to the new owner's holding company.

D. Holding Companies and Corporate Divestitures

A holding company is also useful as a means to minimize tax on the sale of shares of a corporation.

Consider the corporate structure shown in Exhibit 14-10. A holding corporation owned by an individual shareholder is contemplating the sale of shares that it owns in an operating company. The value of the shares to be sold will depend on the strength of the operating company—that is, on the amount of its retained earnings and the value of its assets such as land, buildings, equipment, goodwill, and so on. To the extent that the value of the shares exceeds the shares' original cost, the holding corporation will recognize a taxable capital gain on disposition that will diminish the amount of after-tax proceeds available for reinvestment. However, if before the sale For Sale Corporation distributed all of its retained earnings as a tax-free dividend to the holding corporation, the value of the shares would diminish to the extent of the dividend paid.[20] The shares could then be sold for a lesser amount, resulting in less tax on the disposition and increased after-tax proceeds (from the dividend and share sale) available for reinvestment in another venture. A more detailed example of this procedure was made in Chapter 11. As indicated in that chapter, to the extent that share values are represented by accumulated retained earnings, the potential capital gain from that value can always be delayed by transferring the retained earnings value to a holding corporation before a sale.

All of the above examples demonstrate the significant impact that holding corporations have on cash flow generated from investment returns. It should also be pointed out that a holding corporation does not always have to be in existence from the outset in order for its benefits to be utilized. For example, if, in Exhibit 14-10, the individual shareholder directly owned the shares of For Sale Corporation, a holding corporation could be interposed just before the contemplated sale of shares. This could be achieved using one of the reorganization methods described in the first section of the chapter. Specifically, the individual could sell the shares of For Sale Corporation to a newly created holding company and elect that the transfer price occur at tax values. The proper organization structure would then be in place to pay intercorporate dividends; this would be followed by a sale of shares by the holding corporation.

Exhibit 14-10:
Holding Corporation and Corporate Divestitures

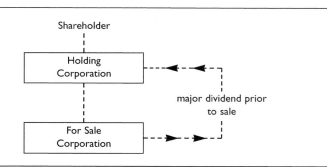

---

20 Special anti-avoidance rules exist that prevent tax-free distributions greater than the defined and realized retained earnings when those distributions are in anticipation of a share sale—ITA 55(2) to (5).

III. Summary and Conclusion

Businesses often divide their operations among several separate corporations in order to satisfy various business objectives and to facilitate changes in ownership participation. The income tax system recognizes that these complex organizations often require restructuring and provides a number of means by which businesses can adapt to the changing business environment. Specifically, the following basic reorganization methods are available:

1. Transfer of assets from one corporation to another.

2. The reorganization of share capital and ownership rights of the corporation.

3. The amalgamation of two or more corporations into a single, combined corporation.

4. The wind-up of a subsidiary corporation into its parent corporation.

With each of the above methods, the reorganization can occur without triggering taxable income, even though assets have been transferred from one entity to another. While no tax occurs on the reorganization, this does not mean that tax has been permanently avoided. The tax positions that existed before the reorganization remain preserved in the new structure and will ultimately be triggered when assets are sold to third parties.

This concept of tax deferral is based on the premise that a reorganization constitutes a change in *form* rather than a change in *substance*, in that all parties to the transaction continue to have an interest in the restructured entity. It is for this reason that independent parties are permitted to use these same reorganization alternatives to combine their operations. As long as the parties have not converted their interest into cash or some other hard asset, and maintain some form of share ownership, the reorganization can occur on a tax-deferred basis.

The details of the tax provisions for completing a reorganization are extremely complex. Even so, managers must strive to understand the nature of reorganization activities—specifically, how those activities are best performed and their impact on immediate and future cash flows. While corporate restructuring is motivated primarily by certain business objectives, the related tax treatment and cash-flow implications must be anticipated so that the related business decision can be fully assessed. When deciding on the method of business reorganization, managers must be able to envision the consequences of the available options. With this in mind, this chapter has stressed the methods available, when to use them, and their general tax impact, rather than the specifics of how to carry out those methods.

This chapter has also demonstrated the important role of holding companies as a means of transferring accumulated earnings from one corporation to another via tax-free dividends. The shifting of after-tax corporate profits from one corporation to another also constitutes a change in form rather than substance and is therefore an important part of corporate reorganization activities. Holding companies have a dramatic impact on after-tax investment returns; they also affect specific decisions relating to business acquisitions and divestitures.

This chapter concludes Part Three of the text, which was devoted solely to corporate structures. While some of the concepts appear complex, they all relate to the corporation/shareholder relationship in a two-tiered tax system that taxes corporate income separately from distributions to the shareholder(s).

Part Four of the text will examine business organizations that are alternatives to the corporation.

Reading List

Income Tax Act References

	Section
Inadequate consideration	69(1)
Transfer of property to a corporation by a shareholder	85(1)
Exchange of shares by a shareholder in the course of a reorganization of capital	86(1) to (3)
Amalgamations	87(1)
Shares deemed to have been received by virtue of a merger	87(1.1)
Amalgamations—rules applicable	87(2)
Taxation year	87(2)(a)
Non-capital losses of predecessor corporation	87(2.1)
Shares of predecessor corporation	87(4)
Control deemed not to be acquired	256(7)
Acquisition of control (losses)	111(4), (5)
Winding up	88(1)
Non-capital losses of a subsidiary	88(1.1)
Net capital losses of a subsidiary	88(1.2)
Deduction of taxable dividends received by a corporation resident in Canada	112(1)
Tax on certain taxable dividends (Part IV)	186(1)
When a corporation is controlled	186(2)
Corporation connected with a particular corporation	186(4)
Deemed proceeds or capital gain	55(2) to (5)

Canada Customs and Revenue Agency Publications

IT-405	Inadequate consideration.
IT-291R2	Transfer of property to a corporation under section 85.
IT-474R	Amalgamation of Canadian corporations.
IT-302R2	Losses of a corporation—the effect on their deductibility of changes in control, amalgamations, and winding up.
IT-488R	Winding up of a 90%-owned taxable Canadian corporation.
IT-269R3	Part IV tax on taxable dividends received by a private corporation.

Other Publications

Dunn, A., "Corporate Consolidations: To Amalgamate or Not to Amalgamate," Report of Proceedings of the 48th Tax Conference (1996), Canadian Tax Foundation, p. 13.1.

Richards, G., "Amalgamations," *Canadian Tax Journal*, Vol. 44, No. 1 (1996).

Roberts and Briggs, "Winding Up: Part I," *Canadian Tax Journal*, Vol. 44, No. 2 (1996); also Part II, Vol. 44, No. 3 (1996).

Review Questions

1. "A corporate reorganization usually involves a change in form rather than a change in substance." Explain this statement.

2. What unique tax treatment does a corporate reorganization provide? What is the logic for permitting this to occur?

3. Is it possible for unrelated corporations to combine their business activities through a reorganization? If it is, what must occur in order to ensure that the transaction will not be treated as an outright sale of property at fair market value?

4. Identify four basic reorganization techniques.

5. Briefly describe two alternative tax treatments when the business assets of one corporation are transferred to another corporation. Are these two alternatives available only if the corporation acquiring the assets is owned by the corporation selling the assets? Explain.

6. If Corporation A wishes to transfer its business operations to Corporation B by way of an asset transfer, must all of the assets relating to that business be transferred? Explain. How will the future income of each corporation be different if some but not all of the business assets are transferred?

7. Describe what takes place when two or more corporations amalgamate.

8. Distinguish between a wind-up of a wholly owned subsidiary corporation and an amalgamation of the parent and subsidiary.

9. What is the tax treatment of a corporation's unused net capital losses and/or non-capital losses after that corporation has been amalgamated with another corporation or has been wound up into its parent corporation?

10. What form of reorganization permits the current common shareholders to retain their existing value in the corporation and, at the same time, alters the ratio relating to the sharing of future growth beyond the existing value? Explain how this reorganization can be accomplished without any immediate tax consequences to the shareholders.

11. What is a holding corporation?

12. Dividends received by a corporation from another taxable Canadian corporation are excluded from taxable income and therefore are not usually subject to tax. However, in certain circumstances, a Canadian-controlled private corporation may be subject to a special refundable tax on the receipt of Canadian dividends. In what circumstances will this special tax apply, what is the rate of tax, and why is it referred to as a "refundable tax"?

13. What is the primary benefit of using a holding corporation to hold investments in shares of other corporations rather than holding those investments personally?

14. Briefly explain why a holding company may be useful when the shares of an active business corporation are being acquired.

15. Briefly explain how using a holding company to own the shares of an active business corporation may be beneficial when the shares of the active business corporation are about to be sold. In what circumstances may using a holding company be disadvantageous when the shares of the active business corporation are being sold? Explain.

Problems

Problem One

Concrete Ltd. is a Canadian-controlled private corporation that manufactures concrete blocks in its Regina plant and also operates a general contracting business.

In 20X1, Concrete acquired 100% of the shares of Little Ltd., which owns a concrete plant in Saskatoon. At the time of acquisition, Little had non-capital losses carried forward in the amount of $175,000 and net capital losses carried forward of $10,000. These losses related to the 20X0 fiscal period.

Both Concrete and Little have a December 31 year end.

The common shares of Concrete are owned 60% by A Ltd., 35% by B Ltd., and 5% by C Ltd. A Ltd., B Ltd., and C Ltd. are owned by Mr. A, Mr. B, and Mr. C respectively. They are all employed by Concrete and are not related to each other.

The three shareholders intend to meet to review the current year's financial results (20X2) and to discuss several other matters. The financial results and other issues that will be discussed are outlined below.

1. After it was acquired, Little continued to lose money. For the year ended December 31, 20X2, it suffered a loss of $60,000. At the time of acquisition the owners planned to make major changes to Little's operations, but they have not been able to complete these on schedule.

2. Concrete had a pre-tax profit of $190,000 for 20X2. Of this amount, $120,000 related to the general contracting business. The contracting business subcontracted all of its work and maintained only a small staff of estimators and administrators.

3. Concrete has accumulated cash reserves that will not be needed for business expansion. The owners are considering paying a $100,000 dividend out of Concrete to the three corporate shareholders. Each holding company will use its share of the dividend for investment purposes.

4. During the year, an agreement was made between A Ltd., B Ltd., and C. Ltd. stating that in the event of the death of A or B or C, Concrete must buy back the shares owned by the deceased's holding corporation. At the time of the agreement, Concrete purchased a life insurance policy on each individual that would provide it with funds to buy back the shares.

5. Several months earlier, A had suggested that Concrete acquire a profitable swimming pool installation business. B and C had vetoed the idea. A intends to inform B and C that he will make the acquisition on his own and intends to acquire the business through A Ltd.

Required:

1. Diagram the financial structure of the shareholders and the corporations described above.

2. What tax advice would you provide with respect to the operations of the subsidiary, Little, considering its poor financial results?

3. Discuss the implications of declaring a dividend of $100,000 from Concrete.

4. If one of the individuals died, what tax implications would arise from the realization of life insurance proceeds?

5. How might the proposed business acquisition by A Ltd. affect B and C? What addition to the shareholder's agreement should B and C propose?

Problem Two

Jimmy Divine owns five of the 100 issued common shares of Poultry Products Ltd. The remaining shares are owned by six other individuals, some of whom are employed by the corporation. The others are passive investors.

Divine has informed the shareholders that he wants to dispose of his shares for their market value, which is $60,000. The shares have a paid-up capital of $50, but Divine had purchased the shares a number of years ago from one of the other shareholders for $10,000. None of the other shareholders has funds to purchase Divine's shares. Unfortunately, the corporation is also temporarily short of cash.

The other shareholders have agreed that the corporation will buy back Divine's five shares at the rate of one share per year over the next five years, but that the total price will remain at $60,000. Divine realizes that the value of the unredeemed shares will grow in the next five years as the company continues to earn profits. He is prepared to forgo these profits provided that the company pays him a fixed dividend on the unredeemed shares of 8% per annum. In addition, he does not want to pay tax on the share sales until he actually receives the cash for them.

Required:

1. What can the company do to buy back Divine's shares at the rate of one share per year so that any unredeemed shares will not change in value before they are redeemed?

2. What amount of net income for tax purposes will Divine earn from the share buy-back in each of the five years?

Problem Three

Betty Borsboom and Walter Good each own 50% of the shares of KM Supplies Ltd. The company has enjoyed steady growth since it began, and all corporate profits have been reinvested in business expansion. The shareholders do not expect this growth to continue, as their market share has reached its peak. In fact, this year, for the first time, the company has generated excess cash flow that is not needed for expansion. Borsboom and Good plan to meet to discuss what they should do with this excess.

Borsboom is 32 years old and Good is 58, and their personal investment strategies are quite different. Borsboom anticipates that as Good reaches retirement age she will have to buy his 50% interest in the company—unless, of course, they decide to sell the entire company to some other party.

The company has invested the excess funds in treasury bills as a temporary measure while the owners decide on a course of action. Good has suggested that the company simply find a more permanent investment; Borsboom has concerns about the future implications of this strategy and may suggest that the company establish a policy of paying a dividend with any excess funds generated.

Required:

1. Identify the problems that may arise if these funds, and future funds, are left in the company and used to acquire a permanent investment.

2. What impact would a policy of regular dividend distributions have on the wealth accumulation of Borsboom and Good?

3. Could their problems be solved if each organized a separate holding corporation, which would in turn acquire their shares in KM Supplies? Explain.

Problem Four

Judy Whyte owns all of the common shares of Danube Manufacturing Ltd. Whyte purchased the shares 10 years ago directly from the corporate treasury at a cost of $50,000. The company regularly earns a pre-tax profit of $180,000.

Whyte has decided to sell the shares of the company to Peter Blue for $700,000. Blue has only $400,000 cash available, but a local bank has agreed to provide a loan of $300,000 for the balance of the purchase price.

Information relating to the company as of the last fiscal year end is as follows:

Paid-up capital of the common shares	$ 50,000
Retained earnings	500,000

Both Whyte and Blue have other sources of income and are in a 46% marginal tax bracket on regular income and 32% on dividends.

Whyte has asked for your advice with respect to the sale of the company. She has mentioned that a friend recently sold his company after transferring his shares to a holding company, and that in so doing he gained some deferral benefits.

You are also the accountant for Blue, and he, as well, has sought your advice.

Required:

1. Compare the tax consequences to Whyte of the following alternatives:
   - Whyte sells shares directly to Blue.
   - The corporation buys back all the common shares from Whyte and issues new shares to Blue.

2. Outline to Whyte the advantages, if any, of first transferring the shares to a holding corporation. Show calculations for each of the alternatives mentioned in 1, and inform Whyte of the short-run and long-run implications.

3. How could Whyte transfer her shares of Danube to a new holding corporation without any immediate tax consequences?

4. Assuming that Whyte will sell her shares directly to Blue for $700,000, answer the following questions with respect to Blue:
   - (a) How will the interest payments on the bank loan be treated for tax purposes?
   - (b) If Blue must obtain money from Danube to repay the principal of the bank loan, what is the fastest possible time period that the loan can be repaid? (You may assume that interest can be paid from personal funds.)

(c) If Blue establishes a holding corporation to borrow money ($300,000) to buy the shares, how fast will he be able to repay the loan principal? (Exclude interest considerations.)

(d) If the holding corporation makes the acquisition, what problem does the interest cost present? How can a later corporate reorganization overcome this problem, and when should this occur?

(e) If Blue uses a holding corporation, he will contribute $400,000 of his own cash to the company to assist with the purchase. Should he loan the $400,000 to the corporation or acquire $400,000 of its common shares? Explain.

Cases

Case One   The Mavis Group

Mavis Corporation, a Canadian company, is a major wholesaler of women's shoes. The company has a history of substantial profits. In 20X7 its net income before tax amounted to $600,000.

Mavis Corporation owns (100%) three subsidiary corporations. The corporate structure is outlined below.

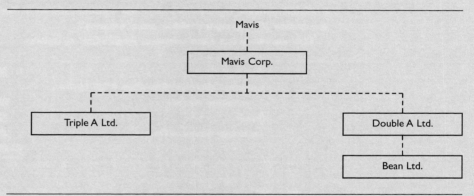

Information relating to the subsidiaries is provided below.

• **Triple A Ltd.**   This corporation was acquired five years ago, in 20X2. The company manufactures women's informal summer shoes and usually earns an annual pre-tax profit of $100,000.

• **Double A Ltd.**   Double A was acquired in 20X3 and manufactures women's high-fashion shoes. The company was profitable for two years after acquisition but has since suffered regular losses. At the end of the current year (20X7) it has unused business losses (non-capital losses) of $400,000. Losses of $50,000 are expected for each of the next three years. The company's assets include land and buildings that have risen in value.

• **Bean Ltd.**   This subsidiary operates a canning business, and its main customer is a large chain of retail food stores. The company was acquired in 20X6, and at the time of acquisition had unused business losses of $150,000 and an unused capital loss of $40,000. In 20X7, Bean suffered a further operating loss of $250,000. Management is concerned about the amount of this loss and is considering whether to close the factory or perhaps sell it.

Bean does not have any significant assets, as it rents its land and building under a short-term lease. It does own the manufacturing equipment, but this has little value.

Required:

Review the existing financial structure of the Mavis Group of companies and discuss what steps might be taken to enhance the company's growth potential.

Case Two   Charles Bert

Charles Bert is a successful Canadian businessman. For the past 15 years he has been president of Bert-Ram Electronics Ltd., a company he started with Peter Ramper. Ramper, who is not employed by the company, obtained shares in the company in exchange for patent rights on one of his inventions.

For many years Bert-Ram suffered the typical growing pains of a new business, including cash-flow shortages. In the past few years, however, the company has generated substantial profits as well as cash flow in excess of expansion requirements.

Bert is not a "high liver," and his annual salary is sufficient to meet his personal needs.

Realco Corporation owns two rental properties and generates rental income of $100,000 annually. Bert owns 25% of the common shares of Realco; the remaining shares are owned 25% by each of three other investors.

Bert currently has a net worth of $1,500,000, as follows:

Personal assets	$ 300,000
Common shares of Bert-Ram (75% of the common shares)	800,000
Bonds	200,000
Common shares of Realco	200,000
	$1,500,000

In 20X1, Bert-Ram earned an after-tax profit of $300,000, of which only $100,000 was required for business expansion. The company currently has $250,000 of cash invested in bank term deposits. Bert and Ramper recently argued about how to invest this cash—Ramper is keen on the stock market, while Bert prefers real estate investments.

Bert's personal income for 20X1 consists of the following:

Salary (Bert-Ram)	$100,000
Interest	15,000
Dividends:	
Bert-Ram	50,000
Realco	15,000
	$180,000

Recently, Bert was given the opportunity to purchase 100% of the common shares of LOBD Software Ltd., a Canadian software wholesaler. The company generates profits of $100,000 after tax and has a strong management team that could run the business without a significant time commitment from Bert. The asking price for the shares is $600,000 cash. The most recent balance sheet of LOBD is shown on the next page.

Bert has decided to purchase the LOBD shares, and his bank has agreed to finance the full $600,000 purchase price. Bert will use his bonds and shares of Bert-Ram as collateral for the loan. The bank requires that at least $80,000 of the loan principal be repaid each year in addition to interest.

Required:

Review Bert's financial structure and outline what steps he can take to maximize his net worth in the future.

LOBD SOFTWARE LTD.
Balance Sheet
May 31, 20X1

Assets:		
Current assets (cash, receivables, and inventory)		$565,000
Fixed assets (at cost):		
Vehicles	60,000	
Equipment	110,000	
	170,000	
Accumulated amortization	(65,000)	105,000
Investment in long-term bonds		100,000
		$770,000
Liabilities:		
Accounts payable		$350,000
Income taxes payable		20,000
		370,000
Shareholder's equity:		
Share capital	10,000	
Retained earnings	390,000	400,000
		$770,000

Other Forms of Business Organization

If you can run a business well,
you can run any business well.
Richard Branson ✍

part four

Chapter 15   Partnerships

To this point in the text, discussions of business structures involving single or multiple owners have been restricted to the two primary taxable entities—individuals and corporations. There are three other forms that a business organization can take: standard partnership, joint venture, and limited partnership.

These three can be referred to as the "secondary" or "non-taxable" entities. *Non-taxable* does not mean that the entity's earned income is not subject to tax, but rather that the entity itself is not directly liable for tax on its earned income.

Each of the three entities is different from the others, but all are structured on similar principles. It is important to recognize that each of the secondary entities can be useful to, and form part of, any business structure, whether that structure involves individuals or corporations, and whether it involves a giant conglomerate or a small business enterprise. The standard partnership form of organization is often considered to be useful only to individuals who practise together in a profession or a small business. Actually, the standard partnership often forms part of the business structure of large public and private corporations.

Each of the three secondary entities is available as an alternative structure whenever a proposed business activity is to be carried out with other parties. The fact that a venture includes other parties complicates the management of cash flows and the related tax variable. The commitment of funds to such ventures requires that a structure be developed which permits the easy return of the original capital invested as well as the return to the investor of any profits for further investment in other ventures.

Cash flow from investments in activities with other parties will be affected by the way in which the profits from the separate venture are taxed and the losses, if any, can be utilized. Cash flow will also be affected by the tax treatment in the event that the original capital is lost and the venture fails, as well as by the tax consequences of repatriating the original capital and accumulated profits. The commitment of funds to any investment activity must take the long view and consider not only the project at hand but also its impact on the investor's ability to participate in other immediate and future activities. This concern is of greater significance when other parties are participating in a venture.

This chapter is devoted solely to the standard partnership form of organization and covers three general areas:

1. The definition and general format of the partnership entity.

2. The taxation of partnership profits and its impact on cash flows.

3. The advantages and disadvantages, in terms of cash flow, of establishing a partnership rather than a corporation.

I. The Standard Partnership—Definition and Format

A. Definition

The *Income Tax Act* does not define "partnership"; it merely outlines the tax treatment of income generated by one. A broad, generally accepted definition is that a partnership is the relationship that exists between entities carrying on a business in common with a view to profit.[1] The entity is created when two or more entities jointly conduct an ongoing business enterprise the scope of which is defined by mutual agreement. It is characterized by the partners sharing in the final net results of the enterprise in an agreed ratio rather than by the mere division of gross receipts.

---

1 IT-90.

Partnerships are often confused with joint ventures or "co-ownership." A joint venture is similar to a partnership in that it involves two or more entities conducting a business activity together, but is different in that it is usually formed for a single purpose or a single transaction (see Chapter 16).[2] A co-ownership usually involves the joint ownership of an investment property rather than an operating business. When several individuals or corporations own a block of rental apartments, that is an example of co-ownership.

This text will not define the legal principles that distinguish these forms of organization from each other; rather, it will demonstrate how these forms can be utilized, and their impact on the decision process. Even so, the reader should appreciate that creating such entities raises complex legal issues that often vary within Canadian and foreign jurisdictions.

B. Partnership Agreement

A partnership venture consists of the *partnership entity*, which conducts its affairs as a separate organization, and a particular number of *partners*. The partners are usually one of the two primary entities (individuals or corporations), although other kinds of entities, such as trusts or other partnerships, may also be participating partners. Exhibit 15-1 demonstrates three simple partnership structures; each consists of the minimum of two partners, with one holding a 60% interest and the other a 40% interest.

The three structures are distinguished by the nature of the participating partners. In structure A both partners are individuals. In structure B one partner is an individual and the other is a corporation. In structure C both partners are corporations. Although individual X and individual Y are directly or indirectly involved in each structure, it is important to recognize that they are not the partners in each of the three partnership ventures; the direct influence of the standard partnership extends from the partnership entity itself to the actual partners and not beyond. In each structure neither partner, whether individual or corporate, is precluded from conducting other activities. In structure C, for example, one or both of the corporate partners may carry on other, unrelated business or investment activities; their involvement in the partnership venture may constitute only a minor part of their separate operations.

A partnership is created by the execution of a *partnership agreement* among the various partners. This agreement becomes the working framework of the entity. Within certain limits, partnership agreements can be tailored to suit the specific needs of the partners. Because of this, the standard partnership is more flexible than the corporation in terms of the procedures for administering the venture's affairs.

The general nature and unique aspects of a particular partnership are developed in the partnership agreement, which gives special attention to three fundamental areas:

1. Each partner's required contributions to the entity.

2. The format and rules for decision making and the management of the partnership's business affairs.

3. How profits or losses are to be shared by the participating partners.

1. Partner's Contribution

A partner can participate in a partnership venture by contributing capital or effort or a combination of the two. It is not always necessary that each partner commit a proportionate amount of financial resources to the venture. When financial resources are required as a contribution, they are usually provided in the form of cash; however, specific assets

---

2 *Woodlin Developments Ltd. v. MNR*, (TCC), 86 DTC 116.

Exhibit 15-1:
Basic Business
Structures Involving
Partnerships

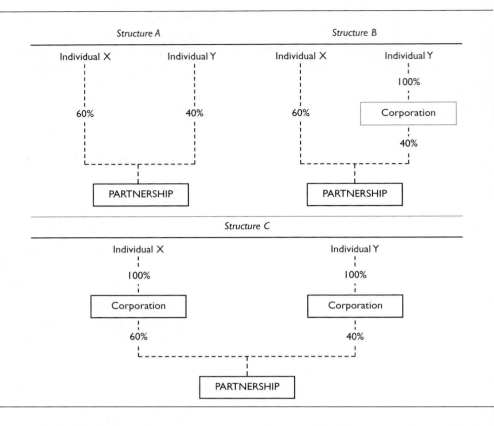

such as land, buildings, equipment, patents, franchises, and the like can also be contributed. The cash or the value of specific assets contributed constitutes the partnership's equity base; if further resources are required, the partnership can incur debt. In summary, a partnership is a self-contained entity holding assets, liabilities, and partner's equity.

2. Management

Usually all partners participate in the management of the enterprise, although by agreement specific partners may be excluded from this process, in which case they are entitled only to share in the operating results.

A special aspect of standard partnerships is that the procedures for decision making can be tailored to the wishes of the participating partners. It is not required that the partner or partners holding a majority financial interest have the final say on all decisions. For example, the agreement may entitle all partners to one vote, whatever the amount of their financial interest, so that a simple majority of votes will settle minor day to-day decisions; at the same time, the same organization may require a unanimous vote for important policy decisions.

Management decision making within a partnership is completely flexible and can be as democratic or as autocratic as the partners wish. This can be contrasted with the corporate form of organization, in which decisions are made by a board of directors, elected by shareholders, whose voting power is determined by the number of voting shares owned. Some flexibility can be achieved in a corporation, but not nearly as much as in a partnership. A minority shareholder of a corporation is often powerless, whereas a minority partner in a partnership can be provided with a great deal of influence if the partners so choose. This flexibility makes a partnership attractive, as its structure can be designed to mirror the specific objectives of the participants.

3. Sharing of Operating Results

The partnership structure also provides significant flexibility in the way profits or losses from operations are shared by the partners. Profits or losses are usually shared as a function of capital contributions, or the degree of effort or participation in the business process, or both. As a partner, an entity may participate in profit sharing on the basis of special expertise or a comparatively greater degree of management effort, even though its financial contribution is non-existent or substantially less than that of other partners. The sharing of profits and losses is a function of the partnership agreement, which can be tailored to the economic realities of the specific situation.

Referring again to Exhibit 15-1, it can be seen that the existence of a 60%/40% partnership interest does not adequately describe the relationship between the two participating partners in any of the three structures, as it is not known if the ratio applies to profit sharing, capital contributions, or decision-making powers. Each of these items may involve a different relationship. This, more than anything else, is what makes standard partnerships unique.

C. Partner Liability

The standard partnership is a separate functioning entity for management purposes. However, it is not a protected *legal* entity that is separate from the affairs of the partners. This means that all obligations and debts incurred by the partnership or by partners acting in the course of partnership business, and all negligent activities performed by them, are the *full responsibility* of *each partner* participating in the venture. Each partner is jointly and severally liable for all partnership activities, which means that every partner's liability exposure not only goes beyond the amount of capital invested in the venture but also goes beyond the proportionate share of partnership involvement. A creditor may seek full satisfaction from any or all of the partners; and it is usual for the partner with the greatest financial strength to be targeted for full satisfaction, even though that partner may hold a smaller partnership interest.

In limited circumstances, risk insurance that limits the partners' exposure may be obtained by the partnership. However, the most common method used to avoid liability exposure involves each intended partner interposing a limited-value holding corporation as the actual partner. Consider the two business structures outlined in Exhibit 15-2. The high-risk structure involves two independent business corporations entering into a 50/50 partnership requiring $1,000,000 of capital. While both corporate partners have contributed $500,000 of capital, their liability exposure is considerably different. Corporation A has a net worth of $1,000,000, whereas Corporation B has a net worth of $8,000,000. Since both partners are jointly and severally liable for the partnership obligation, B bears a greater burden of exposure because of its much higher net worth. For A, which has a net worth of only $1,000,000, the potential consequences of being exposed to the full obligations of the partnership may be catastrophic.

Both partners can limit their risk by developing the low-risk structure outlined in Exhibit 15-2. In this structure, A and B each capitalize a holding corporation with $500,000, that amount being the required contribution to the partnership. Each holding corporation then contributes the $500,000 to the partnership. The partners in this structure are the two holding corporations, not the two business corporations. While each holding company is exposed to the full obligations of the partnership, the liability of each is limited to its net worth of only $500,000. As well, any partnership profits distributed to the partners can in turn be passed on as tax-free intercorporate dividends to the two parent corporations for reinvestment. Usually it is not a good idea to hold the accumulated profits in the holding corporation, since this increases that corporation's net worth and therefore its risk exposure.

Exhibit 15-2:
Partner Liability and
Business Structure

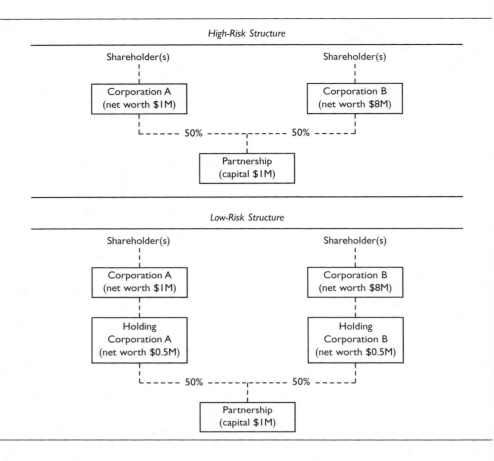

II. Taxation of Partnership Operations

A. Partnership Income and Losses

A partnership is not a taxable entity and bears no responsibility for tax on income generated within its sphere of operations. Instead, income earned or losses incurred by the partnership are allocated to the partners, in accordance with the agreed sharing ratio, for inclusion in each partner's income for tax purposes.[3] The income shared by the partners is allocated for tax purposes regardless of whether such profits have actually been distributed to the partners. Thus, it is conceivable that a partner may bear the full tax liability on its share of income even though the income remains within the partnership for reinvestment.

It is very significant that losses incurred by a partnership are also allocated to the partners and are included in their separate determinations of taxable income.[4] This means that losses can be offset immediately against the partners' other income, provided that other income exists. This is especially advantageous during the start-up period of a new venture, when losses are common. By utilizing losses immediately, the partner can reduce its tax bill and use the extra cash to strengthen the new venture.

The amount of income earned or losses incurred by the partnership is determined for allocation as if the partnership were a separate taxable entity. The partnership can earn business income, property income, and capital gains; all of these are determined according

---

3   ITA 96(1); IT-138R.

4   ITA 96(1); IT-232R2.

to the normal rules for arriving at income for tax purposes. Capital cost allowance, and the amortization of goodwill and other eligible capital property, are determined and applied at the partnership level before allocation.[5]

All partnership income allocated retains its *source and characteristics* when included in the partner's income (see Exhibit 15-3).[6] A dividend to the partnership is a dividend to the partner and is treated accordingly for tax purposes. Capital gains and losses of the partnership become capital gains and losses of the partner. In this sense, the partnership is a *conduit* or *funnel*—it earns income like any other entity but passes it on to the participants as if it had been earned directly by them.

Profits retained in the partnership form part of each partner's capital or equity and are available for distribution whenever the partners so decide. When accumulated profits are distributed to the partner, this constitutes a return of capital, which is not subject to further taxation. Put another way, the repatriation of profits has no tax implications for the members of a partnership; this is not the case for corporate entities, which must distribute their after-tax profits as taxable dividends.

The amount of tax paid on partnership profits depends on the nature of the given partner rather than on the nature of the partnership itself. As a result, the operating results of a particular partnership are subject to various tax implications depending on

(a) whether the separate partners are individuals or corporations;
(b) the rates of tax applicable to the various partners; and,
(c) the other sources of income of each partner.

For example, a partnership loss may be readily offset against the other income of one partner, while sitting idle for another partner who has a minimal amount of income from non-partnership activities. This can result in conflict between the partners. For example, the rate of capital cost allowance is determined by the partnership and, once determined, applies to each partner accordingly. The partner who has other sources of income may want to claim the maximum CCA, while the other partner, who has only losses and no other income, may prefer to claim the minimum in order to reduce the possibility of losses expiring.

Exhibit 15-3:
Example of Partnership
Allocation by Source

Type of activity	Partnership	Allocated 60% Partner A	40% Partner B
Business:			
Retail income	$500,000	300,000	200,000
Manufacturing loss	(100,000)	(60,000)	(40,000)
Property:			
Interest income	10,000	6,000	4,000
Dividend income	40,000	24,000	16,000
Rental income	100,000	60,000	40,000
Capital gains	50,000	30,000	20,000
Capital losses	(30,000)	(18,000)	(12,000)
	$570,000		

5 ITA 96(1)(a) to (c).
6 Political contributions and charitable donations are also allocated to the partners for use in the appropriate manner.

When contemplating forming a partnership, the prospective partners must assess the amount and the timing of future tax costs in terms of their own individual tax status rather than that of the partnership. In effect, the partnership is a component of each partner's own separate organization for tax purposes. Any income earned or loss incurred is simply intermingled with the partner's other sources of income. The profits are not subject to further tax when repatriated to the partners.

It should be noted that if any member of the partnership is an individual, the taxation year of the partnership must be a calendar year (December 31) unless an alternative election is made (see Chapter 5).

B. The Partnership Interest

The participation of an entity as a partner in a partnership venture is recognized through the ownership of a "partnership interest." A partner is considered to own a partnership interest whenever that partner has rights and obligations created by being party to a partnership agreement. The partnership interest is a tradeable asset that can be bought and sold much like a share of a corporation's capital stock. This makes it possible to change the participating partners without disturbing the partnership enterprise itself. In most circumstances a partnership interest is treated as capital property for tax purposes; as such, its disposition results in a capital gain or loss.

Usually a partnership is created when the participants contribute capital in the form of cash or assets in return for a partnership interest, the rights and obligations of which are defined in the partnership agreement. Thereafter, an unrelated entity can become a partner by

(a) purchasing a departing partner's interest, or acquiring a portion of the interest of each remaining partner; or,

(b) contributing cash or specific other assets directly to the partnership in return for a new partnership interest (thereby diluting the earlier partner ratio of participation).

Conversely, existing partners can depart or diminish their percentage of participation by

(a) selling all or a portion of their partnership interest to a new partner or existing partner(s); or,

(b) withdrawing their capital directly from the partnership treasury (thereby enhancing the ownership percentage of the remaining partners).

Notice that in both situations the alternatives involve either a transaction between the partners, which has no effect on the partnership entity, or a transaction between the partnership and a specific partner, which *does* affect the partnership entity. The financial and tax considerations are different for each alternative, as demonstrated in the following example.

Assume that an existing partnership consists of two partners, A and B, who share profits equally. A and B intend to admit a third partner, C, and thereafter share profits on the basis of one-third each. The existing partnership has a net worth of $100,000, of which $50,000 belongs to A and $50,000 to B. New partner C can enter the partnership in one of two ways, as diagrammed in Exhibit 15-4. The transaction under alternative 1 is between new partner C and the partnership. As the existing partnership has a net worth of $100,000, C must contribute $50,000 to achieve a one-third interest. The contribution of $50,000 to the treasury increases the partnership's net worth by $50,000 to a total of $150,000. Partners A and B each retain a $50,000 interest in the entity; however, their interests have been diluted to one-third each as a result of the enhanced financial strength of the partnership arising from C's contribution. Since neither A nor B has directly disposed of any existing partnership interest, this alternative has no tax consequences to the parties.

Exhibit 15-4:
Partnership Structure of
A and B before and
after Admitting C

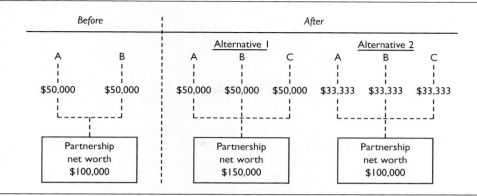

A new partner can also enter the partnership under alternative 2; however, in this case the financial and tax consequences are different. Under this alternative new partner C obtains a one-third interest in the partnership by purchasing some of the partnership interest of both A and B. The transaction is among the partners rather than between a partner and the partnership entity. The cost of a one-third interest is $33,333, which is one-third of the entity's net worth of $100,000. One-half of this amount is paid to A, the other half to B. As a result, A and B receive financial consideration but the partnership retains its former financial strength. Both A and B have disposed of a portion of their partnership interest; this may result in a capital gain or a capital loss depending on the cost of the partnership interest.

The distinguishing features of the two alternatives relate to the financial strength of the enterprise and to how its partners are taxed. In the above example, alternative 1 enhanced the financial strength of the business; alternative 2 did not change the financial strength of the business, but only the original partners' positions in it. In the same way, the departure of a partner will diminish the resources of an enterprise if that partner leaves with his capital; but if the remaining partners use their separate resources to purchase the departing partner's interest, the partnership's resources will be unchanged.

Disposing of a partnership interest, as pointed out previously, will normally result in a capital gain or loss depending on whether that interest's value has increased or diminished in relation to its cost. This, of course, has tax implications. A partnership interest, like a share of a corporation, will increase or decrease in value as a result of

(a) the accumulation, within the entity, of undistributed profits or the occurrence of operating losses; and,

(b) the increase or decrease in the value of assets owned by the partnership such as land, buildings, equipment, goodwill, and so on.

An important feature of partnerships is that any change in value of the partnership interest resulting from *profits retained* or *losses incurred* does not create a capital gain or capital loss when the partnership interest is disposed of. Capital gains or losses on the sale of a partnership interest occur only to the extent that the individual assets owned by the partnership have changed in value. This results from an arbitrary adjustment to the cost base, for tax purposes, of the partnership interest.[7] The actual cost base of a partnership interest (being the contribution amount by the partner to the partnership, or the cost of acquiring another partner's interest) is automatically increased or decreased for tax

---

7   ITA 53(1)(e), 53(2)(c); IT-338R2.

purposes whenever profits or losses are allocated to the partners and whenever accumulated profits are withdrawn.[8] For example, if a partner is allocated $20,000 of profits for inclusion in income, the value of the partnership interest is increased by $20,000 if such profits are not withdrawn. The cost base of the partnership interest is arbitrarily increased by $20,000 and therefore both value and cost increase by the same amount. Later, if the partnership interest is sold, the increase in value from the retained profits of $20,000 is offset by the exact increase in cost of $20,000 and no capital gain occurs.

Partnership profits or losses are funnelled directly to the separate partners for inclusion in income determination and are not taxed again when the partnership interest is disposed of. This treatment must be compared with that given to corporations. Share value increases that result from profits retained in a corporation are included in the determination of capital gains or losses when the shares are disposed of, even though the profits have already been taxed in the corporation. Entities that enter into business ventures with other parties can often choose between organizing the new venture as a partnership or as a separate corporation with shareholders. Not only will the tax impact on the annual income or losses vary between these two basic options, but so also may the tax consequences when the participants' equity is ultimately sold.

C. Transactions with Partners and Reorganizations

A partnership, although a non-taxable entity in terms of income, is considered to be a separate entity for purposes of holding assets. This means that if partners buy property from the partnership, or sell it to the partnership, those transactions are automatically considered to have taken place at fair market value. If, for example, a partner transfers a property that has increased in value to the partnership, that partner is considered to have disposed of the property at fair market value, which may result in taxable income and therefore a tax cost to that partner.[9] The partnership that has acquired the property is considered to have incurred a cost equal to that property's fair market value and consequently may receive certain tax benefits. If, for example, the acquired property is depreciable, capital cost allowance can be claimed by the partnership based on this new cost, thereby reducing the taxable income earned by the partnership and allocated to the partners. In other words, what is lost by the partner may be regained by the partnership, although over a different time period.

As an alternative, a partner can choose, by election, to transfer property into a partnership at a value equal to the partner's cost for tax purposes.[10] This eliminates the creation of taxable income to the partner; but the partnership will also have a lower cost for tax purposes, and capital cost allowance will only be claimable on the lower amount.

Similarly, when an existing partnership transfers its assets to a partner, those assets are considered to have been sold at fair market value.[11] This may also create income to the partnership, which, of course, is allocated to the various partners for inclusion in their taxable income. In limited circumstances, partnership assets can be transferred to the partners without tax consequences; however, such circumstances rarely arise in the normal business process.[12]

---

8 It is possible for the adjusted cost base of a partnership interest to be a negative value. By exception (ITA 40(3.1)), this negative amount does not result in a deemed capital gain (until all partners' rights are satisfied). This exception does not apply to a limited partnership (Chapter 16) or to passive partners in a regular partnership.

9 ITA 97(1).

10 ITA 97(2); IT-413R, -471R.

11 ITA 98(2); IT-338R2.

12 ITA 98(3) to (6).

The areas of tax law affecting transactions between partners and partnerships are complex and normally require professional advice; even so, the reader should be aware that the movement of assets into and out of a partnership has some flexibility, and that the related tax consequences can vary.

It should also be recognized that the choice of a partnership form of organization is not binding on the participants. An existing partnership can be converted into a corporation in which the former partners are shareholders. While the transfer of partnership assets to a new corporation is subject to fair market value rules similar to those discussed above, a partnership can, if it so elects, convert itself into a corporation without immediate tax consequences.[13] In summary, it is not difficult for partners to change a partnership's structure whenever it is in their interest to do so.

D. Small-Business Deduction and Private Corporate Partners

As outlined in Chapters 11 and 13, a Canadian-controlled private corporation is entitled to a lower corporate tax rate (18% in some provinces). This is a result of the small-business deduction that applies to the first $300,000 of annual active business income.

If a Canadian-controlled private corporation is a partner in a partnership activity, it is entitled to use the small-business deduction on the active business income earned by the partnership and allocated to it. However, the active business income earned by the partnership that is eligible for the small-business deduction is limited to $300,000 annually. In effect, the partnership has a separate annual limit which determines the amount of partnership income that is eligible and that can be applied to the partners' separate limits.[14]

Exhibit 15-5 shows a business partnership. The partners are two Canadian-controlled private corporations that share the partnership's profits equally. Each corporate partner has an annual small-business deduction limit of $300,000. The partnership also has a limit of $300,000. The example assumes that the partnership has earned active business income of $400,000.

Only $300,000 of the partnership income is entitled to the lower corporate tax rate; the remaining $100,000 is not. Therefore, each corporate partner must include $200,000 (50% of the total partnership profits) in its income, and of that amount, only $150,000 (50% of the partnership's $300,000 limit) is eligible for the small-business deduction. The balance of $50,000 is subject to normal rates of tax. Keep in mind that each corporate partner has a small-business limit of $300,000 and that the eligible income from the partnership of $150,000 applies against this total. Each partner can earn active business income from other sources that is eligible for the small-business deduction until the $300,000 limit is reached. The $300,000 annual limit of corporate partner 1 is as shown in the table below.

	Available for SBD	Not available for SBD
Partnership income allocated ($200,000)	$150,000	$50,000
Potential business income from sources other than partnership	150,000	unlimited
	$300,000	

If a corporate partner has active business income from non-partnership sources in excess of $300,000, its small-business limit is already fully utilized and none of the income allocated

13 ITA 85(2), (3); IT-378R.
14 ITA 125(1)(a), 125(7)(f); IT-73R5 (paragraphs 20–21).

to it from the partnership qualifies for the low rate of tax. In such circumstances this is a drawback to the partnership form of organization, and one that a corporation must keep in mind when deciding which kind of organization to use as a vehicle to carry on an enterprise with other parties. This is demonstrated in the next two segments of this chapter.

Exhibit 15-5:
Small-Business
Deduction on
Partnership Profits

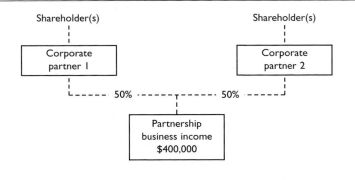

Partnership income:	Partnership		Allocated to	
			Partner 1	Partner 2
Eligible for SBD				
if partner qualifies	$300,000		$150,000	$150,000
Not eligible for SBD	100,000		50,000	50,000
	$400,000		$200,000	$200,000

III. Partnership Structure— Impact on Decision Making

When a choice of business structure is being made, the standard partnership entity cannot be analyzed in isolation; instead, it must be considered in relation to other possible structures. The main alternative to the partnership is the separate corporation, the shares of which are held by the participating entities. Each of the structures has different tax and non-tax implications that must be considered. From a tax perspective, the decision maker should attempt to develop a vehicle that will minimize the cash needed to start up the venture and maximize the return of cash back to the investor for reinvestment. Whenever an entity is considering participating in a venture with other parties, it must consider these four fundamental tax issues:

1. What will be the tax cost on the annual operating profits generated from the new venture? The objective, of course, is to minimize tax on an ongoing basis, but it is especially important to do so during the initial years, in order to improve cash flows and thereby increase the venture's chances of success.

2. If operating losses are expected during the start-up phase, how and when can such losses be utilized against other sources of income of the venture itself or of the participating parties? Even if start-up losses are not anticipated, the investors should consider the implications of unexpected losses. The utilization of losses is as vital to cash flow as the minimizing of tax on profits.

3. What will the tax implications be if the venture fails and is either terminated or sold off at a loss? The loss of all or a portion of an investor's capital will affect that investor's tax position; the resulting tax benefits will reduce the burden of the loss. The participating entities must assess their downside risk by identifying the after-tax cash loss that will occur if the venture fails.

4. How will the capital invested and the accumulated profits be returned to the investor? The investor will want this done in a way that minimizes the amount of tax. The repatriation of capital and profits takes on greater importance when other parties are involved, as their intention is usually to join forces for a specific venture, and surplus funds that are not needed for that specific venture will be distributed.

The tax implications as they relate to each of the above issues will vary with the type of entity—corporation or standard partnership—that is chosen. The amount and timing of the tax cost or benefit must therefore be identified for each alternative so that true cash flows can be determined and a decision made within the normal capital budgeting procedure. Such an analysis is performed in the following case study.

IV. Case Study— A New Venture Organization Structure

Summary of Assumed Facts

1. Krisco Ltd. is a Canadian-controlled private corporation owned by two wealthy Ontario business families. The company has a net worth of $6,000,000 and generates after-tax profits from its clothing import and wholesale business of approximately $1,200,000 annually.

2. Brandi Ltd. is also a Canadian-controlled private corporation. It is owned by a group of Manitoba investors and manufactures denim jeans. The company has suffered losses in the past few years, but a turnaround is imminent and its survival is not in question. Business losses of $2,000,000 have accumulated and are being carried forward for tax purposes over seven years. In spite of the losses, the corporation has a net worth of $3,000,000.

3. Krisco and Brandi intend to jointly develop a new enterprise that will manufacture a special line of clothing for East European countries. Krisco has imported foreign products in the past, and in so doing has developed a network of prominent international contacts that it will contribute to the venture. Brandi will contribute its manufacturing and design experience. Each corporation will commit $1,000,000 to the new venture, which, however, will also require substantial bank financing so that it can acquire the manufacturing assets and fund its operations. Each corporation will own 50% of the new venture.

4. The parties have developed what they consider to be accurate projections of the operating results. While losses are expected in the first three years, the venture should become profitable in the fourth year. By the sixth year profits should level off at about $700,000 annually before tax. The projected operating results are as follows:

	Profit (loss)
Year 1	$(400,000)
Year 2	(200,000)
Year 3	(200,000)
Year 4	300,000
Year 5	500,000
Year 6	700,000 (and thereafter)

Basic Structures Available

The new venture can utilize one of two basic structures.

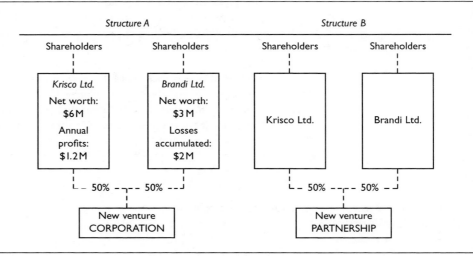

Structure A involves a separate corporation to house the new venture, with Krisco and Brandi each owning 50% of the share capital. Such a structure would require a shareholders' agreement outlining the course of conduct in the event that the shareholders, which have equal voting rights, are stalemated on significant issues.

Structure B is a partnership; the partners are the two corporations, Krisco Ltd. and Brandi Ltd. The decision-making process would be established by the partnership agreement.

Analysis

The following analysis is viewed from the perspective of Krisco Ltd. and is presented in terms of the four fundamental considerations outlined previously.

• **Taxation of operating profits** Although profits are not anticipated until year 4, their impact should be considered before a commitment is made to a particular structure. Under structure A the new venture is a separate corporation and as such will be directly taxed on its annual profits. The new corporation is a Canadian-controlled private corporation. Because the ownership ratio is 50/50 (neither shareholder controls), it is not associated with Krisco or Brandi. The new corporation is therefore eligible for the small-business deduction on the first $300,000 of annual profits. The tax rates on the new venture's profits (assuming a rate of provincial tax of 5% on the first $300,000 profits and 15% on the rest—see Exhibit 11-8 in Chapter 11) are as follows:

	Manufacturing	Non-manufacturing
First $300,000 of annual income	18%	18%
Income in excess of $300,000	35%*	37%

* Due to provincial incentives.

This represents an expansion of the small-business deduction for Krisco, which is also entitled to an annual small-business deduction of $300,000 on its own profits. As a result, Krisco's overall activities are entitled to a low rate of tax on $450,000 of annual income, as follows:

Available directly to Krisco	$300,000
Available indirectly through the new venture (50% of $300,000)	150,000
	$450,000

The availability of the small-business deduction will improve the new venture's cash flow by reducing taxes by up to $57,000 (37% − 18% = 19% × $300,000) annually; this will improve its competitive position and increase its chances of success.

On the other hand, if the new venture is operated as a partnership (structure B), all profits will be allocated directly to the partners. Profits allocated to Krisco will be added to its total income from other operations. As Krisco has already fully utilized its annual small-business deduction, all partnership profits from the new venture will be taxed at the high rates of 35% for eligible[15] manufacturing profits and 37% for non-manufacturing profits.

The impact of the higher tax rates may be softened a little by the formula for determining manufacturing profits. Under the partnership format, Krisco, when determining its manufacturing profits, can include in the calculation its share of the partnership's manufacturing capital and labour (see Chapter 11). This may enhance the arbitrary percentage of manufacturing profits and capture some of Krisco's profits from non-manufacturing activities. This saving, if any, should be viewed as a reduction of tax on the partnership profits.

In terms of profits, Krisco would favour the corporate structure over the partnership.

- **Utilization of operating losses** The new venture expects to incur losses in the first three years of operations that total $800,000. Under structure A the new-venture corporation will have to retain those losses for its own use; they are not immediately available to the participants. The losses will sit within the corporation until profits are generated; according to the projections, they will be fully utilized by the end of year 5. If the full losses ($800,000) from the first three years are applied to the profits of years 4 and 5 (which also total $800,000), they will eliminate tax in each of those years. However, since the tax on the first $300,000 of each year's income is at the low rate, it may be more desirable to use the losses in each year to reduce income to the $300,000 level, thereby eliminating taxes at the high rate. This would, of course, delay utilization of the entire loss into the sixth year.

Under the partnership format, the losses incurred in the first three years are allocated directly to the partners for their own use. From Krisco's point of view this is attractive, as the allocation of $400,000 of losses (one-half of $800,000) will create tax savings to Krisco of about $148,000 over the first three years. The losses from the new venture will be used immediately and the cash-flow benefits will be received in the first three years instead of years 4, 5, and 6.

In terms of loss utilization, Krisco prefers the partnership form of organization. This contrasts with its preference for the corporate form when the venture is profitable.

- **Downside risk** While both parties assume the venture will be a success, the possibility of failure exists, so the tax implications of the loss of the total investment must be considered. Under the corporate structure, overpowering losses from the operations would be locked into the corporation. Each shareholder, as a separate entity, would recognize its loss through the decline in value of the shares acquired in, or the loans made to, the new-venture corporation. In this particular case the loss of the $1,000,000 of share or loan equity by each party would qualify as an allowable business investment loss, one-half of which could be offset against other sources of income. The downside risk of the investment following its total loss is $815,000, as follows:

---

15 Manufacturing profits in excess of $300,000 annually.

Cash invested and lost	$1,000,000
Tax saving on loss utilization	
[37% × ½ ($1,000,000)]	(185,000)
Net cash exposure	$ 815,000

In some cases shareholders may guarantee certain debts within the corporation, and that must be considered as a separate risk factor (see Chapter 20). Losses on the shares or loans to a corporation can be used for tax purposes only when the shares or loans are disposed of. In the case of a loan, a deemed disposition occurs when the owner reasonably considers it to be uncollectible, and therefore an actual disposition is not required. A loss from the decline in value of shares can be recognized only when those shares are sold, or when the corporation is formally bankrupt, or when the corporation is insolvent and has ceased operations. In this case it would be advisable for both parties to invest their $1,000,000 in the corporation by way of a substantial amount of debt and a small amount of share capital. This may, at some time in the future, speed up the loss recognition if the business should begin to falter.

The losses from operations that are locked into the corporation are simply eliminated unless steps can be taken by the shareholders to utilize them. With a 50/50 ownership ratio, this would be difficult to accomplish (see Chapter 14).

When a partnership structure is used, the downside risk has different implications. As the partnership's operating losses are allocated directly to each of the partners, the loss of the investment is effectively recognized as a full business loss. If, for example, the partnership had lost $2,000,000 from operations and then simply terminated, each partner would have lost the $1,000,000 of capital invested. The allocation of an operating loss reduces the cost base of a partnership interest simultaneously with its decline in value; as a result, a capital loss is not incurred. The downside risk to Krisco on the total loss of the $1,000,000 investment in the partnership is therefore $630,000, calculated as follows:

Cash invested and lost	$1,000,000
Tax savings on operating losses allocated	
(37% × $1,000,000)	370,000
Net cash exposure	$ 630,000

Unfortunately, the tax benefits resulting from the loss of the partnership investment may be tempered by the fact that the partners are not limited in liability, and that losses beyond the capital contributions fall to the partners. In this case Krisco has a net worth of $6,000,000, compared with Brandi's $3,000,000. Krisco may ultimately be responsible for the full loss of the venture if Brandi is unable to meet its obligations. Krisco and Brandi may consider establishing holding companies to act as the partners; each holding company would be capitalized with the required $1,000,000 contribution.

This structure (diagrammed on the next page) would limit the liability of each partner to $1,000,000. Unfortunately, the use of holding companies is not without consequences. The losses incurred by the partnership would be allocated to the holding companies and would sit idle, with no other income for offset except that which was generated by the partnership itself. At the same time, although the losses would be locked into the two holding corporations, those corporations would be owned 100% by Krisco and Brandi respectively, and as such belong fully to each party. As a result, each party would have greater flexibility with respect to the use of those losses (see Chapter 13).

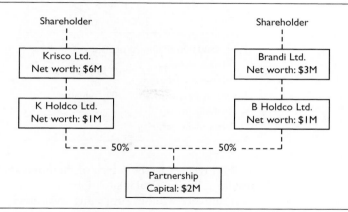

• **Repatriation of capital and profits**   Under a corporate structure, accumulated profits are returned to the shareholders as dividends, which are received by each shareholder corporation free of tax. Consequently, with this structure, 82% of the new-venture profits that are subject to the small-business deduction ($300,000 annually) would be available to Krisco Ltd. and Brandi Ltd. for reinvestment in other ventures. This is calculated as follows:

Profit to the new venture	100%
Tax to new-venture corporation	18
Net retained in new-venture corporation	82%
Tax on receipt of dividend	NIL
Net available for reinvestment	82%

Income in a new-venture corporation that is not subject to the small-business deduction also can be distributed without any further tax; in this case the net profits repatriated to Krisco and Brandi would thus be 65% and 63%, calculated as follows:

	Manufacturing	Non-manufacturing
Profits to the new venture	100%	100%
Tax to new-venture corporation	35	37
Net retained in new-venture corporation	65%	63%
Tax on receipt of dividend	NIL	NIL
Net available for reinvestment	65%	63%

Under the partnership structure there are no tax consequences when profits are distributed to the partners, since all profits have been fully taxed in the hands of the corporate partners (Krisco and Brandi). However, in the case of Krisco Ltd. all partnership profits would be subject to the high rates of tax, as that company's small-business deduction had been used up from other sources, so a lesser amount of repatriated profits would be available for reinvestment purposes.

From Krisco's perspective, the percentage of new-venture profits available for reinvestment after repatriation is as shown next.

	Partnership	Corporation
First $300,000 of annual profits:		
Manufacturing	65%	82%
Non-manufacturing	63%	82%
Profits in excess of $300,000 annually:		
Manufacturing	65%	65%
Non-manufacturing	63%	63%

With respect to the return of the original capital invested, both structures have similar results in this particular situation.

Intuitively, without projecting cash flows over the next several years, it would appear that Krisco would prefer a partnership form of organization during the initial years in order to ensure immediate loss utilization, but would prefer the corporate form once the venture becomes profitable in order to gain an enhanced small-business deduction. If limited liability were not an issue, the conflicting preferences could be overcome by using the partnership in the early years and then incorporating when the venture becomes profitable. However, this would expose Krisco to full liability in the start-up years, when the risk perhaps is at its greatest. At the same time, the full utilization of losses results in a tax advantage that reduces that risk. This risk can be roughly quantified and compared with that of the corporate structure. For example, if Krisco invested $1,000,000 in the corporate structure and it failed, the after-tax cost of that loss would be $815,000, as previously calculated. If, on the other hand, Krisco chose the partnership and exposed itself to greater liability, it could lose approximately $1,294,000 and still be no worse off than if it had invested $1,000,000 in the corporate structure. This comparison is shown in the following table:

	Partnership	Corporation
Actual loss incurred	$1,294,000	$1,000,000
Related tax savings	(478,000)	(185,000)
Net after-tax cash loss	$ 815,000	$ 815,000

It is also worth noting that the tax savings for the partnership would be achieved annually as they occur, whereas the $185,000 tax saving on the corporate investment would be realized much later, when the venture is completely terminated. This analysis throws a completely different light on the liability issue and is very much worth remembering when assessing the overall risk of any venture. All in all, the partnership form of organization is worthy of serious consideration in spite of the liability issue.

To complete the analysis, each party should map the flow of funds into and out of the venture for each alternative and consider the timing differences by measuring the cash-flow impact in net present value terms. The profit returns for each investor will, of course, vary with the venture's need for funds for expansion and debt repayment.

To this point, the position of Brandi Ltd. has not been considered in detail. The available alternatives would not affect its cash flow in the same way they did that of Krisco Ltd. This is primarily owing to Brandi's extensive current-loss position, which effectively makes it a non-taxable entity for several years. The partnership allocation of losses simply adds to Brandi's loss position; as a result, that entity achieves no real benefit in the early years from the partnership format, except that such a format gives it direct ownership of the losses for possible future use.

With respect to the profitable years, Brandi would benefit from the partnership structure, as the allocated profits could be used to offset the major losses that are being carried forward, thereby minimizing tax on the new venture's operations and reducing the risk of the losses expiring. This, of course, is in direct conflict with what Krisco wants, which is to incorporate the profit years in order to gain access to the small-business deduction. In addition, the fact that Brandi's financial strength is significantly less than Krisco's increases the former's concern about unlimited liability, which is a characteristic of the partnership format. Brandi would favour a partnership format that includes a holding company as the direct partner. In the early years the losses locked into the holding company would be of little consequence, in view of Brandi's existing non-taxable position. As the new venture became profitable and the risk of failure was reduced, Brandi and the holding company could easily be amalgamated, which would permit the future allocated profits to be offset directly against Brandi's losses.

In the case study presented here, the participants were private corporations; however, the alternatives considered in the analysis are not restricted to the private corporate sector. Public companies can also give serious consideration to the standard partnership form of organization for ventures involving other participants. In such circumstances the same four basic points of consideration are also relevant; the analysis would be similar to that for Krisco and Brandi, except that the small-business deduction would be omitted as a factor.

V. Summary and Conclusion

The partnership structure is an alternative to the corporate structure for ventures involving multiple owners. Both structures have the same objectives but receive dramatically different tax treatment. The tax treatment of a partnership can be summarized as follows:

1. A partnership is not a separate entity for tax purposes and is not directly subject to tax on income.

2. Income earned by a partnership is allocated for tax purposes and included as income of the partners. Income is deemed to have been allocated to the partners on the last day of the partnership's fiscal year, whether or not those profits were distributed.

3. The profits allocated to partners retain the source and characteristics of the income earned by the partnership.

4. Losses incurred by the partnership are also allocated to the partners and included in each partner's determination of income.

5. The actual distribution of profits to the partners is not taxable income.

6. Although the partnership is not a taxable entity, the partnership *interest* is considered capital property, and its disposition by the owner can result in a capital gain or loss.

The above tax treatment is significantly different from the one given corporations, whose profits are taxed first as corporate income and a second time in the hands of the individual shareholders after distribution. Consequently, both the amount of tax and the timing of the payment of tax are different for each of the two structures.

When contemplating an investment with other partners, the advantages and disadvantages of a partnership should be compared with those of a corporation on the basis of four fundamental issues:

1. What is the annual tax cost on profits earned by the new venture?

2. How and when can operating losses of the new venture be used for tax purposes?

3. What is the maximum after-tax loss to the investor (partner or shareholder) if the investment is a complete failure?

4. What is the tax cost, if any, of repatriating profits of the new venture?

The partnership, as an alternative to the corporation, is a dynamic alternative that can be viable for all business entities regardless of their size.

Reading List

Income Tax Act References

	Section
General rules for partnerships	96(1)
Additions to cost base (partnership interest)	53(1)(e)
Deductions from cost base (partnership interest)	53(2)(c)
Negative adjusted cost base	40(3), 40(2.1)
Contribution of property to a partnership	97(1)
Election by partners—rules	97(2)
Disposition of partnership property	98(1)
Deemed proceeds	98(2)
Partnership ceases to exist—rules	98(3), (4)
When partnership business is carried on as a sole proprietorship	98(5)
Continuation of a predecessor partnership by a new partnership	98(6)
Agreement to share income to reduce or postpone tax otherwise payable	103(1), (2)
Agreement to share income in unreasonable proportions	103(1.1)
Transfer of property to a corporation from a partnership	85(2), (3)
Specified partnership income (loss) of a Canadian-controlled private corporation	125(7)(f), (g)

Canada Customs and Revenue Agency Publications

IT-90	What is a partnership?
IT-138R	Computation and flow-through of partnership income.
IT-338R2	Partnership interests—impact on adjusted cost base resulting from the admission or retirement of a partner.
IT-353R2	Partnership interests—some adjustments to cost base.
IT-231R2	Partnership—partners not dealing at arm's length (unreasonable allocation of income).

IT-232R2	Losses, including limited partnership losses—their composition and deductibility.
IT-278R2	Death of a partner or retired partner.
IT-413R	Election by members of a partnership under subsection 97(2)— transfer of assets to a partnership.
IT-471R	Merger of partnerships.
IT-378R	Winding up of a partnership (includes discussion on conversion of a partnership to a corporation).
IT-73R5	The small-business deduction—income from an active business, etc. (as it applies to a partnership of corporations, see paragraphs 20–21).

Major Court Decisions

Woodlin Developments Ltd. v. MNR, (TCC), 86 DTC 116—Distinction between a joint venture and a partnership.

Marion Estates Ltd. v. MNR, 90 DTC 1369—Distinction between co-ownership and partnership.

Stursberg v. MNR, 90 DTC 1159—Capital contribution by new partner and withdrawal by another partner.

Other Publications

Bernstein, J., "The Use of Partnerships in Private Corporate Planning," Corporate Management Tax Conference (1994), Canadian Tax Foundation, p. 8.1.

McQuillan and Thomas, *Understanding the Taxation of Partnerships*, CCH Canadian, 1991.

Witterich, R., "The Partnership as a Modern Business Vehicle," 1989 Conference Report on Proceedings of the 41st Tax Conference, Canadian Tax Foundation, pp. 21:1–25.

Review Questions

1. Identify three "non-taxable entities." Does "non-taxable" mean that the income earned by these entities is not subject to tax? Explain.

2. What is a standard partnership, and how is it different from a joint venture? and from a co-ownership?

3. What types of entities can be partners in a standard partnership? Does each partner in a partnership have to be the same type of entity? Explain.

4. Must each partner in a partnership contribute an amount of capital that is proportionate to its profit-sharing ratio? Explain.

5. To what extent is each partner liable for the obligations of the partnership? Compare this with the obligations of shareholders in a corporation.

6. How can a partner that has a substantial net worth organize its investment in a partnership so that its liability exposure is limited?

7. "The amount of tax paid on partnership profits depends on the nature of the separate partners and not on the nature of the partnership itself." Explain.

8. "Profits of a partnership are included in the income of the partners only when those profits are distributed to them." Is this statement true? Explain.

9. A partnership may be preferable to a corporation when the business venture is new and expects to incur losses in its early years. Explain why.

10. When net income from business for tax purposes is being determined, the timing of certain expense deductions is discretionary. For example, a taxpayer may claim all of, or some of, or none of the available capital cost allowance. Similarly, the deduction of certain reserves is discretionary. In a partnership structure, is the deduction of discretionary items decided by the partnership as a whole, or can each partner make a separate decision on its proportionate share? What conflict can arise as a result?

11. "Partnership profits or losses allocated to the partners retain their source and characteristics." What does this mean? How does this compare with the manner in which a corporation's profits or losses affect its shareholders?

12. On distribution, for tax purposes, accumulated partnership profits to partners are treated differently from accumulated corporate profits to shareholders. How?

13. What is a partnership interest? What type of property is it considered to be for tax purposes?

14. The value of the shares of a corporation changes when corporate profits or losses are accumulated, and when corporate assets change in value. The value of a partnership interest changes in exactly the same manner. Explain how the tax treatment applied to the sale of a partnership interest differs radically from that applied to the sale of corporate shares.

15. Explain the general tax implications, both to the partner and to the partnership, when a partner transfers property to the partnership that has appreciated in value beyond its cost amount. Is there an alternative treatment? Explain.

16. "A Canadian-controlled private corporation that earns $100,000 from its own active business plus an additional $200,000 from its 50% interest in a business partnership is entitled to apply the small-business deduction to its combined income of $300,000." Is this statement correct? Explain.

17. Identify four factors that managers must consider when deciding whether a new business venture with other parties will be organized as a partnership or as a corporation.

18. An investor may be able to afford to lose more money from a failed business venture if it is organized as a partnership rather than a corporation. Explain why.

Problems

Problem One

George Gingero is a one-third partner in Sweet Tooth, a restaurant that specializes in desserts. Gingero maintains a full-time job and earns a salary of $80,000. In the evenings and on weekends he works at the restaurant, as do the other partners.

The partnership year end is December 31. The financial results for 20X1 are provided in the table below.

Other information is provided below.

1. The amortization expense relates to the restaurant's equipment. At the end of the previous year the undepreciated capital cost of the class 8 equipment was $30,000, and of the class 43 equipment was $20,000.

2. During the year, Gingero received cash distributions of $10,000 from the partnership. In addition, the donations paid by the partnership were designated one-third to each partner.

3. One of the other partners recently offered to buy Gingero's partnership interest for $100,000. Gingero refused the offer, as he plans to continue working in the restaurant. At the end of 20X0 the partnership's accountant had informed him that the adjusted cost base of his partnership interest was $40,000.

Sales		$600,000
Cost of sales		210,000
Gross profit		390,000
Expenses:		
Salaries	150,000	
Rent	50,000	
Maintenance	8,000	
Amortization	12,000	
Donations	3,000	
Supplies	10,000	
Other	17,000	250,000
		140,000
Other income:		
Capital gain on sale of previous franchise		60,000
Dividends from Canadian corporation		4,000
Net income		$204,000

Required:

1. Calculate Gingero's net income for tax purposes for the 20X1 taxation year.

2. If Gingero had sold his partnership interest at the end of the current year for $100,000, how would his net income for tax purposes have changed?

3. Would it be worthwhile for Gingero to set up a corporation to be the partner in the restaurant? Explain.

4. If Gingero sells his partnership interest in Sweet Tooth to his own corporation, how will this affect his tax position?

Problem Two

Conquest Enterprises is a partnership that operates a smallwares wholesale firm. The partners are Cameron Traders Ltd. and Kando Construction Ltd. They share profits equally.

The partnership business has improved this year, and it is anticipated that by year end, profits before capital cost allowance will amount to $420,000 (compared with $190,000 the previous year). During the year the partnership acquired two additional delivery vehicles for $80,000. At the end of the previous year the partnership held the following property:

Class	Undepreciated capital cost
1	$800,000
8	100,000
10	100,000

Cameron Traders is a Canadian-controlled private corporation owned by George Cameron. The company operates an import/export business and earns trading commissions from a wide range of customers. For years it has earned a modest profit ($30,000 last year, after a reasonable salary to Cameron). However, his years of hard work establishing international contacts have finally paid off, and he expects this year's profits to be $250,000, and future years' profits to continue at least at this level.

Kando Construction is owned by Sheila Hampton. Kando has suffered major losses over the past years even after earnings have been allocated from the partnership. Currently, the company has unused non-capital losses of $600,000, of which $300,000 were incurred five years ago. The company appears to have its losses under control and is not in serious financial difficulty, although cash flow has been tight.

The partnership has been seeking to acquire a new warehouse building. Coincidentally, Hampton personally owns a warehouse property, which will be vacated by its tenant in six months. The property has appreciated in value and is worth $80,000 more than its original cost. Hampton has claimed capital cost allowance of $30,000 over the years. She is willing to sell the property to the partnership, as she could use the cash to strengthen Kando. However, she needs all the cash she can get and is not anxious to pay tax on the sale.

Required:

1. Determine the minimum and maximum business income for tax purposes that might be earned by the partnership (Conquest Enterprises) for the current year and allocated to the partners.

2. Which amount of income from the partnership would Cameron Traders and Kando prefer? Explain.

3. Estimate the tax liability of Cameron Traders for the current year.

4. If you owned Cameron Traders, would you recommend that Conquest Enterprises be incorporated? Explain.

5. How would the incorporation of the partnership affect Kando?

6. What can Hampton do to avoid tax on the sale of the warehouse property to the part-nership and generate the maximum amount of cash to help Kando?

Problem Three

Samborski Enterprises Ltd. is a successful Canadian-controlled private corporation operating a plumbing contracting business. The company consistently earns pre-tax profits in excess of $600,000. The profits are typically used to expand the company's own business or to buy out smaller businesses in the same industry. Usually these acquisitions have been successful; they have provided after-tax returns on investment of between 14% and 20%.

Three years ago the company invested $300,000 in common shares of TQ Ltd. This represented a 30% interest in that company. The other shares were acquired by two other investors. Samborski and the other shareholders created TQ to manufacture a new type of pipe that was supposed to revolutionize the plumbing industry. The venture was not successful, and the shareholders decided to shut down the operations. After the assets were sold and the liabilities were paid, there was nothing left for the shareholders. Over the three years, the company had lost $1,000,000, as follows:

Year 1	$ 500,000
Year 2	300,000
Year 3 (including the sale of assets)	200,000
	$1,000,000

The shareholders were relieved to close the business before further losses were incurred, as they would have had to either contribute additional capital or declare bankruptcy. They have instructed their lawyer to wind up the corporation.

At the time the venture was organized, the investors had considered structuring the venture as a partnership. But after only a brief discussion, the idea was rejected because of the potential risk associated with the venture; as well, none of the parties had wanted exposure beyond their initial investment.

Required:

1. Considering that Samborski Enterprises invested $300,000 in share capital three years ago, what after-tax cash loss has it suffered from this investment? Determine the loss on a net present value basis.

2. How much would Samborski Enterprises have lost if it had chosen a partnership structure for TQ rather than a corporate structure?

3. "If the partnership structure had been used, the new venture could have lost even more money and Samborski Enterprises would have been no worse off than if it had used the corporate structure and lost $1,000,000." Is this statement true? If it is, how much would the amount of this extra loss have been?

4. Assume the following scenario: TQ was organized as a partnership, but to ensure limited liability, Samborski Enterprises organized a subsidiary corporation, to which it contributed capital of $300,000; the subsidiary corporation then invested the $300,000 as a partner of TQ. Explain how Samborski Enterprises might have utilized its $300,000 loss, and calculate the amount of its after-tax cash loss in a manner similar to that used in 1 and 2 above.

Case   **Dart and Silver**

Heather Dart owns 100% of the shares of Dart Ltd., a Canadian-controlled private corporation. The company operates a successful printing business that produces advertising flyers and catalogues. Dart Ltd. has retained earnings of $1.5 million and earned profits of $500,000 in the previous year.

David Silver is the editor of a local newspaper and earns a substantial salary. For years, he has envisioned publishing a high-quality magazine that would capture the interests of western Canadians. Silver has had many discussions with Heather Dart, and they have decided to develop and publish *People West.* Silver will quit his job and work full-time on the new venture, for which he will be paid a good salary. Heather Dart will not work for the venture but will provide production advice, especially in the start-up phase.

The new venture will require owners' capital of $600,000. As the venture will be shared on a 50/50 basis, both parties must provide $300,000 at the outset. This is not a problem for Heather Dart, as she has decided that Dart Ltd. will provide her share of the capital and will be the owner of her portion. But obtaining the $300,000 is not so easy for Silver: he has personal savings of only $280,000 and will have to obtain a second mortgage on his house for the balance.

The venture will require, in addition to the owners' capital, financing of $400,000, which a local bank has agreed to advance.

A financial advisor has developed financial projections after discussions with David Silver. These are summarized in the following table:

Year	Income (loss)
1	$(200,000)
2	(120,000)
3	80,000
4	250,000
5	400,000

In addition, Heather Dart has asked that the financial advisor prepare a report outlining alternative organization structures for the venture.

Required:

As the financial advisor, prepare the report.

Chapter 16   Limited Partnerships and Joint Ventures

While the standard partnership is the primary alternative to the corporation, both limited partnerships and joint ventures are also viable alternatives in certain circumstances. In particular, limited partnerships are becoming more common now that the limited partnership statutes have been revised in most provinces.

The tax treatment of limited partnerships and joint ventures is very similar to that of standard partnerships, which was described in detail in Chapter 15. However, both structures have special attributes that distinguish them from standard partnerships. It is these unique aspects that make the limited partnership and the joint venture attractive alternatives in certain types of ventures that involve a group of investors.

This chapter defines the limited partnership and joint venture entities, describes the unique aspects of their tax treatment, and discusses their appropriate use and their impact on cash-flow decision making.

I. The Limited Partnership

A. Definition of Limited Partnership

The limited partnership is a formal entity created, as are corporations, by legal statute. In general terms, a limited partnership has all the attributes of a standard partnership except that certain partners are entitled, by law, to enjoy limited liability.

To qualify as a limited partnership, the entity must have two separate classes of partners —*general* partners and *limited* partners.[1]

The general partner is fully liable for the obligations of the partnership and is responsible for managing its business affairs. In effect, the general partner is treated in the same fashion as a partner in a standard partnership.

The limited partners, on the other hand, are responsible for the obligations of the limited partnership only to the extent of their investment in the partnership.[2] Therefore, a limited partner who has contributed $10,000 of capital to the partnership can lose no more than $10,000 in the venture, whatever the financial condition of the partnership.

In order to qualify as a limited partner, that partner must not take part in the management and control of the business carried on by the partnership. By definition, the limited partner is a passive investor; the general partner is an active participant.

A basic limited-partnership structure is diagrammed in Exhibit 16-1. Each partner, whether general or limited, can be either an individual or a corporation. Notice that the limited partnership has been capitalized with $40,000 of partner contributions, of which $30,000 came from the limited partners and $10,000 from a single general partner. Although the general partner has invested only $10,000, it is, nevertheless, responsible for the full obligations of the limited partnership's business in the event of financial failure. As this imposes a substantial risk to the general partner, it is common for that partner to

Exhibit 16-1:
Limited-Partnership
Structure

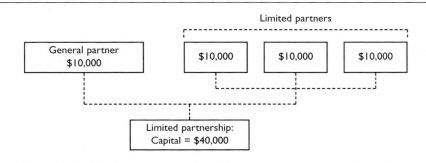

1 McQuillan and Thomas, *Understanding the Taxation of Partnerships*, CCH Canadian, 1991.
2 ITA 96(2.4); IT-232R3.

arrange its affairs so as to limit that risk. It usually does this by establishing a separate corporation with a limited amount of capital to act as the general partner.

For example, consider the structure in Exhibit 16-2. Corporation 1, which has a net worth of $500,000, has entered into a limited partnership as a general partner by creating a subsidiary corporation to act as that general partner. The subsidiary, Corporation 2, is capitalized with only $10,000 of share capital and uses those funds to purchase a standard partnership interest. Although Corporation 2, as the general partner, is fully liable for the debts of the partnership, it can only lose $10,000 because it is itself a limited liability corporation.

In effect, the limited partnership described in Exhibit 16-2 is a complete limited-liability entity similar to a corporation, in that both the limited partners and the general partner are fully protected. In substance, a limited partnership is a partnership with limited liability for its partners.

B. Tax Treatment of Partnership Income and Losses

A limited partnership, like a standard partnership, is not a taxable entity. Instead, the net income or loss of the limited partnership is allocated for tax purposes directly to the partners, in accordance with their profit-sharing ratio.[3] The limited partnership simply acts as a conduit.

Income or loss is allocated to the partners at the end of each fiscal year (normally December 31 if one or more of the partners is an individual), and included in their income whether or not an actual cash distribution has been made. If, at some later time, the accumulated profits are distributed to the partners, those profits are not taxed again. The limited partnership's income is, therefore, taxed only once—at the partner level—unlike a corporation's income, on which two levels of tax are imposed.

Exhibit 16-2:
Limiting the General Partner's Liability

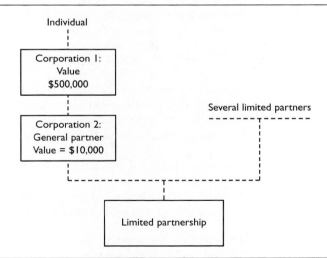

Income allocated by the limited partnership retains its source and characteristics. Accordingly, active business income earned in the partnership is allocated as active business income to the partners. This is so even though the limited partners are, by definition, passive partners that are not active in the management of the limited partnership's business.[4] The tax treatment of a limited partnership's income and losses therefore depends on the tax position of each separate partner. If the partner is a corporation, the active business

---

3   ITA 96(1).
4   ITA 125(7)(f); IT-73R5.

income is eligible for the small-business deduction, subject to the limitations described in Chapter 15. If the partner has losses accumulated from other sources, the partnership profits allocated to that partner can be offset against those losses.

A special restriction applies to the use of losses allocated under the limited-partnership structure. Notwithstanding the amount of losses allocated to them, limited partners are entitled to claim those losses *only* to the extent of their investment in the partnership.[5] For example, a limited partner who has invested $30,000 in the limited partnership is entitled to claim losses for tax purposes only up to a maximum of $30,000, which is the amount that he or she is at risk for. This restriction is not imposed on the general partners because they do not have limited risk.

C. Impact on Decision Making

The limited partnership, like the standard partnership, cannot be analyzed in isolation when a business structure is being chosen for a new venture involving several parties. Instead, it must be compared with the possible alternatives—a separate corporation owned by a group of shareholders, or a standard partnership as described in Chapter 15.

As was the case in previous discussions, the decision maker's goal is to develop a structure that will minimize the cash requirements to start up the venture and maximize the return of cash back to the investor for reinvestment. The following considerations are appropriate:

1. What is the annual tax cost on profits earned by the new venture?

2. How and when can operating losses of the new venture be used for tax purposes?

3. What is the maximum after-tax cash loss to the investor if the new venture should fail?

4. What is the tax cost, if any, of repatriating profits of the new venture?

Each of these considerations was reviewed in detail in the previous chapter, so they will not be re-examined in this chapter except to the extent that they have a bearing on the unique aspects of the limited partnership. Below, the limited partnership is compared with both the standard partnership and the corporation.

1. Limited Partnership versus Standard Partnership

The limited partnership is different from the standard partnership in three ways:

1. Some of the partners in a limited partnership have limited liability; all of the partners in a standard partnership are fully exposed to the partnership's obligations.

2. A limited partnership must have some partners (the limited partners) who are passive investors and do not participate in management. The standard partnership does not face this restriction.

3. In a limited partnership, the use of tax losses allocated to the passive limited partners is restricted to a maximum of the "at risk" amount, whereas all partners in a standard partnership can use the full amount of losses allocated.

The above differences have a significant impact on a new entity's ability to attract investment capital. Because of the unlimited-liability feature of the standard partnership,

---

5   ITA 96(2.1) to (2.7); IT-138R (paragraph 20).

that structure tends to attract partners who want to participate actively in management in order to protect their investment and gain full utilization of the partnership losses if those should occur. While standard partnerships can and do attract passive investors in spite of the risk, such investors tend to be few in number, and of the type who can afford the related risk owing to their substantial wealth. It is rare that a standard partnership can gather capital from a large number of small investors, each of whom invests a small amount for a minor partnership interest, because the risk of unlimited liability is too great.

In comparison, the limited partnership provides broader access to sources of capital. Since limited partners are passive investors with limited liability, the partnership base can be divided into a larger number of smaller-sized units. Since small investors can participate in the entity with limited risk, the venture can tap a whole new source of capital.

2. Limited Partnership versus Separate Corporation

The tax impact on cash flow from establishing a corporation rather than a limited partnership is similar to the impact discussed in Chapter 15 in relation to standard partnerships. However, this issue is briefly re-examined below in the context of limited partnerships, in particular as it pertains to the limited partners, who receive special treatment.

• **Loss utilization** New ventures often suffer start-up losses as part of their development. In order to fund such losses, the venture must have a sufficient capital base. For example, assume a new venture requires $10,000 of capital from a passive investor, of which $6,000 will be used to acquire new-venture assets and provide working capital and $4,000 will be used to fund the anticipated start-up losses. Whether a corporation or a limited partnership is used, the new entity must receive $10,000 in absolute-dollar contributions.

However, the amount of cash required by the passive investor to make the $10,000 contribution is different under each structure. If the investor (assumed to be an individual) makes the $10,000 contribution to a limited partnership, the new venture will have its $10,000, but the cash cost to the investor may be only $8,200, calculated as follows:

Cash contributed	$10,000
Tax savings in year 1 from allocation of $4,000 loss	
(45% × $4,000)	(1,800)
Net cash required in year 1	$ 8,200

The flow-through of the venture's start-up loss to the passive investor permits an immediate use of the loss; the resulting tax savings are enjoyed by the investor rather than by the new venture itself. If a corporation had been utilized instead, the investor's cash requirements would have been the $10,000, as the loss incurred would have been locked into the company, and unusable until the venture became profitable.

This makes limited partnerships extremely attractive to small passive investors, in that less cash is required to join in the venture, which makes it easier to participate. This, along with the limited-liability feature and the option to utilize losses immediately, makes it easier for a new venture to raise capital to get the project started. (Immediate loss utilization is itself a source of capital.)

• **Distribution of profits** A corporation's profit distributions are taxed in a different manner than those of a limited partnership. This is particularly significant when the recipients consist of a large number of passive investors. In most cases many of those investors will be individuals who are subject to high marginal tax rates. Under the corporate structure, the corporation and the shareholders are automatically subject to two levels of tax when profits are distributed. When the corporation is a public company, or a Canadian-controlled private corporation earning business income not subject to the small-business deduction, double taxation will occur as described in previous chapters. As indicated in Chapter 13, a Canadian-controlled private corporation can overcome this problem by paying the shareholder in the form of a deductible salary or bonus. However, this option is not available when the shareholder is a passive investor and has no basis for receiving this form of payment.

Under the limited-partnership structure, no double taxation can occur when profits are allocated to individual passive investors. They are simply taxed once at the partner level. While this structure avoids double taxation automatically, it may present cash-flow problems to the limited partner if profits are allocated but no cash distribution is made. However, most limited-partnership agreements require that some portion of profits be distributed whenever taxable income is allocated.

Limited partnerships are known primarily for their ability to flow losses through to the passive investors; the benefit that double taxation is avoided when the venture becomes profitable is often overlooked. Obviously, the elimination of double taxation will, in the long run, enhance the investors' returns.

• **Capital structures** One of the major features of a corporation is that it can raise equity capital or debt capital from the general public. It can raise debt capital by issuing bonds, debentures, or mortgages; or share capital by issuing a wide variety of classes of shares—common or preferred, voting or non-voting, and so on. This feature, along with the feature of limited liability, is the reason the corporation is the primary business entity. This is so even though investing in a corporation may result in double taxation, and investors may find it difficult to utilize any losses.

The limited partnership also provides considerable flexibility when it comes to raising funds from the public. Limited partnership units offer limited liability to equity investors. In addition, those units can be divided into a number of different classes, each of which has different rights relating to the sharing of profits and losses. In effect, limited-partnership units can be designed with the same flexibility as corporate shares, with some unit holders having preference over others. Similarly, the limited partnership can also issue debt securities such as debentures and mortgages.

A major distinction between the corporation and the limited partnership exists with respect to the feature of limited liability for the equity investors. Limited liability in a corporation is automatic, whereas in a limited partnership it is granted only if certain conditions exist as specified by the limited-partnership statutes of the province in question. One result is that there is a risk that the limited-liability feature may be lost if the partnership later stops complying with those conditions. This has restricted the use of limited partnerships as an alternative to the corporation.

D. Uses of the Limited Partnership

The limited partnership has a wide range of business applications. In general terms, it can be used in any venture that requires a significant amount of equity capital from outside passive investors. It is especially valuable where the venture anticipates losses, as such losses can be flowed through to the passive investors to create immediate tax savings that minimize the risk of their investment.

1. High-Risk Ventures

The limited partnership is extremely valuable as a means of raising capital for a high-risk venture. Ventures such as oil and gas exploration and drilling, mining exploration, and scientific research and development all have the following common elements:

• A high risk of failure.

• A need for a significant amount of initial capital.

• A likelihood of substantial losses in the early years.

- If ultimately successful, a long wait before profits are realized.

- Special incentives with respect to the timing of deductions for tax purposes.

It is difficult for the initiator of a high-risk project to raise capital by debt financing. A limited partnership enables the venture to raise equity capital from a large number of investors, who are provided with the security of limited liability and who can quickly recover a large portion of their investment by immediately using the venture's tax losses.

In addition, the initiator can set up a separate limited partnership for each separate project. In this type of structure, different investors can participate in either some of the projects or all of them. The initiator would participate in and manage each limited partnership as the general partner.

2. Medium-Risk Ventures

While medium-risk ventures have greater access to borrowed funds, this access may be restricted until a reasonable track record is established. The accessibility of borrowed funds may be further diminished if the initiator does not have sufficient capital or collateral and the venture anticipates losses in its first few years of operation.

Consider, for example, a situation where the initiator wants to expand a chain of hotels rapidly but cannot provide all of the necessary capital. Each new hotel will probably incur start-up losses and, as well, will have a high capital cost allowance base in the building and hotel furniture and equipment. The available capital cost allowance (see Chapter 6) will remain unused unless it can be passed on to the investors. In situations like this one, a limited partnership is especially attractive to the passive investor, and as a result there is a greater potential for raising funds.

3. Low-Risk Ventures

Low-risk ventures have substantial access to borrowed funds and therefore require less equity capital. In addition, they often do not suffer any substantial initial losses. Consequently, the flow-through of losses is not an important issue. Because of all this, limited partnerships are not often used in low-risk ventures. However, one should consider that the limited partnership does not lead to double taxation. Therefore, highly profitable low-risk ventures that require outside equity capital should give serious consideration to the limited-partnership structure, since it increases the after-tax returns to the investor, who for this reason may be willing to pay a higher price for the security.

For example, consider the situation in which a corporation must raise additional equity capital to fund an expansion. The anticipated corporate profits are $1,000,000 annually, but to achieve them, the existing owners must give up 40% of the share equity to new investors. Assume the corporation's tax rate is 37% and the individual investor's tax rate is 45%. The ultimate after-tax return to the new investor under the corporate structure can be compared with the return under a limited-partnership structure, as follows:

	Corporation	Limited partnership
Investors' share of profits	$400,000	$400,000
Tax to the business entity	$148,000	NIL
Tax to the investor	76,000	180,000
	$224,000	$180,000
After-tax return	$176,000	$220,000
Combined tax rate	56%	45%

Under the corporate structure, the company pays 37% tax on its earnings and the shareholder incurs additional tax either when dividends are distributed or when the shares are sold at a capital gain that reflects the undistributed profits. Under the limited-partnership structure, only the investor is subject to tax on the venture's profits, with no further tax when profits are distributed. If the limited partner sold the partnership interest before profits were distributed, no additional capital gain would result on the value increase pertaining to the undistributed profits (see Chapter 15). Keep in mind that because the limited partnership pays no tax but shifts this burden to the investors, a policy would need to be established that distributes a portion of the venture's profits to provide cash to investors to meet their personal tax liability.

The difference in results in the above example is dramatic. If the investors are willing to accept an after-tax return of $176,000 under the corporate structure (being 40% of the venture's profits), they may also be willing to accept the same after-tax return from a limited partnership, as the risk factor has not changed. To receive a $176,000 after-tax return from the limited partnership, they need share in only $320,000 of the venture's profits ($320,000 − 45% tax = $176,000). Therefore, under the limited-partnership structure, the existing owners would be required to give up only 32% of their equity, compared with 40% under the corporate structure.

E. Example of a Business Expansion Using a Limited Partnership

The following case situation is presented to demonstrate the significant impact of the tax variable when capital is raised by means of a limited partnership. The facts have been simplified in order to stress the importance of the organizational structure and its effect on return on investment.

The Problem

Diamond Ltd. is a Canadian-controlled private corporation that owns and operates two successful Toronto restaurants. The company is wholly owned by one individual, who provides general management services to both restaurants. The owner wants to develop several new restaurants in Toronto. However, Diamond Ltd. has limited resources that will not permit rapid expansion to several new locations simultaneously. A decision has been made to expand as quickly as possible by raising additional equity from passive investors.

Projected financial information for each new location is summarized in the following table:

Land, buildings, and equipment:	
Cost	$800,000
Mortgage financing	(600,000)
Net cash requirement	$200,000
Permanent working capital	$ 50,000
Initial opening costs:	
Cutlery, tableware, glasses, menus, staff training,	
testing, and opening advertising	$200,000
Operating projections:	
Opening year (loss)	($100,000)
2nd year (loss)	($ 50,000)
3rd year (break even)	–0–
4th year (profit)	$ 30,000
5th year (profit)	$100,000

Based on the number of locations available, Diamond Ltd. can afford to contribute only $50,000 to each location. It is anticipated that each restaurant will eventually produce annual profits of $100,000.

The Organization Structure Used

The capital requirements for starting up each new location total $600,000, as follows:

Equity in building and equipment	$200,000
Working capital	50,000
Initial opening costs	200,000
Cash losses in first two years	150,000
	$600,000

In order to further reduce this requirement, a decision was made at the outset to lease the land, buildings, and equipment. An arrangement has since been made with a local developer, who will acquire the land, and construct and equip the building to specifications. The developer will then sell the building with a long-term lease to a group of real estate investors. The cash requirement for each location is thereby reduced to $400,000, which will be obtained as follows:

From Diamond Ltd.	$ 50,000
From outside investors	350,000
	$400,000

Initially, Diamond Ltd. attempted to attract one or two wealthy investors to provide the outside equity. This proved to be unacceptable, because in return for making a large investment, these investors demanded a high percentage of the ownership; as well, they wanted control over major operating decisions. While Diamond Ltd. is prepared to give up some equity, it is not prepared to give up decision-making control. Diamond Ltd. has decided to seek out a larger number of small investors in order to spread the risk and maintain control. After considering both a corporate structure and a limited-partnership structure, it has decided to organize a separate limited partnership for each new location. The details of each limited partnership are outlined below.

1. Contributions to the partnership are divided as follows:

General partner	$ 50,000	13%
Limited partners	350,000	87
	$400,000	100%

2. The general partner is a subsidiary corporation of Diamond Ltd. and is capitalized with $50,000. The general partner will manage the restaurant and receive a fee of 4% of gross sales. In addition, the general partner will receive a 30% share of the operating profits.

3. The limited partners constitute 35 separate units of $10,000 each ($10,000 × 35 = $350,000). An investor may purchase more than one unit if it wishes. The limited partners are entitled to share in 70% of the profits and will be allocated 70% of the losses.

4. The limited partnership must distribute at least 50% of its annual profits to the partners, although it is a stated objective that all profits will be distributed.

A diagram of the above structure is shown in Exhibit 16-3.

Analysis

Under the limited-partnership structure described above, Diamond Ltd. will achieve its objective—immediate expansion—without giving up management control and without giving up too much of its equity. As a general partner, Diamond retains full control of management decisions. Notice that it contributes only 13% of the total capital ($50,000) but receives 30% of future profits. As future profits are anticipated to be $100,000 annually, Diamond's share is $30,000, which represents a pre-tax return on investment of 60% ($30,000/$50,000).

On the assumption that Diamond Ltd. has substantial profits from its existing two restaurants, the profits allocated to the general-partner corporation will be taxed at the high corporate rate of 37%, as the small-business deduction limit will have been used up (see Chapter 13). If the new entity had been a corporation rather than a limited partnership, a new small-business deduction could have been created provided that Diamond Ltd. did not control the new corporation. Remember, however, that the initiator considered it important to retain control, so a small-business deduction base would not have been achieved under either structure.

By establishing a separate subsidiary corporation, capitalized with only $50,000, to act as the general partner, Diamond Ltd. limits its risk exposure in the new venture. Consequently, in the first two years of operations, the general partner will have no other income that can be used to offset the anticipated losses. However, after the risk of failure has lessened, the general-partner corporation can be wound up into Diamond Ltd. (see Chapter 14); this will transfer the losses to Diamond Ltd. for use against income from its operations.

From the outside investors' perspective, the limited-partnership structure is also attractive, even though they contribute 87% of the capital ($350,000) but share in only 70% of the profits. This is because they can use the allocated losses in the first two years of operations to create tax savings.

The amount of the loss allocated for tax purposes in the first year is magnified because of the initial opening costs. Recall that each venture will spend $200,000 for glasses, tableware, cutlery, advertising, and staff training. Even though these items are capital in nature (because they have a long-term benefit), they are, nevertheless, fully deductible for tax

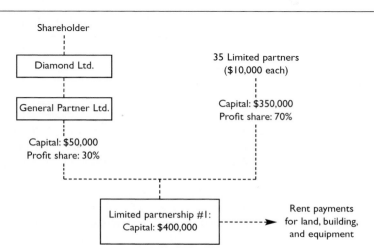

Exhibit 16-3:
Limited Partnership
Structure for Restaurant
Expansion

Shareholder

Diamond Ltd.

General Partner Ltd.

Capital: $50,000
Profit share: 30%

35 Limited partners
($10,000 each)

Capital: $350,000
Profit share: 70%

Limited partnership #1:
Capital: $400,000

Rent payments
for land, building,
and equipment

purposes in the first year. For example, the glasses, tableware, and cutlery are all class 12 assets that have a capital cost allowance rate of 100% (the one-half rule is not applicable—see Chapter 6). Therefore, the partnership's tax losses in years 1 and 2 will total $350,000, as follows:

Year 1:	
Opening costs	$200,000
Operating loss	100,000
	300,000
Year 2:	
Operating loss	50,000
	$350,000

Assuming that the limited partners are in a 45% tax bracket, the cash cost of their investment and subsequent cash returns will be as follows:

	Total	Per investor
Cash invested	$350,000	$10,000
Early tax savings:		
$350,000 × 70% × 45%	(110,000)	(3,150)
Net cash invested	$240,000	$ 6,850
Expected future profits:		
70% of $100,000	$ 70,000	$ 2,000
Pre-tax return on cash invested	29%	
After-tax return on cash investment:		
29% − 45% tax	16%	

In this way the limited-partnership structure permits the new venture to raise $350,000 from outside investors at a cash cost to those investors of only $240,000. If a corporate structure were used, the losses would not be available to the investors, and their cash requirements for acquiring the shares would be $350,000, or $10,000 per investor.

The limited partners receive a relatively high after-tax return because double taxation has been eliminated. Profits attributed to the passive investors are taxed only once, at their personal marginal tax rates. Under the corporate structure, double taxation would occur if Diamond Ltd. chose to maintain voting control over the new venture. For example, Diamond Ltd. might still own 30% of the equity shares (leaving 70% to the passive investors) but might issue itself a special class of shares having full voting authority over the passive investors. Consequently, Diamond Ltd. and the new corporation would be associated (see Chapter 13) and would have to share the small-business deduction. If the new venture were not entitled to a small-business deduction, the venture's profits would be first taxed at 43% and then taxed again on distribution to the passive shareholders. The after-tax return to the passive investors would, therefore, be considerably lower than under the limited partnership structure.

A final point: the limited partnership structure provides the lowest-downside risk to the passive investor. In the event of a complete business failure resulting from excessive operating losses, each limited partner stands to lose no more than $5,500 after tax ($10,000 less 45% tax savings = $5,500) because all operating losses up to $10,000 per investor are allocated as they occur. Under the corporate structure, the passive shareholder would recognize a loss from business failure as a capital loss when the shares were sold or the corporation became insolvent. As only one-half of a capital loss is recognized for tax purposes as an allowable business investment loss (see Chapter 8), each investor would stand to lose a maximum of $7,750 ($10,000 less 45% tax savings on ½ of $10,000 = $7,750).

In summary, the limited-partnership structure in the above example has the following benefits:

1. It permits the project initiator to raise capital by spreading the risk of the investment among a large number of small investors.

2. It permits the venture to raise $10,000 per unit holder at a real cost of only $6,850 to each investor, because of the way that start-up costs are allocated.

3. It provides limited liability to the passive investors, who face a downside risk of only $5,500 for each $10,000 invested.

4. It permits the initiator to give up a minimum of equity (70% of profits for 87% of the capital), because the elimination of double taxation combined with the lower cash cost of entry ($6,850 rather than $10,000) gives the passive investors an acceptably high after-tax return.

5. It permits the initiator to retain absolute management control of the venture as the general partner, who by law must have full responsibility for management decisions.

The limited partnership is a viable and appealing business structure. While it is more complicated to establish and maintain than a corporation, it also significantly improves after-tax cash flow and must be seriously considered for all business expansions that require capital from outside passive investors.

It should be pointed out that the preceding case was given only a superficial analysis. It was presented primarily to show the results of choosing the limited partnership structure. A proper review would involve comparing the after-tax cash flows under a proposed corporate structure with those under a limited-partnership structure, taking into account the timing of both loss utilization and the anticipated distributions to the investors.

II. Joint Ventures

The term "joint venture" is commonly and loosely used in the financial community in situations where partners join together to conduct a common business or investment activity. The term is often used even when the entity is actually a partnership or separate corporation. For tax purposes, the term must be confined to its narrow legal meaning.

A. Definition of Joint Venture

There is no legal statute governing joint ventures, nor does the *Income Tax Act* define the term or describe its specific tax treatment. Even so, joint ventures do exist and are recognized in Canada as a distinct type of entity.

A joint venture is not the same thing as a corporation or partnership. Generally, it can be described as "an association of two or more entities for a given limited purpose without the usual powers and responsibilities of a partnership."[6] What distinguishes a joint venture from a partnership is the concept of "limited purpose." A partnership usually represents an ongoing business relationship, whereas a joint venture is formed for the purpose of a single transaction or an activity of limited duration.

---

6 *Encyclopedic Dictionary of Business Finance*, Englewood Cliffs, New Jersey: Prentice-Hall, 1960; IT-90; McQuillan and Thomas, *Understanding the Taxation of Partnerships*, CCH Canadian, 1991.

Joint ventures are commonly found in the construction industry, when two or more construction companies, each having special expertise, join together to bid on and complete a single construction project. Joint ventures are also widely used in the resource industry for conducting exploration activities, as well as in research and development projects, and in the entertainment industry for financing concerts, plays, and movies.

In some cases limited-purpose or limited-duration projects are referred to as "syndicates." This term reflects the fact that there are many participants in the specific project. In this sense, a syndicate is usually a joint venture having a relatively large number of participants.

A joint venture is represented by a joint-venture agreement that describes the nature of each participant's role in the project and the extent to which each is entitled to the project's revenues and responsible for the project's expenses.

B. Tax Treatment of Joint Ventures

A joint venture, like a partnership, is not itself subject to tax. Instead, each member of the joint venture includes its share of the venture's revenues and expenses as part of its own taxable income or loss. The joint venture simply funnels its profits or losses directly to its separate members.

While the tax treatment of joint ventures is very similar to the tax treatment of partnerships, there are some distinguishing features.

One major difference relates to the method of calculating the income or loss that is allocated for tax purposes. A partnership, even though it is not a taxable entity, is considered to be a separate entity for the purposes of determining the income or loss that is allocated; the partnership itself determines the extent to which discretionary items are used, and each partner must then follow that approach. For example, the amount of capital cost allowance to be claimed is discretionary. Under the partnership structure, the partnership decides on the amount of capital cost allowance claimed in a particular year; each partner is subject to that decision whether it is in its interest or not (see Chapter 15). A joint venture, however, does *not* constitute a separate entity for determining income; because of this, each member of the joint venture is free to choose the amount of capital cost allowance on joint-venture property in accordance with its own particular needs.

The process for determining business income for tax purposes (see Chapter 5) permits a number of discretionary deductions aside from the one for capital cost allowance. These include reserves for doubtful debts, other types of reserves, and the amortization of eligible capital property. Up to a point, the taxpayer can also choose its preferred method of valuing inventory. Under a joint venture, which is an informal entity, each member can control the timing and use of these items.

Joint ventures are also distinguished by the way property is transferred into and out of the venture. A partnership is a formal, separate entity, and any transfer of assets into or out of it must result in a deemed disposition at fair market value, which may create taxable income. While certain elective provisions are available, they are not without complications and may not apply in certain situations. The joint venture, as an informal structure, has no such fair market value rules. Therefore, a joint venture can easily be created and dismantled without significant tax problems relating to the transferring of assets between the joint venture and its members.

Finally, the joint venture and the partnership differ in the way the small-business deduction is applied to the active business income allocated to the members. The amount of active business income earned by a partnership that is available for the low rate of corporate tax when allocated to corporate partners is restricted to $300,000 and divided among the partners according to their profit-sharing ratio (see Chapter 15). This means that a corporate partner owning a 50% interest in a partnership earning $600,000 is entitled to use the low rate of tax on only $150,000 of its share of the profits, even though its actual share of the profits is $300,000. Under a joint-venture structure, this limitation does not apply; the joint venturist corporation is entitled to use the full $300,000 small-business limit provided it has not been used for other sources of business income. Of course, this special tax treatment applies to smaller joint-venture activities only when the joint-venture member is a Canadian-controlled private corporation.

It is important to recognize that the joint-venture structure has limited use and a relatively narrow application. It does, however, create greater flexibility than a partnership and should be considered as an alternative when the nature of the project indicates that a joint venture may be permitted. In some cases it is unclear whether the specific venture qualifies as a joint venture or a partnership. In these circumstances the parties should be aware of the tax consequences in the event that CCRA rules that an intended joint venture is in fact a partnership.

III. Summary and Conclusion

This chapter has introduced two additional non-taxable business entities. The limited partnership and the joint venture, like the standard partnership, are not directly taxable on their income; rather, they funnel their operating results directly to the participants.

The limited partnership, like the corporation, is a formal organization having statute recognition. In general terms it has all of the attributes of a standard partnership except that certain partners have limited liability.

The limited partners are passive investors and do not participate in the management of the partnership's business. In turn, their liability is limited to the extent of their investment in the partnership. The general partners are fully liable for the debts of the partnership and have full responsibility for managing the partnership's business.

A limited partnership restricts the investors' liability and allows them to utilize the partnership's operating losses against their other sources of income. As a consequence, this type of entity is particularly attractive to an initiator who must raise capital from a large number of passive investors for a high-risk venture or for a venture that is expected to incur losses in its start-up years. Because a limited partnership flows losses through to the passive investors, those investors can immediately reduce their taxes and increase their cash flow. This substantially diminishes the amount of risk attached to the investment, which makes it easier for the project's initiator to raise capital from the marketplace.

Joint ventures have a restricted purpose. In effect, a joint venture is a partnership formed to complete a particular transaction or to carry on a limited activity for a specific period of time. It is often difficult to distinguish between a joint venture and a partnership. If it can be shown that an entity is, in fact, a joint venture, the partners in that entity will have greater flexibility when it comes to determining their taxable income and creating or demolishing the entity.

This chapter concludes Part Four of the text, which examined the secondary business structures that flow their income directly to the participants. In Chapter 1 it was indicated that while only individuals, corporations, and trusts are taxable entities, there are, nevertheless, five basic business structures—proprietorships, corporations, partnerships, limited partnerships, and joint ventures. We have now examined and compared all five in terms of their individual characteristics. All five differ dramatically regarding the amount and timing of the related tax. Consequently, choosing one structure over another will alter the related cash flows and have an impact on the ultimate return on investment.

The choice of business structure is a vital component in investment decisions. Before choosing the form of business organization, one must examine each option and anticipate its impact on future cash flows. A venture receives capital and invests it with a view to generating a profit, and ultimately must realize a cash return to the investor. By anticipating and following this path of activity, an informed analysis can be made of any proposed business structure, and structures can be created that best suit the particular situation.

All forms of organization except the proprietorship are applicable to both large and small business ventures. Ventures may differ in size, but all conform to similar tax concepts and require the same basic method of analysis.

The remaining chapters of this text examine specific types of business decisions. Very few new tax concepts will be introduced in these chapters, which apply the basic principles developed in Chapters 3 to 16 to the specific decisions under consideration.

Reading List

Income Tax Act References

	Section
General rules—for partnerships	96(1)
Limited partner (defined)	96(2.4)
Limited-partnership losses (at-risk amount)	96(2.1)
At-risk amount (defined)	96(2.2)
Limited-partnership losses	111(1)(e)
Limitation on deductibility (losses)	111(3)(a)
Specified partnership income	125(7)(f)
Partnership interest acquired by another person	96(2.3)

Canada Customs and Revenue Agency Publications

IT-73R5	The small-business deduction—income from an active business, etc. (allocation to limited partners).
IT-138R	Computation of flow-through of partnership income.
IT-232R2	Non-capital losses, net capital losses, etc., and limited partnership losses—their deductibility in computing taxable income.
IT-90	What is a partnership? (See paragraph 4 of IT-90 on joint ventures.)

Major Court Decision

General Construction Co. Ltd. v. MNR, 59 DTC 1169—Joint-venture status.

Other Publications

Dwyer, B., "A Comparison of the Income Tax Implications of Using Partnership or a Joint Venture," Corporate Management Tax Conference (1994), Canadian Tax Foundation, p. 10.1.

McQuillan and Thomas, *Understanding the Taxation of Partnerships*, CCH Canadian, 1991.

Witterick, R., "The Partnership as a Modern Business Vehicle," 1989 Conference Report on the Proceedings of the 41st Tax Conference, Canadian Tax Foundation, pp. 21:1–25.

Witterick, R., "Syndicated Acquisitions and Financing of a Business," 1990 Corporate Management Tax Conference, Canadian Tax Foundation, pp. 3:1–35.

Review Questions

1. A limited partnership consists of two general classes of partners. Identify these classes and describe the rights and obligations of each.

2. What can be done by a general partner to limit the extent of its obligations to the limited partnership?

3. "The tax treatment of limited partnership income and losses depends on the tax position of each partner." Explain.

4. What key factors distinguish the limited partnership from the standard partnership?

5. "A limited partnership provides broader access to sources of capital." Is this statement true? Explain.

6. Why is there less risk for the passive investor when a business venture is organized as a limited partnership rather than a corporation?

7. Why is it that the passive investor in a profitable business venture may receive a higher rate of return if the venture is organized as a limited partnership rather than a corporation?

8. What is a joint venture, and how is it different from a partnership?

9. With respect to the following, how does the tax treatment applied to a joint venture differ from that for a partnership?
   (a) Determination of capital cost allowance.
   (b) Active business income eligible for the small-business deduction.

Problems

Problem One

Georgio Enterprises is a limited partnership that operates a chain of family restaurants. The partnership was profitable from its inception and is now generating consistent annual pre-tax profits of $800,000.

The partnership includes 20 limited partners, each of whom contributed $60,000 when the venture began. The limited partners, as a group, share 40% of Georgio's annual profits. As the partnership has not expanded for several years, most of the annual profits are distributed to the partners within six months of the year end.

Most of the limited partners are individuals who are subject to a marginal personal tax rate of 45%.

Required:

1. What is the annual after-tax return on investment for each limited partner?

2. If Georgio Enterprises had been organized as a corporation, how would the rate of return to the investors now differ? Show calculations.

3. Assume that Georgio Enterprises (as a limited partnership) made an annual cash distribution sufficient only to cover each limited partner's tax liability, and retained

the balance for expansion. How would the investors' after-tax returns be affected by this, considering that in order to realize their investment they may have to sell their partnership interest for an increased value? Would the return on investment be different if Georgio were a corporation and paid no dividends?

Problem Two

A new business venture requires $600,000 of equity capital from passive investors in addition to the $400,000 of capital that is being provided by the initiator of the project. The $600,000 will be raised by selling 30 units for $20,000 each. The 30 unit holders will participate in 60% of the venture's profits.

It is anticipated that business operations will begin on October 1, 20X1. The entity will use a December 31 year end. Investors must contribute their funds on October 1, 20X1.

The equity capital of $1,000,000 will be used as shown below.

Working capital	$ 200,000
Equipment	300,000
Start-up costs, staff training, and opening advertising	200,000
Operating losses:	
20X1 (for the 3-month period)	250,000
20X2	50,000
	$1,000,000

The initiator is uncertain how to organize the new venture and is trying to decide between a separate corporation that will issue shares, and a limited partnership.

Required:

Which type of entity will make it easier for the initiator to raise the $600,000 of equity capital from passive investors? Explain, using a single investor as an example.

Cases

Case One   Contesso Travel Inns Ltd.

Contesso Travel Inns Ltd. is a successful Canadian-controlled private corporation that owns and operates a small chain of eight hotels in western Canada. The hotels offer high-quality lodging at economy rates and provide only limited services to their guests.

Contesso has succeeded because of its unique approach to the lodging industry and its strong hotel-management expertise. The company has designed and constructed all of its existing units—in fact, a sister corporation owned by the same shareholders (Contesso Developments Ltd.) maintains a small staff whose sole function is to develop new hotels. Contesso Developments has made a profit on each of the eight hotels it has developed over the past five years.

Contesso's success has been noticed in the hotel industry, and a number of similar hotels have sprung up across the country. The executives of Contesso realize that a race is on that will see a number of other companies competing for the most suitable sites for expansion. They estimate that within eight years, the number of remaining quality sites will decline considerably as more hotels are developed across the country.

Contesso seriously considered going public and raising a large amount of capital to embark on a major expansion program. However, it rejected this proposal because it would have had to give up a significant percentage of its equity and because it could not project a realistic expansion plan in view of the increasing competition. At the same time, the company cannot expand rapidly while still owning each new hotel, as each unit requires more than $2,000,000 in equity capital, as well as mortgage financing.

Contesso, therefore, has decided to concentrate on its two strengths—hotel management and hotel development—and to permit outside investors to own each unit.

The expansion plan is as follows:

- Contesso will identify and secure the right to acquire suitable sites.

- The equity requirement for each new hotel is approximately $2,000,000. This will be obtained for each project by the issuing of 200 ownership units to private investors. Each investor may acquire any number of the 200 units. Contesso will receive a fee for organizing the investors and issuing the ownership units.

- Contesso Developments will develop the hotels and assist with the acquisition of all equipment. In addition, the company will arrange mortgage financing for a fee.

- Each hotel will be managed by Contesso under a long-term contract (12 years) in exchange for a fee of 5% of the hotel's gross revenue.

Contesso's executives are satisfied that this plan will result in rapid expansion and, as well, provide their company with significant income from management fees and development profits. Also, after the expansion program is complete, the company will be in a solid position to acquire ownership of the hotels if the outside investors wish to sell.

Each new hotel will be sold to a different investor group in a different city, and the company executives are uncertain about which organization structure to choose. Each new hotel could be organized as a separate corporation, in which case 200 common shares would be issued; or each could be organized as a limited partnership, in which case 200 limited partnership units would be issued.

Financial information relating to each expansion unit is provided in Exhibits I and II.

Required:
Prepare an analysis of the financial information and advise Contesso which organization structure will be most attractive to prospective investors for each of the hotel units.

Exhibit I
CONTESSO TRAVEL INNS
Financial Requirements and Cost Allocations

1. Project cost and financing

Cost:	
Land, building, equipment, and start-up costs	$4,500,000
Financing:	
1st mortgage (35-year amortization), interest at 12%	$2,500,000
Investors' contributions:	
200 × $10,000	2,000,000
	$4,500,000

2. Cost allocations

Land	$ 400,000
Building	2,600,000
Furniture and equipment	500,000
Landscaping	50,000
Linens and supplies	90,000
Costs of arranging mortgage	70,000
Opening advertising and staff training	290,000
Agent's fees for selling equity units	350,000
Expense of issuing units (prospectus, legal, etc.)	150,000
	$4,500,000

Exhibit II
CONTESSO TRAVEL INNS
Anticipated Operating Information

Year	1*	2	3	4
Average room rate	40	42	44	46
Occupancy percentage	60%	63%	66%	70%
Gross revenue	$400,000*	$900,000	$1,100,000	$1,200,000
Operating profit before debt service and depreciation	200,000	400,000	480,000	520,000

* Note: The entity's year end will be December 31. Information for year 1 represents a half-year operation period. Also, the operating profits exclude any of the start-up cost allocations of $4,500,000.

Case Two   Realco*

Realco, a real estate developer, is proposing to obtain land and build a small mall that will house five stores. The five stores that lease the property will be responsible for all operating costs (maintenance, property taxes, utilities and repairs, and so on). The project will be constructed in 20X1 on behalf of a group of investors and will cost $700,000, as follows:

Building	$430,000
Land	120,000
Parking lot	40,000
Interest during construction period	30,000
Landscaping	20,000
Mortgage finder's fee	6,000
Legal fees:	
Land purchase	4,000
Mortgage documents	2,000
Investor offering	6,000
Appraisal fee for mortgage	4,000
Broker's fee for finding investors	38,000
	$700,000

* Adapted, with permission, from the 1989 Uniform Final Examination© 1989 of the Canadian Institute of Chartered Accountants, Toronto, Canada. Any changes in the original material are the sole responsibility of W.J. Buckwold and have not been reviewed or endorsed by the CICA.

The maximum mortgage available on the proposed property is $450,000. The annual interest rate will be 11%. The only security required for the mortgage is the property itself.

Realco has found 10 individuals who are each prepared to borrow $25,000 personally to invest. Its role in the project is now simply to develop the property on behalf of the investors. The ownership structure has yet to be determined. It is expected that the property will be rented beginning in January 20X2 for ten years at $75,000 per year, and that the property will be sold to the tenants at the end of the lease. The sale price will be based on the fair market value at that time. After the property is sold, the ownership structure will be liquidated, with all proceeds going to the investors.

Realco has asked you to prepare a report that analyzes alternative structures for holding the property and recommends the best from a tax perspective. The investors are interested in paying the minimum amount of tax over the life of the investment. Indicate in your report what the maximum tax write-off would be in 20X1 and 20X2, as well as the possible ramifications if one of the investors decides to dispose of his or her interest before the end of 10 years.

Required:
Prepare the report.

Selected Topics

The promises of yesterday
are the taxes of today.

Mackenzie King ✍

part five

Chapter 17   Business Acquisitions and Divestitures— Assets versus Shares

The decision to sell or acquire an existing business is subject to a number of different influences. Obviously, price is a key factor, in that the vendor wants to achieve a maximum realization and the purchaser wants to obtain the highest possible return on investment.

The price paid for a business, although established primarily by market conditions, is influenced by tax considerations. The vendor's real proceeds from a sale are the selling price less the related tax costs resulting from the sale. A vendor that can reduce or defer the amount of tax otherwise payable may be willing to accept a lesser purchase price provided that the after-tax value is the same as or greater than what would normally be expected. The purchaser is actually acquiring a stream of future profits that will be subject to tax. A purchaser that can reduce the amount of tax otherwise payable on that income may be prepared to pay a higher price. The amount of tax payable by the vendor as a result of the sale, and by the purchaser on future earnings, may be influenced by the form of the transaction.

While business acquisitions and divestitures can take many forms, there are only two fundamental options—the sale of specific business assets, or the sale of the corporation that owns those specific assets. The tax implications of these two alternatives have a significant effect on both the purchaser and the vendor, and, in turn, on the price of a business.

This chapter examines both alternatives—the asset sale and the share sale—and their impact on the selling price of a business. Specifically, it examines the tax implications to both the purchaser and the seller, presents the method of analysis for equating the two, and reviews part of the decision process for the purchaser.

I. Assets versus Shares

Before examining the specific tax implications of asset sales and share sales, it is important to establish the nature of each type of transaction.

Consider the diagram in Exhibit 17-1. Shareholder X owns 100% of the shares of For Sale Corporation, which operates an active business. For Sale Corporation owns a number of assets, which may include inventory, land, buildings, equipment, goodwill, patents, and franchises. In addition, it has liabilities. Shareholder Y owns 100% of Buyer Corporation, which also operates an active business. Buyer Corporation wants to buy the business operated by For Sale Corporation.

There are two basic possible ways to transfer For Sale's business to Buyer Corporation. The first possibility is for shareholder X to sell the shares of For Sale Corporation to Buyer Corporation. In this case, payment of the purchase price will flow directly to shareholder X. Buyer Corporation will own For Sale Corporation as a wholly owned subsidiary that will continue to operate its business with the same assets and related liabilities. It is important to recognize that nothing has changed within For Sale Corporation—the balance sheet and the tax values of its assets remain the same. Only the shareholder has changed.

Exhibit 17-1:
Alternative Methods
of Selling a Business

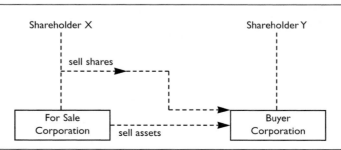

The second possibility is for For Sale Corporation to sell each individual business asset directly to Buyer Corporation. In other words, For Sale Corporation would sell its inventory, land, buildings, equipment, goodwill, and franchises for a specific price for each asset. In this case, payment of the purchase price flows directly to For Sale Corporation, which continues to be owned by shareholder X. In purchasing each specific asset, Buyer Corporation may or may not be assuming the related liabilities of the business. It is not uncommon for specific assets to be purchased and paid for by a combination of cash, an amount owing, and the assumption of the attached liabilities.

Both alternatives result in a tax liability to the vendor when the selling price is greater than the cost for tax purposes of the property sold. Referring again to Exhibit 17-1, a sale of shares at a price in excess of their original cost would result in a taxable gain to shareholder X, leaving the after-tax proceeds available for investment. However, after a sale of specific assets, For Sale Corporation would incur a tax liability. While this would leave after-tax proceeds in the corporation for possible investment, those proceeds would ultimately have to flow to shareholder X, at which time a second level of tax would occur. Clearly, the amount and timing of tax to the vendor is different under each alternative.

The question arises whether this difference in tax treatment also leads to a difference in sale price. If the price established for an asset sale is the same as for a share sale, it follows that considering that the tax implications are different, the vendor would prefer the method that provides the greatest after-tax proceeds for reinvestment. Similarly, in order for the vendor to receive the same after-tax proceeds from each method, it will be necessary to establish one price for an asset sale and another for a share sale. In this case the purchaser would prefer the price that provided the greatest after-tax return on investment.

In order to establish the relationship between an asset price and a share price, one must first examine in greater detail the tax implications to the vendor and the purchaser for each of the basic alternatives.

II. Implications for the Vendor

A. Sale of Assets

As mentioned previously, the sale of specific assets by a vendor corporation will usually result in two levels of tax. It is, therefore, important to establish the following:

1. The amount of tax payable by the corporation, and the timing of the payment of tax.

2. The amount of tax payable by the shareholder, and when that tax may occur.

The types of income or loss generated from the sale of specific assets may vary with the nature of the assets sold; consequently, the resulting tax treatment may also vary.

The sale of capital property may result in a capital gain, of which one-half is taxable (see Chapter 8). The sale of depreciable property may result in recapture of capital cost allowance as well as a capital gain (see Chapter 6). On a sale of business assets, the recapture of capital cost allowance constitutes business income. The sale of intangibles, such as goodwill or patents, franchises, and licences having an unlimited life, may result in eligible capital property income (see Chapter 6), which is classified as business income.

The amount of tax payable on the above types of income depends on the nature of the corporation. A public corporation pays a high rate of tax on all types of income. On the other hand, if the selling company is a Canadian-controlled private corporation, the tax payable on profits classified as business income may be eligible for the lower small business rate if other sources of income have not already used up the annual $300,000 limit. Often a Canadian-controlled private corporation will choose to sell its assets on the first day of a new taxation year in order to achieve an additional small-business deduction base. Taxable capital gains earned by a Canadian-controlled private corporation are subject to a high rate of tax but eligible for a partial refund when the gains are distributed to the shareholders as a dividend (see Chapter 13).

In most cases a corporation must recognize any income from asset sales in the year of disposition. However, income derived from capital gains may be realized over future years if the related proceeds from the sale are deferred over future years. As was indicated in Chapter 8, the option to realize taxable capital gains over a period of years is subject to certain limitations.

The amount and timing of the tax to the corporation can be determined with relative certainty; the amount of the second level of tax on corporate distributions is more difficult to determine precisely. When assets are sold, the corporation that previously housed the business continues to exist unless the shareholder chooses to wind it up. Immediately after the sale, the corporation will continue to own assets in the form of cash or amounts due from the purchaser. If the after-tax proceeds from the sale are retained in the corporation for investment purposes, the second level of tax to the shareholders can be delayed until some future time. When possible, shareholders often delay the second level of tax to gain maximum tax deferral, even though the rate of tax that may apply in the future is uncertain. As will be seen later, this complicates the comparative analysis of asset and share sales.

B. Sale of Shares

In contrast to the sale of assets, the sale of the shares of the entire corporation is relatively simple, because it involves the sale of only one type of asset and usually results in only one level of tax.

The shares of the vendor corporation constitute capital property to the shareholder. Consequently, any gain realized from a sale is a capital gain, only one-half of which is taxable to the vendor. In addition, an individual shareholder may be eligible for the $500,000 capital gain deduction if the vendor corporation's shares are qualified small business corporation shares (see Chapter 10).

When the shareholder of the vendor corporation is an individual, the after-tax proceeds from the sale of shares are not subject to any further taxation and are fully available for reinvestment or for personal use.

As the sale of shares results in the complete sale of the corporation, no tax consequences result to the corporation itself. Even though the price of the shares reflects the fact that certain assets within the corporation have increased in value, such increase is not recognized in the corporation.

III. Implications for the Purchaser

The purchaser's return on investment from a business acquisition results from the future stream of annual profits generated by the acquired business. The amount of pre-tax cash flow that will be generated will be identical whether the purchaser acquires the specific assets of the business or the shares of the corporation which houses that business. However, the purchaser's return on investment is determined not from pre-tax but from after-tax profits. In most situations the after-tax profits arising from an asset purchase will differ considerably from those arising from a share purchase.

A. Purchase of Assets

The most important feature of an asset purchase is that the purchaser can deduct from future income all or a portion of the purchase price by claiming capital cost allowance on depreciable property and amortization of eligible capital property such as goodwill. Because the purchaser is acquiring each individual asset of the business and not the corporation itself, the cost base of each asset for tax purposes is equal to the price paid.

Consider the specific list of assets being acquired under an asset purchase in Exhibit 17-2. Note that each of the assets has a fair market value in excess of the vendor's tax cost. On sale, each asset would create taxable income for the vendor corporation in the form of capital gains and the recapture of capital cost allowance. From the purchaser's perspective, the cost amount of each asset acquired is the fair market value price paid, and therefore the cost of the building ($900,000) can be deducted from future income at a rate of 4% annually. The manufacturing equipment ($500,000) is a class 43 asset available for a 30% write-off rate. The limited life franchise ($150,000) is a class 14 asset, the full cost of which can be deducted at 10% annually on a straight-line basis or faster if justified economically. Notice that no annual deduction is available for the land because it is not depreciable property. However, if the purchaser sells the land at some future time, its cost for tax purposes will be the purchase price of $75,000.

Exhibit 17-2:
Assets Acquired in
an Asset Purchase

Asset	Vendor's tax value	Fair market value	Write-off rate
Land	$ 50,000	$ 75,000	—
Building	600,000	900,000	4% (declining balance)
Manufacturing equipment	300,000	500,000	30% (declining balance)
Franchise (life 10 y)	100,000	150,000	10% (straight line)
	$1,050,000	$1,625,000	

The amount of capital cost allowance available to the purchaser is significantly higher than was available to the vendor prior to the sale. For example, the vendor corporation could claim capital cost allowance on the manufacturing equipment based on its undepreciated capital cost of $300,000, whereas the purchaser will be able to claim capital cost allowance on $500,000. Therefore, while pre-tax profits were the same for the vendor as they are now for the purchaser, the after-tax profits are considerably different. As discussed below, the same variance would not occur if the purchaser acquired the shares of the vendor corporation rather than the specific assets.

In an asset sale of a business, the purchaser and seller may find it easy to agree on a total purchase price but may have difficulty agreeing on how to allocate that total price among the individual assets. When the vendor wishes to minimize tax on the sale and the purchaser wishes to maximize future capital cost allowance, a conflict occurs. For example, referring to Exhibit 17-2, it is in the purchaser's interest to allocate more of the total price to the manufacturing equipment rather than to the land or building, because the manufacturing equipment can be written off at 30%, whereas the write-off on the building is only 4% and no deduction is available on the land. The vendor, however, will want to allocate more of the total price to assets that will result in a capital gain, rather than to those that will create more recapture of capital cost allowance, because only one-half of capital gains are taxable.

In many cases, purchase and sale agreements avoid the allocation problem by simply listing the assets as a group and providing a total purchase price for that group. Each party can then determine its own allocation. However, decision makers should be aware that CCRA can reallocate the total purchase price in accordance with the reasonable fair market values of each separate asset.[1] When making an acquisition, the purchaser is advised to make a reasonable attempt at establishing a fair allocation; this will provide an accurate picture of cash-flow savings from capital cost allowance.

---

1   ITA 68; IT-220R2 (paragraphs 4–7); *The Queen v. Waldorf Hotel (1958) Ltd. et al.*, 75 DTC 5109 (FCTD).

As the amount of capital cost allowance available to the purchaser is an important factor, consideration should also be given to the capital cost classifications of the various assets being purchased. The capital cost allowance classes reviewed in Chapter 6 often change over time. For example, manufacturing equipment has been moved from class 8 (20%) to class 29 (50%) to class 39 (25%), and more recently to class 43 (30%). This means that the classification for the vendor corporation may not be the same as for the purchaser.

B. Purchase of Shares

Purchasing a business by acquiring the shares of the vendor corporation disturbs neither the asset base nor the activity within the vendor corporation. As only the shares have changed ownership, the vendor corporation continues, without interruption, in the same manner as it did before the change in ownership.[2] Consequently, the following tax treatment occurs:

1. The assets within the corporation remain at their tax values even though their fair market values are higher, as indicated in the price of the shares.

2. Capital cost allowance after the acquisition continues from the same tax base as existed before the acquisition.

As a result, the after-tax cash profits of the acquired business following a share purchase will usually be lower than the after-tax cash profits following an asset purchase. When the reader refers again to Exhibit 17-2, the magnitude of this difference becomes obvious. If the shares of the vendor corporation are purchased, the amount of future deductions from income from capital cost allowance is $1,000,000 (building $600,000 + equipment $300,000 + franchise $100,000). If the specific assets are purchased, the total deductions from future income amount to $1,550,000 (building $900,000 + equipment $500,000 + franchise $150,000). Even though these deductions occur over a number of years, this difference has a dramatic impact on after-tax cash flow.

In effect, under the share purchase method, the purchaser simply takes over the tax position of the vendor corporation. This means that in addition to having lower capital cost allowance, the purchaser may be liable for tax in the event that the acquired vendor corporation should subsequently sell some of its assets. For example, if after acquisition the new owner decided to sell the franchise at its fair market value of $150,000, the corporation would have taxable income because its tax value was inherited at $100,000.

Because the share purchase method results in lower after-tax cash flow, *and* because the purchaser inherits a potential tax liability if it later sells some of the corporation's assets, the purchaser will attempt to establish a price for the shares that is lower than would have been paid for the assets. The amount of this discount is not always easy to establish and is subject to negotiation with the vendor. The relationship between the asset price of a business and its share price is examined in Parts IV and V of this chapter.

C. Structure after Acquisition

It is important to recognize that the form of the purchase—assets or shares—does not dictate the nature of the organization structure after the purchase has been made. For example, consider a share purchase similar to the one diagrammed in Exhibit 17-1.

---

2   Except when the acquired corporation has loss carry-overs (see Chapter 11—change in control).

Immediately after the purchase, For Sale Corporation becomes a wholly owned subsidiary of Buyer Corporation. If the purchaser wishes, this structure can continue, with the business operations of the parent and subsidiary in two separate taxable entities. Or the purchaser can, by means of a wind-up or amalgamation, combine the two entities and operate them within one taxable entity (see Chapter 14). Similarly, if a business is acquired by an asset purchase, the new business can be operated as part of the purchaser's business, or it can be turned into a subsidiary corporation.

The post-acquisition structure may have an impact on the tax cost of future activities. For example, when a manufacturing business purchases a non-manufacturing business, the amount of income available for the lower manufacturing rate of corporate tax will vary depending on whether the entities were combined or kept separate. This is because manufacturing income for tax purposes is determined arbitrarily in accordance with the ratio of manufacturing capital and labour to the entity's total capital and labour (see Chapter 11). Therefore, combining or separating the two entities may have a positive or negative impact on the rate of tax payable.

IV. The Relationship between Asset Price and Share Price

As described above, for both the seller and the purchaser, the tax impact of an asset sale is different from that of a share sale, regarding both the amount of tax payable and the timing of the tax payment. Both parties must recognize that the price attached to the sale of a business will vary with the form of the transaction.

The degree to which the price varies cannot be measured with certainty. A vendor can accurately anticipate the tax liability to the corporation if the assets are sold, but cannot be as certain with respect to the amount and timing of the subsequent level of tax when the corporation distributes its earnings to the shareholder. Similarly, a purchaser can accurately anticipate the capital cost allowance available after acquisition under either method, but with the share purchase method will find it difficult to determine the tax liability in the event that the acquired corporation disposes of some of its assets. Any negotiated purchase and sale of a business has some risk with respect to the tax impact. However, this risk can be diminished if both parties understand the tax consequences that would result from an assumed worst-case scenario.

From the vendor's perspective the worst-case scenario is most likely an asset sale whereby the vendor corporation pays tax on the sale of its assets and then immediately winds up the corporation by distributing all of its earnings. The worst-case scenario for the purchaser would involve a purchase of the shares of the vendor corporation and, immediately afterwards, a sale of all of the assets of the newly acquired corporation. Both scenarios would result in full tax liability for the respective parties. Once the worst-case scenarios are known, both parties can assess the likelihood of their occurrence in view of the particular circumstances, and build that factor into the negotiation process.

A. Establishing the Worst-Case Scenario

Once a business has been targeted for acquisition, it is important to establish the worst-case scenario for the vendor. Both the vendor and the purchaser are interested in this analysis. For example, if the worst-case scenario for a vendor is an asset sale, and the net after-tax proceeds from this form of sale are known, the vendor can establish the share price that would provide the same after-tax proceeds. This information is critical to vendors because it permits them to establish a minimum share price that corresponds, on an after-tax basis, to an asset price. Presumably a vendor would not accept a share price that is below this minimum.

At the same time, a purchaser who knows the tax position of the vendor, and also knows the share price that corresponds to the asset price in the worst-case scenario, has a starting point from which to begin negotiations.

The process of establishing the worst-case scenario for the vendor will vary depending on whether the vendor corporation is a small company or a large company, and whether it is a public corporation or a private corporation. Consider the two vendor structures outlined in Exhibit 17-3.

Structure A shows a closely held private corporation. Because the corporation and the shareholder are so closely tied, the worst-case scenario involves

(a) sale of assets at fair market value;
(b) payment of corporate taxes on taxable gains from the sale of assets; and,
(c) distribution of all cash to the shareholder, who incurs an immediate second level of tax.

Structure B is quite different. Under structure B a large number of shareholders own a large public corporation that intends to continue operations indefinitely. The corporation for sale is a subsidiary of the public corporation. If the subsidiary corporation sold its assets, it would incur tax on the sale; however, no second level of tax would occur even if dividends were paid to the parent public corporation, as intercorporate dividends flow tax-free. One could compute the tax effect if dividends were flowed straight through to the large number of individual shareholders, but this would be unrealistic, as the public corporation is not likely to alter its normal dividend policy. Therefore, the worst-case scenario under structure B is different from that under structure A.

It is important that the decision maker involved in a business acquisition or sale establish a realistic worst-case scenario in order to ascertain which investor will be directly affected by the transaction. In structure A it is the individual shareholder; in structure B it is the public corporation, which will reinvest the funds for an indefinite time period.

Exhibit 17-3: *Worst-Case Scenario* *under Alternative* *Structures*	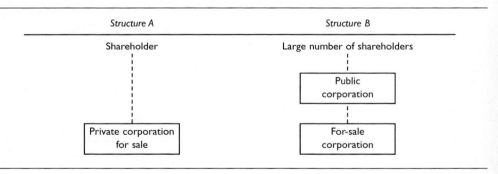

B. Equating the Asset Price with the Share Price

The calculations for determining the tax impact of the worst-case scenario for a vendor corporation, and for determining an equivalent share price, are presented and analyzed below. *The facts in the situation are greatly simplified in order to stress the method of analysis rather than the details that may be required for the computations.*

Summary of Facts

For Sale Corporation is a Canadian-controlled private corporation that operates a small wholesale business. The company is owned directly by two individual shareholders, neither of whom participates in the management of the business. A recent balance sheet of the corporation, presented below, indicates the tax values of the assets, together with their fair market values.

For Sale Corporation: Current Position

	Tax value	Fair market value
Assets:		
Current assets	$400,000	$ 400,000
Equipment:		
Cost	600,000	
Capital cost allowance	(400,000)	
Undepreciated capital cost	200,000	500,000
Goodwill	–0–	200,000
	$600,000	$1,100,000
Liabilities	$200,000	
Shareholders' equity:		
Share capital	50,000	
Retained earnings	350,000	
	$600,000	

The following additional information is provided:

1. If a sale of assets occurs, the transaction date will be one month before the corporation's year end. Normal operating profits to that date will exceed the small-business deduction limit of $300,000. The rate of tax on additional business income is 40%. (Note: This rate is higher than the 37% rate developed in Chapter 11.)

2. Both shareholders are subject to a personal tax rate of 45% and to a dividend tax of 30%, net of the dividend tax credit.

3. The two shareholders, who are the original shareholders of the corporation, acquired their shares from the corporate treasury at a cost of $25,000 each for a total of $50,000, which is the same amount as the share capital on the corporation's balance sheet. After the sale of the business, the shareholders do not intend to continue investing together.

4. The sale would be made in cash. If assets are sold, the purchaser will assume the liabilities of the corporation.

Analysis
In the above situation the worst-case scenario for the vendor would be a sale of assets at fair market value followed by a wind-up of the corporation so that the after-tax proceeds from the sale were distributed to the shareholders. It is now necessary to anticipate the tax liability to the corporation and to the shareholders. On a sale of assets followed by a wind-up of the corporation, the shareholders would receive a total of $563,000 after the payment of all taxes, as follows:

Value of assets sold:	
Current assets	$ 400,000
Equipment	500,000
Goodwill	200,000
Total asset price	1,100,000
Liabilities (assumed by purchaser)	(200,000)
Net cash received from purchaser	900,000
Corporate tax on asset sales (below)	(160,000)
Net cash available for wind-up	$ 740,000
Cash received by shareholders	$ 740,000
Tax on dividend distributions (below)	(177,000)
Net after-tax cash to shareholders	$ 563,000

The amount of corporate tax and shareholder tax noted above requires an explanation. The sale of assets created the following income and tax for the corporation:

Current assets	–0–
Equipment:	
Recapture of capital cost allowance	
($500,000 – $200,000)	300,000
Goodwill:	
Eligible capital property gain (½ of $200,000)	100,000
Total income	$400,000
Corporate tax (40% × $400,000)	$160,000

In order to compute the personal tax to the shareholders, one must first determine the nature of the cash distribution on wind-up. The $740,000 available for distribution consists of $50,000 of share capital and retained earnings of $690,000. It is not necessary to reconcile the pre-sale and post-sale retained earnings in order to arrive at the $690,000, because any amount available for distribution other than the share capital can only be retained earnings. However, the following reconciliation is presented for further clarity:

Retained earnings before the sale	$350,000
Gain on sale of equipment ($500,000 – $200,000)	300,000
Gain on sale of goodwill ($200,000 – 0)	200,000
	850,000
Tax on sale	(160,000)
Retained earnings after the sale	$690,000

Notice that the actual gain on the sale of goodwill is $200,000 although only one-half, or $100,000, is taxable (see Chapter 6). The $100,000 tax-free portion of the goodwill gain can be distributed as a special tax-free capital dividend to the shareholders, as described in Chapter 12. As $50,000 of the distribution represents share capital and a further $100,000 represents a tax-free dividend, the remaining portion of the $740,000 is a taxable dividend to the shareholders.[3] A summary of the distribution and related tax is offered below.

---

3   ITA 88(2); IT-149R4.

Distribution:		
Share capital		$ 50,000
Retained earnings:		
Tax-free dividend	100,000	
Taxable dividend	590,000	690,000
		$740,000
Tax to shareholders ($590,000 × 30%)		$177,000

It should also be pointed out that the return of share capital for $50,000 results in a disposition of the shares to the shareholders. In this case no capital gain or loss occurs because the cancellation price of $50,000 is equal to the cost of the shares to the shareholders.[4]

So, under the worst-case scenario, the shareholders will achieve net after-tax proceeds of $563,000. A share price can now be computed that yields the same $563,000 after the tax on the sale of the shares.

The sale of shares will result in a capital gain, one-half of which is taxable at a rate of 45%. As the gain is the difference between the selling price and the cost of the shares (which is $25,000 for each shareholder for a total of $50,000), the selling price necessary to yield net proceeds of $563,000 can be determined by making the following calculations:

(a) Selling price − tax = $563,000
(b) Selling price − 45% (½) (selling price − $50,000) = $563,000
(c) Selling price = $712,000

The above analysis indicates that under the worst-case scenario, the vendor could accept a price of $712,000 for the shares, or $900,000 for the net assets of the corporation (value of assets sold [$1,100,000] − liabilities assumed [$200,000] = $900,000), and receive the same after-tax proceeds of $563,000. Having established these values, the vendor could be sure that a corporation with assets valued at $1,100,000 would not sell all of its shares for less than $712,000.

At the same time, the vendors can argue that the equivalent share price should be higher than $712,000, because after selling the assets they would not immediately wind up the corporation; rather, they would hold off doing so in order to delay the second level of tax until some future time. This scenario is possible even though the two shareholders have indicated that after the sale they will not continue to invest together. For example, after a sale of assets, but before the distribution to the shareholders, both shareholders could transfer their shares to their own separate holding corporations (see Chapter 14). They could then wind up For Sale Corporation by distributing its $740,000 of after-tax proceeds to those holding companies, which would receive the dividends tax-free. Both shareholders would thus have their share of the $740,000 in their own holding corporations available for reinvestment. The second level of tax would thus be delayed until they transferred the funds from their own holding companies to themselves for personal use.

The purchaser, on the other hand, would argue that avoidance of the second level of tax is not permanent, that the tax will ultimately be incurred, and that any adjustment to the share price should reflect only the value of the delay. And so the negotiations would proceed, until an acceptable share price was established.

---

4   ITA 54.

It is important to recognize that the above result is specific only to the circumstances provided, and that in other roughly similar situations, the tax impact of a worst-case scenario may be different. For example, the income from the sale of assets may be subject to the lower rate of corporate tax if the small-business deduction is available. Further, when a private corporation is subject to high rates of tax, an element of double taxation may be avoided on wind-up if additional salaries or bonuses are paid to those shareholders who also manage the business (see Chapter 13). Each particular business must be examined with an eye to identifying its unique attributes so that the tax consequences resulting from its sale can be anticipated.

This part of the chapter stressed the implications to the vendor; the following part compares the impact of an asset purchase with that of a share purchase from the purchaser's perspective.

V. The Decision to Purchase

The impact of taxation on future cash flow and return on investment is a vital factor in the decision to acquire a business. The concept of business valuations is not discussed until a later chapter; however, it is generally understood that the value of a business to a purchaser is directly related to the after-tax profits that the acquired business will generate.

There are three major tax issues that the purchaser must examine when contemplating a business acquisition in the form of an asset or share purchase. The purchaser must

(a) anticipate the rate of tax that will apply, after the acquisition, on expected future profits;
(b) determine how much extra cash flow will be generated as a result of deducting capital cost allowance and amortizing eligible capital property; and,
(c) when the purchase is by way of a share acquisition, assess the likelihood of incurring additional tax liabilities if the acquired corporation should later dispose of any of its assets.

Each of these three major considerations is examined below.

A. Future Rates of Tax

The rate of tax on business income after acquisition can differ considerably from the rate that was applicable before the acquisition. For example, a business that was entitled to the low corporate tax rate on its first $300,000 of annual business income may be subject to the high rate of corporate tax after the acquisition, if the purchaser is a public corporation or another private corporation that has substantial other sources of business income.[5] The reverse may apply when a corporation that cannot use the small-business deduction (because of its association with other companies) becomes eligible for the lower rate of tax after acquisition. In addition, tax rates may be altered as a result of a combining of the purchased business with the business operations of the purchaser. For example, the combining of manufacturing and non-manufacturing activities will alter the amount eligible for the special manufacturing rate of tax, as was discussed previously in this chapter and Chapter 11. Similarly, combining operations in different provincial jurisdictions will alter the results of the arbitrary formula that establishes provincial tax rates.

When after-tax profits are factored in, the value of a business to the vendor may well be different from its value to the purchaser. This is because different tax rates may apply to each party. As well, the rates of tax, and therefore the value of the business, may vary among

5 ITA 125(3).

potential purchasers. If the post-acquisition tax rates are particularly favourable to a purchaser, that purchaser may have a competitive advantage, since it can afford to pay a higher price than other potential buyers.

It is important for the purchaser to anticipate the post-acquisition tax rates as part of its acquisition strategy; it is equally important for the vendor to attempt to anticipate the purchaser's position. Targeting a purchaser that will receive a special tax benefit from the acquisition may result in a higher sale price.

B. Asset Price or Share Price—Impact on Cash Flow

After examining the potential future profits and the anticipated rates of tax, the purchaser must make the following two decisions:

1. Should the target business be purchased or not?

2. If the purchase is made, what form should it take—assets or shares?

While many factors influence the decision to purchase, it is a key requirement that the acquisition provide an acceptable rate of return in relation to the purchase price. One method of determining whether this requirement will be met is to compare the anticipated future after-tax cash flows on a net present value basis with the required purchase price. The future cash flows are discounted at the acceptable return rate; if their present value is greater than the purchase price, the acquisition is justifiable, at least in monetary terms. Because the price for an asset purchase will be different than for a share purchase, the analysis should be completed for both methods to determine which provides the highest result.

The most difficult aspect of this analysis has to do with estimating the amount of pre-tax profit that will be generated. In the example that follows, this process is grossly simplified—by assuming a constant profit for an indefinite time period—in order to stress the tax aspects and method of analysis. The example uses the *same information* given in the situation described in Part IV of this chapter, which calculated an asset price and a share price in a specific situation.

Summary of Facts

The situation in Part IV of this chapter concluded that under the worst-case scenario for the vendor, a net asset price of $900,000 (fair market value of assets less assumed liabilities) would provide the same after-tax return to the vendor as a share price of $712,000. However, as the vendors can avoid the worst-case scenario by delaying the payment of the second level of tax, they have decided that they will only accept a share price of $820,000. The following additional information is provided:

1. The business is expected to generate pre-tax cash profits of $225,000 annually for an indefinite period of time. Pre-tax cash profits consist of profits before any capital cost allowance or amortization of eligible capital property.

2. The purchaser will make the acquisition only if it can achieve a return on investment in excess of 21% before tax. The purchaser's tax rate is assumed to be 40% (higher than the 37% rate developed in Chapter 11), and so the after-tax minimum acceptable rate of return is 13%.

Analysis

Having analyzed its own tax structure and having proceeded with negotiations, the vendor presents the purchaser with two clear options:

1. Purchase the individual assets for the following values and payment terms:

Current assets	$ 400,000
Equipment	500,000
Goodwill	200,000
	1,100,000
Liabilities assumed	(200,000)
Cash required	$ 900,000

2. Purchase the shares of For Sale Corporation at a price of $820,000.

Both options will provide pre-tax cash profits of $225,000 annually for an indefinite period of time. To calculate the net present value of this stream of cash flow, an arbitrary time period of 20 years will be used here (see following table). A longer time period would diminish the degree of certainty and would not change the results significantly.

Present value of future profits:	
Annual profit	$225,000
Tax @ 40%	(90,000)
After-tax profit	$135,000
Present value of $135,000 annually for 20 y, discounted at 13%	$948,000

Notice that both the annual profit and the discount rate are on an after-tax basis to reflect real cash flows. The calculation of tax has ignored capital cost allowance and the amortization of goodwill even though both will enhance cash flow by reducing taxes. As these items will affect cash flow for a share purchase differently than for an asset purchase, they are examined separately below.

The present value of the cash flow generated from capital cost allowance and amortization of eligible capital property can be determined using the formula introduced in Chapter 6.

$$\frac{C \times T \times R}{R + I}$$

Where:
C = Cost of the asset acquired.
T = Rate of corporate tax.
R = Rate of capital cost allowance or eligible capital property amortization.
I = After-tax discount rate or acceptable rate of return.

If the purchaser acquires the individual assets, the tax base that is eligible for future tax deductions is $500,000 for the equipment and $150,000 for the goodwill. (Only three-quarters of the goodwill's $200,000 cost is eligible for amortization, as explained in Chapter 6.) As the equipment is not used for manufacturing, it falls within class 8 and has a 20% capital cost allowance rate (diminishing balance). The $150,000 tax base of the goodwill is eligible capital property, which has an amortization rate of 7% (diminishing balance). Therefore, the present value of future tax savings from these two items under an asset purchase is approximately $142,000, calculated as follows:

Equipment: $\dfrac{\$500{,}000 \times .40 \times .20}{.20 + .13} = \$121{,}000^*$

Goodwill: $\dfrac{\$150{,}000 \times .40 \times .07}{.07 + .13} = \underline{21{,}000}$

$ \underline{\underline{\$142{,}000}}$

* The formula does not include the effect of the one-half rule for new acquisitions of depreciable property (in this case, equipment). To include this the formula would be:

$$\frac{C \times T \times R \times (1 + I/2)}{(I + R) \times (I + 1)}$$

On the other hand, the purchase of *shares* does not increase the cost base of the assets held within the corporation. Although the value of the equipment and goodwill is reflected in the price of the shares, the cost of the shares to the purchaser is not eligible for a tax deduction until the shares are sold. Therefore, the equipment within the corporation will continue to have an undepreciated capital cost of only $200,000 (see page 569). As the goodwill had no cost within For Sale Corporation, no tax deductions will be available after the acquisition. Because the purchaser, under a share purchase, inherits the tax values of the vendor's assets, the present value of future tax savings is only $48,000, calculated as follows:

Equipment: $\dfrac{\$200{,}000 \times 40\% \times .20}{.20 + .13} = \$48{,}000^*$

Goodwill: $\phantom{\dfrac{\$200{,}000 \times 40\% \times .20}{.20 + .13} = } \underline{-0-}$

$ \underline{\underline{\$48{,}000}}$

* The one-half rule does not apply, because the corporation has owned the equipment for several years.

The relative positions of an asset purchase and a share purchase can now be summarized and compared on a net present value basis as follows:

	Purchase of assets	Purchase of shares
Cash inflow:		
Future profits	$ 948,000	$948,000
Tax savings from:		
Equipment	121,000	48,000
Goodwill	21,000	–0–
Total cash inflows	$1,090,000	$996,000
Cash outflow:		
Purchase price	(900,000)	(820,000)
Excess cash inflow	$ 190,000	$176,000

The above summary indicates that both the asset purchase and the share purchase provide a return on investment significantly greater than the required minimum return of

13% after tax. It also indicates that a marginally greater return will be achieved if assets are purchased even though an asset purchase requires an $80,000 higher purchase price. More than compensating for this higher purchase price are the tax benefits resulting from the higher levels of capital cost allowance and goodwill amortization.

It is clear that the tax treatment relating to business acquisitions has a major impact on the return on investment. It is, therefore, important that the purchaser thoroughly analyze the tax treatment of the specific assets involved in an acquisition.

C. Potential Tax Liability after Share Acquisition

A share acquisition results in the buyer assuming the tax position of the vendor corporation. In such cases there is always a possibility that, after acquisition, the acquired corporation will dispose of all or some of its assets, thereby incurring taxable income. For example, in the previous situation the purchaser, by acquiring the shares of For Sale Corporation for the lower price of $820,000, inherited a potential tax liability of $160,000, calculated as follows:

	Tax value of assets in For Sale Corporation	Fair market value	Potential taxable income
Equipment	$200,000	$500,000	$300,000
Goodwill	–0–	200,000	100,000
			$400,000
Potential tax liability ($400,000 × 40%)			$160,000

An extreme worst-case scenario for the purchaser is one in which, immediately after buying the shares for $820,000, it is forced to sell the acquired corporation's assets at fair market value. The acquired corporation would be left with $740,000, as calculated in the table below.

Fair value of assets sold:	
Current assets, equipment, goodwill	$1,100,000
Liabilities	(200,000)
Net cash received	$ 900,000
Tax on sale of assets	(160,000)
Cash remaining in corporation	$ 740,000

So, a purchase price of $820,000 for shares bears a risk of an $80,000 loss ($820,000 – $740,000 = $80,000). It should be noted that if the shareholder is an individual, a further tax may result if the corporation is wound up.

The extent of this type of risk varies with the particular circumstances. In the preceding situation the business would not likely sell the equipment and goodwill shortly after acquiring it. In addition, the purchaser has the option of selling the shares in the same fashion as they were purchased. However, in some cases the potential tax liability is of greater concern. For example, a purchaser may make a share acquisition of a company that has extensive real estate holdings, and then later have to sell some of that property to raise funds for business expansion or to meet financial obligations. Similarly, certain property may face a strong possibility of being expropriated. Whenever a purchase of shares is contemplated, in the course of establishing an acceptable price the purchaser must try to anticipate possible future events relating to the assets that are held within the acquired corporation, and decide whether or not the risk requires a further discounting of the share price.

VI. Summary and Conclusion

The tax implications relating to the purchase and sale of a business are numerous and play an important role in maximizing return on investment. Chapter 14 examined the important role of the holding company for both the purchaser and vendor in structuring acquisitions and divestitures. This chapter has examined the two fundamental methods of completing a sale and purchase of a corporate business—the sale of assets by the corporation, and the sale of shares of the corporation that houses the business.

The tax treatment relating to each method varies for both the vendor and the purchaser; this results in a different price structure for each method. The effects on the seller and on the purchaser for the two basic methods can be summarized as follows:

Sale of Assets

Effects on the vendor:

1. The sale of assets at fair market value creates taxable income or losses to the vendor corporation.

2. Although the after-tax proceeds from the sale of assets can be retained by the corporation for reinvestment, they ultimately must be distributed to the shareholders, at which time a second level of tax may be incurred.

Effects on the purchaser:

1. Having purchased specific assets at fair market value, the purchaser obtains a cost base for the assets acquired that is equal to the price paid.

2. The new cost base of the assets purchased provides future tax savings from the deduction of capital cost allowance and amortization of eligible capital property. Consequently, the after-tax profits for the purchaser will be higher than they were for the vendor corporation.

Sale of Shares

Effects on the vendor:

1. The vendor disposes of the entire corporation and therefore sells a single asset.

2. The sale of shares results in a capital gain or loss to the vendor, leaving the after-tax proceeds available for reinvestment.

Effects on the purchaser:

1. The purchaser, by acquiring the entire vendor corporation, assumes the tax status of the assets within the corporation; there is no increase in the cost base of these assets even though the asset values are reflected in the price of the shares.

2. Future tax savings from capital cost allowance and amortization of eligible capital property are the same as they were before the acquisition.

Because of these differences in tax treatment, a vendor will normally accept a lower price for shares than for assets. Similarly, a purchaser is normally prepared to pay a higher price for assets, knowing that additional tax benefits will occur. One often hears the generalization that the purchaser prefers an asset acquisition whereas the vendor prefers a share sale. The analysis presented in this chapter indicates that this generalization is invalid. The preference depends on the particular circumstances as they relate to the corporate structure, the nature of the assets, and the tax status of both vendor and purchaser. While a reduced share price may seem attractive to the purchaser, it is worth considering only if the future after-tax return on investment is greater than it would be for an asset purchase.

The vendor must understand the relationship between the share price and the asset price before realistic negotiations can begin. It is equally important for the vendor to determine, to the extent possible, the tax treatment to the purchaser after the acquisition so that a maximum price can be achieved. Similarly, the purchaser must anticipate the future tax impact of each method on the vendor, as well as on itself, in order to establish the parameters of the price negotiation.

Although the examples presented in this chapter have been simplified, the basic concepts developed in them apply equally to all business acquisitions and divestitures, whatever their complexity or size.

Reading List

Income Tax Act References

	Section
Allocation of proceeds	68
Sale of accounts receivable	22
Sale of inventory	23
Ceasing to carry on business	24(1)
When partnership has ceased to exist	24(3)
Fiscal period for an individual proprietor of a business disposed of	25
Winding-up dividend	88(2)
Associated corporations	125(3)

Canada Customs and Revenue Agency Publications

IT-220R2	Capital cost allowance—proceeds of disposition of depreciable property (see paragraphs 4–7 for discussion on allocation of purchase price, and section 68).
IT-149R4	Winding-up dividend.
IT-287R	Sale of inventory.
IT-313R2	Eligible capital property—ceasing to carry on a business.
IT-188R	Sale of accounts receivable.
IT-442R	Bad debts and reserve for doubtful accounts.

Major Court Decision

The Queen v. Waldorf Hotel (1958) Ltd., 75 DTC 5109, (FCTD)—Effect of evidence of hard bargaining on section 68 (allocation of proceeds).

Other Publications

Kroft, E., "Tax Aspects of Buying or Selling Assets or Shares," Corporate Management Tax Conference (1996), Canadian Tax Foundation, p. 1.1.

Weinstein, J., "Sale of a Partnership Business," Corporate Management Tax Conference (1996), Canadian Tax Foundation, p. 12.1.

Howick, W., "Assets Versus Shares: An Approach to the Alternatives," 1990 Corporate Management Tax Conference, Canadian Tax Foundation, pp. 1:1–35.

Review Questions

1. "The sale of business assets by a vendor corporation normally results in two levels of tax rather than a single level of tax, as is the case when the shares of the business corporation are sold." Explain this statement.

2. In general terms, what types of gains or losses may occur for tax purposes when specific business assets are sold?

3. If a business is to be sold on terms that require deferred payments, why may the timing of the related tax cost to the vendor be different if the specific business assets, rather than the shares of the business corporation, are sold?

4. If a group of business assets is sold with specific values attached to each item, what difference, if any, does it make whether the terms of payment (that is, the amount of cash and deferred payments) are expressed separately for each asset sold or as a total for the group of assets sold?

5. When a corporation sells its business by disposing of its business assets, the amount of tax to the corporation resulting from the sale can be determined with relative certainty. Does the same degree of certainty exist with respect to determining the second level of tax when the proceeds of the asset sale are distributed to the shareholder? Explain.

6. The after-tax cash flow from earnings of the acquired business may be different for the purchasers if they acquire the shares of the vendor corporation rather than its specific assets. Explain why.

7. Why is it important for the purchaser to establish an accurate value for each individual asset acquired when a group of business assets is being purchased for an agreed-upon total price?

8. "When a purchaser acquires the shares of a vendor corporation, it may be assuming a potential tax liability of the vendor corporation." What is meant by this statement? To the extent that such a potential liability exists, what impact may this have on the purchase price, and how can it be measured?

9. To what extent, if any, should the vendor to be concerned about the tax status of the purchaser when contemplating the sale of a business?

10. Why is it important for the purchaser of a business to anticipate the post-acquisition organization structure before making the acquisition?

11. When a business can be sold under either an asset sale or a share sale, why is it important that both the vendor and the purchaser attempt to determine the vendor's tax cost from the sale under a worst-case scenario?

12. What is the worst-case scenario when an individual who owns the shares of a business corporation is considering the sale of that business? How is that individual's tax position affected if the business for sale is held within a corporation that is a subsidiary of a large public corporation?

13. What are the three major tax issues that a purchaser must examine when deciding whether to acquire the assets or shares of a business?

Problems

Problem One

Carl owns 100% of the common shares of Extra Ltd., a CCPC operating a wholesale business in eastern Canada. Extra's fiscal year end is May 31, 20X8. It is now April 15, 20X8, and Carl has just signed a letter of intent to sell the wholesale business to Q Ltd.

The initial discussions involved the sale of specific assets of Extra, but a sale of the shares of the company may also be considered. Carl has requested your assistance in estimating the tax liability to Extra *if the business assets are sold*. Information relating to the sale and to the current year's operating income is provided below.

1. The balance sheet of Extra at May 31, 20X8, is estimated as follows:

Accounts receivable	$ 120,000
Inventory, at cost	400,000
Land, at cost	30,000
Building, at book value	280,000
Equipment, at book value	170,000
Licence, at book value	40,000
	$1,040,000
Liabilities	$600,000
Share capital	1,000
Retained earnings	439,000
	$1,040,000

2. Net income before income tax and net gains from the sale of assets for the year ended May 31, 20X8, is estimated as follows:

Income from wholesale operations	$190,000
Dividend income	1,000
Net income before tax	$191,000

The following additional information relates to the net income:

• The dividend income is from a Canadian public corporation, the shares of which were sold during the year for proceeds equal to their original cost.

• Expenses deducted from revenues included the following items:

Legal fees for collection of bad debts	$ 2,000
Donations to registered charities	3,000
Meals and beverages to entertain customers	4,000
Dividend paid to Carl on March 31, 20X8	20,000
Contributions to a registered federal political party	1,000
Replacing a broken window in the building	2,400

3. The 20X7 income tax return indicates the following tax account balances:

RDTOH	NIL
Capital dividend account	NIL
Cumulative eligible capital	NIL
Undepreciated capital cost	
Class 1	290,000
Class 8	140,000
Class 14	42,000

4. The letter of intent regarding the sale of the business indicates that the closing date will be May 31, 20X8. The letter included the following list of assets to be sold, together with each asset's estimated market value. For information, the original cost of each asset is provided.

	Market value	Cost
Accounts receivable	$120,000	$120,000
Inventory	410,000	400,000
Land	40,000	30,000
Building	400,000	320,000
Equipment	90,000	200,000
Licence	45,000	50,000
Goodwill	100,000	
	$1,205,000	$1,120,000

Payment for the above assets would consist of cash plus the assumption of Extra's liabilities.

5. You have suggested to Carl that he consider selling the common shares of Extra rather than the specific assets. You have estimated the market value of the shares to be $600,000. The shares were acquired in 20X1 for a cost of $100,000. In previous years, Carl had used $120,000 of his total capital gain deduction. His cumulative net investment loss (CNIL) at the end of 20X8 is estimated to be $40,000.

Required:

1. Under Part I of the *Income Tax Act*, determine the *minimum income for tax purposes* and the *minimum taxable income* for Extra for the 20X8 taxation year, assuming that all assets are sold.

2. Based on your answer to Requirement 1, calculate the *minimum Part I and Part IV federal income tax* (ignore surtaxes) for the 20X8 taxation year. Your answer should include a calculation of the RDTOH and dividend refund, if any.

3. If an agreement is made to sell the assets of Extra, would you recommend the planned closing date of May 31, 20X8, or a delay of one day to June 1, 20X8? Explain.

4. Briefly outline what the purchaser should consider when choosing between the purchase of assets and the purchase of shares.

5. If Carl decides to sell the shares of Extra, what amount will be added to his net income for tax purposes in his 20X8 taxation year?

Problem Two

Subpump Limited is an active business corporation owned 50% by Simpson and 50% by Clowes. The owners have been attempting to sell the company for several years and have recently received an offer from a serious buyer.

As of December 31, 20X1, the company's financial position was as follows:

Assets

Accounts receivable		$200,000
Inventory (at cost)		70,000
Land		100,000
Building (at cost)	150,000	
Accumulated capital cost allowance	(60,000)	90,000
Equipment (at undepreciated capital cost)		40,000
Goodwill (at cost)		30,000
		$530,000

Liabilities and Shareholders' Equity

Current liabilities		$250,000
Shareholders' equity:		
Common shares	1,000	
Retained earnings	279,000	280,000
		$530,000

Additional information

1. Relevant asset values are as follows:

	Fair market value	UCC	Cumulative eligible capital
Inventory	$ 75,000	–0–	–0–
Land	120,000	–0–	–0–
Building	170,000	90,000	–0–
Equipment	35,000	40,000	–0–
Goodwill	50,000	–0–	4,000

2. On December 31, 20X1, the company's retained earnings consisted of $270,000 of after-tax business profits. The remaining amount of $9,000 represents the non-taxable portion of a previous capital gain.

3. Each owner acquired his shares of Subpump 10 years ago for $50,000.

4. Clowes once owned shares of another small business corporation. He sold them last year and realized a capital gain of $600,000. He claimed the maximum capital gain deduction at that time.

5. The purchaser has stated two alternatives in his purchase offer:
   - A purchase of all assets at fair market value and an assumption of all liabilities. The balance will be paid in cash immediately.
   - A purchase of the shares for $340,000 in cash.

6. Both shareholders want to go their separate ways after the sale. Because of this, Clowes thinks the sale of shares is the best alternative, as it avoids additional tax costs.

7. Both shareholders are in a 45% marginal tax bracket. Both expect to remain in that bracket in the future. The combined (federal and provincial) marginal tax rate for both shareholders is 33% on dividends received (net of the dividend tax credit) and 45% on other income. Subpump's tax rate is 40% on business income not subject to the small-business deduction, and 20% on earnings subject to the small-business deduction. Investment income is subject to a 45% tax rate, plus a $6\frac{2}{3}$% refundable tax.

Required:

1. Which offer should the shareholders accept? Show all calculations (ignore surtaxes).

2. If the assets are sold, is there any way that the two shareholders can divide the cash remaining in the company without paying personal tax? If so, what is it?

Problem Three

Cole and Barker each own 50% of the shares of NRS Ltd., a Canadian-controlled private corporation. NRS had conducted a small active business, which was closed down two years ago, in late 20X0. The corporation sold its assets at that time and used the resulting cash to purchase several commercial real estate properties. At present, the corporation owns three parcels of real estate, as follows:

	Cost	Current fair market value
Parcel 1 (acquired 20X0):		
Land	$10,000	$16,000
Building	40,000	60,000
Parcel 2 (acquired 20X0):		
Land	30,000	40,000
Building	70,000	80,000
Parcel 3 (acquired 20X1):		
Land	15,000	23,000
Building	30,000	42,000

Barker has recently informed Cole that he intends to withdraw as a shareholder of the company and wants to convert his shares to cash. In addition, he wants to own outright all of the real estate known as parcel 3. The shareholders' agreement calls for a wind-up of the corporation when one shareholder wishes to leave; however, Cole wants to keep NRS for himself. The shareholders have therefore agreed to the following:

1. Barker will dispose of his shares for cash at fair market value (transaction date: January 1, 20X3).

2. Immediately thereafter, Barker will purchase from NRS, for cash, the parcel 3 real estate (transaction date: January 2, 20X3).

At December 31, 20X2, the year end of NRS, the corporate balance sheet is as follows:

Assets

Cash		$ 10,000
Land (parcels 1, 2, 3) at cost		55,000
Buildings (parcels 1, 2, 3) at cost	140,000	
Accounting depreciation	(25,000)	115,000
		$180,000

Liabilities and Shareholders' Equity

Mortgage payable		$ 40,000
Shareholders' equity:		
Common shares (paid-up capital)	2,000	
Retained earnings	138,000	140,000
		$180,000

Barker had acquired his shares for $5,000. The paid-up capital of his shares is $1,000, as indicated on the balance sheet (1/2 of $2,000).

The corporation's retained earnings of $138,000 consist of a number of items from past years, as follows:

	Income before tax	Tax	Income after tax
Previous business operations	$103,500	$20,700 (20%)	$ 82,800
Net rentals on real estate (after capital cost allowance)	4,552	2,352 (45% + 6⅔%)	2,200
Taxable capital gain	68,280	35,280 (45% + 6⅔%)	33,000
Non-taxable portion of capital gain	20,000	–0–	20,000
	$196,332	$58,332	$138,000

Barker's personal marginal tax rate is 33% on dividends received (net of the dividend tax credit) and 45% on other taxable income. He has already used up his capital gain deduction.

Required:

1. In view of the shareholders' agreement, determine the value of the common shares owned by Barker.

2. What action should NRS take before Barker disposes of his shares? What effect will this have on the value of those shares and on the related tax when the shares are sold?

3. Describe the two basic ways in which Barker can dispose of his NRS shares, and recommend the best alternative. Show calculations to support your recommendation.

4. What are the tax consequences to NRS in 20X3 as a result of the sale of the parcel 3 real estate?

Problem Four

For several years, Conrad Stone had wanted to acquire the Pineview Motel. The motel had a prime location and was thriving. Part of its property was adjacent to a scenic river, which was used as a picnic area for guests.

Stone felt that if he acquired the property he could continue to operate the motel business but could also piece off its excess land along the river and develop a condominium project. Although the river frontage was not zoned for that purpose, Stone felt that with some effort, this could be changed.

The motel and the land were owned by Henson Enterprises Ltd., a corporation owned by Sheila Henson. She had refused two previous offers from Stone for the land, building, and equipment of the motel, partly because her corporation would have been heavily taxed on the sale.

After further pressure from Stone, Henson agreed to sell, provided that Stone purchased her shares of Henson Enterprises. In this manner, she would be able to claim the maximum capital gain deduction on the sale.

The most recent balance sheet of Henson Enterprises is shown at the top of the next page.

The retained earnings of the corporation are relatively low because Henson has withdrawn most of the earnings through regular dividend distributions.

Over the years, Henson has claimed accounting amortization at a rate equal to the capital cost allowance rate permitted for tax purposes. At the end of the most recent year, the undepreciated capital cost was $350,000 for the building and $30,000 for the equipment.

To determine the share price, Henson first obtained an independent appraisal of the land, building, and equipment. She then suggested a price of $530,000, calculated as follows:

Asset values:		
Current assets		$ 15,000
Land (appraised)		150,000
Building (appraised)		850,000
Equipment (appraised)		30,000
		1,045,000
Liabilities:		
Current liabilities	15,000	
Mortgage payable	500,000	515,000
Share price		$ 530,000

Stone realized that buying the shares at that price would be a problem, because the corporation would retain a potential tax liability in the event that its property were ever sold. After negotiations, Henson dropped the price to $450,000 and Stone purchased the shares for that amount of cash. Stone was not overly concerned about the corporation's

Balance Sheet
Assets

Current Assets		$ 15,000
Land (at cost)		100,000
Building (at cost)	700,000	
Equipment (at cost)	100,000	
	800,000	
Accumulated amortization	(370,000)	430,000
		$545,000

Liabilities and Shareholder's Equity

Current liabilities		$ 15,000
Mortgage payable		500,000
		515,000
Shareholder's equity:		
Common shares	1,000	
Retained earnings	29,000	30,000
		$545,000

tax liability, as the reduced price would provide some relief and he had no intention of selling the property. He would continue to operate the motel and begin to develop the condominium project.

To purchase the shares, Stone used $50,000 of his savings and borrowed $400,000 from his bank, using his personal residence and the acquired shares as collateral. The bank loan is payable on demand.

Two months after Stone purchased the shares, the city announced that it intended to expropriate all of the motel's property to develop a riverbank park. The city had the property appraised and told Henson Enterprises that it would pay the appraised amount for the land, building, and equipment. The appraisal values arrived at by the city were the same as those obtained by Henson two months earlier.

Henson Enterprises has a tax rate of 20% on income subject to the small-business deduction, of 40% on other business income, and of $51\frac{2}{3}$% on investment income. Stone has a marginal tax rate of 30% on dividends received (net of the dividend tax credit), and of 45% on other income.

Required:

1. Determine the tax liability of Henson Enterprises as a result of the expropriation.

2. Determine what Stone's financial position will be after he repays his bank loan.

3. Would the result in 2 have been different if Stone had organized a holding corporation to borrow from the bank and purchase the shares? Explain, providing the calculations.

Problem Five

Kronin Enterprises Ltd. is a Canadian-controlled private corporation operating a successful retail business that generates profits in excess of $600,000 annually. The company is about to acquire a wholesale business operated by KTL Ltd. A recent balance sheet for KTL is presented below.

Assets

Current assets		$ 100,000
Land (at cost)		50,000
Building (at cost)	400,000	
Equipment (at cost)	700,000	
	1,100,000	
Accumulated amortization	(400,000)	700,000
Goodwill (at cost)		200,000
		$1,050,000

Liabilities and Shareholders' Equity

Liabilities		$ 600,000
Shareholders' equity:		
Common shares	20,000	
Retained earnings	430,000	450,000
		$1,050,000

For tax purposes, the building (class 1) has an undepreciated capital cost of $300,000, and the equipment (class 8) has an undepreciated capital cost of $350,000. With respect to the goodwill, the amount of cumulative eligible capital is $100,000.

KTL has offered to sell the assets to Kronin for the following values and payment terms:

Values:	
Current assets	$ 100,000
Land	75,000
Building	550,000
Equipment	600,000
Goodwill	400,000
	$1,725,000
Terms of payment:	
Assumption of KTL liabilities	$ 600,000
Cash	1,125,000
	$1,725,000

Last year KTL earned a pre-tax accounting profit of $220,000 after deducting $30,000 of amortization. Kronin is confident that it can achieve at least the same level of profits after acquisition.

Kronin has virtually decided to purchase the assets of KTL, provided that the investment will generate a minimum acceptable return on investment of 12% after tax.

At a recent meeting, the KTL executives stated that they may want to sell the shares rather than the assets, and do so at a price different from the asset price. They will present an offer to Kronin shortly. Kronin thinks it would be useful to learn what share price would provide the same rate of return as would be achieved after a purchase of assets. The company could then make a quick assessment of the forthcoming share price.

Kronin is subject to a 40% corporate tax rate.

Required:

1. Assuming that an acquisition would be in the form of an asset purchase, should the purchase be made, considering Kronin's minimum return-on-investment requirement?

2. What share price would provide Kronin with the same rate of return as on a purchase of assets? Show calculations.

Case **Bayly Corporation**

Bayly Corporation owns and operates a successful chain of retail pipe and tobacco stores. Bayly is a private corporation owned 100% by a large venture capital corporation.

During 20X1 Bayly earned a net profit *before* tax of $2,000,000, and its most recent balance sheet (see Exhibit 1, next page) shows its financial strength.

Bayly has accumulated large cash reserves for the purpose of acquiring a pipe-manufacturing business. Initially, Bayly was going to construct its own manufacturing plant, but recently it has targeted TOTO Pipes Ltd., a manufacturer of bluestem pipes, as a possible acquisition.

Donna Rose has been given the assignment of reporting to the VP Finance on the feasibility of acquiring TOTO.

Rose attends a meeting with the shareholders of TOTO Pipes and the vice-president of Bayly Corporation. The meeting is short, as its purpose is to get acquainted and gather preliminary information. Rose is able to gather the following information:

1. The common shares of TOTO are owned equally by John Drabinsky and Walter Scully. They started the corporation 15 years ago, when pipe smoking was again becoming popular.

2. In addition to providing the initial share capital, Scully had provided a substantial shareholder loan to TOTO Pipes that enabled the company to survive during its critical start-up years. This loan was paid off two years ago. Scully is a director of TOTO Pipes but is only partly active in its management. He also owns another business, with his son and daughter, where he spends most of his time. Walter Drabinsky is the president and senior manager.

3. Both Drabinsky and Scully are 62 years of age.

4. Drabinsky indicates that he and Scully are prepared to sell all of the assets of TOTO Pipes for the values indicated under "Additional Information" in Exhibit II. If, however, Bayly wants to acquire the shares, they are willing to consider a price of $2,600,000.

5. Certain financial information is provided by Drabinsky (see Exhibit II, page 590).

After the meeting, Bayly's vice-president instructs Rose to prepare a preliminary report on the proposed acquisition.

"First of all we want to know if the prices indicated make sense considering that Bayly's parent company insisted on a 13% after-tax return before approving any major capital acquisitions. I'm a little concerned about the life expectancy of the business because the patent on their major product has a life of only 10 years. They seem to be willing to accept a lower price for the shares than for the assets, and I wonder if they may be willing to accept an even lower share price. It would be useful to have this information before we enter serious negotiations. In addition, provide any other analysis that might help us make a decision."

Donna begins her assignment by gathering certain tax information, and determines that the maximum personal tax rates are 45% on most types of income. Dividends, however, are subject to a 30% rate (net of the dividend tax credit). The corporate rates of tax are 20% for income subject to the small-business deduction, 40% for non-manufacturing income not subject to the small-business deduction, and 37% for manufacturing income. The tax rate on investment income is $51\frac{2}{3}\%$, which includes the $6\frac{2}{3}\%$ refundable tax.

Required:
Prepare the preliminary report.

Exhibit I
BAYLY CORPORATION
Balance Sheet
December 31, 20X1

Assets

Current assets:		
Cash		$ 200,000
Bank term deposits		3,000,000
Accounts receivable		400,000
Inventory		2,400,000
Fixed assets:		
Land		400,000
Buildings and equipment (at cost)	1,600,000	
Accumulated amortization	(700,000)	900,000
		$7,300,000

Liabilities and Shareholders' Equity

Current liabilities:		
Accounts payable		$ 700,000
Bank loan		600,000
		1,300,000
Mortgage payable		2,000,000
Shareholders' equity:		
Common shares	100,000	
Retained earnings	3,900,000	4,000,000
		$7,300,000

Additional information

1. The building and equipment are all used to house the retail outlets and management staff.

2. Total wages paid in 20X1 amounted to $500,000.

Exhibit II
TOTO PIPES LTD.
Balance Sheet
December 31, 20X1

Assets

Current assets:		
Cash and receivables		$ 600,000
Inventory		700,000
Fixed assets:		
Land		100,000
Building (at cost)	400,000	
Equipment (at cost)	800,000	
	1,200,000	
Accumulated amortization	(500,000)	700,000
Patents (on bluestem pipes, at cost)		–0–
Goodwill (at cost)		100,000
		$2,200,000

Liabilities and Shareholders' Equity

Liabilities:		
Accounts payable		$ 500,000
Bank loan (7-year term)		300,000
		800,000
Shareholders' equity:		
Capital shares	100,000	
Retained earnings	1,300,000	1,400,000
		$2,200,000

Additional information

1. Over the past three years the company profits have averaged $750,000 before depreciation, amortization, and income taxes. This average is expected to continue in future years.

2. The company operates solely in Manitoba.

3. Total salaries paid in 20X1 amounted to $400,000, of which $300,000 related directly to manufacturing and $100,000 was for management.

4. All fixed assets were used for manufacturing purposes.

5. The patent on a special pipe filter has 10 years of legal life remaining.

6. Inventory shows a cost of $700,000. However, the company has indicated that the actual cost was $800,000, as the company intentionally lowered its inventory to reduce taxes.

7. The fair market values of other assets are as follows:

Land	$200,000
Building	700,000
Equipment	600,000
Patent	300,000
Goodwill	400,000

8. The UCC of the depreciable assets is as follows:

Class 3	$150,000
Class 43	300,000
Class 44	—0—

The balance in the cumulative eligible capital account is $40,000.

Chapter 18   Business Acquisitions and Divestitures— Tax-Deferred Sales

Most business acquisitions and divestitures are completed on a fully taxable basis by one of the two methods described in the previous chapter. Fully taxable divestitures in the form of share sales or asset sales are characterized by the complete separation of the vendor from the business being sold; in other words, the vendor maintains no continued interest in the ongoing operations of the transferred business.

However, sometimes the vendor chooses or is forced to maintain an ongoing equity interest in the business that is sold. In these cases it is possible to structure the transaction so that the vendor's tax liability is deferred until that continued interest ceases.

This chapter examines the methods available for achieving a tax-deferred sale of a business, the circumstances in which they are relevant, and the resulting general tax treatment to both the vendor and the purchaser. The tax-deferred methods are then examined in two contexts: the sale of a closely held corporation to a third-party purchaser, and the sale of a similar entity to family members.

I. Tax-Deferred Sales and Acquisitions

A. The Nature of and Reasons for a Tax-Deferred Sale

In order for the vendor to achieve a continued tax deferral on the sale of a business, it must be prepared to maintain a continuing equity interest in the purchaser's corporation or the vendor corporation. This equity interest can be in the form of common shares or preferred shares. A vendor who receives common shares as part of the sale transaction incurs continued risk but also the opportunity for continued growth in value. A vendor who receives preferred shares with a fixed dividend rate incurs a lesser risk but also no potential for future growth.

A tax-deferred sale is distinguished from a taxable sale by the nature of the payment received for the property. A *taxable* sale involves the payment of cash, or a deferred payment of cash secured by notes bearing interest. A *taxed-deferred* sale involves payment in the form of shares issued by the purchasing corporation.

There are three basic reasons that a vendor may be prepared to accept a greater risk by receiving shares rather than cash or other secure assets:

1. The vendor wants to participate in the continued growth of the business. In such a case the sale actually constitutes a business combination or merger (see Chapter 14). Increased profits can result from enhanced sales opportunities and from reduced expenses owing to improved economies of scale.

2. The vendor simply wants to enhance its after-tax return on investment. For example, by accepting the full purchase price in the form of preferred shares of the purchaser corporation together with a reasonable fixed dividend rate, the vendor will receive an annual return on the full selling price. If the payment were in the form of cash or notes, the vendor would be able to reinvest only the after-tax proceeds, which would provide a lower annual return.

3. The purchaser may not have sufficient cash to make the acquisition, or perhaps no other acceptable buyers are present. When the vendor accepts preferred shares in the buyer corporation, the purchaser can pay for the business over a period of time by gradually redeeming the preferred shares as future profits and cash flow are generated. This type of situation is common when a business is sold to employees or to family members.

When arranging a tax-deferred sale of a corporate business, one must utilize the special provisions of the *Income Tax Act* that are designed to provide tax relief when corporations are reorganized. Corporate reorganizations were reviewed extensively in Chapter 14 in the context of the combining or separating of business activities within a related group of companies. These same methods apply equally to the sale of a business to an independent third party. When arranging the tax-deferred sale of a business, the following alternative courses of action are available:

1. A sale of assets by one corporation to another at an elected transfer price for tax purposes equal to the assets' tax values.

2. A sale of the corporation's shares to a corporate purchaser at an elected transfer price equal to the tax value of the shares.

3. An amalgamation of two or more corporations.

4. A reorganization of share capital.

Each of these methods is re-examined below in the context of a sale to arm's-length purchasers. The following situation, which is both common and simple, is used as the basis for examining and comparing each method.

Buyer Corporation, which is owned entirely by shareholder X, intends to acquire the business operated by Seller Corporation. Seller Corporation is 100% owned by shareholder Y. The corporate structure prior to the acquisition is diagrammed below.

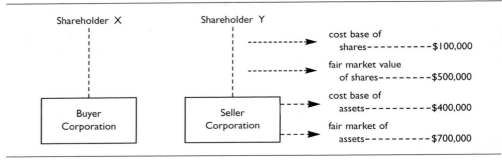

Notice that the cost base to Y of the shares of Seller Corporation is $100,000 and that the fair market value is $500,000. Therefore, a sale of shares would usually result in a capital gain on disposition. Also notice that the assets in Seller Corporation have a fair market value in excess of their tax values; this would usually create taxable income to the corporation if the individual business assets were sold.

B. Sale of Assets   A tax-deferred sale can be achieved by arranging for the vendor corporation to sell individual assets to the buyer corporation at a price for tax purposes equal to the assets' cost amount.[1] This can be done even though the actual selling price for legal purposes is equal to the assets' fair market value. In the sample situation the assets of Seller Corporation have a tax cost of $400,000 and a fair market value of $700,000. In this scenario the assets are sold for $700,000 for legal purposes but only $400,000 for tax purposes. In accordance with the elective rules described in Chapter 12, Seller Corporation can be paid in the form of cash or notes to a maximum of $400,000 (the elected amount), with the balance in the form of shares of Buyer Corporation. The sale and payment terms are summarized as follows:

---

1   ITA 85(1); IT-291R2.

Sale price of assets	$700,000
Payment consideration:	
Cash or notes	$400,000
Shares of Buyer Corporation	300,000
	$700,000

The shares received from Buyer Corporation can be common shares or preferred shares depending on whether the vendor intends to participate in the future growth of Buyer Corporation. This transaction is diagrammed below.

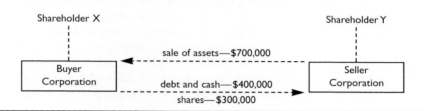

Notice that by electing $400,000 as the tax transfer price, Seller Corporation avoids tax on the asset values in excess of their tax cost ($700,000 – $400,000 = $300,000). Consequently, the shares received as consideration are deemed to have a tax cost of zero even though their fair market value is $300,000.[2] At some future time, when Seller Corporation disposes of the shares, taxable income may be created, although the nature of that income may be different from what would have been created from a normal sale of assets at fair market values.

The tax deferral permits the vendor to fully invest the pre-tax proceeds of the sale to provide a return on investment. In this example the vendor will receive a return on investment from the $400,000 of cash and notes, as well as from the $300,000 of shares received; this is more than it would have received if it had sold the assets at normal fair market values, thereby incurring immediate taxable income. The vendor achieves a tax deferral and the potential for increased returns, but also assumes an additional risk by accepting shares of the purchaser corporation as payment. The ability to recover a value from these shares depends on the future success of Buyer Corporation.

This form of purchase has both advantages and disadvantages to the purchaser. The major advantage is that the purchase can be achieved with a minimum of cash and debt, because of the requirement that shares be issued as part of the payment terms. As a result, a greater amount of future cash flow is available to ensure the success of continued business operations. In addition, the company's ability to borrow operating funds, should those be required, is not significantly disturbed. How much of an advantage this is depends on the terms attached to the shares issued to the vendor. For example, the issuing of non-participating preferred shares to the vendor may carry with it an obligatory redemption program, or may provide the vendor with the option of having the preferred shares redeemed in certain portions after a specified time period.

A major disadvantage to the purchaser is that the cost base of the assets acquired is deemed to be equal to the transfer price elected for tax purposes rather than to the assets' fair market value. As a result, future capital cost allowance on depreciable property will be

2   ITA 85(1)(f) to (h); IT-291R2. The paid-up capital is also reduced to a nominal amount—ITA 85(2.1); IT-463R2.

less than would have been available if the assets had been purchased in the normal fashion (see Chapter 17). In addition, the lower cost base of the assets creates a potential tax liability for the purchaser if, after acquisition, all or some of the assets are disposed of at fair market value. Also, funding the purchase by issuing preferred shares usually requires a fixed obligatory dividend payment that is not deductible from the purchaser's income. Although the dividend rate will be less than the rate of interest on a debt, it may still result in an after-tax cost to the purchaser that is greater than the after-tax cost of interest (see Chapter 21). The purchaser must, therefore, weigh the impact of reduced funding requirements against the impact of reduced capital cost allowance and dividend requirements.

The above disadvantages are of less concern to the purchaser when the acquisition of assets on a tax-deferred basis is actually a business combination as opposed to a buy-out. For example, in the preceding situation, if Buyer Corporation had purchased the assets by issuing $700,000 of common shares to Seller Corporation, with the intention that Seller Corporation continue as a participating shareholder of the larger entity for an indefinite time, the transaction would have signified a business combination rather than a complete takeover. As no cash or debt was exchanged, both parties would have continued to bear a proportionate share of the risk, and the negative aspects described above would have been of little consequence.

C. Sale of Shares   A vendor that wishes to sell a business by selling the shares of the vendor corporation rather than assets can obtain a tax deferral by using the same elective provisions as for an asset sale. Referring again to the sample situation, notice that shareholder Y holds shares of Seller Corporation that have a cost base of $100,000 and a fair market value of $500,000. If Y sells the shares to Buyer Corporation in the normal manner, a capital gain of $400,000 will result, one-half of which will be taxable. This realization of a capital gain can be deferred by electing that the sale price for tax purposes is $100,000 (equal to the cost base), provided that at least $400,000 of the $500,000 purchase price is paid in the form of shares of Buyer Corporation.

After this transaction the corporate structure would be as follows:

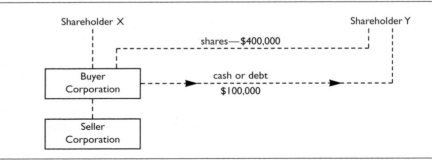

If the elective option is used, the shares of Buyer Corporation that are owned by the vendor, shareholder Y, will have a fair market value of $400,000 but a cost amount for tax purposes of zero. However, when shareholder Y disposes of those shares at some future time, a tax liability will occur.

As with the sale of assets, the vendor can receive either common shares or preferred shares or a combination of the two, depending on the nature of the takeover. In this particular situation, notice that the ratio of cash and debt to share consideration for the asset sale was different than it was for the share sale, assuming that each transaction involved the maximum permitted cash and debt. This difference is as follows:

	Asset sale	Share sale
Total price	$700,000	$500,000
Consideration:		
Cash and debt	$400,000	$100,000
Shares	300,000	400,000
	$700,000	$500,000
Percentage as shares	43%	80%

The above result occurs because the relationship between asset cost and fair market value is usually not the same as the relationship between share cost and fair market value. The vendor's risk is increased when a greater portion of the payment is in the form of the buyer's shares. The vendor should consider this when deciding whether to accept a share sale rather than an asset sale under the elective provisions.

For both the vendor and the purchaser, the advantages and disadvantages of a tax-deferred sale of shares are similar to those for a tax-deferred sale of assets, and no further comment is necessary. However, it should be noted that one problem arises from the sale of shares; it has to do with the formal process involved in making the election to transfer shares at their tax values. To utilize this election, both the purchaser and the vendor must formalize their intentions by signing a tax agreement. While this is not a problem when there are few shareholders, it may be difficult when there are many shareholders, and virtually impossible when the corporation being sold is a public corporation. The parties can overcome this problem by using a less formal tax-deferred method of selling shares, referred to as a *share-for-share exchange*.

A share-for-share exchange has been made when a purchasing corporation acquires the shares of another corporation and the payments consist entirely of shares issued by the purchaser. In these circumstances, and provided that certain other conditions are met, each separate vendor is entitled to declare that its shares have been sold at their cost amount, thereby deferring tax on the sale.[3] This decision is made solely by the vendor when all other conditions are met. Consider the previous sample situation: a share-for-share exchange would occur if shareholder Y sold all of the shares of Seller Corporation to Buyer Corporation for $500,000 worth of shares of Buyer Corporation. Shareholder Y can choose to recognize all or part of the $400,000 capital gain, or none of it, in the year of sale. If shareholder Y chooses to recognize none of the gain, the $500,000 of shares in Buyer Corporation received in exchange are deemed to have a tax cost of $100,000 (equal to the cost of shares sold); any subsequent sales of those shares would trigger the recognition of the capital gain.

Unfortunately, for the purchaser, the share-for-share exchange method is not so attractive. This is because the purchaser's adjusted cost base of the shares acquired in a share-for-share exchange is equal to the lesser of the shares' paid-up capital or their fair market value. As the acquired shares' paid-up capital is normally lower than fair market value, the result is that the purchaser's cost for tax purposes is lower than the market value of the shares. This may result in additional taxes if the shares are subsequently sold. Therefore, when private corporations are involved, they usually prefer to use the elective option described earlier rather than the share-for-share exchange option. However, the share-for-share exchange format may be useful when public corporations are involved.

---

3   ITA 85.1(1) to (3); IT-450R.

D. Amalgamation

As described in Chapter 14, an amalgamation involves the combining of two or more corporations into a single entity housing the business activities of the former corporations. As part of the amalgamation, the shareholders of the separate corporations must become shareholders of the amalgamated corporation, and maintain a continued interest in the combined operations.

The amalgamation process combines a share sale with an asset sale, in that the shareholders of the former corporations exchange their shares for shares of the new corporation, and all of the former corporations transfer their assets to the new corporation. This type of business combination automatically results in a tax-deferred exchange of shares and assets.[4]

Although, by definition, an amalgamation of two business corporations is a business combination, it is often referred to as a "takeover," which is an acquisition that results in one company significantly dominating the other. For example, assume that Buyer Corporation has a net worth of $2,000,000. The amalgamation of Buyer Corporation ($2,000,000) and Seller Corporation ($500,000) would result in the following structure:

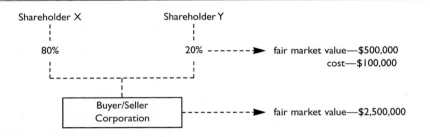

Although the two companies have joined their economic resources in a business combination, shareholder X, with its 80% holdings, clearly dominates shareholder Y, which has become a minority shareholder in the combined entity. In effect, the amalgamation amounts to a takeover by Buyer Corporation and its shareholders.

Business acquisitions using the amalgamation method are most common among public corporations, because the former shareholders of the acquired company can dispose of the publicly traded shares of the new entity on the open market, and in so doing realize their investment under the most favourable conditions.

E. Share Reorganization

A tax-deferred sale of a business can also be achieved by a reorganization of share capital as described in Chapter 14.[5] In this scenario, shareholder Y, before the acquisition, would convert the common shares, which have a value of $500,000 and a cost of $100,000, into fixed-value preferred shares of the same value. The purchaser would then acquire newly issued common shares for a nominal value. The corporate structure immediately after the acquisition would be as shown on the next page.

This method involves considerable risk for shareholder Y, as the opportunity to realize the value of the preferred shares depends entirely on the continued success of the vendor corporation. This method is quite different from the previous ones, all of which provided the vendor with shares of the purchaser corporation and thereby enhanced the vendor's security.

---

4   ITA 87(1) to (4); IT-474R.

5   ITA 86(1) to (3).

The share reorganization method is appropriate when the vendor has significant confidence in the purchaser's ability to manage the acquired business.

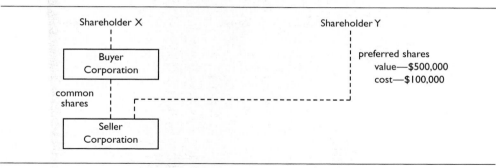

F. Conclusion The above review indicates that several alternative methods are available to achieve a tax-deferred business sale and acquisition. It is clear that each method follows one of the two basic alternatives, which are the asset sale and the share sale. All tax-deferred acquisitions involving a share sale, an asset sale, an amalgamation, or a share reorganization have similar results for both vendor and purchaser. The vendor defers tax on the sale by accepting payment, in whole or in part, in the form of the purchaser's shares; in doing so, that vendor incurs greater risk. The purchaser assumes the disadvantage of a lower cost base for the assets acquired, but is also able to issue shares as payment for the acquisition, which reduces the related cash and debt requirements.

The tax-deferred methods are almost always used when the transaction is a business combination in which two or more entities are joining forces and both or all will be participating in future operations. When the transaction is actually a takeover, the decision to use the tax-deferred method rather than the taxable method is based on the existing circumstances. The tax-deferred method is especially attractive when the vendor has confidence in the purchaser's management abilities. For example, a vendor may be more than willing to sell the business to its managers or employees, in the knowledge that the purchasers will continue to run the business successfully. However, in such a sale the purchaser must usually look to the vendor for financing. The tax-deferred methods of payment by shares suit this type of transaction.

Similarly, the sale of a family business to children is usually highly leveraged; that is, the vendor provides the purchasers with the necessary financing in exchange for a long-term payout. In such cases the tax-deferred methods are an appropriate way to match the tax liability with the receipt of payments. By maintaining a continued share interest, the parent can defer tax until the business generates sufficient funds that the purchasers can buy out the shares.

Because so many options exist, both tax-deferred and fully taxable (see Chapter 17), there is considerable flexibility in structuring a business divestiture and acquisition. The choice of method will depend on the needs of the vendor and purchaser in the given circumstances. Every potential purchase and sale has its obstacles. The wide range of options makes it easier to overcome these and complete a successful sale transaction.

Because the best form of transaction for a particular situation is not always obvious, the decision-making process must involve examining each of the alternatives in terms of both its immediate and its long-term impact. This process is reviewed below in the context of the sale of a closely held corporate business.

II. Sale of a Closely Held Corporation

A. Distinguishing Features

A closely held corporation has either a single shareholder or a relatively small number of shareholders so that the relationship between the shareholders and the corporation is very close. This type of corporation often develops a financial structure that mixes the affairs of its primary business with those of its shareholders. Consequently, special circumstances may exist that affect the manner in which the business is ultimately sold, whether the sale is to independent third parties or to related family members.

Often, but not always, a closely held corporation will have the following features, which will affect any later sale of the business:

1. The corporation that houses the business has, in addition to the business assets, a number of investment assets that are not related to the operation of the business. The existence of investment assets is a result of the corporation's dividend policy, which normally involves distributing to the shareholder only the amounts he or she needs, with any remaining amount being held in the corporation to delay the incidence of tax.

   In addition, the corporation may also own certain business assets such as land, buildings, and equipment, although the ownership of these assets may not be essential to the business, as their use could be secured by way of lease arrangements.

2. The owner of the business is usually under greater pressure to sell the business to immediate family members of the next generation, or to senior managers or other employees who have given long service to the business. Typically, such employees and family members do not have the cash necessary to make the acquisition.

3. The business of a closely held corporation is often sold in response to the owner's wish to retire. Usually, this means that the vendor has a strong need to maximize future income from investment of the proceeds of sale. Obviously, taxation of the proceeds from a sale of assets or shares will diminish the after-tax funds available for reinvestment, and any subsequent income.

So the sale of a closely held corporation must be structured in such a way that the vendor's security is assured and that the purchaser can make the acquisition. One such sale is demonstrated below. It is reviewed first as a third-party sale and then as a sale to family members.

B. Sale to Third Parties

The sale of a business to third parties may involve negotiations with a number of potential buyers, each of which faces a different financial situation, and each of which has a different reason for making the acquisition. The following analysis examines only one particular negotiation, and shows how the form of a sale can be structured to deal with all parties' particular circumstances.

Summary of Facts

Mr. X is the sole shareholder of For Sale Corporation, a Canadian-controlled private corporation that operates a medium-size business. He acquired the shares at a nominal cost when the company was incorporated, and the shares have increased in value substantially. Mr. X has decided to sell the business and retire. While a number of potential buyers are available, he has decided to sell the business to a small group of its senior managers provided that a workable arrangement can be made.

The managers can raise a limited amount of funds from their personal savings, and from loans that would be secured by their personal assets.

The assets of For Sale Corporation are listed below. Except for the current assets and the bonds, the values of the assets exceed their cost amounts. The company does not have a substantial debt load and is heavily financed by retained earnings that have not been distributed to the shareholder.

Assets Related to the Business

Current assets:
   Accounts receivable
   Inventory
Fixed assets:
   Land
   Buildings
   Equipment
Other assets:
   Goodwill

Assets Not Related to the Business

Bonds
Real estate investments

Analysis

When this situation is examined, a number of things immediately become clear.

From the point of view of the vendor, a normal taxable sale of the entire corporation, by way of either an asset sale or a share sale, will create a tax liability that will reduce the after-tax proceeds that are available for generating a retirement income. It is also clear that a sale to the managers is going to require some funding by the vendor, and that Mr. X must be concerned about the degree of security attached to the deferred payments.

The purchasers have limited resources, which means that a flexible, long-term payout must be arranged so that the purchase can be funded from future profits. The purchaser might obtain additional funding from venture capitalists; however, this would mean giving up a portion of the ownership and result in reduced repayment flexibility. Therefore, this is considered an alternative of last resort.

It is also clear that the purchasers do not need all of the assets within For Sale Corporation in order to operate the business they are acquiring. This presents two possibilities. The new owners could acquire the shares of For Sale Corporation, dispose of some or all of the redundant assets, and use the proceeds to fund part of the purchase price (see Chapter 14 on the use of holding companies). Alternatively, those owners could keep all the assets in the corporation and borrow against the redundant assets. For example, For Sale Corporation has a low debt load, and the new owners may be able to pledge the real estate or bonds as collateral in return for favourable long-term financing.

A second possibility is for the purchaser to reduce the overall purchase price by acquiring only the specific assets essential to operate the business. This would leave the remaining assets in the hands of the former owner. In this case, there would be no need to purchase the bonds and investment real estate, and therefore the price could be lowered so that it was more in line with the purchaser's resources. In addition, the land, buildings, and equipment needed for the business could be leased by the business rather than purchased.

It is extremely critical that the purchasers examine the nature of the asset base of the entity they are acquiring. This is especially true when the entity is a closely held corporation and the shareholder is more flexible in terms of alternative buy-out arrangements.

The Sale and Acquisition Structure Chosen

In this situation the purchaser and the vendor met their needs by means of a tax-deferred asset sale of only those assets required to operate the business. Specifically, the transaction involved the following:

1. The new managers created a new corporation (referred to as Purchase Corporation), to which they contributed their available funds in exchange for common share capital.

2. Purchase Corporation then acquired the following assets from For Sale Corporation:

> Current assets:
>   Accounts receivable
>   Inventory
> Other assets:
>   Goodwill

   Payment for these assets consisted of a limited amount of cash, the assumption of current liabilities, and a note payable (with interest) to For Sale Corporation, as well as the issuance of preferred shares to For Sale Corporation.

3. Both parties elected that, for tax purposes, the transfer price of the goodwill was equal to an amount that would create no taxable income to the vendor. In accordance with the election provisions, the value of the preferred shares represented the difference between the fair value of the goodwill and the elected price for tax purposes.

4. The preferred shares paid a fixed dividend that was acceptable to both parties. While the purchaser could redeem the preferred shares at any time, those shares had to be fully redeemed by the end of 10 years. In addition, the preferred shares provided limited voting rights so that although the vendor did not control the new company, he could exercise a significant influence. In addition, the vendor had the option of calling for the immediate redemption of his shares in the event that Purchase Corporation failed to pay an annual dividend.

5. Purchase Corporation did not purchase the land, buildings, and equipment used to operate the business. Instead, it signed long-term leases that provided For Sale Corporation with net rents equal to 12% of the property's fair market value at the time. Purchase Corporation was granted an option to acquire the property at the end of the lease for a price equal to the fair market value of the assets at that future time. The above sale and purchase structure is shown on the next page.

Completing the sale in the preceding format met the needs of both the vendor and the purchaser in this specific situation. The vendor has maximized his future income, in part by deferring the tax that would have resulted from an asset sale. By retaining the land, buildings, and equipment, he has deferred recapture of capital cost allowance and (perhaps) capital gains. The lease arrangement provides a rental return based on the assets' fair

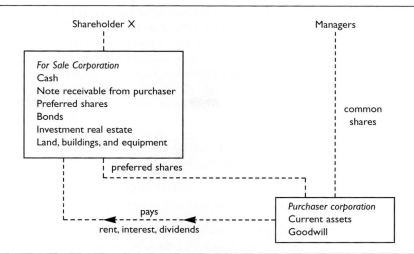

market values; this return is much higher than it would have been if the assets had been sold and the resulting after-tax proceeds invested. Also, the goodwill that was sold on a tax-deferred basis provides a dividend return based on its fair market value rather than its after-tax value.

As well, the vendor has achieved significant security for the following reasons:

1. Retaining the land, buildings, and equipment under a lease arrangement fully protects that property from any risk associated with a possible failure of the business after it is taken over by the managers. In particular, the land and buildings will likely continue to increase in value and can be sold at any time.

2. Although part of the sale price is reflected in preferred shares, the nature of those shares provides For Sale Corporation with significant power, which can be exercised if the purchasers fail to meet their commitments.

3. The business is being sold to managers who have a keen knowledge of the business; their management skills are a known quantity.

4. The purchasers have shown a commitment to the purchase by investing a large portion of their own assets in the new corporation in the form of common shares, which are subordinated to the preferred shares.

The purchasers also achieved their objective, which was to acquire the business with limited capital resources. They have purchased only those assets that are absolutely necessary to run the business and have arranged favourable terms with the vendor, so their chances of success are high. In this case, what is good for the vendor is also good for the purchaser—which is important to any successful sale and acquisition.

It is important to recognize that the consideration of tax factors played a major role in the successful sale negotiation. Both the vendor and the purchasers reviewed all the basic alternatives—asset sale, share sale, and tax-deferred sale—and found a satisfactory solution.

C. Sale to Family Members

The sale and purchase of a business within a family unit has all of the fundamental aspects of a sale to third parties. It can be an asset sale or a share sale as a fully taxable transaction, or it can use the various tax-deferred methods discussed earlier. However, unlike a sale to third parties, a family transaction is influenced by the dynamics of family relationships.

In some cases the nature of the family relationship is such that a sale of a business by a parent to a child is treated as if it were a sale to a third party, in which case the discussion in the previous section is relevant. In most cases, however, the vendor in a family transaction is prepared to give preferential terms that will ensure a successful acquisition by the purchaser.

The sale of a family business to children may appear unnecessary considering that on the death of the parent, the business will likely pass to the children as a succession gift. There are two reasons that a parent may want to sell a family business to children well before an estate transfer:

1. An early transfer may minimize the tax liability that would otherwise occur on the death of the original owner.

2. The early transfer of a family business from one generation to another provides an orderly succession and a continuity of management responsibility.

Obviously, the sale of a business to family members is often motivated by personal factors, which in turn influence the form of the transaction. A sale to a third party must result in the best possible security for the vendor so that he or she can ultimately realize the full value of the business. The vendor will therefore use one of the tax-deferred methods (which require a continued share interest) only if the security of the transaction is more than adequate. In a sale to children, however, the vendor is less concerned about security, as the value of the business will likely pass to the children in any event through the vendor's estate. This means that the deferral and minimization of tax may be the primary concern when the method of transaction is being chosen.

Consider, for example, the same situation described previously involving the sale of a business to third parties, with this change: shareholder X's objectives are to transfer ownership of the business to an only child who is active in the business, and to minimize taxes that may occur on death.

Both of shareholder X's objectives can be satisfied by utilizing the tax-deferred method of share reorganization. Under this method, shareholder X exchanges all common shares owned for fixed value preferred shares having a value equal to the common shares exchanged. As the full value of For Sale Corporation is locked up in the preferred shares, X's child can acquire the new common shares for a nominal cost. This form of transaction has the following results:

1. The parent, shareholder X, has fully financed the change in ownership by accepting fixed-value preferred shares in exchange for the former common shares.

2. The parent has received full value for the company in accepting preferred shares as payment; however, no immediate tax liability results. The parent will be subject to tax if he or she redeems the preferred shares or should die holding the shares.

3. The parent will have a continued source of income from the predetermined dividend attached to the preferred shares.

4. Although the preferred shares will eventually be subject to tax, their value will not grow beyond the value at the date of issuance; this means that the parent's potential tax liability is "frozen" at the date of the sale transaction. Consequently, the parent's ultimate tax liability is considerably less than it would have been if he or she had continued to hold the common shares, allowed them to grow in value, and left them to the child on death.

5. All growth in the value of For Sale Corporation beyond its value at the transaction date will accrue to the benefit of the child as the new common shareholder.

Notice that in this form of buy-out, the child gained entitlement to all property owned by For Sale Corporation—the business assets as well as the investment assets. This may not always be desirable when there are several children in a family and some of those children will not be involved in the business activity. In such cases, an alternative form of transaction could be utilized. For example, the business could be transferred to one child by having For Sale Corporation sell only its business assets, on a tax-deferred basis, to a new corporation created by the child. (This is similar to what was done in the sale to employees that was described earlier.)

As with third-party sales, it is important that in a family sale, the vendor and the purchaser investigate a number of alternative sale-transaction methods to determine which one best satisfies the needs of all parties concerned while maintaining the integrity of the transaction.

III. Summary and Conclusion

A business sale and acquisition can take a number of different forms. In addition to the normal taxable methods that involve selling shares or assets, there are tax-deferred methods.

The tax-deferred methods examined in this chapter are not new; they were also examined in Chapter 14 in the context of corporate reorganizations within a related group of companies. These methods apply equally well to arm's-length acquisitions and divestitures. It is important to recognize that the tax-deferred methods involve particular trade-offs. From the vendor's perspective, the attractiveness of delaying tax on the sale is lessened somewhat by the increased financial risk, which results from the requirement that all or some of the payment be in the form of a continued equity interest in the business. From the purchaser's perspective, the attractiveness of a lesser cash or debt requirement to complete the acquisition is moderated by the reduced deductions available from capital cost allowance on assets purchased, and by the requirement that share capital be issued (as opposed to debt), which must be serviced by non-deductible dividends (as opposed to deductible interest).

Notwithstanding these trade-offs, the tax-deferred methods are viable and often-used alternatives. In the proper circumstances they can be applied to the acquisition and divestiture of large businesses as well as small businesses, and to public corporations as well as private corporations. It is vitally important that the decision maker who is responsible for making an acquisition or sale investigate all of the available transaction forms. Every purchase and sale has unique characteristics; among the array of alternatives, a method can usually be found that meets the particular needs of both the vendor and the purchaser.

The discussion in this chapter confined itself to the purchase and sale of a business involving both a corporate vendor and a corporate purchaser. Similar tax-deferred methods are also available when a business is sold by a corporation to a partnership, by one partnership to another, or by a partnership to a corporation.

Reading List

Income Tax Act References

	Section
Transfer of property to a corporation by a shareholder	85(1)
Computation of paid-up capital	85(2.1)
Share-for-share exchange	85.1(1) to (3)
Exchange of shares by a shareholder in the course of a reorganization of capital	86(1) to (3)
Amalgamations	87(1) to (11)

Canada Customs and Revenue Agency Publications

IT-291R2	Transfer of property to a corporation under section 85.
IT-463R2	Paid-up capital.
IT-450R	Share-for-share exchange.
IT-474R	Amalgamation of Canadian corporations.

Other Publications

Harris, D., "'T' for Two: Estate Planning in a Two Family Business," Report of Proceedings of the 50th Tax Conference, Canadian Tax Foundation, p. 35.1.

Rocchi, R., "Succession of Family Businesses," 1989 Conference Report of Proceedings of the 41st Tax Conference, Canadian Tax Foundation, pp. 15:1–27.

Bernstein, J. "Sale of a Business to Employees," 1985 Corporate Management Tax Conference, Canadian Tax Foundation, pp. 1.16–64.

Ross, D., "Management Buyouts," Corporate Management Tax Conference (1996), Canadian Tax Foundation, p. 14.1.

Review Questions

1. While vendors may gain a tax advantage by selling a business using a tax-deferred method, they may be subjecting themselves to more risk in terms of ultimately realizing the proceeds from the sale. How is a tax-deferred sale of a business distinguished from a taxable sale? Why does a tax-deferred sale involve greater risk?

2. Give three basic reasons that a vendor may be prepared to accept a greater risk in exchange for a tax deferral on the sale of a business.

3. What four basic methods can be used to achieve a tax-deferred sale?

4. What advantages and disadvantages may arise for the purchaser when the specific business assets are acquired from a vendor corporation and the parties elect transfer prices for tax purposes at amounts that will defer tax to the vendor?

5. What is a share-for-share exchange? How does it differ from a sale of shares in which the vendor and the purchaser elect a specific price for tax purposes?

6. Why is a business acquisition using the share-for-share technique attractive to both the purchaser and the vendor?

7. A tax-deferred sale of a business by a reorganization of share capital may present more risk to the vendor than a sale of its shares to a corporate purchaser and an election of a transfer price for tax purposes. Explain why.

8. When a business owned by a closely held corporation is being sold, the vendor is often persuaded to use tax-deferred methods to structure the sale. What is a closely held corporation? What features may such a corporation have that make a tax-deferred sale attractive?

9. Why may the owner of a business want to transfer a business to children during his or her lifetime rather than by way of an estate transfer on death?

10. What feature is often found when a business is being transferred to a family member? How is the tax-deferred method of sale consistent with this feature?

11. How may the sale of a corporation's specific business assets to a purchaser with limited resources provide greater flexibility than the sale of shares of the corporation?

Problems

Problem One

For the past 30 years, Janice Kalinsky has been the president and owner of JK Wholesale Ltd. In contemplation of retirement, she has entered negotiations to sell the shares of JK to Kaplan Brothers Ltd., a company that has been her major competitor. Although Kalinsky's planned retirement date is still five years away, she is prepared to sell now so that she can have a defined amount of capital available to provide a retirement income.

Kaplan Brothers has offered to purchase her shares in JK for $700,000. The shares have a cost base of $200,000. Kalinsky intends to invest the proceeds from the sale in interest-bearing securities that yield a 10% return for five years. The accumulated funds will provide her with a retirement income at the end of five years. In the meantime, she will be employed as the executive director of a national trade association.

Kalinsky is concerned about the amount of tax payable on the sale and has had discussions with Kaplan Brothers about using the elective provisions of the *Income Tax Act* to defer her tax on the sale of shares. Kaplan Brothers has agreed to this and has presented her with two options:

1. Purchase of her shares for $700,000, payable immediately in cash.

2. Purchase of her shares for $700,000, using the elective provisions of the *Income Tax Act* to defer her tax liability. Payment would consist of debt with 10% interest and preferred shares with an annual cumulative dividend rate of 8%. Kaplan Brothers would repay the full amount of the debt and redeem the preferred shares at the end of five years.

Kalinsky's personal marginal tax rate is 30% on dividends (net of the dividend tax credit) and 45% on other income. She used up her full capital gain deduction several years ago while selling a related business corporation.

Kaplan Brothers has earned profits of $400,000 before tax for the past two years.

Required:

1. Determine the amount of capital that Kalinsky will have for retirement purposes at the end of five years under each of the alternative buy-out methods.

2. What other factors must Kalinsky consider before she decides which option to accept?

3. What are the benefits and costs of option 2 for Kaplan Brothers?

Problem Two

Shane Plastics Ltd. is a Canadian-controlled private corporation. All of its outstanding common shares are owned by KS Holdings Ltd., a company owned by Karl Shane. KS Holdings also owns several real estate investments. Shane wants to sell the plastics business to four senior employees, one of whom is his son. Shane realizes that none of the employees has substantial financial resources, and that they may be able to contribute only 25% of the purchase price. Even to obtain this amount, the four employees would likely have to take out personal loans.

A financial institution is prepared to finance the balance of the purchase price provided that Shane agrees to be the guarantor of the loan. Shane may be prepared to do this, even though it would leave the business with a severe debt load and no flexibility should the business have temporary problems.

The employees have asked Shane to finance the purchase by permitting a flexible, eight-year payment schedule. Shane is not averse to this offer provided that he can continue to have some say in the major decisions of the business until most of the payments have been made.

The most recent balance sheet of Shane Plastics is summarized in the following table:

Current assets (cash, receivables, inventory)		$ 500,000
Land		50,000
Building	600,000	
Equipment	350,000	
	950,000	
Accumulated amortization	(400,000)	550,000
Marketable securities (bonds)		100,000
		$1,200,000
Current liabilities		$ 300,000
Mortgage on land and building		400,000
Shareholders' equity:		
Share capital	10,000	
Retained earnings	490,000	500,000
		$1,200,000

The following additional information is available:

1. The undepreciated capital cost of the depreciable property is as follows:

Building	$490,000
Equipment	100,000

2. The asset values are as follows:

Current assets	$500,000
Land	100,000
Building	720,000
Equipment	300,000
Marketable securities	100,000

In addition, the value of goodwill has been estimated at $400,000.

3. KS Holdings acquired the shares of Shane Plastics a number of years ago at a cost of $200,000. Recently, a competitor had offered to purchase the shares of Shane Plastics for $1,200,000; Shane had refused the offer because he wanted to sell to the employees.

Shane is prepared to accept the deferred payment schedule suggested by the employees but has concerns about the immediate tax liability associated with the sale. Shane is 50 years old and intends to maintain KS Holdings to hold his investment portfolio. He will also continue to be employed by Shane Plastics after the business has been acquired by the employees.

Required:

1. Assuming that either an asset sale by Shane Plastics or a share sale by KS Holdings will be made at fair market values, with deferred payments over eight years, which method should Shane prefer? You may assume a corporate tax rate of 40% on all income.

2. Suggest and briefly discuss several alternative methods for deferring the tax liabilities on the sale, and that will also assist the purchasers in making the acquisition, considering their limited resources. Be as specific as possible, given the information provided.

Cases

Case One   Delwin Corporation Ltd.

Carla Delwin has requested that you review her current financial position and her proposed plans, and provide her with tax advice. In response to her request, you have gathered together the following information.

Delwin Corporation Ltd. is a Canadian-controlled private corporation that owns several retail clothing stores. Its common shares are owned 80% by Delwin and 20% by one of her senior managers. Information relating to the shares is as follows:

	Delwin	Manager
Number of shares	800	200
Paid-up capital	$8,000	$ 2,000
Cost	8,000	25,000

In the current year, DCL earned taxable income of $340,000 from the retail operations. It is expected that this level of profit will be maintained next year.

DCL is planning to expand into the manufacturing business and is currently negotiating for the purchase of equipment that will be used to manufacture winter ski jackets. Because the ski jackets have a ready market in her retail stores, profits are expected to be at least $40,000 in the first year.

The expansion will be funded by cash generated from the sale of a building. The building was sold last year and resulted in a capital gain of $200,000 to DCL. The funds are currently invested in short-term bank certificates.

After a major dispute with the senior manager, it was agreed that early in the new year the manager would sell his shares for $120,000, leaving Delwin with 100% of the company. The parties have not discussed how to structure the transaction. However, Delwin has indicated to the manager that the full price will be paid in cash.

Delwin personally owns a commercial building that has generated rental revenue for several years. The current lease will end in the near future, and she has decided that rather than renew the lease, she will use the building to open a new retail location. The property was acquired a number of years ago for $100,000 ($80,000 for the building, $20,000 for the land). To date, she has claimed capital cost allowance totalling $30,000. A recent appraisal indicates that the land is worth $30,000 and the building $90,000. Delwin wishes to transfer the land and building to DCL.

In addition, Delwin personally owns several investments that generate Canadian dividends and interest income. She has been wondering if there would be any tax advantage to incorporating these investments.

Delwin contributes the maximum to retirement plans, and her RRSP currently has a value of $200,000, consisting solely of common share investments.

Delwin's son Eric, who had managed one of the retail stores, has recently been promoted to take on greater management responsibilities. Delwin has promised Eric that after a two-year period he can become a 50% shareholder in DCL. She wants to know how this can be achieved, considering that Eric will have no money to make the acquisition. Also, Delwin is not anxious to pay tax when she restructures the ownership within the family.

Required:

Prepare a report to Delwin providing the tax advice she has requested. Include the tax implications to the manager on the proposed sale of shares.

Case Two*   Mattjon Limited

Matthew and Jonathan have owned a manufacturing company, Mattjon Limited, for 20 years. Matthew, who is 55 years old, retired from the business on December 31, 20X0. He and his wife plan to travel throughout Canada during his retirement.

It is now January 5, 20X1. Jonathan would like to purchase Matthew's 50% share of Mattjon. A recent appraisal put the value of the company at $1.5 million. Jonathan does not have the cash resources to complete the purchase and is concerned about his ability to meet the debt service costs if he has to borrow money to purchase Matthew's shares. As the two men are friends, Jonathan would like to structure the purchase so that it provides the greatest possible tax deferral to Matthew.

Jonathan has heard that holding companies are sometimes used in these situations, but he does not know what such an arrangement would involve. He has also heard about the capital gains deduction and wonders whether it could be applied to this transaction. Neither Jonathan nor Matthew has disposed of any capital property in the past. Extracts from the balance sheet of Mattjon are provided in Exhibit I.

The owners of Mattjon have asked you to prepare a memo suggesting how this transaction might be structured.

Required:

Prepare the memo.

---

* Adapted, with permission, from the 1990 Uniform Final Examination ©1990 of the Canadian Institute of Chartered Accountants, Toronto, Canada. Any changes to the original material are the sole responsibility of W.J. Buckwold and have not been reviewed or endorsed by the CICA.

Exhibit I
MATTJON LIMITED
Extracts from Balance Sheet
As at December 31, 20X0
(unaudited)

Assets (Note 1)

Current:		
Cash	25,000	
Accounts receivable	150,000	
Inventory	300,000	$ 475,000
Fixed:		
Land (note 1)	50,000	
Building (net of accumulated amortization)	100,000	
Machinery and equipment (net of accumulated amortization)	75,000	225,000
Long term:		
Government bonds		300,000
		$1,000,000

Liabilities

Accounts payable	70,000	
Income and other taxes payable	30,000	$100,000

Shareholders' Equity

Capital stock (Note 2):		
2 common shares	200	
600 class A preferred shares	60,000	
600 class B preferred shares	60,000	
Retained earnings	779,800	900,000
		$1,000,000

Note 1: Mattjon is considering relocating its facilities to cheaper industrial land, as a recent appraisal valued the company's land at $550,000. The market value of all other assets approximates book value. Mattjon uses capital cost allowance rates for purposes of financial-statement amortization.

Note 2: For tax purposes, all shares have paid-up capital, and an adjusted cost base, equal to $100 per share. Matthew owns the class A preferred shares and Jonathan the class B preferred shares. Both classes of preferred shares are non-voting, non-participating, and redeemable at their paid-up capital of $100 per share.

Chapter 19   Business Valuations

The previous two chapters discussed the impact of taxation on business acquisitions and divestitures. It is now appropriate to briefly examine the process of valuing a business entity. The previous chapters indicated that the price of a business may be adjusted as a result of the different tax treatments applicable to the vendor and purchaser under the various methods of completing the transaction. However, those chapters did not indicate how the initial price was determined.

Tax factors influence the initial valuation process, though not as much as they influence the form of the transaction. The topic of business valuations is extremely complex and is the subject of complete texts. The purpose of this chapter is to review the basic principles of business valuations to demonstrate the influence of taxation on the process.

I. Basic Principles and Methods of Business Valuations

The very essence of a business operation is that it consists of a number of assets, both physical and intangible, that work together for the purpose of generating a long-term stream of profits. The value of a business as a going concern is tied to and dependent on its income-earning potential.

It should be pointed out that a business does not have to be sold as a going concern. Presumably, a vendor will take whatever steps are necessary to obtain the highest price from the disposition of the business. The sale of a business can, therefore, involve the cessation of business operations followed by the sale of the individual assets that were used in the business. In such cases the value of the business is tied not to its income-earning potential but rather to the value of each of its separate individual assets.

This means that there are two fundamental approaches available to business valuations —the earnings approach and the asset approach.

A. Earnings Approach

A purchaser usually acquires a business for the sole purpose of operating it as a going concern. In essence, it is paying a price for a group of assets that will generate a future stream of profits. While the real value of the future profits will eventually be known, the process of valuing those future profits before the actual purchase is extremely speculative.

Assuming that future profits can be anticipated, the value of the business is determined by capitalizing those anticipated earnings based on a rate of return that reflects the nature and relative risk of the particular business. For example, if anticipated profits are $100,000 annually, and if the purchaser considers that a 25% rate of return is normal for that business or industry, the value of the business is $400,000 ($100,000/.25 = $400,000). In other words, a price of $400,000 would yield a 25% return on investment, or $100,000 annually.

This value of the business does not reflect any particular asset of the business, but rather represents the total value of all assets working together. The total value may in fact be higher than the sum of the values of the individual identifiable assets; in such cases it is clear that an intangible asset referred to as "goodwill" is present (see Chapter 6).

The earnings approach to business valuations is based on the principle that assets in use have a different value than assets being held for liquidation or sale. For example, a delivery truck can be purchased for $25,000, but its in-use value—that is, its value when used to produce delivery revenues—may be substantially higher because of the returns that it generates.

B. Asset Approach

The asset approach to valuations involves the separate valuation of each individual asset within an entity rather than the valuation of a group of assets together as a productive economic force. This method is often referred to as the "adjusted book value method" because it simply takes each asset on the entity's balance sheet and adjusts its recorded book value to an appraised market value in anticipation of liquidation.

The asset approach has limited application. Usually it is used to value investment companies, or a business entity that will not be sold as a going concern because it isn't profitable enough.

- An investment company may own several assets, each of which produces income on its own but does not act in concert with other assets in a specific economic operation. The value of such a company will be equal to the sum of the values the individual assets would realize if disposed of separately.

- A business that consists of a number of assets and that has a poor profit potential may find that the sale of its individual assets to different buyers will result in a higher sale price than if those assets were sold as a going concern. In such cases a simple appraisal of each separate asset would provide a liquidation value for the entity.

C. Earnings Approach and Asset Approach Combined

It is important to recognize that there may be a difference between the value of the business operations and the value of the entity that houses those operations. For example, a single corporation may operate more than one distinct business as well as maintain a portfolio of passive investments. In this situation the value of each business might be determined using the earnings approach based on its own separate profit potential, but the investment portfolio would be valued using an asset approach. The value of the total entity would consist of the combined values of the separate sub-entities; this would reflect the unique structure of the entity's operations and the diversity of its asset composition.

Even when valuing the business operations based on potential earnings, a separate asset valuation may have to be performed. Consider the situation in which a business operation will be sold by means of an asset sale rather than a sale of shares of the entire corporation. The total value of the business operations will be based on profit potential, but once that price is agreed on, the total value will have to be distributed among the various assets to determine the price of each separate asset in order that the related tax implications to the vendor as well as to the purchaser can be determined (see Chapter 17).

D. Other Valuation Methods

A number of other specific valuation methods exist. Some industries and professions often use rule-of-thumb formulas to establish business value. Insurance brokers, certain types of bars and restaurants, grocery stores, retail jewellery stores, professional businesses such as legal, accounting, and medical firms, real estate brokers, and so on, often base business value on a multiple of annual gross revenues earned. For example, an accounting firm may be valued at 125% of gross annual fees plus the appraised value of specific tangible assets.

In some industries a rule-of-thumb multiple is applied not to gross sales or net profits but rather to annual cash flow, which can be defined as profits before depreciation and debt service. Hotels and motels are often valued in this manner; this reflects the fact that the major asset in the business operation is real estate, which normally appreciates in value and is capable of servicing a wide range of debt capacity.

Rule-of-thumb formulas must be considered as having limited usefulness in valuing a specific business because they do not take into account the changing economic variables that constantly affect the profitability of a particular business within any industry. The rule-of-thumb methods are, however, a valuable starting point in the valuation process, as long as it is kept in mind that adjustments must be made to reflect the unique character of the specific business operation being valued.

It is clear that these other methods of valuation are still based on the fundamental principle that the value of a business is mainly a function of its profit potential. The primary method of valuing a business is examined in greater detail below.

II. The Capitalization of Earnings Method

The most widely used and accepted method of valuing a business as a going concern is the capitalization of earnings method. This method is based on the premise that a purchaser is prepared to invest a certain amount of funds now in order to achieve a continued return on that investment in the future. When using this method, two things must be determined:

1. The potential profits that can be achieved from the business.

2. The rate of return required to compensate for the risk involved in achieving those profits.

If this information is known, the value of the business is easy to calculate. However, as indicated at the beginning of this chapter, determining both the amount of potential profits and the risk attached to earning those profits is a speculative task that involves a considerable amount of subjective appraisal. Consequently, the views of the purchaser and the vendor may be wide apart with respect to these issues, in which case the true value of the business will be established by the marketplace.

A. Capitalization Rate or Earnings Multiple

The rate of return necessary to compensate for the risk of the investment is referred to as the "capitalization rate." The higher the risk attached to a specific business, the higher the rate of return required to justify the investment. For example, a business with a high risk factor may be purchased only if the purchaser can obtain an after-tax return on investment of 40% annually. If that business is capable of earning $80,000 annually, its value is $200,000, calculated as follows:

$$\frac{\text{Annual profit} - \$80,000}{\text{Required return} - .40} = \$200,000$$

Similarly, if a lesser-risk business can earn $80,000 annually, a minimum return of only 25% may be acceptable, in which case the value of the business would be $320,000 ($80,000/.25 = $320,000).

The capitalization rate, which reflects the relative risk of the investment, can also be expressed in terms of an earnings multiple. Notice that the business value of $200,000, reflecting a 40% rate of return annually, is equivalent to two-and-a-half times the annual profit of $80,000 ($200,000/$80,000 = 2.5). In other words, the investment of $200,000 can be recovered in two-and-a-half years if normal profits are achieved. Similarly, the business value of $320,000 reflecting a 25% rate of return is equivalent to four times the annual profit of $80,000. It is common to express the value of a business in terms of a multiple of its earnings. It is important to recognize that the stated multiple is simply an expression of the capitalization rate, which is tied to the relative risk of the operations.

The relationship between the capitalization rate, earnings multiple, and business value is shown in Exhibit 19-1 for various levels of risk. Notice that the capitalization rate has an inverse relationship to the earnings multiple: a high capitalization rate reflects a low earnings multiple, whereas a lower capitalization rate reflects a higher earnings multiple.

It is easy to understand what the capitalization rate represents, and how it is used in the valuation process; the method for determining an appropriate capitalization rate is not so obvious. It is one thing to say that the value of a business depends on how risky that business is relative to other businesses; it is quite another to determine the exact degree of risk. To determine future profits with any degree of precision is virtually impossible; the best a decision maker can hope to do is establish a range of capitalization rates that reflects the realities of the specific business being valued. To arrive at this range, the decision maker must consider at least the following general factors pertaining to the business:

Exhibit 19-1: Business Values under Varying Capitalization Rates	Annual profit	Capitalization rate	Business value	Earnings multiple
	$80,000	40%	$200,000	2.5 ×
	80,000	30	267,000	3.3 ×
	80,000	25	320,000	4.0 ×
	80,000	20	400,000	5.0 ×
	80,000	10	800,000	10.0 ×

1. The short-run and long-run market potential for the primary products sold or services provided.

2. The production capacity of the plant and equipment, as well as the potential impact of technological changes, which may affect production efficiency.

3. The availability and security of suppliers of raw materials and/or specially trained and skilled employees.

4. The state of the competition, both short-term and long-term, and the potential impact of that competition on market prices.

5. The strength and depth of management personnel and the quality of labour relations in the industry.

6. Domestic and international economic trends and their possible impact on the company's products or services.

7. The life cycle of the primary products manufactured and sold, as well as the potential for researching and developing new and advanced products within the industry.

8. The quality and quantity of tangible assets (land, equipment, and so on) owned by the business.

Even after considering these factors, different parties may attach different degrees of risk to the specific business. For example, a purchaser who is acquiring a business that is similar to its existing business, with the intention of integrating the two operations, may assess less risk to the target business than a purchaser who is in a different line of business and who has less knowledge of the particular industry. This means that a vendor, in establishing an initial price for a proposed business sale, must consider the types of potential buyers with the goal of obtaining the highest earnings multiple.

In summary, the process of establishing a capitalization rate that reflects the degree of risk attached to profit potential is very subjective and complex. To some extent this explains the apparent preoccupation with rule-of-thumb formulas for arriving at quick business valuations. However, as indicated previously, industry rule-of-thumb formulas are valuable only as a starting point and must be adjusted after the factors listed above have been considered.

B. Determination of Expected Profits

As the purchaser is acquiring a stream of future profits, it is necessary to project the entity's earning capacity. This process, like the one for determining capitalization rates, is speculative and requires that the decision maker accept certain assumptions. Profit projections are often determined under three general scenarios—optimistic, most likely, and worst case.

The reasonableness of the projection depends to some degree on the maturity of the business. A business that has a significant history of proven profitability can project its future income with greater confidence than a business in the early stages of growth. In established businesses for which a proven track record exists, past earnings are commonly used to estimate future earning capacity. Typically, the business earnings of the previous five years are averaged to arrive at the anticipated future profit. In arriving at the average profit, greater consideration is often given to the most recent earnings; to this purpose, a weighting formula is applied to the years included in the review. An example of this procedure is provided below.

Year	Normal earnings	×	Weighting factor	=	Weighted earnings
2003	$100,000		5		$ 500,000
2002	90,000		4		360,000
2001	80,000		3		240,000
2000	60,000		2		120,000
1999	70,000		1		70,000
			15		$1,290,000

Weighted average earnings:

$$\frac{\$1,290,000}{15} = \$86,000$$

The above weighting scheme is referred to as the "sum of the years' digits" method and is based on the number of years being averaged. Because the calculation is averaging five years, the most recent year is given a weight of five, the second most recent year, four, and so on. A three-year average would weight the most recent year by a factor of three, and so on. Although this weighting method is commonly used, there is no requirement that it be strictly adhered to. Much depends on the circumstances; if certain years are more relevant to the future, then greater weight should be attached to them.

Notice that the above calculation used the normal earnings of prior years to determine the average profits. It is important to recognize that the financial statements of prior years do not necessarily reflect the normal profits from the business operations and may include a number of items (in both revenue and expenses) that are unusual or non-recurring. Because of this, past profits must be examined and adjusted to eliminate those items which distort the true profits earned from the business operations. The extent of such adjustments can vary considerably with the nature and size of the particular company. In particular, closely held private corporations often include a number of discretionary expenses in their statements, and follow accounting policies that are more consistent with taxation rules than with economic realities. The following are some typical areas that may require adjustment when normal past profits are being established for predictive purposes:

• **Owners' compensation**   The owner/managers of private corporations often establish their salaries according to need or for tax planning purposes. As a result, owners' salaries may be too high or too low and should be adjusted to reflect the normal salary payable for the management services provided.

• **Excessive reserves** In an attempt to defer taxation, many businesses apply an overly conservative approach to establishing reserves such as allowance for doubtful accounts. They may also take liberties with inventory valuations. Consequently, reported profits in the valuation years may be substantially lower than the actual profits.

• **Amortization policies** Amortization methods vary considerably. In some cases, accepted taxation methods are used for accounting purposes even though they may not reflect the economic realities of the particular assets being amortized. For valuation purposes, an amortization policy should be substituted that reflects a reasonable cost allocation over a realistic time period.

• **Lease terms** The past costs for the use of leased assets may not reflect future lease costs, especially if major leases are coming up for renewal in the near future.

• **Debt service** Similarly, debt financing may have had preferential interest rates in past years; those rates may be up for renegotiation in the near future. Also, in private corporations, debt provided by the shareholders may have an unusually low or non-existent interest rate that will not continue after the sale is completed.

• **Non-recurring expenses and gains** The past profits may include unusual gains or losses from the sale of assets, or abnormal expenses that are not likely to recur.

• **Investment income** If a company has significant investment income such as interest, or dividends, or rents from property that is not connected to the business operations, that income should be removed from the reported profits to isolate the profits attributable to the normal business operations. The earnings multiple should be applied only to those business profits. If the proposed sale will include the investments, a separate valuation must be made for those assets, as their risk factor will be completely different.

• **Income tax** Profit potential is, of course, expressed in after-tax terms, so normal profits should be adjusted to reflect the rates of tax that will apply in the future.

It is important to remember that including past profits in the valuation process is useful only to the extent that those profits can be used to predict the future. A business may have a history of growth and profits; it does not always follow that the future will be similar. In many cases the analysis of past profits simply represents a starting point from which realistic projections can be developed.

C. Sample Valuation

The capitalization of earnings method is demonstrated below. The situation is greatly simplified in order to emphasize the basic method of calculation, and so that the overall valuation can be related to the asset composition of the particular company.

Summary of Facts

Ms. X is the sole shareholder and manager of Retail Corporation, a Canadian-controlled private corporation that operates a retail store from leased premises. Recently she received two inquiries regarding the possible sale of the business. One inquiry was from a large company that operates a chain of similar stores; the other was from a local individual who recently acquired some capital and wants to purchase a business. X is aware that if she decides to sell, she can sell either the shares of the corporation or the individual business assets. But before the negotiation begins, she wants to know the overall value of the company. The following additional information is available:

1. The most recent corporate balance is as follows:

Assets:		
Current assets, including accounts receivable and inventory		$400,000
Display fixtures and other equipment, at cost	160,000	
Accumulated amortization	(70,000)	90,000
Investment in bonds		50,000
		$540,000
Liabilities		$280,000
Shareholder's equity:		
Share capital	1,000	
Retained earnings	259,000	260,000
		$540,000

2. The display fixtures and other equipment were recently appraised and have a market value of $120,000.

3. The business has been in operation for nine years; however, sales and profits increased substantially three years ago after a shopping centre opened across the street. Income statements for the past three years are summarized as follows:

	20X1	20X2	20X3
Sales	$1,000,000	$1,100,000	$1,200,000
Cost of sales	600,000	660,000	720,000
Gross profit	400,000	440,000	480,000
Operating expenses	280,000	300,000	320,000
Operating profit	120,000	140,000	160,000
Interest income	3,000	4,000	5,000
Net income before tax	$ 123,000	$ 144,000	$ 165,000

4. For the past three years X has been paid a salary of $100,000. Mature managers of chain stores in a similar line of business normally earn a salary of $70,000.

5. The current lease for the premises requires annual payments of $60,000. The lease expires next year. The company has an option to renew the lease for a further 10 years at a revised rent of $75,000 annually.

6. A retail trade association, of which X is a member, publishes industry statistics which indicate that over the past five years, retail stores of this nature and of varying sizes have been sold for an average of seven times retail after-tax profits.

Analysis and Valuation

The asset composition of Retail Corporation consists of a group of business assets (accounts receivable, inventory, fixtures, and equipment) and an investment portfolio consisting of interest-bearing bonds. In order to value the company as a whole, two separate valuation methods must be used: the business operation will be valued by the capitalization of earnings approach; the investment portfolio will be valued by the asset approach, which will determine the market price of the particular bonds. (For purposes of the overall valuation, it is assumed that the investment bonds are worth their stated face value of $50,000.)

In order to value the business, an estimate of future maintainable earnings must be made. Using only the information provided, this can be done by adjusting the previous three years' earnings to normal income. In this case it is appropriate to go back only three years, because the nature of the business changed when the shopping centre opened.

Adjusted pre-tax earnings are as follows:

	20X1	20X2	20X3
Business profit before investment income	$120,000	$140,000	$160,000
add			
Excessive owner's salary ($100,000 − $70,000)	30,000	30,000	30,000
deduct			
Additional lease cost ($75,000 − $60,000)	(15,000)	(15,000)	(15,000)
Adjusted profit	$135,000	$155,000	$175,000

Notice that past profits have been adjusted to reflect a more typical manager's salary and a revised lease cost for the premises, as the buyer will be subject to these amounts. When these adjustments are made, the average normal after-tax profits are $130,000, calculated using the weighted average method, as follows:

Year	Income	Weighting	Total
20X3	$175,000	3	$525,000
20X2	155,000	2	310,000
20X1	135,000	1	135,000
		6	$970,000

Weighted average earnings:

$$\frac{\$970,000}{6} = \qquad \$162,000$$

Estimated income tax (20%) (assumed)	(32,000)
After-tax average profits	$130,000

If we accept the industry standard of seven times earnings as the normal risk factor for this type of business, the total value of the company is $960,000, calculated as follows:

Value of the business operations ($130,000 × 7)	$910,000
Value of investment portfolio	50,000
Total value of the company	$960,000

Before discussing the limitations of these calculations, it is important to relate the company's value of $960,000 to its asset composition. The balance sheet provided indicates that the shareholder's equity of Retail Corporation is $260,000, yet the value of this equity is $960,000. This increase in value of $700,000 relates to the apparent value increases of the business assets within the corporation. Assuming that the fair value of the current assets (accounts receivable and inventory) is the same as the stated value, the $700,000 must be allocated to the fixtures, equipment, and goodwill. As the fixtures and equipment were recently appraised at $120,000 (being $30,000 higher than their book value of $90,000), the remaining portion of the value increase must be attributable to the intangible asset, goodwill. The balance sheet stated in terms of fair market values is as follows:

Assets:	
Current assets	$ 400,000
Fixtures and equipment	120,000
Goodwill	670,000
Investment in bonds	50,000
	$1,240,000
Liabilities	$ 280,000
Shareholder's equity	960,000
	$1,240,000

It is clear that if the potential buyer were to acquire the specific assets of the business rather than the shares, he or she would receive additional tax benefits because of the increased deductions relating to capital cost allowance on the equipment and the amortization of goodwill (see Chapter 6). This would improve future after-tax profits for the buyer, who might be prepared to pay a higher price than indicated above (see Chapter 17).

In this example, the procedure for calculating the total company value of $960,000 is subject to a number of limitations. First of all, notice that the average pre-tax earnings of $162,000 are less than the most recent year's income of $175,000. In the three years since the shopping centre opened, profits and sales have enjoyed a steady growth. By obtaining additional economic data relating to the impact of the shopping centre, the vendor may be able to argue successfully that this growth pattern will continue and that average future earnings should therefore be increased. The reverse may also be true if the traffic volume created by the shopping centre has already peaked and is likely to decline when more recent retail developments in other neighbourhoods begin to draw customers away from the area.

Second, it may not be appropriate to use the industry's average-earnings multiple if this particular business is different in a few or many ways from others in the industry. Such things as location, established reputation, product mix, and supplier strength may make this business unique, thereby justifying the use of a different multiple.

And third, the two potential buyers are considerably different. If the large chain operation acquires the business, the corporate tax rate on profits will not be 20% as used in the calculation. At the same time, its operating costs and costs of buying merchandise may be lower, with the result that its calculation of after-tax profits may well be quite different from the one made above. On the other hand, the other potential buyer would be entitled to pay the low rate of tax after acquisition.

These limitations indicate that the standard methods of valuing a business should be viewed with caution and tailored to suit the specific situation.

D. Appreciating Business Assets

The capitalization of earnings approach may result in a misleading valuation if certain business assets do not reflect their real costs when future income streams are being projected. This is particularly the case when the asset may be subject to appreciation for reasons other than its contribution to the business operations. Real estate is a prime example of this. Consider the following situation:

Situation:

For Sale Corporation conducts an active business from premises that have been owned by the corporation for many years. The financial statements indicate only $10,000 of expenses associated with the building for amortization and insurance. (The $10,000 excludes property taxes, utilities, and normal maintenance.)

The fair rental value of the property is $22,000 per year, which, according to the assumed current real estate market, makes the property worth $220,000 (i.e., to yield a 10% net rental).

The business earns a pre-tax annual profit of $100,000 before the above costs associated with the building. Its tax rate is 20%. For Sale Corporation is about to sell the business and expects to achieve a value of eight times normal profits.

Analysis:

The annual reported earnings of the business do not reflect the building's real occupancy cost. If the business were sold at eight times earnings, including both land and buildings, the following overall price would be achieved:

Profit before building costs	$100,000
Building costs	(10,000)
	90,000
Income tax @ 20%	(18,000)
Net earnings	$ 72,000
Value of business ($72,000 × 8)	$576,000

However, this profit reflects the preferential occupancy cost of the building, which is $10,000 rather than the real cost of $22,000. In other words, if the business were sold without the land and buildings but with a proper lease, the business value, separate from the real estate, would be only $499,000, as follows:

Profit before building costs	$100,000
Lease costs	(22,000)
	78,000
Income tax @ 20%	(15,600)
Net earnings	$ 62,400
Value of business ($62,400 × 8) (rounded)	$499,000

Therefore, the value of the enterprise actually consists of two values—the business value and the property value, calculated as follows:

Business value	$499,000
Land and building value	220,000
	$719,000

This analysis indicates that the capitalization of earnings approach should be confined to business operations only, and that when particular assets used in the business have an alternative use, those assets should be examined to determine whether their alternative use has a greater value. In this situation the land and building have a greater value as rental property and, therefore, should either not be sold as part of the business or be sold only after an adjustment has been made to the business valuation.

E. Shareholders' Loans —Debt or Equity?

In closely held private corporations, a shareholder may contribute capital to the corporation by a combination of share capital and loans. As indicated in Chapter 12, shareholder loans, notwithstanding what they are called, may constitute either a true debt of the corporation or part of the shareholder's equity in the corporation. Their true nature is determined by the marketplace in relation to the overall capital structure of the entity. When a corporation is being sold, it is important to determine whether a shareholder loan constitutes debt or equity. Consider the following situation:

Situation:

For Sale Corporation, which is owned by shareholder X, is about to be sold. Below is the portion of the company's balance sheet indicating the shareholder loan and the shareholder's equity.

Due to shareholder		$100,000
Shareholder's equity:		
Common shares	1,000	
Retained earnings	299,000	300,000
		$400,000

No interest is paid on the shareholder loan. The company usually earns $100,000 before tax. Its tax rate is 20%. X intends to sell the company for the typical earning multiple in this particular industry, which is six times earnings.

Analysis:

The matter of the shareholder loan must be resolved when the value of the business is being established. If the capital structure of the company is such that the shareholder loan must be regarded as equity, then X is selling the shares and loan together as an equity package for a value based on the company's earnings. If the shareholder loan is truly a debt obligation of the company, then the debt will remain after the sale and X is selling only the shares. As a debt, the loan must bear interest in accordance with its relative risk and terms of repayment. If we assume that a reasonable interest rate on such a loan is 10%, the following valuation alternatives result:

	As debt	As equity
Profits	$100,000	$100,000
Interest (10%)	(10,000)	–0–
	90,000	100,000
Income tax @ 20%	(18,000)	(20,000)
Normal earnings	$ 72,000	$ 80,000
	× 6	× 6
Business value	$432,000	$480,000

> An assumption that the shareholder loan is debt results in a share value of $432,000; however, X still has continued ownership of the loan, which amounts to a further $100,000, for a total value in the company of $532,000. On the other hand, if the shareholder loan is part of the equity package, the total value of the shares and loan is only $480,000.

This analysis indicates that the treatment of shareholder loans has an impact on the entity's value as determined by the capitalization of earnings approach. The example is simplistic in that it does not consider what impact the debt may have on the risk of the business and therefore on the earnings multiple used. However, it does highlight the importance of the issue. It is an area that is often overlooked, particularly by a vendor who is contemplating the sale of a closely held corporation.[1]

III. Contingent Business Values

A contingent business value is one that establishes a price based on events after the takeover date. The major problem with business valuations is this: how to determine what the future maintainable earnings will be. The purchaser, of course, is going to be pessimistic about potential earnings, while the vendor is likely to be overly optimistic.

A. Definition and Purpose

The setting of a contingent selling price eliminates a considerable amount of doubt because it involves establishing an initial price that will be altered if certain defined expectations are met. Those defined expectations usually relate to later profits; for this reason, a contingent business valuation is often referred to as an "earn-out."

An earn-out purchase and sale often benefits both vendor and purchaser. For the vendor, a contingency agreement is a means to achieve the highest price by proving any assertions made about the business's profit potential. For the purchaser, it is much like an insurance policy, in that a price reduction will result if the acquired business does not perform as predicted by the vendor.

B. Basic Earn-Out Methods

Every business purchase-and-sale transaction presents different risks and contingencies. The nature of a contingent buy/sell agreement is determined in accordance with the circumstances that are the source of doubt in the given situation. The agreement usually sets a base price and provides for increases to that price if future profits are maintained as expected or are greater than expected. Consider the following situation:

Situation:

The shareholders of For Sale Corporation have agreed to sell the shares of the business for the following terms:

1. An initial sales price equal to seven times the average of the previous three years' earnings will be paid in cash on the transaction date.

2. For a period of five subsequent years, the vendor is entitled to a further payment equal to the annual after-tax profits in excess of the earnings established in the initial price.

3. The average of the previous three years' earnings is $500,000.

---

1 If a business is overcapitalized or underleveraged, the resulting effect on value must be considered. See McCallum, T., "Redundant But Necessary," *CGA Magazine*, October 1990, pp. 52–55.

Analysis: The initial price for the shares is $3,500,000 ($500,000 × 7). The additional price adjustment is determined in the following table under assumed future results:

Year	Actual earnings	Base earnings	Price adjustment
1	$ 520,000	$ 500,000	$ 20,000
2	510,000	500,000	10,000
3	560,000	500,000	60,000
4	590,000	500,000	90,000
5	600,000	500,000	100,000
	$2,780,000	$2,500,000	$280,000

Notice that the preceding agreement increased the price by the actual amount of excess profits for a five-year period. A variation on this basic method is to base the additional price on an earnings multiple for average future earnings. For example, the actual average earnings for the five years following the takeover is $556,000 ($2,780,000/5). The revised price, based on an earnings multiple of 7, would be $3,892,000, which is $392,000 higher than the initial price of $3,500,000.

In some situations a contingent contract will use the reverse approach, and establish the initial price at the highest value, with the potential for a price *reduction* if profits fall below a defined minimum. Regardless of the method used, the contingent business valuation is an accepted means of bridging the gap between buyer and seller, and does much to solve the most difficult problem in most business valuations.

While the contingent valuation has significant benefits, it is not without its problems. In particular, it is often difficult for the parties to agree on the method of determining future earnings for purposes of the transaction. Accounting principles can be applied in different ways, and profits may be affected by a number of discretionary items such as owner remuneration, inventory valuation policy, and so on. In many cases a contingent valuation is rejected because the problems associated with policing the agreement are overpowering.

C. Tax Treatment of Contingent Prices

The vendor who sells shares under a contingent price agreement does not know what the final price will be. Because a portion of the price is directly related to actual future profits, an argument can be made that the portion represents regular business income rather than a capital gain.[2] However, when the sale of shares would normally result in a capital gain, CCRA permits the gain on the contingent portion to be treated as a capital gain and recognized whenever the contingent amounts are determinable. This treatment is permitted only if the following conditions are met:[3]

1. The vendor and purchaser are dealing at arm's length.

2. It is reasonable to assume that the earn-out feature relates to the underlying goodwill of the business, the value of which cannot be agreed upon by the vendor and the purchaser.

3. The duration of the sale agreement does not exceed five years.

---

2   ITA 12(1)(g); IT-462.

3   IT-426.

4. The vendor submits a copy of the contingent agreement to CCRA when filing a tax return for the year of the sale.

The tax treatment permitted is referred to as the "cost recovery method," as a capital gain is recognized only when determinable proceeds exceed the cost of the shares sold. For example, if shares having a cost of $600,000 are sold for a base price of $800,000, and if contingent amounts of $100,000 are determined in each of years 3 and 4 after the sale, the recognition of capital gains will be as follows:

Year of sale:		
Proceeds	800,000	
Cost	600,000	
Capital gain	$200,000	
Taxable capital gain (½ of $200,000)		$100,000
Year 3:		
Contingent amount—$100,000		
Taxable capital gain (½ of $100,000)		50,000
Year 4:		
Same as year 3		50,000
Total taxable capital gain		$200,000

Notice that the gains are recognized when the contingent proceeds are determined to exist. If payment of the determined adjusted price is delayed further, the taxpayer may claim the normal capital gain reserve (see Chapter 8).

IV. Summary and Conclusion

A business consists of a group of assets, both tangible and intangible, working together to generate a future stream of profits. The value of a business depends, therefore, on its profit-making potential.

Each asset within a business may have a specific disposable value if sold separately in liquidation; however, it is important to realize that business assets are held not with the intention of disposal, but in order to conduct business operations. For this reason these separate asset values usually have little impact on the valuation process.

The primary method of valuing a business is the capitalization of earnings method. This method weighs the earnings potential of a business against the risk associated with those potential earnings. The value of the business is equal to the estimated future profits capitalized to yield a rate of return consistent with what is required to justify the risk. Although the calculation itself is simple, the process of estimating future profits and the rate of capitalization is not. Both these estimates are extremely subjective, and prone to wide variations among different valuators.

For the sake of more accurate profit projections, and to eliminate risk, a purchaser can analyze the company's past earnings performance. However, past earnings must be substantiated, and then adjusted after a thorough appraisal of these factors: related markets, production capability, management expertise, competition, and economic and environmental influences.

The speculative aspect of business valuations can be diminished if buyer and seller enter into a contingent price agreement, which establishes a base price and allows for adjustments to that price after future performance is assessed.

The process of valuing businesses is an art and not a science, and requires considerable investigation and foresight.

Reading List

Income Tax Act References

	Section
Dispositions subject to warranty	42
Payments based on production or use	12(1)(g)

Canada Customs and Revenue Agency Publications

IT-426	Shares sold subject to an earn-out agreement.
IT-330R	Dispositions of capital property subject to warranty, covenant, or conditional or contingent obligations.
IT-462	Payments based on production or use.

Other Publications

Wise, R., "Valuations and Price Adjustment Clauses," Report of Proceedings of the 50th Tax Conference, Canadian Tax Foundation, p. 33.1.

McCallum, T., "The Going Concern Approach," *CGA Magazine*, January 1991, pp. 40–44.

McCallum, T., "Redundant But Necessary," *CGA Magazine*, October 1990, pp. 52–55.

Moeller and Tapper, "Principles of Income (Loss) Determination," *Journal of Business Valuation*, 1991, pp. 271–280.

Campbell, Low, and Murrant, *The Valuation and Pricing of Privately Held Business Interests*, CICA, 1990.

Review Questions

1. What is the key factor influencing the value of a going-concern business?

2. Distinguish between the earnings approach and the asset approach to business valuations. When is it appropriate to use each?

3. What is the capitalization of earnings method of valuing a business? Why is it that the value determined by this method may vary considerably between the purchaser and the vendor?

4. Explain how the capitalization of earnings method takes into account the relative risk of the particular business being valued.

5. What is the relationship between a capitalization rate and an earnings multiple?

6. How is the capitalization rate of a particular business determined?

7. "Because a purchaser is acquiring a business that will earn future profits, the amount of profits earned in the past is not relevant to the valuation of the business." Is this statement true? Explain.

8. Given that reported past profits reflect future expectations, why may it be necessary to revise those past profits for such items as owner's compensation, occupancy costs (rent), interest costs, income taxes, and so on?

9. How is the capitalization of earnings method affected when the entity being valued has profits from business operations and, in addition, income from passive investments (for example, interest income)?

10. Why is it that the value of a specific business may vary from purchaser to purchaser, even though all prospective purchasers have the same degree of certainty with respect to the earnings potential of the business?

11. Often, certain assets that a business uses have the potential for an alternative use by the owner. What impact may this have on the capitalization of earnings method for valuing the business operations?

12. What is the contingent business value or "earn-out" method of valuing a business?

13. What benefits can be achieved by using the contingent business value method? What problems may occur when it is chosen?

Cases

Case One   Little Boy Ltd.

Little Boy Ltd. is a Canadian public corporation whose shares are traded on the Alberta Stock Exchange. The company operates a chain of grocery stores in western Canada.

Little Boy began as a small family business owned by the three Hardy brothers, but grew rapidly due to the brothers' aggressive business policies and their ability to choose prime locations for their stores. Ten years ago the company became a public corporation; it raised substantial equity and used it to fund a major expansion. Much of the funding was used to acquire land and construct stores according to the particular specifications that suited their business.

Even after the public share issue, the Hardy brothers maintained 60% of the company's common shares. The company's shares traded actively on the Alberta Stock Exchange. The share values have increased steadily along with the company profits. Historically, the shares have traded at 10 times the after-tax earnings per share—a value consistent with that of other public companies in the same industry.

Last year one of the brothers died. His estate has gradually disposed of his shares in Little Boy by selling them on the open market. This has left the remaining two brothers with 40% of the common shares. The remaining shares are widely held.

Not long ago, Joel Hardy, the president of Little Boy, received information that a particular investor was showing an unusual interest in the corporation's shares and was quietly buying them in large blocks. After further investigation he discovered that the investor was a holding corporation owned by an individual with a history of taking over and liquidating corporate businesses.

The most recent balance sheet of Little Boy is shown in Exhibit I. Additional financial information is provided in Exhibit II.

Exhibit I
BALANCE SHEET
20X1

Current assets		$ 6,000,000
Equipment (at cost)	3,200,000	
Accumulated amortization	(1,000,000)	2,200,000
Land		1,000,000
Buildings	10,000,000	
Accumulated amortization	(2,000,000)	8,000,000
		$17,200,000
Current liabilities		$ 4,200,000
Long-term debt:		
Mortgage bonds (10% interest)		
secured by real estate; due 20X3		2,000,000
		6,200,000
Shareholders' equity:		
Common shares	3,000,000	
Retained earnings	8,000,000	11,000,000
		$17,200,000

Exhibit II
Additional Financial Information

1. After-tax corporate profits for the current year amounted to $2,000,000. The corporate tax rate is 45%.

2. Amortization expense deducted in arriving at the above profit is as follows:

Equipment (12% straight line)	$347,000
Buildings (4% diminishing balance)	320,000

3. The company occupies a total of 150,000 square feet of building space. Of this amount, 10,000 square feet is leased at the current rental rate of $10 per square foot. This property was leased from a real estate investor who had purchased land and constructed a building according to the company's specifications. The property had cost the investor $1,000,000. Little Boy is responsible for all expenses associated with the leased property. The remaining stores occupy space in buildings that are owned by Little Boy.

4. The undepreciated capital cost of the buildings for tax purposes is not significantly different from book value.

Required:

Analyze the financial information and explain why Little Boy may be the target of a takeover bid.

Case Two Blakey's Enterprises Ltd.

Blakey's Enterprises Ltd. is a Canadian-controlled private corporation that has operated a small retail men's clothing store in rural Ontario for 70 years.

Like his father before him, Charlie Blakey is a conservative businessman who believes that personal service and a choice of inventory is the key to success. In fact, he is so concerned with attempting to keep customers happy that he seldom holds after-season sales for fear of offending those customers in a small town who have paid the full retail price.

His banker often says, "Charlie, you've got to get that inventory down. You turn that stock only three times a year, which is much less than the norm for your industry." Blakey knows this to be true, but always says he would rather keep unsold stock after the end of season than unload it at a discount. His interest costs are understandably high, and during the last economic crisis, when interest rates reached an all-time high, he had some concern for the store's survival.

Blakey's daughter also works in the business but has little interest in it. Most of her time is spent on a few administrative matters and outside business interests.

There are four staff on the payroll—Blakey, his daughter, George (near retirement), and Fred. Their salaries are given below.

Blakey	$24,000
Blakey's daughter	16,000
George	16,000
Fred	20,000

Fred is the most enthusiastic of the group and is constantly coming up with new ideas, only to see them put aside by Blakey. As Blakey reaches retirement age, Fred approaches him with the idea of purchasing the business. After discussing the matter with his daughter, Blakey decides to sell the store to Fred provided that a reasonable price can be established and that Fred can raise the necessary cash to meet the full purchase price.

Blakey has provided Fred with the most recent financial statements (see exhibits) as well as the following information:

1. Profits during the recent recession were nominal, according to the past financial statements. However, the most recent year was profitable, and in order to avoid an excessive tax burden, Blakey undervalued the closing inventory by $20,000. Blakey's tax rate is 20%.

2. Blakey is satisfied that the current level of profits reflects future expectations and that the past year's results, during the recession, should be ignored.

3. The outstanding shareholder's loan is non–interest-bearing and is payable on demand.

4. For years, Blakey has obtained his personal clothes from the store without cost. The amount has varied from year to year; in the previous year the cost value of clothing taken was $4,000.

5. In addition, certain expenses have always been paid by the store. Blakey's car is leased by the store at a cost of $380 per month and is used primarily to get him to

and from work. From time to time, Blakey drives to Toronto on buying trips. The store also owns a four-wheel-drive Jeep used exclusively by the daughter.

6. Travel expenses include a trip to Ithaca, New York ($1,200), for Blakey and his wife to attend a bowling tournament. Blakey's great love is bowling, and his store annually gives away a fine suit as a prize for a bowling tournament, which is usually held in the United States.

7. Blakey's daughter will obtain another job before the sale. Fred does not intend to hire a replacement for her. Fred asks Blakey to remain on staff after the sale for a salary of $24,000 per year. Fred will manage the store. (A friend of his, the local manager of a department-store men's wear department, earns a salary of $30,000.)

8. The building and land was acquired years ago for $47,000. The building has been depreciated to $15,000 since acquisition. A recent appraisal indicated that the property is now worth $90,000. The building consists of 1,500 square feet. Space of similar quality is usually leased for $6 per square foot net of all building expenses and property taxes.

9. Published statistics indicate that stores of this nature are currently valued based on a normal after-tax return of 20%.

10. Fred is anxious to proceed because a national men's wear chain has also approached Blakey to discuss a buy-out.

Required:
Assist Blakey and Fred in establishing a value for the business. Also, consider how this value may be affected if the purchaser is the clothing store chain rather than Fred.

Exhibit I
BLAKEY'S ENTERPRISES LTD.
Balance Sheet
May 31, 20X1

Assets		
Current assets:		
Cash on hand		$ 12,000
Accounts receivable		60,000
Inventory (lower of cost or market)		155,000
Prepaid expenses		3,500
		230,500
Land, building, and equipment:		
Land	7,000	
Building	40,000	
Fixtures	12,000	
Auto	11,000	
	70,000	
Accumulated amortization	(44,000)	26,000
		$256,500

Liabilities and Shareholders' Equity

Current liabilities:

Accounts payable		$ 36,000
Bank loan payable on demand		70,000
		106,000
Mortgage payable (interest @ 10%)		40,000
Due to shareholder (payable on demand)		60,000
Shareholders' equity:		
Share capital	1,000	
Retained earnings	49,500	50,500
		$256,500

Exhibit II
BLAKEY'S ENTERPRISES LTD.
Statement of Retained Earnings
Year Ended May 31, 20X1

Balance May 31, 20X0	$51,000
Profit for the year	30,720
	81,720
Dividends paid	32,220
Balance for May 31, 20X1	$49,500

Exhibit III
BLAKEY'S ENTERPRISES LTD.
Statement of Income
May 1, 20X1

Sales		$501,000
Cost of goods sold		318,600
Gross profit		182,400
Expenses:		
Insurance	$ 3,600	
Wages and salaries	76,000	
Travel	4,000	
Donations	1,200	
Heat	2,200	
Hydro	1,800	
Property taxes	1,100	
Advertising	8,000	
Auto	10,660	
Depreciation:		
Building	500	
Fixtures	600	
Auto	1,800	
Promotion	1,200	
Supplies (bags, boxes, etc.)	4,600	
Signs and window displays	7,200	
Delivery and other	7,440	
Interest	12,100	144,000
Net profit before taxes		38,400
Income taxes (20%)		(7,680)
Net income		$ 30,720

Chapter 20   Domestic and International Business Expansion

A business enterprise grows throughout its life. It does so by expanding existing product lines or services into new domestic markets, developing new products or services, and reaching into international markets. While an entity's expansion strategy is a function of its ability to exploit opportunities in accordance with its relative strengths and weaknesses, tax factors play a vital role in the decision-making process.

Every entity, in everything it does, tries to minimize risk and maximize after-tax returns on investment. After-tax cash flows are significantly influenced by the structure utilized to conduct the expansion. In Chapter 17 the influence of taxation on business expansion through *the acquisition of an existing business* was demonstrated. This chapter will review the tax implications of expansion through *internal growth and development*. Specifically, this chapter will

(a) briefly examine domestic expansion by consolidating a number of issues discussed in previous chapters; and,

(b) develop the fundamental interrelationships between foreign taxation and Canadian taxation, as they relate to international business expansion activities.

I. Domestic Business Expansion

The process of expanding existing business operations usually involves committing capital and human resources. As with any investment decision, the decision maker must attempt to create an expansion structure that will minimize the start-up cash requirements and maximize the return of cash to the business for reinvestment. As indicated in previous chapters, the following fundamental tax considerations are relevant:

1. What will be the annual tax cost on new profits generated from the expansion?

2. How and when can operating losses during the start-up period be offset against other taxable income to generate cash flow?

3. What are the tax implications if the expansion fails and is discontinued?

4. How can the original capital invested, and accumulated profits, be returned from the expansion with a minimum amount of tax?

The choice of structure depends on whether the expansion is to be funded completely with internal equity and borrowing power or by a combination of internal equity and new outside equity. When an expansion opportunity exists but the entity's resources are limited, that entity must either limit the expansion, or grasp the opportunity more fully by raising additional equity capital from new participants. Many of the alternative structures, and their related tax implications, have already been examined in this text; this section of the chapter simply summarizes and consolidates those discussions in the context of expansion decisions.

A. Expansion with Existing Resources

Expansion in Canada may be limited to the home province or involve activity in other provincial jurisdictions, each of which imposes a different rate of tax. In either case, two fundamental structural alternatives are available: the expansion activity can be operated as a division of the existing corporation, or within a separate corporation that is a subsidiary of the parent corporation.

• **Loss utilization** A major difference between the divisional structure and the corporate structure relates to the ability to use any losses in the start-up years. As a division is housed within the existing structure, all losses incurred can immediately be offset against income from other, profitable divisions within the corporation. Consequently, immediate additional cash flow is generated from tax savings, which can be used to help fund the expansion. However, utilizing the division structure also means forgoing limited liability, so that the obligations of the new division become the obligations of the enterprise that established it. Using a separate corporation may limit liability, but it also limits the utilization of the start-up losses, since those can be used only by the separate corporation that was created to house the expansion. Therefore, when the expansion activity will involve start-up losses, the cash funding requirements for a corporation are greater than for a corporate division.

• **Expansion failure** If the expansion activity fails and is discontinued, either the losses and related obligations will be funded by the initial capital invested, or the losses will require further funding to meet the obligations.

If the potential losses are limited to the capital invested, both the division structure and the separate corporation structure permit the eventual use of the incurred losses for offset against other income. Under the division structure, the losses would generate tax savings as they occur. Under the corporation structure, the losses would accumulate but could be used after a corporate reorganization that amalgamates the parent with the expansion corporation (see Chapter 14). The difference is timing.

However, when potential losses may exceed the capital invested, the impact of limited liability must be weighed against the after-tax cost of absorbing the losses. If a corporation structure were used and losses exceeded the capital invested such that bankruptcy was imposed, the owner would forgo the opportunity of amalgamating the loss company with a profitable company, and instead recognize the loss as a capital loss of the initial capital provided to the expansion corporation. Only one-half of the initial capital loss could be offset against other capital gains, unless the expansion corporation was a small business corporation, in which case one-half of the loss could be offset against other income (see Chapter 8). An example of the impact of this on cash flow is demonstrated in the following situation:

Situation: An existing business invests $100,000 in an expansion project. The project loses $30,000 each year for five years (total losses $150,000) and is then discontinued. The existing entity is subject to a tax rate of 40%. If the company uses a division structure, an additional cash contribution of $50,000 is made at the end of year 4 to fund the excess losses. If a corporation structure is used, no additional contribution is made and bankruptcy of the separate corporation occurs.

Analysis: Under the division structure, the existing corporation pays out cash of $100,000 initially, plus $50,000 at the end of year 4, which creates cash tax savings of $12,000 annually for each of the five years ($30,000 × 40% = $12,000). Under the corporation structure, the existing corporation pays out only $100,000 initially and incurs a capital loss on the investment of $100,000 in year 5, which creates a cash tax saving of $20,000 (½ of $100,000 = $50,000, × 40% = $20,000), assuming the capital loss can be utilized.

The cash flows from each alternative, together with the net present values, are summarized in the table on the next page.

This analysis indicated that although the division structure was exposed to greater losses in absolute terms ($150,000 compared with $100,000 for the corporate structure), the net after-tax consequences for that structure were lower in net present value terms. This is because the losses available for use receive preferential treatment under the division structure regarding both *timing* and *amount*. In summary, the apparent benefit of limited

	Division structure	Corporation structure
Initial investment	$100,000	$100,000
Year 1—tax saving	(12,000)	–0–
2—tax saving	(12,000)	–0–
3—tax saving	(12,000)	–0–
4—tax saving	(12,000)	–0–
—additional investment	50,000	–0–
5—tax saving	(12,000)	(20,000)
Net cash outflow	$ 90,000	$ 80,000
Net present value of cash outflows discounted at 12%	$ 88,000	$ 89,000

liability must be weighed against a realistic estimate of potential cash flows, and the related tax effect, when it is being decided which structure to use for expansion activities.

• **Taxation of expansion profits**   The amount of tax paid on profits from the expansion activity can vary depending on whether a division or a separate corporation is established, if the expansion activity crosses provincial boundaries, and/or the nature of the expansion profits differs from existing profits. As explained in Chapter 11, the rates of provincial corporate tax vary from province to province. In addition, manufacturing profits are subject to a lower rate of federal tax and, in some provinces, a lower rate of provincial tax. It was also indicated in Chapter 11 that when income is determined by province for tax purposes, an arbitrary formula is applied that provides different results under the division structure and the separate corporation structure. The same is true when manufacturing income is separated from non-manufacturing income for tax purposes.

For example, consider the following situation, which concerns an expansion into another province:

Situation: Sask Ltd. is a Saskatchewan-based corporation that operates a wholesale distribution business. The company is contemplating an expansion into Alberta and projects the following results:

	Saskatchewan operations	New Alberta operations		Total
Sales	$1,000,000	$300,000	(23%)	$1,300,000
Salaries	300,000	70,000	(19%)	370,000
Profits	200,000	20,000	(9%)	220,000

Provincial tax rates at the time of expansion are 17% of taxable income in Saskatchewan and 15% in Alberta. (These are artificial rates.)

Analysis: If the above expansion uses a division structure, there are two basic possibilities:

1. A direct sales approach from the Saskatchewan head office, with customers in Alberta serviced by Saskatchewan-based personnel.

2. A permanent place of business in Alberta (i.e., a sales office and/or warehouse) staffed by Alberta-based personnel.

If the expansion involves a separate corporation, an Alberta-based corporation can be established to provide a permanent location and staff.

Assuming operating results as projected above, the amount of provincial tax under each method is as follows:

Direct Sales

Expansion profits are earned by the Saskatchewan corporation and are subject to Saskatchewan tax rates unless a permanent establishment exists in another province.

Tax: 17% × $20,000	$3,400

Branch Location

Branch profits also belong to the Saskatchewan corporation. However, the Alberta tax rate applies because the expansion operations are carried out from a permanent establishment there. Alberta profits are determined for tax purposes by an arbitrary formula based on sales and salaries (see Chapter 11), as follows:

Profits attributed to branch:		
Branch sales	23%	
Branch salaries	19	
Average: (23% + 19%)/2	21%	
Total profits	$220,000	
Allocated to Alberta branch		
(21% × $220,000)		$46,200
Tax from expansion:		
Alberta tax ($46,200 × 15%)		$ 6,930
Less tax saved on profits shifted to		
Alberta from arbitrary formula:		
Alberta allocation	$ 46,200	
Actual Alberta profits	(20,000)	
	$ 26,200	
Tax saved ($26,200 × 17%)		(4,454)
Incremental tax from expansion		$ 2,476

The reduced tax amount under the branch approach is a result of two things: the lower rate of Alberta tax, and the fact that the income allocation formula arbitrarily allocated more profits to Alberta than were actually earned there ($46,200 rather than $20,000).

Separate Corporation

If a separate Alberta corporation is used, all actual profits in Alberta belong to the Alberta corporation, which is a separate entity, so only the Alberta rate of tax applies on the actual expansion profits.

Tax: 15% × $20,000	$3,000

This situation demonstrates how the amount of tax varies significantly according to the expansion method employed. The three methods can be summarized as follows:

	Expansion profit	Tax	Effective rate
Direct sales	$20,000	$3,400	17%
Branch location	20,000	2,476	12
Separate corporation	20,000	3,000	15

Similar variances may occur when the expansion process involves manufacturing income. Expanding a non-manufacturing business by adding on a manufacturing component, or vice versa, may involve an arbitrary allocation of manufacturing and non-manufacturing income that may well affect the tax reduction available for manufacturing and processing profits. The impact of utilizing a division structure rather than a separate corporation structure in a situation involving manufacturing activities was shown in Chapter 11.

• **Repatriation of capital and accumulated profits** The process of repatriating the original capital invested, as well as accumulated expansion profits, is similar under both structures—division and separate corporation—for domestic expansion that does not involve new equity participants. As the division structure combines the expansion activity with existing activities within the same entity, repatriation is not an issue. However, when the expansion is housed in a separate, wholly owned subsidiary corporation, any dividends normally flow tax-free between the corporations, with the result that no tax implications arise on repatriation (see Chapters 11, 13, and 14).

B. Expansion with New Equity Participants

It is common for an existing business enterprise to encounter expansion opportunities when existing financial resources are inadequate. In such situations the decision maker must choose between two strategies: limited expansion and slow growth, or rapid expansion through the raising of additional equity from new participants. Choosing the latter course raises a number of questions:

1. Will the new equity members share in the existing operations as well as the expansion activity, or just the expansion activity?

2. Will the new participants be active in the business or be passive investors?

3. Will the new participants consist of a small number of large investors or a greater number of smaller investors?

4. Can the expansion be divided into several separate operations with different participants for each?

5. How much equity must be given up to achieve the desired level of expansion?

Clearly, once a company decides to involve additional equity participants in a business expansion, it must then choose between alternative business strategies and then choose between alternative business structures. The choices it makes will be influenced greatly by the nature of the expansion business and the financial circumstances of the existing business. Regarding structure, the decision maker has three alternatives available, each of which was discussed in previous chapters:

- separate corporation
- standard partnership
- limited partnership

Because each of these three structures has different tax implications that lead to different cash flows, it is important to match the alternative structure with the range of alternative strategies for including new equity participants. In most cases the strategy will influence the structure, but in some cases the structure will influence the strategy. The process of determining potential cash flows is basically the same whether one is expanding an enterprise with new equity or with internal resources; in either case, the process centres on determining how future profits will be taxed, how operating losses will be used, how losses will be treated if the expansion fails, and how capital and accumulated profits will be repatriated for reinvestment. However, when new equity participants are included, the analysis is more complex because it includes the new participants as well as the initiator.

The tax implications of the alternative structures were examined in detail in two separate case studies in Chapters 15 and 16. In Chapter 15 a corporation that operated a clothing wholesale business expanded into clothing manufacturing with a new equity participant, who provided both capital and manufacturing expertise. In this particular case the expansion strategy was predetermined—it required a single active participant with specific expertise. As a result, the alternative structures for the expansion were limited to either a separate corporation or a separate partnership, and the cash-flow implications were different for each participant.

The example of an expansion provided in Chapter 16 was quite different. The initiator wanted to expand his chain of restaurants and could do so by seeking out a small number of large, passive investors or a larger number of smaller passive investors. Also, it was possible to recruit different investors for each new location. In this case the different attributes of the available structures significantly influenced the strategy chosen—the limited partnership, which provides a minimum of risk to passive investors along with preferential treatment of tax losses. Choosing this structure meant seeking out a larger number of smaller, passive investors for each location. By choosing this structure, the initiator, as well as the investors, achieved an enhanced return on investment. Also, by leasing the required real estate and equipment, the initiator—who had limited financial resources—was able to grasp the opportunities at hand and maintain control of the organization while giving up a minimum of equity.

• **Expansion of the small-business deduction** In some expansion situations it may be desirable to give up more equity rather than less in order to achieve higher after-tax returns. This is especially desirable in private corporations if the expansion structure can increase the amount of income subject to the lower rate of corporate tax. Consider the following situation:

Situation: Roller Ltd. operates a number of amusement centres, each of which includes a roller rink and an indoor miniature golf facility. The existing operations generate profits in excess of $300,000 annually. Three new location opportunities exist, each of which has an annual profit potential of $150,000 and requires a capital investment of $500,000. It is important to expand rapidly; otherwise, the locations may be lost to competitors. Roller Ltd. has the financial strength to raise $1,000,000, which is two-thirds of what is required to expand to three new locations. Roller Ltd. also needs strong managers to run the locations. This introduces the possibility of raising equity capital from people who will also be active in the business. For demonstration purposes, Roller's top tax rate is assumed to be 40%.

Analysis: One obvious possibility is to obtain three separate active participants (one for each location). Each participant would contribute one-third of the $500,000 required for a given location. Each location would be owned 67% by Roller Ltd. and 33% by the manager-participant, and could be organized as either a separate partnership or a corporation. By following this course of action, Roller Ltd. would achieve the following return on investment:

Profits ($150,000 × 3)	$450,000
Tax @ 40%	(180,000)
After-tax profit	$270,000
Roller's share (⅔ of $270,000)	$180,000
Return on investment:	
$\dfrac{\$180,000}{\$1,000,000} =$	18%

This return would be the same whether a given location was run as a partnership or a corporation. If partnerships were used, profits would be allocated to Roller Ltd. and taxed at the high corporate rate. If separate corporations were used, each new corporation would be associated with Roller Ltd. because it controls each corporation, and therefore no additional small-business deduction would be achieved (see Chapter 13).

The small-business deduction base could be expanded by varying the ownership ratios and using a separate corporation structure. This would provide greater after-tax returns to all parties. For example, if Roller Ltd. relinquished 50% ownership of each separate location and used separate corporations, none of the corporations would be associated (see Chapter 13) and each would be entitled to the lower corporate tax rate of approximately 20% (for demonstration purposes). This structure (see the top of next page) would provide a greater after-tax profit to Roller Ltd. and require a reduced capital investment of $750,000 ($250,000 × 3).

This structure would provide a 24% return to Roller Ltd., as shown below.

Profit from each location	$150,000
Tax @ 20%	(30,000)
After-tax profit	$120,000
After-tax profit of three locations	
($120,000 × 3)	$360,000
Roller's share (50%)	$180,000
Return on investment:	
$\dfrac{\$180,000}{\$750,000} =$	24%

By giving up one-half rather than one-third of the equity, Roller Ltd. has maintained its share of after-tax profits of $180,000, increased the after-tax return on investment from 18% to 24%, and saved $250,000 of cash resources, which can be used for other expansion opportunities.

The above discussion and examples show that cash returns on domestic expansion activities, whether funded with internal resources or additional equity, can be significantly affected by the structure chosen to implement the activities. In many cases the optimum structure is not obvious and the decision maker must explore and test a number

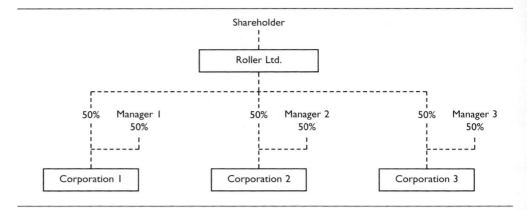

of alternatives before determining which is best in terms of cash flow, tax treatment, and other non–tax-related factors.

II. International Business Expansion

The expansion of a Canadian business enterprise into foreign markets is complicated because tax is imposed in the foreign jurisdiction as well as in Canada. Ultimately, cash will flow from the foreign operations back to Canada for reinvestment. It is vital to determine the amount and timing of tax when projecting future returns from such expansion. A Canadian business entity can utilize a number of alternative organization structures when expanding into a foreign jurisdiction. This part of the chapter briefly identifies and examines the fundamental tax implications of foreign business structures.

A. Basic Issues

There are two fundamental approaches to conducting foreign business operations. The foreign activity can be conducted from the home base in the form of direct export sales to consumers or distributors, or the foreign activity can be conducted by developing a formal foreign structure that involves a physical presence in the foreign jurisdiction. Formal structures can include the following:

1. A simple branch location.

2. A separate foreign corporation as a subsidiary of the Canadian parent corporation.

3. A separate foreign joint venture, partnership, or limited partnership.

4. An advanced, broadly based, foreign structure that includes foreign holding corporations, finance companies, and sales and manufacturing entities.

The primary business structures for foreign expansion activities are diagrammed in Exhibit 20-1. These basic structures were reviewed briefly in Chapter 3 and are discussed in more detail later in this chapter. Each has different business, legal, and tax consequences. From a tax perspective, the main issues are these:

1. To what extent is tax imposed by the foreign jurisdiction on foreign business operations?

2. How does Canadian tax apply on the foreign business profits? And how can losses on foreign operations be utilized, should they occur?

Exhibit 20-1:
Basic Structures for
Foreign Expansion

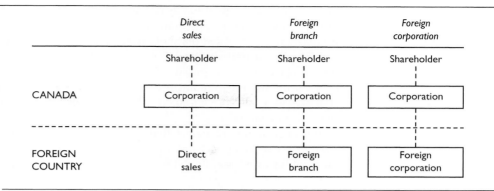

3. What tax treatment is applied to transactions between the foreign operation and the Canadian owner? The following types of transactions may occur:

- Intercompany sales of products and services between the Canadian and the foreign entity (intercompany pricing).

- The transfer of tangible and intangible assets from the Canadian entity to the foreign entity.

- The payment of rents or royalties on property leased by the Canadian entity to the foreign entity.

- The receipt of dividends from the repatriation of profits of a foreign subsidiary corporation.

- The payment of interest by the foreign entity to the Canadian entity on loans advanced to finance the foreign operations.

- Inter-entity management fees.

- The allocation of costs incurred by the home entity on behalf of the foreign entity.

- The reorganization of foreign structures; for example, the converting of a branch operation into a foreign subsidiary.

These issues are discussed below in terms of the three primary structures outlined in Exhibit 20-1. The discussions identify only the general tax principles relating to foreign operations, as the specific tax treatment will vary from country to country. As described in Chapter 3, Canada has entered into bilateral tax agreements with many countries, and each agreement identifies which jurisdiction has authority to impose tax on cross-border activities.

B. Direct Export Sales

From a tax perspective, direct sales by a Canadian company to a foreign market are treated quite simply. Recall from Chapter 3 that Canadian taxpayers are subject to Canadian tax on their world income. This means that direct sales by a Canadian business corporation to a foreign market are treated as if they were domestic sales, and are fully taxable in Canada as business income.

For foreign tax purposes, most foreign countries tax only those nonresidents who carry on business in the foreign country. At issue is what constitutes "carrying on a business." The tax treaty between Canada and the particular country will define the term more specifically.

Usually, the term applies to business activity implemented from a permanent establishment in the foreign country. For example, the Canada–U.S. tax convention defines "permanent establishment" as a fixed place of business through which the foreign business operation is carried on; it includes a place of management, a branch, an office, and a factory.[1] However, a fixed place of business used solely for the storage, display, or delivery of merchandise is deemed not to be a permanent establishment. Using this definition as a yardstick, expansion activities into foreign markets by direct export sales usually are not subject to tax in the foreign country.

It is important to recognize that the definition of a "permanent establishment" may vary from treaty to treaty. Because of this, the specific definition used by the particular country targeted for expansion should be examined before export activities are undertaken.

C. Foreign Branch Location

A Canadian business corporation, rather than penetrating foreign markets by direct export sales, may decide to establish a physical presence in the foreign country in the form of a branch location (see Exhibit 20-1). A Canadian corporation can establish a foreign branch simply by renting office space to house foreign personnel, who then perform sales, service, and administrative functions relating to the development of the foreign operations.

It is important to recognize that the foreign branch location is part of the Canadian corporation and does not constitute a separate legal entity. The tax treatment of profits earned by the foreign branch location is as follows:

1. Because the branch constitutes a permanent establishment in the foreign country, branch profits will be subject to the income taxes applicable in the foreign jurisdiction.

2. The foreign branch profits form part of the world income of the Canadian corporation (see Chapter 3), and are therefore also taxable in Canada as normal business income.

3. Canadian taxes payable on the business profits of the foreign branch can be reduced by the foreign tax credit (federal and provincial), which, within limits, provides for a Canadian tax reduction by the amount of foreign taxes paid.[2] The foreign tax credit calculation is discussed later in this chapter.

The impact of this tax treatment is demonstrated in the following example:

Situation: Canadian Ltd. maintains a branch business operation in a foreign country, from which it earns business income in a particular year. The foreign country imposes two rates of tax on corporate income—30% on the first $100,000 of income and 45% on income in excess of $100,000. The Canadian corporation is subject to a 40% tax rate (assumed), and its shareholders pay tax at the highest personal rate.

Analysis: The profits earned by the foreign branch are subject to three levels of taxation. First, the foreign profits are taxed in the foreign country. Second, the foreign profits are taxed within the Canadian corporation. And third, the Canadian shareholders are taxed when the profits are distributed as Canadian dividends from the Canadian corporation. The three levels of tax are calculated as follows, using the two foreign tax rates of 30% and 45% and assuming $1,000 of business profits in each category:

1 Article V, Canada–U.S. 1980 Tax Convention (1997 protocol).
2 ITA 126(2): IT-270R2.

	1st $100,000 of profits 30%	Profits over $100,000 45%
Foreign tax:		
Foreign income	$1,000	$1,000
Foreign tax	(300)	(450)
	700	550
Canadian corporate tax:		
Federal and provincial tax @ 40% of $1,000	(400)	(400)
Foreign tax credit	300	400
Net corporate tax	(100)	–0–
After-tax profit to Canadian corporation	600	550
Shareholder tax:		
Tax on dividend to shareholder net of dividend tax credit (30% of dividend)	(180)	(165)
Net cash to shareholder	$ 420	$ 385

Notice that in this calculation, the tax on branch profits that were subject to a 30% foreign tax rate was fully credited against the Canadian tax rate of 40% by the foreign tax credit. The Canadian corporate tax simply represents the difference between the Canadian tax rate of 40% and the foreign tax rate of 30% (40% − 30% = 10%). However, on foreign profits taxed at the foreign rate of 45%, the Canadian foreign tax credit was limited to the amount of Canadian taxes paid on the foreign income (40%), so the higher foreign tax rate of 45% prevailed. As a result of the limitation applied to the foreign tax credit in Canada, foreign branch profits are always taxed at the higher rate, whether foreign or Canadian.

The total of the taxes paid in the above example on $1,000 of foreign-branch income is calculated in the following table:

Foreign tax rate	30%	45%
Foreign tax	$300	$450
Canadian corporate tax	100	–0–
Canadian shareholder tax	180	165
Total foreign and Canadian taxes	$580	$615
Effective rate of tax	58.0%	61.5%

It is interesting to note that the foreign income earned by the branch ultimately is translated into a Canadian dividend when it is distributed to the Canadian shareholders. Consequently, the Canadian shareholder is entitled to a dividend tax credit for corporate taxes paid even though all or at least some of the corporate taxes were paid to a foreign jurisdiction.

This example indicates that the foreign branch structure does not provide any tax benefits when the entity is operating in a country that imposes lower tax rates than Canada. A lower foreign tax rate of 30% simply means that a portion of the normal Canadian tax of 40% (assumed) is paid to the foreign jurisdiction.

However, the branch structure does provide one major advantage over the foreign corporation structure: losses incurred by the foreign branch can immediately be used to off-set profits made in Canada, thereby reducing Canadian taxes otherwise payable. This resulting increased cash flow can be retained in Canada or reinvested in the branch to enhance the opportunity for long-term success.

Future profits accumulated in the foreign branch operation usually can be repatriated to the Canadian corporate owner without further tax consequences. As the branch is part of the Canadian company, profit distributions do not constitute a dividend payment and therefore do not attract any foreign withholding taxes, as they would if a foreign subsidiary corporation had been established. (This is discussed below.) However, some foreign countries *do* impose a special additional *branch tax* equivalent to the tax imposed on the payment of dividends; decision makers should investigate this before choosing the branch structure.[3] Normally, the foreign branch tax is eliminated by the Canadian foreign tax credit.

D. Foreign Subsidiary Corporation

A company that expands into foreign markets by establishing a foreign corporation as a subsidiary of the Canadian corporation faces entirely different tax consequences than does a company that chooses the branch structure. Business profits earned by a foreign subsidiary corporation are subject to the following tax treatment:

1. The subsidiary corporation, being incorporated in the foreign jurisdiction, is subject to the prevailing income taxes of the foreign country.

2. As the foreign corporation is not a resident of Canada, it is not subject to Canadian tax on business profits earned within the corporation.

3. After-tax profits accumulated within the foreign corporation can be distributed to the Canadian parent corporation as a dividend. As described in Chapter 11, dividends received from a foreign affiliate are excluded from corporate taxable income and are therefore not subject to Canadian corporate tax.

4. Most countries impose a special tax on dividends paid to a foreign shareholder. The tax is withheld and remitted to the foreign jurisdiction by the payer. For example, the United States imposes a 5% withholding tax on dividends paid to Canadian share-holders.[4] Rates in other countries range from 5% to 25%. As the dividend is not subject to Canadian corporate tax, no foreign tax credit can be claimed to offset the foreign withholding tax on the dividend.

The impact of this tax treatment is demonstrated in the following example:

Situation: Canadian Ltd. carries on business operations in a foreign country through a wholly owned foreign subsidiary corporation. The foreign country imposes a tax rate of 30% on the first $100,000 of business profits, and of 45% on profits in excess of $100,000, as well as a 5% withholding tax on dividends paid to Canada. In Canada, both the Canadian corporation and its shareholders are taxed at the high rates of tax, which is assumed to be 40% for corporations and 45% for individuals.

3 The concept of a branch tax is described in IT-137R3; see also ITA 219.

4 Article X, Canada–U.S. Tax Convention; IC 76-12R4. The 5% rate applies when the recipient of the dividend is a company owning 10% or more of the voting shares; otherwise the rate is 15%.

Analysis: The business profits of the foreign corporation are subject to three levels of tax—foreign corporate tax, foreign tax on dividend distributions to the Canadian corporation, and Canadian tax on dividend distributions from the Canadian company to the Canadian shareholders. The three levels of tax are calculated in the following table, using the two foreign tax rates of 30% and 45% and assuming $1,000 of business profits in each category.

	1st $100,000 of profits 30%	Profits over $100,000 45%
Foreign tax:		
Foreign income	$1,000	$1,000
Foreign tax	(300)	(450)
After-tax income to foreign corporation	700	550
Foreign withholding tax:		
When dividends are paid (5%)	(35)	(28)
Net received by Canadian corporation	665	522
Canadian corporate tax:		
Corporate tax on foreign dividend	–0–	–0–
Funds available to Canadian corporation	665	522
Canadian shareholder tax:		
Tax on dividends to shareholders net of		
dividend tax credit (30% of dividend)	(200)	(157)
Net cash to shareholders	$ 465	$ 365
Summary of taxes paid:		
Foreign tax:		
On business income	$ 300	$ 450
On repatriation of dividends	35	28
Canadian corporate tax	–0–	–0–
Canadian shareholder tax	200	157
	$ 535	$ 635
Effective tax rate	53.5%	63.5%

This analysis indicates that the types of tax payable, the amounts of tax payable, and the timing of the tax payments are dramatically different when foreign expansion is implemented through a foreign corporation. Exhibit 20-2 compares the branch structure with the corporation structure under two rates of applicable foreign tax by summarizing the two examples given previously.

• **Foreign profits subject to 30% foreign tax** The assumed 30% foreign tax rate is substantially lower than the assumed Canadian tax rate of 40%. In this situation the corporation structure provides the lowest tax cost and therefore the highest after-tax cash flow. Because utilizing the corporation structure involves separating the expansion profits from the Canadian corporation, the expansion profits are subject only to the foreign tax rate of 30%; this leaves 70% of the profits available for further foreign expansion activity. In comparison, the branch structure imposes the Canadian rate of tax of 40%; this leaves only 60% of foreign profits for further foreign expansion.

Exhibit 20-2: Tax Treatment of Foreign Branch versus Foreign Corporation	Foreign tax 30%		Foreign tax 45%	
	Branch	Corporation	Branch	Corporation
1. Tax paid when foreign profits are earned	$400	$300	$450	$450
2. Tax paid when foreign profits are repatriated*	–0–	35	–0–	28
	400	335	450	478
3. Tax paid when distributed to Canadian shareholders	180	200	165	157
Total	$580	$535	$615	$635
4. Effective tax rate	58.0%	53.5%	61.5%	63.5%

*Ignores possible foreign branch tax that is normally eliminated by the Canadian foreign tax credit.

Similarly, the amount of after-tax profits available for repatriation to the Canadian corporation is higher under the corporation structure when the foreign tax rate is substantially lower than the Canadian tax rate. The total tax after repatriation under the corporation structure is 33.5%; 66.5% of the foreign profits are thereby available for reinvestment in Canada. When the branch structure is used, however, total taxes are 40% after repatriation; in this case only 60% of foreign earnings are available for Canadian reinvestment.

And finally, the corporation structure increases the ultimate returns available to the shareholders of the Canadian corporation when dividends are declared, in that it increases their overall yield by 4.5% as a result of Canadian reduced taxes (58.0% – 53.5% = 4.5%).

• **Foreign profits subject to 50% foreign tax**   As indicated in Exhibit 20-2, the reverse results occur when foreign tax rates are higher than the Canadian rates—the branch structure creates *greater* cash-flow returns. When foreign tax rates are 45%, both the branch structure and the corporation structure create immediate tax on foreign profits earned at a rate of 45%; this leaves the same after-tax funds available for further foreign expansion. However, when profits are being repatriated, the foreign corporation is subject to a withholding tax whereas the branch is not. Therefore, under the corporation structure, the Canadian parent incurs total taxes of $478, or 47.8%, upon repatriation, leaving only 52.2% of the foreign profits available for reinvestment or for distribution to the Canadian shareholders. Notice, as well, that the foreign corporation structure results in overall taxes of 63.5% after distribution to the Canadian shareholders because of the high foreign taxes paid on expansion profits.

Although the choice of foreign structure may be influenced by a number of non–tax-related issues—business and legal considerations and so on—it is important to examine how tax treatment affects expansion cash flows under the basic alternatives, keeping in mind the anticipated cash requirements for further foreign expansion, the repatriation requirements, and the effect on distributions to Canadian shareholders. A number of other tax issues aside from this one arise when a foreign structure is being developed. These are discussed briefly below.

E. Alternative Cash Flows from a Foreign Subsidiary   The establishing of a foreign entity often requires significant support by the home-based entity. For example, the Canadian corporation may provide assets such as equipment, capital, rights to use patents and licences, and management services to the foreign operation. If a branch structure is used, these types of support usually have no tax implications, as the foreign branch is simply a part of the Canadian corporation. However, establishing a subsidiary corporation as a separate legal entity results in a different relationship. Consider the structure outlined in Exhibit 20-3 on the next page.

The structure indicates that the Canadian parent corporation, as well as providing equity capital, supplies the foreign corporation with the following: capital funds (through inter-corporate loans), equipment for use in the foreign operations, production technology, and certain management services. Consequently, the foreign entity, as a separate corporation, may be required to pay for the use of those assets and services. This payment may take the form of interest, rents, royalties, and management fees.

Such payments are deductible from the foreign corporation's income and result in reduced profits to the foreign corporation and increased profits to the Canadian parent corporation. In effect, foreign income is shifted to Canada before foreign income tax is applied. Because of this, foreign countries impose a special withholding tax on such payments to nonresidents. The amount of withholding tax varies from country to country and is often modified by the applicable international tax treaty.[5] For example, the following tax rates apply to payments from an American subsidiary to its Canadian parent:

Interest	10%
Rent	25
Royalties	10
Management fees	–0–

Any interest, rent, royalty, or management fee received by the Canadian corporation from its foreign subsidiary is fully taxable in Canada as property income or business income. The combination of Canadian tax and foreign withholding tax usually does not result in double taxation because the amount of Canadian tax is reduced by the foreign tax credit. For example, the payment of $10,000 of interest from the foreign subsidiary to the Canadian parent would normally be taxed as shown in the following table:

Foreign tax:		
Interest paid	$10,000	
Withholding tax @ 10%		$1,000
Canadian tax:		
Income	$10,000	
Corporate tax @ 40% (assumed)	$ 4,000	
Foreign tax credit	(1,000)	$3,000
Total foreign and Canadian tax		$4,000

Notice that the total tax of $4,000 corresponds to the Canadian tax rate of 40%. The imposition of the withholding tax merely results in an allocation of the Canadian rate of tax between Canada and the foreign jurisdiction. Also notice that the treatment of interest, rents, royalties, and management fees is different from the treatment of dividends. As explained previously, the dividends are not taxable to the Canadian corporation, so the foreign withholding tax on dividends is not available for a Canadian foreign tax credit.

---

5   IC 76-12R4 (summary of withholding tax rates for treaty countries).

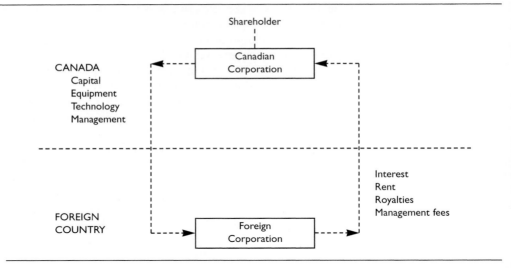

Exhibit 20-3:
Cash Flows between
Foreign Subsidiary and
Canadian Parent

All of this indicates that the manner in which a Canadian parent corporation provides support for its foreign subsidiary corporation can affect the ultimate cash returns on investment. For example, when the foreign subsidiary corporation is subject to a much lower tax rate than the Canadian parent, it may be advisable to provide additional capital to the subsidiary in the form of share capital bearing dividends as opposed to loans bearing interest. The payment of loan interest reduces foreign profits and shifts income to Canada, where it is taxed at the higher rate; whereas the providing of additional share capital leaves greater profits in the foreign subsidiary, which takes advantage of the lower corporate tax rate. The cash-flow analysis is the same as the one that was used to compare the corporation structure with the branch structure earlier in this chapter. Conversely, when foreign tax rates are much higher, funding by debt shifts income from the foreign entity to the Canadian corporation, in the form of interest payments, the result being lower overall tax rates.

In order to avoid excessive shifting of profits from one country to another, most foreign countries have special tax provisions that limit the deductibility of expenses paid to non-resident parent corporations when such expenses are unreasonably high. In other words, fair pricing rules generally prevail. However, within limits, support for foreign operations can be designed in such a way that the amount of foreign and Canadian tax payable is minimized and the timing of that tax is optimized.

F. Foreign Tax Credit

Both the taxation of foreign branch income and the payments from a corporate subsidiary of dividends, interest, rent, royalties, and management fees are significantly affected by the application of this country's foreign tax credit. As indicated previously, the foreign tax credit is designed to limit the total tax to an amount that is no greater than the one imposed by the country with the higher rate of tax. (The actual formula can be obtained by examining the appropriate interpretation bulletins and is not discussed in this chapter.[6])

While the concept appears simple, the actual calculation of the foreign tax credit is rather complex. As well, it is important to recognize that the calculation does not always provide the intended result. The Canadian foreign tax credit can only be applied to the foreign taxes on foreign income as determined by Canadian tax law. Income, however, may

---

6   ITA 126(1), (2); IT-183, IT-270R2.

be determined differently in other countries in accordance with their procedures for calculating income and recognizing expenses. For example, a foreign branch operation that holds depreciable property may be subject to one rate of capital cost allowance in the foreign country and a considerably different rate in Canada. In such cases the annual branch profits from which foreign tax is calculated may be different from those from which Canadian tax is calculated. This difference may result in a combined foreign and Canadian tax that is greater than the conceptual maximum of the highest tax rate of either country.

Canadian tax law deals with this problem by permitting companies with unused tax credits on foreign business income to carry those credits back three years and forward seven years.[7] While this reduces the risk of losing foreign tax credits, it also alters the normal timing for the tax payments, which in turn affects cash flow and return on investment.

The carry-over provisions do not apply to unused foreign tax credits on non-business income. As a result, rents, interest, and royalties paid by a foreign subsidiary, when those items constitute property income to the Canadian parent, cannot be carried back or forward if they cannot be used in the current year. However, foreign taxes on non-business income that are not offset by a foreign tax credit can be deducted as a normal business expense.[8] This provides partial, though not total, relief from double taxation.

In summary, decision makers who are contemplating a foreign expansion must consider not only the type of structure but also the nature of the transactions between Canada and the foreign entity when studying the resulting cash-flow implications.

G. Intercompany Transfer Pricing

An important aspect of international expansion involves the treatment applied to sales of products from the Canadian parent to its foreign subsidiary corporation. Consider the following three simple examples:

1. A Canadian manufacturing company sells finished products to its foreign subsidiary for distribution in the foreign market.

2. A Canadian company manufactures component parts in Canada and sells them to a foreign subsidiary for assembly and foreign-market distribution.

3. A Canadian company sells raw materials to a foreign subsidiary for processing, manufacturing, and foreign-market distribution.

In each of these examples, some of the business process is begun in one country and completed in another country. The question arises as to how much profit belongs to each country. Whenever there is a difference in tax rates between the Canadian parent corporation and the foreign subsidiary corporation, there is a desire to shift profits to the country with the lowest tax rate. The Canadian parent may attempt to either "underprice" or "overprice" such transactions—in other words, to manipulate the prices. Profits can also be shifted by means of service charges, commissions, interest charges, rents, and royalties.

Canadian tax law has adopted a reasonableness test with respect to the pricing of goods sold to foreign subsidiary corporations. As a result, products sold to a foreign subsidiary, whatever their stage of completion, are deemed to have been sold at a price that would reasonably have been expected in similar circumstances had the parties been dealing at arm's length.[9] It is often difficult to determine what constitutes "reasonable." Canada and many other countries have endorsed the pricing methods recommended by the

---

7   ITA 126(2); IT-520.

8   ITA 20(11), (12); IT-506.

9   ITA 69; IT-468R.

Organization for Economic Cooperation and Development for establishing reasonable transfer prices.[10]

The most common method is to base the transfer price for non-arm's-length transactions on comparable arm's-length selling prices. In effect, a company is deemed to have sold the goods to its subsidiary at the same price at which it sells the goods to outside parties. When appropriate comparables are not available, two other specific methods are endorsed. One is the "cost plus" method, which is based on a reasonable mark-up over the vendor's actual cost for the product sold. The other is the "resale price" method, which starts with the foreign subsidiary's ultimate customer selling price and works backward by deducting an appropriate profit margin.

It is important to recognize that in order to avoid double taxation on international transfers, a pricing policy must be established that is based on normal commercial considerations rather than on tax considerations. While some flexibility exists in the system, the consequences of extreme variations are significant and undesirable.

H. Converting a Foreign Branch to a Foreign Subsidiary

Foreign business expansion often involves a progression from one structure to another. For example, when expansion requires a physical presence in a foreign country, the branch structure may initially be used because of its simplicity and low cost, and because branch losses in the start-up years can be offset against the Canadian corporation's other taxable income. However, at some point, it may be necessary to convert the foreign branch into a foreign subsidiary corporation. As diagrammed in Exhibit 20-4, this procedure involves the transfer of assets such as inventory, equipment, and goodwill from the branch to the foreign corporation. As the branch is part of the Canadian corporation, the transfer of assets is actually between the Canadian corporation and the newly established foreign subsidiary corporation.

In Chapter 12 it was established that assets can be transferred from one corporation to another at tax values rather than at fair market values. However, this option, under Canadian tax law, is available only when the assets are being transferred to another Canadian corporation. Usually, foreign-branch assets can be transferred to a foreign corporation only at fair market values; this results in Canadian tax if the values of those assets exceed their tax costs.

If the branch assets will result in a significant tax liability on incorporation, the Canadian corporation can choose to retain ownership of certain assets. For example, the Canadian corporation can retain ownership of physical assets such as buildings and equipment and lease them to the foreign corporation. The same corporation can also retain intangible assets such as patents and goodwill, in which case the foreign corporation will pay royalties for their use. Such payment of rents and royalties amounts to a shifting of profits from the

Exhibit 20-4:
Incorporation of a
Foreign Branch

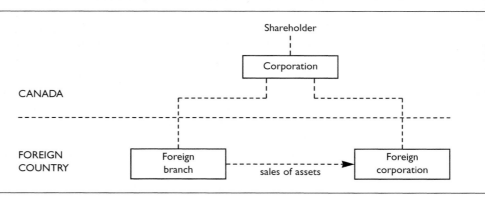

10 IC 87-2R; ITA 247.

foreign company to Canada, and the Canadian corporation will be subject to a foreign with-holding tax as previously described. This may or may not be advantageous—it depends on the income tax rates applicable on foreign income.

The process of deciding which form of business structure to utilize for foreign expansion must include consideration of the potential tax implications should it become necessary to alter the structure at some future time. International reorganizations do not have the same flexibility as domestic reorganizations.

The preceding discussions have provided a general perspective on the taxation issues relating to the expansion of a business to foreign jurisdictions. Clearly, the decision to embark on international business activities has cash-flow implications, and a significant amount of advance consideration is required when it comes to choosing the most appropriate organizational structure.

III. Summary and Conclusion

This chapter has examined the tax implications relating to the expansion of a business enterprise. An expansion can be conducted using any of a number of alternative business structures, each of which affects in a different manner how and when expansion profits are taxed, how operating losses may be used to generate tax savings, how tax savings are created if the expansion is discontinued, and how accumulated profits are taxed on repatriation.

Expansion can be domestic or foreign. A domestic expansion using internal resources can be structured utilizing either a division of the existing corporation or a separate operating corporation. Each of these structures has its own tax consequences relating to the timing and nature of tax savings resulting from expansion losses. As well, each affects in a different manner the application of provincial taxes and the taxes on manufacturing and processing activities.

When domestic expansion cannot be funded with internal resources, it may be necessary to include additional new equity participants. Such expansion activities can utilize a separate corporation, a standard partnership, or a limited partnership. These structures can be matched to alternative strategies that determine whether the new participants will be active or passive investors; whether there will be a small number of large investors or a greater number of smaller investors; and whether those investors will participate in all or only parts of the expansion program. In some cases it may be preferable to give up more equity than is necessary, in order to achieve tax savings from an expanded small-business deduction base and thereby greater after-tax returns on investment.

Expansion across international boundaries is even more complex because of the imposition of foreign income taxes and the need to integrate those taxes with the Canadian tax system. The three basic methods of achieving a foreign expansion are these: direct export sales, the establishment of a foreign branch location, and the formation of a separate foreign subsidiary corporation. Direct export sales are taxed only in Canada. Foreign profits earned by a foreign branch are subject to both foreign and Canadian income tax; but the Canadian foreign tax credit can be applied to ensure that the combined rate of tax is no more than that of the country with the higher tax rate. In addition, foreign branch losses can be offset against Canadian profits. Income earned by a foreign subsidiary corporation is at first taxed only in the foreign country, and after-tax profits are available for further foreign expansion. However, profits distributed by a foreign corporation as dividends are subject to a further foreign withholding tax.

While the decision to expand a business enterprise is based primarily on business and economic considerations, the methods chosen to implement that expansion can significantly affect the eventual cash returns. The expansion process therefore must involve examining alternative business structures and anticipating possible future results and scenarios; only in this way can the potential economic benefits be properly assessed.

Reading List

Income Tax Act References

	Section
Foreign tax deduction	126(1), (2)
Rules relating to unused foreign tax credits	126(2.3)
Employees of an international organization	126(3)
Foreign tax	126(5)
Business income tax (defined)	126(7)(a)
Non-business income tax (defined)	126(7)(c)
Tax for the year otherwise payable (defined)	126(7)(d)
Unused foreign tax credit (defined)	126(7)(e)
Foreign taxes on income from property exceeding 15%	20(11)
Foreign non-business income tax	20(12)
Unreasonable consideration	69(2) to (7)

Canada Customs and Revenue Agency Publications

IT-506	Foreign income taxes as a deduction from income.
IT-270R2	Foreign tax credit.
IT-183	Foreign tax credit—member of a partnership.
IC 76-12R4	Withholding tax rates to persons in treaty countries.
IT-468R	Management and administration fees paid to non-residents.
IC 87-2R	International transfer pricing and other international transactions.

Other Publications

Brodie, J., Glaser, M., "Transfer Pricing in Canada and the United States: Differences in Legislation, Policies and Practices," *Beyond Numbers (CA Magazine),* June/July 1999, pp. 22–23.

McAskile, A., "Acquiring, Holding, and Financing U.S. Businesses by Canadians," Corporate Management Tax Conference (1996), Canadian Tax Foundation, p. 17.1.

Webb, G. "Tax Factors Affecting the Choice Between a U.S. Branch and U.S. Subsidiary," 1988 Report of Proceedings of the 40th Tax Conference, Canadian Tax Foundation, pp. 45:1–46.

Review Questions

1. Domestic and international expansion decisions, like any investment decisions, should attempt to utilize a structure that will minimize the start-up cash requirements and maximize the cash returns to the initiator. Briefly outline the fundamental tax considerations that are relevant to the expansion process.

2. What are the two basic organization structures that can be used for domestic expansion activities without the participation of new equity investors? What is the major difference between these structures, regarding tax?

3. The rates of applicable provincial tax and tax on manufacturing profits may be different solely as a result of the expansion structure chosen for new activities. Explain why.

4. What are the basic organization structures that can be used for domestic expansion activities requiring additional capital from new equity participants?

5. When new equity participants are required in order to complete an expansion, what decisions must be made before an analysis of the organizational structure is performed?

6. Is it possible to increase the after-tax rate of return by choosing to give up more equity rather than less when new equity participants are required for expansion? Explain.

7. What are the primary business structures used to conduct foreign expansion activities?

8. In most cases, what must be true before a Canadian entity will be subject to foreign taxes on foreign business activities?

9. When the tax rates in a foreign country are lower than Canadian tax rates, will the use of a foreign branch structure to conduct the Canadian entity's foreign activities be advantageous? Explain.

10. In what circumstances is a foreign branch structure preferable to a foreign corporation structure?

11. Assume that a Canadian individual owns a substantial portion of a foreign corporation's shares and receives a dividend from them. Would the tax treatment applied to that dividend be different if it were first paid to a Canadian corporation owned by that individual?

12. "If foreign tax rates are the same as Canadian tax rates, a Canadian corporation conducting profitable foreign activities will not care whether a foreign branch or a foreign corporation is used to house the foreign operations." Is this statement true? Explain.

13. A Canadian business corporation may, in addition to providing equity capital, also support its foreign operations by providing loan capital, management services, technology, and equipment. What general implications does the foreign organization structure (branch versus corporation) have on these additional support activities?

14. Why may a Canadian business entity attempt to underprice or overprice products sold to its foreign subsidiary corporation? How do Canadian tax laws treat such transactions?

15. What tax consequences may result when the business operations of a foreign branch are transferred to a newly created foreign subsidiary corporation? How does this compare with the tax treatment resulting from the transfer of a Canadian branch operation to a Canadian subsidiary corporation?

Problems

Problem One

Sanford Pipe Ltd. is a Canadian corporation operating a profitable business in eastern Canada. Four years ago the company attempted to expand its operations to northern Mexico. At that time, Sanford invested $700,000 in a newly created Mexican subsidiary corporation. That corporation used those funds to acquire special equipment and as working capital for the new venture.

From the beginning, the foreign operations were plagued with a number of unexpected setbacks, including labour and production problems. As these setbacks occurred, Sanford contributed additional cash to keep the operations afloat. Sanford finally recognized that the Mexican subsidiary was a hopeless case and decided to close it. After the equipment was sold and all liabilities were paid, the Mexican corporation was wound up and Sanford received $200,000.

The financial results of the Mexican venture are summarized below.

Year	Losses incurred	Cash provided by Sanford
20X1	$300,000	$ 700,000
20X2	200,000	100,000
20X3	200,000	200,000
20X4	100,000	–0–
	$800,000	$1,000,000

The president of Sanford regretted the decision to undertake the foreign expansion. Not only did it result in a substantial loss, but, as well, the cash requirements resulted in the company forgoing a number of other opportunities that could have yielded 15% after tax. Assume Sanford is subject to a 40% corporate tax rate.

Required:

1. Determine the after-tax loss in cash flow terms to Sanford as a result of the foreign venture.

2. If the foreign venture had been organized as a foreign branch of Sanford, how much would it have lost?

Problem Two

Kronston Ltd. is a Canadian-controlled private corporation that imports irrigation equipment from Taiwan for distribution in southwestern Ontario. Last year the company achieved a profit of $600,000 after tax.

Kronston is interested in expanding its operations to the Okanagan region of British Columbia. It recognizes that to be successful, it will require a committed manager who is familiar with the area and understands the special problems of irrigation in that region.

The Okanagan region is capable of generating profits of $250,000 annually. Sonia Harapiuk lives in Vernon, B.C., and has been active in the irrigation business for many years. She is interested in managing the Okanagan expansion provided that she can have an equity interest in the venture. Kronston is not averse to this, as Harapiuk has proven expertise in the industry and her equity participation would ensure a long-term commitment. She has requested 50% equity in the venture and has sufficient funds to provide her share of the capital required to start the venture.

Kronston had been thinking of allowing Harapiuk to purchase a 25% interest in the Okanagan activity. The company feels that her participation is important, but also sees other alternatives. Before making a decision, the president of Kronston has asked his financial manager to determine the financial cost of allowing Harapiuk to own 50% instead of 25% of the new venture. The project will require a total capital investment by the owners of $800,000. Kronston has other opportunities for investing its funds, and these opportunities can yield pre-tax returns of 25% annually.

Required:

What would be the financial cost to Kronston of permitting Harapiuk to have the equity interest in the new venture that she has requested? Assume corporate tax rates are 20% on income subject to the small-business deduction and 40% on other business income.

Problem Three

Jean Dumenil is a senior executive for Dentex Ltd., a Canadian company operating a national chain of retail stores. His colleague and friend, George Watson, recently gave up his job as marketing manager with Dentex and has moved to the United States to start his own chain of retail stores.

Watson is trying to raise equity capital by selling shares of his new American corporation. He has approached Dumenil and offered him a 25% interest in that corporation in exchange for a $250,000 cash investment. Dumenil has confidence in Watson's abilities and has agreed to the investment. Watson has assured Dumenil that the American corporation will pay regular dividends of $20,000 annually as soon as adequate cash flows permit.

Dumenil is subject to a personal marginal tax rate of 45% on income, except on Canadian dividends, which are taxed at a rate of 30%. Watson has informed Dumenil that the American corporation will pay tax at a rate of 40% on its business income. U.S. withholding tax on dividends is 15% if paid to an individual and 5% if paid to a Canadian corporation owning more than 10% of the shares.

Required:

1. Determine the amount of tax that Dumenil will be required to pay if annual dividends of $20,000 are paid.

2. What is the combined rate of foreign tax and Canadian tax that will be paid on Dumenil's share of the American business profits after they are distributed to him as dividends?

3. Would you advise Dumenil to create a Canadian holding corporation to own the shares of the American corporation? Explain, and provide supporting calculations.

4. If Dumenil uses a holding corporation but is going to require the annual dividends for personal use, how should he capitalize the holding corporation with his $250,000? Explain.

Cases

Case One   Klondike Carpets Ltd.

Klondike Carpets Ltd. is a large Winnipeg retailer of home and office flooring. The company is a success because it keeps abreast of market changes and provides personalized service to its customers.

The company is owned by three brothers, each of whom plays a major role in the business operations. George, a CA, handles financing. Walter heads up the buying department and travels extensively. Ken is the primary marketing person, the one who instills the concept of "personal service" in the sales organization.

Klondike's profits for the last fiscal year amounted to $450,000 after reasonable salaries to the three managing shareholders. The company has accumulated large cash reserves.

Recently, the brothers have been discussing what to do with their successful business. They have listened to offers to sell the company that, if accepted, would give them sufficient net capital to live a comfortable life. But they have also considered just staying the way they are (that is, a successful local business) and letting their wealth accumulate. This sounds attractive, but they are all young enough to seriously entertain expansion possibilities.

Recently, Ken completed a tour of Canada and targeted 10 cities that he thought could support a successful operation like the one in Winnipeg.

The Winnipeg operation has two locations—the main store on Portage Avenue and a branch in Polo Park. The branch is managed by Shirley Friesen, who is exceptional in that she runs the business as if she owns it. The previous year she was rewarded with a bonus of 10% of profits.

Walter has expressed concern that Shirley, with her expertise and personality, may soon open her own store in competition. Although she does not currently have any substantial amount of capital, Walter is aware that she saves her entire bonus as well as a portion of her regular salary.

The brothers plan to meet to discuss these current issues. In preparation, George has assembled the following information:

Winnipeg branch store

Current profits	$120,000
Major assets:	
Working capital and inventory	300,000
Fixtures and leaseholds	nominal

Expansion stores
- New stores would be in rented premises.
- Possible good locations: 10.
- Capital required per store:

Working capital	$300,000
Leasehold improvements and fixtures	250,000
Start-up costs (opening advertising, giveaways, etc.)	50,000
	600,000
Available bank financing on new store	200,000
Net capital required	$400,000

- Profits are expected to be 30% of capital invested, or $120,000 per store (after amortization, etc.).

- Klondike can raise about $2,000,000 for expansion by combining its cash reserves with a small amount of bank financing. The required bank financing is separate from the bank financing for each new store described above.

- Corporate tax rates are 20% on income subject to the small-business deduction, 40% on other business income, and $51\frac{2}{3}\%$ of investment income.

Required:
Recommend a course of action for

(a) the Polo Park branch operations; and,

(b) a possible expansion to the target cities.

Case Two   Cargill Transport Ltd.

Cargill Transport operates a Canada-wide trucking operation hauling commercial freight. In the past several years a number of Canadian customers have had requirements involving shipments to their American operations.

Cargill does not have operating facilities or licences to operate in the United States and so, until now, has basically ignored this potential market.

Cargill's Winnipeg operation, however, has had so many requests for foreign hauling that it has set up an arrangement with a Minneapolis-based hauler. The arrangement is that Cargill hauls Canadian freight to the American border and leaves the trailer at the border to be picked up by the American hauler. Likewise, the American hauler brings American freight to the Canadian border and leaves the trailer for a Cargill truck to pick up.

The arrangement is cumbersome for two reasons:

1. It is difficult to coordinate freight loads to match delivery deadlines, and often the trucks are returned from the border without a trailer.

2. It is difficult to accurately allocate the fee between the two carriers, as the distance travelled by each is different and operating costs also vary.

Cargill wants to expand its operations into the entire United States. This will have to be done gradually, as Cargill's resources for expansion are limited.

Cargill is owned 50% by a British corporation and 50% by Turnbull Holdings Ltd., a Canadian investment corporation. Turnbull is entirely owned by the Pickle family of Toronto.

Cargill's executives in Toronto have recently decided to begin expanding into the United States. Winnipeg has been chosen to spearhead the expansion because it is the only location that has any foreign activity and connections.

Obtaining a licence to operate in the United States is rather complicated, especially in the highly regulated transportation industry. It is necessary to obtain both state and federal licences. One option, of course, is to acquire a major existing American company that is already licensed throughout the United States, but this is not practical because of Cargill's financial limitations.

Charles Wheeler, the vice-president (finance), is given the task of developing the American expansion. He wants to establish a base in Minneapolis and obtain a licence permitting hauls from there to Winnipeg.

The Winnipeg division of Cargill has 12 vehicles and trailers that are not being fully utilized, and Wheeler decides to relocate these to the United States to establish the company's presence there. The American base will require a small freight depot as well as parking and repair facilities; however, all major administration, such as accounting and payroll, will still be carried out at the administration office in Winnipeg. An American bank account will be established to collect American fees and pay American expenses.

Wheeler does not know how long it will take for the operations to become profitable, although he is reasonably certain that the route will eventually be lucrative. Wheeler is certain that as the operation grows and experience is gained, more American personnel will be hired to assist in the expansion program. In the meantime, market studies are to be carried out to determine where the next thrust should be.

Before investigating the expansion, Wheeler gathers together what limited information the company has on international taxation, and on business organizations in foreign countries (see below).

CARGILL TRANSPORT LTD.

1. Canadian tax rate for Cargill (assumed)	40%
2. American tax rates for American corporation*	
First $40,000 profit	25
Next $60,000 profit	35
Profit over $100,000	43
3. American withholding tax on dividends	5
4. Canadian withholding tax on dividends to the United Kingdom	10

* The American tax rates are not actual American rates. They have been arbitrarily chosen to demonstrate various levels of foreign tax that may occur.

Required:

How should Wheeler proceed with the expansion so as to maximize the profits and returns for the entire organization?

Comprehensive Cases (Chapters 12–20)

Comprehensive Case One   Seacourt Restaurants Ltd.

Charles Court owns and operates the Seacourt Restaurant as a proprietorship. The restaurant has gained a reputation for offering quality food, good service, and moderate prices in a cozy, relaxed setting. It is a distinctive restaurant well known to the people of Winnipeg. Court often brags about the competence of his bar and restaurant staff and about the efficiency of his kitchen.

Profits in the past year amounted to $120,000 before draws by Court, who lives modestly and requires only about $50,000 before tax for living expenses. Over the years, he has invested excess profits in public securities, so he has substantial investment income, which in itself puts him in the maximum tax bracket.

Court has asked you whether he should incorporate. He is aware that incorporation has some advantages but has also read in the newspapers that double taxation occurs when a corporation structure is used.

Required:

Outline the benefits that may be achieved by incorporation of this business, and provide Court with information that will help him to understand the relationship between corporations and their shareholders.

Some time later ...

After incorporation, Court's business continues to prosper, and he hires Charles Spud to work as an assistant manager. Spud is young and aggressive. He has good marketing skills but his real strength lies in cost control and staff efficiency. With Spud's help, the restaurant's pre-tax profits increase to $240,000 after both Spud and Court have been paid fair salaries.

Court begins to spend less time at the restaurant. In his place, Spud efficiently manages the whole operation. Court continues to take a $50,000 salary.

Spud approaches Court and asks if he can acquire part ownership. Spud feels that he contributes substantially to the generating of profits and that a 20% equity interest would be reasonable.

Court approaches you for advice. He feels that he might be able to satisfy Spud by establishing some bonus arrangement but that he will likely have to let Spud own 20% of the operations. He also mentions that the land and building have increased greatly in value. Their current value of $800,000 is $300,000 higher than the original value. Usually, in the restaurant industry, land and building can be leased at 12% of their original value on a net-net basis (that is, the tenant pays all of the costs associated with the building). Currently, the company deducts about $30,000 annually for amortization on the existing building. If Court shares ownership, he does not want Spud to share in any continued appreciation of the building, as Court regards this as a "fortuitous gain."

It is common in the restaurant business to value the business at six times normal after-tax profits.

Court has also indicated that Spud has no money with which to make a purchase of equity.

Required:

1. Outline alternatives that will permit Spud to acquire a 20% interest in the business, and briefly evaluate each alternative. Recommend a course of action.

2. What value should be used for the transfer of 20% ownership?

Some time later ...

After suffering a heart attack, Court asks Spud to purchase his remaining 80% interest. Spud agrees. Court will keep the building as an investment. They agree on a price of $600,000, to be paid in cash on closing, for the remaining 80% of the shares. By now the company has built up $200,000 of cash reserves. The bank has agreed to loan Spud $400,000 for the balance (the $400,000 to be repaid over an eight-year period).

Retained earnings at the time of sale amount to $300,000.

Required:

Advise both Court and Spud on how the transfer of 80% of the shares can best be structured to maximize cash flows.

Some time later ...

Seacourt continues to prosper, and good profits are maintained, although most of the cash generated goes to reduce the bank debt.

A local businessman approaches Spud to see if Spud would purchase his failing restaurant, the Butcherchop. While Spud feels he could turn the business around, he wisely backs away because of the amount of cash that would be needed to redecorate the restaurant.

The Butcherchop Ltd. has accumulated losses of $300,000, which the present owner can use if the company combines its operations with those of a successful venture. He therefore returns to Spud and proposes the following:

1. A new entity would be set up that would share profits or losses 50/50.

2. The new entity would rent the building and equipment from the Butcherchop Ltd.

3. Spud would develop a new concept and oversee renovations costing $150,000.

4. Spud would contribute $25,000 equity. The Butcherchop Ltd. would provide the remaining $125,000 required to meet the cash needs in 3 above.

5. Spud would not be liable except to the extent of $25,000.

Spud realizes that losses may result in the early years, but is reasonably certain that his ideas will be successful.

Required:
Outline alternative methods of organizing the new entity, and evaluate each.

Some time later …
Finally, the bank loan is paid off. Spud realizes that the Seacourt concept is distinctive enough to market in other locations. He has two young managers who are aggressive and want an opportunity to help expand the business. They envision Seacourts across the country.

Spud realizes that expansion would require extensive resources. It would take about $1,000,000 to erect a building comparable to the one in Winnipeg; an additional $200,000 would be needed for fixtures. In addition, a new restaurant might incur several years of losses before profits begin to come in.

Of course, each location could be financed in some manner, but equity requirements still appear high.

Spud realizes he must address two fundamental problems:

1. How to reduce the equity cash requirements.

2. How to raise sufficient capital and minimize risk to the existing successful operation.

With regard to 2, Spud lists the following alternatives:

1. Expand slowly by developing one restaurant and not expanding further until the first is generating positive cash flows. (This way, Spud would retain 100% control.)

2. Raise a large amount of capital from many local investors to open several restaurants at once. These investors would be equity holders but not active in management.

3. Find one wealthy investor to provide most of the cash, with Spud providing management and development expertise.

4. Seek out separate capable managers, each of whom has the resources to be part owner, for the individual new restaurants.

Required:

1. What can be done to reduce the equity requirements of each new restaurant?

2. For each of the preceding alternatives, outline a form of organization that may be suitable, and briefly comment on why it appears suitable.

Comprehensive Case Two   Cambell Enterprises Ltd.

Cy Cambell is chairman of the board of Cambell Enterprises Ltd. The company originally operated a successful car dealership, which was sold in 20X4. When it was sold, Cambell talked several of the key employees into staying on and assisting in the management of new ventures in the auto industry. The employees acquired shares in Cambell Enterprises; shortly thereafter, the company purchased the shares of Borex Distributors Ltd., a company that distributes specialty parts to retail auto-accessory stores. Borex last year earned profits of $400,000 before tax but after salaries had been paid to each manager. The profits of Borex have been funnelled to Cambell Enterprises and reinvested in other business ventures, one of which is not related to the auto industry. An organizational chart for the current year (20X9) is shown on page 665.

The shareholders have some major decisions to make with respect to their holdings, and the vice-president (finance) has prepared the following summary:

• **Winnipeg Moon Publishers Ltd.**   Winnipeg Moon operates a daily tabloid newspaper in Winnipeg. The company was acquired in 20X5 and had accumulated business losses of $100,000 at that time. Since acquisition, the *Moon* has lost an additional $500,000, mainly because it can't find enough readers. Management is convinced that substantial losses will continue for another three to five years before circulation reaches a break-even level. They are prepared to sustain losses for two more years, but if they find no alternative solutions, they will take no further risks. During this time, they will consider the following:

1. Selling the company.

2. Finding new additional equity investors to share the risk until profits are attained.

3. Winding up the operations.

The second alternative is the most desirable, but given the risks and losses, it may be difficult to attract participants.

• **Kronin Tire and Rim Ltd.**   Kronin operates a tire retreading plant that converts old used tires into "like new" tires. The process is capital-intensive, and the plant has recently been retooled with modern equipment. Profits of Kronin amount to about $350,000 annually.

• **Patrick's Jack and Jump Ltd.**   The shares of Patrick's were acquired in 20X6 at a cost of $1,200,000. Even after dividends have been paid, the company has accumulated retained earnings of $1,400,000. An offer of $2,800,000 for the shares was received last week, and Cambell feels this offer reflects the proper fair value. The details of the transaction have yet to be worked out, and a meeting is planned for early next week to complete the sale.

• **Borex Distributors Ltd.**   Borex has been successful in distributing accessories in Manitoba and Ontario for the past several years. Last year two salespeople were sent into North Dakota and Minnesota for a three-month selling tour. They then completed a similar tour of western Canada. The number of orders generated convinced the executives that these markets could be exploited. The expansion plans could be carried out by dividing the new territories among the Winnipeg-based sales representatives, or by establishing sales offices in both Alberta and Minnesota serviced by salespeople living in those territories. Ultimately, a more formal organization may be required.

• **QuickStart Co.**   One of the biggest selling items for Borex is a remote-control car starter, which is supplied by an American company. Borex has learned that a local businessman plans to establish a business named QuickStart to manufacture the product in Winnipeg but is short of funds for establishing and starting up the plant. Borex has offered to put up half the money ($600,000) to start the venture in return for a 50% equity ownership. Borex is convinced the operation will eventually be profitable, though it will likely suffer losses for at least the first four years.

• **Julio Car Stereo Systems Ltd.**   Cambell Enterprises is attempting to purchase this company, and has completed a series of meetings with Julio, which has agreed to sell its net assets for $1,200,000, or its shares for $1,140,000. Julio is a profitable company and either of these prices would be satisfactory as a purchase price. (Last year Julio earned a pre-tax profit of $500,000.) Julio's most recent balance sheet is as shown in the following table:

Assets		Liabilities and Equity	
Current assets	$600,000	Bank loan	$200,000
		Share capital and	
Goodwill (at cost)	–0–	retained earnings	400,000
	$600,000		$600,000

The fair market value of Julio's current assets is the same as stated on the balance sheet. A decision must be made regarding which offer to choose. The decision to buy has already been made. The cash received from the sale of Patrick's Jack and Jump will provide more cash than is required for the above acquisitions.

Cambell has proposed a new investment in the book-publishing industry, but the other shareholders have strongly argued against it because of their problems with the *Moon*. Cambell has decided to make the investment on his own, and intends to propose that a large cash distribution be made to shareholders so that he will have the funds to finance the venture on his own.

Required:
Review the above financial structure and business plans of Cambell Enterprises. How might Cambell and the other shareholders maximize their wealth?

Exhibit 1
ORGANIZATIONAL CHART

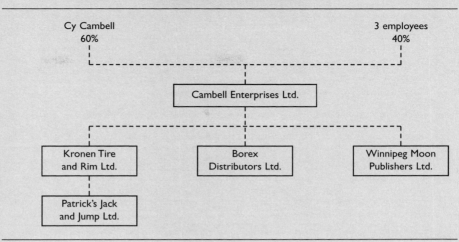

Chapter 21   Tax Aspects of Corporate Financing

Corporations, and in particular public corporations, can obtain capital funding in a great number of ways. The basic capital funding alternatives are these: debt, equity, and leasing. Within each of these basic categories, there are numerous sub-alternatives, including bonds, debentures, common shares, various types of preferred shares, and lease arrangements with varying terms and conditions.

Each of the basic financing methods has different tax implications, to both the corporation and the investor who provides the capital. These varying tax treatments affect the after-tax cost of obtaining corporate capital. The corporation's goal is always to develop a cost-efficient financial structure. While the financing treatment chosen may be influenced mainly by the existing financial structure and by market conditions, tax is also an important consideration.

An efficient capital structure is one that minimizes the after-tax cost of financing to the corporation and, at the same time, maximizes the after-tax returns to the investor. It is therefore critical that the decision maker examine financing options on a global basis by integrating corporate and investor tax considerations.

This chapter will examine the tax consequences of the basic financing alternatives. Specifically, this chapter will examine

(a) the tax implications of choosing debt rather than equity, from the perspective of both the corporation and the investor;

(b) the tax treatment of financing charges relating to the issuing of debt and equity securities; and,

(c) the tax implications of leasing assets rather than purchasing them.

I. Debt versus Equity

As already mentioned, the cost of financing is influenced by the tax treatment to both the corporate issuer of securities and the investor who purchases those securities. The potential investors in corporate securities include individuals, private corporations, other public corporations, and an array of pension and other investment funds; each of these entities is subject to a different tax treatment. A particular type of security that will enhance the tax position of a particular type of investor may be in greater demand, so that a corporation can issue it at a higher price, the result being lower financing costs. For example, investors with capital losses may prefer securities that pay nominal dividends but offer greater capital growth, because this maximizes capital gains, which can then be offset against capital losses.

In order to take advantage of a tax-sensitive marketplace, the corporation must be familiar with investor tax concerns and, whenever possible, attempt to satisfy those concerns. A corporation must consider its finance costs in the context of investor needs.

A. Cost of Corporate Debt and Equity

The real cost of financing is the after-tax cost. Debt is serviced by the payment of interest, which is fully deductible by the corporation in arriving at its taxable income.[1] On the other hand, equity capital is serviced by the payment of dividends, which are not deductible and must be paid from after-tax corporate income. From the investor's perspective, interest income on debt is fully taxable, whereas dividend income receives special treatment.

The implications of this are shown in the following simplified situation:

---

1   ITA 20(1)(c).

Situation: A corporation that is subject to a tax rate of 40% intends to raise $100,000 of capital for expansion purposes. Current market conditions indicate that debt funding would require an interest rate of 10%. As an alternative, the company could raise the capital by issuing preferred shares having a fixed dividend rate of 8%.

Analysis: While the dividend rate of 8% on the preferred shares is less than the interest rate of 10% on debt, this is not reflected in the resulting tax consequences to the corporation. When comparing the two alternatives, it is useful to determine the amount of corporate income required to service the dividends and the interest respectively.

If debt is issued, the corporation can service the interest payments with $10,000 of corporate income, as follows:

Corporate income required	$10,000
Interest paid (10% of $100,000)	(10,000)
Net income to corporation	$ –0–
Tax to corporation	$ –0–

However, if preferred shares are issued, the corporation must pay $8,000 of dividends from after-tax corporate profits. This means that the corporation must earn $13,333 to service $8,000 of dividends, calculated as follows:

Corporate income required	$13,333
Corporate tax: $13,333 @ 40%	(5,333)
Net after-tax income	$8,000
Dividends paid	(8,000)
Net cash to corporation	$ –0–

In order to fund debt interest of 10%, the corporation must invest the borrowed funds to return at least 10%. In comparison, to fund a dividend of 8% the corporation must invest the funds obtained to return at least 13.3%. In other words, the cost of a 10% debt is 10% but the cost of an 8% dividend is actually 13.3%.

This analysis indicates that debt financing has a considerable advantage over equity financing. This advantage stems from the fact that by choosing to pay interest, and thereby shifting income directly to the investor, the corporation avoids double taxation. Note that in this example, if the corporate tax rate had been 18 to 20%, the cost of equity capital would have been more in line with the cost of debt capital. In Chapter 11 it was shown that the high corporate tax rate on business income in 2004 was 37%. If this 37% rate is applied to the above situation and analysis, the corporate cost of an 8% dividend is reduced to 12.7% from 13.3%. The anticipated reduced tax rate will reduce the cost of equity from the current level but it remains significantly more expensive than the cost of debt.

The above comparison of debt and equity was examined in the context of equity in the form of preferred shares, which bear a stated dividend rate but do not otherwise participate in corporate profits. In this context, except for the fact that the tax treatment is different, preferred share financing and debt financing are similar from the perspective of the holder of common shares. Because common share equity participates in corporate profits, it is difficult to compare the cost of debt with the cost of common share financing.

In comparing the cost of debt with the cost of preferred share financing, the difference between the required interest rate and the required dividend rate is obviously important. In the previous example, the cost comparison was made by arbitrarily choosing a 10%

interest rate as an alternative to an 8% dividend rate. The required dividend and interest rates are influenced by the financial strength of the company and by market conditions, but also by how the investor is taxed on the different types of returns received. This variable in financing costs is discussed below.

B. Tax Treatment to Investors

Capital markets that provide financing to corporations are sensitive to how investment returns are taxed. Interest, dividends, and capital gains are all taxed in a different manner when received by the investor. Also, the tax treatment of each type of return may vary depending on the nature of the investor. Investors can be taxable entities such as individuals, private corporations, and public corporations; or they can be non-taxable entities such as pension funds, retirement savings funds, and charitable organizations.

The marginal tax rates for the different types of investment returns were developed in previous chapters and are summarized in Exhibit 21-1. It is important to remember that these rates are based on assumed federal and provincial rates of tax applicable in the particular year, and should be updated by the reader for current decision making.

Exhibit 21-1:
Tax on Investment Returns by Type of Entity*

	Interest	Dividend	Capital gain
Individuals:			
Low bracket	26%	7%	13%
Second bracket	34	17	17
Third bracket	40	24	20
Top bracket	45	30	23
Canadian-controlled private corporations	51⅔	33⅓	26**
Public corporations	37	0	19

* These rates include an assumed provincial tax rate and ignore federal and provincial surtaxes (see Chapters 10 and 13).
** ½ (51⅔%).

Exhibit 21-1 indicates that interest income is taxed at the normal rates applicable to individuals and corporations. The tax rate on capital gains is simply one-half of the tax rate on interest, reflecting the fact that only one-half of capital gains are taxable (subject to the lifetime capital gain deduction for individuals). The tax rate on dividend income for individuals is the normal rate of tax less the dividend tax credit (see Chapter 10). Portfolio dividends received by private corporations are subject to a special refundable tax of 33⅓% (see Chapter 13), whereas dividends received by public corporations are not taxable at all (see Chapter 11).

By applying the varying tax rates given in Exhibit 21-1, both the investor and the corporation issuing securities can determine which investment yields provide equivalent after-tax returns. For example, an individual in the top tax bracket can receive a 10% interest return or a 7.9% dividend or a 7.1% capital gain, and achieve the same after-tax rate of return, calculated as follows:

	Interest	Dividend	Capital gain
Tax rate	45%	30%	23%
Income	$100	$79	$71
Tax	(45)	(24)	(16)
After-tax return	$ 55	$55	$55
Rate of return	5.5%	5.5%	5.5%

Therefore, ignoring at this time the relative risk of each investment, individual investors in the highest tax bracket would be indifferent to whether they receive 10% interest, a 7.9% dividend, or a 7.1% capital gain, as each alternative provides an after-tax return of 5.5%.

The equivalent yields for a different type of investor may be quite different. For example, if the investor is a public corporation, a 10% interest return will result in the same after-tax income as a 6.3% dividend or a 7.8% capital gain, calculated as follows:

	Interest	Dividend	Capital gain
Tax rate	37%	NIL	19%
Income	$100	$63	$78
Tax	(37)	–0–	(15)
After-tax return	$ 63	$63	$63

Notice that because intercorporate dividends received by a public corporation are not taxable, a 6.3% dividend received by such an entity provides the same after-tax return as 10% interest; whereas an individual would have to receive a 7.9% dividend to achieve what is equivalent to a 10% interest return.

A profile of equivalent yields is presented in Exhibit 21-2. It is based on the assumed tax rates provided in Exhibit 21-1. This exhibit shows the pre-tax returns required to yield equivalent after-tax returns on interest, dividends, and capital gains for each type of investor. A 10% interest rate is used as the base rate of comparison. Similar comparisons can be made using different rates of interest.

The type of information provided in Exhibit 21-2 is essential to corporations that are examining various financing alternatives, as it indicates how potential investors will view the security being considered for issue. For example, if current interest rates are 10% and the corporation is considering issuing preferred shares with a fixed dividend rate of 7%, it will be wise to note that those shares will be less attractive than an interest-bearing security for all potential investors *except* other public corporations. This is because for an investor that is a public corporation, a 7% tax-free dividend yield is equivalent to a taxable interest yield of 11.1% (11.1% – tax @ 37% = 7%).

Similarly, when contemplating different types of equity issues, the issuing corporation should recognize that dividends and capital gains receive different tax treatment. Equity issues of common shares, or of preferred shares that are convertible into common shares, can provide the investor with both dividends and capital gains because they participate in corporate earnings. However, when the investor is an individual, the tax rate on dividends is less than on capital gains provided that the investor does not have a capital gain exemption. Because of this, some investors prefer greater dividend returns even though capital growth will be lower, whereas other investors prefer capital growth despite the resulting reduced dividends. A corporation that issues both common shares with low dividends and

Exhibit 21-2: Equivalent Pre-Tax Yields		Interest	Dividend	Capital gain
Individuals:				
	Low bracket	10%	7.9%	8.5%
	Second bracket	10	7.9	7.9
	Third bracket	10	7.9	7.5
	Top bracket	10	7.9	7.1
Canadian-controlled private corporations		10	7.2	6.5
Public corporations		10	6.3	7.8

higher growth potential, and convertible preferred shares with a high dividend rate and a lower growth potential, can attract a larger group of investors. This in turn results in a tax-efficient capital structure, which ultimately reduces the overall costs of financing.

The tax relationship between interest, dividends, and capital gains often changes when tax laws are revised. The amount of the dividend tax credit, for example, has been changed several times in the past few years. Similarly, the treatment of capital gains has undergone numerous changes. When such changes occur, corporations must re-evaluate their financial structures and develop alternative methods of obtaining capital that are consistent with the new tax regime.

C. Preferred Share Financing

The offering of preferred shares as an alternative to debt financing is severely constrained owing to the non-deductibility of dividend payments. With corporate tax rates being in the range of 33 to 40%, corporations must earn a substantially higher dividend rate in order to meet their commitments on preferred share dividends.

Also, preferred share financing may be subject to a further tax burden, the nature of which was not discussed in previous chapters. Under Part VI.1 of the *Income Tax Act*, all Canadian corporations are subject to a special tax on preferred share dividends in excess of $500,000 annually.[2] This tax is payable by the payer of the dividend rather than the recipient. The rate of tax varies depending on the nature of the preferred shares; however, in most cases the tax is 40% of dividends paid in excess of $500,000. While this tax appears excessive, it is fully recoverable against the normal income tax to which the company is subject. For example, if the corporation is usually subject to 37% tax on income, the special tax on preferred shares reduces the normal income taxes by an equivalent amount, thus completely eliminating the tax on the preferred share dividend. Provided that the corporation is subject to normal rates of tax, the preferred share dividend tax is effectively eliminated. The special tax is not eliminated if the corporation has no taxable income, but even in this case, through a carry-forward mechanism, it can be recovered in future years when taxable income is earned.

The purpose of the special tax on preferred share dividends is to prevent corporations that are not taxable from paying dividends to other public corporations that receive the dividends on a tax free basis. In such circumstances, if it were not for the special tax, neither the payer nor the recipient would be subject to tax.

The special preferred share dividend tax prevents a narrow form of tax abuse; at the same time, however, it creates a risk for all large corporations issuing preferred shares. Although the tax is non-existent if the payer is normally taxable, the payer cannot be certain that future circumstances will be the same. Consider, for example, a company that has issued preferred shares but at some future time incurs losses that cause the company to be temporarily non-taxable. When dividends are paid on the preferred shares, the special tax applies, although it may be recoverable through the carry-over mechanism. Of course, the tax could be avoided by not paying the dividend in those particular years, but that in turn would lessen the attractiveness of the security to the investor.

There is no doubt that current tax laws make preferred share financing difficult for corporations. In spite of this burden, corporations still consider preferred share financing viable when debt loads reach their maximum. From the common shareholder's perspective, preferred share issues are always viable if expected returns are greater than the related high financing costs.

---

2   ITA 191.

In particular, "perpetual" preferred shares, which have no fixed redemption requirements, increase the equity base of the corporation; this adds to its financial strength, which in turn permits it to obtain additional debt financing at a lower cost. In other words, the disadvantages of preferred share equity must be weighed against the benefits, which are increased borrowing power and lower debt-financing costs.

Perpetual preferred shares with no fixed redemption date may be less attractive to investors if the shares have a fixed dividend rate, as such shares are subject to value changes if market interest rates fluctuate significantly. In recent years this problem has been overcome with the emergence of "floating rate preferred shares," which have a dividend rate that fluctuates in relation to the prime rate of interest. This built-in mechanism stabilizes the value of the shares, which are thus more attractive to the investor.

In summary, in spite of the tax burden to the corporate issuer, preferred share financing is a viable alternative to debt financing, especially if the share issue is designed so that it enhances the after-tax returns of potential investors.

II. Tax Treatment of Financing Charges

In addition to the normal costs of interest (on debt) and dividends (on equity issues), the process of obtaining capital funding may incur other types of costs. For both debt and equity securities, the corporation may incur certain costs in the process of implementing and selling the securities on the open market. Also, it may be necessary to issue the securities at a price other than the stated price of the security, the result being a discount or premium on sale. The tax treatment of these items is discussed briefly below.

A. Expenses Incurred to Issue Shares or Borrow Money

The corporation may incur certain costs in the process of developing securities and issuing them to investors. Such costs include the following:

1. Legal fees for the preparation of a prospectus.

2. Accounting and auditing fees to certify the financial statements and prepare other financial information.

3. Costs of printing the security certificates and the related prospectus.

4. Fees paid to a registrar or transfer agent.

5. Costs of filing information with any regulatory body.

6. Commissions and fees for the services of salespeople, agents, or dealers in securities.

7. Mortgage registration, processing, and appraisal fees.

8. Premiums on life insurance policies assigned as a collateral requirement of a debt obligation.

These and other similar costs are of a capital nature because they provide a long-term benefit over the life of the securities. As capital expenditures, these costs would not usually be permitted as a current deduction for tax purposes. However, by specific exception (see Chapter 5), expenses other than life insurance premiums, if incurred in the process of issuing shares or borrowing money, can be deducted in arriving at net income for tax purposes over a five-year period at the rate of one-fifth of the total cost per year.[3] Premiums

---

3   ITA 20(1)(e), (e.2); IT-341R3.

on life insurance policies used as collateral for a debt are fully deductible when incurred, provided that the premium is an annual amount.

The after-tax cost of financing is, therefore, affected by the tax treatment of the associated costs. While the cost of interest or dividends is spread out over the life of the security, the implementation costs are arbitrarily subjected to a five-year allocation, even though the costs are incurred at the outset. When making business expansion decisions that involve financing by new capital, the decision maker must determine the after-tax cost of financing; this means considering the tax treatment of both the implementation costs and the ongoing service costs of interest or dividends.

B. Securities Issued at a Discount or Premium

In some circumstances a corporation issuing a debt or equity security may receive a price less than or greater than the stated value of the security. This discount or premium affects the issuing corporation's financing costs. The related tax treatment of the discount or premium is an important factor in establishing those costs.

Debt and equity securities can be issued at amounts greater than or less than their stated amount. This normally occurs as a result of a change in economic conditions between the time the security is developed and the time it is put on the market. For example, a $100 bond bearing a 9% interest rate may end up selling for only $98 if interest rates have increased between the time the bonds were developed and the date of their issue. A price variance may also result if the investors' perception of the security's attractiveness is different from what was anticipated by the issuing company.

A premium or discount on equity issues for common and preferred shares has no tax impact on the issuing corporation. As the cost of equity financing through dividends is not tax deductible, the related discount or premium is similarly treated. Therefore, when a $100 preferred share bearing a 7% dividend is issued at $98, it simply means that the dividend rate is actually 7.14% ($7/$98) and must be financed from after-tax profits. However, in the case of debt securities such as bonds and debentures, since the interest cost is deductible, the tax treatment of a premium or discount affects the after-tax cost of such securities. Because of all this, the comments that follow apply only to debt securities, and examine discounts and premiums separately.

1. Issuing Debt Securities at a Discount

When a debt security is issued at a discount, the borrowing corporation receives an amount that is less than it is obliged to repay at the end of the debt. The issuing company is also obliged to pay interest at the stated rate times the face value of the security. The issuing company therefore has two costs—the cost of interest, which is paid annually, and the cost of the discount, which is paid at the end of the debt term.

The tax treatment of the discount depends on the amount of the discount.[4] For tax purposes, debt issued with a discount of 3% or less is referred to as a "shallow" discount, while a discount of more than 3% is referred to as a "deep" discount. The full amount of a shallow discount is deductible as a business expense when it is repaid (which is usually at the end of the term of debt). However, only one-half[5] of a deep discount can be deducted as a business expense. In effect, a deep discount is treated as if it were a capital loss, except that it is deductible from business income.

In this way, the issue of debt at a discount changes the timing of the tax deduction; in the case of deep discounts it also changes the amount of the tax deduction. Consequently,

---

4   ITA 18(1)(f), 20(1)(f).

5   Department of Finance—stated intention from October 2000 Economic Statement.

the after-tax cost of financing debt issued at a discount is different from the after-tax cost of financing debt issued at face value, even though the pre-tax cost may be the same. Consider the following situation:

Situation: A corporation issues a $100,000, ten-year bond paying interest annually. Market conditions dictate that investors require an interest return of 9.25%. The after-tax cost of financing the debt is analyzed below. It is assumed that the corporation issued the bonds bearing an interest rate of 9.25%, 9%, or 8.5%. Assume a corporate tax rate of 40%.

Analysis: If the bonds are issued with an interest rate of 9.25%, which is the same as the market demands, they maintain their face value of $100,000 and incur annual interest costs of $9,250 before tax.

If the bonds are issued with a 9% interest rate, they are discounted to $98,000 in order to yield 9.25% to the investor, and the company pays $9,000 interest annually (9% × $100,000) for 10 years. While the company pays lower annual interest costs ($9,000 rather than $9,250) it has an additional up-front cost of $2,000 from the discount ($100,000 − $98,000 = $2,000). The discount of $2,000 constitutes a shallow discount, which is fully deductible for tax purposes *at the end of year 10*.

If the bonds are issued with an interest rate of 8.5%, they are discounted to $95,000 in order to yield the investor 9.25%. Annual interest costs decline to $8,500 (8.5% ×$100,000). However, because the discount amount of $5,000 is greater than 3% ($5,000/$100,000 = 5%), this constitutes a deep discount, of which only one-half ($\frac{1}{2}$ of $5,000 = $2,500) is deductible for tax purposes at the end of year 10.

In each case, the company incurs a pre-tax cost of financing of 9.25%. However, each alternative results in a different rate of cash flow and a different tax result, and therefore a different after-tax cost in cash-flow terms. This is summarized in the following table:

	9.25%	9.00%	8.50%
Interest rate	9.25%	9.00%	8.50%
Face value of bond	$100,000	$100,000	$100,000
Issue price	$100,000	$ 98,000	$ 95,000
Financing costs:			
Interest (years 1–10)	$ 9,250	$ 9,000	$ 8,500
Tax saving (40%)	(3,700)	(3,600)	(3,400)
Annual cost	$ 5,550	$ 5,400	$ 5,100
Discount (year 1)	$ –0–	$ 2,000	$ 5,000
Tax saving (in year 10)	–0–	(800)	(1,000)
	$ –0–	$ 1,200	$ 4,000
Pre-tax cost	9.25%	9.25%	9.25%
After-tax cost, considering timing			
of cash flows	5.55%	5.61%	5.69%

This analysis shows the impact of financing costs on after-tax cash flow. A discount tends to increase the cost of financing, and this must be considered when a debt issue is contemplated. The tax treatment outlined above is applied to most interest-bearing debt securities. In some cases corporations will issue debt securities with no stated interest rate, which allows those securities to be substantially discounted in accordance with prevailing interest rates. In such cases the discount is considered to be interest and is allocated over the term of the security based on a simple compound-interest approach.

2. Issuing Debt Securities at a Premium

When a debt security is issued at a premium, the borrowing corporation receives a price greater than the security's stated amount. For example, a $100,000 bond bearing 10% interest may be issued at $102,000 if the market interest rate at the time of issue is less than 10%. The issuing corporation will pay a higher rate of interest in exchange for a premium gain, because it is required to repay only the stated value of the security ($100,000 in the above example).

The tax treatment of a premium to the corporation issuing the security is extremely favourable. Unless the issuing corporation is in the business of lending money, the premium is not taxable. Therefore, issuing debt securities at a premium will usually reduce the after-tax cost of financing; this is the opposite of what happens when securities are issued at a discount. For example, consider the issue of a $100,000 ten-year corporate bond bearing interest at 10% at a time when market interest rates are only 9.5%. To yield 9.5%, the bond could be issued for $103,000; this would provide the issuer with a $3,000 tax-free gain. The combination of a tax-free $3,000 gain and annual interest costs of $10,000 ($6,000 after tax, assuming a 40% tax rate) would result in a net after-tax financing cost of 5.6%. If the security had been issued at its par value of $100,000, with interest at the market rate of 9.5%, the after-tax cost of financing would have been 5.7% (9.5% – tax savings of 40% = 5.7%).

Both discounts and premiums are designed to compensate for interest-rate fluctuations. However, since they are subject to special tax treatment, they must be considered a distinct item of financing costs; this means that their impact must be anticipated before any type of debt security is developed and issued. Premiums and discounts may also have tax consequences for the investor who purchases the securities.

3. Tax Treatment of Discounts and Premiums to the Investor

An investor who purchases a debt security at a discount will receive a lower-than-normal rate of interest but will also receive a gain when the security is repaid at its face amount. The reverse is true when the security is purchased at a premium. From the investor's perspective, as from the issuing corporation's, the discount or premium represents an adjustment of the interest rate and is subject to varying tax treatment.

When the lender (investor) is in a position to negotiate the terms of the loan, the premium or discount is treated as income and is fully taxable when the debt is repaid. When the security is a public issue (for example, a corporate bond or a debenture), the investor cannot usually dictate terms but can only react to the market situation. If this is the case, the tax treatment to the investor varies with the nature of the investor. When the purchasing of bonds and debentures is part of the investor's business, the gain or loss on a discount or premium is fully taxable at the time the debt is repaid. When the investor is not in the business of acquiring securities, but rather is simply investing savings, and when the investment in such securities is infrequent and forms a minor part of that investor's income-earning activity, the gain or loss is considered to be a capital gain or loss, only one-half of which is taxable.

An investor may generate more after-tax income by purchasing a bond at a discount (and thus achieving a capital gain) than by purchasing a bond at face value with a higher interest rate. The yield on a given corporate debt security varies with the tax position of the investor who purchases the security. While issuing bonds at a discount may be more costly to the issuer (as demonstrated above), it may also attract those investors who will receive favourable tax treatment as a result of purchasing that security, and increase the likelihood that the debt issue will be successful.

Both the corporate issuer and the investor are sensitive to the tax treatment of discounts and premiums. Any decision to raise debt capital must include an analysis of the impact of discounts and premiums on both the company and the potential investors.

III. Leasing— An Alternative to Debt Financing

The value of an asset to a business arises from its use in the income-earning process. The right to use an asset can be obtained through ownership or through a lease arrangement. When a business secures the right to use an asset for a desired period of time in exchange for rental payments, it relieves itself of the financing costs required for ownership. In this way, leasing is an alternative to debt financing.

When a business is choosing between owning and leasing, it must consider a number of factors, of which a primary one is the effect on cash flows. Accordingly, the method of payment and the related tax treatment are both vital components in the decision process. This section of the chapter compares the after-tax cost of leasing with the after-tax cost of owning in the context of financing *equipment*. The analysis that follows can also be applied to real estate; however, such analysis is complicated by the fact that real estate is usually an appreciating asset.

A. Types of Leases

The right to use equipment can be obtained through an operating lease or a financial lease. A *financial lease* provides the business (the lessee) with the right to use the asset for a long period of time—usually for most of its useful life. In most cases the lessee will be the only user of the equipment. The lease term and the rental payments under a financial lease are structured so that the leasing company can recover the full cost of the asset and, in addition, achieve a normal return on its investment; in this way, financial lease payments are similar to amortized loan payments. Most financial leases also provide the user with the option to purchase the asset either at the end of the lease term or during the term, or to re-lease the equipment after the initial term for a substantially reduced rental. This is possible because the leasing company has recovered the full cost of the asset and earned a normal return over the initial time period. Because a financial lease provides a right of long-term use, and because the rental rates are tied to the cost of the equipment and normal interest rates, it is considered to be a direct alternative to purchasing assets with debt financing.

Operating leases are usually short-term and are used to obtain the use of short-lived, lower-cost assets such as office furniture, equipment, and automobiles. Because such assets have a short life span, it makes little difference, in taxation terms, whether they are owned or leased. In such cases, the advantages of leasing have to do with the simplified administration of frequently changed assets.

B. Tax Treatment of Financial Leases

The tax treatment of leasing costs is not complex. Annual rental payments are fully deductible in arriving at net income for tax purposes. Therefore, provided that the business has taxable income, the rental payments will directly reduce taxable income by the amount of the lease payments. In other words, cash payments and tax savings occur simultaneously.

In comparison, if assets are purchased, the tax deductions may not occur at the same time the debt payments are made. Cash payments must be made for both the principal and the interest on the loan. At the same time, tax deductions for owned assets are determined by the applicable rate of capital cost allowance and the payment of interest. Payments relating to loan principal are not deductible.

When a business can choose between leasing and owning, it must compare the after-tax cash flows of each alternative. This analysis is demonstrated in the following situation:

Situation: A company requires new equipment that has a cost of $100,000. If the asset is purchased, the company must borrow the full $100,000; this will require principal repayments of $20,000 annually for five years, as well as interest payments at 11%. The equipment is a class 8 asset for tax purposes, and so has a capital cost allowance rate of 20% (see Chapter 6). It is estimated that the equipment has a useful life of 10 years and no apparent salvage value.

Alternatively, the company can enter into a financial lease that requires an annual rent (payable in monthly instalments) of $27,000 over a five-year lease term. The company can renew the lease for a further five years at a substantially reduced annual cost of $2,260. The payment of $27,000 per year in the first five years reflects the fact that the leasing company will recover its full cost of $100,000 and, in addition, earn 13% before tax.

The company pays tax at an assumed rate of 40%.

Analysis: If the company purchases the equipment with a $100,000 loan bearing 11% interest, it will be required to make the following pre-tax payments in the first five years:

Year	Principal	Interest	Total
1	$ 20,000	$11,000	$ 31,000
2	20,000	8,800	28,800
3	20,000	6,600	26,600
4	20,000	4,400	24,400
5	20,000	2,200	22,200
	$100,000	$33,000	$133,000

However, the above annual cash costs are reduced by tax savings at 40% of the interest component and by the capital cost allowance. The 20% capital cost allowance is applied on a diminishing-balance basis (see Chapter 6), and only one-half of the normal rate is applied in the first year. In addition, the capital cost allowance will continue beyond five years, creating continued tax savings after the loan is fully paid off.

Under the lease arrangement, pre-tax cash costs in the first five years total $135,000 ($27,000 × 5 y). As well, if the equipment is used for a further five years, additional lease costs of $11,300 ($2,260 × 5 y) will be incurred. As the lease costs are fully deductible, tax savings in each year amount to 40% of the annual lease payments.

The after-tax cash cost, together with a net present value analysis, is summarized below for each alternative.

Year	Net Cash Out Purchase	Net Cash Out Lease	Leasing advantage (disadvantage)
1	$22,600	$16,200	$ 6,400
2	18,080	16,200	1,880
3	18,200	16,200	2,000
4	18,032	16,200	1,832
5	17,634	16,200	1,434
	94,546	81,000	13,546
6–10	(14,746)	6,780	(21,526)
	$79,800	$87,780	$ (7,980)
Net present value cost	$64,436	$62,847	$ 1,589

This analysis indicates that an asset purchase will result in after-tax costs in the first five years of $94,546, but will result in cash *savings* in the second five years (from capital cost allowance) of $14,746; thus, the total after-tax cost of this arrangement is $79,800. In comparison, the lease alternative results in higher total after-tax costs of $87,780. However, it is important to recognize that the timing of these costs is different for each alternative. In the first five years, leasing costs are lower by $13,546, whereas in the latter five years they are higher by $21,526. When these timing differences are analyzed on a net present value basis (discount at the borrowing cost of 11%), it can be seen that leasing holds a marginal advantage over owning ($62,847 as opposed to $64,436).

In the above example, leasing presents only a marginal advantage over owning; however, the cash-flow situation in the early years is important. Notice that in the first year, leasing provides $6,400 of additional cash flow to the business; over the first five years, it provides a total of $13,546 of additional cash flow. Every business expansion involves risk, and that risk is usually higher in the early years. In this particular case, the leasing option reduces the risk of expansion failure by creating more cash flow in early years when it may be most needed. This advantage is difficult to quantify but is an important consideration when a choice is being made between the two alternatives.

There is no general rule that can be used to decide between leasing and owning. Each particular situation has its own unique circumstances. The terms attached to financial leases are negotiable, just as the terms of debt financing are negotiable. The decision-making process involves analyzing the after-tax cost of each alternative on a net present value basis.

Recent changes in the tax rules offer a second option relating to the tax treatment for leased equipment.[6] Under certain conditions the lessee can treat a lease contract for tax purposes as if it were a purchase—in effect, the lessee can forgo rent payment deductions and claim capital cost allowance and an imputed interest deduction. This treatment requires agreement with the lessor; even so, it provides added flexibility to the financial lease alternative.

IV. Summary and Conclusion

This chapter has examined the impact of taxation on the cost of corporate financing through debt, equity, and leasing. All of these methods raise corporate capital by providing a return to an investor. These returns can take the form of interest, dividends, or rents. Each of these forms has a different tax treatment to the corporate issuer, and so results in a different after-tax cost. Similarly, the tax treatment of the returns for the investor that provided the financing also varies.

Raising capital by issuing debt requires the payment of interest, which is fully deductible against the corporation's income for tax purposes. Therefore, debt can be serviced without profits being affected as long as the borrowed funds can be used by the corporation to earn a return equal to the interest rate on the debt.

In comparison, raising capital by issuing new equity in the form of preferred shares requires the payment of dividends, which are not deductible in arriving at net income for tax purposes. This means that in order to service equity, the corporation must use the funds to earn a substantially higher amount of income, because it must fund the dividend payment with after-tax dollars. As a result, the cost of equity is usually higher than the cost of debt.

From the investor's perspective, interest received on debt is fully taxable; whereas dividends are tax-free to other public corporations, but subject to a special refundable tax of $33\frac{1}{3}\%$ to other private corporations, and taxable at a reduced rate (net of the dividend tax credit) when received by individuals. All of this means that the relationship between interest and dividends depends on the nature of the investor, so there are different market demands for different securities.

---

6 ITA 16.1; Regulations 8200 and 1100 (1.13); IT-233R.

In addition to the cost of interest and dividends, the issuing corporation may incur costs for developing and issuing the securities. Even though these costs are incurred in the year of issue, most of them are deductible for tax purposes in equal amounts over a five-year period.

In some cases corporate debt is issued at a price less than or greater than the face value of the security. Such premiums or discounts arise when the stated interest rate is different from the market interest rate. When debt is issued at a discount, the issuer receives less money up front but pays a lower rate of interest. However, because the cost of the discount is deductible only when the security is paid off, there is a significant gap between the time the cost is incurred and the time it can be deducted for tax purposes. Also, if discounts are greater than a defined limit, the future deduction is limited to one-half of the discount cost. This increases the overall costs of debt financing. When debt securities are issued at a premium, the reverse is true: the issuer receives more money up front but the interest costs are higher. The premium received is usually not taxable, so the after-tax cost of debt issued at a premium is reduced.

The right to use an asset can also be obtained through a financial lease. Because a financial lease bases the required rental payment on the full repayment of the asset's cost plus a reasonable return to the lessor, it is comparable to purchasing an asset with borrowed funds. However, the after-tax cost of leasing is different from the after-tax cost of owning because of the timing of the related tax deduction. Lease payments in the form of rentals are deductible when incurred; when an asset is purchased, only interest and capital cost allowance can be deducted.

Since different financing schemes receive different tax treatments, the decision maker must examine the related costs on an after-tax basis, taking timing differences into account. The decision maker must also anticipate the tax positions of the various types of investors in the marketplace, since they also calculate their rates of return on an after-tax basis. This global approach will assist in developing an efficient financial structure that minimizes financing costs to the issuer and maximizes returns to the investor.

Reading List

Income Tax Act References

	Section
Interest (expense)	20(1)(c)
Expenses re: financing	20(1)(e)
Premiums on life insurance used as collateral	20(1)(e.2)
Leasing properties	16.1
Payments on discounted bonds	18(1)(f)
Discount on certain obligations	20(1)(f)
Cost of borrowed money	21(1) to (5)
Tax on corporations paying dividends on taxable preferred shares (Part VI.1)	191, 191.1 to .3

Canada Customs and Revenue Agency Publications

IT-121R3	Election to capitalize cost of borrowed money.
IT-265R3	Payments of income and capital combined.
IT-341R3	Expenses of selling shares, units in a trust, and interests in a partnership or syndicate; and expenses of borrowing money.
IT-309R2	Expense of borrowing money—life-insurance premiums.
IT-233R	Lease option agreements; sale-leaseback agreements.

Other Publications

Ashton, R., "Leasing: Recent Developments," 1997 Corporate Management Tax Conference, Canadian Tax Foundation, pp. 11.1–46.

Richardson, E., "Financing Business Acquisitions: an Update," 1990 Corporate Management Tax Conference, Canadian Tax Foundation, pp. 7:1–75.

Review Questions

1. Why is it important to examine the corporate cost of financing alternatives in conjunction with the tax position of the potential investors?

2. If a corporation is subject to a 37% tax rate, why may it be advantageous for it to issue debt as opposed to preferred shares?

3. If the corporate tax rate is 18%, what difference does it make whether the corporation issues debt bearing 10% interest or preferred shares with an 8% dividend rate?

4. A corporation issues 11% bonds as well as preferred shares with an annual 8% dividend rate. Excluding the risk factor, what type of investor would prefer the bond and what type would prefer the shares? Explain.

5. An investor who is an individual could earn a 10% return either from shares that pay a low dividend and have high growth, or from shares that pay a high dividend and have low growth. Assuming that the risk related to each is the same, which investment would the individual prefer?

6. If the cost of preferred share financing is so much greater than debt, why are such securities issued by public corporations?

7. Briefly describe the tax treatment applied to expenses incurred to issue shares or borrow money (the cost of a prospectus, commissions to brokerage firms, and the like). What impact does this tax treatment have on the after-tax cost of financing?

8. If a corporation issues a bond at a price less than the face value of the security, the discount is amortized, for accounting purposes, over the life of the bond. How does this treatment of the discount compare with the treatment for tax purposes?

9. If a corporation issues a bond at a discount, will the after-tax cost of financing to the issuing corporation be higher or lower than if it had issued the bond at its face value? Explain.

10. Is the after-tax return to a casual investor who purchases a bond at a discount greater than or less than the after-tax return on a bond purchased at its face value? Explain.

11. How does the issuing of a bond at a premium affect the after-tax cost of financing to the corporate issuer?

12. Explain the difference between a financial lease and an operating lease.

13. What is the difference, in tax terms, between leasing and owning?

Problems

Problem One

The Canadian Queen's Bank of Industry Ltd. is a large national Canadian bank. It has significant expansion opportunities. However, its ability to raise additional debt capital from bonds or debentures is restricted because of the debt/equity regulations of Canada's *Bank Act.*

The bank has decided to issue preferred shares. The financial highlights of the prospectus are as follows:

Proposed issue 4,000,000 floating rate, class A preferred shares (cumulative, redeemable, and without par value).

Price $100 per share.

Dividends Dividends will be payable monthly. The dividend rate will float in relation to changes in the prime interest rate as set by the bank. The initial annual dividend rate will be equal to $\frac{2}{3}$ prime plus $\frac{1}{2}$% per annum. As dividends will accrue and be payable monthly, the normal dividend payment will be $\frac{1}{12}$ of the annual rate.

Redemption The shares will be redeemable at the option of the bank in whole or in part from time to time.

At the time the prospectus was issued, the bank published the following interest rates for its customers:

Prime lending rate	7.5%
Savings account (interest monthly)	3.0
One-year term deposits	5.5
30-day term deposits	4.0

The bank is subject to an income tax rate of 40%.

Required:

1. Assume that the bank will issue all of the preferred shares proposed in the prospectus. What amount of additional income must the bank earn in order to service the preferred shares without diminishing the amount of earnings currently available to the common shareholders?

2. How would your answer to 1 be different if the bank could issue bonds with an interest rate equal to 1.5% less than the prime rate?

3. Are the preferred shares attractive to investors? Explain.

Problem Two

Orpin Industries Ltd. is about to make its first bond issue in the public market. Orpin is a small but growing company, and its shares are starting to be recognized. For the past two years, they have consistently traded at a price equal to 12 times the after-tax earnings per share.

The proposed bond issue will raise $20,000,000, which will be used to expand the corporation's retail operations into western Canada. The expanded operations should provide a minimum return on investment of 22%.

After receiving financial advice, the company decides to issue the bonds in units of $1,000 with an annual interest rate of 10% (interest payable annually). The financial advisor indicates that at this interest rate, the bonds can be sold (with a 10-year term) at their par value.

Just before the issue date, long-term interest rates in the market increase by half a percent. Orpin realizes that it will have to issue its bonds at a discount in order to obtain the full $20,000,000. Alternatively, the company could delay the issue for a short time, revise the prospectus, and print new bonds to reflect the higher interest rate. This would, of course, create additional costs. Before making the decision, Orpin wants to know if there would be any benefit to revising the interest rates.

Orpin is subject to a 40% tax rate.

Required:

1. If Orpin issues the bonds as originally proposed (that is, with an interest rate of 10%), how much will it have to discount them? Ignore any tax implications to the potential investors.

2. Based on your answer to 1, determine the after-tax cost of financing the bond issue under both the discount option and the revised interest-rate option.

3. Assuming that the interest rate on the bond is revised, how may this affect the trading value of Orpin's common shares?

4. If the company chooses to issue the bonds at a discount, could the amount of the discount be affected by the tax treatment to the potential investor? Explain.

Problem Three

Anderson Enterprises Ltd. is a Canadian corporation wholesaling auto parts in eastern Canada. The company has decided to begin manufacturing a product that it currently wholesales.

The expansion will require manufacturing equipment costing $80,000. Anderson's bank has agreed to provide a term loan to finance the entire purchase. The terms of the loan call for monthly payments of $1,235 for eight years. The payment includes interest at 10½%. The bank provides the company with a payment schedule, which is roughly summarized on an annual basis in the table below.

Year	Principal	Interest	Total
1	$7,000	$7,820	$14,820
2	7,500	7,320	14,820
3	8,500	6,320	14,820
4	9,000	5,820	14,820
5	10,000	4,820	14,820
6	11,000	3,820	14,820
7	13,000	1,820	14,820
8	14,000	820	14,820

It is estimated that the equipment will have a useful life of 10 years and will be scrapped at the end of that time.

Anderson has also obtained some quotes for leasing the equipment. The quote with the most favourable terms involves a six-year lease with monthly payments of $1,565 and an option to renew on an annual basis for a mere $2,000 per year. Anderson likes this alternative because his company would not have to renew after six years if it wanted to acquire more modern equipment.

However, at this point, the company anticipates that it will use the equipment for its useful life of 10 years, at which time it will acquire replacement equipment.

The company is subject to a 40% tax rate. It has expansion opportunities that can yield a minimum before-tax return of 22%.

Required:
1. Determine the financial cost to Anderson of leasing rather than owning the manufacturing equipment. Assume that at the end of 10 years the company will scrap the equipment and purchase new equipment.

2. How would your answer to 1 change if, after 10 years, Anderson Ltd. leased rather than purchased the equipment?

3. What other factors, if any, should the company consider when making the decision?

Problem Four

Brandi Manufacturing Ltd. has decided to expand. To raise additional capital, the company is considering selling $300,000 of its present manufacturing equipment to an insurance company and leasing it back for eight years, which is the estimated useful life of the equipment. The equipment will have no residual value after eight years. The annual rent on the lease-back would be $54,000.

The equipment to be sold under the sale-and-lease-back arrangement is not all of the equipment owned by the company. The undepreciated capital cost of all of the company's manufacturing equipment (class 43) was $800,000 at the end of the previous year. Of this $800,000, approximately $100,000 relates to the equipment that the company is thinking of selling.

The equipment that would be sold is used to manufacture a single specialized product. The equipment generates annual pre-tax revenues of $60,000 and is expected to continue to do so in the future.

Brandi is interested in the sale-and-lease-back arrangement because it will enable the company to obtain $300,000 of immediate funds with a related annual payment of $54,000, which appears to be equivalent to a low rate of interest. The company is subject to a corporate tax rate of 40%. The company considers 12% to be a reasonable after-tax rate of return.

Required:
1. If Anderson does not sell the equipment, how much cash flow will be generated, in net present value terms, from the ownership and operation of that equipment?

2. What rate of interest is reflected in the lease arrangement?

3. What net present value cash flow would be obtained as a result of the sale-and-lease-back arrangement?

Chapter 22   Employee Compensation

One of the more significant costs associated with conducting a business is employee compensation. Employers face various types of decisions when paying employees. They must decide if they will pay more or less than other employers, which employees within the organization will be paid differently, whether the compensation will provide short-term or long-term incentives, and which methods of compensation will be used. While managers approach compensation as a major expense that must be minimized, they also recognize that providing a flexible compensation program which meets the various needs of employees will enhance long-term profitability. A strong compensation package is a positive influence on employee attitudes—it attracts the best employees, enhances efficiency, reduces staff turnover, and improves union relations.

A major influence on compensation decisions is the tax treatment associated with the various methods of compensation. This chapter will discuss the tax treatment of the most common methods of employee compensation and examine the impact of those methods on costs (to the employer) and value (to the employee).

I. Basic Objectives and General Tax Principles	A fundamental objective of the compensation program of any business is to provide maximum satisfaction to the employees at the least possible cost. From the employer's perspective, the real cost of compensation is measured in after-tax terms. Similarly, the employees judge the value of compensation they receive in terms of available after-tax disposable income for acquiring the necessities of life and creating savings. Too often, compensation programs are negotiated only in pre-tax terms; the result of this is greater after-tax costs for the employer and reduced after-tax disposable income for the employee.

The general tax principles relating to employment income received by employees were developed in Chapter 4. Chapter 5 examined the tax treatment of compensation expenses incurred by the employer. These chapters explained that an employee's employment income is calculated in a different way than is the employer's business income. In general terms, compensation expenses are fully deductible from the employer's business income when they are incurred, whereas the related employment income, in the form of wages or benefits, is fully taxable to the employee when received. However, not all forms of compensation follow these basic principles. Certain types of benefits are not taxable to the employee; others are taxable on a deferred basis even though they remain deductible by the employer.

The employer can offer non-taxable or tax-deferred compensation items to create increased after-tax value. This increased value can be transferred entirely to the employee, retained by the employer, or shared by both parties (see Part II). In order to make fullest use of the available tax preferences, the decision maker must take into account the employee's tax position. This involves acquiring a thorough knowledge of how employment income is taxed.

The employer can achieve further cost savings from economies of scale. For example, when an employer purchases group life insurance for its employees, the normal premium rate can be substantially reduced. As with tax savings, the savings from economies of scale can be fully passed on to employees, kept by the employer as a cost advantage, or shared by both parties.

It is also important to recognize that different forms of compensation may have different values to different employees within the organization. For example, a tax-free benefit such as family health insurance may be more attractive to an employee with a family than to a single employee, who may prefer some other type of benefit such as the payment of club dues in a sporting facility. It is therefore important that a range of compensation forms be made available, so that employees can choose those which best suit their particular needs.

The various forms of compensation are usually categorized in terms of their desired influence on employee behaviour; however, they can also be categorized in terms of the nature of payment. The compensation categories by nature of payment are as follows:

- direct
- indirect
- deferred

Direct compensation consists primarily of salaries, hourly wages, commissions, bonuses, and other base-pay methods. Direct compensation is fully deductible by the employer and fully taxable when received by the employee. This form of compensation does not require further analysis because of its obvious impact on both parties. When a 10% wage increase is awarded by an employer who pays tax at the rate of 40%, the actual after-tax cost to that employer is 6% (10% – 40% tax = 6%). However, as employees are subject to a progressive tax rate, the after-tax value of that 10% wage increase will vary among employees. A 10% raise in pay to an employee in a 45% tax bracket amounts to 5.5% after-tax, whereas an employee in a 26% tax bracket will receive 7.4% after-tax. This information is valuable because it helps employers identify which employees within the organization would prefer forms of compensation that offer reduced tax costs.

The tax consequences of indirect and deferred compensation are now reviewed.

II. Indirect Compensation

Indirect forms of compensation provide employees with specific benefits and/or per-quisites. In most cases indirect compensation is fully deductible by the employer. However, the tax to the employee varies—some benefits are fully taxable, others are tax-free.

A. Taxable Indirect Compensation

As discussed in Chapter 4, the *Income Tax Act* states that, with certain exceptions, all benefits employees receive or enjoy, if incurred by virtue of their employment, are taxable. Below are some of the common types of indirect compensation that are fully taxable to the employee:

- Personal use of employer's automobile.
- Holiday trips, other prizes, and incentive awards.
- Free personal travel derived from frequent-flyer programs.
- Travel expenses of an employee's spouse.
- Interest-free and low-interest loans from the employer.
- Premiums under provincial hospitalization and medical-care insurance plans. (Plans obtained from the private sector are not taxable.)
- Tuition fees paid by an employer.
- Gifts. (Certain gifts below $500 are not taxable.)
- Board and lodging, except at remote locations.
- Life insurance.
- Employee counselling services, such as financial planning and tax services, unless such service is provided by the employer's in-house staff.

Considering that the above types of indirect compensation are fully taxable to the employee, this question arises: What value is gained by the employer and by the employee from such types of compensation? Overall cash savings can result if two conditions are present:

1. The employee needs the particular benefit and would acquire it in any case from after-tax disposable income if it were not provided by the employer.

2. The employer can acquire the particular benefit at a lower cost than can the employee because of its greater purchasing power and financial strength.

As indicated previously, the cash flow gained can be transferred to the employee, kept by the company as a cost saving, or shared between the two. Consider the following situation:

Situation: An employee who is in a 45% marginal tax bracket needs to acquire additional life insurance of $100,000. The annual premium cost to the employee is $1,000. The employer, by establishing a group life insurance program for a large number of employees, could provide the additional insurance at a substantially reduced premium cost of $600 per annum. The employer is contemplating a raise in pay for the employee in the form of a $2,000 increase in annual gross salary.

Analysis: If the employer provides a $2,000 salary increase, the employee will first pay tax on the salary and then use the after-tax proceeds to acquire life insurance at a cost of $1,000. The result is shown below.

Salary received	$2,000
Tax @ 45%	(900)
After-tax salary	1,100
Life insurance cost	(1,000)
Net cash to employee	$ 100

Assuming that the employer is subject to a 40% tax rate, the after-tax cost of awarding a $2,000 salary increase is $1,200 ($2,000 − 40% tax saving = $1,200).

As an alternative to a $2,000 salary increase, the employer could offer a salary increase of $673 and, in addition, provide $100,000 of life insurance at a cost to the company of only $600 (for a total pre-tax cost of $1,273). The after-tax positions of the parties involved would be as follows:

Employee:		
Salary received		$ 673
Less tax:		
Salary	673	
Insurance benefit	600	
	$1,273	
Tax (45% of $1,273)		(573)
Net cash to employee		$ 100
Employer:		
Salary paid		$ 673
Insurance premium paid		600
		1,273
Tax saving @ 40%		(509)
After-tax cost		$ 764

These two positions are summarized in the following table. Under both alternatives, the employee receives $100,000 of additional life insurance in addition to $100 of disposable income; in effect, that employee has achieved an overall remuneration increase equivalent to $2,000 in pre-tax terms. However, the employer, by using the benefit form of remuneration, has reduced its annual after-tax cost from $1,200 to $764. When applied to a number of employees, this approach can result in significant cost reductions in employee compensation.

	Salary only	Salary plus benefit
Employee (net cash received)	$ 100	$100
Employer (after-tax cash cost)	1,200	764

In the above example the cost savings achieved by providing equivalent benefits were retained fully by the employer. As an alternative, the employer could pass the entire cost savings on to the employee. For example, the employer could provide the employee with a salary increase of $1,400 and also pay the $600 life insurance premium for a total cost of $2,000. This cost, on an after-tax basis, would amount to $1,200 ($2,000 – tax savings of 40% = $1,200), which is identical to the cost of a $2,000 salary increase. However, the employee would achieve much higher after-tax remuneration, as shown below.

Cash salary received		$1,400
Less tax:		
Salary	1,400	
Benefit	600	
	$2,000	
Tax (45% of $2,000)		(900)
Net cash to employee		$ 500

Notice that the employee would receive after-tax cash of $500 and still have $100,000 of life insurance. In order to achieve this position without the enjoyment of the employer's benefit program, the employee would have needed to receive a salary increase of $2,500, as shown below.

Salary	$2,727
Tax @ 45%	(1,227)
After-tax salary	$1,500
Life insurance cost	(1,000)
Net cash to employee	$ 500

In summary, for an after-tax cost of $1,200 to the employer (which in pre-tax terms is $2,000), the employee can receive a remuneration increase equivalent to $2,727. This constitutes a raise in pay higher than was originally contemplated.

As a third alternative, the cost savings from the benefit program could be shared by the employer and the employee in some ratio. For example, the employer could pay an increased salary of $1,000 and, as well, provide $100,000 of insurance at a cost of $600, for a total pre-tax cost of $1,600 and an after-tax cost of $960 ($1,600 – tax savings of 40% = $960). The employee would receive net cash after tax of $280 in addition to the value of the life insurance. In this case the employer's cost would be reduced from $1,200, and the employee's cash position would be improved from $100.

The three alternatives analyzed were all compared with a straight salary increase of $2,000 for a particular employee. The results are summarized below.

	Salary only	Salary and Benefit		
		Cost saving retained by employer	Cost saving shifted to employee	Cost saving shared
Cost to employer	$1,200	$ 764	$1,200	$ 960
Benefit to employee:				
Cash	$ 100	$ 100	$ 500	$ 280
Insurance value	1,000	1,000	1,000	1,000
	$1,100	$1,100	$1,500	$1,280
Salary equivalent	$2,000	$2,000	$2,727	$2,327

Clearly, the use of fully taxable employee benefits as an alternative form of compensation can result in significantly increased cash flow for the employer or the employee, or both.

It is very important that the employer examine compensation costs in after-tax terms. In addition, the value of alternative forms of compensation must be communicated to employees in terms of salary equivalents. For example, it is important that the employee (in the above summary) realize that a salary increase of $1,000 plus a $100,000 life insurance policy is equivalent to a pre-tax salary increase of $2,327, in that both provide the same benefits and disposable income. Many employers fail to communicate this information to their employees, with the result that salary and wage negotiations become more difficult.

B. Non-Taxable Indirect Compensation

Although, as a general rule, benefits provided by the employer are fully taxable to the employee, the *Income Tax Act*, by exception, permits certain benefits to be received tax-free.[1] In addition, by administrative policy, CCRA considers certain other types of benefits also to be non-taxable.[2] Listed here are some of the common benefits that qualify for special treatment (see Chapter 4):

- Group sickness or accident insurance plans.

- Private health services plans.

- Supplementary unemployment benefit plans.

- Counselling services relating to the mental or physical health of the employee.

- Membership fees for a social or athletic club, if the membership is principally for the employer's advantage. (Note that the employer cannot deduct the cost of such fees under any circumstances—Chapter 5.)

---

1   ITA 6(1)(a).

2   IT-470R.

- Moving expenses for transferring employees to a new location. When an employer compensates an employee for a decrease in value or impairment of the employee's residence, 50% of the compensation in excess of $15,000 is a taxable benefit.
- Discounts on merchandise.

While the above benefits are not taxable to the employee, all of them, with the exception of club memberships, are fully deductible by the employer as compensation expenses against business income. These types of benefits can create additional cash flow in two ways:

1. Eliminating tax on the amount of benefits received by the employee.

2. Reducing costs resulting from economies of scale when services are purchased for a large number of employees.

Consider the following situation:

Situation: An employer is prepared to pay an extra $2,000 to an employee who is subject to a 35% tax rate. The employee needs additional family health insurance and disability insurance. The employer, who pays tax at the rate of 40%, can purchase these types of insurance under a group plan at a 20% discount.

Analysis: The employer can provide the additional remuneration as a salary increase or in the form of a benefit package to the employee. The cost of each alternative to the employer is $2,000 before tax and $1,200 after tax ($2,000 − 40% tax savings = $1,200). However, each alternative has a dramatically different value to the employee. A $2,000 salary will provide the employee with the following:

Salary	$2,000
Tax @ 35%	(700)
After-tax value	$1,300

On the other hand, providing the employee with $2,000 of benefits that are not taxable to that employee is equivalent to providing after-tax benefits of $2,500, calculated as follows:

Cost of benefits provided	$2,000
Add discount obtained by employer	500
Retail value of benefits	2,500
Personal tax	–0–
After-tax value to employee	$2,500

In other words, a benefit package with an after-tax value of $2,500 for the employee is equivalent to a salary increase of $3,846 ($3,846 − tax of 35% = $2,500). In this particular case an employer who provides $2,000 of the desired tax-free benefits incurs an after-tax cost of $1,200, while rewarding the employee with the equivalent of a gross salary increase of $3,846.

This analysis indicates that it is highly worthwhile to provide employees with tax-free benefits that can be purchased at a discount. Again, this increase in after-tax value can be shared between the employer and the employee, thereby reducing the employer's remu-neration costs and increasing the employee's after-tax disposable income.

Always remember that the value to employees of tax-free benefits will vary from group to group according to income levels and the corresponding rates of personal tax. All tax-free benefits create some amount of value; together, they form a vital part of compensation programs. It is important to stress to employees again and again the value of tax-free bene-fits in terms of pre-tax salary equivalents. Otherwise, it is difficult to maximize the cost effi-ciency of such programs. Communicating the value of employee benefits should start when wage settlements are being negotiated and should continue thereafter. A simple annual statement to each employee pointing out the pre-tax value of all of the components of remuneration can have a positive impact on employee relations and on future wage nego-tiations.

III. Deferred Compensation

The highly progressive tax rates imposed on individuals constitute a strong inducement to utilize compensation methods that provide tax-free benefits. There are few such forms of compensation, however. A next-best alternative is to compensate employees on a deferred basis; that is, by delaying the payment until some future time. From the employee's perspective this may present two advantages:

1. Taxing income later rather than sooner may result in lower tax rates under the progressive system, especially if payments are delayed until retirement.

2. If the delayed payments are invested on the employee's behalf, investment returns will be achieved on pre-tax income rather than on after-tax income.

Deferred compensation programs are established on the assumption that employees will attempt to save some portion of their annual income for retirement. As the annual personal living expenses of each employee vary, so does the general attractiveness of the different deferred compensation programs. When analyzing the benefits to employees of deferred compensation, one must compare the wealth accumulation and investment returns from a deferred program with what would be achieved if employees attempted to save and invest a portion of their normal after-tax salary.

A number of deferred compensation programs are available. Not all are subject to the same tax treatment. There are three categories of deferred plans: registered plans, non-registered plans, and stock-based plans. Each of these categories is discussed briefly below.

A. Registered Plans

The *Income Tax Act* sanctions two specific registered deferred compensation plans that provide preferential tax treatment. As indicated in Chapter 4, these are the registered pension plan (RPP) and the deferred profit sharing plan (DPSP). Both plans permit the employer to deduct, for tax purposes, a limited amount of contributions on behalf of specified employees. In neither case is the value of the benefit to the employee taxed until the funds are removed from the plan. This removal usually occurs at retirement. In addi-tion, investment returns on accumulated contributions are not taxable until they are distributed to the employee.

Because contributions to registered plans are deductible by the employer, the after-tax cost of such contributions is the same as the after-tax cost of compensation in the form of normal salaries. However, receiving the compensation as a registered plan rather than as salary makes a vast difference to the employee. As explained in Chapter 4, an employee who receives $3,500 annually for 30 years in the form of an RPP or DPSP and who earns compound interest on it at 10% accumulates $633,000. In comparison, an employee in the 45% tax bracket who receives salary of $3,500 annually for 30 years and invests the after-tax amount ($3,500 – 45% tax = $1,925) to earn interest at 10% (5.5% after-tax) accumulates only $147,000.

While the difference between these two plans is significant, one must recognize that the $633,000 accumulated under the deferred option is fully taxable when paid to the employee, whereas the $147,000 accumulated under the salary option is not subject to further taxation. It is difficult to estimate the future tax liability on the deferred option because it depends on the manner in which the funds are paid to the employee (lump-sum or a monthly pension payment), and on the future applicable tax rate. However, even when the worst-case scenario is assumed—which is, that the employee will withdraw the deferred amount in a lump sum that is taxable at a high rate of 45%—the deferred option still amounts to $348,000 ($633,000 – 45% tax = $348,000).

The value of deferred compensation can be expressed as a pre-tax salary equivalent, using this worst-case scenario. The following calculation shows that a deferred compensation amount of $3,500 annually is equivalent to an annual taxable salary of $8,278:

Salary received	$ 8,278
Tax @ 45%	(3,725)
Net after-tax salary	$ 4,553
Compound value of investing $4,553 annually for 30 y	
at 5.5% after-tax (10% – 45% tax = 5.5%)	$348,000

This means that an employer (with a 40% tax rate) who provides $3,500 annually to a registered deferred compensation program at an after-tax cost of $2,100 ($3,500 – 40% tax saving = $2,100) is, in effect, providing the employee with a salary equivalent of $8,278. Of course, the pre-tax salary equivalent will vary with the tax bracket of the given employee. However, deferring tax on the benefit and on the investment returns accumulated will always result in a significant value spread between the benefit cost and its salary equivalent.

B. Non-Registered Plans

The *Income Tax Act* makes reference to the following non-registered deferred compensation plans:[3]

- Employee profit sharing plans.[4]

- Employee trusts.[5]

- Salary deferral arrangements.[6]

- Retirement compensation arrangements.[7]

While these plans exist to provide a formal deferral of compensation, they are seldom used because there is no tax relief for the amounts deferred. For example, under an employee profit sharing plan and an employee trust, the employer contributes amounts on

---

3   IT-502.

4   ITA 6(1)(d), 144(1), (3), (5).

5   ITA 6(1)(h), 6(1)(a)(ii), 248(1).

6   ITA 6(1)(i), 6(11), (12), (14), 20(1)(oo), 56(1)(w), 248(1).

7   ITA 6(1)(a)(ii), 56(1)(x), 248(1).

behalf of the employees to an intermediary or trustee, who invests the funds for the employees' benefit. The payments to the plan are deductible from the employer's income but must also be included, along with any investment returns, in the employees' income in the year in which they are received by the plan.

In effect, the rules applicable to non-registered deferral plans are anti-avoidance provisions designed to prevent the deferral of tax on employee compensation.

C. Stock-Based Plans

To provide employees with long-term incentives and rewards, corporate employers can develop compensation plans that give the employee an opportunity to purchase shares, which will grow in value as corporate profits increase. There are several such plans available. Some are described briefly below, together with their general tax treatment.

1. Stock Options

Stock option plans provide the employee with the right to purchase shares from the corporate treasury at a specified price for a specified period of time. In many cases the option price offered is less than the shares' value at the time. The tax treatment to the employee from stock option benefits was described in detail in Chapter 4. In general terms, the employee is taxed on the benefit received at the time the option is exercised and the shares are purchased *if* the option price is lower than the market value of the share on the date the option is granted.[8] For example, an employee may be granted an option to purchase treasury stock for $10 per share at any time over the next five years. Because the option price is fixed, but the shares' value may grow, the employee can receive a growth in value without actually purchasing the shares. However, when the shares are purchased, the employee will incur a taxable benefit equal to the difference between the shares' value and the option price. After exercising the option, the employee can retain the shares or sell them on the open market. When the option price is the *same as* the market value of the shares on the date the option is granted, the employee can delay a benefit recognition until the date the shares are sold.

From the employer's perspective, this form of incentive is attractive because it does not involve a cash payment, although it does result in dilution of ownership. In addition, stock option plans are an incentive to employees to enhance the long-term profitability of the business.

2. Stock Purchase Plans

Employees working for a public company can purchase shares in their employer's corporation on the open market at any time. However, they are usually constrained by a lack of funds to do so. A stock purchase plan permits employees to purchase a specific number of shares from the corporate treasury at fair market values using funds loaned to them by the employer.[9] Because the funds loaned to the employees come back to the company in exchange for the shares, there is no cash cost to the employer.

From an employee's perspective, stock purchase plans provide an investment opportunity without a financial burden. In many cases the corporation issues the employee preferred shares that are convertible into common shares; such shares have little downside risk but do have an opportunity for growth. As the employee does not purchase the shares at a discount, no taxable benefit occurs. When the shares are sold, the employee will incur a capital gain if the shares have increased in value.

3. Stock Bonus Plans

Under a stock bonus arrangement, an employer simply issues shares to an employee in lieu of a cash bonus. Usually the number of shares issued is a function of the profitability of the business, and awards are given to employees based on their particular contributions.

The full value of all shares received as a stock bonus is taxable to the employee as

---

8 ITA 7.

9 ITA 15(2), IT-119R3 (paragraph 19).

employment income in the year the shares are issued.[10] Therefore, while the stock bonus results in no cash cost to the employer, it results in a tax cost to the employee.

4. Phantom Stock Plans

A phantom stock plan does not actually provide employees with shares; rather, it is an elaborate deferred bonus agreement. It is called a "phantom stock plan" because the amount of the bonus is tied directly to changes in the value of the corporation's shares. For example, an employer may award points to an employee, having tied the value of those points to the value of the common shares traded on a stock exchange. Although the points are awarded, the employee does not cash them in until the end of a specified vesting period. Points may be forfeited if the employee is dismissed for cause. Once the vesting period is over, the employee will receive a cash bonus that is taxable at that time. The employer will receive a tax deduction in the year the bonus is paid.

A phantom stock plan is beneficial to the employer because it preserves cash flow until the end of the vesting period. It is also beneficial to the employees in that the company shares its profits with them on a tax-deferred basis. A phantom stock plan requires careful planning to avoid being classified as a salary deferral arrangement; the latter, as described previously, would result in the employee being taxed on the benefit when it is earned rather than when it is received.

Each of these four stock-based plans was reviewed in a superficial manner; it should be clear, however, that each provides long-term incentive rewards, which in turn can enhance the cash flow of the employer while enhancing the employee's wealth.

IV. Summary and Conclusion

This chapter has examined how the tax system affects decisions relating to employee compensation. Employers and employees are separate taxable entities and determine their taxable income by different principles; however, they also interact in ways that bind them together in a common decision process. Employers who are sensitive to the tax status of their employees can develop compensation programs that maximize the after-tax income of those employees and, at the same time, minimize the company's after-tax cost.

There are a number of compensation methods available besides the basic ones, which are salaries, commissions, and bonuses. Employers can compensate employees indirectly by providing benefits that those employees would otherwise have to acquire on their own from after-tax salaries. Although some of these benefits are taxable to the employee, the amount taxable may be less than the value to the employee. For example, when employers can purchase benefits for less than retail cost, the employee is taxed only on the discounted cost. Certain other benefits are not taxable to the employee. The savings the employer gains by obtaining benefits at a lower cost and by the reduction of income taxes can be passed on to the employees or shared between the employer and the employees.

As well, employers can help to maximize their employees' long-term wealth accumulation. By utilizing tax-deferred compensation methods such as RPPs, DPSPs, and stock-based investment plans, employers can substantially increase their employees' savings, as well as the returns on those savings.

Whenever possible, the employer should offer a range of compensation alternatives so that it meets the needs of the greatest possible number of employees. At first glance, this may seem more costly to the employer; however, in the long run, the providing of benefits that have greater after-tax value to the employee will result in a more cost-efficient compensation program. In this regard, it is important to explain to employees the value, in terms of cash equivalents, of each alternative form of compensation. Flexible and creative compensation programs can improve productivity and in so doing make the business more competitive.

---

10 ITA 5; treated in the same manner as a cash bonus.

Reading List

Income Tax Act References

	Section
Value of benefits	6(1)(a)
Employee profit sharing plans	144
Allocations, etc., under profit sharing plans	6(1)(d)
Employee benefit plans	6(1)(g)
Employee trust	6(1)(h)
Salary deferral arrangement payments	6(1)(i)
Employee trust, salary deferral arrangement, retirement compensation arrangement (defined)	248(1)
Salary deferral arrangement	56(1)(w)
Retirement compensation arrangement	56(1)(x)
Agreement to issue shares to employees	7
Shareholder debt (loan for shares)	15(2)

Canada Customs and Revenue Agency Publications

IT-529	Flexible employee benefit programs.
IT-470R	Employee fringe benefits.
IT-63R4	Benefits, including standby charge for an automobile.
IT-428	Wage loss replacement plans and employee trusts.
IT-227R	Group term life-insurance premiums.
IT-119R3	Debts of shareholders.

Other Publications

Tunney, W., "Taking Stock: The Pros and Cons of Stock-Based Compensation," 1991 Corporate Management Tax Conference, Canadian Tax Foundation, pp. 3:1–28.

Dath and Fuoco, "Flexible Employee Benefit Arrangements," 1991 Corporate Management Tax Conference, Canadian Tax Foundation, pp. 6:1–13.

Review Questions

1. Why is it important for an employer to be familiar with the marginal tax rates that apply to its employees?

2. A number of indirect compensation benefits are considered to be taxable benefits to the employee. What advantage can the employer and/or the employee gain by including such benefits as part of a compensation package?

3. When an employer provides a taxable benefit to an employee at a cost that is lower than the normal retail price, what amount is included in the employee's income for tax purposes?

4. Certain indirect forms of compensation are deductible by the employer but not taxable to the employee. Does this special tax treatment provide a benefit to the employee or to the employer? Explain.

5. How should the employer describe the value of benefits provided in a compensation package to an employee?

6. What is deferred compensation? How can it be of value to the employee?

7. An employer contributes $2,000 annually to a deferred profit sharing plan on behalf of an employee for 10 years. The plan invests the funds and earns an annual return of 12%. What is the pre-tax annual salary equivalent of such a benefit for an employee who is subject to a marginal tax rate of 40%?

8. Explain what benefits the employer and the employee can achieve by establishing
   (a) a stock option plan;
   (b) a stock purchase plan; and,
   (c) a stock bonus plan.

Case   **Sapasco Industries Ltd.**

Sapasco Industries Ltd. is a Canadian private corporation that manufactures a small line of plastic containers. The company has been in existence for only nine years but has grown rapidly. Last year, sales reached $8,000,000, and a record high profit of $750,000 was achieved.

The company now employs 41 staff in addition to the president, who is the sole shareholder. The current annual payroll, exclusive of the shareholder/president, is $1,730,000 and consists of salaries, bonuses, and compulsory benefits such as Canada Pension Plan and Employment Insurance contributions. The company is concerned about its increasing payroll costs, especially since recent wage increases in their industry have averaged 10%. The company's year end is approaching, and Sapasco must soon decide on salary adjustments for its existing staff.

Not long ago, Sapasco was approached by an insurance company, which suggested that it start up an employee benefit plan, to include a deferred profit sharing plan and three basic insurance plans. The insurance company indicated that if the insurance plans were accepted as a group, it could reduce the annual premiums by 20% of the normal retail rate. Also, it could invest the DPSP funds to yield an average return 1% higher than that earned by individuals who invest separately in RRSPs.

The president of Sapasco has asked Carol Asaki, the personnel manager, to review the insurance company's proposal. The president tells her, "I have always felt that excessive benefit programs create more administrative headaches than they are worth. But I'm willing to look at them further in view of the large wage settlements we may be facing. Let me know the value of the proposal to us as well as to the employees."

To prepare her report to the president, Asaki gathers together certain information, which is summarized in Exhibit I. In addition, she pulls the personnel file on one of the company's employees. The information in this file is summarized in Exhibit II.

Required:

On behalf of Asaki, prepare a draft report for the president.

Exhibit I
SAPASCO INDUSTRIES LTD.
Selected Financial Information

PAYROLL SUMMARY

# of employees	Salary range	Payroll
2	$100,000 and over	$ 240,000
4	$60,000 – $100,000	320,000
9	$40,000 – $60,000	450,000
14	$25,000 – $40,000	460,000
12	$18,000 – $25,000	260,000
41		$1,730,000

Tax rates

Sapasco Industries Ltd.	40%
Employees (by income range):	
0 – $30,000	26%
$30,000 – $60,000	34%
$60,000 – $100,000	40%
$100,000 and over	45%

Proposed benefit plan

DPSP:

Contributions will range from $0 to $3,500 and should average $2,000 annually per employee. Currently, DPSP funds can be invested to yield 12% annually.

Insurance plans

	Average premium per employee
Group term life insurance:	
Basic ($25,000 coverage)	$100
Additional ($75,000 coverage)	300
	$400
Group health and dental plan	$500
Group accident and sickness plan (disability)	$600

Exhibit II
SAPASCO INDUSTRIES LTD.
Summary of Personnel File

Jason Steiman

Age: 33
Family status: Married, three children
Current salary: $38,000
Amounts withheld from salary
- Canada Pension Plan
- Employment Insurance
- Monthly contributions made directly to employee's bank for the purchase of his private RRSP ($200 per month).

Appendix   Administration of the Income Tax System

It was indicated in Chapter 3 that the design and ongoing development of income tax law is the responsibility of the Department of Finance. However, the monumental task of administering the law and ensuring that taxpayers comply with it is the responsibility of Canada Customs and Revenue Agency (CCRA). The *Income Tax Act* includes many provisions that deal with the following administrative issues:

- Who must file tax returns and when they must be filed.

- Procedures for assessing returns that have been filed.

- Deadlines for income tax payments.

- Penalties for failing to meet the compliance provisions.

- Taxpayers' rights, and procedures for appealing disputed assessments.

This appendix briefly reviews the most important provisions relating to each of these areas.

I. Filing of Returns

Every taxpayer, whether an individual, a corporation, or a trust, must file an income tax return. However, the filing deadline is different for each of these entities.

A. Corporations

A corporation must file an annual income tax return within six months of its taxation year end, even if it has no income or has no financial activity.[1]

B. Individuals

Every taxpayer who is an individual must file an income tax return by April 30 for the most recent calendar year.[2] This date is extended to June 15 if the individual or his or her spouse carries on a business. However, unlike a corporation, an individual is usually not required to file a return in a year in which no tax is payable. Even so, taxpayers should be aware that a penalty may be imposed if no return was filed as a result of an incorrect determination that no tax was payable. For this reason, every individual is well advised to file a return every year.

The April 30 filing requirement usually applies to the final return of a deceased taxpayer. However, if the date of death is after October in the year and before May of the following year, the individual's legal representatives must file within six months of the date of death.[3] It should be noted that certain portions of a deceased person's income may be filed in separate tax returns.[4]

C. Trusts and Estates

Every trust must file an income tax return within 90 days of its taxation year.[5] The taxation year of a trust created by an individual during his or her lifetime (*inter vivos* trust) is the calendar year. A trust created upon an individual's death (testamentary trust) can choose a fiscal period as its taxation year.

---

1 ITA 150(1)(a); IC 85-3R2.
2 ITA 150(1)(d); IC 91-1.
3 ITA 150(1)(b).
4 IT-326R3, -212R3.
5 ITA 150(1)(c).

II. Assessment

After receiving an income tax return, CCRA is required to assess it "with all due dispatch."[6] Usually this means within two to four months of the date the return was filed, which is only enough time for CCRA to scrutinize the calculations. However, CCRA has the right to reassess returns at a later time. This right is subject to the following limitations:[7]

1. A filed return can be reassessed *at any time* if the taxpayer has made any misrepresentation that is attributable to neglect, carelessness, or wilful default, or has committed any fraud in filing the return or supplying information.

2. In all other circumstances, individuals, trusts, and Canadian-controlled private corporations can be reassessed within three years of the date the original assessment was mailed. For public corporations the time limit is extended to four years. It should be noted that any taxpayer has the right to waive these time limits.

When a taxpayer files a return that shows no taxable income, CCRA issues a statement that no tax is payable. However, this statement does not constitute an assessment. Often there was no taxable income because there was a loss for the year in question. The taxpayer may be able to apply that loss against an earlier or later year's income, so it is in the taxpayer's interest to establish that the loss has been accepted by CCRA, and that its availability is certain. A taxpayer can request that CCRA make a determination of the non-capital loss, net capital loss, restricted farm loss, or limited-partnership loss for the particular year.[8] Once determined, it is binding on the parties as if it were an assessment.

III. Payment of Tax

Usually, all taxpayers must pay tax at various times throughout and after the taxation year. Those times are different for individuals and corporations.

A. Individuals

Individuals must pay tax on certain types of income at the time such income is received; with other types of income, payments must be made on an instalment basis.

The most important type of income for most individuals is employment income. For this type of income the employer is required to withhold the appropriate amount of tax and remit it to CCRA on the employee's behalf.[9] Tax must also be withheld on a number of other types of income, such as retiring allowances, Employment Insurance benefits, pension benefits, and payments from a registered retirement savings plan.

Income that is not subject to withholding taxes at source may be subject to quarterly tax instalments. This is required whenever the individual's federal tax owing (after deducting taxes withheld at source) exceeds $2,000 for both the current year and either of the past two taxation years.[10] These instalments are due on the 15th day of March, June, September, and December. The amount of tax payable for each instalment is calculated using one of the following methods:

---

6 ITA 152(1).
7 ITA 152(4); IC 75-7R3.
8 ITA 152(1.1); IT-512.
9 ITA 153(1).
10 ITA 156(1), 156.1(1).

(a) one-quarter of the estimated tax payable that is not withheld at source; or

(b) one-quarter of the previous year's tax liability that was not withheld at source; or

(c) for the March and June instalments, one-quarter of second preceding year's tax liability that was not withheld at source, and for the September and December instalments, one-half of the preceding year's tax liability that was not withheld at source, minus the March and June instalment payments.

CCRA provides each taxpayer with a calculation of his or her required instalments; this calculation is based on the prior year's tax liability. It is up to each individual to estimate the current year's tax if he or she wants to pay a lower instalment. Instalments need not be made when the federal tax for the current year or the previous year is less than $2,000.[11] Also, special rules exist for taxpayers whose chief source of income is farming or fishing.[12]

B. Corporations

Corporations usually do not earn income that is subject to withholding tax. Consequently, instalment payments are the primary method of remitting corporate tax. A corporation must make 12 instalments per year beginning at the end of the first month of the taxation year. Unless the current year's taxes will be lower than in the previous year, the monthly instalment is equal to one-twelfth of the previous year's tax liability. Often, the previous year's tax liability is not known when the first and second instalments are due. In such cases, the first two instalments can be based on the total tax paid in the second previous year, and the remaining 10 instalments are adjusted after the tax liability of the previous year is known.[13]

If more tax is owing after all of the required instalments have been made, the amount must, for most corporations, be paid within two months of the taxation year end.[14] This period is extended to three months if the corporation is a Canadian-controlled private corporation whose taxable income does not exceed the $200,000 annual business limit, and if during the year or previous year a small-business deduction was claimed.

For both individuals and corporations, CCRA charges interest on any tax that is due and payable but not paid. Interest is also charged on late or deficient tax instalments. The rate of interest is the rate prescribed by the regulations and is adjusted quarterly.[15] The rate prescribed by CCRA is compounded daily, so the effective annual rate is higher than the published prescribed rate. Such interest costs are not deductible for tax purposes. Worth noting is that CCRA will *pay* interest on overpayments of tax.[16] Interest on overpayments is usually calculated from the date that the return was required to be filed or that the tax was paid. However, no interest is paid on excess tax instalments.

IV. Penalties and Offences

To ensure compliance, the *Income Tax Act* imposes a number of penalties. These penalties are over and above any interest costs on late payments of tax. Some of the more relevant penalties are outlined below.

• **Failure to file an annual return**   Five percent of the tax unpaid for the year, plus 1% for each month after the due date, to a maximum of 12 months.[17]

---

11 ITA 156.1(1).

12 ITA 155.

13 ITA 157(1); IC 81-11R3.

14 ITA 157(1)(b).

15 ITA 161(1), (2); Regulation 4301.

16 ITA 164(3); Regulation 4301.

17 ITA 162(1).

- **Repeated failures to file an annual return**   Ten percent on a second or further late filing. This relates to returns applicable to the three years after a 5% penalty has been assessed. This 10% penalty is increased by 2% for each month after the due date, for a maximum of 20 months.[18]

- **Failure to report an item of income**   Ten percent of the unreported income *if* the failure to report occurs more than once in a three-year period.[19]

- **Knowingly making a false statement or omission**   Fifty percent of the tax owing on the excluded or understated amount.[20]

- **Late or insufficient instalments**   Fifty percent of the interest payable on the late or deficient instalment, if that instalment interest is more than $1,000; or, more than 25% of the interest that would have been payable if no instalment had been made, if that amount is greater than $1,000.[21]

The total of penalties and interest can be a significant amount. It should be noted that CCRA has the authority to waive or cancel the interest and penalties if the non-compliance resulted from circumstances beyond the taxpayer's control, such as a major illness.

Regarding some of the above activities, a taxpayer may, in addition to the penalty, be liable to a fine and/or imprisonment. For example, a taxpayer who fails to file a return as and when required may, upon conviction, be subject to a fine of between $1,000 and $25,000, or to a fine and imprisonment for a term not exceeding 12 months.[22] In addition, a person who has participated in making a false statement, or who has destroyed documents to evade the payment of tax, is liable to a fine of between 50% and 200% of the tax that he or she sought to evade, or to a fine and imprisonment for a term not exceeding two years.[23]

V. Objection and Appeal

Taxpayers who receive an assessment with which they do not agree have the right to appeal. Such appeals are subject to certain formalities and must conform to certain time limits.

The first step is to request a formal review of the items in dispute. At this review the taxpayer makes a representation to CCRA. CCRA then confirms or alters the assessment.

To obtain this review, individuals must file a formal notice of objection within one year of the required filing date of the year in question, or within 90 days of the day the notice of assessment was mailed, whichever is later. All other taxpayers must file the objection within 90 days of the date the assessment was mailed.[24]

A taxpayer who is not satisfied with the result of this first appeal may make a second appeal, this to the Tax Court of Canada, within 90 days of the day CCRA confirmed its assessment or made its reassessment.[25] A taxpayer who is still not satisfied can then appeal (within time limits) to the Federal Court of Canada, and perhaps to the Supreme Court of Canada.

Visit the Canadian Income Taxation Web site at **www.mcgrawhill.ca/ college/buckwold7** to view any updated tax information.

---

18 ITA 162(2).

19 ITA 163(1).

20 ITA 163(2).

21 ITA 163.1.

22 ITA 238.

23 ITA 239.

24 ITA 165.

25 ITA 169.

Index